Becoming Aware

Katie Barwick-Snell

Velma Walker

Cover image courtesy of Bonnie L. Peruttzi, MHR Executive Director, Transition House.

Transition House, Inc., is a private non-profit organization founded in 1982 in Norman, OK. Our Vision is changing lives by creating pathways for mental wellness. Our Mission is improving our community by providing tools for sustaining mental wellness with skills development, supportive care, and advocacy. The hands in the cover photo are of people who are working to overcome a disease that society often sees as a character flaw. Transition House visit www.thouse.org.

www.kendallhunt.com
Send all inquiries to:
4050 Westmark Drive
Dubuque, IA 52004-1840

Copyright © 1976, 1977, 1981, 1986, 1992, 1995, 1998, 2001, 2004, 2007, 2010, 2013, 2017, 2021
by Kendall Hunt Publishing Company

ISBN 978-1-7924-0892-2
Text ISBN 978-1-7924-0891-5

Published in the United States of America

Brief Contents

Contents

CHAPTER 2
Self-Awareness 85

CHAPTER 3

Who's in Control? 161

CHAPTER 4

Dealing with Emotions 223

CHAPTER 5

Interpersonal Communication 301

CHAPTER 6

Developing Relationships 373

CHAPTER 7

Resolving Interpersonal Conflict 451

CHAPTER 8

Managing Stress and Wellness 505

CHAPTER 9

Values, Ethics, and Choices 571

Preface

You will discover that the new fourteenth edition of *Becoming Aware: A Text/Work-book for Human Relations and Personal Adjustment* will assist each learner in the process of becoming more aware of yourself and others through an interactive learning.

This new edition is a text/workbook with online components that will give students the opportunity to become active learners in the process of exploring human relations and personal adjustment. Learning should be a "hands on" experience. This new edition will explore, experiment, test, and apply the scholarly theories and ideas within the world of human relations. The art of developing relationships that improve personal skills and effectiveness uses a combination of theories from Human Diversity, Psychology, Social Psychology, Communications, Theology and Sociology. Personal adjustment is the process of balancing conflicting needs, or needs challenged by obstacles in the environment. We feel this text/workbook will allow the learner to think critically, work through problems logically, and make connections with the real world and thus become an active learner. We know the more you become actively involved within the subject matter of human relations and personal adjustment, the more you will learn. **Human Relations** is a multidisciplinary field that promotes democratic values, advocacy and social justice. **Human relations** can also be defined as the art of developing relationships that improve personal skills and life effectiveness. It offers insight into how you fit into the world and feel about race, class, and gender issues. Basically you have to understand yourself before you can understand others effectively and **"become aware"** of how you fit into the world.

Knowing human relations skills and knowledge helps you to confront systemic social and organizational social inequites.

Personal adjustment is the maintenance of emotional equilibrium in the face of internal and external stressors by acceptance and adaptation. This new edition will give you and the other students within the class many new opportunities to get actively involved in learning about yourself and others.

About the Book

The approach in *Becoming Aware* is humanistic and personal; that is, it stresses developing a healthy and effective personality and understanding the common struggles we all have in developing a greater awareness of self and establishing more meaningful relationships with others. It especially emphasizes taking risks in accepting personal responsibility for achieving a greater awareness of self and deciding whether and how we want to change our lives.

What is more important to us than our personal adjustment and our relationships with other people? This new edition is written for college students of all ages and for all others who wish to explore the world of self-awareness and discover new avenues for personal growth and adjustment and the development and continuance of personal relationships.

The book was written for learners who are looking for a practical course: one that deals with issues in everyday living and that may also provide a catalyst for their own personal growth. *Becoming Aware* has been adopted in courses dealing with the psychology of adjustment, human relations, applied psychology, personal growth and awareness, communication, etc. It has also been fortunate to have had numerous adoptions from technical and vocational programs, ranging from nursing to electronics. In addition, instructors in teacher-training courses as well as management-development courses have found *Becoming Aware* a practical guide for their students.

Organization of This Edition

This is a personal interactive book. Within each chapter, the reader is encouraged to examine scholarly, relevant ideas and issues pertaining to their understanding of self and their relationships with others. These skills are highly sought after in the workplace, combined with diversity and technology knowledge make them ready for the todays world. We have emphasized using scholarly resources and have included numerous videos to reinforce learning.

This book is designed to be a personal workbook as well as a classroom text. Each chapter has a minimum of five activities for the reader to pause and reflect on the personal application of the concepts and theories presented in the chapter. Most of the activities will allow the reader to get personally and individually involved in completing the tasks, while a few of the activities will require each person to get involved in a small group process in order to complete the task. It is important for all learners to participate in individual projects as well as group activities to retain the knowledge learned. In today's world of business we all have to learn to function as a team (within groups) and as individuals. The better we learn to do it now, the better we will survive in the world.

Active learning is emphasized throughout the text. Each chapter contains a Learning Journal, which will allow the reader to write and assess the personal value or meaning gained from the concepts presented. The activities, as well as the Learning Journals, will be available online, specifically designed for more convenient classroom participation in work outside of class that can be used for evaluation and assessment. Additionally, there are numerous thought-provoking quotations, from well-known sources, and numerous short videos, links, poems and words of wisdom designed to further promote insightful awareness. A journal project can be used as a final project grade.

The learning process is an important aspect of this book. The reader gets more involved within the subject matter of the text through the use of beginning reflections that help them note key ideas and chapter test review questions, which will allow learners to relate directly to the important concepts and ideas within each chapter. Reflection questions are designed to help them to develop critical thinking skills and work through problems logically.

To emphasize the need for critical thinking skills, many of the important concepts and ideas are highlighted through use of elements titled—"Think about This"—"Check This Out"—"Consider This"—and "How To." Also in class activities like Think...Pair... Share and Pause and Reflect.

The sociocultural perspective within the field of human relations and personal adjustment is having a much greater impact on our lives, and it needs to be emphasized more and more. There is continued emphasis on diversity, including additional information on ethnicity, along with culture and gender. You will note the continued emphasis on the elements titled "Focus on Diversity" and "Gender and You." Since technology has impacted the way we now interact we have included new information on Becoming aware of how technology impacts each chapter topic.

What's New in This Edition?

The fourteenth edition of Becoming Aware reflects significant updating. This text was originally created about 30 years ago and in this 14th edition we have made efforts to include inclusive language, new terminology and updated technology. We may have missed some so please forgive us... technology and research changes quickly ... Each chapter has been extensively reviewed and updated including using gender neutral language. New current references, updated glossary terms, and interesting quotations have been added. Engaging media, activities and links to audio and video have been added to the text so if you are using this textbook on your computer or tablet or in the classroom you can enjoy the supplemental media to visually explain the information along with your reading the text. We are certain the engaging presentations designed to enhance discussion and encourage critical thinking. Since Relationships in families, classes and workplace are all important. Different styles of communicating: ethnic and cultural differences and understanding gender differences will be explored.

Relationship management. Dating and romantic-consent,(including the me-too movement) negotiation and maintenance. You will find new or additional information in the following areas:

* New Sections on Becoming Aware of Technology in every chapter.
* Online activities added in selected chapters and updated media links including online quizzes, videos, activities and podcasts.
* Several revised chapter activities and new chapter activities.
* New section: What is Human Relations and how you will be able to use it in your life and career.
* New coverage of tolerance, acceptance, and appreciation of differences.
* Inclusive gender-neutral language throughout the text.
* Discussion of gender identity.
* Expanded importance of self-concept with mindset discussion.
* Extended discussion of the Big Five Personality Factors, with the addition of the HEXACO model.
* Enhanced discussion of the Myers Briggs type psychology.
* Increased discussion of strengths-based psychology.
* New Gender and You discussion—Where Did You Learn Your Gender?
* New section: A look at social psychology.
* New discussion of cyberbullying, sexting and Internet privacy.
* Expanded section on helping people grieve with introduction of the Ring Theory.
* New Focus on Diversity: Microaggressions.
* Modernized discussion of technology and communication.
* New discussion of the concept of implicit bias.
* Strengthened discussion of becoming friends with the addition of friendship traits.
* Updated discussion of Internet dating and social networking.
* Broadened discussion of "Should I remain single?"
* Think/pair/share an activity for class or to use independently.
* Increased discussion of realities of conflict.
* New information on mistakes to avoid in a conflict.
* New discussion on cross-cultural relationships.
* Updated information on Millennials, Generation Z and stress.
* Revamped discussion of physical effects of stress.
* Revised tips on managing stress.
* Expanded discussion on the nature of prejudice.
* Howard's seven-step method of values clarification.
* Updated discussion of honesty/ethics in professions.
* Steps for intelligent-risk taking.
* Expanded discussion on why goal setting is important.
* New coverage of research on happiness and wellbeing.

Acknowledgments

We are grateful to the reviewers for their insightful suggestions and innovative ideas: Dr. Barwick-Snell: Thank you to Rev. Anna Holloway from Langston University for her ideas and her expertise in content, editing and gender neutral language; Dr. Joanna Harris, Psychology, East Central Oklahoma University; Abigail Klumpenhouwer, Jessica Fuchs, Staff and students from Bridges in Norman, Oklahoma; Dr. Janna Martin, University of Oklahoma; Dr. Cheryl Walker Esbaugh; James Barwick-Snell, LSU; Bridges staff and student , Transition House wellness class members, and OU students who are on the cover photo; and poet/administrator Colton Snead. I am grateful for all of your insightful suggestions and innovative ideas. A special thank you for Dr. Velma Walker for her guidance and mentoring. Finally, I would especially like to thank my family for all the support and ideas they gave me and all the experience and help from my wonderful husband/editor Dr. Daniel C. Snell (a writer of numerous Near Eastern history and religion texts) and my family, James, Abby, & Andrew, and my foster kids Jessica, Will and Brittany. Thanks to all my friends for their support, ideas, contributions, and suggestions.

Finally, we would like to acknowledge those individuals and publishers who kindly gave us their permission to reprint their materials. In several instances, we regret that even after diligent searching, we have not been able to properly credit material being used. Some of the material has been used for many years in classes and workshops with the result that proper identification has been lost, or we no longer are able to provide source information as we would like. Because the material has proved to be of great value, it is included in the book. We trust that eventually we will be able to credit these authors with proper recognition for their work.

Dr. Katie Barwick-Snell and Dr. Velma Walker

About the Authors

Dr. Katie Barwick-Snell University of Oklahoma Professor Emeritus has been a faculty member at the University of Oklahoma, Norman, since the early 1990s. She is currently retired but still teaching graduate students in Human Relations, and Women and Gender Studies. She helped develop and implement the undergraduate Human Relations program at the University of Oklahoma and was the first academic advisor of the popular undergraduate major in Human Relations. She has won numerous advising and teaching awards. Her B.S. is in Home Economics from Mississippi State University, her M.S. in Human Development from the University of Oklahoma, and her Ed.D. in Occupational and Adult Education from Oklahoma State University. She was on faculty in the former Home Economics Department at USAO in Chickasha, Oklahoma and the former School of Home Economics at the University of Oklahoma. She was also cook on an archeology dig in Syria in the late 1980s and has lived in Australia and Scotland.

She is a long-time volunteer for Transitions House, Board of Directors, Norman Public Schools, Norman's Center for Children and Families, the Women's Resource Center Board of Directors, and most recently a community volunteer with Parents Helping Parents, an organization for parents of substance abuse, to offer hope and help to other parents. She is married and has two fantastic grown children, a wonderful son in law, two delightful "other daughters," and three geriatric dogs.

Let us remember: One book, one pen, one child, and one teacher can change the world.
—MALALA YOUSAFZAI

Dr. Velma Walker is a Professor Emeritus of psychology at Tarrant County College, Northeast Campus in Hurst, Texas. Although she has specialized in human relations courses for 39 years at the college level, she has also been a counselor and coordinator of student job placement and career information. She has a bachelor's degree in business administration/education, a master's degree in counseling and psychology, and a doctor of education degree, with emphasis in counseling, psychology, and administration. Dr. Walker is also a certified mediator for conflict resolution.

Dr. Walker has given human relations training seminars in the areas of communication, motivation, stress management, time management, and personality lifestyles for educators and business and professional groups for over 36 years. She has also served as a teacher consultant for the Educational Division of the Zig Ziglar Corporation. Dr. Walker is a multiple year honoree in *Who's Who Among America's Teachers*.

chapter 1

Getting Acquainted with Ourselves and Others

Rawpixel/Shutterstock.com

I expect to pass through this life but once; therefore if there be any kindness I can show or any good thing that I can do for any fellow being, let me do it now, not defer, or neglect it, for I shall not pass this way again.

Think About This...

Write a paragraph answering the following thoughts in your class journal

After everyone has finished the assignment get into small groups of 4 to discuss.

Think for a minute about your greatest experiences in life. Most likely, you were probably with another person.

- What would we do without other people?
- What would you do without friends?
- What would it be like?
- Where would you go?
- Would you have fun?
- How do you react in a group? Do you feel shy or do you speak out?

- Would you know what love is?
- Have you ever had a close friend or close relative die? How did you feel when it happened?
- Have you ever experienced or had a close friend or relative experience a divorce? Did they feel lonely? Were they depressed? What did they experience?
- Have you had any interesting positive experiences with technology? Have you been phubbed or spammed?
- How did you feel when your best friend or lover returned after being gone for a long period of time? Overjoyed? Excited?

It is obvious that personal relationships and friendships are important to us. We need merely to reflect for a moment on the source of our greatest pleasure and pain to appreciate that nothing else in our life has aroused the extremes of emotion more than the relationships that we have experienced with other human beings.

What is Human Relations?

Human relations (HR) has many meanings to many people, but for this text **human relations** can be defined as the art of developing relationships that improve personal skills and life effectiveness. It offers insight into how people fit into the world and feel about race, class, and gender issues. We have to understand ourselves before we can understand others effectively and "**become aware**" of how we fit into the world. In looking at ourselves and how we relate to others, we can build better relationships and succeed at school and work. Human relations has an emphasis on such skills as behavior, empathy, cooperation, intergroup development, and interpersonal development. The field of study incorporates sociology, psychology, communications, human diversity, and other areas like management and human development into the social psychology curriculum. Another definition of human relations is the study of improving interpersonal relationships among people or groups of people. Clearly, the basic study of human relations includes a great deal of attention to the emotional needs of oneself as well as to the emotional needs of others. Emotional adjustment (also referred to as personal adjustment or psychological adjustment) is the maintenance of emotional equilibrium in the face of internal and external stressors. This is facilitated by cognitive processes of acceptance and adaptation. This is also addressed in this textbook about human relations and personal adjustment.

According to Dr. George Henderson, Sylvan N. Goldman Professor of Human Relations at the University of Oklahoma, "Human relations encompasses all the many ways in which people interact with each other to form social units. Unlike social scientists, who are interested primarily in describing *what is*, students of human relations are also concerned with determining *what may be done* to foster positive group interactions" (Henderson, 1996, p.17). He also states that the conflicts that grow out of human relationships may take many forms, positive and negative, such as age and sex rivalry, racism, and, possibly, violence. Microaggressions may also occur as a subtle interaction. Human diversity/human relations refers to many sources of differences among people, including ethnic or racial, gender, disability status, and sexual orientation. People need to understand others' differences and be willing to to embrace them or tolerate those differences.

Becoming Aware of Human Relations: Finding Common Ground
https://www.youtube.com/watch?v=umwMb-21qzM

Dr. George Henderson, founder of the Human Relations program at the University of Oklahoma, speaks about human relations.

As mentioned above, human relations is the study of improving interpersonal relationships among people or groups of people. Dr. Lowell Lamberton defines HR as "the skill or ability to work effectively through and with other people" (Lamberton, 2014, p. 4). Human relations includes a desire to understand others, their needs and weaknesses, and their talents and abilities. For anyone in a workplace setting, human relations also involves an understanding of how people work together in groups, satisfying both individual needs and group objectives. If an organization is to succeed, the relationships among the people in that organization must be monitored and maintained (Lamberton, 2014). Again, the basic study of human relations includes a great deal of attention to the emotional needs of oneself as well as the emotional needs of others.

Human relations begins with self-understanding. The self is about being a total person or individual. We each have a **public self**—that is, how we communicate about ourselves and what others actually perceive about us are a **private self,** which is the actual person that we may be (Dubrin, 2016). In a perfect culture, cultural messages provide scripts for how people should interact with each other; these scripts include expectations about gender. Gender expectations and the gender composition of a friendship influence a relationship. People of all genders regularly face a host of media images that romanticize and sexualize their routine encounters, and confront an array of societal expectations and constraints that make a rewarding friendship with another person challenging (Baumgarten, 2002). Everyone needs to feel that we have someone to help us out or take care of us and support us. This is called an *emotional attachment*. Many people consider their family and/or friends as their emotional attachments, or supporters. People are heavily involved with social groups, like religious organizations or support groups, or create a "family of close friends." Some people have social ties on social media or in their workplace and these are their emotional attachments. Wherever we find them, **having close healthy relationships is a good thing**.

Human relations also involves emotional adjustment (also referred to as personal adjustment or psychological adjustment), the maintenance of emotional equilibrium in the face of internal and external stressors. This is facilitated by cognitive processes of acceptance and adaptation. Social cognition is a sub-topic of social psychology that focuses on how people process, store, and apply information about other people and social situations. It focuses on the role that cognitive processes play in our social interactions.

Relationships are the foundation for meaning and success in life.
—DOUGLAS DAFT

Human relations is the art of developing relationships that improve your personal skills and life effectiveness. It offers insight into how you fit into the world. Basically, you have to understand yourself before you can understand others effectively and "become aware" of how you fit into the world.
—KATIE BARWICK-SNELL

In order to become a healthy and happy person, an individual needs to form close, caring interpersonal relationships. How do we learn to do this? Perhaps the words of John Hope Bryant, founder and CEO of Operation HOPE, will provide some thoughts worth remembering:

> People meet you where you are. If you're open, they tend to be open. If you're closed, they tend to be closed. If you're vulnerable, they tend to be vulnerable. And people are often a little insecure and afraid of themselves. They're afraid to tip their hand. It's just human nature, self-preservation. People will generally only tip their hand when they see you tip your hand. (Bryant, 2009)

BECOMING AWARE OF RELATIONSHIPS—THINK ABOUT IT

10 Commandments of Relationships:

Choose Your Tribe Wisely: Are you hanging with chickens or eagles? We must surround ourselves with people who pull the best out of us … instead of the worst. Some people will keep us all penned up … others help us soar!

Make Relationship Building a Priority: We might think we are not good at building relationships. That's OK. If it is important, we can get better at it. Start with this fundamental truth: PEOPLE MATTER!

Balance Care and Candor: Our relationships should be characterized by truth and care. Do we know when to challenge our friends with the truth, versus when we share the truth with empathy and compassion?

Make it a Habit: This might sound very "cold and robotic," but we are extremely busy. If we don't make it a habit to reach out in our relationships, we will only do so when we need something. I don't think that is how we want to be known in our relationships.

Like-Mindedness Matters: Find people with common goals, values, interests and aspirations. This doesn't mean that we shouldn't have experiences with diverse groups. Those experiences are key to our growth. However, the people we grow closest to often share core things in common with us.

Be A Giver: If we enter into a relationship thinking it is all about ourselves, then the relationship probably won't last, or at best be very shallow. Seek opportunities to serve others first.

Be a Plus: John Maxwell talks about this in his book *The 21 Irrefutable Laws of Leadership in the Law of Addition*. Be the person someone wants to run into at the grocery store … not the person people run from. Be positive and encouraging, not critical and a downer.

Shut Your Mouth, Open Your Ears: We will build much stronger relationships with people based on what we hear them say, not what they hear us say. If you are a great listener and ask great questions, people will be blown away by your conversation skills. Try it.

Be grateful: When was the last time you told someone you were grateful for the relationship you had with them? You understand as well as I do how rare healthy, strong relationships are in this world. Take time today to let those people know how much you value them.

Right the Wrongs: Relationships are hard and messy. That is probably why we don't engage in them like we should. If you mess up, own up and apologize. If someone wrongs you, forgive them and move on.

Friends … it is all about relationships. They are key to our success in every aspect of our lives, even professionally. If you want to find your dream job, you are going to have to master relationships.

—R.Cook (2020) Rennie Cook.com

Becoming Aware of your Educational Skills: Learning Styles & Multiple Intelligences: Theory Integration
https://www.youtube.com/watch?v=FVg9n0l0Gf0

Dr. Carol Gilligan believes "the truths of relationships return in the rediscovery of connection, in the realization that self and others are interdependent and that life, however valuable in itself, can only be sustained in relationships" (Gilligan, 2016).

Self-Disclosure is a Tool for Building Relationships

BECOMING AWARE OF WHO WE ARE—WHAT GENERATION ARE YOU?

JANUARY 2019 Pew Research
DEFINING GENERATIONS: WHERE MILLENNIALS END AND GENERATION Z BEGINS
The generations defined

**https://www.pewresearch.org/wp-content/uploads/2019/01/
FT_19.01.17_generations_2019.png?w=640**

Where are you in the generations? How do you think this affects you in relationship building and technology use?

Do You Know Yourself?

Self-awareness is necessary in order to fully understand others. Psychologists have found that a person must gain an understanding of themselves before they can become acquainted with and understand others. There are some basic questions concerning self-discovery and getting acquainted with others that we can ask ourselves. How well do I know myself? Is it easy for other people to get to know me? How well do other people really know me? How much of myself do I reveal to those with whom I want to have a close, personal relationship? How much do I want them to know about me regarding my innermost thoughts, feelings, and actions? I also have to ask myself, how interested am I in learning the innermost thoughts, feelings, and actions of those with whom I desire to have a close relationship? This chapter and the whole book will cover the importance of self-disclosure and how special relationships are.

> *If I tell you who I am, you may not like who I am, and it's all that I have.*
> —JOHN POWELL

The revealing of the inner-self is called self-disclosure. This means talking to another person about our innermost thoughts and feelings, our aspirations and dreams, our fears and doubts. It is talking about things of which we are ashamed and proud. Self-disclosure is a crucial part of relationship building. Dr. Sidney Marshall Jourard, a Canadian psychologist from the 1960-70s, is also known for his "Self-Disclosure Theory" of humanistic therapy. The process was originally defined as telling others about yourself. Since then, an extensive amount of information about disclosure has been produced. Decision making behind the act of disclosing private information is an extremely complicated process, especially when we are considering close personal relationships and family interactions. According to Reiss (2006), sexual self-disclosure is likely to bring about greater bonding between intimates. We also know that, although intimacy often increases the possibility of revealing information, there are times when disclosure is counterproductive for the relationship or family.

© michaeljung/Shutterstock.com

How do we learn to form close relationships?

A Vlog is a "video- blog" that features mostly videos rather than text or images. Many people follow popular YouTube video creators (or "vloggers") posting candid testimonials about personal experiences with mental illness and treatments. Thousands have used the platform to discuss depression, OCD, trichotillomania, eating disorders, bipolar disorder, panic attacks, severe social anxiety, and more (Lanning 2019).

Why study self-disclosure? The evolution of a relationship—getting acquainted, becoming friends, and developing intimacy—is based on how much we are willing to disclose about ourself and how much the other person is willing to disclose about themselves to us. The more we know about another person and the more he or she knows about us, the more effective and efficient the relationship will be. People who share their ideas, interests, experiences, expectations, and feelings with others will generally have more friends and develop long lasting relationships more easily than those who do not (Lanning, 2019; Lynch & Daniels, 2000; Delerga et al., 1993). It can be hard when a lack of self-disclosure makes people suspicious and uncomfortable to be around.

In turn, they will not talk about themselves, and finding those common interests on which to base a relationship will become difficult.

Is self-disclosure important in a relationship? Good self-disclosure skills are fundamental to relationships for many reasons, including the following:

- **Defining Yourself.** Disclosing personal information lets you be known to others. If you do not define yourself, misunderstandings are more likely to occur. Others may perceive you based on their own interpretation, rather than on information you give them.
- **Knowing Yourself.** As you disclose information about yourself, you can get deeper insight and understanding about the kind of person you are. You also give others the opportunity to give you feedback.
- **Getting Acquainted.** Talking about yourself and letting other people talk about themselves gives each of you the opportunity to understand and know the other as an individual. Each is given the opportunity to understand and trust the other. **Reciprocity** (a positive response from the person with whom one is sharing information) often happens. Then the other person who received the disclosure self-discloses in turn.
- **Developing Intimacy.** As you begin to share and receive, a deeper feeling of trust and understanding will evolve and a mutual feeling of closeness will develop.
- **Being Responsible.** Behaving responsibly with that knowledge and not betraying your friend's confidence is another key element in self-disclosure.

> *No one can develop freely in this world and find a full life without feeling understood by at least one person.*
> —PAUL TOURNIER

Before we can engage in self-disclosure, there must be an atmosphere of goodwill and trust. An individual is not likely to engage in much self-disclosure if the situation involves too much personal threat, or even a threat to anyone with whom he or she is closely associated.

People around the world view more than 1 billion hours of YouTube videos per day in 2019—more than any major television network or streaming service can deliver. Millennials view an average of 12.1 hours of YouTube videos per week. This potentially massive audience gives popular creators a real opportunity to engage peer-to-peer with fans about previously taboo topics.

After filmmaker Anna Akana lost her younger sister to suicide, she began using her channel to speak out about mental illness, becoming one of the first highly followed vloggers to address her own depression publicly. In a 2013 video, "Please Don't Kill Yourself," she said, "I've been pretty open about the fact that my sister committed suicide in 2007, and I've been getting a lot of questions from people, like, 'I want to kill myself. What should I do?' If you commit suicide, I don't even know, I don't even know what would happen to you. All I really know is what happens to the people around you after you die." Some feel that many people today do not have as much privacy because of social media disclosing information about them. Public self/private self is the term used for this phenomena. **Some people misuse technology**—such as photos, videos, social media, and dating apps—to engage in harassing, unsolicited, or non-consensual sexual interactions violating someone's private space . It can leave

FOCUS ON DIVERSITY

RESPECTING SELF-DISCLOSURE AND DIVERSITY IN RELATIONSHIPS

Researchers often study communication behaviors of various cultures, and have noted that self-disclosure tends to be high in mainstream North American society. People from various cultures, including ones within the United States, have learned different communication styles. What Westerners consider openness and healthy self-disclosure may feel offensively intrusive to people from some Asian societies. The dramatic, assertive speaking style of many African Americans can be misinterpreted as abrasive within a Western Caucasian perspective. **The best way to understand what another's behavior means is to ask.** This conveys the relational message that they matter to us, and it allows us to gain insight into the interesting diversity among us. For Americans, Japanese, and Koreans, self-disclosure was directly associated with online relationship development. However, the relationship between self-disclosure and trust was positive only for Americans (Yum & Hara, 2005). Americans' online relationships might be too open and trusting for other cultures.

the person on the other end feeling manipulated, unsafe, exposed, and worried about their online reputation. The laws pertaining to these situations vary from state to state as well as on on the platforms used, and they are evolving rapidly. Learn more about these situations so you can feel better prepared to report and protect your privacy if they happen. So be careful of disclosing too much on social media. Sociologist Dr. Brené Brown believes that we all need to define our boundaries. Boundaries are not fake walls or divisions, but *respect for yourself and your friends* (Brown, 2010).

Do you need to disclose?

Self-disclosure usually involves the sharing of private information, and it is generally of such a nature that it is not something one would normally disclose to everyone who might inquire about it. Therefore, we are not expected to bare the innermost secrets of our souls to casual acquaintances—we can save that information for the significant others in our lives. Self-disclosure is a rewarding experience, comparable to those of food and sex (Tamir & Mitchell, 2012). People enjoy self-disclosure if they know other people are listening; talking is a means of catharsis toward good feelings. **Catharsis** is a release of emotional tension that can be achieved through sharing and self-disclosure with others. Self-disclosure promotes attraction. People feel a sense of closeness to others who reveal their vulnerabilities, innermost thoughts, and facts about themselves. The sense of closeness increases if the disclosures are emotional rather than factual. Self-disclosing in vlogging (video-blogging) hinges on the idea that confessional videos bring psychological benefits to their creators, and is based on foundational research on the power of expressive writing to help people come to grips with personal issues.

In 1997, James Pennebaker of the University of Texas asked a group of students to write for 20 minutes at a time over the course of several days in response to a prompt about traumatic experiences; other students were told to write in the same fashion about a neutral topic. Those who responded in writing to the prompt about traumatic experiences reported better psychological health months later and had made fewer visits to the campus health center. The "Pennebaker effect" has since been confirmed by other studies, including a number of studies evaluating individuals who blogged about their experiences. The exercise enables people to build a structure around their difficult experiences and regain a sense of control—much as the vloggers have (Lanning, 2019).

It is extremely important to ask ourselves some important questions before disclosing. Balance in disclosing your information is important … but not too much; remember TMI, or "too much information," is not a good idea (Punches, 2010):

- Can I trust this person with this information?
- How could this information be used against me? Misconstrued?
- Is this the right time and place to disclose?
- Am I sharing things about myself incrementally and slowly, or too much, too soon?
- How has the person received private information in the past?
- What could happen if I share too much too fast?

What should you reveal to another person? A few examples might be:

- Likes and dislikes
- Fears and anxieties
- Attitudes and opinions
- Tastes and interests
- Ideas about money
- Work perceptions
- Personality choices
- Feelings and reactions about events that have just taken place
- Perceptions of self and others

There are some disadvantages to self-disclosure as well, particularly if there is too much of it. Talking too much about ourselves early in a relationship may not facilitate the development of friendship. People might view high self-disclosure as an indication that we are too immature, insecure, or phony, or even that we tell everyone such things. Other people like to think that they are special to us (O'Connel & O'Connel, 2005).

What is the greatest risk of self-disclosure? Personal disclosures that are too general reduce the sense of openness, thus reducing the feeling of closeness. Disclosures that are too intimate often highlight character and personality flaws, thus decreasing likeability. People who make intimate disclosures too early in relationships are often perceived as insecure, which further decreases likeability (Shafer, 2015). Self-disclosure involves taking risks. *The greatest risk is one of rejection—not being liked or accepted.* This may cause us to hide behind a mask—a *facade*—and try to be something we know we are not. In this state, effective communication cannot occur and the growth and maintenance of those deep, special, and meaningful relation-

BECOMING AWARE OF TECHNOLOGY

WOMEN DISCLOSE MORE THAN MEN

More research is needed to understand changing relationships and if disclosure research of communication messages between same-sex couples is the same as that of traditional couples.

Several studies have looked at how men and women disclose online. Overall, they have found that women disclose online more than men (Kleman, 2007). When looking at the content of messages, Li (2006) found that computer-mediated communication messages sent by males were more confrontational and autonomous, while female messages were supportive and rapport-building (Sheldon, 2013). Women tend to have more friends and closer relationships than men. These friendships tend to provide them with more social support. Most research shows that women tend to be more openly self-disclosing than men, although the disparity seems smaller than originally believed. Because women tend to value "personal talk" more than men, they tend to share more personal information and feelings with their female friends (Kilmartin, 2015). Previous studies have shown that women disclose to their close friends more than men. Results of testing gender differences in self-disclosure suggest that women disclose to their exclusive face-to-face and exclusive social media friends more than men, but men have more intimate discussions with their recently added social media friends than women do (Sheldon, 2013).

Males tend to disclose more to strangers than females do, and are more willing to disclose casual things about themselves, such as their work, accomplishments, attitudes, and opinions. Males are also less intimate and less personal than females. Males are expected not to disclose; it's not "manly." In peer/friendship relationships that emphasize competition and challenge, males often avoid revealing weaknesses, and at times associate self-disclosure with loss of control and vulnerability. Research shows that men often become closer by doing things together or doing things for each other, rather than just talking with each other (Wood, 2017). Byers and Demmons (2010) found that women disclose more than men do, both sexually and non-sexually. However, sexuality is a highly personal and private topic for self-disclosure. Women may be less comfortable than men are in discussing sex, especially their own sexual satisfaction, because the double standard of sex roles inhibits them from admitting to being knowledgeable about sex (Huong, 2010).

ships with friends and spouses cannot occur. Risk nothing, gain nothing. We have a choice—to withdraw from honest encounters, to hide our feelings, to falsify our intentions—or to be transparent, open, and real through self-disclosure.

What are the advantages of self-disclosure? Self-disclosure has the potential to improve and expand interpersonal relationships, but it serves other functions as well. One advantage is that *self-disclosure improves relationships.* We prefer to be with people who are willing to disclose to us and we are more willing to be open with them. Self-disclosure is a reciprocal process. Disclosure leads to trust and trust leads to more disclosure, and, thus, the relationship will grow and develop into a mature and long-lasting, loving interaction. There is a strong positive correlation between self-disclosure and marital satisfaction. Research has shown that the more a couple is willing to disclose about themselves, the greater the marital satisfaction and the greater the chance the marriage will last over a longer period of time (Santrock, 2006).

Self-disclosure promotes mental health. The second advantage is that *self-disclosure promotes mental health*. Withholding important information can create stress and thus lead to less effective functioning and even possible physical problems (Jourard, 1976, Hyman, I. Self 2008). We all need a release, and for many of us "talking out" our feelings, problems, and thoughts will relieve us of the stresses and anxieties that are interfering with our everyday functioning. This release of emotional tension through talking is known as a ***catharsis***. As many of us have discovered, we feel relieved after sharing our problems with another person. This is the reason counseling and therapy are so effective for many individuals. Sidney Jourard used the concept of transparency to mean self-disclosure. He felt that the only way one could come to understand himself or herself was through disclosure to significant others. This requires a dropping of defenses, pretense, social performance, and other protections against authenticity.

Transparency requires honesty and courage. Becoming more transparent is an ongoing process. So in this sense, the transparent self is not the parts of self that are revealed, but the dynamic process of moving toward authentic self-disclosure (Pegg, 2018).

Self-disclosure online. There were 3.48 billion social media users in 2019, with the worldwide total growing by 288 million (9 percent) since this time last year. Given the continued growth in its popularity, social media is becoming another avenue for initiating and maintaining interpersonal relationships. A number of studies have found that relationship maintenance and social interaction (Sheldon, 2008; Smock, Ellison, Lampe, & Wohn 2011) are the primary motivations for using social media. Social network users tend to rely more on self-disclosures to create a sense of closeness because they do not receive verbal and nonverbal cues that would be otherwise exchanged in face-to-face communications. The veracity of information exchanged online is suspect, thus forcing online daters to spend more time verifying information from their online counterpart. Once veracity has been established, the lack of a physical presence increases the probability of more intimate disclosures online, leading to the illusion of a close relationship, and, likewise, increases the intensity of the disappointment when a relationship goes wrong (Shafer, 2015). Think: Are these relationships illusionary in closeness or are they just too fast? Emojis are used by generation Z and millennials, and often older adults aren't sure how to use them. This has caused some funny disclosures from all generations and could lead to confusion and misunderstandings. 😉

Self-validation. Another advantage of self-disclosure is that periodically we need ***self-validation***. We sometimes need an assessment from family and friends that we are okay or have done a good job. Sometimes this can be manipulative, by looking for validation that you have done a fantastic job or look good. If we disclose information such as "I think

> *If I expose my nakedness as a person to you, do not make me feel shamed.*
> —JOHN POWELL

> *Long-distance relationships are hard no matter what. When you don't have face-to-face time, it's just different.*
> —VANESSA HUDGENS

I may have made a mistake …" with the hopes of obtaining the listener's agreement, we are seeking validation of our behavior—confirmation of a belief we hold about ourselves. On a deeper level, this sort of self-validating disclosure seeks confirmation of important parts of our self-concept (Adler & Proctor, 2016).

BOUNDARIES

Jillian Roberts, a child/adolescent psychologist and professor of educational psychology, developed a way to explain the concept of boundaries. These include personal boundaries, interactions with others and sexual consent. It is called **Smart Boundaries, Concentric Rings**. Roberts says, "It's always hard to describe this psychological concept so that individuals can wrap their minds around the idea of protecting themselves, so Concentric Rings are a visual representation of the different ways we interact with those around us and the ways we respect ourselves and our fellow human beings.'"

The Self Ring Roberts believes every person has a center, where their true self resides. This core could be called our moral compass and internal boundary; when it gets stretched too far, we can feel it in our "gut." This is why we need to protect ourselves by listening to our gut feelings. This could be when we are with our family and friends or on our own.

The Family Ring represents the bond between people who love one another and will always protect, respect, and nurture one another. In this ring, there is respecting others and insisting on respect from others. Your individual situation determines who is included in this ring, like immediate, extended, or adopted family.

The Community Ring represents the larger community in which we live: friends, classmates, teachers, teams, coaches, even extended family. It includes people seen on a semi-regular basis. Bumping into or breaking rules in the community helps us learn where the community boundaries are. (For some, those lessons must happen quite often before they are remembered.)

The Online Ring is the final ring that encompasses the billions of humans in our global society. In earlier generations, there weren't many ways to interact with the world, and this ring didn't really exist. But today, the Online Ring is extremely important to navigate successfully through, because the social, emotional and sexual connotations online can quickly challenge our boundaries. Know your boundaries! (Roberts, 2019)

Eight Quick Tips for Interpersonal Communication and Relationship Building

When approaching any interaction with another person, try these eight things:

1. Assume the best intentions of the other person. I like the phrase "start new." Trust that they have your best interests at heart.
2. Understand the other person's perspective in the situation.
3. Truly listen and ask questions to learn more.
4. Share your perspective of the situation.
5. Find the commonalities.
6. Leverage those commonalities for the common good.
7. Keep communication open as you move forward (to minimize frustration and to create trust).
8. Speak up if things go awry.

Becoming Aware of how technology impacts your life.

What do you think about being a child of the digital age? Many of your teachers grew up with less technology than you have or maybe not any at all. I expect you have often helped your teachers or parents with technology issues.

The reality of our times is that unless we try hard to communicate face to face with our friends and relatives, technology can dominate our communications. We can be maneuvered by technology, marketing, corporations, society, and media.

Some can say we consume everything, but rarely listen. We are permanently connected to our devices, but rarely to ourselves. That is why we need to practice the human relations techniques discussed in this textbook. We strive to be better versions of ourselves, to be all we can be, but we may never really allow ourselves to savor idle time and just be.

It seems that in this day and age, we are overwhelmed with information and our very own overwhelming choices: to quit or try to change, keep or let go, shop or save, sleep or get up. We have all the tools to be who we are, to look and eat better, but many are more anxious and depressed than ever before.

How much of your attention do you grant to eye contact versus screen contact? Some believe that over the past 40 years, technology has had a major impact on most areas of life. Besides the obvious advantages of being able to share our current plate of food with the rest of the world, technology is literally changing the way we meet, work, travel, research, and do countless other activities.

Technology supports all major aspects of life. The danger that comes with it is the fact that it can be very distracting and occupies a lot of our lives. Having big ideas does not require any technology—their implementation or verification, on the other hand, usually does.

Think about it using Einstein as an example; he came up with the most mind-boggling ideas, yet did not have any access to advanced technology (at least based on current understanding). It took armies of researchers another 100 plus years (and counting) to simulate his ideas. And that's where technology played a crucial part. So, how do we stay curious in today's digital world? The main point is to build a healthy relationship with technology. In the near future (and even in the present), it will be a skill to know **when to use technology** and when to access your very own curiosity. We should not forget that although technology simplifies a lot of work, it does not provide new ideas (yet). That's our job as humans!

From driverless vehicles to algorithms controlling our dating lives to simply Google finishing our sentences, it can seem hard to know where free will and the authentic self are. Some believe that it all started with the dream of machines doing what we can't do, like exploring the heights and the depths of our planet, followed by inviting technology into our daily lives so we can improve what we've been doing for centuries: agriculture, war, art, sports, etc. Today we are seeing competition every step of the way, but this kind of competition comes with a twist: who can do everything faster?

Never have we been so connected yet mobile, having so much information at our disposal. While technology can enhance our lives, it can also paralyze it. There is no doubt about the fact that use of technology can become a very compulsive behavior. It is not about how often we access the digital world, but rather when and why we do so. Always question your intent and understand the cause-effect relationships between the submersion of technology in our daily lives and its impact on being human.

Our society moved into a techno-economic era in the 1990s with the start of the internet, and this caused a shift from a stable and slow-paced world to an unstable and fast-paced world, and also a shift from information scarcity to information abundance according to Rosling & Rosling-Ronnlund (2018). This is called a paradigm shift. It is defined by Merriam-Webster (2019) as an important change that happens when the usual way of thinking about or doing something is replaced by a new and different way. Moving to a more technical world has been a paradigm shift for teachers and parents, too, and as they embrace this new paradigm shift in life and work principles, they will help you feel more at ease in this new world, too.

Now think about it.

While the previous generations used to be taught to aim for stability and status early in their career, it is much more crucial for your generation that believes that technology opens new doors of possibility to look—first—for your purpose. Knowing yourself is essential. This unstable and fast-paced world also requires us to embrace a lifelong learning mentality. With new technology knowledge you are constantly bombarded with information and you need to learn fundamental knowledge, the ability to make sense of information, and the power to speak up. (Anne Loehr 2016)

The Johari Window

The Johari Window was introduced in 1955 and is a classic tool developed by and named after psychologists Joseph Luft and Harrison Ingram in the mid-20th century, and can be looked upon as a communication window through which you become more aware of yourself and your potential as a communicator, as you give and receive information about yourself and others. It is currently used as an easy tool for trainers and educators in business, communication theory, and human relations to discuss who you think you are. In order for a relationship to develop into a quality relationship, there needs to be trust and mutual sharing of information and feelings, also known as *openness*. An *open communicator* is one who is willing to seek feedback from others and to offer information and personal feelings to others. Open communication involves both giving and receiving. According to the Window, a person's communication behavior can be viewed by looking at the size of each of the four windowpanes—Open Area, Hidden Area, Blind Area, and Unknown Area.

Figure 1.1   THE JOHARI WINDOW

	Known to Self	Unknown to Self
Known to Others	Open	Blind
Unknown to Others	Hidden	Unknown

Adapted from Joseph Luft, *Of Human Interaction*, by permission of Mayfield Publishing Co., Copyright 1969 by the National Press.

See Figure 1.1 for the four areas in the Johari Window:

1. The *Open Area*, which represents information you know about yourself that is also known to others.
2. The *Hidden Area*, which represents all that you know about yourself that is private and not known to others. Information in the Hidden area becomes public primarily through self-disclosure.
3. The *Blind Area*, which represents information about yourself that others can see, but you do not. An example would be a mannerism in speech or gesture of which you are unaware but that is quite obvious to others, such as constantly saying "you know" or constantly playing with your keys.
4. The *Unknown Area*, which represents information that is unknown to both you and others. This represents the new things we are all constantly discovering about ourselves: an unrecognized talent, strength, or weakness can develop at any given point in time.

Your Johari Window will look quite different based on the nature of a relationship. For example, in a relationship with your very best friend or your significant other, you will probably have a very large Open area (see Figure 1.2). However, someone you have just recently met will have a very small Open area (see Figure 1.3). As the relationship evolves and you become closer to that person, the Open area will grow, as you share more about yourselves. Likewise, as you listen to comments and feedback from this person, the size of your Blind area will decrease.

Figure 1.2 THE JOHARI WINDOW IN A CLOSE RELATIONSHIP

	Known to Self	Unknown to Self
Known to Others	Open	Blind
Unknown to Others	Hidden	Unknown

Adapted from Joseph Luft, *Of Human Interaction*, by permission of Mayfield Publishing Co., Copyright 1969 by the National Press.

Figure 1.3 THE JOHARI WINDOW EARLY IN A RELATIONSHIP

	Known to Self	Unknown to Self
Known to Others	Open	Blind
Unknown to Others	Hidden	Unknown

Adapted from Joseph Luft, *Of Human Interaction*, by permission of Mayfield Publishing Co., Copyright 1969 by the National Press.

The Johari Window *is a simple and useful tool for understanding yourself and others* in a variety of contexts:

- self-awareness
- personal development
- improving communications
- interpersonal relationships
- group dynamics

- team development; and
- intergroup relationships.

The Johari window and other similar tools are great for Human Relations professionals because they have has an emphasis on "soft skills" such as behavior, empathy, and cooperation; inter-group development; and interpersonal development. It's a great model to use because of its simplicity and also because it can be applied in a variety of situations and environments. Involve other people and ask for feedback about yourself. Be prepared to seriously consider the feedback. That doesn't mean that you have to do everything that's suggested, but you should at least listen and think about it. Then give the person who provided the feedback some acknowledgement or thanks for making the effort. Depending on how confident you are, you might prefer to do this as either a group exercise or on a one-to-one basis. Remember that giving effective feedback is a skill, and some people may be better at it than others. When receiving feedback, be respectful, listen, and reflect on what has been said. It may be that, upon receiving feedback, you may want to explore the issue further, and that can lead to discovery about yourself.

The Johari Window as a tool can help to reveal these types of issues:

- Some things are perhaps better not communicated with others.
- People may pass on the information they received further than you desire or use it in a negative way.
- Some people or cultures have a very open and accepting approach to feedback, and some do not. People can take personal feedback offensively, so it's important when facilitating to exercise caution and start gradually.

Johari is a classic model, and, as with other powerful ideas, simply helping people to understand is the most effective way to optimize its value to people. When people really understand it in their own terms, it empowers them to use the thinking in their own way, and to incorporate the underlying principles into their future thinking and behavior.

Now think about it.

There are various ways you can use a Johari Window to evaluate your relationships and increase your self-knowledge. Think about your interactions with family, friends, people at work, school, etc. Generally, your strongest and closest relationships have a very large Open area because being open with the other person and listening to feedback builds trust. You will have an opportunity to draw several Johari Windows at the end of this chapter.

Now, think about a particular person with whom you interact: Is it possible that you keep many parts of yourself hidden from this person? Why are you doing this, and is it healthy for the relationship?

How open are you with people at work, school, acquaintances, friends, your nearest neighbors, and even family members?

In order to reduce the size of the Blind area and the Unknown area in some of your relationships, are there any individuals you may need to ask for, and be open to receive from, some honest feedback?

Are there any modifications you need to make in any of your relationships to increase your overall effectiveness?

We need to understand why relationships are important. We are all social beings and seek social relationships. We all have a need for other people. Relationships satisfy needs. We are motivated not only to seek the company of others, but also to form close and lasting relationships. Many people have difficulty forming relationships and do not seem to have any friends. What happens to these people?

Building Intimate Relationships

According to Daniel and Lynch (2000) there are many kinds of relationships, and a given kind may fit a given person at one stage of development but not at another. Driven by our personal history, we choose partners/spouses who help us meet our present needs, fulfill our expectations, and, if we're lucky, work through our issues and grow in the directions in which we need to grow. For a person or couple, recognizing these can open doors to a broader spectrum of ways of being with ourselves and each other.

Five Dominant Patterns of Couples Relationships

Daniel and Lynch (2000) found that there are **Five Dominant Patterns of Relationships**. Sharpening and deepening our awareness of we're doing, and how we're doing it, can help us change our behavior in ways that make a relationship more nourishing and supportive, and less toxic and painful, or it can help us see what we're not going to find in a relationship. In either case, a clearer perception of our present reality can help us move toward doing a better job of meeting our own needs and the needs of others.

1. **Survival Relationships.** These exist when partners feel like they can't make it on their own. In this type of situation, the choice of a partner tends to be undiscriminating, made out of emotional starvation—almost anyone available will do. This involves relating at its most basic: "Without you I am nothing; with you I am something." Often partners think in terms of what the other person wants them to want, and are out of touch with what they themselves want. They may have little tolerance for independence and aloneness, and "go everywhere together and do everything together."

2. **Validation Relationships**. A person may seek another's validation of his or her physical attractiveness, intellect, social status, sexuality, wealth, or some other attribute. Many teenagers and young adults who are looking for a sense of identity form relationships based on physical or sexual validation. If no deeper basis for connection materializes and the partners drift apart, there is a strong chance

that the needs for validation have been met and the partners have begun seeking something different. And the relationship is over. The partners have learned to validate in themselves the qualities they were insecure about and they are ready to connect along other dimensions.

3. **Scripted Relationships.** This common pattern often begins when the partners both are just out of high school or college. They seem to be "the perfect pair," fitting almost all the external criteria of what an appropriate mate should be like. They often marry, living out their traditional expectations for the sex roles they learned they were supposed to play. He has the "right" kind of job and she is the "right" kind of wife, and they have the "right" kind of house or apartment or condo in the "right" place. Partners in these relationships need to look at all the things they've wanted to do in life but haven't, because these things didn't fit their stereotypes about themselves and their expectations about their partners. They need to learn to communicate at an emotional level, to disclose their feelings and listen to those of their partner. They may need to learn to work less and play more.

4. **Acceptance Relationships**. This is what many of us thought we were getting into when we entered a relationship, including many people in the three categories above. In an acceptance relationship we trust, support, and enjoy each other. And within broad limits, we are ourselves.

5. **Individuation-Assertion Relationships.** These relationships are based on the assertion of each person's wants and needs, and on respect for the other person's process of personal growth. Often they are focused on partners' struggles with what is missing or lacking in terms of self-discovery, becoming whole, and developing their potentialities. They require each person's acknowledgment and appreciation of their differences.

For some couples in other forms of relationships, it's easier to move into an acceptance relationship, while for others it's easier to move into an individuation-assertion relationship. In a scripted relationship where partners have very different interests but genuinely care for each other, loosening the role expectations and creating space for each person to follow his or her own pursuits is one way to step out of chronic power struggles.

Living Alone. The experience of living alone deserves a few words in the context of relationships. The reasons people live alone include:

- First, some processes are "loner" processes, such as grieving, or exploring oneself in a variety of contexts with a variety of people.
- Second, people may keep their distance from others because of fears and insecurities. Some kind of counseling or therapy is often appropriate here.
- Third, they may keep their distance because of a desire to learn to stand alone and be independent, or to work through issues which caused trouble in a past relationship before moving into a new one.
- Fourth, a person may be available, but face a supply-and-demand inequality of acceptable partners. In this case, a network of supportive friends can be invaluable.
- Finally, someone may be fulfilled enough on his or her own and feel no strong need for a partner. Some highly creative artists fall into this category. A network of supportive friends can be valuable.

FOCUS ON DIVERSITY

PUT YOURSELF IN SOMEONE'S SHOES: A DIVERSITY THOUGHT

My mother would always remind me, "Put yourself in the other person's shoes. Don't think you know how they feel and what they have to go through daily." We have added to this text a number of concepts and ideas that you may not believe in or agree with. They include sensitive ethnic, cultural, and gender issues. It is so important to consider different sides of an issue in a contemplative, analytical way. Our world needs more people to feel open to others and meet new people who are not like them. This is the only way we will end the racial and gender turmoil, such as violence against women. Unless we can educate ourselves about others, be aware of information about sociocultural issues from more than one perspective, develop relationships, and "walk in another's shoes," we will not be truly educated.

Loneliness

Have you ever felt lonely? What causes loneliness? Answer the questions on the following page before you continue to read this section.

Most people experience occasional loneliness, and it's an especially common experience among people who find themselves in an unfamiliar environment with a completely new social scene. Loneliness isn't necessarily about being alone—we can be surrounded by people and still feel alone. It's the *feeling* of being alone that counts, along with feeling empty, unwanted, or isolated. The lack of relationships can create loneliness.

Loneliness occurs when a person has fewer interpersonal relationships than desired or when the relationships are not as satisfying as desired. Loneliness is one of the most serious problems in our society today, "Loneliness isn't a feeling to be ashamed of, but simply a way for your body to tell you that you need more connections, just like hunger means you need food," says Shasta Nelson, founder of Girlfriend Circles.com, a women's friendship matching site, and author of *Frientimacy: How to Deepen Friendships for Lifelong Health and Happiness (2016).* Research shows that when a person reports feeling lonely, their close family and friends are 52 percent more likely to say they're lonely too, and others can "catch" loneliness up to three degrees of separation (i.e., your friend's friend's friend), according to a study in the *Journal of Personality and Social Psychology.*

Loneliness is complex and usually unpleasant. Loneliness typically includes anxious feelings about a lack of interpersonal connection with other beings, both in the present and extending into the future. Loneliness can be felt even when surrounded by other people, and one who feels lonely, *is* lonely. The causes of loneliness are varied and include social, mental, emotional, and physical factors. Among other findings, loneliness was also linked to smoking, being less physically active, compulsive use of digital technology, having low qualifications, and being less likely to talk about problems with others, although it was not related to job hunting efforts (Davis, 2018).

Research has shown that loneliness is prevalent throughout society, including in people in marriages and relationships, in families, in veterans, and in those with successful careers (Cacioppo & Patrick 2008). Social isolation is a state of complete or near-complete lack of contact between an individual and temporary and involuntary lack of contact with other humans in the world. Social isolation can be an issue for individuals of any age, though symptoms may differ by age group (Pittman & Reich, 2016).

Loneliness is **not** something that happens only when we are physically alone. It can also happen when we are with people. Online friends, followers, or "likers" don't necessarily add up to much when you crave fulfilling interaction, and satisfying, long-term relationships are not a mystery to be left up to chance (or technology). The good news is that, according to relationship coach Kira Asatryan, loneliness has a reliable antidote: the feeling of closeness. We can and should cultivate closeness in our relationships using the steps outlined in this book: knowing, caring, and mastering closeness.

> *Connected, but alone?*
> *https://www.ted.com/talks/sherry_turkle_connected_but_alone/transcript?language=en*
>
> *Sherrie Turkle describes how, in this age of near-constant digital "connection," loneliness is a challenge that faces us all.*

If you're feeling lonely, try taking Turkle's advice and start a conversation with someone. School is a great place to meet new people and develop new and interesting relationships. Others in school are new, just like you, and will welcome the chance to connect with and get to know another classmate. Try joining a campus interest group or club, play a team sport, or just ask another student if they'd like to meet for coffee or to study. If feelings of loneliness persist, and especially if you also feel depressed, you should get help from a counselor or health services.

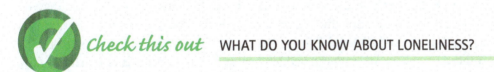 **Check this out** WHAT DO YOU KNOW ABOUT LONELINESS?

TRUE OR FALSE?
_____ Loneliness is more predominant during adolescence.
_____ Loneliness varies with the time of day and day of the week.
_____ Loneliness may be a sign of personal problems.
_____ Loneliness may be the cause of depression, suicide, and other mental disorders.
_____ The elderly are less lonely than most groups of individuals.
_____ Loneliness is not the same as aloneness.
_____ Most people assume other people have more friends than they do.

Based on research and literature, all of the above statements are mostly true, and we will address them in the following information.

The truth is that between two-thirds and three-fourths of Americans believe there is more loneliness in today's society than there used to be, report dissatisfaction in their current friendships, and feel they have fewer meaningful relationships than they did five years ago. Another statistic comes from a study, published in the *American Sociological Review*, that looked at two decades of social isolation in the United States. To the question of how many confidants one has, in 1994 the common answer was two to three confidants; as of 2004 the answer was closer to zero (Nelson, 2016). Much more than half of the world's populations are chronically depressed or lonely, and everyone will experience some type of depression at some point in their lives. But the good news is you don't have to go it alone (Creole, 2016).

> *Maybe the biggest problem with loneliness is that we walk around thinking we are the only ones suffering from it.*
> —JEANNE MARIE LASKAS

You can learn strategies to alleviate the symptoms of depression and loneliness. Talk to your medical doctor about these feelings and they can decide if you need a counselor, a support group, or maybe medication. With so many people in the world who are depressed and taking antidepressants, there is no shame. Another treatment for both loneliness and depression is pet therapy, or animal-assisted therapy, as it is more formally known. While pets as companions have been popular for hundreds, if not thousands of years, an Emotional Support Animal is a fairly new concept. An emotional support animal is a pet that has been "prescribed" by a psychologist, psychiatrist, or therapist to a patient as part of their plan toward wellness. The aim is to provide comfort to the patient, and something positive for them to focus on. The overall goal is that the animal will provide emotional support for patients during times of need, when they may not have any nearby friends or family to rely on (2019, https://esadoctors.com/emotional-support-animal-anxiety/). Studies and surveys, as well as anecdotal evidence provided by volunteer and community organizations, indicate that the presence of animal companions such as dogs, cats, rabbits, and guinea pigs can ease feelings of depression and loneliness among some sufferers. Beyond the companionship the animal itself provides, there may also be increased opportunities for socializing with other pet owners. Many university classes will allow service animals or emotional support animals with proper paperwork in the classroom to give support and ease anxiety for their owners.

Can people be lonely in the presence of others? The answer is a resounding **yes**, and the feeling can be dreadful. Mara commented, "You can be in the center of a crowd and be dreadfully lonely." Some people can feel lonely even when surrounded by others. Debbi, whose husband had left her, said, "I have periods of loneliness now, but it's nothing compared to how lonely I felt when my husband was sitting in the same room with me." Being married offers no protection from the dangers of loneliness: Studies indicate that roughly 20% of the general population suffers from chronic loneliness at any given time, and in one recent study of older adults, 62.5% of people who reported being lonely were married and living with their partner. In addition to the emotional anguish loneliness creates, it also has devastating effects on our mental and physical health. Loneliness depresses our immune system functioning, increases inflammatory responses that put us at greater risk for cardiovascular disease, and can literally shorten our longevity. On the mental health front, loneliness puts us at risk for depression and anxiety and causes us to distort our perceptions such that we view ourselves, our lives, and our relationships more negatively, which in turn influences our behavior in damaging ways (Winch, 2013).

Becoming Aware of Loneliness: A video game that helps us understand loneliness

https://www.ted.com/talks/cornelia_geppert_a_video_game_that_helps_us_understand_loneliness

Step into artist Cornelia Geppert's visually stunning video game "Sea of Solitude," which explores how battling the "monsters" of loneliness and self-doubt can help us better grapple with the complexity and struggles of mental health.

Being lonely is not the same as being alone. Some people prefer solitude and are content with fewer social interactions. Many of us have a need to be alone at times in order to maintain our mental health. Loneliness is a highly subjective and personal feeling. Guy Winch in his article "Together But Lonely" (sometimes referred to as Living Together Lonely LTL) offers three strategies to overcome loneliness. The first is to take the initiative and ask your partner about something they care about, and really listen to what they say. The second is to try to make shared memories. You might try certain activities that require little effort, like a walk in the neighborhood. And lastly, try to take their perspective. Often couples who have been together a while assume they know what the other is thinking (Winch, 2013).

Who is lonelier? Loneliness is found in all groups. Loneliness is most prevalent among teenagers, unmarried young adults, the divorced, and the widowed. Adult learners are among thousands of peers who suffer more loneliness than any other group (Wiseman et al., 2006). Though we may know a lot of people, that doesn't mean we feel we have meaningful connections. But if we don't acknowledge our need—and admit that we lack meaningful connections, that we feel disconnected—we limit our chances of getting our needs met. In other words, if we don't identify the problem, we can't do anything about it. To admit we wish for more meaningful friendships is the first step to inviting us to then ask the all-important question, "What could I do to develop more fulfilling relationships in my life?" (Nelson, 2016). Everyone needs a confidant. A **confidant** is a person with whom one can share problems and worries and who gives one feelings of being understood and accepted (Wills & Ainette, 2012).

 Check this out

Students in Dr. Janna Martin's University of Oklahoma Human Relations classes decided to make buddy benches for a few of the neighboring elementary schools to promote good human relations skills.

The Friendship Bench is a tool for positive mental and emotional health used in various settings. In a school setting it may also be known as a "buddy bench," and is a special place in a school playground where a child can go when they want someone to talk to. So if you see someone sitting alone, please join them and make a new friend.

Preventing and reducing loneliness is crucial to well-being and good health. Social relationships protect people against loneliness. Friendship qualities like intimacy and frequency of contact may vary throughout a person's lifespan (Nicolaisen & Thorsen, 2016).

Loneliness makes a person vulnerable to unhealthy different situations. These may include more depression, use of drugs as an escape, and higher blood pressure. There is even some evidence that points to loneliness being associated with higher risks for heart disease, lessened longevity, and increased risk for recurrent illness (Hafen et al., 2005).

Weiss and Schneider also found that making new connections impacts not only society as a whole, but also more specifically communication in relationships and across generations (2014).

Zhou, Sedikides, Wildschut, and Gao (2008) found that we can counteract loneliness with nostalgia by increasing perceived social support similar to what we had in our early years. Think about how music from when you were young makes you feel, or play music for your parents or grandparents from their high school or college years and see if it lifts their spirits. Renowned scientists Christakis and Fowler present compelling evidence for our profound influence on one another's tastes, health, wealth, happiness, beliefs, and overcoming loneliness, as they explain how social networks form and how they operate (2009).

Becoming Aware of Loneliness: How to get rid of loneliness and become happy
https://youtube.com/watch?v=vZT-bB66iIk

Olivia Remes share her insights on loneliness and how to beat it.

What Should a Relationship Provide?

Once a friendship is established through **self-disclosure and reciprocity**, the glue that binds is **intimacy**. According to Beverly Fehr's research, people in successful same-sex friendships seem to possess a well-developed, intuitive understanding of the give and take of intimacy (2008). "Those who know what to say in response to another person's self-disclosure are more likely to develop satisfying friendships," Fehr says (2008). Hefty helpings of emotional expressiveness and unconditional support are ingredients here, followed by acceptance, loyalty, and trust. Our friends are there for us through thick and thin, but rarely cross the line: A friend with too many opinions about our wardrobe, our partner, or our taste in movies and art may not be a friend for long (Karbo, 2016).

Why do our society and many other cultures put so much emphasis on marriage? Why are there clubs for single people, escort services, singles bars, dating services, and social networking websites, people advertising for partners in local newspapers, and using 1-900 telephone services to meet new people? Why—because people are lonely.

Friendship
Voluntary personal relationship typically providing intimacy and assistance, in which the two parties like each another and seek each other's company.
–BEVERLY FEHR, 2006

Relationships with others lie at the very core of human existence.
—ELLEN BERSCHEID AND LETTIA PEPLAU

We have a strong need for relationships. The following needs must be satisfied in order to have a fulfilling life and overcome feelings of loneliness.

Emotional attachments. We all need to know that no matter what the situation is or whatever we do, good or bad, there will be someone around to take care of us or help us out. As long as we know this, we feel comfortable and secure. A child who knows that their mother or father is available whenever they need one of them will feel secure enough to explore the world around them. They will be willing to take some chances and risks in life. A child who is insecure and not sure if the parents will be available when needed will be clinging and unsure of other people. How would you feel if you were told by your parents, "If you ever get in trouble with the law," or "If I ever hear about you taking drugs," or "If you ever get someone pregnant or get pregnant, don't step a foot back in this house?" Most people who have been told this when they were young feel very insecure and lonely, since they are not sure anyone will be there for them in a time of need.

Where do we get emotional attachments? Most people will receive their emotional attachments from their parents and pets, especially during their early years of development. And if you think about it, many individuals continue to rely on their parents for this support for most of their lives. This is why you will hear stories about married couples who, when they are having marital problems, will go back to their parents' home, because parents still provide that individual with the feeling of security. As we tend to mature and start to detatch from our environments, becoming more independent, we begin to find this emotional support from others—our best friend, boyfriend, girlfriend, spouse, pastor, etc. For some people, their dog or cat will provide them with this feeling of security.

People and animals have a long history of living together and bonding. Perhaps the oldest evidence of this special relationship was discovered on a dig in Eynan in 1978, by Simon J.M. Davis and Francois Valla. They found evidence dating back 12,000 years that a human skeleton had been buried with the hand resting on the skeleton of a 6-month-old wolf pup. "The bond between animals and humans is part of our evolution, and it's very powerful," says Dr. Ann Berger, a physician and researcher at the NIH Clinical Center in Bethesda, Maryland. Today animal companions are more popular than ever. The pet population nationwide has been growing dramatically for nearly a half century, from about 40 million pet cats and dogs in 1967 to more than 160 million in 2006. About two-thirds of U.S. households now own at least one pet (NIH, 2016).

Inanimate objects can also be a source of security. Items such as teddy bears, dolls, or imaginary companions are examples. Other sources could be certain belief systems, religious beliefs, or a philosophy of life. Even confidence within one's self may satisfy the need for emotional attachments for some people. A young child's blanket or teddy bear may be a source of security; if you take the blanket or bear away from some children even for a short time, to be washed, the child may go into a rage and become very insecure and lonely.

What happens to a person who has been relying solely on their spouse for the satisfaction of this need, especially when the spouse announces that the relationship is over? This person will become insecure, lonely, and vulnerable. A newly divorced or separated individual who has lost his or her emotional support is very open and vulnerable to another person or belief system that tends to show support for the individual. This is why many individuals can find themselves in a negative relationship, sometimes with a cult, or gang that purports to provide emotional support.

Social ties. *Social ties* provide us with the feeling of belonging—a feeling that we are part of a group and have an identity. During early childhood this feeling of belonging and developing an identity is, for most children, provided by their parents. This is expressed with statements like, "I'm a member of the Smith family or Adams family or Sanchez family." Later in childhood, the peer group becomes more important to them than the family, especially during adolescence. Social ties can also be within the community, such as social groups, religious affiliations, or even neighborhood gangs. Just having a small group of friends that we know from the neighborhood or school we attend helps us to have that feeling of belonging. We all need an identity, and we can have many identities.

How does the person feel who is not able to join a club or be a member of a team? This person feels "left out" and feels that there is something missing in their life. They will do whatever it takes to satisfy this need. The end result of not having this need satisfied is the same as for those whose emotional attachment needs are not satisfied. This person will feel lonely, depressed, and vulnerable.

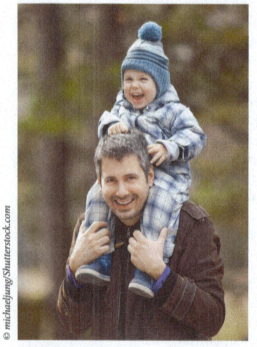

Who provides you with a feeling of belonging?

How can we satisfy this need? *Social ties* may be satisfied through positive as well as negative means, including marriage—a legal bond that makes you feel like you belong to a family and have a recognized identity. A person's job or career may also give some people a feeling of identity and belonging. Ask a person the question, "Who are you?" and the response is generally, "I'm a student, a banker, a plumber, a salesperson, an attorney," etc. These titles give the individual an identity, and the organization the person works for gives the person a feeling of belonging.

During the high school and college years, a person's identity may be found in many different ways. Some students find their identity by being on an athletic team, by being an excellent student, playing in the band or orchestra, dating a cheerleader, being in a sorority or fraternity, or just working a job to pay the bills. If a student does not find their identity or feeling of belonging through "normal" or acceptable means, they will attempt to satisfy this need through other means, such as drugs, non-traditional clothing, a unique hairstyle, promiscuous behavior, gang activity, or delinquent behavior; or some people delve into the Internet or social media, which can narrow their world. Remember we can have many identities.

© michaeljung/Shutterstock.com

MUTUAL REWARD THEORY (MRT)

The Mutual Reward Theory (MRT) states that a relationship between two people is enhanced when there is a satisfactory balance of rewards between them (O'Neil & Chapman, 2008). Actually, if any meaningful relationship is to remain healthy over a long period of time, the individuals involved must benefit from the relationship. The more equally the rewards balance out, the stronger and more permanent the relationship becomes. The relationship will quickly weaken if one individual suddenly realizes that they have been contributing significantly more than they have been receiving.

The discussion of emotional support and social ties should demonstrate to all of us that we should not rely only on one person or one source for the satisfaction of our emotional and social needs. We all need to work at developing a good support system. Yet, is there anything we can do to enhance our personal, meaningful relationships?

Emotional support and social ties are not only important to young people; they are vital to all of us and will continue to be important throughout our lives. We will be in a constant state of stress and anxiety if our emotional support and social ties change too much. Divorce, death of a loved one, changing jobs or being fired from a job, retirement, breaking up with a boyfriend or girlfriend, or a serious illness may be the cause of our needs changing. People with adequate social support are also less likely to suffer from depression, anxiety, and numerous physical problems. And, in a four-year study of 823 people, Dr. Robert Wilson (2007), senior neuropsychologist, Rush University Medical Center, reported that seniors who feel disconnected from other people are twice as likely to develop an Alzheimer's-like form of dementia as those who are not lonely.

Now that we understand the need for relationships, many of us still find it difficult to get to know other people and develop good relationships. Why do we fear getting acquainted?

> *You can make more friends in two months by being interested in other people than you can in two years trying to get others interested in you.*
> —ZIG ZIGLAR

Becoming Aware of Jung: Introduction to Carl Jung—Individuation, the Persona, the Shadow, and the Self
https://www.youtube.com/watch?v=uhAeXyVDDTc

An introduction to Carl Jung's philosophy from the Academy of Ideas.

How to control shyness and not let it control you!

Meeting people and forming relationships should be fun, but for a lot of people it is a difficult process full of stress and anxiety. "It seems so easy for other people, but for me, it's one of the most difficult things I do in life." Because of the complexity of our society, we have made getting acquainted and developing relationships an involved process. "How can I make meeting people and forming relationships more fun and less stressful? Why do I feel so uncomfortable meeting people?" Shyness is a descriptor of how you feel in a situation, and not a negative personality trait. Shyness is something that can be controlled. Remember shy people are slow to warm up and want to be around people; an an introvert often does not want to be there.

WHAT IS SHYNESS?

Am I shy? How did you answer the above questions? If your answer to any of the questions is that you feel uncomfortable, anxious, inhibited, and excessively cautious, then you showed signs of *shyness*. Shyness is universal. Nearly one of two Americans say they are shy. In addition the incidence seems to be rising, and the use of technology may be turning our society into a culture of shy people (Carducci & Zimbardo, 2016). It affects young and old, men and women, celebrities and people like you and me. It is a very common condition. The consequences of shyness can be devastating. If you mistake having alone time for shyness, remember that everyone needs alone time, but some need more of it.

What is shyness? The APA Encyclopedia of Psychology (2019) says shyness is the tendency to feel awkward, worried, or tense during social encounters, especially with unfamiliar people. Severely shy people may have physical symptoms like blushing, sweating, a pounding heart, or upset stomach; negative feelings about themselves; worries about how others view them; and a tendency to withdraw from social interactions.

Most people feel shy at least occasionally. Some people's shyness is so intense, however, that it can keep them from interacting with others even when they want or need to—leading to problems in relationships and at work.

Stein and Walker (2009) believe many people are not happy being shy because they find it prevents them from expressing themselves, making friends and enjoying themselves to the fullest. Shyness can be like a cocoon which is warm and safe but it can be confining and lonely. It is a normal personality trait. That means everyone has that trait, some just more than others. It is inherited from your genes, but it is not influenced only by your genes, but by choices you make.

Social anxiety is closely affiliated with but not identical to shyness. Anxiety is an uncomfortable internal state usually associated by the unknown. Anxiety is an emotion, and it is a lot like fear. Anxiety is wondering what bad could happen, not that it will, but you wonder if it will (2009).

How common is shyness? Researcher Dr. Bernardo Carducci (2000), in his popular book *Shyness: A Bold New Approach*, makes it very clear that between 75 and 95% of people have felt shy at one point in their lives. In fact, Dr. Carducci has compiled the following statistics on the pervasiveness of shyness:

- About 80% of American college students report they have been shy at some point in their lives.
- Almost 50% of our population says that they're shy.
- About 89% of shy people claim that they've been shy all their lives.

- Of people who are not shy now, 75% have been shy at some point in the past.
- Only 11% of our population claims that they are not shy now and have never been shy in the past.
- About 21% of shy people feel shy daily or almost daily, while almost 60% of the people say that they're shy feel shy at least once a week.
- About 78% of shy people believe that they can overcome shyness, while 3% say that they cannot.

Dr. Carducci also comments that the three most common shyness-provoking situations are: 1) being around strangers, 2) the presence of people in positions of authority by virtue of their role or knowledge, and 3) being with potentially romantic partners, either one-on-one or in a group (2000).

Shyness refers to a tendency to withdraw from people, particularly unfamiliar people. Shyness involves *feelings, physical reactions,* and *thoughts* that create a state of anxiety, discomfort, and inhibition. Extremely shy individuals are typically low in self-esteem and largely preoccupied with what others think of them. Driven by a fear of rejection, shy people often engage in self-sabotage to prevent themselves from growing closer to others and avoid social situations when possible (Stein & Walker, 2009).

What are the consequences of intensive shyness? Feelings of shyness can start very early. Shy children are at greater risk of being bullied and rejected by their peers. Those friendships they do succeed in making are often of lower quality than the friendships made by children who are less shy. Shy children are more likely to internalize problems such as depression, anxiety, and loneliness. Gender identity or uncertainty of gender issues can contribute to shyness. There are also gender differences, with shy boys being more likely to have socio-emotional difficulties than shy girls. This is probably due to shyness being less socially acceptable for boys than for girls, since boys are expected to be more dominant and self-confident (Vitelli, 2013). For some people shyness may become a "mental handicap" that is as crippling as the most severe of physical handicaps. Its consequences can be devastating. What are the consequences of shyness?

1. *Shy people can become preoccupied with themselves and thus become self-conscious.* Because of this, they are not aware of other people's feelings and needs.
2.. *Shyness can make it difficult for us to become acquainted with new people and thus make new friends.*
3. *Shyness can keep us from experiencing new situations.* This could affect our career prospects or higher education. Shy young adults are also less likely to date, get married later (if at all), and are less likely to enter into stable relationships. Through different relationships, most young adults learn what they are looking for in a permanent partner and also become more experienced in handling a stable relationship. When shy people who do not gain these experiences, their ability to form permanent intimate relationships later in life may be impaired.

Something to Think About

REFLECT ON HOW YOU FEEL IN THE FOLLOWING SITUATIONS:

- Meeting people for the first time.
- Asking someone for a date.
- Giving a talk in front of a group of people.
- Going to a party or going to a dance or nightclub.
- Asking someone for help—for example, your boss or professor.
- Being interviewed or participating in a discussion group.
- Situations requiring assertiveness—for example, asking for your money back.
- Showing your body in a nonsexual context.
- Are you slow to warm up to people (possibly shy)?
- Do you want to be there or not want to be there (possibly an introvert)?
- Shyness is universal.

4. *Shyness can prevent people from standing up for their own rights and as individual; it can keep them from expressing their own feelings and beliefs.*

5. *Shy people tend not to demonstrate their personal strengths capabilities. As a result, they often prevent others from making positive evaluations. If you have two employees, equal in all abilities except that one is shy and the other is not shy, which of the two would you promote? In most situations the non-shy person would be promoted because we are more aware of his or her potential than that of the shy person.*

6. *Some people are not really shy— shyness is about more about feelings than behavior, and they may be presenting respect from their culture or they might need time to know you before they interact* Zimbardo (1990); Carducci & Zimbardo (2015); Duffy (2007/2008); Henderson, Lynne & Zimbardo, Phil. (2010); Vitelli (2013).

> *Shyness is a series of choices that gradually cement into a lifestyle.*
> —BERNARDO CARDUCCI

What is the difference between a shy and non-shy person? It may surprise many of you to learn that the major difference between the two is a matter of *self-evaluation*. How do you compare yourself to others? Do you see yourself as capable, intelligent, or as attractive as the person next to you? If the answer is no, then would you interact with them? Or, if you did have to interact with them, how would you feel? Would you feel inferior or inadequate? Many people would feel this way. Why? The shy person is more likely to feel inferior comparing themselves to others. The not-shy person is more likely to have a positive self-evaluation. This reveals that shyness is often connected to illusion; there is no objective reason to see oneself as "better" or "worse" than another. One person may have formal education and no common sense, while the other is practical and self-taught; everyone brings gifts.

Over the past 30 years, estimates of the prevalence of SAD (Social Anxiety Disorder) in the general population have increased from 2% to over 12%, with 26% of women and 19% of men reporting they were "very shy" growing up. The highest levels of shyness in the US samples were also found among Asian Americans, while Jewish Americans were typically least shy. Culturally based self-definitions mediate social anxiety, and particular self construal are related to particular types of social anxiety. Treatments for shyness, social anxiety, and SAD generally include cognitive restructuring, social skills training, and role-plays of threatening situations (Henderson, Lynne & Zimbardo, Phil,. 2010).

Technology and shyness. Technology is continually redefining how we communicate. We no longer engage in as many face-to-face interactions on a daily basis as we once did. How often do you call a friend or colleague when you know they are not in so you can leave a message on their machine? How often do you see a bank teller or gas station attendant? Voice mail, faxes, banking online, text messaging, and email give us an illusion of being "in touch," but what is to touch but the keyboard or keypad?

Today's teens and college students are what researchers call "digital natives," or the "iGeneration," a generation constantly connected to the Internet and social media, texting, and instant messaging. Certainly, there are both positive and negative effects of social networks. However, research by Larry Rosen (2011), a social media researcher at California State University, indicates that online social networking can give shy people an easier experience building relationships, by connecting through media instead of in person. Technology has made us time-efficient and redefined our sense of time and its value. It is not to be wasted, but to be used quickly and with a purpose. As a result encounters have become barren of personal social interaction. They are information-driven, problem-oriented, and solution-based. No pleasantries. No backs slapped. We cut to the chase: I need this from you. Says Zimbardo, "You have to have an agenda." Some people don't work at the office at all; they telecommute and have less personal contact (2016).

Carducci and Zimbardo also state "that the dwindling opportunities for face-to-face interaction put shy people at an increasing disadvantage. They no longer get to practice social skills within the comfort of daily routine" (2016, pg 7). Dropping by a colleague's office to chat becomes increasingly awkward as you do it less and less. Social life has shrunk so much it can now be entirely encapsulated in a single, near-pejorative

FOCUS ON DIVERSITY

DEFINING GENERATIONS: WHERE MILLENNIALS END AND GENERATION Z BEGINS

The generations defined- where do you fit in?
https://www.pewresearch.org/fact-tank/2019/01/17/where-millennials-end-and-generation-z-begins/ft_19-01-17_generations_2019/

phrase: "face time," denoting the time employees may engage in eye-to-eye conversation. Electronic, hand-held video devices, used alone and played solo, now crowd out the time-honored social games of childhood. "Even electronically simulated social interactions can't substitute—they do not permit people to learn the necessary give and take that is at the heart of all interpersonal relationships" (2016, pg 7).

If technology is ushering in a culture of shyness, it is also the perfect medium for the shy. The Internet is a conduit for the shy to interact with others; electronic communication removes many of the barriers that inhibit the shy. You prepare what you want to say. Nobody knows what you look like. The danger, however, is that technology will become a hiding place for those who dread social interaction. The first generation to go from cradle to grave with in-home computers, faxes, and the Internet is entering adulthood. We are just beginning to accurately assess shyness in the wake of the new electronic age. In order to do a serious study, we must find a group of infants—shy and not-shy—and follow them through their life, as well as observe different people, from different generations, in different periods of their lives. Only then will we see the course of shyness over a lifetime (Carducci & Zimbardo, 2016).

What causes shyness? There is no one cause of shyness. Many diverse causes include brain chemistry and reactivity (inborn temperament), harsh treatment from teachers or classmates, overprotective parents, faulty self-perceptions, poor adaptability, intolerance for ambiguity, physical appearance, life transitions (such as going to school, divorce, a new job), and even cultural expectations. Furthermore, some people are simply more sensitive about their behavior and are more easily embarrassed than others (Carducci, (2019); Casriel, 2007). According to Vitelli, research into shyness has suggested different causes including genetic influences, prenatal influences, environmental factors (including the effects of emotional abuse in childhood), or the result of a traumatic social episode. While usually not severe enough to merit a diagnosis of social phobia or social anxiety, shyness can have a powerful effect on a person's sense of well-being along with being linked to depression or other emotional problems due to isolation (2013). Research is ongoing between many cultures, and whether different cultures accept shyness and parent children to be shy (Gudino and Lau, 2010). Something to think about is why many people think shyness is a trait that is not wanted. Consider shyness in different cultures. In some cultures being reserved is proper, but in other cultures it can be thought of as "being stuck-up". In the business world in

America you are urged to "work" the crowd, and meet new people. Being shy might lose you business. Personal issues like uncertainty in gender identification can contribute to shyness because of uncomfortable situations or bullies. Remember shyness is not a negative personality trait or a character flaw. It is a description.

Overcoming shyness. How can a person overcome shyness? It would be naive to pretend that shyness can be overcome easily. It is important, however, to emphasize that with time and intention, shyness can be overcome successfully. There are three steps in the process of dealing with shyness (Carducci, 2016, Zimbardo, 2018; Pelusi, 2007). These steps are: 1) analyzing shyness, 2) building self-esteem, and 3) improving social skills.

Analyzing Shyness

- Try to pinpoint exactly what social situations tend to elicit feelings. Or do you appear shy because of cultural expectations? Some Asian or Native American cultures have cultural expectations that might appear like shyness.
- Try to identify what causes your shyness in that situation. Use a diary or journal to keep track of the times you experience this feeling.
- Have a friend or relative give you feedback. Discuss how you interact with others and how you can improve.

Building Self-Esteem

- Learn to take compliments.
- Recognize that you ultimately control how you see yourself.
- Eliminate self-criticism and introduce self-compassion.
- Set your own standards. Do not let others tell you how to live your life. Identify your competencies and develop them.
- Set realistic goals. Do not set your goals too high or too low. Many people demand too much of themselves.
- Talk positively to yourself. Tell yourself that you can do it and that you are a good person.
- Use affirmations that are achievable, like "I am going to persevere until I succeed!"
- Affirm your real worth.
- Learn to take rejection. Rejection is one of the risks everyone takes in social interactions. Try not to take it personally; it may have nothing to do with you.

Improving Social Skills

- Follow a role model. Select someone you respect and observe how they interact. Imitate their behavior.
- Learn to listen.
- Talk to one new person every day about something.
- Volunteer at a place of interest to you.
- Reinforce yourself for each successful interaction.
- Use your imagination. Rehearse in your mind new situations and how you will respond.
- Practice with a friend—interviews, dating situations, etc.

> *Attract what you expect. Reflect what you desire ... Become what you respect ... and Mirror what you admire.*

> *Most of us feel that others will not tolerate emotional honesty in communication. We would rather defend our dishonesty on the grounds that it might hurt others; and having rationalized our phoniness into mobility, we settle for superficial relationships.*
> —JOHN POWELL

- Find your comfort zone. Not all social situations are for everyone. Go where your interests are. You might be happier at an art gallery, book club, or on a volleyball team than you are at a cocktail party or bar.

It takes time to change. Do not expect to overcome shyness overnight; it is a gradual process.

According to psychologist Bernardo Carducci (Casriel, 2007), conversation with strangers typically moves through five stages:

1. Opening comment (keep it simple) and introductions,
2. Trying out topics and exploring for common ground,
3. Closing, in which you tell the person that you're going,
4. Summing up what you learned, and
5. Possibly exchanging contact information.

Remember, once you internalize these steps, you will always have a mental map of where to go next. Shy people who are determined to develop their social skills can make themselves interact despite the nervousness it provokes, and they can also end up garnering great satisfaction from the effort, even if some bashfulness remains (Rodgers, 2006).

One aspect of social interaction for everyone is perceptual awareness. Becoming aware of how we see others is part of interacting effectively with others. As we begin to reach out and meet new people, many will eventually become our friends and lovers. We begin the process of getting acquainted and finding friends through *perceptual awareness*.

Perception refers to how we mentally organize and interpret the world around us. Because we all have different backgrounds and experiences, we perceive the world around us in different ways—and thus many of us misinterpret and misunderstand the people around us. We need to increase our perceptual awareness.

Why we all need to practice emotional first aid.
https://www.ted.com/talks/guy_winch_the_case_for_emotional_hygiene

Guy Winch makes a compelling case to practice emotional hygiene.

Perceptual Awareness

How can we prevent misunderstandings due to the inaccuracy of our own perceptions? Serious problems can arise when people accept their misinterpretations as if they were a fact of life, while we tend to get upset with others when they jump to conclusions about our own behavior. For example:

A friend says, "You really look tired today!" (You were feeling great until they said that.)

"What's the matter with you today?" (Who said anything was wrong?)

"Why are you mad at me and not talking to me?" (You are concerned about your final exam that you are not prepared for.)

How can we become more aware of our misinterpretations and make people more aware of their personal perceptions? The *perceptual awareness process* will provide us with a technique that will help us deal with these misperceptions. What is this process?

- Make note of the **behavior you are observing**. Describe the behavior.
- **Interpret the behavior**. Why is that person acting that way? (Write down at least two interpretations.)
- Ask yourself what you would do in the same situation and look at their **point of view**. Put yourself in the other person's place.
- Ask for **clarification** about how to interpret the behavior. Do not jump to conclusions. Ask the person why they are acting that way or ask someone else how they would interpret the situation.

The perceptual awareness process will help us understand others more accurately instead of assuming that our first impression is correct. Our goal is a mutual understanding and acceptance of others.

Now, let us take a closer look at how we perceive the people we meet and interact with on a regular basis through the process called *people perception*. This section will be somewhat longer.

> *Fair isn't everybody getting the same thing ... Fair is everybody getting what they need in order to be successful.*

CONSIDER THIS

APPLICATION OF THE PERCEPTUAL AWARENESS PROCESS

Your roommate, Stephanie, has been quiet for the last two days and has not been talking to you (Behavior). You are sure that she is mad at you (First interpretation). She may have had a fight with her boyfriend (Second interpretation). "Why would I be acting that way?" (Put yourself in that situation). Ask Stephanie, "You seem very quiet lately, can you tell me why?" (Request for clarification).

Jim stomped out of the room and slammed the door (Behavior). Jim must have not liked what I said and got mad (First interpretation). Jim sure must be in a hurry and accidently slammed the door (Second interpretation). "Why would I have acted that way?" (Put yourself in that situation). "Jim, how did you feel when you left the room yesterday?" (Request for clarification).

Think of some situations you have been in and go through this process.

People Perception

Imagine yourself alone at a large party that you are attending. You look around and see nothing but unfamiliar faces. As you look at each individual, you immediately make a judgment of what you think each person is like. Your perception of each individual is based on many things, such as your past experiences, prejudices, and stereotyping. Since your past experiences, prejudices, and stereotypes are different from those of others, your perception of each individual will be different from other people's interpretations. You may perceive someone as serious and studious, while someone else may perceive the same individual as depressed and slow intellectually. Sometimes we discover that our perception is not always accurate. Initiating interactions is a valuable skill to have. Being open-minded is the best way to approach it. Some recent psychological studies indicate that our perception may be distorted at the time we first see the behavior because we are using our own past experiences, prejudices, and stereotyping to interpret what we see.

As we encounter people daily, we form an impression or perception of them. The term *social perception* describes the way we perceive, evaluate, categorize, and form judgments about the qualities of people we encounter (Nevid, 2015). These *social perceptions* have a critical influence on our interactions. In fact, they are more important in guiding our feelings, thoughts, and behaviors than the actual traits or attitudes of the people around us. The factors that seem to influence our social perceptions are *first impressions, stereotyping*, and *prejudices*.

First impressions. First impressions can have a tremendous influence on our perception of others. The initial impression we have of another person may have a strong impact on our future interactions with them. If you go to a party and see someone who looks just like the boss who fired you last week, what is your impression of that person? What is the likelihood of you approaching that person? You will most likely avoid that person even though they seem to be very friendly and not at all like your boss. The ***primacy effect*** occurs when the first impression carries more weight than any subsequent information. That first impression of the person who looks like your previous boss will be difficult to change even if you see them in a new and different situation (Myers, 2013).

Our first impressions are formed quite rapidly—often within a matter of seconds. Research indicates that negative first impressions are often quickly formed and hard to overcome. This is why they say "getting off on the wrong foot" may be particularly damaging to a person (Hutson, 2016). The opposite tends to be true of positive first impressions, which are often hard to earn but easily lost. If the person we are meeting for a first date is late, what is our first impression? Since this is our first encounter, would we think that they are unreliable and must be a flake? A negative first impression? Many would feel this way; this kind of impression will be difficult to change. If the new date is on time, we are less willing to say that this person is reliable and conscientious. Research indicates that, indeed, a perceived early wrong is the greater offense and can permanently cripple a relationship, even after repeated apologies (Hutson, 2016). Most of us will take more time to make that judgment even though the first impression was positive.

You never get a second chance to make a first impression
—GARY WILLIAMS

What do we notice first? While walking down the street one day, you see a person whom you have never seen before. In your mind you immediately form an impression of what you think this person is like. What has the greatest impact on the formation of an opinion? Was it the way the person was dressed, their hairstyle, their size or shape, their facial expression, or their physical attractiveness? In the article "6 Myths about Men and Women and Relationships," Gwen Seidman indicated that data reveals that *both* men and women think perceived attractiveness are important, with men rating it somewhat higher than women (Seidman, 2012). Some people feel that we seem to be influenced more by *physical appearance* than anything else. This may be due to the fact that mass media puts too much emphasis on these factors and, thus, has a great influence on our perception of the world. A major factor in our attraction to others is the way they make us feel. We are drawn to people who make us feel happy, hopeful, and optimistic, and when they are gone, we want to see them again (Patrick, 2019). We know we'll be judged, as we judge in turn, by what happens the moment we and a stranger see each other for the first time (Hutson, 2016).

Other factors that seem to have an impact on our first impressions of others include what the individual is doing (their behavior) at the time we perceive them and what the **interactional possibilities** are with that person (whether or not they would be a good date, tennis partner, study partner). If we see someone acting odd or different the first time we see them, what kind of person do we think he or she is? What will we think of that person the next time we see them? Most of us would continue to perceive them as different, because of what we observed them doing the first time we saw them. If we see someone who we think would be fun to date, will we approach them? If we think the person sitting in the corner would help us study psychology, will we ask them to help? If we perceive someone as "stuck-up," or as having an "attitude," will we approach them? Based on our first impressions of these individuals, we have already determined how we will respond or not respond to them. We are making decisions based on how we perceive the *interactional possibilities* (Aronson et al., 2015).

What about the impressions we leave on the Internet, via webpages and social media? Any information you post on those sites is quite public and long-lasting. It may be taken down, but there is still a record of it that someone could use against the author. Employers often have Internet services that do new employee searches before they hire a person. They may search many sites, including those that might be considered private. The lesson is to remember that the Internet is available to millions of people— just think before you post.

Tolerance, Acceptance, and Appreciation of Differences

Tolerance is a fair, objective, and permissive attitude toward those whose opinions, beliefs, practices, or racial or ethnic origins differ from one's own; freedom from bigotry (Websters Dictionary, 2019).

Tolerance is also defined as sympathy or indulgence for beliefs or practices differing from or conflicting with one's own (Merriam Webster Dictionary, 2019)

Acceptance is defined as agreement with or belief in an idea, opinion, or explanation. (Merriam Webster Dictionary, 2019)

Appreciation is defined as a feeling or expression of admiration, approval, or gratitude (Merriam Webster Dictionary, 2019)

These topics can be considered steps tolerating someone, accepting them and then appreciating them.

From a brain perspective, we cannot really learn and internalize something if we aren't aware of it or change it. Becoming aware of something is essential for memory development. Becoming aware of something, and then engaging deeply in that thing is how our identity is shaped and eventually, our personality.

What we focus on expands and shapes how we view ourselves, our future, and our past. It is a key that provides learning experiences but also helps us observe people who model what successful behavior looks like. Clearly, modeling is one of the ways people learn.

The following discussion can help you examine your attitudes and commit to any positive change. Keep your mind open to new ideas. Classifying people into social groups is called *social categorizing*. The categories are often based on characteristics such as race, ethnicity, class, and gender. You can find yourself over-categorizing, and that is called **stereotyping**. The information learned and modeling tolerance and acceptance will provide a enlightened way to engage with the world. (See the discussion below on stereotyping.) Social justice issues like racism, sexism, feminism, heterosexism, classism, ableism, and privilege need to be thought about so you can address societal issues with knowledge. Definitions are found in the glossary. Also other current terms for gender and sexuality have been added to the glossary for you to become aware of and add to your knowledge base, such as **affirmed gender**, **cisgender,** and **androgynous.**

Check out the Heroic Imagination Project that psychologist Phillip Zimbardo has researched, at https://www.heroicimagination.org. It provides lessons and tools to encourage "**everyday heroism**," or the power of individuals or networks of individuals to neutralize negative social influences. The mission of the Heroic Imagination Project is to teach young people how to "stand up, speak out and act courageously in challenging situations." (Zimbardo, 2017).

Becoming Aware of Technology: Creating a New Generation of Youth Super Heroes
https://youtu.be/oMMhgJ_Vpwk

At TEDxRoma, Philip Zimbardo discusses carrying out small social-centric gestures that inspire others to do good.

THE "HOW" OF POSITIVE SOCIAL CHANGE:

- **The Power of One** — How to **be the first** and specific in helping others in need;
- **The Power of Two** — How to **be an ally** to others who are doing the right thing;
- **The Power of Three** — How to **use group psychology to promote prosocial behavior.**

Prejudices Our perceptions of other people may be influenced and distorted by our prejudices. Prejudices predispose us to behave in certain ways toward other people and groups. *Prejudice* is when we prejudge a person or group of people prior to having all known information and facts. Being prejudiced does not always have a negative meaning; it can also be positive. If we see someone dressed as a nurse, we might automatically perceive that person as kind and generous, even though we do not know anything else about the individual. When prejudice is negative, it can lead to *discrimination*, which involves negative behavior in the form of unfair treatment toward members of a group.

Stereotyping Many people think people with red hair have hot tempers, that police officers are mean, that Irish people drink a lot, that Japanese people are intelligent, and that Jewish people are rich. These are *stereotypes*—preconceived, inaccurate, rigid beliefs about individuals or groups of people. The habit of stereotyping people is so common that almost any personal characteristic leads to the formation of stereotypes and *labeling* (note that "all" is often implied in each stereotype). For example, what are your feelings about overweight people, old people, short people, Black people, women, or LGBTQ people. (Lesbian, Gay, Bisexual, Transgender, and Questioning)? Leo Buscaglia once said, "a loving person does not label others." Labeling can happen often and is mainly what you see. "The eye can be the most inaccurate, most inconsistent, and the most prejudicial organ we have in the body. What is truly essential is invisible to the eye" (Buscaglia, 1982, p. 94).

Labeling theory This theory of how the self-identity and behavior of individuals may be determined or influenced by the terms used to describe or classify them. It is associated with the concepts of self-fulfilling prophecy and stereotyping. Labeling theory holds that deviance is not inherent in an act, but instead focuses on the tendency of majorities to negatively label minorities or those seen as deviant from standard cultural norms The theory was prominent during the 1960s and 1970s, and some modified versions of the theory have developed and are still currently popular. Often labeling happens mainly based on perception.

According to Dr. Susan Fiske, tall people are more apt to get hired first and get paid more than short people. Also according to her research, attractive students tend to get better grades than less attractive students. Are you aware that women in the US earned just 79 cents for every dollar men made in 2019? The perception that women cannot do an equal job for equal pay still persists. Is this because tall people are better qualified than short people, attractive students are more intelligent than the less attractive students, and women are not as good employees? No, it is because we have allowed our prejudices and stereotyping to influence our behavior. We must learn to overcome these influences and accept people as they are, and we must be aware of how we learned to perceive them (Fiske, 2014). We will have more to say about prejudice and stereotypes and how they affect our values in Chapter Nine.

> *We slaughter one another in our words and attitudes. We slaughter one another in the stereotypes and mistrust that linger in our heads, and the words of hate we spew from our lips.*
> —NELSON MANDELA

Becoming Aware of Terminology

"Gender identity" is often conflated with sexual identity

According to David Schmitt 2017), cultural psychology, and new studies of transsexuality, along with our evolutionary heritage, all point to the same conclusion: There are psychological differences between men and women. But, just as the evidence is mounting that psychological sex differences are real, denial of differences have become rampant. Whether you identify as a man or a woman is your ***sexual identity***.

When they study differences in the way self-identified men and women think (such as how they read a map), feel (the degree to which they experience empathy), and behave (say, their likelihood of committing homicide), psychologists are said to be investigating psychological **sex differences**.

Gender, or gender psychology, according to the American Psychological Association, reflects the *attitudes, feelings, and behaviors that a given culture associates with biological sex*. The term ***gender*** refers to whether a person is typically masculine and/or feminine as defined by their local culture. (Sometimes this is called *gender-role or sex-role orientation* or *gender expression.* but we need to be clear when discussing sex differences.)

Inaccuracy in social perceptions. This is both a cause and an effect of prejudice. We will examine a few sources of inaccuracy that we discussed earlier that contribute to prejudice in important ways.

- *Stereotyping.* Stereotyping seems to contribute more than any other factor in determining our prejudices. Many people subscribe to derogatory stereotypes of various groups. Although studies suggest that racial stereotypes have declined over the last several decades, they are still not a thing of the past (Plous, 2002). The **stereotype content model** (SCM) is a psychological theory arguing that people tend to perceive social groups along two fundamental dimensions: warmth and competence (Fiske, Cuddy, Glick, & Xu, 2002). The SCM was originally developed to understand the social classification of groups within the population of the United States. However, the SCM has since been applied to analyzing social classes and structures across countries and history (Fiske, 2012).

    Becoming Aware of prejudice, bias, and social perception: Social perception - Primacy recency
    https://www.khanacademy.org/test-prep/mcat/individuals-and-society/perception-prejudice-and-bias/v/social-perception-primacy-recency

- *First Impressions.* One of the problems with the power of first impressions is that many people's first impressions of minorities come not from actual interactions, but from the media or disparaging remarks made by parents, neighbors, and others. Thus, many impressionable children develop unfavorable opinions toward **people of color, people with disabilities,** or **lesbian, gay, bisexual, transgender, and questioning (LGBTQ) people** before they have any opportunity for rewarding interactions with members of these groups. Even though these negative first impressions may eventually be overridden by contradictory experiences, the *primacy effect* probably contributes to prejudice. In other words, trusting based on false impressions is a pervasive consequence of our initial reactions to other people—these reactions encourage often inaccurate stereotypes about races and ethnic groups other than our own, women, old people, overweight people, and many other negatively stigmatized social groups (Pingitore et al.,1994; Brownell, 2005). Psychologist Dr. Susan Fiske developed a **continuum model of impression formation** which describes the process by which we form impressions of others. Impression formation is framed as depending on two factors: The available information and the perceiver's motivations (Kruglanski, 2012; Fiske, Lin & Neuberg, 2018; Fiske, Lin, & Neuberg, 1999). According to the model, these two factors help to explain people's tendency to apply stereotyping processes in preference to individuating processes when forming social impressions.

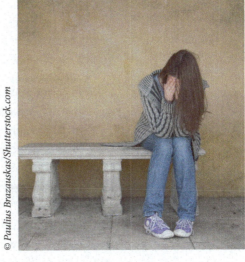

What is your impression of this person?

- *Categorizing.* People frequently categorize others on the basis of *inherited traits* (culture, gender, ethnicity, physical features) or *acquired traits* (education, occupation, lifestyle, and customs). **In-group—out-group bias** explains the tendency to hold less favorable opinions about groups to which we do not belong, often over-emphasizing the negative aspects *(out-groups)*, while holding more favorable opinions that are often exaggerated about groups to which we do belong *(in-groups)* (Jackson, L. M. 2011; Hewstone et el, 2002). The tendency of people to favor their own group, known as "in-group bias," has been found in cultures around the world (Van Vugt, M., De Cremer, D., P. Janssen, D. 2016; Aberson, Healy & Romero, 2000). We perceive people like ourselves to be members of the "in-group" and those who are different to be part of the "out-group." We tend to have more favorable attitudes toward "in-group" members than "out-group" members. We tend to explain the behavior of people in the "out-group" on the basis of their membership in what we might consider the "out group." When you make a point of getting to know people in your "out group" you might find you like them and they like you. It is important to remember that our prejudices are always present. Maybe you have had preconceived ideas about each other and the barriers are not like you thought they were.

Watch this brief video to explain in and out group perception.
https://www.khanacademy.org/test-prep/mcat/individuals-and-society/ perception-prejudice-and-bias/v/ethnocentrism-and-cultural-relativism-in-group-and-out-group

As we continue the process of **people perception**, we discover that it is common for us to make many mistakes in our perceptions of others. We have found that our prejudices and our stereotypes often lead to unfair treatment of others. We will now take a look at one characteristic—appearance—that seems to have the greatest impact on our perception of others without substantial evidence to support its accuracy—another distortion in perception. The better we get to know someone, the more beautiful he or she becomes in our eyes. We often perceive the people we love as being beautiful, regardless of what anyone else may think.

Becoming Aware of Prejudice and Unconscious Bias: How to Hack Your Brain's Prejudice with Veggies
https://greatergood.berkeley.edu/video/item/how_to_hack_your_brains_prejudice_with_veggies

The Greater Good Science Center presents research that suggests a quick trick you can use to combat your unconscious biases.

Physical attractiveness. Are you more likely to seek out an attractive person as a friend or someone who is perceived as less attractive? If you were an employer, would you be more likely to hire the most attractive applicant? Do you perceive physically attractive people to be more poised, likeable, sexy, competent, happy, interesting, and socially skilled than people of average or unattractive appearance? Many of you would answer *no* to these questions, but when it comes time for you to act on these questions it could be a different story. Research indicates that physical attractiveness has a profound influence on our impression of others and our interactions with them Plight, J., & Vliek, M. (2017); (Berscheid 2006; Baron et al., 2012).

Men (both gay and straight) seem to consciously recognize the importance of physical attractiveness more than women (both straight and lesbian; see Lippa, 2007). However, experimental research, as well as evidence from online dating and speed dating, shows that physical attractiveness is equally important to men and women. Attractiveness tends to be a more important factor in our dating decisions than traits like personality, education, and intelligence (Eastwick et al., 2011; Eastwick and Finkel, 2008; Luo and Zhang, 2009; Kurzban and Weeden, 2005; Sprecher, 1989; Thao et al., 2010).

In general, people tend to believe that what is beautiful is good (Atwater et al., 2013). This stereotype seems to start early in life. When preschool children were asked to pick whom they liked best and who they thought was the best behaved in their class, they selected for both categories of their classmates with the same group of children adults judged to be the most attractive physically (Berscheid, 2000).

We have all been told, "Beauty is only skin deep, and it's what's inside the person that counts." A person's character and behavior are more important than looks. Most of us would probably agree that physical attractiveness should not be a major factor in interpersonal attraction. Then, why is physical beauty such a powerful influence in attracting us to others?

Becoming Aware of Diversity

Do you know what colorism is? Watch this video and learn more about colorism.

Confessions of a D Girl: Colorism and Global Standards of Beauty | Chika Okoro | TEDxStanford

https://www.youtube.com/watch?v=fvoWoMIwr-g#action=share%20 %22https://youtube/fvoWoMIwr-

One reason is that we all want to be accepted and liked, and we perceive attractive people as being more friendly, liked more by others, and thus, if we hang around them more we will also be perceived in the same way. People tend to see themselves as being more similar to attractive people than to unattractive people. Another reason is that, beginning early in life, we have been told that beautiful things are good and that ugly things are bad, so we have generalized this belief to include our perception of people. Later, we discover that attractive people tend to receive more positive reinforcement than less attractive individuals, and, thus, they will be more likely to feel good about themselves. Finally, if they feel good about themselves, other people will also perceive them as more positive and they will continue to receive more and more reinforcement. As a result of such cultural conditioning, most people do associate physical attractiveness with a wide variety of desirable characteristics (Myers, 2013).

People's attractiveness is surprisingly unrelated to their self-esteem. One reason may be that, except after comparing themselves with super-attractive people, few people view themselves as unattractive. As time goes by, we become accustomed to our own face and perceive it on a positive basis (Gosling, 2016).

Intimate Relationships When selecting a person to date, does physical attractiveness influence our selection? Research has shown that people desire to date the most attractive person possible. But when given the opportunity to choose a date, people tend to choose someone of attractiveness nearly equal to their own (Berscheid, 2000). We may desire the more attractive date, but we may be afraid that they would reject us. In order to maintain a positive self-concept, we are more likely to select someone we think would be more likely to say "yes." That person will most likely be someone whom we perceive as equal to us in physical attractiveness. The **matching hypothesis** proposes that people of similar levels of physical attractiveness gravitate toward each other (Worchel et al., 2000). There seems to be evidence to support this in regard to selecting friends, dating partners, and marriage partners. But no matter our personal level of attractiveness, or our partner's, as we get to know, like, and respect each other more, our attraction naturally grows and deepens (Kniffin and Wilson, 2004). The longer we know each other, the less important physical attractiveness becomes to beginning and maintaining a long-term relationship (Hunt et al., 2015).

What is important to you? Your best friend wants to find you a date. Your friend asks you to list the three most important characteristics you would like that date to have. **Kindness, loyalty, and understanding** (not looks, status, and excitement) are the key points research has found for essential qualities in a partner (Seidman, 2017). Take a minute and write down the three characteristics that are most important to you in a potential date. Most people would say *intelligence*, *friendliness*, and *sincerity* are the most important qualities. But when you actually make your selection, you base your selection on physical appearance.

> *The only way to live happily with others is to overlook their faults and admire their virtues.*
> —DAVID GOODMAN

According to Weeden and Sabini (2005), physical attractiveness may serve as a gatekeeper directing us toward partners who are healthy, age appropriate, and able to reproduce. When we make real-life dating and mating decisions, research indicates, physical appearance dominates and we choose to pursue relationships with those who are attractive to us (Fugère, 2017, Luo and Zhang, 2009; Kurzban and Weeden, 2005; Thao et al., 2010).

Physical attractiveness is not correlated with intelligence, mental health, or even self-esteem. However, our tendency is to perceive beautiful people as healthier and just plain better than others (Burris, 2018).

The more aware we are that characteristics, like physical attractiveness, influence our perceptions of others, the less chance that these characteristics will have on influencing our perceptions of others. Thank goodness that *beauty is in the eye of the beholder* and what is beautiful to one person is not considered beautiful to another person. This gives all of us a fair chance.

Another important aspect of *people perception* is the judgment we make about why people behave as they do. Our responses to other people are strongly influenced by these judgments, and we are constantly attempting to understand the reasons for other people's behavior. This leads us to the *attribution process*.

CONSIDER THIS

APPLICATION OF THE PERCEPTUAL AWARENESS PROCESS

What would you do and think in the following situation? Class is over, and as you are walking to your next class you see your boyfriend or girlfriend on the other side of campus talking to a member of the opposite sex. Many of you would feel your emotions take control of your mind and body and react aggressively toward your partner and accuse them of flirting with the other person. Are you jealous? What would you say when your boyfriend or girlfriend finds you talking to a member of the opposite sex? It tends to be a different story when the shoe is on the other foot, doesn't it? Why?

In the situation above, you attributed your romantic partner behavior to his or her personality and not being a trustworthy person. You forgot to consider the situation they were in. Remember, yesterday they were sick and missed their classes, and they were talking to the other person in order to get the notes for class. Your response to this event was inappropriate because you did not consider the situation your partner was in. Have you ever done this? We are more likely to respond this way to people we do not know than people we do know. Hopefully, you are secure enough in your relationship with your romantic partner that you would trust them talking to a person of the opposite sex.

Attribution Process *Attribution theory* shows that we frequently over-estimate the influence of a person's personality and under-estimate the impact of the situation he or she is in (Worchel et al., 2000).

- *Attribution Error.* When we observed Juan for the first time, he was studying by himself in the cafeteria using a laptop computer. What is our first impression of Juan?

What label do you give him? He must be a loner. He must be an intellectual. He must be a "nerd." Are we right about our perception of Juan? The next day we are walking by the soccer field and we notice a very fast, aggressive player scoring a goal, and we discover that it is Juan. Was our first impression of Juan correct? We then further discover that Juan is also a very outgoing individual with lots of friends. We definitely made an error based on our first impression. Remember, a person's behavior at a given time may or may not reflect their personality—but we tend to assume that it does. Attribution is concerned with how we make sense of our world, because we wonder why people say and do the things they do (Reeder, 2013).

Inaccuracy in our perceptions tends to persist because first impressions can be very difficult to overcome. Evidence seems to demonstrate that we tend to see what we expect to see in our interpersonal interactions. Now that you are more aware of how your perceptions are influenced, we hope that you can begin to accept people as they really are.

Another variable that has a powerful influence on our perception of others and our interaction with them is *the power of expectations.*

We like to think that predicting the future is usually the work of astrologers or others who claim to be a prophets. In reality, each of us predicts what will be, and we also make it come true. A self-fulfilling prophecy is "an expectation that helps to bring about the predicted events, which consequently strengthens the expectation" (Myers, 2013). Psychologists are aware that these expectations can affect the behavior and outcome of others.

The self-fulfilling prophecy. We see what we want to see; we become what others expect of us. This is the premise of the *self-fulfilling prophecy*. This is such a powerful force in our life that it not only determines how you see yourself in the present, but can also actually influence our future behavior and that of others. A *self-fulfilling prophecy* occurs when a person's expectations of an event makes the outcome more likely to happen than would otherwise have been true.

Rosenthal and Jacobson (2003) found that teacher expectations can have a tremendous effect on students. For example, a teacher was told that certain students had more intellectual potential than the other students in the class. The class was given a test prior to the teacher's first day of class and another test a few months later. The results were surprising, because all of the students started with about the same potential. The students who were recognized as having "high potential" by the teacher improved at a much higher rate than those recognized as "average" students—apparently as a result of the teacher's higher expectations. The **Pygmalion effect**, or **Rosenthal effect**, is the phenomenon whereby others' expectations of a target person affect the target person's performance, A corollary of the Pygmalion effect is the **golem effect**, in which low expectations lead to a decrease in performance (Mitchell, Terence R.; Daniels, Denise (2003); Rosenthal and Jacobson (2003).

Types of self-fulfilling prophecies. There are two types of self-fulfilling prophecies. The first type that we will discuss is *imposed* by one person on another, so that the expectation of one person seems to control another's action. We described this in the Jacobson and Rosenthal study of a teacher's expectations of their students.

> *If you think you can do something, or you think you cannot, you are usually right.*
> —HENRY FORD

The X teacher expected certain students to do well, and as a result they did better than the low-expectation students. To put this phenomenon in context with self-concept, we can say that when a teacher communicates to a student the message "I think you're bright," the student accepts that evaluation and changes their self-concept to include it. In contrast, we realize that the reverse is also true for students whose teachers send the message "I think you're stupid."

The second category of self-fulfilling prophecy is the *self-imposed prophecy* that occurs when your own expectations influence your behavior.

Expectations are the basis of the self-fulfilling prophecy. We find that expectations are the foundation of our success, but they can also be the basis of our failure. If we believe that we can succeed, we can do it. If we believe that we are incompetent and not capable, we tend to do badly. Which do you want? This type of self-fulfilling prophecy can become a vicious circle (Schultz, W. & Oskamp, S. (2000, 2005). A thought about oneself is carried out in behavior, which then brings about an even stronger confirming thought. If the descriptor is a positive one which increases our self-esteem, the self-fulfilling prophecy is a friend. For example, if you wake up and immediately think—perhaps for no particular reason at all—that today is going to be a terrible day, your attitude might make your prediction come true. You may unconsciously work to **affirm your belief** by ignoring the positive, amplifying the negative, and behaving in ways that are unlikely to contribute to an enjoyable day. Too often, though, our thoughts are limiting and serve as our enemy. Figure 1.4 demonstrates this vicious cycle.

Self-fulfilling prophecies are powerful. They can have a positive or negative impact on our self-concept, or they can influence us in the business world, or in how our family operates. What kind of effect has a self-fulfilling prophecy had on you?

Figure 1.4

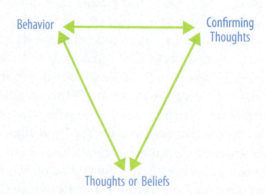

Adapted from Person to Person: Positive Relationships Don't Just Happen, 5th Edition by Sharon L. Hanna © 2008.

Can I Change My Image?

Can I change how others perceive me? Can I change my expectations? Change is not easy. We are constantly projecting ourselves to others as being a capable, good, bad, inferior, successful, happy, sad, depressed, or superior type of person. Social psychology literature deals with strategic self-presentation, and if we don't like the way others perceive us, we can change our image through *impression management*.

Impression management. Impression management is a conscious or subconscious process in which people attempt to influence the perceptions of other people about a person, object, or event. There is a strong correlation between the *self-fulfilling prophecy* and *impression management*. If we project our image of ourselves as successful people, others will perceive us as being successful, and if they expect us to be successful, we become more successful. ***Impression management*** refers to our conscious effort to present ourselves in socially desirable ways (Worchel et al., 2000; Santrock, 2006).

Have you ever been interviewed for a job? Most people would dress differently for the interview. We would make sure to say the "right" things and respond positively to the interviewer. This is doing what we call *impression management*. We are attempting to portray ourselves in a way that we think the interviewer expects us to be. *Impression management* is necessary if we want people to like us, respect us, hire us, or buy something from us.

How can we influence the impressions we make on others?

If you do not like how others perceive you, you can change your image. You can change the way you dress, the way you act, your hairstyle, your posture, or whatever it takes to change your image. You can do it. "People are sensitive to how they are seen by others and use many forms of impression management to compel others to react to them in the ways they wish" (Giddens, 2005). An example of this concept is easily illustrated through cultural differences. Different cultures have diverse thoughts and opinions on what is considered beautiful or attractive. As we begin to understand the process of people perception, we are now ready to begin the process of getting acquainted. "Confidence is the necessary spark before everything that follows," says educator and activist Brittany Packnett. In an inspiring talk, she shares three ways to crack the code of confidence—and her dream for a world where revolutionary confidence helps turn our most ambitious dreams into reality (Packnett 2019).

> *We inherit our relatives and our features and may not escape them, but we can select our clothing and our friends, and let us be careful that both fit us.*
> — VOLNEY STREAMER

Become Aware of Confidence.

Brittany Packnett- How to build your confidence and spark it in others. *https://www.ted.com/talks/brittany_packnett_how_to_build_your_confidence_and_spark_it_in_others?utm_campaign=tedspread&utm_medium=referral&utm_source=tedcomshare*

The best remedy for a lack of faith in one's abilities is not blind optimism, but rather a more realistic look at the landscape. There is a big difference between astute and arrogant. Confidence that's based firmly on what is actually known may not only be a better personal guide than exaggerated certainty; studies suggest it's also more likely to earn the faith of others (Markman, 2018). You might want to pay attention to the way you come across to other people. Work on standing straight and making eye contact. Make an effort to speak loudly and clearly and to put force behind your words. Often, you'll find you get the benefit of the doubt from other people. (Tenney, E.R., Meikle, N.L., Hunsaker, D., Moore, D.A., & Anderson, C. 2019)

In her TEDTalk, Meaghan Ramsey, who works on the Dove Self-Esteem Project, presented key ways she and her colleagues have learned that our society needs to educate for **body confidence** and encourage nurturing and supportive conversations about body image and behavior. The influence of family, friends, and other relationships is essential for how boys and girls, men and women treat each other especially in relation to "body talk." We all need to help young adults develop lasting strategies to overcome appearance-related stresses. We all need better role models. In a media and celebrity obsessed society—with size zero models, airbrushing and online trends such as #thighgap and #thinspiration—we all need to talk to our friends, parents and teachers about impression management. It can be hard balancing style, high fashion and comfort. Collaboration throughout our society. Communities, governments, businesses and other organizations need to work together to influence the above contributing factors and help revert the negative effects of a constantly changing culture, online and offline media messages, personal relationships and so on.

It's up to every one of us to be astutely conscious of the way we talk, to change the negative conversation, to promote individual beauty inside and out, to admire differences, and to truly embrace our own personal presentation to the world. We should all feel accountable for the messages we endorse through various channels. Communication takes many forms and every individual effort matters to create change. It should never be okay to stop loving how we look.

How To Make Favorable Impressions

Most of us make a conscious effort to influence the way others think of us. When we present ourselves to others, we usually try to make ourselves look better than we really are. We spend billions of dollars rearranging our bodies, our faces, our minds, and our social skills.

To increase the odds of making a good first impression, Valerie White and Ann Demarais (2007), authors of *First Impressions: What You Don't Know about How Others See You*, offer these tips:

1. Make eye contact at least half to two-thirds of the time (any more than this and you may come on too strong). And pay attention to your body language. Lean toward others when they speak. Nod every now and then. (Remember this is based on American culture—other cultures may be different.)
2. Smile, even if you aren't in the mood. Just going through the motions of showing some teeth may make you—and others—feel better, says the research.

3. Be careful about "oversharing," i.e., disclosing too much personal information about yourself. Keep it light. Keep it positive.
4. Try a little flattery. People warm to others who pay them compliments even if they know they're false. It is best when done sincerely.
5. Got a prepared opening line as an ice-breaker? Ditch it, or you risk coming across as shallow, aggressive, and calculating. Ask the interviewer about the job so you might gain insight into questions to ask.
6. Check your impulse to use the other person's name repeatedly. Once or twice might work, but overplaying the name game can make you seem "salesy" and forced.
7. Think a neutral, inscrutable style makes you appear thoughtful, deep, or cool? Forget it. Aloof behavior like kicking back at the table, crossing your arms, or showing zero emotion makes you look bored or arrogant.

Marty Nemko (2019), career and personal coach, believes the key to making a good first impression is making the other person feel good about him or herself. But that must go beyond smiling and praising. The conventional advice "Don't put yourself down" is usually wrong, according to Nemko. Self-effacement, as long as it's not self-eviscerating, is a plus because the less amazing you appear, the better the person feels about him- or herself in comparison. That's why you usually make a more positive connection by saying, "I'm clueless about this. Can you help?" than by dazzling 'em with your expertise.

Standard advice for networking at events or classes is to start conversations. If you find that challenging, you may attract sufficient people just by conveying openness: wearing a hint of a smile, open body language, and occasional half-seconds of eye-contact with appealing people. That passivity even confers an advantage: If someone initiates conversation with you, they're automatically more invested in making it work, because of commitment (Nemko 2019).

Remember that first impression techniques that work in one cultural setting may not work in another. For example, the nonverbal "thumbs up" gesture, which means in the United States that everything is OK, or that we would like to hitch a ride, means something very different in Greece—an insult similar to a raised middle finger. In the Native American culture of the Sioux, it is considered courteous to open a conversation with a compliment. In some Eastern European countries, if one person expresses great admiration for another's wristwatch, courtesy dictates that the watch is given to the admirer. When interacting with people from different backgrounds and different cultures, remember that they may be interpreting the situation or event differently.

Our values can also color "the facts." Our preconceptions can bias our observations and interpretations. Sometimes, we see what we are predisposed to see. Even the words we use to describe a person or an event can reflect our values.

Developing New Relationships

Unfortunately, it is not easy to meet or get acquainted with others. If we wait for others to initiate the encounter, we may become very lonely. It is up to you, and only you, to initiate the encounter and get the ball rolling in order for your friendships to grow and develop into long-lasting relationships. Seek friends who enjoy similar activities and have several interests. Have many circles of friends and enjoy a diverse group of friends.

If we understand the steps that are involved in initiating new relationships, we will be more likely to begin to incorporate them into our everyday life. What are these steps?

Listen to the podcast on Living in a lonely world.
https://www.apa.org/research/action/speaking-of-psychology/lonely-world

Initiating new relationships. Here are some steps you can take to initiate new relationships.

- **Communication** underlies all relationships, but in order to communicate with others we must first make contact with them. Whatever the nature of the situation, an encounter will usually begin with some communicative act that invites a response from another person. In order to do this, we must develop good communication skills. We find that the people who seem to have lots of friends also seem to have good communication skills. These skills can be learned. The communication chapter will help you learn these skills.

- **Being active** may give us the opportunity to get acquainted with someone we would like to get to know by allowing them to see and get to know us more often. The more familiar we become with someone the more apt we are to interact with that person. The first time you walk by a stranger, what do you do? Most of us would ignore the stranger. The next time you walk by the stranger, you may smile. The next time you see one another, you say, "Hi," and from then on, the more you encounter this person, the more you begin to interact. All of a sudden—you're friends. Depending on the town or city you are in—in major cities (like NYC or Paris) you might not try this on the street, but in the elevator of your apartment or in your place of worship, you might have more positive interactions.

Research reveals that most people are more likely to like, and even marry, an individual who lives, works, or goes to school within close proximity to them. *Proximity—* geographical nearness—is perhaps the most powerful predictor of friendship. Of course, *proximity* also provides opportunities for fights, assaults, rapes, and murders. But much more often it instigates liking. If you live in a college dormitory, your friends are more likely to live down the hall than across campus. Your earliest friends were probably children who lived next door or even in the same neighborhood.

What about the saying, *absence makes the heart grow fonder?* As long as we isolate ourselves from other prospective dates or mates, the saying is accurate. But, for most of us the saying goes, *"Absence makes the heart grow fonder for someone else."* There is another saying that is appropriate here: *"When I'm not with the one I love, I love the one I'm with."* What happens when friends and lovers move away? Eventually most of these relationships will slowly dissolve to nothing more than a periodic phone call or card.

Evidence shows that familiarity does not breed contempt; it breeds fondness. The more we are exposed to novel stimuli—a new person or new product—the more our liking for such stimuli will increase. This phenomenon, called the ***mere-exposure effect***, explains in part why we are attracted to people in close proximity to us (Wood et al., 2013).

Table 1.1

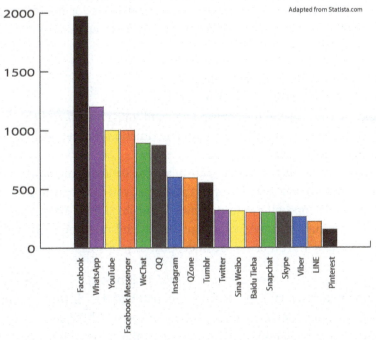

Most famous social network sites worldwide as of April 2017, ranked by number of active users (in millions)

Adapted from Statista.com

If it seems as though you are having difficulty getting acquainted with others, you may want to join a singles club, or even try a social networking website. The Internet has tremendously expanded opportunities for people to meet and develop relationships through social networking services. Facebook was the first social network to surpass 1 billion registered accounts and 2.41 billion monthly active users as of June 30, 2019. More than 2.1 billion people use Facebook, Instagram, WhatsApp, or Messenger every day on average (Facebook website, August 2019) Distance was once a huge obstacle to developing and fostering friendships, but social media has changed that. See Table 1.1 for more detail on who uses social networking sites.

Be careful when joining a club, dating service, or social networking website—check their references. How long have they been established? How much will they cost you? Talk to other friends who have joined or used their services. You want to make sure that you can benefit from their services and not let them take advantage of you.

Social skills enable you to create situations to meet new people and to maintain their friendship. Some ways to enhance your social skills in initiating relationships are:

*Practice the skills you observe other people using that enable them to interact well among others.
*Practice role playing with a friend—your friend will also be able to provide you with beneficial feedback that will enable you to change.

Everyone can be great because everyone can serve.
—DR. MARTIN LUTHER KING, JR.

*Practice different situations in your mind. Picture yourself asking someone out for a date or imagine yourself being interviewed for a job. The more you practice, the better you will be able to handle the situation.

*Practice verbal and nonverbal skills.

*Another idea would be to have someone record video of you in different situations. This is a lot of fun and provides great feedback when you watch yourself on film. Examples of social skills:

*Being confident with conversations.

*Being aware and sensitive to others feelings.

*Recognize when to end the conversation and doing it without being abrupt.

*Don't expect to be smooth and deft in any situations but be aware and apologize when you make mistakes.

Classes in communication skills, human relations, or acquiring assertiveness skills will provide you with new techniques and skills that you can apply in developing new relationships while improving your present relationships. Take classes at a community college, museum, or through community parks and recreation. You will probably meet people in class who otherwise do not appear in your social or work environment.

These are just a few steps you can use in initiating new relationships. What about meeting and interacting with people from different cultures? If you see someone who is struggling to make friends or being bullied or ignored because they do not dress like others, *please* step up and say Hi, or at least smile at them. You never know what someone is facing. You might end up with a great friend. You may find that you get to know yourself better and get to know another person with a shared exchange regarding what we know about ourselves—*self-discovery*.

Becoming Aware of who we are- What generation are you?

JANUARY 2019 Pew Research

DEFINING GENERATIONS: WHERE MILLENNIALS END AND GENERATION Z BEGINS

The generations defined

https://www.pewresearch.org/wp-content/uploads/2019/01/FT_19.01.17_generations_2019.png?w=640

Where are you in the generations? How do you think this effects you in relationship building and technology use?

Successful interactions with people from other cultures. In the world today, it is important that we learn to relate successfully with people from other cultures. *"Culture" refers to a group or community with which we share common experiences that shape the way we understand the world.* It includes groups that we are born into, such as gender, race, national origin, class, or religion. It can also include groups we join or become part of. For example, we can acquire a new culture by moving to a new region, by a change in our economic status, or by becoming disabled. We all belong to many cultures at once. Building relationships with people from different cultures, *often many different cultures,* is key in building diverse communities that are powerful enough to achieve significant goals. Relationships are powerful. Our one-to-one connections with each other are the foundation for change. We need to move beyond prejudicial thinking that affects our interactions with different types of people. We all want to experience success in our efforts in developing intercultural relationships.

In order to work with people from different cultural groups effectively, we will need to build sturdy and caring relationships based on trust, understanding, and shared goals. We must show respect, seek out activities of mutual interest, work cooperatively on projects, spend part of our time with others, and so forth.

> *Friendship is a plant we must often water.*
> —GERMAN PROVERB

"STEP OUTSIDE YOUR BOX"

People tend to bond more easily when out of their comfort zone. The experience will provide an instant group of people with whom you share a unique memory. Try new things alone or with friends.

- **TRAVEL** with a group.
- **TAKE A CLASS** in something you love; enthusiasm is contagious.
- **GET A DOG** (a pet is also good for your health) and show up every morning at your local dog park. People love to chat about their pooches.
- **TAKE A FRESH LOOK** at your neighbors, co-workers, classmates, fellow gym bunnies—the people you meet and greet on a regular basis. If you've been standoffish, say hello. If you've traded hellos for months, engage them in conversation.
- **SMILE**

Karbo (2016)

BUILDING RELATIONSHIPS WITH PEOPLE FROM OTHER CULTURES

In the Community Toolbox developed by The Kansas Health Foundation there are many ways that people can learn about other people's cultures and build relationships at the same time.

Here are some steps you can take.

- Make a conscious decision to establish friendships with people from other cultures.
- Put yourself in situations where you will meet people of other cultures.
- Examine your biases about people from other cultures.
- Ask people questions about their cultures, customs, and views.
- Read about other people's cultures and histories.
- Listen to people tell their stories.
- Notice differences in communication styles and values; don't assume that the majority's way is the right way.
- Risk making mistakes.
- Learn to be an ally.

Make a conscious decision to establish friendships with people from other cultures.

Making a decision is the first step. In order to build relationships with people different from yourself, you have to make a concerted effort to do so. There are societal forces that serve to separate us from each other. People from different economic groups, religions, ethnic groups, and races are often isolated from each other in schools, jobs, and neighborhoods. So, if we want things to be different, we need to take active steps to make them different.

Once you have made the decision to make friends with people different from yourself, you can go ahead and make friends with them in much the same way as with anyone else. You may need to take more time, and you may need to be more persistent. You may need to reach out and take the initiative more than you are used to. People who have been mistreated by society may take more time to trust you than people who haven't. Don't let people discourage you. There are good reasons why people have built up defenses, but it is not impossible to overcome them and make a connection. The effort is totally worth it.

Examine your biases about people from other cultures.

We all carry misinformation and stereotypes about people in different cultures. Especially, when we are young, we acquire this information in bits and pieces from TV, from listening to people talk, and from the culture at large. We are not bad people because we acquired this; no one requested to be misinformed. But in order to build relationships with people of different cultures, we have to become aware of the misinformation we acquired.

http://ctb.ku.edu/en/table-of-contents/culture/cultural-competence/culture-and-diversity/main

> *When I meet someone from another culture, I behave in the way that is natural to me, while the other behaves in the way that is natural to him or her. The only problem is that our "natural" ways do not coincide.*
> —RAYMONDE CARROLL

These feelings must be perceived as positive and be reciprocated by those culturally diverse individuals. Some people report that they have many friends and that these friends are gracious and cordial, but others report that those same people are abrasive, unfriendly, and should be avoided.

We discover that most intercultural interactions often involve tasks of some kind. The tasks that people want to accomplish while interacting with people from other cultures involve such things as: community projects, completing a degree in school, wanting to start or maintain a joint venture, completing forms that have to be filled out, visiting a foreign country and finding your way to a strange location, communicating with someone you cannot understand, and dealing with government agencies, medical facilities, or legal hassles. These tasks need to be accomplished in an efficient manner and within a reasonable amount of time.

People also experience minimal stress due to the fact that they are dealing with individuals from other cultures rather than from their own culture. Life is stressful enough, and successful intercultural relations suggest that there should be no additional stress brought on by the fact that the others with whom people work and/or interact are from a different cultural background (Community Toolbox developed by The Kansas Health Foundation, 2019).

Becoming aware of Technology and Culture

It has been noted that social media and the Internet are very powerful tools that can influence and shape human behavior. Social media has played a significant role in recent outbreaks of social protest and resistance in many countries. The mushrooming of protests and the mobilization of resistance against the governments of other countries have been heavily dependent on the resources provided by citizen's social media reports and television reporting. Observers have concluded that in a networked world social media possesses the potential to promote public participation, engagement, and the process of democratizing public life (Furedi, 2015). There has been abuse from other countries using social media to give misinformation and inflame hatred in the political world of the United States. (Shane, 2017).

The creative use of social media is a response to aspirations and needs that already exist or at least exist independently of it. This technology is a resource that can be utilized by social and political movements looking for a communication infrastructure or people trying to create chaos or harm.

As we close this chapter, perhaps the words of Winston Churchill are worth remembering:

You haven't learned life's lesson very well if you haven't noticed that you can give the tone or color, or decide the reaction you want of people in advance. It's unbelievably simple. If you want them to take an interest in you, take an interest in them first. People will treat you as you treat them.

Chapter Review

Our greatest pleasures and our most traumatic experiences have evolved around relationships.

- *Human relations* can be defined as the art of developing relationships that improve personal skills and life effectiveness.
- *Social control*—within sociology, refers to the many ways in which our behavior, thoughts, and appearance are regulated by the norms, rules, laws, and social structures of society. Some believe revealing personal information may increase control over people or situations. Society uses certain sanctions to enforce a standard of behavior that is deemed socially acceptable; this is called social control. Individuals and institutions utilize social control to establish social norms and rules, which can be exercised by peers or friends, family, state and religious organizations, schools, and the workplace. The goal of social control is to maintain order in society and ensure conformity in those who are deemed as deviant or undesirable in society (Carmichael, Jason "Social Control." Oxford Bibliographies. 26 June 2012).
- *Self-discovery*—to get to know yourself
- The revealing of the inner self is called *self-disclosure*.
- The evolution of a relationship is based on how much you are willing to disclose about yourself and how much the other person is willing to disclose about themselves to you—this process is also called self-disclosure.
- Good self-disclosure skills are fundamental to relationships for many reasons: defining yourself, getting acquainted, developing intimacy.
- The greatest risk of self-disclosure is rejection.
- There are many advantages of self-disclosure, including improvement of relationships, promotion of mental health, self-validation, social control, and impression management.
- The *Johari Window* is a tool that illustrates how self-disclosure operates and allows you to become more aware of yourself and your potential as a communicator in a given relationship/situation.
- The size of the window pane in the Johari Window may vary depending on your communication behavior and the quality of your relationship.
- *Loneliness* is one of the most serious problems in our society today—it is a feeling of longing and emptiness that is caused by the lack of emotional attachments and social ties.
- Loneliness makes a person vulnerable to many different situations, including the use of drugs and alcohol, suicide, medical problems, sexual promiscuity, mental illness, and negative relationships.
- What should a relationship provide? *Emotional attachments and social ties* must be satisfied in order to have a fulfilling life and overcome the feeling of loneliness.
- Most people will receive their emotional attachment from a combination of parents, relatives, mates, friends, pastors, animals, and comfort objects.
- *Social ties* provide us with the feeling of belonging, a feeling that we are part of a group and have an identity.
- *Shyness* is universal; it involves feelings, physical reactions, and thoughts that create a state of discomfort, and possible anxiety. Shyness is not a negative personality trait, it's not a character flaw, and it's not a disease. It's simply a description of how an individual responds and behaves.
- The consequences of shyness may be devastating. Only the person can know if a desire for alone time is not the same as shyness; remember everyone needs alone time but some need more of it.
- The major difference between a shy person and a not-shy person is a matter of *self-evaluation*; only the person can know what they need.
- There are three steps in the process of overcoming shyness—1) analyzing your shyness; 2) building your *self-esteem*; 3) improving your social skills.

- The perceptual awareness process will help us understand others more accurately instead of assuming that our first impressions are correct.
- When thinking about sensitive ethnic, cultural, and gender issues, it is important to consider different sides of issues in a contemplative, analytic way, as the *perceptual awareness* process explains.
- *Technology* changes may diminish actual personal interaction, or they may be helpful in meeting new people. Technology is also being used in many new ways to connect to other cultures and ideas.
- *Social perception* describes the way we perceive, evaluate, categorize, and form judgments about the qualities of people we encounter.
- The factors that influence our *social perceptions* are *first impressions, stereotyping,* and *prejudices.*
- First impressions can have a tremendous influence on our perceptions of others. The initial impression we have of another person may have a strong impact on our future interactions with them. The *primacy effect* occurs when the first impression carries more weight than subsequent information.
- The inaccuracy of social perception is both the cause and effect of prejudice. *Stereotyping* seems to contribute more than any other factor in determining our prejudices.
- The *attribution process* allows us to make sense out of other people's actions, figure out their attitudes and personality traits, and, ultimately, gain some control over subsequent interactions with them through our increased ability to predict their behaviors.
- The *self-fulfilling prophecy* is a powerful force in our life that not only determines how you see yourself in the present but can also actually influence your future behavior and that of others. (We see what we want to see; we become what others expect of us.)
- You can change. *Impression management* allows you to consciously present yourself in socially desirable ways.
- Developing new relationships is not always an easy process. The steps involved in initiating new relationships include communication and self-disclosure. The *mere-exposure effect* explains why we are attracted to those who are in close proximity.
- The *Mutual Reward Theory* (MRT) states that a relationship between two people is enhanced when there is a satisfactory balance of rewards between them.

You can learn to make your social life rich and rewarding by taking an active role in changing yourself. Your knowledge and beliefs about relationships will influence your enjoyment. You learn from experience, so take charge of your life, and take a few risks and chances. Enjoy life and appreciate each and every relationship you have.

Learning Outcomes

1. Describe the risks involved in getting acquainted with others.
2. Describe what a person can do to overcome shyness.
3. Why do we need to study self-disclosure? Why is self-disclosure important in a relationship?
4. What are the greatest risks of self-disclosure? Explain.
5. What are the advantages of self-disclosure? Explain.
6. What is the purpose of the Johari Window? How can the Johari Window be of benefit to you?
7. What is loneliness? What effects will loneliness have upon an individual?
8. How can a person overcome the effects of loneliness?

9. Define emotional attachments and social ties and explain their importance in relationship to loneliness.
10. Explain what shyness is and discuss the consequences of shyness.
11. Explain why technology has positive and negative consequences in relationships.
12. Explain the perceptual awareness process.
13. Explain what gender is.
13. Why do we need to study people perception?
14. Explain how first impressions, stereotyping, and prejudices influence our perception of others.
15. How does physical attractiveness influence our perception of others?
16. Explain the attribution process.
17. What is the self-fulfilling prophecy? What influence can it have on a person?
18. Explain how you can change your image. Why should we study impression management?
19. What are the qualities necessary to have a close, personal relationship with another person?
20. Explain the Mutual Reward Theory (MRT).
21. Explain the four steps in initiating new relationships.
22. How can we have successful interactions with people from other cultures?
23. Does technology enhance social connections? How? How not?
24. Define human relations.
25. Identify the three most common shyness-provoking situations, according to Dr. Bernardo Carducci.
26. Explain what LTL (Living Together Lonely) means.

Key Terms

Attribution Error
Attribution Theory
Categorizing
Catharsis
Continuum Model of Impression
Confidant
Depression
Discrimination
Diversity
Emotional Attachments
First Impressions
Generations
Human Relations
Impression Management
Intercultural Communication/
    Interactions
In-Group—Out-Group Bias
Johari Window

Open Area
Blind Area
Hidden Area
    Unknown Area
Living Together Loneliness (LTL)
Loneliness
Matching Hypothesis
Mere-Exposure Effect
Mutual Reward Theory
Openness
Open Communicator
People Perception
Perceptual Awareness Process
Physical Attractiveness
Public Self and Private Self
Prejudice
Primacy Effect
Proximity

Self-Disclosure
Self-Discovery
Self-Esteem
Self-Evaluation
Self-Fulfilling Prophecy
Self-Validation
Shyness
Situational Shyness
Social Control
Social Dominance
Social Networking
Social Perception
Social Ties
Stereotyping
Tolerance
Technology

Reflections: Critical Thinking Activities

Answer the following questions and turn them into your instructor for grading. (All questions answered = A; 13 questions answered = B; 8 questions answered = C).

1. Discuss the risks involved in getting acquainted with others.
2. Describe what a person can do to overcome shyness.
3. Why is self-disclosure so important in a relationship and what are the advantages of self-disclosure?
4. What is the purpose of the Johari Window? How can the Johari Window be of benefit to you?
5. What effects will loneliness have upon an individual?
6. How can a person overcome the effects of loneliness?
7. What is the self-fulfilling prophecy? What influence can it have on a person?
8. What are the qualities necessary to have a close, personal relationship with another person?
9. If you knew someone was moving to a new town and did not know anyone in that town, what would you tell this person about meeting and getting to know others? Explain the three steps in initiating new relationships.
10. Describe Impression Management and give examples of how it can be used. How have you applied it in the past?
11. Give some examples of how first impressions have influenced your interactions with others. Were they accurate or inaccurate?
12. Why is the Mutual Reward Theory (MRT) important in relationships?
13. How can we have successful interactions with people from other cultures?
14. Explain how a person can be married or move to a foreign country and still feel lonely.
15. Why are human relations skills needed?
16. What are the public self and private self?
17. How would you explain self-esteem? Why would you want to build it up? Why might you want to lose it?
18. How do you explain tolerance? Is it different from stereotyping? Does mere-exposure effect have a part in these explanations?
19. How has technology impacted your life? What rules does your household have about your phone & computer use? What would you do if you had someone online bully you? What if someone started sexting you? What would you do?

Technology Resources and Activities

RESOURCES

www.shyness.com/

The Shyness Institute offers this Web site as "a gathering of network resources for people seeking information and services for shyness." It is an index of articles, associations, and agencies that work with shyness. This page is a gathering of network resources for people seeking information and services for shyness. It is sponsored by The Shyness Institute, Berkeley, California (an institute for research and public education in shyness and social fitness, developing Social Fitness Training, including mindfulness exercises).

www.kevan.org/johari

An interactive Johari Window in which you are asked to describe yourself from a list of adjectives and you can also ask friends and colleagues to describe you and then see the results.

The Loneliness Workbook: A Guide to Developing and Maintaining Lasting Connections by Mary Ellen Copeland (2000)

It's Not Supposed to Be This Way: Finding Unexpected Strength When Disappointments Leave You Shattered by Lysa TerKeurst (2018)

https://www.youtube.com/watch?v=vikkaf0Guyc

Center For Mindfulness (Aug 6, 2017).

A touching and inspiring talk from the so called Dr. Love, Dr. Leo Buscaglia. Leo reminds us that the time to love is now, and he reads the poem "Things You Didn't Do."

https://www.youtube.com/watch?v=DEwnjxPqR6A

Break Away From Negative Thoughts & Experience Life | Kip Hollister | TEDxBeaconStreet Published on Jan 4, 2017

CEO and Mindfulness Expert Kip Hollister spoke at TEDxBeaconStreet on how to be more focused, fulfilled, and successful in both work and life by bringing your vision to fruition. Using her over 30-year history in the staffing industry and her passion for mindfulness in achieving one's full potential, Kip leads listeners on a journey to remove negative thoughts and find happiness. She discusses the roadblock in her life that led her to start the Hollister Institute and start living a more mindful life.

www.authentichappiness.sas.upenn.edu/testcenter.aspx

University of Pennsylvania Questionnaire Center with Emotion Questionnaires like Compassionate Love Scale, which measures your tendency to support, help, and understand other people. Other scales measure depression and happiness. Please note you must sign up with your email and make a password. There is no charge.

https://psychcentral.com/

PSYCHCENTRAL Offers a variety of quizzes and tools. A psychology quiz—like the kind that we offer here—can help a person determine whether there is a concern in their life that should be addressed, whether it be through learning more about it or through professional help. Our psychology tests are free to take, and are largely based upon scientific studies or medical references in the area they focus on. The mental health quizzes below are instantly and automatically scored once completed, giving you immediate results. No registration is required to take a test.

http://psychcentral.com/quizzes/loneliness.htm

The Loneliness Quiz, based on the UCLA Loneliness Quiz.

https://www.researchgate.net/profile/Domina-Petric/publication/339365799_Beauty_Bullying/links/5e4d927ca6fdccd965b3e8ad/Beauty-Bullying.pdf

Body dysmorphic disorder (BDD) is a distinct mental disorder in which a person is preoccupied with an imagined physical defect or a minor defect that others often cannot see. As a result, people with this disorder see themselves as "ugly" and often avoid social exposure or turn to plastic surgery to try to improve their appearance.

https://www.tolerance.org/magazine/spring-2016/toolkit-for-wanted-playground-buddy

This toolkit for "Wanted: Playground Buddy" provides suggestions and activities to help students and educators add a Buddy Bench to the playground and make their school more inclusive. Issue 52, Spring 2016

http://www.understandingprejudice.org/

Social Psychology Network: Check out the Exercises and Demonstrations (2019).

http://heroicimagination.org/

The HIP education programs prepare heroes in training for everyday heroic action. A website developed by Dr. Philip Zimbardo. "Most people want to take effective action in challenging situations, they just don't know how."

–Dr. Philip Zimbardo

https://www.splcenter.org/teaching-tolerance

Southern Poverty Law Center: Teaching Tolerance

Technology-Video links

https://www.ted.com/talks/brittany_packnett_how_to_build_your_confidence_and_spark_it_in_others

TED Talk 2019: How to Build your confidence and spark it in others.

https://www.youtube.com/watch?reload=9&v=MacQtvTYaGI

The Charisma Myth by Olivia Fox Cabane | Animated Core Message

https://www.ted.com/talks/dan_ariely_how_to_change_your_behavior_for_the_better?language=en

Improve Your Behavior/to/TED-Talks-to-Improve-Your-Friendships.htm

https://www.youtube.com/watch?v=MtLVCpZIiNs&feature=youtu.be

Sherry Turkle—Alone Together

https://www.ted.com/talks/meaghan_ramsey_why_thinking_you_re_ugly_is_bad_for_you

Meaghan Ramsey discusses the surprising impacts of low body and image confidence—

https://www.ted.com/talks/anne_lamott_12_truths_i_learned_from_life_and_writing/up-next?utm_campaign=tedspread&utm_medium=referral&utm_source=tedcomshare

Anne Lamott at TED2017: 12 truths I learned from life and writing

https://www.youtube.com/watch?v=3zJHwOwirjA

Three questions to ask yourself about everything you do | Stacey Abrams

https://youtube.com/_0hxl03JoA0

The lethality of loneliness: John Cacioppo at TEDxDesMoines

https://www.youtube.com/watch?v=whjDeFZDEUk

Codependency & Pathological Loneliness: Why We Stay w/ Narcissists. The Lonely Hurt! Expert http://www.ted.com/talks/guy_winch_the_case_for_emotional_hygiene

Guy Winch talks about Emotional first aid

https://www.youtube.com/watch?v=iCvmsMzlF7o

The Power of Vulnerability by Social worker Brene Brown

http://www.ted.com/talks/thandie_newton_embracing_otherness_embracing_myself?language=en

Embracing Others Embracing Self by Thandie Newton

https://www.youtube.com/watch?v=OMGUzXknoVQ

What Social Anxiety Feels Like

https://www.youtube.com/watch?v=2U-tOghblfE

Nicholas Christakis: The hidden influence of social networks

https://www.youtube.com/watch?v=08cYINwQYts

Leo Buscaglia—Speaking of Love

https://www.Documentaryheaven.com/

Documentary Heaven is a site that will help you to become aware of concepts you might be unaware of. It is a site filled with thousands of free online documentaries You will need to enter a keyword; for example, social psychology

http://documentaryheaven.com/discovering-psychology/

The power of the situation—social psychology

https://www.youtube.com/watch?v=rqk-HYTGapI

Trans-forming our thoughts on gender | Katina Sawyer | TEDxVillanovaU

This talk will highlight the experiences of transgender individuals as a way to shed light on a pressing topic which requires a greater amount of attention—the need for greater freedom of gender expression—and will provide guidelines for how to become a true transgender ally.

https://www.youtube.com/watch?v=rv0g8TsnA6c

Sherry Turkle—Connected but alone? (2013)

Watch this video and decide what the main points are and what you think about them. Do you agree with her points? Reflect and discuss with your friends.

Assignment: Create your own Learning Journal

Writing is one of the most favorite methods of self-expression and emotional catharsis. A learning journal is a good idea to do for this textbook. We suggest a notebook or a technological alternative in which you can add graded assignments from the book in one place along with personal writings, reflections, and thoughts from the assignments that interest you from each chapter.

Some of the students from previous classes that this text has been used commented that they kept their journals and read them later and reflected on their personal changes. Writing and reflecting on your life can help you to clarify your ideas and opinions.

Your instructor might assign certain assignments for a grade, but there are many ideas and concepts that may be new to you, and your journal would be a good place to keep all of your personal insights and activities you might want to do again later (or have your friends do and discuss their findings).

The following assignments are to be handed into the instructor or included in your class journal for grading. Make sure each class member participating in your group is listed for each assignment.

Consult your instructor about grading and as to whether instructions for group activity and individual answers are to be turned into instructor or included in your class journal.

Building Community Activities

Building Social ties in the class

How To Play Shh!

Simply announce that you want everyone lined up across the room by birth-date. Only catch: **no talking**. Once they are all lined up, ask certain people their birthdays just to be sure.

The activity can be repeated multiple times but categorized by shoe size, height, month of birthday, etc.

Three of a Kind

Set a time limit and instruct students to find three other students they share something in common with, though not through anything obvious or visible, such as hair color. The idea is to help them make connections that may not be immediately apparent.

Self-Disclosure Activity

Two Truths and a Lie

Divide the class into small groups with 5-6 members. Each group sits in a circle, and each participant self discloses and tells their group three statements; two are true and one is a lie. The other students in the group must guess which is the lie.

Name _____ Date _____

Getting Acquainted Interview

PURPOSE

To interview another person in order to get to know them well enough to introduce them to the rest of the group.

INSTRUCTIONS FOR STUDENT PLUS 2-3 CLASSMATES

1. Each individual should make a list of 10 interview questions that you would not mind someone asking you.

2. Choose a partner and exchange your list of questions with the person.

3. During the next 10 to 20 minutes you have in which to interview each other, each of you should write out your partner's answer as you ask them questions.

4. At the end of interview time, you and your partner join the larger group (if the group is larger than 20, you may want to divide into smaller groups). Each individual will introduce their new friend to the rest of the group using the information you received in the interview. Each partner may correct or modify the information.

DISCUSSION

1. What was the value of this activity?

2. What did you learn about your partner that you did not know prior to the interview?

3. How is an interview different from an ordinary discussion?

4. Do you believe that the information you have gained from your partner is accurate? Is this the same impression you had of your partner when you first saw this person?

5. Were your answers honest, or were you attempting to impress your partner? Explain.

6. Because of this experience in class, will you be willing to talk with this person in the courtyard, sit with this person in the cafeteria, or do something social with this person outside of school?

Name _____ Date _____

Explore Your Community Activity

PURPOSE

Explore online the geography and culture of people in your school, community, or neighborhood. Find ways to help others in your community. If you are able to visit people from other countries and cultures, do so. It really can open your ideas about how others live, work, and play …

INSTRUCTIONS

Write up a brief paragraph of what you found out.

1. What did you find out about your community?

2. What are your ideas that might help the community?

3. What was the value of this activity?

Name _____ Date _____

Who Am I Presentation

PURPOSE

To enable each person to know something about all the other people in the class—including the teacher.

INSTRUCTIONS

1. Construct outside of class a Who Am I Presentation by pasting or gluing fragments, pictures, or words torn out from magazines, newspapers, and so on onto a large poster board (or other chosen object) to form an abstract "picture" or composition. You may also create any of these words/pictures that you use.

   OR

2. You may develop your Who I Am Presentation using a computer generated creative approach, or another creative approach that is JUST **you**. (If in doubt, just check with the instructor.)

3. Each individual is asked to compose the presentation around the following ideas—this is what you will be graded on.

   a. Use at least three people who are the most influential in your life. What cultures impact your life?

   b. Use hobbies and interests you have.

   c. Use three words you would like to have said about you.

   d. Use the part of your personality of which you are most proud.

   e. Use the part of your personality that may create difficulties in your relationship with others.

   f. Use an accomplishment of which you are most proud.

   g. Use your likes and dislikes.

   h. Use the goals and values you have for your life.

   i. Use your background, family, and friends.

   j. Use your greatest lesson learned in life.

4. Give your presentation to the class, commenting on the various pictures or meanings reflected. The timeframe is approximately five minutes.

DISCUSSION

1. If you were to do your presentation again, what changes would you make?

2. What was the most difficult part of this assignment? Why?

Name _____ Date _____

First Impressions

PURPOSE

To utilize feedback in discovering how accurate your judgments are about people. To discover how first impressions influence our perceptions of others.

INSTRUCTIONS

1. Without speaking, select a person you do not know in the class and sit together.

2. Without verbally communicating with your partner, write down predictions and/or impressions about the person for the following items:

   a. Estimated Age: _____

   b. Major: _____

   c. Estimated Education: Did not complete high school _____
   Completed high school _____ Some college _____ College degree _____

   d. Nationality or Culture: _____

   e. Political Preference: _____

   f. Occupation: _____

   g. Marital Status: Married _____ Separated _____ Divorced _____
   Single _____ Widowed _____

   h. Children: Yes _____ No _____ How many? _____

   i. Interests:

_____ Sports, what type		_____ Gambling
_____ Camping		_____ Shopping
_____ Movies		_____ Artistic
_____ Gardening		_____ Music, what type?
_____ Dancing		_____ Reading, what type
_____ Politics		_____ Travel
_____ Exercising		_____ Writing
_____ Civic Activities		_____ Cooking
_____ TV		_____ Other

    j.   List any personality traits or characteristics that might describe this person:

        1)

        2)

        3)

        4)

        5)

DISCUSSION (WITH YOUR PARTNER):

1. Compare your impressions of each other. Discuss where you were correct and where you were incorrect.

2. As you compare your impressions/predictions with your partner for each item, be sure to comment on what clues or cues led you to make the prediction. In other words, why did you predict what you predicted? For example, did any of these concerns have an influence on your observations, impressions, and predictions?

    a.   Clothes/appearance

    b.   Anything you remembered from the first day of class

    c.   Eye contact or lack of eye contact

    d.   Sex and age of partner

    e.   Mannerisms when you first began to observe each other

    f.   Stereotyping according to ethnicity and race

    g.   Your own belief system and values—what you want your partner to believe

    h.   What other concerns had an impact?

3. Honestly, did first impressions because of overall appearance have anything to do with your observations and predictions?

DISCUSSION (WITH ALL OF THE CLASS MEMBERS):

1. How does this exercise apply to our everyday interactions with others?

2. How can we change our impressions of others?

Name _____ Date _____

Evaluating Stereotypes

PURPOSE

To clarify what stereotypes you have been taught about other groups and evaluate how the process of stereotyping works.

INSTRUCTIONS

The instructor will post the following list of words on sheets of paper around the room.

Republicans	Democrats
Gender	Gender
Old people	Teenagers
Blondes	Redheads
African American	Asian American
Native American	Hispanic American
Midwestern	Southern
Protestants	Jews
Higher income	Lower income
Lawyers	Car salespeople

1. Each member of the class is to circulate around the room, read the various categories, and write at least one stereotype he or she has heard under each heading. Be sure to not repeat anything that is already written.

2. After the members of the class have finished writing, they are then asked to go around the room and read all the stereotypes under each category and make note of any of particular interest.

3. The instructor will either divide the members into small groups or conduct a class discussion surrounding the following discussion questions.

DISCUSSION

1. What are your personal reactions to comments written under each heading of stereotypes?

2. How accurate are the stereotypes of their identities?

3. What have you learned about stereotyping others?

Name _____ Date _____

Where Does It Come From?

ASSESSING YOUR EMOTIONAL ATTACHMENTS AND SOCIAL TIES

INSTRUCTIONS

Refer to the definitions of Emotional Attachments and Social Ties in the chapter and then look at the following list. If the item provides you with no support, put a "0." If the item provides you with minimal support, put a "1" in the appropriate space, or if you feel that the item provides you with a lot of support, put a "2" in the appropriate space. For example, for Significant Others, you may have a 2 under Emotional Attachment and a 1 or 0 under Social Ties.

You may also want the people who are important to you to take this inventory and review their means of emotional attachment and social ties. If you have young children, you may want to review the inventory for them to make sure they have adequate means of support.

Attachment	Emotional Ties	Social
Partner: boy or girlfriend, husband or wife, parents, etc.	_____	_____
Friends: school-mates, co-workers, close friends, neighbors, etc.	_____	_____
Extended Family: aunts and uncles, grandparents, brothers and sisters, in-laws, etc.	_____	_____
Support Groups: singles clubs, men's groups, women's groups, 12 step groups, etc.	_____	_____
Teams: sport teams, hobby groups, singing groups, athletic club members, square dance groups, etc.	_____	_____
Service Groups: Rotary, Kiwanis, sororities and fraternities, Elks, Masons, Scouts, etc.	_____	_____
Racial, Ethnic, and Nationality Groups: associations, clubs, etc.	_____	_____
Vocational Groups: unions, firefighters, police associations, etc.	_____	_____
Religious Organizations: church, Bible study group, men's or women's groups, etc.	_____	_____

Community Groups: neighborhood associations, protection groups, etc. _____ _____

Total _____ _____

SCORING

Add your total points under each column. You should have a score of at least five in each column. The higher the score, the better. If your score is below a five in either column you may want to seek help in adding to your means of emotional attachments and/or social ties. Be prepared to discuss in class.

DISCUSSION

1. Explain from where you receive your emotional attachments. How important are these sources to you?

2. Explain from where you receive your social ties. How important are they to you?

3. What would you tell a friend who is lonely how to change in order to find emotional attachments and social ties?

Internet Search Activity

INSTRUCTIONS

The Oxford dictionary defines **"Heterosexual"** as a romantic and/or sexual attraction or behavior between people of opposite genders.

Webster's dictionary defines **"privilege"** as the right or immunity granted as an advantage or favor to some but not to others. **Heterosexual privilege confers unearned and unchallenged advantages and rewards on heterosexuals solely as a result of their sexual orientation.**

Heterosexism is the existence of advantages and rewards on heterosexuals solely as a result of their sexual orientation. Many of the things that heterosexuals take for granted may be unavailable to gay or bisexual or transgender people.

ADVANTAGES SEARCH

What are some of the advantages of being heterosexual "straight"?

Make a list of the advantages a heterosexual "straight" has.

- If you are "straight," what advantages do you enjoy that gay people are less likely to enjoy? Think hard—many of the things that heterosexuals take for granted are not equally available to everyone. Examples include displaying a picture of one's loved one without fear of retaliation or ridicule; not having to hide parts of one's life from family, friends, and co-workers; or having the loved one be legally recognized as the next-of-kin. How many other things can you think of?
- When you have made your list, go to www.yahoo.com or www.google.com and type "heterosexism" into the search box. What items could be added to your list as a result of your search? Why do you think you didn't see them earlier?

Name _____ Date _____

Human Relations Internet Search Activity

INSTRUCTIONS

Make a list of the careers a person can do or get a job doing in the field of Human Relations. Research two you might be interested in.

Looking on the Bright Side Exercise

WHY YOU SHOULD TRY IT

We all tend to ruminate on things that have gone wrong in our lives—a mistake we made at work, an evening that didn't go as planned. We might even think about them so often that our lives seem filled with these mishaps and disappointments. Focusing on them too much, however, can cast a pall over our lives and even be associated with depressive thinking.

Looking on the bright side even when things go wrong is a key component of optimism, which research links to lower rates of depression, a better ability to cope with stress, and more relationship satisfaction, among other benefits. While finding the silver lining on a negative experience might (understandably) make you fear turning into a Pollyanna, many of us have a tendency to look on the bright side too rarely, not too often. This exercise is designed to help you achieve a healthier balance.

WHY IT WORKS

Looking on the bright side of life in general, or of a bad situation in particular, can increase happiness by boosting your sense of self-worth, motivating you to go after your goals, and enhancing your enjoyment of life. Regularly completing the silver linings exercise can help you get in the habit of recognizing positive aspects of your life and seeing the upside to challenging situations rather than fixating on the downsides. With repeated practice, you may find that it comes more naturally to look on the bright side, even when faced with difficulties in your life.

EVIDENCE THAT IT WORKS

Sergeant, S., & Mongrain, M. (2014). An online optimism intervention reduces depression in pessimistic individuals. Journal of Consulting and Clinical Psychology, 82(2), 263-274.

RESULTS OF STUDY

Participants who completed a set of optimism exercises (this exercise and the Goal Visualization task) daily for three weeks reported greater engagement in life and less dysfunctional thinking (e.g., believing that small failures make one a failure as a person) at the end of the study than they had at the start of it. Participants who had a tendency to be pessimistic especially benefited from the exercise and showed fewer depressive symptoms afterward. However, these effects seemed to wear off two months later, suggesting the need to repeat this practice periodically.

Adapted from the Greater Good in Action Science Center: https://ggia.berkeley.edu

Relationships and Generations Activity

The Pew Research Center describes the generations in this chapter in a graph.

This provides the opportunity to look at others both by their place in the life cycle—whether a young adult, a middle-aged parent or a retiree—and by their membership in a cohort of individuals who were born at a similar time.

Where are you on the generation graph in chapter 1?

1. **Make a list of your closest friends.** Where are they on the generations list?

    Are they all on your age cohort?

    What are some of the world, national, and local experiences you have in common?

    List them.

2. **How many friends that are older than you do you have a relationship with?** What generation are they?

3. **How do you feel around other generations?** Are you uncomfortable/comfortable with people older than you?

4. **Do you want to have more friends of different generations?** Discuss this with others to come up with a plan for meeting these people.

Name _____ Date _____

Draw Your Own Johari Window

PURPOSE

To gain a better understanding of yourself and examine the degree of overall "openness" of your communication.

To understand self-disclosure as a situational concept—you respond (communicate) differently in different situations.

To provide insight into your "open self," "blind self," "hidden self," and "unknown self."

INSTRUCTIONS

Draw your own Johari Window for each of the following situations:

1. When you are with your closest friend.

2. When you are with your parent or parents.

3. When you are in this class.

4. When you are at a social gathering with people you do not know very well.

In addition to the above activity, you may want to explain the purpose of the Johari Window to the following individuals: your best friend, one of your parents, another member of this class, and a new acquaintance, and have them draw the Johari Window as they perceive you. This will give you an idea of how others perceive you.

DISCUSSION

1. Compare your windows in the different situations. Do they differ? Why?

2. How could you become a more "open" communicator?

3. How do others perceive you? Do you agree with their perception of you?

4. What could you do to change other people's perception of you?

Name _____ Date _____

Getting Acquainted

LEARNING JOURNAL - CHAPTER 1

Select the statement below that best defines your feelings about the personal value or meaning gained from this chapter and respond below the dotted line.

I learned that I . . .   I was surprised that I . . .

I realized that I . . .   I was pleased that I . . .

I discovered that I . . .   I was displeased that I . . .

Case studies

Self-fulfilling Prophecies Self-fulfilling prophecies occur all the time, although you are not always aware of them.

- John hates math, but registers for a math class anyway, knowing that he will have difficulty learning the material. He ends up dropping the class because he is failing the course.
- Jane expected to become nervous and not do well in her job interview, and later she did actually become nervous during her interview.
- Terry's boss assigns them a new task, saying that Terry will have difficulty completing it. Terry proved him right and did not complete it.
- A parent tells his daughter Dana that they are a brat. Dana proves him right and keeps causing problems.
- You anticipated having a good (or terrible) time at a social affair, and your expectations came true.

In each of these cases, there is a good chance that the event happened because you expected it to happen. How could a change in thought process make the outcomes different in each of these situations?

Chapter 2
Self-Awareness

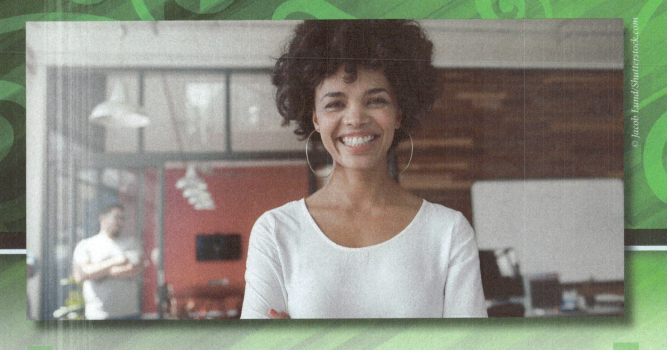

© Jacob Lund/Shutterstock.com

An individual's self-concept is the core of their personality. It affects every aspect of human behavior: The ability to learn, the capacity to grow and change, the choice of friends, mates, and careers. It is no exaggeration to say that a strong, positive self-image is the best possible preparation for success in life. —Joyce Brothers

Think About This...

In my memories of when I was a "little" kid, between the ages of two and four, it seemed like everything I would attempt would be a "No, No." "No" to this, and "No" to that, and "No" to everything. For a while I almost thought my name was "No No." I soon learned that my life was much easier if I just sat and watched television.

Life was not much fun, because I was afraid to try anything since I thought I would get in trouble. I didn't think I was a very good kid, since most of the people around me kept telling me that I wasn't capable of doing anything. I thought it was because I was "no good" and "inferior," but in reality I just wasn't old enough to do what I wanted to do. I didn't realize that.

When I turned six, I was excited because it was time to go to school like the "big kids." It was a new life, and I needed a change. It didn't take long for me to realize that I was not as good as the rest of the kids.

They laughed at my overalls and shiny shoes. When it came time to select teams, I was the last to be picked since I was short, skinny, and wore glasses.

I wanted to be liked by the other students and my teachers, so I became the "class clown." I needed attention and I got it, but it was the wrong type of attention. I became depressed and felt inferior to the people around me, so I withdrew into my own little world and isolated myself as much as I could. I would sit in the back of the room at school, and at home I would go to my room and draw.

My early school years were not fun. In middle school I got mixed up with the "wrong crowd." I wanted to be accepted, so I thought I had to be like everyone else. I wanted to be part of a group with an identity, so I got involved in a gang. In the meantime, I tried a few drugs and got in trouble. It wasn't a happy time in my life.

In ninth grade, I registered for an art class, not knowing what art was all about. The teacher asked the students to draw a picture. I turned mine in and the teacher thought it was great. The teacher thought that I had talent, but I knew better. I had been told that I was "dumb, inferior, and not capable of accomplishing anything," so why try. My teacher encouraged me and kept telling me how good I really was, so I kept trying. All of a sudden the other students were also telling me that I was good, and I began to believe it. I became motivated to succeed in the field of art. I overcame my depression and anxiety, set some goals, and found some friends who accepted me for being me, and not because of my size or looks.

I am now a professional artist and feel good about myself and my life. I like people and accept them as they are, and will allow them the freedom to grow and develop as individuals. I hope you will, too.

"Self-Image" Development

Reviewing the story above, we realize that people acquire a sense of self throughout their life. It is an ongoing process that evolves from our experiences and interactions with others within the environment. Significant adults in our life also provide us with feedback as to who we are. This is the beginning of *self-image development*. In this chapter we will learn ways in which we can identify and better understand our *real selves* and learn strategies to improve self-esteem.

Self-image is the mental picture, generally of a kind that is quite resistant to change, that depicts not only details that are potentially available to objective investigation by others (height, weight, hair color, gender, IQ score), but also items that have been learned by that person about themselves, either from personal experiences or by internalizing the judgments of others. A person's self-image is their answer to the question "What do you believe people think about you?"

Self-Image Most psychologists say that self-image is acquired. During infancy, early emotional experiences form the basis for its development. Our *self-image* is affected by all the experiences we have had—successes and failures, compliments and "put downs," happy times and sad times, personal thoughts and experiences, our own ex-

> *Your only obligation in any lifetime is to be true to yourself.*
> —RICHARD BACH

pectations and others' expectations of us, and the way other people have reacted to us, especially in our early adulthood. As you can see, a person's self-concept is not a singular mental self-image, but a multifaceted system of related images and ideas. A more technical term for self-image commonly used by social and cognitive psychologists is **self-schema**. Self-schemas are also considered the organization of the traits people use to define themselves; the person draws information about the self into a coherent scheme (Schacter, 2016).

> **Who am I?** Before we go on, take a few minutes and try to answer the question by writing ten brief statements that begin with *I am* _____. After you have completed your list, examine it to find ways that your self-image has evolved. It may have developed from your social world or the nature of your interactions with others, with statements such as: "I am a friendly person," "I am a shy person," "I am a family-oriented person," "I am a political activist." Still other statements may refer to traits that you attribute to yourself either because other people have attributed them to you or because you have seen that you stand out in those ways in comparison to other people: "I am short," "I am good at math," "I am conscientious." You probably will not find any self-statements in your list that do not stem in one way or another from your social environment.

WHAT IS EGO IDENTITY?

One of the main elements of Erikson's psychosocial stage theory is the development of ego identity. It is the conscious sense of self that we develop through social interaction, which is constantly changing due to new experiences and information we acquire in our daily interactions with others (Arnold, 2017).

According to the book *Essential Social Psychology* by Richard Crisp and Rhiannon Turner:

© Roman Samborskyi/Shutterstock.com

We learn who we are from the way we are treated by the important people in our lives.

- The individual self consists of attributes and personality traits that differentiate us from other individuals. Examples include introversion or extroversion.
- The relational self is defined by our relationships with significant others. Examples include siblings, friends, and spouses.
- The collective self reflects our membership in social groups. Examples include British, Republican, African-American, or gay.

Since we are talking about self-awareness, let's understand what the terms are, because they cause much confusion. More terms are in the Glossary in the back of the book. There is also more discussion of these concepts throughout the text.

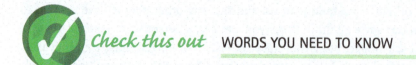
> *I am not what I think I am, I am not what you think I am. I am what I think you think I am.*
> —AARON BLIEBERG AND HARRY LEUBLING

Ableism - Discrimination or prejudice against individuals with disabilities.

Cultural Difference - To be highly skilled in interpersonal relations you must recognize and appreciate individual and demographic (group or category) differences as well as cultural differences. People from the same demographic group often come from many different cultures; respectfully navigating these differences calls for cultural sensitivity, political correctness *(also called PC)*, cultural intelligence, and respect for all workers and cultures.

Gender/Gender Identity - A person's innate, deeply felt psychological identification as a man, woman, transgender, or somewhere on the spectrum, which may or may not correspond to their sex assigned at birth. People are called cisgendered, gender queer, transgendered, or gender fluid. *Gender identity is often conflated with sexual identity.* According to David Schmitt (2017), cultural psychology, and new studies of **transsexuality,** along with our evolutionary heritage, all point to the same conclusion: There are psychological differences between men and women.

(But, just as the evidence is mounting that psychological sex differences are real, denial of differences have become rampant).

Whether you identify as a man or a woman is your ***sexual identity.*** When they study differences in the way self-identified men and women think (such as how they read a map), feel (the degree to which they experience empathy), and behave (say, their likelihood of committing homicide), psychologists are said to be investigating psychological **sex differences.**

Gender, or gender psychology, according to the American Psychological Association, reflects *the attitudes, feelings, and behaviors that a given culture associates with biological sex.* The term ***gender* refers to whether a person is typically masculine and/or feminine as defined by their local culture**. (Sometimes this is called *gender-role or sex-role orientation or gender expression*, but we need to be clear when discussing sex differences.)

Transgender - Transgender is an umbrella term for persons whose gender identity, gender expression, or behavior does not conform to that typically associated with the sex to which they were assigned at birth. Gender identity refers to a person's internal sense of being male, female, or something else; gender expression refers to the way a person communicates gender identity to others through behavior, clothing, hairstyles, voice, or body characteristics. "Trans" is sometimes used as shorthand for "transgender." While transgender is generally a good term to use, not everyone whose appearance or behavior is gender-nonconforming will identify as a transgender person. The ways that transgender people are talked about in popular culture, academia, and science are constantly changing, particularly as individuals' awareness, knowledge, and openness about transgender people and their experiences grow (WWW.APA.org).

Sex Roles - People are born male or female, and their society teaches them how to be masculine or feminine. Also called *sex-role stereotyping.*

Intersectionality - This term started in the 1980s when a lawyer, Kimberly Crenshaw, realized we did not have a way to talk about the experiences of people of color (racial discrimination) and different experiences of men and women (gender discrimination) without looking at the intersections of who we are. Intersectionality refers to the reality that we all have multiple identities. It also gives us a way to talk about impressions and privilege that overlap and reinforce each other. Black men and black women both endure racial discrimination, and black women and white women both endure gender discrimination. A video is included in the back of this section that explains intersectionality visually.

Bias - Positive or negative feelings or opinions about a social group; prejudice.

Implicit Bias - Implicit is unquestioning or unreserved; absolute: implied, rather than expressly stated: implicit agreement. **Bias** is a particular tendency, trend, inclination, feeling, or opinion, especially one that is preconceived or unreasoned: unreasonably hostile feelings or opinions about a social group; prejudice. So **implicit bias** would be an unquestioning preconceived notion or opinion of a social group: predjudice.

Bisexual - Traditionally bisexual has referred to romantic or sexual attraction to two, and not more than two, genders, specifically male and female. However, the term is increasingly being used to refer to a level of sexual fluidity in which an individual moves bidirectionally along a spectrum of sexuality. This newer sense accounts for attraction to people who do not fall within the gender binary.

Disabilities - the consequence of an impairment that may be physical, cognitive, intellectual, mental, sensory, developmental, or some combination of these that results in restrictions on an individual's ability to participate in what is considered "normal" in their everyday society. Many people would rather be referred to as a person with a disability instead of handicapped.

Disabled - Having a physical or mental condition that limits movements, senses, or activities.

LGBTQ - An acronym that originated in the 1990s and replaced what was formerly known as "the gay community." The acronym was created to be more inclusive of diverse groups. **LGBTQ** stands for lesbian, gay, bisexual, transgender, and queer (and/or questioning) individuals/identities.

The "LGB" in this term refers to sexual orientation. Sexual orientation is defined as an often enduring pattern of emotional, romantic, and/or sexual attractions of men to women or women to men (heterosexual), of women to women or men to men (homosexual), or by men or women to both sexes (bisexual). It also refers to an individual's sense of personal and social identity based on those attractions, related behaviors, and membership in a community of others who share those attractions and behaviors. Some people who have same-sex attractions or relationships may identify as "queer," or, for a range of personal, social, or political reasons, may choose not to self-identify with these or any labels.

The "T" in LGBT stands for transgender or gender non-conforming, and is an umbrella term for people whose gender identity or gender expression does not conform to that typically associated with the sex to which they were assigned at birth. Some who do not identify as either male or female prefer the term "genderqueer." While it is important to understand that sexual orientation and gender identity are not the same thing, they do both reflect differing forms of gender norm transgression and share an intertwined social and political history (www.apa.org).

Privilege - a right or benefit that is given to some people and not to others. A special opportunity to do something that makes you proud. The advantage that wealthy and powerful people have over other people in a society (Gender + Equality Center - The University of Oklahoma, 2019).

We will now begin to explore many of the theories and ideas of how we become the people we are. Let us take a look at how other people influence our feelings about ourselves.

Influence. Think about the people who matter in your life, for good or not so good. How have they affected you? How have they affected your self-image? To whom are you a significant other? Think about the kind of influence you are having on their self-image. Is it a positive or negative effect? If you are a parent, a spouse, a boyfriend or girlfriend, a teacher, a son or daughter, a brother or sister, or a person who can have any impact on another individual, you are a significant other.

> *One isn't born one's self. One is born with a mass of expectations, a mass of other people's ideas— and you have to work through it all.*
> —V. S. NAIPAUL

A parent says to a child, "You'd better not try that, I don't think you can do it." You ask your husband, "Can't you ever do anything right?" A teacher tells a student, "Everyone else in the class understands it; what's wrong with you?" A son tells his mother, "You're a rotten parent, you made me this way." Positive reinforcement helps people have a healthy view of themselves. These negative comments, heard frequently enough, can negatively impact a person's view of themselves. If we hear these comments too often, we soon begin to believe them, especially if the person saying them is important or significant to us.

From all of these numerous experiences, we construct a mental blueprint of the sort of person we believe we are. Once an idea or belief about ourselves goes into this mental picture, it becomes "true" as far as we are personally concerned. We generally do not question its validity, but proceed to act upon it as if it were true. Most of our actions, feelings, responses, and even our abilities are consistent with this contracted self-image. If we see ourselves as incapable when we enter a math class, we will most likely experience difficulty and failure. If you view yourself as well qualified and capable as you are interviewed for a job, the interviewer will evaluate you on a positive basis, and this will improve your prospects of getting the job. This is often called the *self-fulfilling prophecy*. For a review of this discussion on the self-fulfilling prophecy, refer to Chapter One.

© New Africa/Shutterstock.com

Becoming Aware of **Privilege: People Learn Their Income Privilege**
https://www.youtube.com/watch?v=752SAKNBMRk
https://www.youtube.com/watch?v=4K5fbQ1-zps

Life of Privilege Explained in a $100 Race

Think/Pair/Share Activity

Do you ever compare yourself to other people? How does this comparison influence your feelings about yourself?

Gaining self-knowledge from our perceptions of others: social comparison. How many times have you asked yourself such questions as, "Am I as good looking as Jake?" "Can I play tennis as well as Anne?" "Am I as smart as Marti?" We gain self-knowledge from our own behavior; we also gain it from others through *social comparison*, the process in which individuals evaluate their thoughts, feelings, behaviors, and abilities in relation to other people. Social comparison helps individuals evaluate themselves, tells them what their distinctive characteristics are, and aids them in building an identity. We tend to compare ourselves with others of our own sex; males compare themselves to other males and females compare themselves to other females. People who are gender fluid or atypical in some way have fewer examples for comparison. Drawing on her work as a professor of cognitive neuroimaging, Gina Rippon unpacks the stereotypes that bombard us from our earliest moments and shows how the question "Do you have a female brain or a male brain?" impacts our ideas of ourselves and even shapes our brains (Rippon, 2019). Students who are questioning their gender may become quite confused from the societal, social, and family messages they are given. Social comparison allows us a way to decide if we are the *same or different, inferior or superior* (Festinger, 1954; Kassin et al., 2016).

> *Our main task in life is to give birth to ourselves.*
> —ERICH FROMM

Alike or different? How did you learn about your ethnicity or that you are male or female? A child who is told that he is a different color than his schoolmates begins to see himself as different. A 6'4" female student compares herself with her female schoolmates and perceives herself as weird. "All my friends are from Vietnam, just like I am, and this makes me feel like I'm part of the group; I'm the same as they are." This perception of sameness or difference in relation to others has a great influence on how we perceive ourselves (Flora, 2005).

Inferior or superior? How often do we label ourselves or others? We tend to decide our social value status by comparing ourselves to others. Are we attractive or ugly? A success or failure? Intelligent depends on those against whom we measure ourselves. In school we compare ourselves with other students: "I'm not as smart as José," or "I'm more intelligent than Gretchen." In sports we tend to compare ourselves with other athletes: "I'm a better racquetball player than Steve," or "Ben's a better quarterback than I am." Some individuals compare themselves to social heroes, rock stars, celebrities, professional athletes, or others' social media (remember, social media is edited for only the best stuff, and no down sides).

Social comparison theory has been modified over the years and continues to provide an important rationale for why we affiliate with others and how we come to know ourselves (Kimmel & Aronson, 2011).

The importance of self-concept. When our *self-concept* is intact and secure, we feel good. When it is threatened, we feel anxious and insecure. When our self-concept is one that we can be wholesomely proud of, we feel self-confident. We feel free to be ourselves and to express ourselves. When it is an object of shame, we attempt to hide it rather than express it—we withdraw inside ourselves. If we have strong, positive feelings about ourselves, we want and feel that we deserve a good loving relationship, or a good job, and even a feeling of freedom—whatever we think of as the highest good for us. On the other hand, if we have a poorly developed, negative, or inferior self-image, we may expect very little for ourselves. We may settle for second or third best because we feel that is all we deserve. In essence, we project to others the way we feel about ourselves. If we cannot like and respect ourselves, how can we ever hope other people will see us as worthy individuals who have something to contribute to the world in which we live?

To gain a better understanding of how the self-image evolves over a life span, we need to study some of the traditional theories of personality that will provide us with a foundation of how we become aware of who we really are.

Personality Development

Throughout our lives, we will attempt to understand other people, such as our boyfriends or girlfriends, our bosses, our husbands or wives, our teachers or anyone we encounter as a part of our routine. In addition, we will also attempt to understand ourselves. The following theories will help us gain an understanding of ourselves and the people around us. We will consider a variety of theories that will help you in the journey of finding yourself and answering the question, *Who am I?*

The theory that has had the greatest impact on the field of psychology was developed by Sigmund Freud in the 19th century. This classic theory has created a lot of controversy, not only within the realm of psychology, but also within our everyday lives—in literature, movies, child-rearing practices, and the feminist movement, among many other areas of life. Let us take a look at some of Freud's ideas—**The Psychodynamic Approach**.

Sigmund Freud. Freud's theory of personality development provided the foundation for many other personality theories. Freud in *A General Introduction To Psycho-Analysis*, 2001 edition, states that a person's personality is made up of three distinct but interrelated parts: the id, ego, and superego.

What is this thing called an id? The ***id*** is composed of the basic biological drives that motivate an individual. This includes the hunger drive, the thirst drive, sexual impulses, and other needs that assure survival and bring pleasure. The id operates according to the *pleasure principle*, which demands immediate gratification of its urges, and some people believe this often leads to a lack of impulse control—much like a preschooler throwing a temper tantrum. Much of the criticism of Freud's theories are related to the emphasis he puts on the sexual impulses, pleasure drives, and their control over our behavior (Larsen & Buss, Personality Psychology: Domains of Knowledge about Human Nature (2017).

The *superego* incorporates the values and morals of society which are learned from one's parents and others. It develops around the age of 3–5 and is acquired from the environment around us. It consists of our values, morals, religious beliefs, and ideals of our parents and society. Another name for the superego would be our *conscience*. The superego tells us what is right and wrong, what we should do and should not do—our *moral compass.* This is the part of our personality that makes us feel guilty and experience anxiety when we do things we should not, and allows us to reward ourselves or pat ourselves on the back when we doing something good. As you can observe, the id and the superego are in conflict. Each characteristic is trying to take control of your life (Freud 1965). Remember the cartoon with the man with the devil on one shoulder and an angel on the other shoulder, both giving him advice? You could use the following analogy—the id is the "devil" and the superego is an "angel," each attempting to control your life. If either the id or the superego takes control of your life, you may develop some form of personality disorder.

Ego, the reality principle. The ego develops before the superego. The ego begins to develop the first time a child understands the word *no.* With that first "no," the ego has begun to develop and begins to moderate and restrain the id by requiring it to seek gratification of its impulses through realistic and socially acceptable means. The conflict between the id and the superego causes anxiety, which, in turn, leads the ego to create defense mechanisms to control the anxiety. Defense mechanisms will be discussed in Chapter Eight. The *ego, the reality principle,* is the rational, logical, and realistic part of your personality that attempts to maintain balance between the id and superego.

Many critics point out that Freud's theories are not supported by any empirical (experimental) data. In fact, as researchers began to take a more scientific look at his ideas, they found that several were unable to be supported: in order for a theory to be scientifically valid, it must be possible to disprove ("falsify") it with experimental evidence, and many of Freud's notions are not falsifiable.

In his singular emphasis on the structure of the human mind, Freud paid little to no attention to the impact of environment, sociology, or culture. His theories were highly focused on pathology, and largely ignored "normal," healthy functioning. He has also been criticized for his myopic view of human sexuality to the exclusion of other important factors (https://courses.lumenlearning.com/boundless-psychology/chapter/psychodynamic-perspectives-on-personality/2019).

Most psychologists today think that Freud put too much emphasis on the biological drives, specifically the sex drive as a major part of the id. For example, Alfred Adler, an early member of Freud's inner circle, argued that the foremost human drive is not sexual, but a striving for superiority (2014). Also, Erik Erikson, an original follower of Freud, realized that the biological drives are important, but that the effects of the environment on our development and on us are as important, if not more important. Let's take a look at Adler's and Erikson's theories.

I do the very best I know how, the very best I can, and I mean to keep on doing it to the end.
—ABRAHAM LINCOLN

I am not what I think I am, I am not what you think I am. I am what I think you think I am.
—AARON BLIEBERG AND HARRY LEUBLING

Adler's Individual Psychology Theory

To Alfred Adler, personality arises from our attempts to overcome or compensate for fundamental feelings of inadequacy. Adler was responsible for coining the popular term **inferiority complex**, a concept, he argued, that underlies and motivates a great deal of human behavior. From his point of view, it is our natural drive for superiority that explains motivation, not sexual gratification as envisioned by Freud. Adler (2016) viewed striving for superiority as a universal drive to adapt, improve oneself, and master life's challenges. He felt that young children understandably feel weak and helpless in comparison to more competent older children and adults. These early inferiority feelings supposedly motivate individuals to acquire new skills and develop new talents (Nevid & Rathus, 2019).

> *Your only obligation in any lifetime is to be true to yourself.*
> —RICHARD BACH

Adler (2016) also noted that everyone has to work to overcome some feelings of inferiority. **Compensation** involves efforts to overcome imagined or real weaknesses, limitations, or inferiorities by developing other areas of our personalities. Adler (2016) believed that compensation is entirely normal. However, in some people, inferiority feelings can become excessive, resulting in what is called an inferiority complex, exaggerated feelings of weakness and inadequacy. Adler thought that either parental pampering or parental neglect could cause an inferiority problem. He also believed that early childhood experiences exert momentous influences over adult personality (2014).

> *Shame corrodes the very part of us that believes we are capable of change.*
> —BRENÉ BROWN

Adler was careful to explain that an inferiority complex can distort the normal process of striving for superiority. He felt that some people engage in overcompensation in order to conceal their feelings of inferiority. Instead of working to master life's challenges, people with an inferiority complex work to achieve status, gain power over others, and acquire the trappings of success (fancy clothes, impressive cars, or whatever looks important to them). Unfortunately, they tend to flaunt their success in an effort to cover up their underlying inferiority complex (Adler, 2009).

© nixki/Shutterstock.com

Birth order. It was also Adler who first focused attention on the possible importance of *birth order* as a factor governing personality. Although his theory created many studies on the effects of birth order, the studies failed to support his hypothesis. In recent years, there has been some revived interest in the relationship between birth order and personality, but the research findings have continued to be somewhat inconsistent (Weiten et al., 2017). Yet, the topic is very interesting to discuss.

Think/Pair/Share Activity

In groups of 4, discuss this question: What is wrong with me? After 10 minutes, report back to the class.

Erikson's Eight Stages

Erik Erikson. Erik and Joan Erikson have identified *eight stages of psychosocial development* that each individual experiences in their lifetime. Joan Erikson was the main collaborator in developing husband Erik Erikson's eight stages of psychosocial development. Her contribution to Erikson's theory of personality could have been neglected, but was nevertheless important: Erik admitted being unable to distinguish between his own contribution and his wife's. Joan had a great influence on the development of the stages and on the inclusion of the eighth stage. Each stage is characterized by specific stages that must be mastered. If these stages are not satisfied, an unfavorable outcome throws us off balance and makes it harder to deal with later crises. As each stage is completed, we continue to build toward a positive, healthy development and a satisfying life. They believed that people who are plagued with unfavorable outcomes will continue to face frustration and conflict while striving to develop as a person. A brief description of Erikson's eight stages of psychosocial development follows (Feldman, 2016).

> *Erikson's Stages of Psychosocial Development*
> *https://www.youtube.com/watch?v=9s2dYVhtFnE*

Erikson's Eight Stages of Psychosocial Development

1. **Trust vs. Mistrust.** Infancy (birth to 18 months). During the first years of life, a child is completely dependent on others for the satisfaction of his or her needs. If a child is parented with secure love and positive encouragement and their needs are satisfied on a consistent basis, the child will feel comfortable and secure. If the child's needs are not satisfied on a regular basis, *mistrust* will develop, and this may become the core of later insecurity and suspiciousness. This child will become *mistrusting* and fearful of others and have difficulty developing close, trusting relationships with others in the future.

2. **Autonomy vs. Doubt and Shame.** Early Childhood (2 to 3 years). During ages 18 months through three, a child is attempting to become more independent. They are learning to walk, talk, explore, and become toilet trained. The people around him or her, especially the parents, help the child to develop a sense of independence and autonomy by encouraging him to try new skills and by reassuring him or her if he fails. Consistent discipline is also important during this time. If the parents are inconsistent, overprotective, or show disapproval while the child is attempting to do things on their own, they may become doubtful, unsure, and ashamed. If a child is told by a *significant* authority figure that they may be able to

read or be toilet trained, they may wonder, "What is wrong with me? My parents say I may be able to do that, but I can't do it." This child may feel doubtful and shamed and thus feel negative about their capabilities. A child who has accomplished some of these tasks and is given encouragement and positive reinforcement will feel confident and independent.

3. **Initiative vs. Guilt.** Preschool (3 to 5 years). During the ages of three through five, the child moves from simple self-management or self-restraint to an ability to take control. This is the *questioning and exploring stage* when a child wants to try anything and everything. The child becomes very curious about the world around them. If they are encouraged to take the *initiative* and explore the world, the child will feel good about themselves and will continue to be curious in the future. If the child's activities and curiosity are not encouraged, the child will feel *guilty* whenever they take the initiative, and this can cause the individual to become passive. Why try to do something if adults keep showing disapproval? This often instills *learned helplessness*.

4. **Industry vs. Inferiority.** School Age (6 to 12 years). Important Events: Schools assume that the child is between the ages of six and twelve and is excited about life and motivated to solve problems and accomplish tasks. These are the early school years when ideally the child is making new friends, joining clubs and teams, and succeeding in school. When a child has a task to complete, such as a homework assignment, or cookies to sell, or a craft project, the child may attempt to accomplish the task with encouragement from others. The parents may not intervene and complete the task for the child. Otherwise, the child will quickly learn that others will complete the task, so why try? Or possibly the child will feel inferior and incapable because their parents are completing the tasks for them. The goal of good parenting is that accomplishment of tasks, when rewarded or recognized, leads to healthy development. Many parents feel like they are being responsible parents by "helping" or correcting children, which in reality, hinders their development. During this stage, the child is becoming involved in the outside world, and other people such as teachers, classmates, and other adults can have a great influence on the child's attitude toward themselves. If someone is there to bail you out, then they are "helicopter parents," and then why would you need to learn independence?

5. **Identity vs. Role Confusion.** Adolescence (12 to 20 years). A person is caught between childhood and adulthood (Biological adolescence ends about 24-28 years). The major task to accomplish during this stage is to answer the question, "Who am I?" Adolescence is a turbulent time for many individuals. Mental and physical maturation brings on new feelings and new attitudes of which people are unsure. Should these new feelings and attitudes be expressed or inhibited—especially one's newfound sex drive?

Our identity evolves from our self-perceptions and our relationships with others. People need to see themselves as positive, capable, and lovable individuals as well as having the feeling that they are accepted by others. Otherwise, they will experience **role confusion**, an uncertainty about who they are and where they are going. Role confusion may lead to a constant searching for acceptance and a feeling of belonging. This search for identity can lead people to unhealthy relationships and to alternatives such as drugs and gangs.

Be yourself; everyone else is taken.
—OSCAR WILDE

The beginning of the adult years. Freud did not put much emphasis on the adult years, but Erikson noticed that we continue to go through different stages as we age.

6. **Intimacy vs. Isolation Young Adulthood (20 to 40 years).** Now that we feel good about ourselves and have an *identity*, we are ready to form intimate, loving relationships and learn to share with others. During the young-adult years we must develop the ability to care about others and express a willingness to share experiences with them. Marriage, committed relationships, and sexual intimacy do not guarantee these qualities. Failure to establish intimacy with others leads to a deep sense of *isolation*. The person feels lonely and uncared for in life. A person who satisfies this stage is capable of developing close, intimate, and sharing relationships with others and feels comfortable and secure in these relationships. Pew research (2017) indicates that young adults are choosing not to marry or marrying later in life, suggesting that they are building close relationships with friends. The median age at first marriage had reached its highest point on record: 30 years for men and 28 years for women in 2018, according to the U.S. Census Bureau. The average age at which U.S. women first become mothers is 26.4—comparable to the age at first birth among Latvian women, but lower than in the 28 other nations in the Organization for Economic Cooperation and Development (OECD) for which data is available (Pew Research 2018).

7. **Generativity vs. Self-Absorption Middle Adulthood (40–65 years).** Important Events: Career and Parenthood. Until middle age, we seem to be preoccupied with ourselves. Even the intimacy stage is primarily for the self to prevent loneliness. Now we are ready to look beyond the self and look to the future, not only for ourselves, but also for others. This seems to be the best time to establish a family, because we are concerned about the development and welfare of others. This is the time in our life when we feel productive and are concerned for the benefit of humankind. What about the individual who does not feel productive and also feels like they are not accomplishing any goals in life? This person feels trapped. Life loses its meaning and the person feels bitter, dreary, unfulfilled, and stagnant. This person becomes preoccupied with the self, personal needs, and interests. Daniel Levinson (1986) wrote before his death in 1994 extensively about stages of adult development. However, most of Levinson's research and work were based on the study of men (Newton, 1994). According to Levinson, if people do not go through a ***mid-life transition stage***, they may live a life of *staleness and resignation*. Some individuals, approximately two to five percent of the population (McCrea & Costa, 2005), will experience a painful and disruptive struggle, which is called the ***mid-life crisis.*** This is similar to the adolescent identity crisis (Erikson stage of identity versus role confusion), where the individual seeks a new identity or to find an identity. Because these individuals have not satisfied their goals they had set for themselves, they experience frustration. It is not uncommon for individuals to divorce their spouses, quit their jobs, buy a convertible, and attempt to start all over again.

> Before his death Rabbi Zusya said, "In the world to come, they will not ask me, 'Why were you not Moses?' They will ask me, 'Why were you not Zusya?'"

What dreams do you have for your life?

© REDPIXEL.PL/Shutterstock.com

8. **Ego Integrity vs. Despair Maturity (65 years–death).** Important Events: Reflection on life. Old age should be a time of reflection, when a person should be able to look back over the events of a lifetime with a sense of acceptance and satisfaction. This is the type of person who has tried to live life to its fullest. The individual who wishes they could live life over again, and also feels cheated or deprived of any of the breaks in life, will live a life of regret and failure. This is the person who keeps saying, "What if …?" or "If I had taken that opportunity …" and because of this, feels depressed and will be unhappy the rest of their life. However, newer research indicates that it is possible to resolve this issue and move into acceptance and end life with integrity.

As most people continue through this stage, they re-evaluate the meaning of life for themselves and ideally find a new meaning that will help reduce fear and anxiety and help prepare them for facing death.

What traits do you think this woman possesses?

© Sergey Mironov/Shutterstock.com

Navigating the Twelve Stages of Life. Thomas Armstrong has written that each stage of life has its own unique "gift" to contribute to the world. We need to value each one of these gifts if we are to truly support the deepest needs of human life. Here are what he calls the twelve gifts of the human life cycle:

Prebirth: Potential – The child who has not yet been born could become anything—a Michelangelo, a Shakespeare, a Martin Luther King—and thus holds for all of humanity the principle of what we all may yet become in our lives.

GENDER AND YOU

MEN OR WOMEN: WHO'S THE BETTER LEADER?

Acccording to Brené Brown, leadership is not about titles, status, and wielding power. A leader is anyone who takes responsibility for recognizing the potential in people and ideas, and has the courage to develop that potential (2018). According to a 2014 Pew Research Center study, Americans believe, in general, that women in high political offices are better than men in several different capacities. For example, when it comes to working out compromises, 41% say women are better at it than men (27% say men are better). Thirty percent say women work harder to improve the quality of life for Americans, as opposed to 22% who say men work harder at it. Thirty percent also believe that women stand up for beliefs despite political pressure, as opposed to 19% for men. Women are rated as being more honest and ethical, with 37% compared to 30% for men. Finally, women are perceived as being more persuasive than men, at 25%. Men rated 18% for persuasiveness.

Brown, *Dare to Lead: Brave Work. Tough Conversations. Whole Hearts* (2018) and Adapted from Pew Research Center. Survey conducted Nov. 12-21, 2014.

Birth: Hope – When a child is born, it instills in its parents and other caregivers a sense of optimism; a sense that this new life may bring something new and special into the world. Hence the newborn represents the sense of hope that we all nourish inside of ourselves to make the world a better place.

Infancy (Ages 0-3): Vitality – The infant is a vibrant and seemingly unlimited source of energy. Babies thus represent the inner dynamo of humanity, ever fueling the fires of the human life cycle with new channels of psychic power.

Early Childhood (Ages 3-6): Playfulness – When young children play, they recreate the world anew. They take what is and combine it with what is possible to fashion events that have never been seen before in the history of the world. As such, they embody the principle of innovation and transformation that underlies every single creative act that has occurred in the course of civilization.

Middle Childhood (Ages 6-8): Imagination – In middle childhood, the sense of an inner subjective self develops for the first time, and this self is alive with images taken in from the outer world, and brought up from the depths of the unconscious. This imagination serves as a source of creative inspiration in later life for artists, writers, scientists, and anyone else who finds their days and nights enriched for having nurtured a deep inner life.

Late Childhood (Ages 9-11): Ingenuity – Older children have acquired a wide range of social and technical skills that enable them to come up with marvelous strategies and inventive solutions for dealing with the increasing pressures that society places on them. This principle of ingenuity lives on in that part of ourselves that ever seeks new ways to solve practical problems and cope with everyday responsibilities.

Adolescence (Ages 12-20): Passion – The biological event of puberty unleashes a powerful set of changes in the adolescent body that reflect themselves in a teenager's sexual, emotional, cultural, and/or spiritual passion. Adolescent passion thus represents a significant touchstone for anyone who is seeking to reconnect with their deepest inner zeal for life.

Early Adulthood (Ages 20-35): Enterprise – It takes enterprise for young adults to accomplish their many responsibilities, including finding a home and mate, establishing a family or circle of friends, and/or getting a good job. This principle of enterprise thus serves us at any stage of life when we need to go out into the world and make our mark.

Midlife (Ages 35-50): Contemplation – After many years in young adulthood of following society's scripts for creating a life, people in midlife often take a break from worldly responsibilities to reflect upon the deeper meaning of their lives, the better to forge ahead with new understanding. This element of contemplation represents an important resource that we can all draw upon to deepen and enrich our lives at any age.

Mature Adulthood (Ages 50-80): Benevolence – Those in mature adulthood have raised families, established themselves in their work life, and become contributors to the betterment of society through volunteerism, mentorships, and other forms of philanthropy. All of humanity benefits from their benevolence. Moreover, we all can learn from their example to give more of ourselves to others.

Late Adulthood (Age 80+): Wisdom – Those with long lives have acquired a rich repository of experiences that they can use to help guide others. Elders thus represent the source of wisdom that exists in each of us, helping us to avoid the mistakes of the past while reaping the benefits of life's lessons.

Death & Dying: Life – Those in our lives who are dying, or who have died, teach us about the value of living. They remind us not to take our lives for granted, but to live each moment of life to its fullest, and to remember that our own small lives form part of a greater whole (Armstrong, 2019).

Armstrong also believes since each stage of life has its own unique gift to give to humanity. We need to do whatever we can to support each stage, and to protect each stage from attempts to suppress its individual contribution to the human life cycle. Thus, we need to be wary, for example, of attempts to thwart a young child's need to play through the establishment high-pressure, formal academic preschools. We should protect the wisdom of the aged from elder abuse. We need to do what we can to help our adolescents at risk. We need to advocate for prenatal education and services for poor mothers, and support safe and healthy birthing methods in developing countries. We ought to take the same attitude toward nurturing the human life cycle as we do toward saving the environment from global warming and industrial pollutants. For by supporting each stage of the human life cycle, we will help to ensure that all of its members are given care and helped to blossom to their fullest degree (Armstrong, 2019).

> Do not be too timid and squeamish about your actions. All life is an experiment.
> —RALPH WALDO EMERSON

All of us need to continue to evaluate our lives on a regular basis. As long as we do this, we will not experience any traumatic transitions that will disrupt our life (Malone JC, Liu SR, et.al., 2016; Gibbs, 2005). As you observe the above eight stages you notice that there is a positive and negative aspect of each stage. Are you able to identify the stage you are in right now? Are you able to identify the stages some of your friends are in? Erik Erikson was one of the first psychologists to put some emphasis on the fact that we continue to go through developmental stages throughout our lives. Freud emphasized that the first six years of life were the most important years.

Erik and Joan Erikson's work not only expanded Freud's theory to later stages of life, but also broadened it considerably, by emphasizing cultural differences and by stressing the development of the ego through identity challenges that were more psychosocial than strictly biological. In couching his theory in terms of these identity crises, Erikson provided a broad framework for viewing development throughout the lifespan. Although based largely on personal observation and intuition, including reflections on his own life, many of these observations were indeed insightful, and have led to many new and fruitful research studies (e.g., de St. Aubin, McAdams, & Kim, 2003; McAdams & de St. Aubin, 1998, on generativity). Erikson's belief that couples who married young were most likely to succeed when each of the individuals has achieved a degree of identity themselves has also received support in empirical research (Helson & Pals, 2000; Pals, 1999), at least in terms of women's self-identity (Fleming, J. S. Psychological Perspectives on Human Development, 2018).

Trait Theory

Your friends ask you to tell them about your brother. You tell them he tends to be domineering, anxious, optimistic, intelligent, and athletic. Are these terms you have used to describe other people? Many of us use terms like moody, smart, stupid, restless, impulsive, passive, careful, aggressive, quiet, reliable, shy, or outgoing to describe people. The words we use to describe other people (and ourselves) are called **traits**, relatively stable and consistent personal characteristics. Trait theorists are interested in measuring how people differ (which key traits best describe them), and then in measuring how much they differ (the degree of variation in traits within the individual and between the individuals).

Think About it

BECOMING AWARE OF YOUR PERSONALITY

According to Dr. Benjamin Hardy, there's no such thing as a personality "type." Hardy believes that's just one of the popular cultural myths of personality. Another connected myth is that your personality is the "real you" which you must "discover," rather than intentionally choose and create. (Hardy, 2019).

Personality Types

The Big Five. The Big Five personality traits, also known as the five-factor model (FFM) and the OCEAN model, is a taxonomy of "personality traits." Trait and type theories were developed by well-known psychologists, such as Gordon Allport, Raymond Cattell, and Hans Eysenck, and gained popularity in the 1980s. They follow a common sense approach, and researchers today still find them attractive. However, rather than speaking of hundreds of traits or of a few types, many theorists now agree that there are five broad categories. These five major dimensions of personality have become known as the *Big Five* (McCrae & Costa, 2005; 2008). The five factors can be remembered with the following mnemonic device by using the first letters of each of the traits, which spell OCEAN. (see Table 2.1) For more information watch this YouTube video about OCEAN Traits Theory: https://www.youtube.com/watch?v=K-CwHV9HCxH0.

Many researchers are now convinced that the best way to describe personality and individual differences is to find where people stand on the following dimensions: 1) openness to experience, 2) conscientiousness, 3) extraversion, 4) agreeableness, and 5) neuroticism. McCrae and Costa agree with Catell that personality can be described adequately by measuring these basic traits. Their bold claim has been supported in many studies by other researchers, and the five-factor model has become the dominant conception of personality structure in contemporary psychology (John & Srivastava, 2008). The five factors are:

> A realistic assessment of my strengths usually turns up several weaknesses also. Becoming more self-accepting involves not only awareness of strengths but also the acceptance of my weaknesses, not in the sense of not wanting to do something about them, but in the sense of not letting them block the use of my strengths.
> —DAVID G. JONES

Openness to experience (inventive/curious vs. consistent/cautious)

Conscientiousness (efficient/organized vs. easy-going/careless)

Extraversion (outgoing/energetic vs. solitary/reserved)

Agreeableness (friendly/compassionate vs. challenging/detached)

Neuroticism (sensitive/nervous vs. secure/confident)

The five factors are represented by the acronym OCEAN (or CANOE). Beneath each proposed global factor, there are a number of correlated and more specific primary factors. For example, extraversion is said to include such related qualities as gregariousness, assertiveness, excitement seeking, warmth, activity, and positive emotions (Deary, M, Whiteman, 2003). This is indicated, in part, by the fact that these dimensions are ones to which most people in many different cultures refer in describing themselves.

Personality traits https://www.youtube.com/watch?v=M2GdRyESoUE

Individuals who score highly on verbal/crystallized intelligence measures have been found to also report being more open to experience (Schretlen, et. al, 2010).

Table 2.1   THE "BIG FIVE" PERSONALITY FACTORS / OCEAN

TRAIT	DESCRIPTION OF HIGH SCORER	DESCRIPTION OF LOW SCORER
Openness to experience	Imaginative	Practical
or	Prefers variety	Prefers routine
Not open	Creative	Uncreative
Conscientiousness	Responsible	Negligent
or	Organized	Disorganized
Undirected	Dependable	Undependable
Extraversion	Talkative	Quiet
Or	Expressive	Reserved
Introversion	Active	Passive
Agreeableness	Good-natured	Irritable
or	Helpful	Stubborn
Antagonistic	Trusting	Suspicious
Neuroticism	Worrying	Calm
or	Anxious	Self-restrained
Emotional stability	Insecure	Secure

Adapted from McCrae & Costa (2005; 2008); 2010.

Trait theories allow us to describe personality, but they do not necessarily help us understand how we developed these traits (Cloninger, 2013). Yet, the above traits are stable across the life cycle; if you're curious when young, you're likely to be curious when older. Five decades of research on the determinants of the Big Five suggests that the heritability of each trait is in the vicinity of 50% (Krueger & Johnson, 2008). What about describing people in terms of temperament and personality type?

HEXACO The **HEXACO personality inventory model** includes six dimensions of human personality: Honesty-Humility, Emotionality, Extraversion, Agreeableness, Conscientiousness, and Openness to Experience. Along each of these six dimensions, the four cardinal virtues (wisdom, courage, temperance, and justice) are represented. The "H" in the H factor stands for "Honesty-Humility," one of the six basic dimensions of the human personality. People who have high levels of H are sincere and modest; people who have low levels are deceitful and pretentious. It isn't intuitively obvious that traits of honesty and humility go hand in hand, and until very recently the H factor hadn't been recognized as a basic dimension of personality. But scientific evidence shows that traits of honesty and humility form a unified group of personality traits, separate from those of the other five groups identified several decades ago. The H factor explores the scientific findings that show the importance of this personality dimension in various aspects of people's lives: their approaches to money, power, and sex; their inclination to commit crimes or obey the law; their attitudes about society, politics, and religion; and their choice of friends and spouse. Drs. Lee and Ashton provide ways of identifying people who are low in the H factor, as well as advice on how to raise one's own level of H. (Ashton & Lee, 2007)

The Big 5 OCEAN Traits Explained
https://www.youtube.com/watch?v=KCwHV9HCxH0

http://hexaco.org/ gives you basic information and materials for the HEXACO Personality Inventory-Revised, an instrument that assesses the six major dimensions of personality.

Mindset A concept from world-renowned Stanford University psychologist Carol Dweck is based on decades of research on achievement and success. Mindset is defined as is the established set of attitudes held by someone. Dr. Dweck found that teaching a growth mindset creates motivation and productivity in the worlds of business, education, and sports.

In 2007 Dweck studied the effect of praise on students in a dozen New York schools. Her seminal work—a series of experiments on 400 fifth-graders—paints the picture most clearly. Dweck sent four female research assistants into New York fifth-grade classrooms. The researchers would take a single child out of the classroom for a nonverbal IQ test consisting of a series of puzzles—puzzles easy enough that all the children would do fairly well. Once the child finished the test, the researchers told each student his score, and then gave him a single line of praise. Randomly divided into groups, **some were praised for their *intelligence*.** They were told, "You must be smart at this." **Other students were praised for their *effort*:** "You must have worked really hard." Why just a single line of praise? "We wanted to see how sensitive children were," Dweck explained. "**We had a hunch that one line might be enough to see an effect.**"

After inducing Dweck's researchers then gave all the fifth-graders a final round of tests that were engineered to be as easy as the first round. Those who had been **praised for their effort significantly improved** on their first score—by about 30%. Those who'd been told they were smart did worse than they had at the very beginning—by about 20%.

Dweck had suspected that praise could backfire, but even she was surprised by the magnitude of the effect. "Emphasizing effort gives a child a variable that they can control," she explains. "They come to see themselves as in control of their success. **Emphasizing** natural intelligence takes it out of the child's control, and it provides no good recipe for responding to a failure." Then the students were given a choice of test for the second round. One choice was a test that would be more difficult than the first, but the researchers told the kids that they'd learn a lot from attempting the puzzles. The other choice, Dweck's team explained, was an easy test, just like the first. Of those **praised for their effort, 90% chose the *harder* set of puzzles**. Of those praised for their intelligence, a majority chose the *easy* test. The "smart" kids took the cop-out. Why did this happen? "When we praise children for their intelligence," Dweck wrote in her study summary, "we tell them that this is the name of the game: Look smart, don't risk making mistakes." And that's what the fifth-graders had done: They'd chosen to look smart and avoid the risk of being embarrassed.

In a subsequent round, none of the fifth-graders had a choice. The test was difficult, designed for kids two years ahead of their grade level. Predictably, everyone failed. But again, the two groups of children, divided at random at the study's start, responded differently. Those praised for their effort on the first test assumed they simply hadn't focused hard enough on this test. "They got very involved, willing to try every solution to the puzzles," Dweck recalled. "Many of them remarked, unprovoked, 'This is my favorite test.'" Not so for those praised for their smarts. They assumed their failure was evidence that they weren't really smart at all. "Just watching them, you could see the strain. They were sweating and miserable."

In follow-up interviews, Dweck discovered that those who think that innate intelligence is the key to success begin to discount the importance of effort. *I am smart,* the kids' reasoning goes; *I don't need to put out effort.* Expending effort becomes stigmatized—it's public proof that you can't cut it on your natural gifts. Repeating her experiments, Dweck found this effect of praise on performance held true for students of every socioeconomic class. It hit both boys and girls—the very brightest girls especially (they collapsed the most following failure). Even preschoolers weren't immune to the inverse power of praise (Bronson, 2007).

"Parents should praise children for their effort, their concentration, their strategies," Dweck said. This view creates a love of learning and a resilience that is essential for great accomplishment. Virtually all great people have had these qualities. Teaching a growth mindset creates motivation and productivity in the worlds of business, education, and sports. It enhances relationships—praising brains and talent does not foster self-esteem and accomplishment but jeopardizes them (Dwerk, 2007).

Achievement and success—a simple idea that makes all the difference. Dweck found that children's performance worsens if they always hear how smart they are. Kids who get too much praise are less likely to take risks, are highly sensitive to failure, and are more likely to give up when faced with a challenge. What mindset do you have? Can you tell what mindset your friends have?

In a fixed mindset, people believe their basic qualities, like their intelligence or talent, are simply fixed traits. They spend their time documenting their intelligence or talent instead of developing them. They also believe that talent alone creates success—without effort. They're wrong.

In a growth mindset, people believe that their most basic abilities can be developed through dedication and hard work—brains and talent are just the starting point. The key is be specific about the praise you give. watch the you tube video of Carol Dweck's explanation.

Check out these two videos on Carol Dweck's mindset theory.

The power of believing that you can improve
https://www.youtube.com/watch?v=_X0mgOOSpLU

Growth Mindset vs. Fixed Mindset
https://www.youtube.com/watch?v=KUWn_TJTrnU

MYERS-BRIGGS TYPE INDICATOR

While there are many personality type indicators and/or tests available, perhaps the best known is the Myers-Briggs Type Indicator° (MBTI°). It is based on the theory of Carl Jung's psychological types. In essence, we have mental or psychological preferences for performing certain tasks. (It is a fun, entertaining test for a classroom activity and, even though questions exist about the use of the test—see "Something to Think About," below—giving the MBTI has proven to stimulate the conversation around the idea and use of personality tests.) According to type psychology, there are 16 basic personality types consisting of four dimensions. We will now discuss these four different dichotomies or dimensions (Myers Briggs Foundation, 2019, Myers & Myers, 1995).

Extroversion (E) or Introversion (I). People who prefer extroversion like variety and action in their work and everyday activities. They are sociable, naturally communicate energy and enthusiasm, and are particularly good at interacting with people. Extroverts prefer having people around them most of the time, and it is not unusual for them to act quickly, sometimes without thinking. Extroversion is characterized by breadth of activities (as opposed to depth), surgency from external activity/situations, and energy creation from external means (Olson, 2012). Surgency is a trait aspect of emotional reactivity in which a person tends towards high levels of positive affect. It has been linked to the Big Five personality traits of extroversion. The trait is marked by pronounced engagement with the external world. Extroverts enjoy interacting with people, and are often perceived as full of energy. They tend to be enthusiastic, action-oriented individuals. They possess high group visibility, like to talk, and assert themselves (Canadian Research & Development Center of Sciences and Cultures, 2012).

Introverts like having a great deal of time for quiet activities so they can concentrate, develop ideas, and reflect on the day. In fact, one of their strong gifts is their natural ability to reflect on decisions they need to make, so it is rare for them not to think through something very carefully before making a decision. Introverts are collectors of thoughts, and solitude is the place where the collection is curated and rearranged to make sense of the present and the future (Helgoe, 2010). They keep their energy and enthusiasm inside, prefer working alone, and are quite comfortable with just a few very close friends.

Sensing (S) or Intuition (N). Individuals who lean toward sensing are practical and realistic and like to use facts, details, and examples to help them solve problems. They may distrust and ignore their inspirations, preferring to just continue with what is, with some fine tuning. Sensing types like established ways of doing things, usually proceed step-by-step, and rarely make errors of fact.

People who lean toward intuition enjoy solving new complex problems and are good at seeing the big picture, new possibilities, and new ways of doing things. It is common for them to rely heavily on insights and imagination. They often follow their inspirations, good or bad, and often may make errors of fact. Intuitive types prefer change, sometimes radical, to continuation of what is and often proceed in bursts of energy, with slack periods in between.

Thinking (T) or Feeling (F). Thinkers lean toward logical analysis and deep thought to make decisions, being careful to review the pros and cons of any decision they need to make. They tend to be brief, concise, firm-minded, and can give criticism when appropriate. It is normal for them to be convinced by cool, impersonal reasoning and tend to use emotions and feelings as the only cognitive data to weigh in the decision-making process.

Feelers tend to use personal values to make their decisions, while taking time to consider how much they care and how much personal investment they have for each of the alternatives. These individuals are sociable and friendly, prefer harmony with others, dislike telling people unpleasant things, and tend to be sympathetic and appreciative. They are convinced by personal information, enthusiastically delivered.

Judgment (J) or Perception (P). Individuals lean toward a judging lifestyle tend to live in an organized, structured, planned way, desiring to regulate life and control it. The J's prefer to "plan their work and work their plan," and like to get things settled and finished. These individuals create lists to keep them on schedule and often focus on the task to be done.

Those who lean toward a perceptive approach tend to live in a flexible, unstructured, and spontaneous manner. They prefer to leave things open for last-minute changes and dislike deadlines, schedules, and may postpone tasks that need to be done. It is common for these individuals to present views as tentative and modifiable. Perceptive individuals use lists to remind them of all the things they have to do someday.

If a man does not keep pace with his companions, perhaps it is because he hears a different drummer. Let him step up to the music which he hears, however measured or far away.
—HENRY DAVID THOREAU

The merit of the MBTI is that it enables us to expect specific personality differences in particular people and to cope with the people and differences in a constructive way.
—ISABEL MYERS

106

Something to Think About

The MBTI is only one type of personality inventory. It was created with the Big Five typology in mind. Check out the website https://www.myersbriggs.org/my-mbti-personality-type/ There have been questions concerning the validity of the MBTI personality inventory. The MBTI does poorly on reliability, says Annie Murphy Paul in *The Cult of Personality Testing.* Also research shows "that as many as three-quarters of test takers achieve a different personality type when tested again, and the sixteen distinctive types described by the Myers-Briggs have no scientific basis whatsoever." In a recent article, Roman Krznaric adds that, "if you retake the test after only a five-week gap, there's around a 50% chance that you will fall into a different personality category." As management researchers William Gardner and Mark Martinko write in a comprehensive review, "Few consistent relationships between type and managerial effectiveness have been found." As Susan Cain explains in *Quiet,* "more than a thousand studies conducted by scientists worldwide" suggest that introverts "are more sensitive than extroverts to various kinds of stimulation, from coffee to a loud bang to the dull roar of a networking event." The vast majority of us are ambiverts; in Dan Pink's words from *To Sell is Human,* most people are "neither overly extroverted nor wildly introverted."

If you are interested in taking the Myers-Briggs questionnaire, check out the link to the Myers Briggs Foundation. Your college counseling service may have a version you can take, or you may have an opportunity in a class or seminar. The book *Please Understand Me* (Keirsey & Bates, 1998) offers a questionnaire that provides scores in the four categories. Also, the Web Resources at the end of the chapter may be useful. Included are videos about the MBTI, the Harry Potter MBTI versions, and also a video questioning the validity of the MBTI test.

Now, it is time to return to our discussion of other theories that will help us understand how we have evolved into the individuals we are today, many of the inventories and tests that different authors create with are based on classic theories that we will now discuss.

Dismissive positivity—also known as toxic positivity

Having an unhelpful cheerful attitude is "dismissive positivity." Instead of acknowledging my friend's anguish, my chipper attitude minimized her anxiety. I can't change how I made her feel, but I will strive to be more compassionate when people share their despair with me in the future.

Psychotherapist Whitney Goodman calls having an unhelpful cheerful attitude "dismissive positivity." In an Instagram post, she explained how to better respond to someone who's in pain.

- Instead of saying, "You'll get over it," to someone in distress, say something to impart validation and hope: "This is hard. You've done hard things before and I believe in you."

- "Think happy thoughts!" becomes, "It's probably pretty hard to be positive right now. I'm putting out good energy into the world for you."
- "Everything happens for a reason!" is updated to, "This doesn't make sense right now. We'll sort it all out later."

(Goodman, Whitney, 2019. https://www.psychologytoday.com/us/therapists/whitney-goodman-miami-/2582310)

THE ART OF PEOPLE: 11 SIMPLE PEOPLE ATTITUDES THAT WILL GET YOU EVERYTHING YOU WANT.

- Sometimes you'll get your way, sometimes you won't.
- While you can't control the outcome, you can choose your attitude.
- Choose positivity.
- Choose gratitude.
- Enthusiasm is contagious.
- Put yourself second.
- Walk in others' shoes before taking action.
- Open your ears—you might connect to someone by really listening, not just waiting your turn to talk.

(Kerpen, 2016; artofpeople.com)

Author Dave Kerpen believes it's actually those with the best *people skills* who win the day—those who build the right relationships, and those who truly understand and connect with their colleagues, their customers, their partners, and those who can teach, lead, and inspire (Kerpen, 2016). In his book *The Art of People*, Kerpen feels that in a world where we are constantly connected, and social media has become the primary way we communicate, the key to gaining influence, getting what we want, and getting ahead is being the person others like, respect, and trust. Because no matter who you are or what profession you're in, success is contingent less on what you can do for yourself, but on *what other people are willing to do for* you. A self-assessment is available at the end of the chapter so you can evaluate yourself. You can also check out the quiz on Dave Kerpin's website to see what you are:

http://www.artofpeoplebook.com/quiz

Strengths-Based Psychology

Tom Rath (2013) began working with a team of Gallup scientists led by the late Donald O. Clifton who was known as the Father of Strength Psychology. Their goal was to start a global conversation about what's right with people, rather than focusing so much on people's challenges. Emphasis is placed on the so-called "strengths" of leadership, also referred to as the "power of leadership." They believed that people have several times more potential for growth when they invested energy in developing their strengths instead of correcting their deficiencies.

Strengths-Based Leadership is aimed at touching the intrinsic needs of employees and giving them the right support, and other leadership qualities to achieve effective leadership. Gallup's research shows that the perfect leader does not exist. Apart from the fact that specific situations determine one's style of management, effective managers generally exhibit overlapping characteristics. They usually have vision and are able to communicate this to their employees. In this way they are passionate and they can stimulate the people around them and involve them in the organization and its management. They focus on the process and quality of the execution of the work. Their performance can be linked to this. Effective leaders follow progress, and in this way support their employees (Mulder, P. 2018).

The Gallup scientists studied leadership over 30 years. To do so, they studied a million work teams, conducted more than 20,000 in-depth interviews with executives, and interviewed more than 10,000 employees worldwide.

Based on Gallup's 40-year study of human strengths, they created a language of the 34 most common talents and developed the Clifton StrengthsFinder assessment to help people discover and describe these talents. *Strengths-Based Leadership* is a book published by the American consultant Tom Rath and the British consultant Barry Conchie in 2013, on behalf of the U.S. research and consulting firm Gallup Incorporated.

A range of strengths evaluation tools are at the end of this chapter. Be sure to review the web resources activity: *Brief Strengths Test*, or *VIA Survey of Character Strengths*, which measures 24 strengths and is free online. You can get an analysis of your scores for your personal evaluation.

There are now several major approaches in the helping professions to facilitate personal growth based on capacity and not limitations.

Positive psychology Martin Seligman is a strong promoter within the scientific community of his theories of positive psychology and of well-being. Seligman's most famous work is his research on the theory of learned helplessness. "Learned helplessness is a term specifying an organism learning to accept and endure unpleasant stimuli, and unwilling to avoid them, even when it is avoidable."

The strengths perspective in social work Dennis Saleebey was a passionate believer in encouraging people to build on their strengths. He translated this into practice with colleagues at The Strengths Institute, which is part of the school of social welfare at the University of Kansas.

Solution oriented therapies Steve de Shazer was a 20th century therapist who was active in the fields of family therapy, social work, and research. He pioneered the practice of solution-focused brief therapy.

These professionals are from some of the most prominent schools of thought. Davidson (2014) developed a model from these traditions with eight principles that can be used for an individual's personal growth or as a guideline for helping others. To make the model easier to remember, Davidson uses an acronym: STRENGTH.

Table 2.2   THE STRENGTH MODEL

S Be "solution-focused" instead of going over and over describing what is wrong. As a helper, listen to problems with empathy and then collaborate to discover new possibilities and do things differently.

T Do a "trajectory preview." Imagine a better future and use that preferred scenario to activate hopes and dreams. Use your new vision of what you want as a way to keep on track with what you will do.

R Begin "resource development." Identify resources that will promote successful outcomes and, with supportive people, put in the effort to access those resources.

E Conduct an "exceptions analysis." Emphasize overlooked strengths and remember what has helped in the past. Under-utilized skills and previous solutions pave the way for exceptions to current problems.

N Practice "noticing positives." Get in the habit of thinking more about what is already good and what is getting better. This helps motivate a person to build on strengths and to recognize progress being made.

G Concentrate on "goal setting." Select a few short-term goals that are likely to lead to quick, small solutions, while also identifying some longer-term goals based on emerging strengths and accomplishments.

T Do a "tenacity review." Remind yourself of times when you have been determined and reinforce a positive image of your abilities to endure difficult times.

H Focus on "human capacity development." Identify skills to develop competence and rely on maximizing the potential within the self, while drawing on strengths of family, group, traditions, and culture.

(Davidson, 2014)

Carl Rogers: Self-Theory—Humanistic Approach

Carl Rogers (1995) defines the development of the self-concept in terms of *self-actualization*, the fulfillment of one's own unique potential. The key to self-actualization is the self-concept. Rogers maintains that the way we regard ourselves depends largely on the kind of regard given by others. In the ideal situation, love is given freely and does not depend on any specific aspects of behavior. Rogers calls this **unconditional positive regard** (Pastorino & Doyle-Portillo, 2019). A general definition is the attitude of complete acceptance and love, whether for yourself or for someone else. When you have unconditional positive regard for someone, nothing they can do could give you a reason to stop seeing them as inherently human and inherently lovable. It does not mean that you accept each and every action taken by the person, but that you accept who they are at a level much deeper than surface behavior. Individuals who have received unconditional positive regard have a positive realistic self-concept, high self-esteem, and feelings of self-respect. Rogers believes that a fully-functioning person lives totally in the present and is continually changing to make full use of their potential.

CARL ROGERS' THEORY

"To be with another in this [empathic] way means that for the time being, you lay aside your own views and values in order to enter another's world without prejudice. In some sense it means that you lay aside your self; this can only be done by persons who are secure enough in themselves that they know they will not get lost in what may turn out to be the strange or bizarre world of the other, and that they can comfortably return to their own world when they wish. Perhaps this description makes clear that being empathic is a complex, demanding, and strong—yet subtle and gentle—way of being" (Carl R. Rogers 1957).

Some difficulties in functioning are caused by a lack of *unconditional acceptance* by others starting at birth. Many parents make their affection and approval conditional on certain kinds of behavior. If the child does what the parent says, the parent will love the child. If the child does not live up to parental expectations, the parent may show disapproval and withhold affection. Consequently, the child attempts to live up to his parents' expectations, but cannot always be successful. This is the beginning of an unrealistic self-concept.

In order to become a self-actualized individual, we must accept ourselves as we are, the positive and the negative, with the potential to grow as a person and to accept others as they are, rather than wishing that they were somehow different. We all need to learn to place a high value on the individuality and uniqueness of ourselves and others.

MASLOW: CHARACTERISTICS OF A SELF-ACTUALIZED PERSON

Maslow describes the good life as one directed towards self-actualization, the pinnacle need. Self-actualization occurs when you maximize your potential, doing the best that you are capable of doing

1. **Self-actualized people embrace the unknown and the ambiguous.** They are not threatened or afraid of it; instead, they accept it, are comfortable with it and are often attracted by it. They do not cling to the familiar. Maslow quotes Einstein: "The most beautiful thing we can experience is the mysterious."
2. **They accept themselves, together with all their flaws.** She perceives herself as she is, and not as she would prefer herself to be. With a high level of self-acceptance, she lacks defensiveness, pose or artificiality. Eventually, shortcomings come to be seen not as shortcomings at all, but simply as neutral personal characteristics.

   "They can accept their own human nature in the stoic style, with all its shortcomings, with all its discrepancies from the ideal image without feeling real concern [...] One does not complain about water because it is wet, or about rocks because they are hard [...] simply noting and observing what is the case, without either arguing the matter or demanding that it be otherwise."

Nonetheless, while self-actualized people are accepting of shortcomings that are immutable, they do feel ashamed or regretful about changeable deficits and bad habits.

3. **They prioritize and enjoy the journey, not just the destination.**

   "[They] often [regard] as ends in themselves many experiences and activities that are, for other people, only means. Our subjects are somewhat more likely to appreciate for its own sake, and in an absolute way, the doing itself; they can often enjoy for its, own sake the getting to some place as well as the arriving. It is occasionally possible for them to make out of the most trivial and routine activity an intrinsically enjoyable game or dance or play."

4. **While they are inherently unconventional, they do not seek to shock or disturb.** Unlike the average rebel, the self-actualized person recognizes:

   "... the world of people in which he lives could not understand or accept [his unconventionality], and since he has no wish to hurt them or to fight with them over every triviality, he will go through the ceremonies and rituals of convention with a good-humored shrug and with the best possible grace [... Self-actualized people would] usually behave in a conventional fashion simply because no great issues are involved or because they know people will be hurt or embarrassed by any other kind of behavior."

5. **They are motivated by growth, not by the satisfaction of needs.** While most people are still struggling in the lower rungs of the 'Hierarchy of Needs,' the self-actualized person is focused on personal growth.

   "Our subjects no longer strive in the ordinary sense, but rather develop. They attempt to grow to perfection and to develop more and more fully in their own style. The motivation of ordinary men is a striving for the basic need gratifications that they lack."

6. **Self-actualized people have purpose.**

   "[They have] some mission in life, some task to fulfill, some problem outside themselves which enlists much of their energies. [...] This is not necessarily a task that they would prefer or choose for themselves; it may be a task that they feel is their responsibility, duty, or obligation. [...] In general these tasks are non-personal or unselfish, concerned rather with the good of mankind in general."

7. **They are not troubled by the small things.** Instead, they focus on the bigger picture.

   "They seem never to get so close to the trees that they fail to see the forest. They work within a framework of values that are broad and not petty, universal and not local, and in terms of a century rather than the moment.[...] This impression of being above small things [...] seems to impart a certain serenity and lack of worry over immediate concerns that make life easier not only for themselves but for all who are associated with them."

8. **Self-actualized people are grateful.** They do not take their blessings for granted, and by doing so, maintain a fresh sense of wonder towards the universe.

   "Self-actualizing people have the wonderful capacity to appreciate again and again, freshly and naïvely, the basic goods of life, with awe, pleasure, wonder, and even ecstasy, however stale these experiences may have become to others

[...] Thus for such a person, any sunset may be as beautiful as the first one, any flower may be of breath-taking loveliness, even after he has seen a million flowers. [...] For such people, even the casual workaday, moment-to-moment business of living can be thrilling."

Viktor Frankl: Search for Meaning

Viktor Frankl (1998) states:

> As humans, we are capable of self-awareness, which allows us to reflect and to decide. With this awareness, we become free beings who are responsible for choosing the way we live and thus influence our own destiny.

This awareness of freedom and responsibility gives rise to existential anxiety, which is a basic human condition. Whether we like it or not, we are free, even though we may seek to avoid reflecting on this freedom. The knowledge that we must choose leads to anxiety. Facing the inevitable prospect of eventual death gives the present moment significance, for we become aware that we do not have forever to accomplish our projects.

> *Life has taught me so many lessons, it's hard to decide which one is of the greatest value, but one of the most important is this: Nobody will believe in you unless you believe in yourself.*
> —LIBERACE (1919–1986), PIANIST

CONSIDER THIS

THE SELF-ACTUALIZED PERSON

- The self-actualized person is a participant in life rather than a spectator.
- They are inclined to be objective, spontaneous, emotional, and intellectually honest.
- They try to understand the interpersonal and environmental problems they face but they also accept their limitations in gaining true insight concerning them.
- They work out the best adjustment to life of which they are capable, often without fully understanding all that is involved.
- However, they are willing to experience the pleasures and discomfort of self-revelation: i.e., they accept the mixed pain and joy that accompanies each change in attitude and feeling toward themselves and others.
- Their claims on life are, for the most part, reasonable. If they want to be a member of the Country Club and yet cannot afford it, they find other social and recreational outlets in keeping with their budget.
- The self-actualized person without special talent or ability is able to emotionally share in the gifts of others without undue regret about their own inborn deficiencies.
- They do not brood about missed opportunities, lost causes, errors, and failures. Rather, they look on them for what they can contribute to doing things differently or better in the future.
- They do not get stuck in the rut of irrational feelings of love, hate, envy, jealousy, suspicion, lust, and greed, because they let each feeling spell out its special message for them.

Adapted from *Self-Acceptance* by McDonald, Smith, and Sutherland. Copyright by The Hogg Foundation for Mental Health. The University of Texas, Austin, Texas.

Holocaust survivor Viktor E. Frankl is known as the founder of logotherapy, a mode of psychotherapy based on man's motivation to search for meaning in his life. Victor Frankl discusses his ideas in the context of other prominent psychotherapies and describes the techniques he uses with his patients to combat the "existential vacuum." in his book *Man's Search for Meaning*.

Frankl wrote that our task is to create a life that has *meaning* and *purpose*. (Meaning, purpose, and self-actualization will be discussed in more detail in Chapters Nine and Ten.) As humans, we are unique in striving toward creating purposes and values that give meaning to living.

This is an existential view of human nature that states that the significance of our existence is never fixed once and for all. Rather, we continually recreate ourselves through our goals. Humans are in a constant state of transition, emerging, evolving, and becoming. Being a person implies that we are discovering and making sense of our existence.

Virginia Satir: Self–Worth

> *I am me and I am okay.*
> —VIRGINIA SATIR

Virginia Satir (1988; 2004) indicates in her writing that the crucial factor in interpersonal relations—what happens inside people and between people—*is the picture of the individual worth that each person carries around.* A person who can appreciate his or her own self-worth will be able to see and respect the worth of others. She describes a human being who is living humanly as a person who understands, values, and develops his or her body, finding it useful and beautiful. This is a person who is honest about himself or herself and others, who is willing to take risks, to be creative, embrace change, who is feeling, loving, playful, authentic, and productive. She says that the person who is living humanly can stand on their own two feet, can love deeply and fight fairly and effectively, and can be on equally good terms with both their tenderness and their toughness.

Self-worth is learned, and the family is where it is initially acquired. Human beings can continue to learn, grow, and change all their lives. Every person has a feeling of worth, which might be higher (positive) or lower (negative).

Virginia Satir uses a pot concept as a metaphor for evaluating self-worth. How many ounces are in your pot today?

36 oz.—
27 oz.—
18 oz.—
9 oz.—

Pot of Self-Worth

If you have low self-worth or know someone with low self-worth, you can change how that self-worth can be adjusted and grows higher. Growth in self may demand a change to a more nurturing environment, where a new environment is also needed. We will be able to develop and grow in an atmosphere where individual differences are appreciated, mistakes are tolerated, communication is open, and rules are flexible—this is a nurturing environment. Satir describes the main points that help human beings change and grow:

1. Communication of feelings: all feelings are honorable. Express your feelings—no one knows how you feel if you do not disclose your feelings to them.
2. Belief that a person is able to grow and change: If you believe you can change, you can.
3. Restoring the use of the senses: Take in the world and see freely, touch freely, and hear freely.

What is in the pot of self-worth? Satir uses a pot concept as a metaphor for available self-worth, and to refer to how you feel about yourself. For example, assuming the maximum capacity of a pot of self-worth is 36 ounces, how many ounces would be in your pot today? And, what kind of self does it hold?

Suppose your pot is full of a feeling you have had since childhood, such as hostility toward one of your parents because they abused you. Your inner thoughts say, "I must be a bad person, since my parents always beat me. I'm no good. I must have deserved the abuse." Your pot of self-worth is low because of your past experience. You are experiencing "self-defeating" thoughts. You can learn to change these feelings. You can change your "self-talk," and tell yourself that you are a "good person." You can read a good self-help book that may help you or you may seek professional counseling.

The self-worth pot is constantly changing. One day you get an "A" on a test and you feel great; your pot of self-worth is full of good feelings. The next day you call someone on the phone for a date and you get turned down. Now your pot of self-worth is low—it has a lot of negative feelings in it. Knowing that you are a good person, no matter what happens to you, will help you maintain a full pot of good feelings and help you succeed in life.

Any feeling you have is a human feeling, and all human feelings are valid feelings. We are free to function fully and free to make choices about what we want and how we act.

How Do Our Thoughts and Our Environment Relate to the Development of Our Personality?

In Chapter Three we will discover how learning theory relates to the development of our personality, but in the meantime we will discover how our thoughts and our relationships with other people interrelate.

How Did I Get to Be the Person I Am Today?

Cognitive theories of personality point out that there are important individual differences in the way people think about and define situations. Cognitive theories stress the mental processes through which people turn their sensations and perceptions into organized impressions of reality. They emphasize that people actively choose their own environments to a great extent. People choose to enter those situations that they expect to be reinforcing and to avoid those that are unsatisfying and uncertain. As many of you have observed, some members of minority ethnic groups "stick together" on college campuses. These members are often/sometimes uncertain about whether they would be accepted if they ventured into different ethnic friendships. Most of us tend to avoid relationships we expect to be uncomfortable or unsatisfying; we do this by avoiding opportunities or refusing to seek opportunities for new relationships outside our comfort zone.

This piece of research suggests that personality is based on or deeply effected by cognitive processes. Cognitive processes is the interaction of one's thoughts and actions and behavior. This perspective assumes that human beings are decision makers, planners, and evaluators of their own behavior. Many contemporary researchers claim that people can change their behavior, their conception of themselves, and their personalities in a short time if they are willing to change their thoughts. More often than not, we hope our cognitions are rational and sensible, thus enabling us to live and make decisions in emotionally healthy ways. But many times, our cognitive processing is irrational and not sensible, and we may be totally unaware of it.

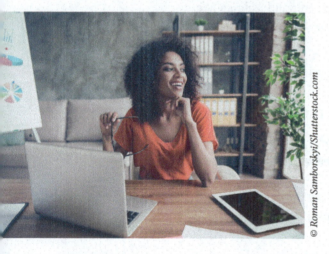

Does positive thinking influence your behavior?

© Roman Samborskyi/Shutterstock.com

Talk to yourself. Holding an inner dialogue is not only very normal, but also useful. In fact, the inner conversations we have with ourselves can have a powerful effect on our emotional well-being and our motivation. Developing an awareness of precisely what we are saying to ourselves and about ourselves can help us understand why we react the way we do to various people and events in our lives.

Building self-esteem is easier with the help of positive self-talk (self-talk is discussed in depth in Chapter Eight). You may have discovered that negative self-talk can have a tremendous influence in the development of someone's feelings about themselves—a poor self-concept. Research shows that talking to yourself positively can make you feel much better.

Thinking positively and optimistically. This kind of thinking can influence your behavior. A positive mood improves our ability to process information efficiently, increases optimism, and raises self-esteem. A positive attitude enhances our sense of comfort in being able to manage our environment, and acting on this optimism can actually lead to a sense of more control over our circumstances. Since many of us are not positive thinkers and are more pessimistic than optimistic, how can we change our attitude?

BECOMING AWARE-THINK ABOUT IT

Let's take a brief look at what is called *cognitive restructuring*—the process of modifying thoughts, ideas, and beliefs. Cognitive restructuring can be used to increase positive and optimistic thinking. This is also known as *self-talk*—the unspoken, mental speech we use when we think about something, solve problems, and make plans. Self-talk is very helpful in cognitive restructuring. Positive self-talk will allow you the freedom to build the confidence you need in order to reach your potential. David Sarwer is a psychologist and former clinical director at the Center for Weight and Eating Disorders at the University of Pennsylvania, now at Temple University. On an NPR,- David Sawyer says that, in fact, a mirror is one of the first tools he uses with some new patients. Dr. Sawyer stands them in front of a mirror and coaches them to use gentler, more neutral language as they evaluate their bodies.

Self-Talk becomes reality
https://www.nhpr.org/post/why-saying-believing-science-self-talk#stream/0

Take a look at what you may be saying to yourself in Table 2.3.

Is there a relationship between the self-fulfilling prophecy and positive self-talk? When you keep telling yourself, "I'm no good," "I'll never amount to anything," "I'm a liar," "Nobody likes me," "Nobody will ever love me," "I will never be able to pass math," etc., you will discover that it unconsciously affects your attitude and behavior. This is why it is so important to monitor your self-talk.

Several strategies are listed below that will help you monitor and fine tune your self-talk.

> *I want you to get excited about who you are, what you are, what you have, and what can still be for you. I want to inspire you to see that you can go far beyond where you are right now.*
> —VIRGINIA SATIR

Table 2.3   WHAT DO YOU TELL YOURSELF?

POSITIVE SELF-TALK: AFFIRMATIONS	NEGATIVE SELF-TALK: NEVER SAY
I sure am a good person.	I am not a very good person.
I know I can do it.	I cannot do anything right.
I am a harder worker than most people think.	I sure am stupid.
I know, if I try hard enough, I can pass that math class.	I will never be able to pass math.
If I do not ask, I will never know if Cassandra will go out with me.	Cassandra would not want to go out with me.
I sure feel good.	I feel depressed.
Sabi and Angie are two of my good friends.	Nobody likes me.

What can you say to yourself to make you feel more confident?

Mental health experts have discovered that this process has a tremendous influence on the development of positive self-esteem for many people. Our thoughts have a great influence on our behavior, but we also need to look at the importance of external events and see how they are interrelated. Ethan Kross is a psychologist at the University of Michigan. He studies the pronouns people use when they talk to themselves silently, inside their minds. He finds that a subtle linguistic shift—shifting from *I* to your own name can have really powerful self-regulatory effects ("Why Saying Is Believing—The Science Of Self-Talk," NPR, 2014).

BECOMING AWARE OF SELF-TALK

Self-talk is important in many ways according to Dr. Tim Legg, MD of Healthline.com. It's the script that we use to frame our lives. If we constantly give ourselves negative messages, then we begin to develop automatic thoughts that take us from a particular incident to a negative emotional reaction. Conversely, if we engage in positive self-talk, we begin to view the world in a more positive manner and will ultimately feel better about ourselves. We can't always control what happens, but we can control how we react to it!

Cognitive and Social Learning Theories

Two somewhat different theories combine an emphasis on cognitive processes and a focus on social learning processes. Some psychologists believe that we learn many of our behaviors either by conditioning or by observing others and modeling our behavior after them. Like cognitive and social psychological theorists, they emphasize the importance of mental processes: How we think and feel about the situations we are in affects our behavior. So instead of focusing solely on how our environment shapes us (learning theory), social-cognitive theorists focus on how we and their environment interact: How do we interpret and respond to external events? How do our schemas, our memories, and our expectations influence our behavior patterns?

Human beings are driven by neither inner forces nor environmental factors, but rather by monitoring the impact of their behavior on other people, on the environments, and on themselves. We learn from our own experience and also learn vicariously by observing other people. We can also evaluate our own behavior according to personal standards and provide ourselves with reinforcers, such as self-approval or disapproval.

Bandura's (2001) theory explains the complex interaction of individual element, behavior, and environmental stimuli. Each element can influence or change the others, and the direction of change is rarely one-way; it is bidirectional. This is an interactive, reciprocal perspective that has inspired researchers to study how the environment shapes the personal element, such as self-control, self management and self-concept, and how these, in turn, influence behavior.

The following categories of cognitive variables may have a tremendous influence on your behavior. Can you identify how these relate to your life?

1. **Expectancies.** What we have learned from our past experience leads us to form different expectations that help to determine our reactions to future events. You expect that your marriage will be the perfect relationship. When you discover that your spouse does not live up to your expectations, how do you feel? You expect to get at least a "B" in your psychology class, but the night before the final exam, you go to a party instead of studying. You only get a "C" for your grade. You tell yourself how dumb you were for not studying and feel disappointed in yourself. You expect to get a "D" in your calculus class, and you receive a "C." How do you feel? Think back on some of your experiences. How have your expectations affected your life?
2. **Competencies.** Each of us has a different combination of abilities and skills that shape our responses to events. Juan and Kyla are both asked to give a speech at a local event. Juan thinks he is a good speaker, so he accepts, but Kyla does not feel competent as a public speaker, so she refuses the offer. What are your competencies and how have they influenced your behavior?
3. **Personal Values.** Our sense of priorities and values also shape our decisions and actions. You refuse the offer for a job in a store where they sell pornographic magazines, but accept the job as a sales clerk in a store that sells religious goods. Your values influenced your decision.
4. **Encoding Strategies.** We also have different ways of perceiving and categorizing experiences that shape our responses. One mother gets very angry at her teenager when she sees his messy room, while another mother takes it in stride and realizes that it is a stage most teenagers go through.
5. **Self-Regulatory Systems.** We also formulate goals, plans, and strategies that influence our actions. You decide to take a physics class because you are majoring in science, and even if you decide to drop science as your major, physics will help you in your other future pursuits. Another student decides that physics would be a waste of time and would not be beneficial (Mischel, 2007).

What is reciprocal determinism? According to psychologist Albert Bandura, **reciprocal determinism** is a model composed of three factors that influence behavior: *the environment, the individual, and the behavior itself.* According to this theory, an individual's behavior influences and is influenced by both the social world and personal characteristics. We have repeated this statement many times, but we cannot recall who we should credit for it: "We react to others as others react to us; others react to us as we react to them." Behavior, internal personal factors, and environmental influences all operate as interlocking determinants of each other. These three components are continually interacting with one another. Just as the environment exerts an influence on individual behavior, a person's actions also play a part in influencing the environment (Bandura, 2006). *Reciprocal determinism* is the interacting influences between person, behavior, and environment. You respond to a new acquaintance as a happy, positive person, and they respond back to you on a positive basis. Your new acquaintance sees you as a friendly, happy person, and you

Figure 2.1

RECIPROCAL DETERMINISM

feel good about yourself because they responded back to you on a positive basis. You have a new friend. You were reinforced positively for being friendly, and in the future you will most likely respond positively to other new acquaintances.

Environments and people interact. We are both the products and the architects of our environments. Let's take a look at some specific ways in which people and environments interact.

1. Our personalities shape how we interpret and react to events. A shy person is most likely to interpret a frown on someone's face as a negative response, even though the person might not be not feeling well.

2. Our personalities help create situations to which we react. You think your roommate is mad at you and you respond negatively to your roommate, and, thus, your roommate responds angrily toward you. Now your actions are being reinforced; you must have been correct about your roommate's feelings. However, your roommate was not mad at you, but because of your response your roommate now is mad. Has this ever happened to you?

3. Different people choose different environments. The type of party you go to, the friends you associate with, the music you listen to, the type of shows you watch on television, the places you hang out, the reading you do for pleasure—all are environments that you have chosen based on your beliefs, attitudes, and moods. The son of one of our colleagues was trying to decide which college to attend. He made his choice based on his liberal political beliefs. Most of the students attending that college will have similar political beliefs and will thus reinforce one another for having those beliefs. A person with a conservative orientation may not feel as comfortable at that college.

> *The person whom you're with most in life is yourself and if you don't like yourself you're always with somebody you don't like.*
> —MARC LEWIS

As you continue to read this book you will see how your thoughts, actions, and environment interact to influence your behavior. We will be studying self-efficacy and social learning theory in Chapter Three.

What kind of environment makes you happy?

We now have some insight into how our personalities have evolved over a period of time. We have looked at a variety of theories that contribute to our development. What theory do you feel has had the greatest influence on you, or do you think that each theory has some valid points that you could use to justify how your personality developed? An interesting project would be for you to write your own personality theory that best describes your development.

Now we need to take a look at the importance of the "self"— your self-concept, self-image, and self-esteem. What kind of influence do these have on your behavior, and how does the "self" develop?

THE SELF

There is new thinking about the self. The *self* is one of psychology's most vigorously researched topics. Every year we see new studies that appear on self-esteem, self-awareness, self-monitoring, and self-efficacy.

Becoming *Aware*

One example of new thinking about the self is the concept of possible selves. Your possible selves include your visions of the self you dream of becoming—the rich self, the thin self, the educated self, the successful self, and the admired self. They also include the self you fear becoming—the unemployed self, the addicted self, the failed self, and the unloved self. Such selves motivate us by laying out specific goals to pursue and the energy to work toward them. As they say: "Those who dream most, achieve most."

The nature of the self.   One of the main factors differentiating humans from other animals is awareness of *"self."* As human beings, we can think, feel, and reflect on who we are. We form an identity and attach a value to it.

The Person That Is Me

If ever you should meet me
    the image you may see
is just a mere reflection
    of the person that is me.

    The person I am really,
the one deep down inside,
    is made of many feelings
that I sometimes try to hide.

Feelings of doubt and worry,
    wondering how I will fit in.
Feelings of hope and longing,
    that someday I might win.

    Feelings of frustration
for answers I don't know.
    Feelings for my loved ones.
Relationships that grow.

Feelings of loss and loneliness,
    of memories left behind.
Feelings of excitement.
    For what I have yet to find.

So remember when you meet me
    the image you may see
is just a mere reflection
of the person that is me.

—Tom Krause

Excerpt "The Person That Is Me" from the book *Touching Hearts—Teaching Greatness* by Tom Krause. Used with permission of Universal Press Syndicate.

Please write short answers for class discussion in triads.

- Who are YOU?
- Where are you headed?
- Does it make a difference that you exist?

© Narith Thongphasuk/Shutterstock.com

How do you see yourself?

> *I often marvel that while each man loves himself more than anyone else, he sets less value on his own estimate than on the opinions of others.*
> —MARCUS AURELIUS, A.D. 121–180 MEDITATIONS

Over 2,000 years ago, the Greek philosopher Socrates advised all seekers of wisdom to *"know thyself."* What Socrates realized and we have discovered since is that the most vibrant, compelling, and baffling reality we can know is our *self*. It is difficult to define and even more difficult to measure or even investigate. Yet, such awareness of *self* is vital in knowing how people adjust to life.

Many ideas about the self have sprung from the humanistic-existential perspective, discussed earlier. Carl Rogers (1995) has summarized a number of important characteristics of the self, as follows:

1. It is organized and consistent.
2. It includes one's perceptions of all that comprises "I" or "me."
3. It includes the relationship among I or me and other people and features of life, as well as the value and importance of these relationships.
4. The self is available to consciousness (we can become aware of it), but it is not always conscious at any given moment.
5. The shape of the self is constantly changing, yet always recognizable.

We are human. We wrestle with our humanness. Some of us struggle with insecurity or inferiority, some deal with emotional problems, while others face mental or sexual problems. Poverty, illness, and physical disability can also test us. Many feel the pain of gender, racial, or ethnic prejudice. It is as if each of us is given a special task or challenge to work on as part of life and part of what will enhance our growth as an individual. It is the joy of discovering ourselves as human beings, our personal growth, sharing our love with others, and the contribution we make to others' lives that makes the process of life so exciting. The journey inward is life. Each of us must find our own way.

Find Your Real Self

The *personal self-image* is the part of the self that includes physical, behavioral, and psychological characteristics that establish uniqueness. It also includes gender, racial or ethnic identity; age, and status. Your personal self-image, who you think you are, is literally a package you put together from how others have seen and treated you and from your conclusions as you compare yourself to others. Your *sense of identity* is the end result of the interaction between your uniqueness and how others have reacted to it. It is the package you call *me*. But it is not the *real self*.

It is never who you are that hangs you up, but rather who you *think* you are. To discover your **real self**, it is important to separate the *real you* from your *personal self-image*. Lining up to fit the "real you" is of the utmost importance. There is probably no more exciting journey than that of *real self*-discovery. Once your *self-belief system* is accurate, you are free of the low self-esteem trap. You are free to be the **real you**.

Personal Self-Image Your personal self-image includes past teachings about yourself. As a child, you build your **sense of self** based on what others told you about yourself. If you were exposed to large doses of *put downs* and **belittlers**, your personal self-image does not feel very pleasant. If you grew up in a very positive climate, your *me* package feels good to live in. Your personal self-image is simply a belief system you have constructed about yourself. These past learnings gel into a *self* which may or may not be accurate. But once past learnings are part of your **self-image**, you see the package you have put together as accurate, regardless of the facts.

Tom, for instance, was repeatedly told as a child that he was ignorant because he was slow to learn to read. Because he bought that label, he ignored or denied any evidence of his academic ability and creativity. Unintelligent and "smart" do not mix; they are mutually exclusive. Tom held onto those negative messages, also called false beliefs, he received from significant people in his life, such as his parents and teachers. He also ignored any contrary evidence, because it did not fit the unintelligent profile.

As an adult, Tom's past learning limited the accuracy of his "personal Self-Image." He saw only evidence of being academically inferior. Years later, despite a college degree and a successful career, Tom still sees himself as unintelligent.

Each of us identifies whatever qualities we learn to place after the words *I am*. Like Tom, we see such traits as truths about ourselves. These truths or *self-beliefs* literally screen out any messages to the contrary. In this way, past teachings, false beliefs, can limit our options. If your self-worth is low or shaky, you are still believing things about yourself that are untrue negative ideas programmed into you about *you*.

False beliefs are created over many years, and people cement these beliefs without questioning their validity—at the time, you were just a kid who had not learned to read as quickly as others; now you consider yourself unintelligent.

> "The greatest task for any person is to find meaning in his or her life."
> —VIKTOR E. FRANKL

> My Mother said to me, "If you become a soldier, you'll be a general. If you become a monk, you'll end up as the pope." Instead, I became a painter and wound up as Picasso.
> —PABLO PICASSO

These belief systems shape our worldview, since:

> "we learn our belief systems as very little children, and then we move through life creating experiences to match our beliefs. Look back in your own life and notice how often you have gone through the same experience." – Louise L. Hay

Becoming aware of the self. Once you become aware that you are not locked into a false belief, a whole new set of choices will open up. You become aware of new ways to see yourself, new ways you can behave, and new ways to relate. Of course, such choices and behaviors have been available to you all along. The problem has been that you did not fully appreciate your capabilities and potential.

Gender and You

These are a few of the gender definitions that you need to be familiar with in our culture today. More can be found in the Glossary.

Affirmed gender (noun): The gender by which one wishes to be known. This term is often used to replace terms like "new gender" or "chosen gender," which imply that a person's gender was chosen rather than simply innate.

Agender (adj.): Describes a person who does not identify with any gender identity.

Ally (noun): A person who does not identify as LGBTQ, but stands with and advocates for LGBTQ people.

Androgynous (adj.), *Androgyne* (noun): Used to describe someone who identifies or presents as neither distinguishably masculine or feminine.

Aromantic (adj.): A romantic orientation generally characterized by not feeling romantic attraction or a desire for romance.

Asexual (adj.): Used to describe people who do not experience sexual attraction or do not have a desire for sex. Many experience romantic or emotional attractions across the entire spectrum of sexual orientations. Asexuality differs from celibacy, which refers to abstaining from sex. Also *ace*, or *ace community*.

Assigned sex (noun): The sex that is assigned to an infant at birth based on the child's visible sex organs, including genitalia and other physical characteristics. Often corresponds with a child's assigned gender and assumed gender.

Binary system (noun): Something that contains two opposing parts; binary systems are often assumed despite the existence of a spectrum of possibilities. *Gender (man/ woman)* and *sex (male/female)* are examples of binary systems often perpetuated by our culture.

Biological sex (noun): A medical classification that refers to anatomical, physiological, genetic, or physical attributes that determine if a person is assigned male, female, or intersex identity at birth. Biological sex is often confused or interchanged with the term "gender," which encompasses personal identity and social factors, and is not necessarily determined by biological sex. See *gender*.

Bisexual, Bi (adj.): A person emotionally, romantically or sexually attracted to more than one sex, gender, or gender identity though not necessarily simultaneously, in the same way, or to the same degree.

Cisgender (adj.): Describes a person whose gender identity (defined below) aligns with the sex assigned to them at birth.

Lack of awareness is the same as having no choice. It is up to you to increase your awareness about the real you, so you can experience inner freedom. By increasing your awareness about yourself, you increase your choices in life. Carl Rogers (2002) described a *fully functioning person* as one who feels inwardly free to move in any direction. Being a fully functioning person can be a reality for you. If you strive for such an inner freedom, little can hold you back.

The benefits of self-esteem. How we feel about ourselves is important. Research studies reveal the benefits of positive self-esteem and the hazards of self-righteous pride. High self-esteem—a feeling of self-worth—pays dividends. People who feel good about themselves have fewer ulcers, fewer sleepless nights, succumb less to pressures to conform, are less likely to use drugs, are more persistent at difficult tasks, and are just plain happier (McKay & Fanning, 2000).

Self-Esteem

How to appreciate your true self. This chapter began with a description of the nature of self. Remember that as human beings, we have the ability to reflect on who we are. We are aware of a unique *identity*. But we are not only aware of *ourself*; we attach a value to that *self*. So we can decide whether we will accept or reject *ourself*, whether we are *OK* or *not OK*, whether we are good or bad. You are either a *self-hater, self-doubter,* or a *self-affirmer*.

So this unique human ability we have—the ability we have to attach a value to our self—can lead to self-rejection and tremendous emotional pain. The term **self-esteem** refers to the overall evaluation of oneself, whether one likes or dislikes who one is, believes or doubts oneself, and values or belittles one's worth. How you evaluate yourself is crucial to your psychological adjustment.

Does your cultural orientation influence your self-esteem?

> There is overwhelming evidence that the higher the level of self-esteem, the more likely one will treat others with respect, kindness, and generosity. People who do not experience self-love have little or no capacity to love others.
> —NATHANIEL BRANDEN

FOCUS ON DIVERSITY

WHAT IS YOUR CULTURAL ORIENTATION?

Answer the following questions Yes or No:

                                                                  Yes   No

1. I like to live close to my good friends and family.
2. To be superior, a person must stand up for themselves.
3. I enjoy meeting and talking to my neighbors every day.
4. If the group is slowing me down, it is better to leave it and work alone.
5. The larger the family, the more family problems there are.
6. It is reasonable for a son to continue his father's business.
7. I can count on my relatives for help if I find myself in any kind of trouble.
8. In the long run, the only person you can count on is yourself.
9. There is everything to gain and nothing to lose for classmates to group themselves for study and discussions.
10. If you want something done right, you have to do it yourself.

If you answered "yes" to questions 1, 3, 6, 7, and 9, you are more than likely from a collectivist orientation. If you answered "yes" to 2, 4, 5, 8, and 10, you are more than likely from an individualistic orientation. What does this mean?

Individualism vs. Collectivism

What groups do you belong to?

Over the years, social scientists have observed that cultures differ to the extent to which they value individualism and the virtues of independence, autonomy, and self-reliance, or collectivism and the virtues of interdependence, cooperation, and social harmony. In a collectivist society, a person is first and foremost a loyal member of a family, team, company, church, state, and other groups. In an individualist culture, however, personal goals take priority over group allegiances. In what countries are these different orientations most extreme? The United States, Australia, Great Britain, Canada, and the Netherlands, in that order, are the most individualistic. People from Venezuela, Colombia, Pakistan, Peru, Japan, Taiwan, and China are the most collectivistic (Matsumoto, 2007). Think about the institution of marriage. With a collectivist perspective of the marriage, the two people involved in it, husband and wife, are looked upon as a group. Their individual values are lost if the marriage is considered more important than the two people. In such a situation, it is the collectivism at work.

© Roman Samborskyi/Shutterstock.com

Table 2.4   INDIVIDUALISM VS. COLLECTIVISM

	INDIVIDUALISM	COLLECTIVISM
Concept of self	Independent (identity from individual traits)	Interdependent (identity from belonging)
Relationships	Many, often temporary or casual; confrontation acceptable	Few, close and enduring; harmony required
Attribution	Behavior reflects one's personality and attitudes	Behavior reflects social norms and roles
Coping methods	Changes reality	Accommodates to reality
Morality	Defined by individuals (self-based)	Defined by the group (duty-based)
Life task	Discover and express one's uniqueness	Maintain connections, fit in
What matters	My personal achievement and fulfillment; rights and liberties	We-group goals, and solidarity; social responsibilities and relationships

Adapted from Myers (2017) and Matsumoto (2007).

Individualism and collectivism are so deeply ingrained in a culture that they mold our very self-conceptions and identities. Take a brief look at Table 2.4 and see how each culture may influence your personality and self-esteem.

What about people from different ethnic groups and cultural backgrounds? Does your cultural orientation influence your **self-esteem**?

A study in 1951 by Leaky showed that when a student's self-esteem changed, so did performance. A later study found a positive correlation between self-esteem and grade-point average. Self-esteem was also related to teacher ratings of students and observations of classroom behavior. Students with higher levels of self-esteem generally performed at higher academic levels and got along more positively in the classroom. In terms of academic performance, a student's IQ score may not be as important as the self-esteem rating. Self-confidence permits a child to perform, whereas brilliance may be trapped in low self-esteem (Krueger & Vohs, 2003).

Briggs also believed that self-esteem is the mainspring that slates every person for success or failure. Self-esteem has a direct influence on the feeling of self-worth, on human relations, productivity, integrity, stability, and uncertainty. "Self-esteem is the armor that protects a person from the dragons of life: drugs, alcohol, unhealthy relationships, and delinquency" (McKay & Fanning, 2000).

Another benefit of self-esteem is the ability to accept criticism and rejection. Those with high self-esteem tend to view criticism as constructive. They do not interpret a "no" as rejection, but instead try harder and use the constructive criticism as a learning tool.

Clearly, self-esteem influences all aspects of life; in fact, it is the foundation upon which happiness and well-being are built.

There is as much difference between us and ourselves, as between us and others.
—MICHEL DE MONTAIGNE, ESSAYS, 1588

The costs of low self-esteem. Low self-esteem exacts costs. People who do not feel good about themselves are vulnerable to depression and failure. Those whose self-image falls short of what they think they ought to be are vulnerable to anxiety. Most counselors will agree that most of the clients that they encounter who are unhappy, frustrated, and in a state of despair are individuals who have impairments in self-acceptance and self-esteem. There seems to be a correlation between self-esteem and life problems, but the opposite can also be true, that life problems may be the cause of low self-esteem. People who are negative about themselves also seem to be thin-skinned and judgmental (Cole et al., 2004).

LYING AND SELF-ESTEEM

Dr. Benjamin Hardy, an organizational psychologist, writes that research shows that people lie, at least in some degree, in almost every conversation they have. Lying is easy.

We all lie to ourselves all the time.

We lie to others.

We do things we don't really want to do.

It takes courage to be honest.

It takes honesty to build intimacy and trust in our relationships.

It takes radical honesty to become *truly* successful, where you feel amazing about yourself and about what you do.

You have to say "no" sooner.

You have to be *way* more honest in your communications, about what you really want. Otherwise, you'll spend your whole life doing what you don't want.

Remember, Say No sooner.

Be more honest about the situation.

Being honest may cost you some friends and money in the short run. But lying will cost you everything. Especially yourself.

Courage is the doorway.

And this is why most people will never truly be successful.

What are you currently saying "Yes" to that you should be saying "No" to?

Changing your life isn't a process, it's a decision. The problem is, most people take way way to long to make their decisions. Indecision is a bad decision.

Dr. Robert S. Feldman, psychology and deputy chancellor of Amherst University, says his years of research show that people lie because it "greases the wheels of social interaction." Feldman also says it isn't easy to tell from body language whether or not a person is telling the truth. One study found that in a 10-minute conversation, over 60% of the people said at least 2–3 lies.

"People tell a considerable number of lies in everyday conversation. It was a very surprising result. We didn't expect lying to be such a common part of daily life," Feldman said (Feldman, 2016).

FALSE MEMORIES AND "TRUTH BIAS"

Lies result from false memories and from truth bias. False memories are not necessarily deliberate, but situations are compounded when someone insists that something did/did not occur. Feldman suggests that "truth bias" occurs because "we tend to assume that other people are being truthful and that leads us to miss many lies." (Feldman, 2016) Now, there are several reasons why we do that.

One reason is that we're cognitively lazy. We don't always want to be thinking, "Is this person telling me the truth, is this person lying?" It takes a lot of cognitive effort to assume people aren't telling the truth. The other reason we assume people are being truthful is because we're hearing things that are relatively agreeable to us.

The concept of truth bias helps to put (some) lies in perspective—certainly in the case of a polite fib concerning a person's appearance or skill levels. Most of us know and even accept that kind of lie. But lies can cross the line into possibly dangerous and certainly damaging territory. It may start with something inadvertent, almost innocuous. (Feldman, 2016)

If you feel good about yourself, you are more apt to succeed in whatever you do. Both Abraham Maslow and Carl Rogers emphasize the point that a "healthy" self-image pays dividends. Accept yourself, and you will find it easier to accept others. See Table 2.5 for the benefits.

BECOMING AWARE-HEALTHY AND UNHELTHY RELATIONSHIPS

Katie Hood talks about self esteem and healthy and unhealthy relationships at TED2019.

The Difference Between Healthy and Unhealthy Love
https://www.ted.com/talks/katie_hood_the_difference_between_healthy_and_unhealthy_love

Table 2.5   HIGH SELF-ESTEEM VS. LOW SELF-ESTEEM

HIGH SELF-ESTEEM TRAITS	LOW SELF-ESTEEM TRAITS
Perceives reality	Avoids reality to avoid anxiety
Relatively undefensive	Defensive
Gives credit to others when it is due	Envies others and puts them down
Natural	Plays a role
Task-centered	Self-centered
Enjoys being alone	Oriented toward approval of others
Self-reliant	Dependent
Feels kinship with humankind	Us vs. Them
Relationships are intimate	Relationships are casual
Non-judgmental of others	Critical of others
Accepts self	Strives to be perfect and avoid mistakes
Well-developed value system	Values not clarified
Philosophical sense of humor	Hostile
Accepts compliments	Rejects compliments or qualifies them
Cooperative with others	Views self as different from others
Makes growth choices	Makes fear choices
Dares to be unpopular	Conforming
Experiences without self-consciousness	Considers what others think

Adapted from Bandura (2006) and McKay & Fanning (2000).

Self-serving bias? Social psychologists have found that most people are not realistic in evaluating themselves, their capabilities, or their behavior. The *self-serving bias* is a person's tendency to evaluate their own behavior as worthwhile, regardless of the situation. Most people consider themselves to be more intelligent, more sensitive, more considerate, more likely to succeed, and more of a leader than they consider most other people. We tend to be self-enhancing, and we often exaggerate positive beliefs about ourselves (Nier, 2004).

People tend to take credit for their successes and blame others for their failures. That is, we may assume that good things happen to us because we deserve them and that bad things happen to other people because they deserve them. Yet, when something bad occurs in our own lives we look for blame and tend to avoid seeing ourselves as responsible. When something bad happens to others, we may blame it on their carelessness or reckless behavior (attribution theory). The combination of attribution error and self-serving bias helps some people maintain their self-esteem and appear competent. However, this may inhibit some people from having realistic goals, thus setting them up for disappointment.

Psychologists have focused on two possible explanations for the development and role of the self-serving bias. First, a self-serving bias meets people's need for self-esteem and need to feel good about themselves in comparison to other people. It allows people to deal with their limitations and gives them the courage to venture into areas they normally might not explore. Self-serving biases allow people to present themselves to other people in a positive light. Psychologists explain self-serving bias as being partly due to an attempt to "save face" and protect self-esteem in the face of failure (Nier, 2004). We all need to feel good about ourselves, and the self-serving bias allows us to do this.

> *The only person who is educated is the one who has learned how to learn and change.*
> —CARL ROGERS

MY DECLARATION OF SELF-ESTEEM

I am me.

I was uniquely created. There's not another human being in the whole world like me—I have my very own fingerprints and I have my very own thoughts. I was not stamped out of a mold to be the duplicate of another.

I own all of me—my body, and I can do with it what I choose; my mind, and all of its thoughts and ideas; my feelings, whether joyful or painful. I am not defined by what I have or what I own.

I own my ideals, my dreams, my hopes, my fantasies, my fears.

I reserve the right to think and feel differently from others and will grant to others their right to thoughts and feelings not identical with my own.

I own all my triumphs and successes. I own also all my failures and mistakes. I choose what I do and am responsible for my own behavior. I will permit myself to be imperfect. When I make mistakes or fail, I will know that I am not the failure—I am still OK—and I will discard some parts of me that were unfitting and will try new ways.

I will laugh freely and loudly at myself—a healthy self-affirmation.

I will have fun living inside my skin.

I will remember that the door to everybody's life needs this sign: Honor Thyself.

I have value and worth.

Review again Table 2.5 illustrating characteristics of low self-esteem and high self-esteem.

Just knowing what traits a person *of high self-esteem* has is not enough for most of us to embark upon the philosophical, emotional, and behavioral change necessary to increase our self-esteem. On the following pages is a list of strategies that provide a good start. This list is by no means complete, because this process is ongoing and will continue your entire lifetime. Remember that this is not an easy process. It not only takes work but also requires the inner strength to put up with the anxiety that goes along with making change and making mistakes. Remember, too, that not all these strategies will work for you. Think of this list as a menu from which you choose what you like, what fits, and from which you reject what you do not like and what does not fit. So, here goes. This is no easy fix, just an aid or guideline for you. And just because you are willing to try to judge yourself less often means you are a courageous person.

STRATEGIES TO IMPROVE SELF-ESTEEM

1. **Recognize That You Are in Control of Your Self-Image.** The first thing you must do is recognize that you ultimately control the way you see yourself. You have the power to change your self-image. You have the choice to accept or reject feedback. Your self-image resides in your mind and is a product of your thinking. Although others may influence your self-concept, you are the final authority.

   People with low self-esteem tend to be more accepting of negative feedback about themselves than of positive feedback. Are they in control of their self-image? As people become aware of this, they can begin to learn to reject the negative feedback and take control of their own self-image.

2. **Be Able to Accept All Parts of Your Physical Appearance Now!**
   Describe your age, height, weight, facial appearance, skin, hair, and specific body areas such as chest, waist, and legs. Then accept your body. Treasure it. It is what you have and it works. Say to yourself, "You are all I have, and I will take care of you." Judy started working on appreciating her body by completing an appearance inventory as follows:

   - large brown eyes
   - clear, young looking skin
   - fat stomach
   - fat hips
   - slim legs
   - 5'5"
   - nice teeth
   - too many fat cells

   Then she went back over her list and put a plus next to descriptions that represented strengths to her, a minus by items she wanted to change, and did not mark the items she considered to be neutral. She also re-worded those minus statements to more accurate, less judgmental statements:

Minus Statement	Less Judgmental
Fat belly	32-inch waist
Fat hips	40-inch hips
Too many fat cells	Slightly overweight

   Remember, *people with low self-esteem* put off *self-acceptance* until they get that unattainable and unrealistic "perfect" body. It is imperative you treasure your body the way it is now.

3. **Affirm Your Strengths.** As a result of cultural and parental conditioning, you may find it anxiety provoking to give yourself credit for your assets. It is now time, however, to toot your own horn. Get a *big* piece of blank paper. List all your strengths. Think of all parts of your *Self-Image*.

- Your physical appearance
- How you relate to others
- Your personality
- How others see you
- Your work/school/daily task performance

It takes a concentrated effort to make this list. If you are having difficulty thinking of strengths, think of how your best friend would describe you in each of these areas. Your list of strengths will be long if you are willing to put forth the effort and willing to experience the anxiety. Once you have listed many of the qualities in yourself you appreciate, that does not mean you will remember them. Remembering your strengths, particularly at the times when you feel most down on yourself, requires a system. The following three strategies may help you really believe in your positive qualities:

A. *Daily affirmations (positive sayings).* Write affirmations for yourself each day using your name. Make them believable, comforting, and supportive. And repeat them to yourself in front of the mirror.
B. *Reminder signs and notes.* Many people who list positive messages report they reinforce and strengthen their personal sense of adequacy.
C. *Active integration.* Recall specific examples and times when you clearly demonstrated your strengths. Transform your strengths into specific memories. This process will help to convince you that your list of positive qualities actually applies to you.

4. **List Your Faults.** Every person has faults; it is normal and human. The problem is that people use their faults for destructive self-attack and to condemn themselves. There are four basic rules to acknowledging weaknesses:

A. *Use non-pejorative language.* This is language that does not make a bad situation worse. Go through your list and eliminate all the words that have negative connotations. Banish certain words from your self-descriptive vocabulary; for example: fat, ugly, dumb, blabbermouth.
B. *Use accurate language.* Confine yourself to the facts.
C. *Be specific rather than general.* Eliminate words such as always, never, anything.
D. *Find and name weaknesses and write them down. No exceptions or corresponding strengths.* This is essential for any item you feel particularly bad about.

5. **Attain Legitimate Accomplishments and Successes.** Accomplishing worthwhile activities is a major contributor to self-esteem. It is also important to remember that accomplishments do not have to be *big*. They just have to be something that you achieved through hard work and commitment. Social science research suggests this sequence of events: Person establishes a goal > person pursues the goal > person achieves the goal > person develops esteem-like feelings (Cole et al., 2004).

> *Those who dream most, achieve most.*
> —ANONYMOUS

> *You will always be in fashion if you are true to yourself, and only if you are true to yourself.*
> —MAYA ANGELOU

6. **Make the Growth Choice Rather than the Fear Choice.** Take responsibility to direct your own life. If you are dissatisfied with your life as it is now, be willing to change. You promote your growth—or not—each time you make a decision. We are constantly making decisions whether to be honest or to lie, to try new things or be safe, to be open or be defensive. If you make each decision a choice for growth, you manifest courage. Take a look at your privilege.

7. **Shed Perfectionistic Demands.** Perfectionism is the tendency to believe that only the "perfect" is acceptable. Real-world success hinges less on getting everything right than on how you handle getting things wrong. There's a difference between excellence and perfection. Excellence involves enjoying what you do. Perfection means not being satisfied—no matter what (Marano, 2008).

8. **Become More Synergistic.** Maslow describes this as being *involved with others*. Become involved with other people and your work and leisure time will become more valuable to you. Make a commitment. Alfred Adler (2009) points out that we greatly promote our health and functioning by cooperation with others.

9. **Observe People You Admire.** Identify at least five qualities that you aspire to and admire in others. Become a careful observer. Think of how you can adapt their behavior to fit your own personal style.

10. **Keep a Diary.** Record what you enjoy about your day. You may be doing things out of habit rather than because you enjoy them. By keeping a diary, you may discover that some of your activities do not make you happy. If this is the case, then you can actively make the attempt not to do these things any longer.

11. **Keep a Sense of Humor.** Laugh easily, enjoy a good joke, have fun in life. Some of us do not know how to play. We take our life and ourselves too seriously. Perhaps we grew up in families in which there was not much fun and happiness. Remember to keep a balance in your life between work and play. Take time for the pleasures in life.

12. **Do Not Be Afraid to Make Mistakes.** You will make thousands of mistakes during your lifetime if you plan to live up to your creative potential. Do a personal mistake check, and then increase the number of mistakes you make each day by 10%. You will take more risks, stretch, grow, and enjoy life more. You learn through experience. If you do not try something, you may lose out on a lot of experiences in your life.

Everyone makes mistakes; do not worry about them. Forgive yourself for making mistakes. If you do not make mistakes, you're not trying. You learn from your mistakes. Remember "friends" who run you down, even in jest, are not friends. Omit them.

The twelve strategies listed here to help you to improve your self-esteem will give you a good start. As your work progresses, you may come up with a few of your own that are not listed here. Remember your sense of self initially comes from others; you were told about yourself and who you are when you were a small child by those around you. As an adult, it is up to you to develop a realistic positive sense of self. To do this, you must be dedicated to the effort for a lifetime. It is not enough to say you will love yourself. Your assumptions about yourself and about your world must be positive, healthy, realistic ones, and self evaluation is lifelong work.

Watch this and explore your own privilege and prejudices.

Your Privilege is Showing
http://www.yourprivilegeisshowing.com/blog/2018/2/6/watch-the-your-privilege-is-showing-tedx-talk

At the beginning of the 20th century, sociologist Charles Cooley described the American identity as a "looking-glass self." Our sense of ourselves, wrote Cooley, is formed by our imagination of the way we appear in the eyes of others. Other people are a looking glass in which we see not merely our own reflection but a judgment about the value of that reflection. ("Each to each a looking glass/reflects the other that doth pass," he wrote.) If we are lucky, we feel pride in that imagined self; if not, we feel mortification (Elliott, 2004).

Growth and change are not a destination, but rather a journey. All through our lives, if we are to function fully, we will continue to grow and change. Self-esteem is really so much more than just feeling good about oneself. Researchers are quick to assert that excessive pride can be dangerous, and too few people really know how to be humble. Remember, **narcissism** is the tendency to regard oneself as grandiosely self-important. Self-esteem is about having respect for yourself and others. Self-esteem is essential for psychological survival. One of the main factors differentiating humans from animals is awareness of self: the ability to form identity and attach a value to it (McKay & Fanning, 2016). Self-esteem is about trusting your ability to make appropriate choices and cope effectively with adversity. According to self-esteem researcher Dr. Nathaniel Branden (2015), author of *The Psychology of Self-Esteem,* building self-esteem requires a lifelong commitment to six principles and daily practices:

BRANDEN'S SIX PILLARS OF SELF ESTEEM

Self-esteem = self-efficacy + self-respect. —NATHANIEL BRANDEN

- **Living consciously.** Maintain an unflinching willingness to face reality even when it is painful. Become aware of how you treat yourself and how others are treating you.
- **Self-acceptance.** Experience and take responsibility for your thoughts, feelings, and actions. Avoid putting yourself down.
- **Self-responsibility.** Realize that you alone are responsible for your life and well-being. You are responsible for your own choices.
- **Self-assertiveness.** Have the courage to stand up for who you are. Do not pretend to be someone you're not to avoid someone else's disapproval.
- **Living purposefully.** Identify your goals and the actions needed to attain them. Organize your priorities to meet those goals.
- **Personal integrity.** Demonstrate personal integrity by telling the truth, honoring commitments, and dealing with others justly and considerately. Conduct your life by merging what you know, what you profess, and what you do.

Authors Linda Sanford and Mary Ellen Donovan (2004) in the classic audio version of *Women & Self-Esteem: Understanding and Improving the Way We Think about Ourselves,* describe the power of self-esteem as follows:

Our level of self-esteem affects virtually everything we think, say, and do. It affects how we see the world and our place in it. It affects how others in the world see and treat us. It affects the choices we make—choices about what we will do with our lives and with whom we will be involved. It affects our ability to take action to change things that need to be changed.

Becoming Aware of Technology and Self-awareness

Human relationships are rich; they're messy and demanding. We have learned the habit of cleaning them up with technology. And the move from conversation to connection is part of this. But it's a process in which we shortchange ourselves. Worse, it seems that over time we stop caring; we forget that there is a difference.

We are tempted to think that our little "sips" of online connection add up to a big gulp of real conversation. But they don't. Email, Twitter, Facebook, all of these have their places—in politics, commerce, romance, and friendship. But no matter how valuable, they do not substitute for conversation.

Your devices provide powerful fantasies:

- that we can put our attention wherever we want it to be;
- that we never have to be alone.

Our new devices have turned being alone into a problem that can be solved.

In her 2012 book *Alone Together: Why We Expect More From Technology and Less From Each Other,* Sherry Turkle said:

> In today's workplace, young people who have grown up fearing conversation show up on the job wearing earphones. Walking through a college library or the campus of a high-tech start-up, one sees the same thing: we are together, but each of us is in our own bubble, furiously connected to keyboards and tiny touch screen.
>
> We live in a technological universe in which we are always communicating. And yet we have sacrificed conversation for mere connection.
>
> At home, families sit together, texting and reading email. At work, executives text during board meetings. We text (and shop and go on Facebook) during classes and when we're on dates.
>
> We think constant connection will make us feel less lonely. The opposite is true. If we are unable to be alone, we are far more likely to be lonely.
>
> Most of all, we need to remember—in between texts and emails and Facebook posts—to listen to one another, even to the boring bits, because it is often in unedited moments, moments in which we hesitate and stutter and go silent, that we reveal ourselves to one another (Turkle, 2012).

Chapter Review

Life is a journey. All through our lives, if we are to function fully, we will continue to grow and change.

- People acquire a sense of self throughout their lives; it is an ongoing process that evolves from our experiences and interactions with others.
- If we are to have a strong self-concept, we need love, respect, and acceptance from the significant others in our lives. Who are the significant others in your life, and what impact have they had on your self-concept?
- The self-fulfilling prophecy has a great influence on a person's image of themselves.
- As we compare ourselves with others (social comparison) we gain a better understanding of ourselves, be it positive or negative.
- When our self-concept is intact and secure, we feel good. When it is threatened, we feel anxious and insecure.
- Self-esteem is essential for psychological survival. One of the main factors differentiating humans from animals is awareness of self: the ability to form identity and attach a value to it.
- **Dwerk's theory of mindset.** Some of the less-bright students are real go-getters, thriving on challenge, persisting intensely when things get difficult, and accomplishing more than they expected. The right mindset and being praised for trying harder, not for how smart they were, made a difference, according to Dwerk. The students who have learning goals—who are concerned with increasing their competence and abilities while mastering new tasks over time—make better grades. Dwerk found that the best mix is a combination of (a) valuing learning and challenge, and (b) valuing grades but seeing them as merely an index of your current performance, not a sign of your intelligence or worth.
- **Freud's theory of personality development** provides the foundation of many other personality theories. Freud stated that the personality is made up of three distinct, but interrelated, parts: the id, the ego, and the superego. The **id** is composed of the basic biological drives that motivate an individual, including the pleasure-seeking part of your personality. The **ego** is the rational, logical, and realistic part of your personality. The **superego** consists of our values, morals, religious beliefs, and ideals of our parents and society.
- To **Adler** (2016), personality arises from our attempts to overcome or compensate for fundamental feelings of inadequacy. Adler was responsible for coining the popular term "**inferiority complex**," a concept, he argued, that underlies and motivates a great deal of human behavior. While he believed that everyone has to work to overcome some feelings of inferiority, Adler believed that some people overcompensate in order to conceal their feelings of inferiority.
- Most recent research studies do not seem to support Adler's idea that birth order is a possible factor regulating personality.
- **Erik Erikson** identified **eight stages of psychosocial development** that each individual needs to satisfy throughout their life. They are:
  1. Trust vs. Mistrust,
  2. Autonomy vs. Doubt,
  3. Initiative vs. Guilt,
  4. Industry vs. Inferiority,
  5. Identity vs. Role Confusion,
  6. Intimacy vs. Isolation,
  7. Generativity vs. Self-Absorption, and
  8. Integrity vs. Despair.

- The **Myers-Briggs Type Indicator** covers four dimensions: Extroversion (E) or Introversion (I), Sensing (S) or Intuition (N), Thinking (T) or Feeling (F), and Judgment (J) or Perception (P).
- Some psychologists have developed a personality theory that identifies personality traits that many of us use to describe other people (and ourselves). These are called **traits**, which are relatively stable and consistent personal characteristics. This is known as the **Big Five Model of Personality**.
- Your personality evolves from the Big Five, these traits include the **OCEAN** traits: Openness, Conscientiousness, Extraversion, Agreeableness, and Neuroticism.
- The **HEXACO Personality Dimensions Inventory** model includes six dimensions of human personality: Honesty-Humility, Emotionality, Extroversion, Agreeableness, Conscientiousness, and Openness to Experience. Each of these six dimensions represent the four cardinal virtues (wisdom, courage, temperance, and justice).
- **Strengths-Based Psychology** is based on the work of Tom Rath and a team of Gallup scientists who set out to start a global conversation about what's right with people, rather than focusing so much on people's shortcomings. Their work was originally led by the late Father of Strengths Psychology, Donald O. Clifton.
- **Carl Rogers' Self-Theory** defines the development of the self-concept in terms of self-actualization, which is defined as the fulfillment of one's own completely unique personality. Unconditional positive regard (unconditioned acceptance) leads to unimpaired growth and the development of positive characteristics.
- **Viktor Frankl** states that our task is to create a life that has meaning and purpose.
- **Virginia Satir's Self-Worth theory** indicates that what happens inside people and between people is the picture of the individual worth that each person carries around.
- Cognitive theories of personality point out that there are important individual differences in the way people think about and define situations.
- **Building self-esteem** is easier with the help of **positive self-talk** and thinking positively and optimistically.
- **Cognitive restructuring**, the process of modifying thoughts, ideas, and beliefs, can be used to increase positive and optimistic thinking.
- **Self-talk** is the unspoken, mental speech we use when we think about something, solve problems, and make plans. Positive or negative self-talk may have an influence on your self-concept.
- Reciprocal determinism is the interacting influences between person, behavior, and environment.
- Your personal **self-image** is the part of the self that includes physical, behavioral, and psychological characteristics that establish uniqueness.
- There are many benefits to positive self-esteem, including better health, feeling happy, etc.
- There are many costs to low self-esteem, including poor health, unhappiness, more frustration, poorer work performance, etc.
- The **self-serving bias** is a person's tendency to evaluate his or her own behavior as worthwhile, regardless of the situation.
- **Individualistic societies** value independence, autonomy, and self-reliance. **Collectivistic societies** value interdependence, cooperation, and social harmony.
- Individualism and collectivism are so deeply ingrained in a culture that they mold our self-concepts and identities.
- There are many **strategies to improve self-esteem**, including:
  1. Recognize that you are in control
  2. Accept your physical appearance—just the way you are
  3. Affirm your strengths
  4. List your faults

5. Attain legitimate accomplishments and successes
6. Make a growth choice rather than a fear choice
7. Shed perfectionistic demands
8. Work well with others
9. Observe role models
10. Keep a diary
11. Keep a sense of humor
12. Do not be afraid to make mistakes

- Self-esteem researcher and author Dr. Nathaniel Branden says that building self-esteem requires a lifelong commitment to six principles and daily practices: living consciously, self-acceptance, self-responsibility, self-assertiveness, living purposefully, and personal integrity. Remember, **narcissism** is the tendency to regard oneself as grandiosely self-important. This attitude is dangerous.
- In terms of technology, many of the experts say digital life will continue to expand people's boundaries and opportunities in the coming decade and that the world to come will produce more help than harm in people's lives.
- Personal growth and self-awareness involve accepting ourselves and enjoying our relationships with others. Only "you" can make the choice whether you will live an enjoyable and fulfilling life, or one of stagnation.

Learning Outcomes Review

1. Why do we need to study about the development of the "self"?
2. Explain how significant others influence a person's self-image.
3. Define and explain Carol Dwerk's theory of mindset. What mindset do you have?
4. Explain Alfred Adler's theory of personality development and the inferiority complex.
5. What do the latest research findings suggest about birth order as a possible factor regulating personality?
6. Describe Erikson's Eight Stages of Psychosocial Development.
7. Briefly explain the four dimensions of the Myers-Briggs Type Indicator.
8. Explain how the Big Five Model of Personality has influenced your perception of others, using the "Big Five" Traits.
9. Define Strengths-Based Psychology.
10. Describe how Carl Rogers' Self-Theory influences the development of your personality.
11. Describe, briefly, Viktor Frankl's Search for Meaning theory.
12. Briefly describe Virginia Satir's Theory of Self-Worth.
13. Define Reciprocal Determinism and explain how our thoughts and our environment influence the development of our personality.
14. Explain how cognitive and social-learning theories explain your self-image.
15. Describe the cognitive variables that influence your behavior.
16. Define collectivism and individualism and explain how they may influence an individual's self-concept.
17. What are the costs of low self-esteem? Explain.
18. What are the benefits of having high self-esteem? Explain.
19. Define the Self-Serving Bias and explain how it influences your behavior.
20. Briefly explain the twelve strategies that will help you improve your self-esteem.

21. Define narcissism and explain how Nathaniel Branden's views of building self-esteem are exactly the opposite from narcissism.

22. Briefly describe Davidson's STRENGTH model for helping yourself and others.
Davidson's Strengths is modeled from Positive Psychology traditions. It can be used for an individual's personal growth or as a guideline for helping others. What is the STRENGTH acronym?

Key Terms

Agreeableness
Autonomy vs. Doubt
Cognitive Restructuring
Collectivism
Compensation
Conscientiousness
Ego
Extroversion or Introversion
Generativity vs. Self-Absorption
HEXACO/OCEAN
Id
Identity Formation
Individualism
Industry vs. Inferiority
Inferiority Complex
Initiative vs. Guilt
Integrity vs. Despair
Interpersonal Relations
Intersectionality

Intimacy vs. Isolation
Judgment or Perception
Mid-Life Crisis
Mid-Life Transition Stage
Mindset
Myers-Briggs Type Indicator
Narcissism
Neuroticism
Openness
Personal Self-Image
Positive Psychology
Pot of Self-Worth
Privilege
Real Self
Reciprocal Determinism
Search for Meaning
Self-Awareness
Self-Esteem
Self-Image

Self-Perception
Self-Serving Bias
Self-Talk
Self-Theory
Self-Worth
Sensing or Intuition
Significant Others
Social Comparison
Stages of Psychosocial
    Development
STRENGTH Model
Strengths-Based Psychology
Superego
Thinking or Feeling
Trait
Trust vs. Mistrust
Unconditional Positive Regard

Reflections: Critical Thinking Activities

Answer the following questions and turn them into your instructor for grading. (All questions answered = A; 13 questions answered = B; 8 questions answered = C).

1. Do we have a choice in determining who we become? Explain.
2. How do our interactions with others help in discovering who we are?
3. Who are the significant others in your life? What impact have they had on your life? Were they a good influence or a bad influence?
4. How does striving for perfection lead to emotional pain?
5. How does social comparison influence our self-image?
6. How have the id, ego, and superego influenced your behavior?
7. How has the concept of inferiority complex impacted your personality development?
8. Discuss the relationship between your life and Erikson's Stages of Development.
9. Discuss your personality type on the Myers-Briggs Type Indicator. Do you think it is open to being wrong or lacking?
10. Why is it so difficult to make changes in our self-concept?
11. Discuss the cultural influences on a person's development.
12. Which theory of personality seems to explain your own development best?
13. How can excessive pride be dangerous?
14. How do you think birth order has influenced your personality development?
15. Do you think tests for Personality Type are true and enlightening? Or are they a bunch of bunk?

Technology Resources and Activities

ACTIVITIES

http://www.mindsetonline.com/testyourmindset/step1.php

> Carol Dweck's mindset website—find out what your mindset is.

http://www.selfgrowth.com/topics.html

> This site provides much information about self-improvement and personal growth.

www.keirsey.com

> This website is dedicated to personality/trait differences. For a free sample you can click on the temperament sorter icon and read the results about yourself.

www.authentichappiness.sas.upenn.edu/testcenter.aspx

> Brief Strengths Test or VIA Survey of Character Strengths—measures 24 character strengths.

https://www.psychologytoday.com/us/tests

If you are interested in taking tests to learn more about yourself- Check out Psychology Today tests

http://hexaco.org/hexaco-online

On this website you can complete the HEXACO Personality Dimensions Inventory-Revised (HEXACO-PI-R).

https://www.apa.org/topics/race

APA on Understanding Racism

https://www.apa.org/topics/lgbt/transgender

APA on Transgender People, Gender Identity, and Gender Expression

https://www.youtube.com/watch?v=_h938XCpI7U

What Is Privilege? on youtube.com

VIDEOS

https://www.cbsnews.com/video/gender-the-space-between/

Video exploring genderfluid and other gender definitions.

https://www.cbsnews.com/news/transgender-gender-identity-terms-glossary/

The gender identity terms you need to know, by Cydney Adama of CBS News.

http://www.ted.com/talks/carol_dweck_the_power_of_believing_that_you_can_improve

Carol Dweck: The power of believing that you can improve

https://www.ted.com/speakers/dan_gilbert

Harvard psychologist Dan Gilbert says our beliefs about what will make us happy are often wrong—a premise he supports with intriguing research, and explains in his accessible and unexpectedly funny book, *Stumbling on Happiness*. Dan Gilbert believes that, in our ardent, lifelong pursuit of happiness, most of us have the wrong map.

https://www.youtube.com/watch?v=w6dnj2IyYjE

Intersectionality

https://www.youtube.com/watch?v=n2kUpKP18z8

Khan Academy on Intersectionality

https://www.youtube.com/watch?v=FeLpvgAVtU8

Self Esteem—Understanding and Fixing Low Self-Esteem

https://www.apa.org/topics/race

https://www.apa.org/pi/oema/resources/ethnicity-health/african-american/stress

https://www.apa.org/pi/oema/resources/ethnicity-health/asian-american/bullying-and-victimization

https://www.apa.org/topics/lgbt/transgender

https://www.youtube.com/watch?v=nHSZ3_VMgjU

Introduction to the Myers-Briggs Personality Test

https://www.youtube.com/watch?v=Q5pggDCnt5M

Why the Myers-Briggs test is totally meaningless

https://www.youtube.com/watch?v=_h938XCpI7U

Watch the video and do the privilege walk activity in class.

https://www.youtube.com/watch?v=R4b_ojKx6UI

Your Privilege Is Showing | Lillian Medville | TEDxBeaconStreet 2018

Whether we acknowledge it or not, race, sex, gender, class, and privilege are all part of our daily lives no matter who we are, what we look like, or where we're from. But too often we don't talk about these issues for fear of saying the wrong thing, or that the conversations will be difficult, bitter, and even painful.

Your Privilege Is Showing is a social justice card game that provides the unique framework that develops the skills needed to have challenging conversations around inclusion, equity, and diversity.

https://www.ted.com/talks/cameron_russell_looks_aren_t_everything_believe_me_i_m_a_model

Cameron Russell: Looks aren't everything. Believe me, I'm a model.

What a recent TED talk teaches us about our hidden stereotypes, and their pernicious effects. With candor and directness, Russell draws on her own experiences as a highly successful model to expose modern manifestations of racism and sexism, where physical appearance dictates who gets seen and heard in the mass media, and how they're perceived.

http://www.glma.org/

Gay/Lesbian Medical Association

http://www.glnh.org/

LGBT National Help Center

https://www.hrc.org/

Human Rights Campaign

https://www.hrc.org/resources/glossary-of-terms

Dictionary of terms about sexual orientation and gender identity or expression

BECOMING AWARE OF DEVELOPMENT ACTIVITY—EXPLORE THESE QUESTIONS

Answer in your journal and be prepared for a class discussion.

1. In the first stage of development—Basic Trust Versus Basic Mistrust—Erikson believes that an anxious mother can transmit her anxiety to her child, with negative consequences for that child's development. Suppose a correlational study was conducted in which a correlation was indeed found between mothers' and babies' anxiety. Correlation, of course, does not imply causation. What alternative explanations might be suggested to account for this finding?

2. If you have (or have had) children at the second stage of development (Autonomy Versus Shame and Doubt), think of the kinds of conflicts you will have had with your children. Make notes on these and share with the class.

3. Pick any two of Erikson's eight stages. Think of someone you know who seems to fit into each of these stages in a positive or negative way. Describe them (share with the class).

4. Class discussion: Erikson and Freud were both very traditional in their ideas about sexual adjustment. Think about how times have changed, and discuss alternative ideas.

5. Think about your own life and where you are going. What kind of an old age would you like to have? (For class sharing.)

6. How does the treatment of elderly people in our culture differ from that of traditional cultures? How might the treatment of elderly people be improved in our society?

7. To what extent do you think that Erikson's framework applies (or fails to apply) to women as well as to men? To what extent do you think it would work or not work with other cultures?

BECOMING AWARE OF DWECK'S MINDSET THEORY

Mindset exercise

Purpose: For an interesting discussion on mindset. Please read this link and reflect on it in your journal. Be prepared for a class discussion with 2 or 3 classmates or friends.

Fixed vs. Growth: The Two Basic Mindsets That Shape Our Lives

https://www.brainpickings.org/2014/01/29/carol-dweck-mindset/

Discussion partner _____

Discussion partner _____

Discussion partner _____

Group discussion report notes:

BECOMING AWARE OF THEORIES ACTIVITY

Reflect on the questions and add to your Class Journal.

What theory do you feel has had the greatest influence on you, or do you think that each theory has some valid points that you could use to justify how your personality developed?

An interesting project would be for you to write your own personality theory that best describes your development.

The "Big Five" Test

PURPOSE

To survey the "Big Five" Personality Traits.

INSTRUCTIONS

1. Using the numbers on the scale from 1 to 5, indicate how true each of the following terms is in describing yourself.

    1 = Not at all true of me: I am never this way.
    2 = Mostly not true of me: I am rarely this way.
    3 = Neither true nor untrue of me, or I can't decide.
    4 = Somewhat true of me: I am sometimes this way.
    5 = Very true of me: I am very often this way.

    1. _____ imaginative
    2. _____ organized
    3. _____ talkative
    4. _____ sympathetic
    5. _____ tense
    6. _____ intelligent
    7. _____ thorough
    8. _____ assertive
    9. _____ kind
    10. _____ anxious
    11. _____ original
    12. _____ efficient
    13. _____ active

    14. _____ soft-hearted
    15. _____ nervous
    16. _____ insightful
    17. _____ responsible
    18. _____ energetic
    19. _____ warm
    20. _____ worrying
    21. _____ clever
    22. _____ practical
    23. _____ outgoing
    24. _____ generous
    25. _____ self-pitying

INSTRUCTIONS FOR SCORING

To compute your score for each of the five scales, simply add your scores for the items that contribute to each of the scales.

Openness to Experience: 1, 6, 11, 16, 21   Your Score _____

Conscientiousness: 2, 7, 12, 17, 22   Your Score _____

Extroversion: 3, 8, 13, 18, 23   Your Score _____

Agreeableness: 4, 9, 14, 19, 24   Your Score _____

Neuroticism: 5, 10, 15, 20, 25   Y   our Score _____

Note: Be sure to review Table 2.1 for a description of high and low scores. Also, review the next page for mean scores of men and women. High scores on neuroticism are not desirable. Discuss this with your instructor.

Mean scores for men and women on each of the scales are listed below:

	Men	Women	Your Score
Openness to Experience	20.3	19.4	
Conscientiousness	18.8	20.2	
Extroversion	18.8	19.0	
Agreeableness	18.8	22.2	
Neuroticism	16.3	18.5	

DISCUSSION

1. Review the descriptions in the text of the five types and answer the following: Do you agree or disagree with your scores? Why or why not?

2. How do you think you could start to improve the areas where you scored the lowest?

Brody, N., & Erhlichman, H. (1998). *Personality Psychology: The Science of Individuality.* Upper Saddle River, NJ: Prentice Hall.

Name _____ Date _____

I Am a Person Who ...

PURPOSE

To become more aware of how you are perceived by others and how accurate you are in your perceptions of others.

INSTRUCTIONS

1. You have two forms—one for you and one for another person. Each person responds to the first scale by circling the number on the continuum that indicates the way you present yourself to others. Do not mark this the way you see yourself, but the way you feel you come across to others.
2. Give the second form to a friend and have him or her evaluate you.
3. Looking at both scales, identify any discrepancies between the two. Ask your friend to discuss the discrepancies in terms of: "I see you this way because . . ."

I AM A PERSON WHO . . .

Personal warmth		Aloofness, coldness
Neat appearance		Careless appearance
Cheerful disposition		Unhappy disposition
Sincerity, genuineness		Insincerity, artificiality
Insecurity in behavior		Confidence in behavior
Reluctancy to talk with others		Eagerness to talk with others
Desire to listen		No interest in listening
Primary concern for self		Primary concern for others
Ability to express ideas and feelings		Difficulty in expressing ideas and feelings
Awareness of what is happening		Lack of awareness of what is happening
Difficulty in making other people comfortable		Ease in making other people comfortable
Talk too much		Talk too little
Not intelligent		Intelligent
Excitement, enthusiasm		Dullness, apathy

Note: If you want more than one person to evaluate you, make several copies of this form.

_____ IS A PERSON WHO . . .

Personal warmth	Aloofness, coldness
Neat appearance	Careless appearance
Cheerful disposition	Unhappy disposition
Sincerity, genuineness	Insincerity, artificiality
Insecurity in behavior	Confidence in behavior
Reluctancy to talk with others	Eagerness to talk with others
Desire to listen	No interest in listening
Primary concern for self	Primary concern for others
Ability to express ideas and feelings	Difficulty in expressing ideas and feelings
Awareness of what is happening	Lack of awareness of what is happening
Difficulty in making other people comfortable	Ease in making other people comfortable
Talk too much	Talk too little
Not intelligent	Intelligent
Excitement, enthusiasm	Dullness, apathy

DISCUSSION

1. Many times we feel we present particular characteristics to others because that is the way we see ourselves. What does this activity show us about our awareness and honesty in conveying our true self to others?

2. Did you have a realistic perception of yourself as compared to how the other person perceived you? Discuss the differences between your perceptions and the other person's perceptions.

3. Discuss how our perceptions of another person affect our interactions with them.

Adjective Checklist

PURPOSE

To provide an opportunity for the class members to reveal themselves to the other group members and to receive feedback on how the other group members perceive them.

INSTRUCTIONS

1. Review the list of words and place a (+) next to the adjectives you think best describe you and a (–) next to the adjectives which are least descriptive of you.
2. Divide into groups of three or four.
3. Each member then shares, with the group, at least four adjectives that are most descriptive and least descriptive of them.
4. Another option is to ask a friend (using the other person's adjective checklist), to place a (+) next to the adjectives they think best describe you and a (–) next to the adjectives they think are least descriptive of you.

_____ accepting	_____ simple	_____ silly
_____ self-accepting	_____ proud	_____ selfish
_____ anxious	_____ adaptable	_____ carefree
_____ aggressive	_____ dependent	_____ determined
_____ original	_____ effervescent	_____ spontaneous
_____ happy	_____ thoughtful	_____ tense
_____ vain	_____ lazy	_____ certain
_____ controlling	_____ dependable	_____ sentimental
_____ irritable	_____ mystical	_____ unpredictable
_____ worried	_____ inconsiderate	_____ patient
_____ rigid	_____ understanding	_____ extraverted
_____ brave	_____ sarcastic	_____ hostile
_____ responsible	_____ dreamy	_____ questioning

_____ remote	_____ loving	_____ serious
_____ shy	_____ ambitious	_____ modest
_____ warm	_____ authoritative	_____ mature
_____ withdrawn	_____ calm	_____ unsympathetic
_____ bitter	_____ conforming	_____ immature
_____ independent	_____ confident	_____ objective
_____ naive	_____ intelligent	_____ religious
_____ complex	_____ observant	_____ organized
_____ sensitive	_____ obsessive	_____ unorganized
_____ insensitive	_____ relaxed	_____ sympathetic
_____ nervous	_____ intuitive	_____ temperamental

DISCUSSION

1. What did you find out about yourself as a result of this activity?

2. What is the one adjective that causes you the greatest amount of difficulty in relationships with other people? Explain.

Name _____ Date _____

Other Person's Adjective Checklist

INSTRUCTIONS

1. Review the list of words and place a (+) next to the adjectives you think best describe your friend and a (–) next to the adjectives which are least descriptive of your friend.

_____ relaxed	_____ confident	_____ adaptable
_____ intuitive	_____ intelligent	_____ dependent
_____ serious	_____ observant	_____ effervescent
_____ modest	_____ obsessive	_____ thoughtful
_____ mature	_____ self-accepting	_____ lazy
_____ unsympathetic	_____ anxious	_____ dependable
_____ immature	_____ aggressive	_____ mystical
_____ objective	_____ original	_____ inconsiderate
_____ religious	_____ happy	_____ understanding
_____ organized	_____ vain	_____ sarcastic
_____ unorganized	_____ controlling	_____ dreamy
_____ sympathetic	_____ irritable	_____ silly
_____ temperamental	_____ worried	_____ selfish
_____ accepting	_____ rigid	_____ carefree
_____ ambitious	_____ brave	_____ determined
_____ authoritative	_____ responsible	_____ spontaneous
_____ calm	_____ simple	_____ tense
_____ conforming	_____ proud	_____ certain

_____ sentimental

_____ unpredictable

_____ patient

_____ extraverted

_____ hostile

_____ questioning

_____ remote

_____ shy

_____ warm

_____ withdrawn

_____ bitter

_____ independent

_____ naive

_____ complex

_____ sensitive

_____ insensitive

_____ nervous

_____ loving

Name _____ Date _____

The Rosenberg Self–Esteem Scale

PURPOSE

The scale below is a widely used research instrument that taps respondents' feelings of general self-esteem.

INSTRUCTIONS

Using the scale below, indicate your agreement with each of the following statements.

1	2	3	4
Strongly Disagree	Disagree	Agree	Strongly Agree

_____ 1. I feel that I am a person of worth, at least on an equal basis with others.

_____ 2. I feel that I have a number of good qualities.

_____ 3. All in all, I am inclined to feel that I am a failure.

_____ 4. I am able to do most things as well as most other people.

_____ 5. I feel I do not have much to be proud of.

_____ 6. I take a positive attitude toward myself.

_____ 7. On the whole, I am satisfied with myself.

_____ 8. I wish I could have more respect for myself.

_____ 9. I certainly feel useless at times.

_____ 10. At times I think I am no good at all.

SCORING

To calculate your score, first reverse the scoring for the five negatively worded items (**3, 5, 8, 9,** and **10**) as follows: 1 = 4, 2 = 3, 3 = 2, 4 = 1. Then sum your scores across the 10 items. Your total score should fall between 10 and 40. A higher score indicates higher self-esteem.

Total Score _____

DISCUSSION

1. Do you agree or disagree with your score? Why or why not?

2. From the strategies to improve self-esteem discussed in the text, what do you think you need to do to improve your self-esteem?

Adapted from *Society and the Adolescent Self-Image* by M. Rosenberg, (2016) Princeton University Press.

Name _____ Date _____

Do Gender Roles Still Exist?

PURPOSE

Discover how you and others perceive gender roles and issues.

INSTRUCTIONS

In the spaces below, list 10 characteristics and behaviors that you associate with being male and female in our society. Note whether you think each is traditional or not used anymore.

1. You may either do this activity individually or with a partner. An interesting alternative would be to divide into groups of 4 with different genders in each group. This will help the class see whether there is a distinct perceived difference or not.

Gender neutral	Males	Females
1. _____	1. _____	1. _____
2. _____	2. _____	2. _____
3. _____	3. _____	3. _____
4. _____	4. _____	4. _____
5. _____	5. _____	5. _____
6. _____	6. _____	6. _____
7. _____	7. _____	7. _____
8. _____	8. _____	8. _____
9. _____	9. _____	9. _____
10. _____	10. _____	10. _____

2. Before you go on, make two copies of the list and set them aside for now.
3. Look at the list of the different characteristics, both male and female, and gender neutral, and circle the ones that best apply to you. You may discover that you identify with some characteristics of the opposite sex. How many of them did you select?
4. Divide into small groups of 3 to 5 individuals and answer the following questions.

Becoming *Aware*

DISCUSSION

1. Did the females in the group circle more of the male characteristics than males circled of the female characteristics? Which characteristics could be gender neutral? If so, why?

2. Are there some characteristics of the opposite sex that you wish could be attributed to members of your sex? Which ones are they? Why would you like them attributed to your sex?

3. Do you feel our definitions of gender roles are preventing you from behaving or developing in the ways you would prefer? Explain.

4. How have gender role expectations influenced your personality development?

5. How could we best make society more accepting of varying gender roles?

6. Now give the copy of the list that you previously made to someone who knows you well and ask them to circle the characteristics that best apply to you, using gender neutral characteristics. When they have completed the list, compare your list with theirs. How we see ourselves is not always how others see us. How closely did your list match your friend's? What might the differences tell you about yourself?

7. Give the other copy of the list to someone who knows you well who is at least ten years or more older or younger than you, and do the same as in previous question. Is there a difference because of age? If there is a difference, why?

Name _____ Date _____

Human Relations Position Paper

PURPOSE

To confidentially analyze your present position, based upon your past experiences and learning, in order to have a better idea of the direction in which you want to move in the future.

INSTRUCTIONS

1. A Human Relations Position Paper should represent a critical analysis of those factors that have brought you to this point in your life and have made you what you are. It should also include your plans for the future.
2. No one but you and your instructor will read your position paper unless, of course, you choose to show it to someone else. Your instructor considers it completely confidential.
3. As a guide for preparing your position paper, the following outline is suggested. This is intended only as a guide, and you may add or delete whatever items you choose.
4. Anything that helps you arrive at your position and chart your course of action (from poetry to pictures to words) is acceptable.
5. Your instructor will determine the length of this paper. We suggest five pages.

   Retain a copy of this to review in ten years. How far have you come?

HUMAN RELATIONS POSITION PAPER OUTLINE

I. The Person I Am (Include the influential factors which have contributed to making you what you are).
   A. Influence of Family Background
      1. Relationship with parents
      2. Relationship with siblings
      3. Socioeconomic setting
      4. Family's expectations
      5. Other
   B. Adolescence
      1. School experience
      2. Peer group (left out/included—Why?)
      3. Successes/Failures and their effect
      4. Influential adults other than parents
      5. Other

C. Personal Sexuality
  1. Dating experiences and their effects
  2. "Facts of life" information or misinformation and its effect
  3. My "role" in life and how people understand me
  4. My attitudes toward the opposite sex
  5. Other
D. Goals for Future
  1. How have I arrived at my goals?
  2. Occupational choice—Why?
  3. Feelings of personal adequacy or inadequacy
  4. Degree of flexibility
  5. Influential people
  6. Other
II. Where Do I Go From Here?
  A. Summary of Present Position
    1. How do I see myself/how do others see me?
    2. How well do I communicate?
    3. Value system
    4. Accepting relationships with others
    5. My view of a meaningful occupation
      a. What I expect
      b. What's expected of me
      c. My chances for success
    6. How I view my sexuality
      a. In relation to marriage
      b. "Role" expectations
      c. Understanding of needs
  B. Plans for Future
    1. What is the Good Life for me?
      a. How I will achieve it
      b. How it relates to my value system
      c. How it relates to my chosen occupation
    2. What are my priorities for the future?
    3. Do I want to "go it alone" or build relationships with others?
      a. How I will do this
    4. Do I want to share my life with someone else in marriage?
      a. My responsibilities
      b. What I expect of others
    5. What will my biggest problems be?

Self–Awareness

LEARNING JOURNAL

Select the statement below that best defines your feelings about the personal value or meaning gained from this chapter and respond below the dotted line.

I learned that I . . .

I was surprised that I . . .

I realized that I . . .

I was pleased that I . . .

I discovered that I . . .

I was displeased that I . . .

....

Chapter 3
Who's in Control?

© Andrey_Popow/Shutterstock.com

The Waters Which Carry Our Ships

We were made for adventure, for love, for excitement, for life.
It won't be easy to set sail into the depths of life. It won't be easy to discover life in the
fullest extent. It may not even be all you wished for. In fact, it will probably be completely
different, completely better than anything you could have imagined.
Remember, the waters are waiting for the first chance to sink you. They'll toss you around,
beat up on your walls, try and break you down. Don't let them.
Find out what your waters are. Find out what's trying to destroy your vessel.
Let them push you to where you want to be.
Never forget, whatever it may be, the water can't sink you unless you let it in inside.
The negative, the tragedies, the bad things in life won't ever stop you unless you let them.
And let the voices of those who doubt you be the wind in your sails. —Colton Snead, 2019

Think About This...

Think for a minute about your greatest experiences in life.

- "How am I ever going to stop smoking?"
- "I hate the way I look. What can I do to change it, or to like myself the way I am?"
- "I need to study more. My grades aren't too good. How can I get myself to sit down and study more?"
- "I would sure like to have more dates; I haven't had a date for two months. How can I get more dates?"
- "I've been married for three years, and the relationship is not as exciting as it was before. What can I do to improve the relationship, or is it time to get out?"
- "My boss is always so critical. Why can't she be more positive?"

Most of us have either asked one or more of these questions, or we have heard many of our friends ask them. Now the question is "If I want to change, can I?" "Am I in control of my own behavior or is someone or something else in control of me?" "How can someone change?" As we all know, change is not easy.

B. F. Skinner (2002), a well-known psychologist, has indicated in much of his writing that all of our behavior is controlled, and that there is no such thing as "free will." Do you agree? This is a philosophical question that people have been discussing for years. We will not attempt to answer this question in this book, but we will be referring to it, directly or indirectly, throughout the book.

Something to Think About

REFLECT ON CONTROL:

Write down your answers:

- What is control?
- Who is control of my life?
- Me?
- My parents/boss/friend/colleague/partner?
- Is it random or is it a combination?

Do you agree with Skinner that your behavior is controlled, or do you believe in free will?

Who is in control of my life? You? Me? Someone else? Our environment? Psychologists have come up with a number of theories to explain how we can develop the capacity to manage our own behavior and to influence other people's behavior. Many psychologists believe that **learning theory** is the answer to all our questions. Check out the youtube videos on the theories that are after this section for a refresher on learning theories. Learning theory underlies all relationships—good, bad, happy, and sad ones.

Locus of control is an individual's belief system regarding the causes of his or her experiences and the factors to which that person attributes success or failure. This concept is usually divided into two categories: **internal** and **external**. If a person has an **internal locus of control**, that person attributes success to his or her own efforts and abilities. A person with an **external locus of control**, who attributes his or her success to luck or fate, will be less likely to make the effort needed to learn (Joelson, 2017).

Locus of Control–Self-Control/Management or External Control

Self-control or self-management is often considered to be the opposite of external control. In self-control, individuals can set their own standards for performance, and will then reward or punish themselves for meeting or not meeting these standards. On the other hand, in external control, someone else sets the standards and delivers or withholds rewards or negative consequences. People with an external locus of control are also more likely to experience anxiety, since they believe that they are not in control of their lives. This is not to say, however, that an internal locus of control is "good" and an external locus of control is "bad." There are other variables to be considered (Joelson, 2017).

MOTIVATION

Discuss the following scenario in triads. Then answer the questions.

Both Angie and Beth took a psychology test last Friday. Angie studied two hours every night for the last five nights, and it paid off for her; she received an "A" grade. Angie knows that she earned her grade; it took a lot of work. On the other hand, Beth only studied two hours total for her test, and she also received an "A" for her grade. Beth knows how hard she really studied and that she was really lucky to receive such a good grade.

- How hard will Beth study for her next test?
- Who will be more motivated to study, Beth or Angie?
- Which person will be most likely to succeed in school and everyday life?

Look at your answers to how hard Beth will study and who is more motivated. Is this a bad example? How can we measure the different strengths and abilities of these students?

Perceived locus of control. Locus of control is often viewed as an inborn personality component. However, there is also evidence that it is shaped by childhood experiences—including children's interactions with their parents. Children who were raised by parents who encouraged their independence and helped them to learn the connection between actions and their consequences tended to have a more well developed internal locus of control (Joelson, 2017). People differ markedly in their feelings about their capacity to control life situations. Some people feel that they are in control of their own destinies. Their general expectancy about what happens to them and what they achieve in life is due to their own abilities, attitudes, and actions. In contrast, other people see their lives as being beyond their control. One of our basic human needs is a sense of control, to know that we have a choice, that our actions make a difference. For decades, psychologists have studied this concept as locus of control (LOC). The more internal our LOC, the more we believe our own efforts determine what happens in our lives; the more external our LOC, the more we feel our lives are controlled by outside forces (chance or powerful others) (Rockstraw, 2006). They believe that what happens to them is determined by external forces, whether it is luck or fate, other people, "Mother Nature," or the stars. Much has been written on the self-perceived ability of individuals to change the nature of their lives (Joelson, 2017; Rockstraw, 2006; Judge & Bono, 2001; Schultz & Schultz, 2012). While many psychologists interpret ideas such as "locus of control" and "self-efficacy" as individually variable personality characteristics, they may actually

Luck is a matter of preparation meeting opportunity.
—OPRAH WINFREY

reflect worldviews of a nation, ethnic group, or geographic community. According to psychologists (Rockstraw, 2006; Zukerman et al., 2004; Schultz & Schultz, 2012), these two types of people are said to be identified as having either an *internal* or an *external* "locus of control."

Internals perceive that their efforts make a difference when they are facing a difficult situation, so they try to cope with it. They take whatever action seems appropriate to solve the problem. "I didn't make an A on that test … I guess I will study longer next time."

Externals perceive that their efforts will not make a difference, so naturally they do not attempt to cope with threatening situations.

The difference in perceived locus of control is important for personal adjustment to the world. People who believe they can control events in their environment will respond to stress quite differently from those who believe the opposite. Schultz indicates that these attitudes are learned from experience prior to the age of nineteen. If you discover that your efforts are repeatedly rewarded, you will believe that you will be able to manage your outcomes in the future. If you discover that your efforts are to no avail, you will become resigned to the lack of control (Schultz & Schultz, 2012).

Can you control events in your environment? Do you feel that you are in control of your environment?

Internal or External Or Both?

© Anna Furman/Shutterstock.com

What implications does research on the locus of control have for you? The most important point is that there is a link between your beliefs about locus of control and your behavior. If you believe your experience is beyond your own control, you may expend less effort than you could. You may not try as hard as you are able, because you believe that your efforts will not make a difference. You may satisfy yourself with poor performance, figuring there is nothing you can do to improve the situation. Certainly some situations are more out of your control than others are, but your overall attitude about challenging situations will affect every aspect of your life.

Are internals or externals more successful? Internals seem to be more successful in more aspects of life than externals. Although an internal locus of control does not ensure success, those who believe they can influence the events in life tend to be the best life managers. These people are more likely to consider the possibility of doing something differently in their lives than people with an external orientation. Research has linked external LOC with poor mental and physical health, passivity, anxiety, depression, and learned helplessness; and internal LOC with greater happiness, health, success, and the ability to cope with challenges (Hahn, 2000). In recent years, unfortunately, external LOC has been on the rise (Twenge, Zhang, & Im, 2004). Fraught with instability and economic inequality, our culture often makes us feel that external forces control our fate (Dreher, 2014).

Internals are more curious than externals about ways to improve their lives. Psychological research has found that people with a more internal locus of control seem to be better off later in life., They tend to be more achievement oriented and get better paying jobs (Joelson, 2017). They see that education and knowledge are personal power. They are more likely to read about problem areas in their lives and attend workshops and classes related to solving these problems. Internals are also better listeners than externals (Worchel et al., 2000). They are more likely to ask questions, give others time to speak, and accurately interpret what others are saying. Internally oriented individuals tend to get better grades and score higher on standardized academic tests than externals (Schultz & Schultz, 2016).

Concerning relationships, internals tend to fare better than externals, especially considering the fact that internals tend to be better listeners and are more willing to work at improving their relationships. During stressful times in life, internals are more likely to seek social support than externals. Numerous studies have found that having an internal locus of control is associated with positive functioning and adjustment (Roden, 2004). Another study found that the less internal locus of control an individual perceives, the greater the likelihood for stress and depression (Kormanik & Rocco, 2009).

Take a look now at the following Consider This.

> *For the weak, it is impossible. For the fainthearted, it is unknown. For the thoughtful and valiant, it is ideal.*
> —VICTOR HUGO

CONSIDER THIS

INTERNALS AND EXTERNALS

How would you respond in this situation?

Event
Wanda's boyfriend and Jeff's girlfriend just announced to each of them that the relationship is over.

Response
Jeff's response: "What did I do wrong?" "What can I do to get her back?" "Why doesn't she like me anymore?" "I'll do anything for her." "My whole life is ruined."

Wanda's response: "My boyfriend has sure been depressed lately," "He sure has changed in the past few months," "I really like him, but I could tell that things weren't going well between us recently," "I know it will be tough, but I know I can get along without him."

Imagine what you would say to yourself if your partner were to tell you today that your relationship is over. **Think/pair/share your answer.**

Perceived Control or Lack of Control

Jeff continues to call his girlfriend to find out what he can do to get her back. He sends her gifts, pleads with her, but his efforts are to no avail. Whatever he does seems to have no effect on her. He feels he does not have any control over the situation.

Wanda seems to understand that she has no control over her boyfriend's behavior, but she does have control over her own life. She accepts the fact that the relationship is over and she needs to get on with the rest of her life. She has respectful acceptance.

Outcome

Jeff develops a negative feeling about himself and his life. He sees himself as no good, not worthy, and that nobody will ever love him, so what is the use of living? He becomes depressed, passive, and develops *learned helplessness*. That is the assumption—based on past failures—that one is unable to do anything to improve one's performance or situation, and he just gives up.

Wanda's not happy with the situation, but realizes that she does not have any control over her boyfriend, so she looks to the future. She sets new goals and actively begins to work to achieve them ("There are other fish in the sea."). In the course of her activities, she meets new people.

Who's in Control?

We would define Jeff as an "external" because he feels that he is not in control of his own destiny, that outside forces are determining his fate, and that whatever effort he puts into changing the situation will not make any difference. (A quick note: Remember that we do not get to control other people. We can only have control of ourselves.)

Wanda would be defined as an "internal," since she perceives herself as in control of her destiny, and her success is dependent upon her efforts, and not on others. She also realizes that she does not have control over other people's behavior.

Personal control versus learned helplessness. Helpless people often perceive that control is out of their hands, and this perception may deepen their feelings of resignation. They are sometimes victims of their own self-talk. This is what Martin Seligman (2006) and others found in experiments with both animals and humans. When dogs are strapped in a harness and given repeated shocks, with no opportunity to avoid them, they learn a sense of helplessness, now called "learned helplessness."

When people are faced with repeated traumatic events over which they have no control, they too, will come to feel helpless, hopeless, and depressed. You can see the importance of parents teaching their children to have the feeling of some control over their lives and their behavior. Parents who do everything for their children are not doing their children a favor; the children begin to show learned helplessness, because "Daddy will take care of it." Seligman's research now shows that people's *cognitive interpretation* of aversive events determines whether they develop learned helplessness (Weiten et al., 2014).

Life out of your control. *Learned helplessness* is the passive behavior, self-taught, produced by the exposure to unavoidable aversive events. For example, in concentration camps, prisons, work environments, or nursing homes where people are given little control, they will experience a lowering of morale, a feeling of increased stress, depression, and a feeling of helplessness. Increasing control—allowing workers to have some participation in decision making, allowing inmates to make decisions about when they want to watch TV or exercise, letting nursing home patients make choices about their environment—noticeably improves morale along with mental and physical health. Perceived control is vital to human functioning. Thus, for young and old alike, we should create an environment that enhances a sense of control and self-efficacy (Aronson et al., 2018).

According to Gwen M. Scott RN, MC, RCC, human beings are born in the External Control position. Survival is contingent on their being taken care of in every way. As children grow and mature, they naturally move toward the Internal Control position. At first, the parents are grateful and proud of their child's signs of independence (i.e., feeding themselves, clothing themselves).

The parents' pride turns into discomfort when the child begins to hold differing views from their parents. There are arguments between parent and child over who is "right" and what is "normal." A submissive child tends to become the "obedient/good child" and a noncompliant child tends to become rebellious, and is deemed the "disobedient/bad child."

Scott believes the goal in parenting is to nurture children to assume an **Internal Control** position, thus assuming responsibility for choices and consequences. When adults remain mostly in the **External Control** position, they feel "used" and angry, not in control of their own destiny:

- they feel responsible for other people's irresponsibility
- blame others for what is "not right in my life," feel victimized
- this perpetuates the dysfunctional environment, where no one is in charge of themselves, but everyone feels obliged to control others.

Challenge: To recognize what is happening and move toward the more functional position of Internal Control, becoming your own "CEO":

- set and maintain reasonable boundaries with self and others, thus assuming responsibility for your own destiny
- allow others to influence your decisions, then choose the decision that makes the most sense to you, and live with the consequences of your decisions (Scott, 2013).

> *You draw nothing out of the bank of life except what you deposit in it.*
> —W. CLEMENT STONE

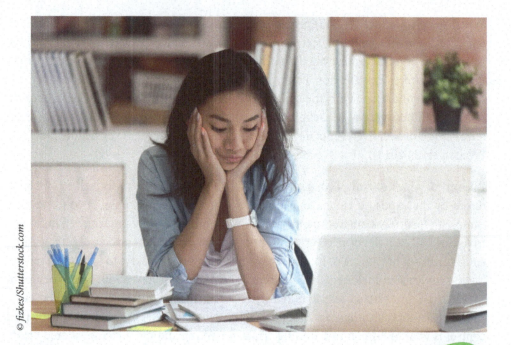
© fizkes/Shutterstock.com

Are you an *internal* or an *external*? Which of these do you want to be? Can you change your behavior? Who's in control?

Something to Think About

REFLECT ON CONTROL:

Consider these questions:

- Who/what is controlling your life?
- Where would you plot yourself between the two positions of External vs. Internal Control?

The book *How to Ikigai: Lessons for Finding Happiness and Living Your Life's Purpose* by Tim Tamashiro explains a simple but abstract map for living a meaningful life. After reading this book, you will understand how to implement Ikigai's four directions in your own life:

Do what you love
Do what you're good at
Do what the world needs
Do what you can be rewarded for

How can we take control? In the following activity, we will give you some helpful hints on managing and taking control of your life. In order to increase the probability of you developing an internal locus of control, you will want to work on the following items (Watson & Tharp, 2006; Santrock, 2006 Chowdhury, S.F., Pychyl, T.A. (2018)):

> **Developing your Locus of Control Activity** In your journal, write on the subject "*Who am I?*" Please make a section about your LOC and think about the following concepts. Write your thoughts on how you are incorporating these into your life and how you might incorporate them.

1. *Consider changing aspects of your environment.*

   Ask yourself some of the following questions: What types of people in my life contribute to my locus of control beliefs? What is it about school or my job that contributes to my LOC? How do my current friends, acquaintances, and other people in my life contribute to my locus of control? What can I do about these situations in order to take control of my life?

2. *Try new activities rather than the usual safe and secure ways of doing things.*

   Take some risks, do something different, try a new restaurant, do not travel the same route home or to school each day, try new food, wear different clothes, or try anything that will help you break old habits that may be harming you. **Externals** have difficulty trying something new and breaking old habits. Trying to enjoy something new will help you see that you can control aspects of your life.

3. *Begin to assume more responsibility for tasks at home, work, and school.*

   Volunteer to do things that you do not usually do. Join a committee, volunteer to help someone, and offer to take responsibility for some tasks to be completed. Start slowly and then keep adding on responsibilities. You will feel much better about yourself and see that you are in control.

4. *Notice new things so you stay anchored in the present, engaged, and mindful.*

   Dr. Ellen Langer (2014) and CT Ngnoumen (2014) have determined that the mindless following of routine and other automatic behaviors leads to much error, pain, and a predetermined course of life. Mindful living helps you to have an increase of learning, and decrease in accidents. You notice new things when you are in the present. Mindfulness, which is derived from Zen Buddhism, is basically a skill one can use to better tolerate and cope with emotional distress. You become engaged. Working on your mindfulness with even small amounts of meditation or just "being in the moment" doing your routines in life will help you when you have those ruminations which are aggravating negative thoughts running through your head that will not leave you alone. Being mindful during routines can help many individuals. For example "I failed that test"... "I could kick myself for not studying more" ... "My dad is going to ream me out for this" ... "My teacher made it too hard" ... "I failed that test... ."

5. *Work to get things done and try not to procrastinate, but manage your emotions.*

   A study, coauthored by Dr. Chowdbury and Dr. Pychyl, found links between procrastination and negative emotions like frustration and resentment. It becomes more difficult to cope with the potential negative emotions we predict our task will create. So, instead of feeling even worse, we opt for something that makes us feel good. "Giving in to feel good" is the term given to this phenomenon in willpower or forcing yourself to do something you hate; it's about managing your emotions so they don't get hijacked by your inner critic (Chowdhury, S., & Pychyl, T.A. (2018). You could also work to be a Precrastinator. Precrastination is the urge to start a task immediately and finish it as soon as possible. If you're a serious precrastinator, progress is like oxygen and postponement is agony (Rosenbaum, Gong, Potts, 2014).

Dr. David Allen (2014), a professor of psychiatry, believes that mindfulness is relevant to the first part of of the Serenity Prayer—"accepting things that one cannot change." What about changing the things that need changing? How do we know which things can be changed and which ones cannot, and how does one go about changing them? He explains that people feel emotional pain for the same reason they feel physical pain: It is a signal to the person that something in that person's body or mind is wrong and needs attention. Sometimes this needs the help of a trained therapist.

It is important to note that the newest findings from neuroscience show that the prefrontal cortex plays a major role in our ability to understand behavior and impulses. This research demonstrates that because the prefrontal cortex matures later than other brain systems (around the mid-20s), adults should be better than children at controlling themselves. Likewise, other research shows when our self-control is depleted and our brain becomes fatigued by too much restraint, we may, in fact, experience even less control than we ordinarily would (Ackerman et al., 2009).

As you continue to read this chapter you will discover new ways to take control of your life. One of the ways that you will discover to take control of your own life is by developing a high level of *self-efficacy* (which is your belief that you can do anything you put your mind to!).

What is self-efficacy? *Self-efficacy* is our belief about our ability to perform behaviors that should lead to expected outcomes. Believing that you can direct your behaviors is fundamental to self-management. Individuals having high self-efficacy for particular behaviors or skills are likely to work longer and try more strategies to develop these

Why do women tend to focus on interdependence and good relationships? Could this be culturally mandated in their environment?

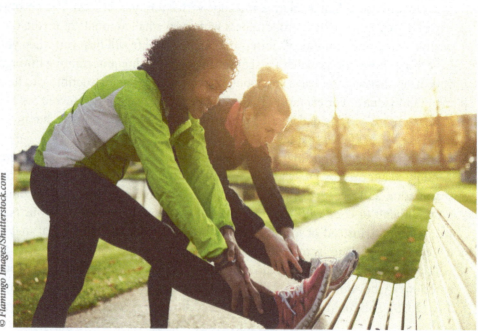

© Flamingo Images/Shutterstock.com

skills than those with low self-efficacy (Bandura, 2008). When self-efficacy is high, we feel confident that we can execute the responses necessary to earn reinforcers. When self-efficacy is low, we worry that the necessary responses may be beyond our abilities.

Perceptions of self-efficacy are subjective and specific to different kinds of tasks. For instance, you might feel extremely confident about your ability to handle difficult social situations, but very doubtful about your ability to handle academic challenges (Baron, 2004; Kolbe, 2009). Perceptions of self-efficacy can influence which challenges we tackle and how well we will perform them. One thing is certain: good outcomes increase self-efficacy; they fuel an appetite for future risk (Webber, 2010).

Becoming Aware of Self Efficacy: Why Self-Efficacy Matters
https://www.youtube.com/watch?reload=9&v=agwsjYg9hJ8

Mamie Morrow shows us how our belief in our own ability to succeed is critical to actually succeeding.

Gender and self-efficacy. Men and women develop differently, both physiologically and socially. This difference affects their self-efficacy. As children, girls are more likely than boys to play in small groups in which interpersonal awareness is more likely to be heightened. In contrast, boys are more likely than girls to play in large groups where opportunities for discussion are minimized. In addition, boys, more than girls, may be encouraged to become involved in competitive, achievement-related activities (Deaner et al., 2012).

Perceived Self-efficacy Bandura believes you should try to exercise control over the events that affect your life (2008). You have a strong incentive to act if you believe that control is possible—that your actions will be effective. Perceived self-efficacy, or belief in your personal capabilities, regulates human functioning in three major ways:

1. **Competency, or self-efficacy.** A person's sense of competence, or *self-efficacy*, and their trust in a positive support system will help to limit the levels of stress or degree of depression they may feel/experience in a difficult or threatening situation.
2. **Motivational.** A person's belief in their own ability to achieve a goal, and their trust in their flexibility in the face of obstacles, will strengthen their motivation to complete the goal. Motivation will be stronger if individuals believe they can attain their goals and then adjust them based on their progress.
3. **Cognitive.** People with positive thoughts, feelings and beliefs and higher aspirations will have higher self efficacy (Bandura, 2008).

"It all comes out all right in the end. If it's not all right, it's not the end."
—ANONYMOUS

Check this out   RATE YOUR SELF–EFFICACY

Remember that self-efficacy is the extent or strength of one's belief in one's own ability to complete tasks and reach **goals**.

Place a check mark in the column that best applies to you for each item: (1) not at all true, (2) barely true, (3) moderately true, and (4) exactly true.

Items	Self–Rating			
	1	2	3	4
1. I can always manage to solve difficult problems if I try hard enough.	_____	_____	_____	_____
2. If someone opposes me, I can find the ways and means to get what I want.	_____	_____	_____	_____
3. I am certain that I can accomplish my goals.	_____	_____	_____	_____
4. I am confident that I could deal efficiently with unexpected events.	_____	_____	_____	_____
5. Thanks to my resourcefulness, I can handle unforeseen situations.	_____	_____	_____	_____
6. I can solve most problems if I invest the necessary effort.	_____	_____	_____	_____
7. I can remain calm when facing difficulties because I can rely on my coping abilities.	_____	_____	_____	_____
8. When I am confronted with a problem, I can find several solutions.	_____	_____	_____	_____
9. If I am in trouble, I can think of a solution.	_____	_____	_____	_____
10. I can handle whatever comes my way.	_____	_____	_____	_____

Total Score: _____

Scoring

Total your score for the 10 items. Total scores can range from 10 to 40. The higher your score, the more general self-efficacy you are likely to have. If you scored 31 or higher, you likely have a reasonably strong sense of self-efficacy. If you scored 20 or lower, you may want to think of ways that you can improve your self-efficacy.

Scale adapted from Santrock (2006).

Two Explanatory Styles

Researchers like Martin Seligman have been studying optimists and pessimists for years, and they have found that an **optimistic worldview carries certain advantages** (Seligman, 2018). *Optimism* is defined as a general tendency to expect positive outcomes, while *pessimism* is defined as a general tendency to envision the future as unfavorable. To understand why someone becomes an optimist or a pessimist, it helps to understand what distinguishes them. Optimistic people tend to feel that bad things won't last long and won't affect other parts of life. Pessimists tend to believe one negative incident will last and undermine everything else in their lives.

Also important, researchers say, is the story or causal attributions you construct about why things happen—your *explanatory style*. Psychologist Martin Seligman (2006) suggests that people who have an *optimistic explanatory style* tend to use external, unstable, and specific explanations for negative events. People who have a *pessimistic explanatory style* use internal, stable, and global or pervasive explanations for negative events.

To pessimists, the "movie of life" is a documentary that has an unchangeable script. Optimists grab the story line and become directors. They edit, refocus, and add color to concoct a brighter, happier picture. This hopeful, in-control attitude shields them from outside influences and inner emotional turmoil. Positive thinkers feel powerful. Negative thinkers, Seligman says, feel helpless because they have learned to believe they're doomed, no matter what.

More than any other major personality trait, optimism is a matter of practice.
—KATHLEEN MCGOWAN

OPTIMISTS SEE POSSIBILITIES

Optimists roam the earth searching for opportunities. There is ample evidence that optimists do better in most areas of life. Studies show they are more successful, have happier relationships, get depressed less, make more money, and are generally healthier than pessimists. Optimists are forward-looking; that is, they have a positive view of the future (Knittel, M.G., 2016).

PESSIMISTS SEE PROBLEMS

Pessimists roam the earth expecting things to turn out worse than they really are. They think about things in terms of "always" and "never." They often feel they are victims of circumstance. Studies show pessimists perform better when they think negatively. They set low expectations for themselves and by imagining the whole range of bad outcomes use this knowledge as motivation (Knittel, M.G., 2016).

Are you an optimist or a pessimist? Do you look at the bright side and expect good things to happen, or do you tend to believe that if something can go wrong, it will? Check out the Pessimist/optimistic activity on the next page.

Don't try to figure out what other people want to hear from you; figure out what you have to say. It's the one and only thing you have to offer.
—BARBARA KINGSOLVER

Health, happiness, and success. Studies show that optimists are better at coping with the distress associated with everything from menopause to heart surgery. Furthermore, scientists at UCLA discovered that optimists have more disease-fighting T cells. Not surprisingly, positive thinkers live longer. Mayo Clinic researchers recently compared the scores of a personality test taken by 839 men and women three decades ago with their subsequent mortality rates. Those who had a pessimistic explanatory style in their younger years had a significantly higher risk of dying than their optimistic peers (Mayo Clinic, 2019). Optimism as it relates to stress will be discussed in Chapter Eight. Optimistic thinking tends to lead us to a more successful, happier, and healthier life.

Optimism is also a remarkable predictor of achievement and resilience. For example, studies have found that optimistic Olympic-level swimmers recover from defeat and later swim even faster, whereas pessimistic swimmers, following defeat, get slower (Seligman, 2006). When faced with serious problems—such as deciding about a risky operation, coping with traumatic events, or overcoming drug abuse or alcoholism—optimists tend to focus on what they can do rather than on how they feel. They keep their sense of humor, plan for the future, and reinterpret the situation in a positive light.

Optimists, by definition, expect to eventually recover from adversity, and they expect to be successful at whatever they do, so they work differently to reach their goals than pessimists do. Thus, another *self-fulfilling prophecy* is created (Myers, 2013). Suzanne Segerstrom, a University of Kentucky psychologist, indicates that optimism leads to increased well-being because it leads you to engage actively in life (Neimark, 2007).

Optimistic thinking tends to lead us to a more successful, happier, and healthier life.

© michaelheim/Shutterstock.com

ARE YOU AN OPTIMIST OR PESSIMIST?

Are you an Optimist (hopeful and confident about the future or the successful outcome of something) or a Pessimist (a person who tends to see the worst aspect of things or believe that the worst will happen)?

A MINI-QUIZ TO HELP YOU DECIDE IF YOU LEAN TOWARD PESSIMISM OR OPTIMISM

1. Do you view most things are your fault?
2. Do you have "all or nothing" thinking?
3. Do problems become catastrophes?
4. Are you a perfectionist?
5. Do you have a hard time accepting compliments?
6. Do you seek the approval and opinion of others before acting?
7. Do you tend to over-generalize?
8. Do you focus on the negative minutiae?

(If you answered "yes" to four or more of these questions, you are more of a pessimist than an optimist.)

BECOMING AN OPTIMISTIC PERSON

Here are a few simple ways to become a more optimistic person, according to Barrie Davenport, author of *Live Bold and Bloom* and other books.

1. Avoid catastrophic thinking. Avoid the use of words like awful, disgusting, horrible, dreadful, revolting, repulsive, etc.
2. Give yourself credit for your own success.
3. Be persistent and "act as if" you are an optimist. Some would say, "*fake it till you make it.*"
4. Re-frame disappointment. When you fail, think about the lessons you learned.

Martin Seligman in his book *Learned Optimism* believes that changing how we think changes how we feel, and that we choose the way we think.

So if we think like an optimist, we probably will be optimistic, and if we think like a pessimist, we probably will be pessimistic.

Learned optimism. Martin Seligman (2006) defines *learned optimism* as a learned way of explaining both good and bad life events that in turn enhances our perceived control and adaptive responses to them. In learned optimism, the real emphasis is on interpreting life events in a reasonably accurate way to enhance our perceived control and, thus, our adaptive responses. According to Seligman (2006), people can train themselves to make optimistic explanations by the following three steps:

- First, think about situations of adversity (being turned down for a date, doing poorly on a test, losing a sports competition);

- Next, consider the way you normally explain these events, and, if it is pessimistic (Nobody likes me, I'm not very smart, I really choked in the game),
- Then dispute these explanations by looking closely at the facts and alternative explanations (she probably had plans with her family, I need to spend more time studying, my opponent played a great game).

Practice this exercise over and over again. And, be sure to consider the following advice from David Myers (1993), author of *The Pursuit of Happiness*:

> The recipe for well-being requires neither positive nor negative thinking alone, but a mix of ample optimism to provide hope, a dash of pessimism to prevent complacency, and enough realism to discriminate those things we can control from those we cannot.

In order to understand yourself better and to discover different ways to improve your life, psychologists have developed many different theories. Many of these theories evolve from or revolve around learning theory.

THE BOTTOM LINE

Nobody owes us a living.

What we achieve or fail to achieve in our lifetimes, is directly related to what we do, or fail to do.

No one chooses their parents or childhood, but we can choose our own direction.

Everyone has their own problems and obstacles to overcome, but comparisons don't help.

Nothing is carved in stone; we can change anything in our lives, if we want to badly enough.

Excuses are for losers: Those who take responsibility for their actions know what to do to make progress in life.

Winners meet life's challenges head on, knowing there are no guarantees.

It's never too late or too early to change our approach. Time plays no favorites and will pass whether we act or not.

Dare to dream and take risks . . .

Becoming aware of Terminology:
Gender Identity

Dr Robert Weiss Ph.D., MSW gives the quick definition of gender identity terms: it is the degree to which a person *self-identifies as male or female (or something in between)*. Gender identity can differ from a person's biological gender at birth, though often it does not. **Gender expression** is the degree to which society might identify a person as *masculine or feminine* (regardless of that person's biological gender and gender identity). The term for individuals whose *birth gender and gender identity match is* **cisgender**. The term for individuals whose *birth gender and gender identity do not match is* **transgender**. If you were born with male genitalia and self-identify as male, you are cisgender. If you were *born with male genitalia and self-identify as female*, you are **transgender**. The term for individuals who do *not identify as male or female*, regardless of genitalia, is **non-binary**.

Some people express themselves via a mix of masculine and feminine traits. Gender expression is not always fixed over the lifespan. Some people choose to disguise the style of gender expression with which they are most comfortable to avoid stigma—effeminate men acting more masculine, masculine women acting more feminine. In actuality, **gender expression** and **sexual orientation** are unrelated.

A person can choose to hide who he or she is, especially with gender expression, but that person cannot change his or her core sense of self. No amount of talk therapy, aversion therapy, prayer, or any other tactic will make a sensitive boy feel comfortable being butch, or a person who self-identifies as male feel comfortable as a female, or a gay man straight (Weiss, 2019)

Social Learning Theory

Albert Bandura is one of several behaviorists who have added a cognitive flavor to learning theory. Bandura points out that humans obviously are conscious, thinking, and feeling beings. He feels that some psychologists like B. F. Skinner ignore these cognitive processes. An important aspect of *social learning theory* that may have an important impact on our lives is *observational learning*—the fact that much of personality is learned in social situations through interactions with and observations of other people, including family members (Mischel, 2004).

Observational learning. This occurs when an individual's behavior is influenced by observing others, who are called models. Observational learning requires that you pay attention to someone who is *significant* to you, a parent, or a friend. You observe their behavior and understand its consequences, and then store this information in your memory. It is not always conscious; sometimes we emulate observed behavior to fit

> *Children need models more than they need critics.*
> —JOSEPH JOUBERT, *PENSÉES*, 1842

in (at work, at school, at church) without thinking about it. We can be led to act out without understanding where the impulse to act originated (Bandura, 1965; Ferguson, 2010; Cherry, 2019).

Some role models are more influential than others. Children and adults tend to imitate people they like and respect more so than people they do not. We also are especially prone to imitate the behavior of people whom we consider attractive or powerful, such as rock stars, movie stars, sports heroes, or politicians. It is a bit scary to discover that we are also more likely to model ourselves after the individual who is the most aggressive, especially if that aggression leads to positive reinforcement. If you observe your mother yelling at your father in order to get him to do something, and he does do it, you are more likely to yell at someone the next time you want something. Without that experience, you most likely would have not yelled at someone in order to get your way. A five-year-old boy goes to the store with a seven-year old. The older boy picks up a candy bar and does not pay for it and on the way home shares it with his friend. Did he get positive reinforcement for stealing? What is the likelihood of the younger boy attempting to pocket a candy bar the next time he goes to the store? What we learn through modeling is not always positive. That is why our parents keep saying, "Do what I say, not what I do."

According to *social learning theory*, modeling has a great impact on personality development. Children learn to be assertive, conscientious, self-sufficient, aggressive, fearful, and so forth by observing others behaving in these ways.

Bandura's research with the Bobo doll in the 1960s noted that in social learning theory, learning occurs through observations and interactions with other people. Essentially, people learn by watching others and then imitating these actions. The Bobo experiment involved exposing children to two different adult models; an aggressive model and a non-aggressive one. After witnessing the adult's behavior, the children would then be placed in a room without the model and were observed to see if they would imitate the behaviors they had witnessed earlier.

Bandura's experiment remains one of the most well-known studies in psychology. Social psychologists continue to study the impact of observed violence on children's behavior today. In the 50 years since the Bobo doll experiment, there have been hundreds of studies on how observing violence impacts children's behavior (Cherry, 2019).

Many of you are familiar with the classic cartoon TV program called *The Simpsons*. Matt Groening, the creator, decided it would be funny if the Simpsons' eight-year-old daughter Lisa played the baritone sax. Do you think this would have an influence on the audience of this program? Sure enough, across the country little girls began imitating Lisa. Cynthia Sikes, a saxophone teacher in New York, told the *New York Times* (January 14, 1996) that when the show started, she got an influx of girls coming up to her saying, "I want to play the saxophone because Lisa Simpson plays the saxophone." Groening says his mail regularly includes photos of girls holding up their saxophones.

Think/Pair/Share Activity

Please discuss the question in triads.

- What do you think about Bandura's research?

How Does Learning Theory Influence Your Life?

When you do something you enjoy, what is the likelihood that you will do it again?

If you try something and fail at it, what are the chances that you will attempt it again?

If you ask someone out for a date five times and the answer is "no" each time, are you going to ask again?

If you make a nasty comment to a classmate who responds by telling the teacher, will you make that comment next time?

If someone you do not know very well embarrasses you in front of a large group, are you going to avoid that person in the future?

If you drink something that tastes good, will you drink it again?

You hate green peas because you were forced to eat them as a kid. Do you eat them now?

All of these situations can be explained by learning theory. In order to understand learning theory, we need to define the term *learning*. **Learning** is defined in psychology as a relatively permanent change in behavior as a result of experience or practice (Gardner, 2002).

Before you can begin the process of learning, you have to pay attention. Are you aware of all the different types of stimuli that get your attention?

What Gets Your Attention?

You are concentrating on reading a book and the phone rings. What do you do? A person whom you perceive as attractive enters the room. Do you notice that person? What gets your attention? Before you can learn something, you have to pay attention to it. Attention is the most important aspect of learning, because we have to pay attention to something before we can respond. Another aspect of attention that may surprise you is that **you can only pay attention to one thing at a time**. You cannot watch TV and study at the same time. Again, to what do you pay attention? We find that there are three kinds of stimuli that attract our attention. They are *novel*

What gets your attention?

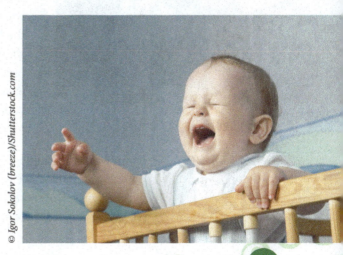

© Igor Sokolov (breeze)/Shutterstock.com

stimuli, significant stimuli, and *conflicting stimuli.* We find that these three different kinds of stimuli are not only important to learning, but also vital to our relationships with others.

Novel stimuli. We tend to pay attention to people, places, or things that are new, different, unique, or original. You tend to pay more attention to the student who is new to your school than a student who has been going to your school for the past few years. When reading the newspaper, you tend to notice an advertisement that is in color more than in black and white, because the color ad is unique. The person with a Mohawk haircut will generally be noticed before someone with a "normal" hairstyle. A person wearing the latest in fashion will tend to get more attention than someone wearing last year's style of clothing. Why? Because it is unique, different, or *novel.* The more familiar we become with the "new" person, the "unique" hairstyle, or the "latest" fashion, the less we are apt to pay attention. We tend to begin to take them for granted. When you begin to date someone, you tend to give the individual a lot of special attention, but what happens after you have been dating that same individual for years? Many times you find that you begin to habituate or get bored with that individual when the novelty wears off, and you no longer pay as much attention to him or her.

What else gets your attention?

Significant stimuli. So, you like to listen to music? Do you like ice cream? Are you interested in sex? Do you like money? If your answer to all of these questions is *yes,* then all of these things are *significant* to you, and you will pay attention to them. If you are a teacher and want to get your students to learn, you had better make sure the material is *significant* to your students. Otherwise, you may find it difficult to keep your students' attention. You need to make the material relate directly to your students' needs, wants, interests, and desires, and if you do this, you will be surprised to discover that your students are paying attention and learning.

© Dima Sidelnikov/Shutterstock.com

Do you get bored in relationships after the novelty wears off?

How important is this in a relationship? When you first start knowing someone, do you consider your friend's needs, wants, interests, and desires when deciding where to go and what to do? If you do, you will find that your friend's will respond more positively to you, and you both will be much happier. If you send your friend or date flowers for the first time and he or she likes them, will you receive more attention? Are the flowers *significant?* Are the flowers *novel?* Since they are both *novel* and *significant,* they should increase the attention paid to you by your friend. Long-term friendships are valuable, and it is worth investing time and energy in keeping up with your circle of friends. You reinforce your friends, and your friends reinforce you. It tends to make life more interesting to you and your friends.

If you want a romantic relationship to continue on a positive basis over a long period of time, you must make sure that you provide *kind, novel* and *significant* stimuli in the relationship—otherwise the relationship will become stale and boring. This is why that old saying is appropriate here; *the grass always looks greener on the other side of the fence.*

You wonder why your friend's romantic partner, husband, wife or significant other is always interested in others? You wonder why students are not paying attention to the teacher? Could it be that the other people are novel and maybe even more significant?

Conflicting stimuli. What if we were to tell you that, "All of your behavior is controlled!"; "There is no 'God'!"; "It is all right to steal!" And "It's okay to cheat on your spouse, boyfriend, or girlfriend!" Are these statements in conflict with any of your beliefs?

Conflicting stimuli can be useful to create a challenge, which can be exciting in its own way. Discovering how you and your relationship partner come to terms with a difference can be both fun and a little daunting. There are many techniques for navigating this process; if the relationship is precious to you, it is advisable to go carefully and get assistance when dealing with conflicting stimuli. We have discovered that you will not only pay attention to *novel* and *significant* stimuli, but also to anything that is in conflict with your *values, needs, or morals*. It has been found that in many relationships the only time that two people pay attention to one another is when they are in conflict—arguing, fighting. We do not recommend this form of stimuli in order to get attention, because it can create more problems than it solves. If this is the only time you find that you and your relationship partner pay attention to one another, you might want to change this by seeking counseling, reading a good self-help book, or changing your behavior in order to provide more kind, novel or significant stimuli in your relationships.

With all the technology and equipment we have today and with all the activities available to us, many of us still get tired of just sitting around. We get bored with life.

Make life more exciting! We all seek change in our lives. Kids get bored, teenagers get bored, and adults get bored. If you take your kids to the zoo every Saturday, eventually they will not enjoy going any longer. If you take your date to the movies every Friday night, it just is not as exciting as it used to be. You have your favorite dessert, a hot fudge brownie sundae, every night for two months. Believe it or not, even that sundae will not be enjoyed as much as it was when you could have it only once a month. Using novel and significant stimuli in your life will help you and those around you have an exciting, non-boring life.

We learn throughout life. We all need to change in order to adapt to the world that we must live in. What we have learned in the past is not always the best for us in the future. Consider using novel and significant stimuli and sometimes conflicting stimuli as you relate to others in business situations, in relationships, in family situations, and in teaching-learning environments—which is the laboratory of life. If you do, you will discover that your life and the lives of the people around you will improve.

Now that we have your attention, it is time to learn.

> *Learning is the eye of the mind.*
> —THOMAS DRAKE

Learning Theory

> *Life's greatest achievement is the continual remaking of yourself so that at last you know how to live.*
> —W. RHODES

Why study learning theory? Learning theory is the basis of all interactions—we are applying it constantly and it is constantly being applied on us, most of the time without our knowledge. Learning theorists believe that our behavior, including our personality, is shaped through classical conditioning, operant conditioning, and observational learning. If you have a better understanding of learning theory, it will help you understand the relationships you have with others and hopefully you will be able to improve the relationships you are involved in, and help you acquire new relationships.

An understanding of learning theory will also allow you to understand yourself as well as others. You will learn how to manage your own behavior as well as discover ways in which you can influence other people's behavior.

> *No law or ordinance is mightier than understanding.*
> —PLATO

Most aspects of learning begin with *classical conditioning*. Let's take a look at this process and then discuss *operant conditioning*.

Classical Conditioning

HOW DOES CLASSICAL CONDITIONING WORK?

Ivan Pavlov, a Russian physiologist, is considered the founder of *classical conditioning*. To make a long story short, Pavlov was experimenting with the salivary response of dogs. At first, a bell was rung and the dog emitted no response or an irrelevant response, such as the ears perking up. Therefore, the tone of the bell is a *neutral stimulus (NS)* in that it does not evoke the desired response (salivation). When the food was placed in the dog's mouth, the dog would automatically salivate. Food is called the **unconditioned stimulus (UCS)** because it is the cause of the salivation, the **unconditioned response (UCR)**. After ringing the bell a few times prior to feeding the dog, Pavlov noticed that the dog was salivating in response to the bell, before the food was brought in. The bell now becomes the **conditioned stimulus (CS)** and causes the dog to salivate, the **conditioned response (CR)**. Was there a change in the dog's behavior as a result of its experience? If the answer is yes—learning has taken place and the dog has been conditioned (Nairne, 2010). Figure 3.1 outlines the classical conditioning process.

As most of you know, when a child goes to the clinic for the first time for an injection, the child is not hesitant to go. Again, as you know, the injection, the *unconditioned stimulus (UCS)*, causes pain and anxiety, the unconditioned response. Will the child willingly go to the clinic next time? The answer is most likely, no way! As soon as the child sees the clinic or smells the odor in the clinic, the child will get very upset and attempt to get away from there as quickly as possible. The sight of the clinic or the odor causes fear and anxiety, which is the *conditioned stimulus (CS)*. So, the child tries to avoid the pain of the injection, the *conditioned response (CR)*. Do you now understand why many children don't want to go to the clinic or doctor's office? They have been *classically conditioned* to fear these situations.

Figure 3.1 THE CLASSICAL CONDITIONING PROCESS

CONDITIONING
Pavlov's Dog Experiment

BEFORE CONDITIONING

| Unconditioned stimulus | Unconditioned response | Neutral stimulus | No response |

DURING CONDITIONING

Food + Bell   Unconditioned response

AFTER CONDITIONING

Conditioned stimulus   Conditioned response

© VectorMine/Shutterstock.com

Has this ever happened to you? Did you ever drink too much of a specific kind of alcohol one evening and then later that night get very sick? As many of you know, since that night, you have never touched that kind of alcohol and most likely never will again, but you will still drink other forms of alcohol. Why? You associated getting sick with a specific kind of alcohol, not alcohol in general. This one experience conditioned you to dislike that specific kind of alcohol. Sometimes you can be conditioned very quickly, as many of you have learned.

WHY DO I HATE PEAS?—STUDENT STORY

When I was a baby I was fed peas. At that time, I tolerated them, since I really didn't have a choice. As I got a little older, I could decide what I liked and disliked, but at the dinner table I was told that I had to "clean" my plate and eat every one of the peas. I hated the taste of them, but I had to eat them anyway. Every time I took a bite of them, I thought I was going to get sick, and a time or two when I did eat them, I did get a little ill. I always associated the feeling of sickness with the peas. Twenty years later, I will still not eat peas. Now, when I look at them, I still get a weird feeling in my stomach. Why do I still dislike peas? You will discover that this was learned through **classical conditioning**.

It's amazing how classical conditioning has created many of our emotions, including fears, phobias, likes, dislikes, attractions, and bonding experiences.

Have you heard about Albert? Most fears and phobias are learned through the process of *classical conditioning*. The famous experiment of John B. Watson and Rosalie Rayner (1920) demonstrates how fears and eventually phobias are easily learned.

An eleven-month-old boy named Albert was classically conditioned to fear a variety of furry things. Before the experiment, Albert enjoyed playing with a white rat. One day as the rat was handed to Albert, the experimenters made a loud terrifying noise that startled Albert and made him cry. They continued to do this six more times, until Albert showed a strong fear of the rat, crying and shrinking away whenever the rat was placed near him. As the experiment continued, the experimenters presented Albert with other objects that were similar to the white rat, such as a white stuffed animal, a furry white blanket, and a Santa Claus mask.

To their surprise, Albert showed the same fear response to the different furry objects as he did the white rat. This process is called *stimulus generalization*. A day later, Albert was released from the hospital where the experiment took place. So, if you are walking down the street one day wearing your white fur coat and a seventy-year-old man starts yelling and running the other way, say, "Hi, Albert." Albert should have gone through a reconditioning process called *desensitization* in order to extinguish him of the fears.

Classical conditioning helps explain the formation of fears, attitudes, prejudices and feelings that may seem quite irrational. For example, you don't understand why you have such an uneasy feeling around your red-haired boss. You can't think of any logical, rational reason for this feeling. You have also noticed that you feel uneasy around other red-haired individuals. One day while you were reminiscing about elementary school, you remembered that your second-grade, red-haired teacher slapped your hands with a ruler every time you made a mistake. At this time, this was a very painful, embarrassing experience to be hit in front of all your friends. This one early experience that you repressed is still having an effect upon your present life, especially your interactions with red-haired individuals. You were conditioned to dislike red-haired individuals. Prior to second grade, you liked people with red hair, but since this one experience, red-haired individuals have become the *conditioned stimulus* for your fear (uneasy feeling), the *conditioned response*. Have you ever had an experience like this?

Table 3.1   CLASSICAL CONDITIONING: LEARNING THROUGH ASSOCIATIONS

NEUTRAL STIMULUS PLEASANT OR PAINFUL STIMULUS BEFORE CONDITIONING	DURING CONDITIONING	AFTER CONDITIONING
Pavlov's Experiment Bell– Food– Bell elicits no response Bell is paired with food which elicits salivation Bell alone without food elicits salivation	McDonald's Advertising Goal Golden arches– Food– Arches elicit no response … Arches are paired with tasty food, which elicits salivation … Arches alone without sight of food elicits salivation.	A Child Learning Dog bite– Dog elicits pleasant response– Dog bite is paired with pain– Sight of dog instills feeling of fear and avoidance

So you now understand how fears, prejudices, phobias, dislikes, stereotypes, and uneasy feelings can be learned through classical conditioning. Each one of these can have a negative effect upon our relationships with others. The more we are aware of how these feelings develop, the greater the chance we have to unlearn them through the same conditioning process. Most aspects of learning begin with classical conditioning, but as learning evolves, classical conditioning develops into another form of learning—operant conditioning (Weiten et al., 2012).

We Learn from Our Experience

Operant conditioning. Why do you work? Why do you continue going out with the person you are dating? Why do you still have certain friendships that remain strong over the years and other friendships that have waned? You receive positive reinforcement for working, so you continue to work. Your date satisfies your needs, so you continue to date that person. Your friends satisfy some of your other needs, and in return, you reinforce them and the friendship continues, while the relationships that are not reinforcing or satisfying will wane over a period of time. All of these interactions involve operant conditioning.

Operant conditioning is based on the premise that we are controlled by the consequences of our behavior. Operant conditioning relies on the *law of effect*, which states that behaviors followed by positive consequences are more likely to be repeated, and behaviors followed by negative consequences are less likely to be repeated (Hamilton,

2007). Many psychologists will say that most of our behavior is learned through operant conditioning. If you cry and then get what you want, are you going to cry the next time you want something? The cry was reinforced, and the reinforcement will increase the probability of you crying the next time you want something. The class clown gets attention for acting out in class, even though it is considered by most of us as negative attention, so the individual continues acting out. If this person did not get any attention, would he or she continue to be the class clown? Most likely, this individual would not. If you change your hair style and receive a lot of compliments, will you continue to wear it that way? If you receive a lot of stares or negative comments on your new outfit, will you wear it again? We tend to like people who compliment us more than people who ignore us or make negative comments. These are all examples of operant conditioning. We make a response and the consequences of that response determines whether or not we make that response again.

WHAT ARE THE CONSEQUENCES?

Reinforcement. In behavioral terminology, pleasant or unpleasant stimuli that strengthen a behavior are called *reinforcers*, and their effect is called *reinforcement*. The simplest type of reinforcer, called *primary reinforcer*, is a pleasant or unpleasant one to which we respond automatically without thinking (food, drink, heat, cold, pain, physical comfort or discomfort). For example, a kiss is a *primary reinforcer*, it can be pleasant or unpleasant, depending on who is doing the kissing: your sweetheart, or a vampire. The vast majority of our reinforcers, however, are not primary reinforcers, but *conditioned or secondary reinforcers*—stimuli to which we have attached positive or negative value through association with previously learned conditional reinforcers. For example, money is a secondary reinforcer. When you were a youngster and someone gave you a dollar bill, what did you do with it? Most likely you tried to eat it or make an airplane out of it. In order for the dollar to gain reinforcing value, you had to take it to the store and trade it for candy or food, and at that time you realized it had reinforcing value. Other secondary reinforcers would be a smile, a grade you receive in school, a trophy, etc. Negative consequences need not be physical punishment, but giving options that have consequences. If you need help with negative consequences, the book *Parenting With Love And Logic* (2006) by Jim Fay and Foster Cline (2004) has a formula that involves three things: the child makes a mistake, the adult responds with empathy and compassion instead of anger, and the child learns from the consequences of his or her actions.

Reinforcers act to strengthen behavior through two different types of consequences. These two consequences are positive reinforcement and negative reinforcement. Consequences can also weaken or eliminate a behavior through the use of punishment (Lefton & Brannon, 2007).

Positive reinforcement. This is anything that increases a behavior by virtue of its presentation. If you help a stranger who responds by giving you five dollars, what is the chance of you helping other strangers?

Failure is positive reinforcement.
—ANONYMOUS

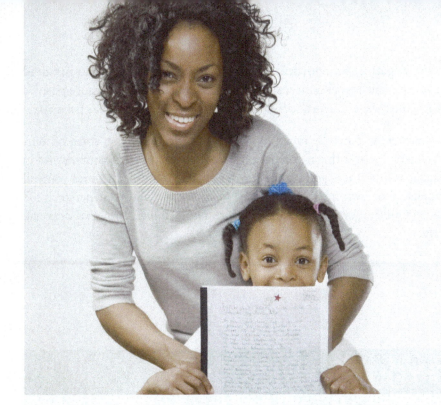

© AVAVA/Shutterstock.com

Positively reinforce
the good responses—
not the bad ones.

POSITIVELY REINFORCE THE GOOD RESPONSES—NOT THE BAD ONES

You were given five dollars (positive reinforcement) for helping the stranger, and that five dollars will increase the probability of you helping other strangers in the future. If you had not received the money, you are not as likely to help in the future. A child cries at the store, and the father gives the child a candy bar to be quiet. Now the father discovers that the child cries every time they go to the store. What is happening here? The father is giving the child positive reinforcement for crying. We need to be careful about what behaviors we are reinforcing. As you can see, it is easy to reinforce improper behavior. A partner may ask us very nicely to do a favor for them, and we ignore the request. Later, when our partner yells and screams at us to do something, we immediately respond and do it. What is happening here? We are positively reinforcing our partner for yelling. And, now we wonder why our partner is always yelling at us. **Remember, positively reinforce the good responses, not the bad ones.**

Negative reinforcement. This is anything that increases a behavior by virtue of its termination or avoidance. My employer yells at me for not producing enough work, so now I work harder to produce more in order to avoid being yelled at. In this situation, the yelling would be defined as *negative reinforcement*. I received a ticket for speeding once, and now I find that I am obeying the speed limit more often in order to avoid getting any more tickets. *The ticket is negative reinforcement.* We avoid people who are not nice to us and avoid classes we have difficulty with because of negative reinforcement. Negative reinforcement may have positive consequences, because it allows us to avoid painful and dangerous situations. Can you think of any examples?

Punishment. This is anything that decreases a behavior by virtue of its presentation. You drink too much scotch one evening and get very sick. To your amazement, you do not ever want to drink scotch again. Getting sick is the *punishment* for over-drinking.

Everything should be made as simple as possible, but not simpler.
—ALBERT EINSTEIN

Should you use negative consequences? Psychologists suggest that we do not need to use negative consequences as a means of disciplining our children, because positive reinforcement is the most effective and best means of controlling someone's behavior.

Positive reinforcement is generally much more effective than any other form of reinforcement. You will discover that if you use positive reinforcement on yourself and in your relationships with others you will be much happier, and those around you will be much happier. Your own life, your business relationships, and your personal life will be richer and much more positive and effective. *Life is change. Growth is optional.* **Choose wisely.**

GENDER AND YOU

WHERE DID YOU LEARN YOUR GENDER?

How do we acquire our gender roles? Being a boy or a girl, for most children, is something that feels very natural. At birth, babies are assigned male or female based on physical characteristics. This refers to the "sex" of the child. When children are able to express themselves, they will declare themselves to be a boy or a girl (or sometimes something in between); this is their "gender identity." Most children's gender identity aligns with their biological sex. However, for some children, the match between biological sex and gender identity is not so clear. The World Health Organization (WHO) uses gender incongruence to describe people whose gender identity is different from the gender they were assigned at birth. Gender role socialization operates through learning processes of reinforcement and punishment, observation, and self-socialization. But these days it is not as cut and dried as it was in the past. Times have changed. See https://www.psychologytoday.com/us/basics/genetics

Our expectations of "what girls do" and "what boys do" have changed. Girls frequently excel at sports and school subjects traditionally thought of as masculine. Boys frequently excel in artistic subjects once traditionally thought of as feminine. All children show some behaviors that were once thought of as typical for the opposite gender—no one shows exclusively male or female traits—and this is normal. For some young children, expressing a wish to be or identifying as another gender may be temporary; for others, it is not. Only time will tell. Some children who are gender non-conforming in early childhood grow up to become transgender adults (persistently identifying with a gender that is different from that assigned at birth), and others do not. Many children grow up to identify with a gay, lesbian, or bisexual sexual orientation (i.e., attracted to the same or both genders, as opposed to feeling they are a different gender). There is no way to predict how a child will end up identifying themselves later in life. This uncertainty is one of the hardest things about parenting a gender non-conforming child. It is important for parents to make their home a place where their child feels safe and loved unconditionally. **Research suggests that gender is something we are born with; it can't be changed by any interventions. It is critically important that children feel loved and accepted for who they are.**

Self-Control and Self-Management in Everyday Living

A look at social and positive psychology. In "Becoming Aware" of yourself, you will find that *social psychology* is the scientific study of how people's thoughts, feelings, and behaviors are influenced by the actual, imagined, or implied presence of others. Social psychology is a discipline that has traditionally bridged the gap between psychology and sociology. It looks at the individual and group dynamics which are at work in Human Relations (Moscovici, 2006). ". . . positive psychology is not to be confused with untested self-help, footless affirmation, or secular religion—no matter how good these may make us feel. Positive psychology is neither a recycled version of the power of positive thinking nor a sequel to *The Secret.*" (2008) Social Psychology is the branch of psychology that deals with social interactions, including their origins and their effects on the individual. Human Relations also contains the newer field of positive psychology. "Positive psychology is the scientific study of what makes life most worth living", it is a scientific approach to studying human thoughts, feelings, and behavior, with a focus on strengths instead of weaknesses, building the good in life instead of repairing the bad, and taking the lives of average people up to "great" instead of focusing solely on moving those who are struggling up to "normal" (Peterson, 2008). Martin Seligman proposed a new subfield of psychology with a focus on what is life-giving rather than life-depleting. The foundational paper of this new field, positive psychology, was published in 2000 by Seligman and the "founding father" of flow, Mihaly Csikszentmihalyi. As you learn more about the field, social psychologists such as Carol Dweck at Stanford in the field of "mindsets"; Claude Steele, Gregory Walton, and Geoff Cohen at Stanford University in the fields of "stereotype threat, belonging, and values affirmation"; Timothy Wilson of University of Virginia in the field of "core narratives"; and Peter Gollwitzer of New York University in the fields of "action triggers" and "implementation and goal intentions" are theorists who might influence you.

The most important thing to understand about positive psychology is that it is indeed science—it is a subfield of psychology, and although it is sometimes derided as a "soft science" or a "pseudoscience," it is still based on the scientific method of evaluating theories based on the evidence. As University of Michigan professor and positive psychology legend Christopher Peterson put it:

Do you have grit? *Grit* is defined as "perseverance and passion for long-term goals." It is a positive trait based on an individual's passion and perseverance. People with grit also possess "zeal" and "persistence of motive and effort." This characteristic derives from a person's research coupled with a powerful motivation to achieve their respective objective. This perseverance of effort promotes the overcoming of obstacles or challenges that lie within a gritty individual's path to accomplishment, and serves as a driving force in achievement realization. *Grit: The Power of Passion and Perseverance*, (2016) by Angela Duckworth, is an excellent resource on grit. Another social psychologist, Dr. Carol Dwerk, also has been doing research about mindset, which you learned about in Chapter Two.

If you don't like what you're getting, change what you're doing.
—ZIG ZIGLAR

All of us are engaged in a variety of everyday activities simply to survive. We must eat, drink, sleep, and take care of basic biological needs. It turns out that all of these activities can pose challenges to successful personal adjustment to our environment, and we must be careful to control them and not let them control us. For some people, their eating habits, drug use, sleeping habits, or alcohol use control their lives.

Use the If- then to create your own list.

include it in your "Who am I" paper.

What other challenges do we have that seem to control our everyday lives? Do any of you need to study more? Would you like to stop smoking?

Would you like to exercise more? Do you watch TV too much? Are you shy? Would you like to make more friends? These and many of your other habits that you would like to change can be modified. You can do it! Find out how.

An implementation intention is a self-regulatory strategy in the form of an "if-then plan" that can lead to better goal attainment, as well as help in habit and behavior modification. It is subordinate to goal intentions as it specifies the when, where, and how portions of goal-directed behavior. The concept of implementation intentions was introduced in 1999 by psychologist Peter Gollwitzer.

Implementation intentions, a term coined by Peter Gollwitzer, is a specific type of intentional statement that defines when and where a specific behavior will be performed. "If- then" This will possibly help you avoid procrastination by initiating a goal action. **It's time to make your own implementation intention for an important goal intention in your life** (Pychyl, 2008 & 2010).

Psychologists have also devised a number of different theories to explain how we develop the capacity for self-control. There is one technique that has been very successful for many individuals (Martin & Pear, 2010). This technique includes the application of learning theory to improve your self-control. If we stop and think about it, self-control—or the lack of it—underlies many of the personal challenges that we struggle with in everyday life. *What we learn can be unlearned.* Before we learn about the self-change program, perhaps the wonderful words from psychologist Robert Leahy (2006), the author of *The Worry Cure,* might be worth remembering:

> If you want to whip yourself into shape, or renovate your apartment, don't wait until you feel ready, because no such time will come. Instead, commit to doing something that you don't want to do each day. After all, if your goal is to lose 15 pounds, you'll have to consistently deny your desires in order to achieve it. Resourceful people are not having fun all of the time. But they do feel empowered when they force themselves to do what is needed (Flora, 2016).

© samjapan/Shutterstock.com

What challenges do we have that seem to control our everyday lives?

STRATEGIES TO SELF-CHANGE: A FIVE-STEP PROGRAM

Step 1: Identify the behavior to be changed.

Step 2: Observe the behavior to be changed.

Step 3: Set your goal.

Step 4: Design your program.

Step 5: Monitor and evaluate your program.

> It's the friends you can call up at four a.m. that matter.
> —MARLENE DIETRICH

A Self-Change Program

Step One-Identify the behavior to be changed. Changing habits, not "breaking" or not having "willpower" implies that those who struggle are "weak." **Not true!** The first step in any systematic program of self-modification is to identify the specific behavior that needs to change. We must be specific and clearly describe the problems and identify the exact nature of the behavior we want to change. For example:

- I want to exercise more
- I would like to have more friends
- I need to stop procrastinating

Which of the statements above is too vague, and would not be easy to observe? Can you measure and observe how much you exercise? Definitely. But, can you observe yourself procrastinating? Identify what things you are not doing, so you can get them completed in a timely manner.

> Not everything that is faced can be changed, but nothing can be changed until it is faced.
> —JAMES BALDWIN

Some changes need support! Drug abuse, physical abuse, eating disorders, and other serious negative habits that are detrimental to your health can be changed through this process of self-modification—with a lot of willpower. Recent studies have called the idea of "willpower" into question; it is possible to will a behavior change for a time, but it is rarely permanent without support. Research has found that it is easier to change these serious habits with the benefit of professional help and support. So, please seek professional help, or if you know anyone else having a serious problem, please help them find professional help. Talk to your instructor, counselor, medical doctor, pastor, or therapist. There are many kinds of programs for drug/alcohol, physical abuse, and weight issues in many areas, and many of them are free. Many meet daily, or weekly, and usually a sponsor at the meetings will help you.

Step Two-Observe the behavior to be changed. The second step in your self-modification project is to observe the behavior to be changed in order to discover your *operant level* (baseline), the number of responses prior to beginning the project. I kept a food diary for a week to record what I was eating. i made sure to note the time and location. People are often tempted to skip this step and move ahead. In order to evaluate your progress you must not skip this step. You need to know the original response level, the starting point. You cannot tell whether your program is working unless you have a baseline for comparison. While observing your behavior in order to find your **operant level,** you need to monitor these three things: 1) the initial response level of the target behavior, 2) the events that precede the target behavior, and 3) the typical consequences (reinforcement or punishment).

Baseline Data

I kept a food diary for a week to record what I was eating. I made sure to note the time and location. I found that I was eating chips and candy after school. I also found that I usually didn't eat breakfast, but my dinners included a healthy protein and at least one vegetable.

1. **Initial Response Level.** You need to keep track of each and every time the targeted behavior that occurs within a specified period of time—usually five to seven days. Write down on a piece of paper attached to your cigarette package each and every cigarette you have each day for a week. Keep a diary of the number of dates you have within a three-week period, the amount of time you study each day for five days, the number of times you yell at your kids, the amount of time you spend exercising each day for six days, or whatever the targeted behavior happens to be. As soon as you can identify a *pattern of behavior,* you are ready for the next step. If you discover that you do not exercise, there is nothing to observe; you are ready to begin. Your *operant level* for exercise is "0," no responses prior to conditioning. You may discover that your *operant level* for cigarette smoking is "23 cigarettes" per day, "42 minutes" of studying each day, "3,100 calories" each day, or "2 dates" per month. Now to the next step.

2. **Events That Precede the Target Behavior.** The events that precede the target behavior can play a major role in governing your target response. Where you study may affect how much time you actually study. When you study at the library, you find that you study more than when you study at home on the kitchen table or

> *Sometimes we miss a workout or eat something that isn't ideal, but if you had a flat tire on your car would you get out and puncture the other three? Of course not! If you slip, shake it off and do better the next day!*
> —JILLIAN MICHAELS

on your bed. You may discover that you smoke more when you drink coffee. You may find that you may have to give up coffee in order to stop smoking, because coffee seems to create the urge to smoke. You may find that you eat the greatest number of calories late at night after you have a couple of beers; the beers seem to stimulate the hunger drive. Once you are able to pinpoint the events that seem to cause the behavior, you can design your program to circumvent these behaviors or break the pattern down.

3. **Consequences.** Finally, you need to identify the reinforcement that is strengthening the targeted behavior or the punishment that is decreasing or suppressing it. We eat so we don't die, and we sometimes eat to be indulgent—the food becomes reinforcing within itself; just like smoking, we enjoy it. It is easier not to study than to study. Bad habits are self-reinforcing. I do not have to worry about being turned down for a date if I do not ask anyone out. Most of the behaviors we would like to change are being reinforced and are very difficult to change.

Stimulus Conditions

I don't have much time in the morning to eat breakfast, which is why I always skip this meal. At the end of the school day, I'm very hungry and get something readily available which usually ends up being junk food from the vending machines at school.

Step Three-Set your goal. The most important factor in the third step is that when you set your goal, make sure that it is a realistic goal that can be accomplished. Losing twenty pounds in four weeks is not realistic, but four to five pounds could be realistic. Studying five hours a day, seven days a week is not realistic for many students, but studying three hours a day, five days a week would most likely be accomplished by most students, depending on how many courses you are taking and how many hours you work per week. Try to set behavioral goals that are both challenging and realistic. You want your goals to be challenging, so that they lead to improvement in your behavior. **Setting unrealistically high goals—a common mistake in self-modification—often leads to unnecessary discouragement.**

Setting A Goal

Since skipping breakfast results in less-desirable choices in the afternoon, I decided it would be important for me to eat breakfast every day. I also decided to bring healthy snacks to school every day. Hopefully, that would result in buying less junk food

Step Four-Design your program. Now that you have identified the targeted behavior to be changed, found your operant level (remember, it is intentional actions that have an effect on the surrounding environment), and set your goal, you are ready to design your program.

Design a Program

Since time is an issue in the morning, I decided to make hard-boiled eggs and keep them in the refrigerator. I could just take one every morning to eat on my way to school for my breakfast. I also decided to keep an apple, banana, and almonds in my backpack to snack on instead of buying junk food.

You have now discovered that many of your bad habits and behaviors that you have identified to change are self-reinforcing. In order for you to change, you must find something that is more reinforcing to you than the previous reinforcement. You must find something that will motivate you and make you want to change. If you intend to reward yourself for increasing a response, you need to find an effective reinforcer. What is reinforcing to one individual may not be reinforcing to another. Your choice will depend on your unique personality and situation. How can you discover what is reinforcing to you?

Select reinforcers. What is reinforcing enough to you to motivate you to change? Is it money, sex, free time, concert tickets, praise, or tickets to the ball game? An easy way to discover what is reinforcing to you is to observe your own behavior for a while (Watson & Tharp, 2006).

- Observe what you enjoy doing for a few days.
- Observe what you spend your money on each week.
- What kind of praise do you like to receive: from yourself and from others?
- What are your major interests?
- What do you do for fun?
- What people do you like to be with?
- What do you like to do with those people?
- What would be a nice present to receive?
- What makes you feel good?
- What would you like to do for your next vacation?
- What would you buy if you had an extra $20? $50? $100?

Punishers and Reinforcers

My reinforcer is simply that I felt better and healthier when I ate less junk food. My punisher is that I felt sick when I ate too much junk food.

Any or all of the above could be used as reinforcers to motivate you to change. As B. F. Skinner's early research demonstrates, reinforcement—*not punishment*—is necessary for permanent change. Reinforcement can be intrinsic, or extrinsic—not part of the essential nature of someone or something; coming or operating from outside. According to Dr. Carol Sansone, a psychology professor at the University of Utah, one type of reinforcement must be present for self-change; two would be better than one, and *three* would be best (Goldberg, 2002).

Administer the reinforcers. Receiving the reinforcement has to be contingent upon you first making the appropriate response. Once you have chosen the reinforcer, you then have to set up reinforcement contingencies. Your reinforcement contingencies will describe the exact behavioral goals that must be met and the reinforcement that may then be awarded. Do not administer too much reinforcement and receive it too often. If you receive too much of something or receive it too often, you soon get bored or habituate to it. If a chocolate milkshake was used as reinforcement five times a day for three weeks, you would soon get tired of having milkshakes and habituate to them. They will soon lose their reinforcing value.

Generally, rapid reinforcement works better than delayed reinforcement. If we delay reinforcement, we discover that we do not realize what behavior is being reinforced. You may find it easier to have a friend or relative administer the reinforcement. It may also commit you more to your project if you make up a behavioral contract for you to sign and give to your friend.

Results

I had eggs every morning, which definitely resulted in less junk food in the afternoons. I only bought chips twice during the week, instead of every day. I ate my healthy snacks as an alternative three of the days.

Trying to modify behavior is a difficult task. Sometimes it helps to have someone we can talk to or who might assist us to do this. It is difficult to change some of our actions by ourselves. We might benefit from a person who can offer advice or encouragement. Or, we might need another person to know about our plan because it keeps us honest and committed to our project. It is sometimes easy to fool yourself about your progress, but another person may not be as easily deceived.

© Jacob Lund/Shutterstock.com

What do you do for fun? Reward yourself when you make progress with a reinforcer!

Self-Change Project—A happy ending

Remember, today is wide open. I will decide on a course of action and move ahead. All around me help is available for the asking.

Step Five-Monitor and evaluate your program. Now that you have designed your self-change project, you are ready to "try it." As you begin the project, you need to monitor your progress as you begin to achieve your goal. Monitoring your progress will allow you to assess if your plan is working. Start with your **operant level (baseline)** and continue to accurately record the frequency of your targeted behavior so you can evaluate your progress. If your behavior shows improvement, keep up the good work; however, if there is no improvement or you begin to regress, you need to reevaluate **your reinforcers**, since they do not seem to be motivating you to improve. You may need to strengthen your **reinforcement** or the delay between the time you emit the behavior and the time you receive the reinforcement may be too lengthy. Do not reward yourself when you have not actually earned it. Many people end up giving themselves the reinforcers no matter what they do. They rationalize it by saying, "I needed that new dress anyway" or "I just need a vacation, even though I'm not going to stop smoking." Another problem you may have in not reaching your goal is that you are trying to do too much too quickly by setting unrealistic goals.

> *A bad habit never disappears miraculously— it's an undo-it- yourself project.* —ABIGAIL VAN BUREN

CONSIDER THIS

A SAMPLE CONTRACT

Target behavior: I want to lose five pounds in the next six weeks.

Contract between: Sally Sane

Amy Abler (roommate of Sally Sane)

Agreement: Sally Sane—I agree to stop eating candy bars and drinking soda between meals. I will write down each and every candy bar and soda that I consume for the next seven days. I will weigh myself each day and record it. After the observation period, for the following two weeks, I will eat only one candy bar each day and two cans of soda. During the second two weeks, I will eat one candy bar every other day and one soda each day. On the final two weeks, I will have only one candy bar and one soda every three days. From that day following, I will substitute pieces of fruit and vegetables and glasses of water for my snacks between meals.

Agreement: Amy Abler—I agree to help Sally Sane lose five pounds and stop eating candy bars and drinking soda between meals. I will review her program with her weekly, and do whatever I can to help her reach her goal.

Consequences: Sally Sane—For each week that I reach my goal, I will buy a movie I want or the jewelry I really want... If I fail to reach my goal during the week, I do not get the movie I want, and I will have to clean the apartment without Amy's help. When I reach my final goal, I will receive two tickets to the concert that I have wanted to attend.

Consequences: Amy Abler—I will praise Sally for keeping her schedule and offer encouragement. I will review her program with her weekly and give her feedback. If she reaches her goal by the end of the six weeks, I will clean the apartment the next two weeks without Sally's help.

Signed: _____   Date: _____

When set into action, **self-modification** also known as **behavioral modification** programs often need some fine-tuning. So do not be surprised if you need to make a few adjustments. Often, a small revision or two can turn a failing program around and make it a success. Don't give up!

A *habit* is the intersection of *knowledge, skill,* and *desire. Knowledge* is the what to do and the why. *Skill* is the how to do. And *desire* is the motivation, or the want to do. In order to make something a habit in our lives, we have to have all three. In other words, you have to want to change a habit, have a desire to learn a new way of doing something, and have the ability to do the task the new way. All of this, of course, takes time and energy because you must engage in a particular behavior at least 30 consecutive days before it becomes a habit. Furthermore, it may take six weeks to a year for the habit to become stabile in your life (Aamodt & Raynes, 2001).

Often a new and improved pattern of behavior becomes self-maintaining. When you feel good about yourself and know that you are successful, keeping up your change becomes self-reinforcing. Responses such as eating right, not smoking, exercising regularly, or studying diligently may become so habitual that they no longer need to be supported by an elaborate program. But you may find it important to periodically reinforce yourself for *doing the right thing* and not slipping back to your old patterns of behavior. You did a good job! Keep up the good work!

As you work on your self-change program, just remember the words of novelist Louis L'Amour:

> Up to a point, a [person's] life is shaped by environment, heredity, and movements and changes in the world about [them]; then there comes a time when it lies within [their] grasp to shape the clay of [their] life into the sort of things [they wish] to be . . . Everyone has it within [their] power to say, "This I am today; that I shall be tomorrow."

BECOMING AWARE OF TECHNOLOGY-WHO'S IN CONTROL?

Taking a little bit of time to consider who or what agency put information on the Internet makes a difference in making sure your information and source is legitimate. This can make the difference between a failing paper and an excellent one!

EVALUATING WEB SITES IS A S.N.A.P.!

S = Source—Somebody created this site. Who?

N = Nature—Why does this site exist? Purpose?

A = Appearance/Accessibility—Does this site function efficiently?

P = Page Content—Is the information accurate and reliable?

© 1999 by Jo Monahan, M.S., Coordinator of Electronic Information Services, University of North Texas. All rights reserved. Permission to reprint granted.

The **World Wide Web** has increased accessibility to massive amounts of information on virtually every topic imaginable. Because online information is largely uncensored and unverified, the increasing use of the Internet poses new challenges to students.

There are five general steps that outline the **process of critical thinking**. The following brief description of the critical thinking process underscores the value of these skills in assessing information obtained through the Internet (Guffey, 1996):

1. **Identifying and clarifying the issue.** Clearly articulating the main question that is being considered, as well as the secondary questions that are implied by the topic; seeking and generating additional questions relating to the issue.
2. **Gathering information.** Learning more about the issue and context in which the issue is presented; researching the history surrounding the issue; accessing different sources of information to collect a balanced perspective.

3. **Evaluating evidence.** Unwillingness to accept information gathered at face value; consideration of the sources of information and their accuracy; questioning whether information is fact or opinion and whether the source has biases or ulterior motives that might prevent complete objectivity.

4. **Considering alternatives and implications.** Analyzing and synthesizing information and drawing conclusions from the evidence gathered; listing potential solutions or perspectives and weighing the advantages and disadvantages of each.

5. **Creative thinking.** Achieving distance from information or material and striving to develop unique and original perspectives.

Chapter Review

We learn throughout life. What we learn is not always positive, but we have also learned that we can take the negative and turn it into a positive and rewarding experience.

- Self-control is the opposite of external control.
- In **self-control**, the individual sets his or her own standards for performance, and will then reward or punish themselves for meeting or not meeting these standards. On the other hand, in **external control**, someone else sets the standards and delivers or withholds the rewards or punishment.
- People differ markedly in their feelings about their capacity to control life situations.
- People who perceive that their efforts make a difference when they are facing a difficult situation and take whatever action seems appropriate to solve the problem are referred to as **Internals.**
- People who perceive that their efforts do not seem to make a difference and they seem to be controlled by such things as luck or fate are referred to as **Externals.**
- **Learned helplessness** is the passive behavior produced by the exposure to unavoidable aversive events.
- **Operant level** is intentional actions that have an effect on the surrounding environment,
- **Self-efficacy** is our belief about our ability to perform behaviors that should lead to expected outcomes.
- Men and women develop differently, both physiologically and socially. This difference affects their self-efficacy.
- **Optimism** is defined as a generalized tendency to expect positive outcomes, while **pessimism** is defined as a general tendency to envision the future as unfavorable.
- Psychologist Martin Seligman (2006) suggests that people who have an **optimistic explanatory style** tend to use external, unstable, and specific explanations for negative events.
- Optimists, by definition, expect to eventually recover from adversity, and they expect to be successful at whatever they do, so they work much harder to reach their goals than pessimists do.
- People who have an **optimistic explanatory style** tend to use external, unstable, and specific explanations for negative events.
- People who have a **pessimistic explanatory style** tend to use internal, stable, and global explanations for negative events.
- **Learned optimism** is a learned way of explaining both good and bad life events that in turn enhance our perceived control and adaptive responses to them.
- According to **Social Learning Theory**, **modeling** (imitation) has a great impact on personality development.
- **Learning** is defined as a relatively permanent change in behavior as a result of experience or practice.
- **Self-efficacy**, or belief in your personal capabilities, regulates human functioning in three major ways: *Mood or affect, Motivational,* and *Cognitive.*
- **Grit** in psychology is a positive, non-cognitive trait based on an individual's passion for a particular long-term goal or end state, coupled with a powerful motivation to achieve their respective objective. This perseverance of effort promotes the overcoming of obstacles or challenges that lie within a gritty individual's path to accomplishment, and serves as a driving force in achievement realization.
- Before you can begin the process of learning, you have to pay attention. We find that there are three kinds of stimuli that attract our attention: 1) **Novel stimuli**, 2) **Significant stimuli**, and 3) **Conflicting stimuli**.
- **Cognitive behavior** is the theory that behaviors and emotions are the result of negative patterns of thinking which have adapted over time. It is the basis of the counseling approach called **Cognitive Behavioral Therapy** or **CBT**.

- What is **Behavior Modification**? A common topic in psychology classes and theory, behavior modification involves altering behavior to encourage a desired behavior or discourage an undesired behavior. To do this, you might use positive or negative reinforcement. Positive reinforcement is adding something (like a reward or punishment), while negative reinforcement means you're taking something away.
- **Personal Energy** is about being aware of how much mental, emotional, and physical energy is used during a day. Often in time management the emotional, mental and physical energy it takes to accomplish the tasks are not factored in or focused on (Martin, 2018).
- Another aspect of attention that may surprise you is that you can only **pay attention to one thing at a time.**
- Why study learning theory? Learning theory is the basis of all interactions—we are applying it constantly, and it is constantly being applied to us, most of the time without our knowledge.
- In most of our daily interactions, we are using operant conditioning. **Operant conditioning** is based on the premise that we are controlled by the consequences of our behavior. It relies on the **law of effect**, which states that behaviors followed by positive consequences are more likely to be repeated, and behaviors followed by negative consequences are less likely to be repeated.
- **Reinforcers** strengthen behavior. A **primary reinforcer** is a pleasant or unpleasant stimulus that has immediate reinforcing value: food, water, heat, pain, etc. A **secondary reinforcer** is a stimulus to which we attach positive or negative value through association with previously learned conditioned reinforcers.
- Positive reinforcement, negative reinforcement, and punishment all have a tremendous impact on our life. **Positive reinforcement** is defined as anything that increases a behavior by virtue of its presentation. **Negative reinforcement** is defined as anything that increases a behavior by virtue of its termination or avoidance.
- We can change! We all have bad habits and things that we would like to change. If you apply your program to your daily life, you will discover that you will be able to modify your behavior.

Learning Outcomes Review

1. Define "perceived locus of control" and explain the difference between an internal and an external.
2. Explain what learned helplessness is and how it can influence someone's life.
3. What are the recommended "helpful hints" mentioned in the text for developing an internal locus of control?
4. What is learned optimism? What does Seligman suggest for learning to be more optimistic?
5. What is self-efficacy? Explain how you can increase your self-efficacy.
6. Define optimism and pessimism and explain how optimistic explanatory and pessimistic explanatory styles can influence someone's behavior.
7. Define Social Learning Theory and explain the importance of imitation (modeling) in a person's development. For example, if you are a teacher and want to get your students to learn, you had better make sure the material is *significant* to your students.
8. Explain the importance of novel, significant, and conflicting stimuli in our life. Why is it important to study learning theory in relation to understanding yourself and in your relationships with others? Explain.
9. Define **grit** and explain if you have it.
10. What are primary and secondary reinforcers?

11. What is a self-change program? What are the steps involved in a self-change program? Explain.
12. Explain why the perseverance of effort called grit promotes the overcoming of obstacles or challenges.
13. What is behavior modification?
14. What is CBT?

Key Terms

Behavioral Contract
CBT-Cognitive Behavioral Theory
Cognitive Learning
Consequences
External Locus of Control
Grit
Initial Response Level
Internal Locus of Control
Law of Effect
Learned Helplessness
Learned Optimism
Learning Theory
Mental Health

Modeling
Negative Reinforcement
Novel Stimuli
Observational Learning
Operant Conditioning
Operant Level
Optimism
Optimistic Explanatory Style
Personal Energy
Pessimism
Pessimistic Explanatory Style
Positive Reinforcement
Primary Reinforcer

Punishment
Reinforcement
Reinforcer
Secondary Reinforcer
Self-Change Program
Self-Control
Self-Efficacy
Significant Stimuli
Social Learning Theory
Target Behavior
Violence

Reflections: Critical Thinking Activity

Answer the following questions and turn them into your instructor for grading. (All questions answered = A; 13 questions answered = B; 8 questions answered = C).
1. Why do you think it is important to study learning theory in regard to human relations?
2. Do you feel you are in control of everything in your life?
3. What are the benefits of having an internal locus of control? What are the benefits of having an external locus of control?
4. What do you think determines whether you become an internal or external?
5. What do you think causes learned helplessness?
6. What is self-efficacy and how can you increase your self-efficacy?
7. Discuss the benefits of being an optimist compared with being a pessimist.
8. Who has been a role model in your life? What influence have they had on you?
9. Are there any positive role models in our society? Who are they, and what characteristics do they have that make them a positive role model?
10. Name some negative role models. What influence are they having on our youth today?
11. What can you do to your relationships to make them more interesting and exciting?
12. If you were a teacher, what would you do in order to keep your students' attention?
13. Using operant conditioning, how would you change one of your bad habits? Explain.
14. Why is mindfulness helpful to some people?
15. How would you change your anxious behavior with CBT?

Technology Resources and Activities

MEDIA

https://www.howatthronline.com/quicksurveys/locusintro.a5w

Locus of Control Quick Survey
William Howatt Ph.D., Ed.D.
2003 © Howatt HR

https://podsearch.com/listing/happier-with-gretchen-rubin.html

Happiness Podcast

https://www.youtube.com/watch?v=YMPzDiraNnA

Learned helplessness

https://youtu.be/zxkaLQwl34c

B. F. Skinner operant conditioning

https://www.youtube.com/watch?v=4XQUJR4uIGM

Ellen Langer: Mindfulness over matter

https://www.youtube.com/watch?v=nXixMXDPv6g

Dr. Ellen Langer on Mindfulness and the Psychology of Possibility.

https://www.headspace.com/andy-puddicombe

Andy Puddicombe is a meditation and mindfulness expert and an accomplished presenter.

https://www.ted.com/talks/angela_lee_duckworth_grit_the_power_of_passion_and_perseverance?language=en

Angela Lee Duckworth: Grit: The power of passion and perseverance.

https://www.youtube.com/watch?v=BzuawrFE1xM

The Happiness Project with Gretchen Rubin.

https://www.youtube.com/watch?v=HTfYv3IEOqM

The effect of trauma on the brain and how it affects behaviors, a presentation by John Rigg at TEDx-Augusta 2015. In his work with trauma patients, Dr. Rigg has observed how the brain is constantly reacting to sensory information, generating non-thinking reactions before our intelligent individual human brains are able to process the event and formulate a self-driven response.

https://www.ted.com/talks/cameron_russell_looks_aren_t_everything_believe_me_i_m_a_model? language=en

Cameron Russell: Looks aren't everything. Believe me, I'm a model.

https://www.youtube.com/watch?v=PTlmho_RovY

Killing Us Softly 4: Image of women.

https://www.youtube.com/watch?v=jryCoo0BrRk

Rethinking anxiety: Learning to face fear | Dawn Huebner | TEDxAmoskeagMillyardWomen

http://www.glnh.org/

LGBT National Help Center

https://www.hrc.org/

Human Rights Campaign

https://www.hrc.org/resources/glossary-of-terms

Dictionary of terms about sexual orientation and gender identity or expression

https://www.youtube.com/watch?v=WLMJHdySgE8

Violence: A family tradition, a presentation by Robbyn Peters Bennett at TEDxBellingham on November 23, 2013. Robbyn Peters Bennett, LMHC, CMHS is a psychotherapist, educator, and child advocate who specializes in the treatment of trauma-related mental health problems resulting from the effects of early childhood stress, abuse and neglect.

TRANSGENDER AND GENDER EQUITY HELPING RESOURCES

https://forge-forward.org/

"**FORGE** is a national transgender anti-violence organization, founded in 1994. Since 2009, we have been federally funded to provide direct services to transgender, gender non-conforming and gender non-binary survivors of sexual assault. Since 2011, FORGE has served as the only transgender-focused organization federally funded to provide training and technical assistance to providers around the country who work with transgender survivors of sexual assault, domestic and dating violence, and stalking. Our role as a technical assistance provider has allowed us to directly see key continued and emerging challenges many agencies are experiencing in serving sexual assault survivors of all genders."

https://www.genderspectrum.org/

"Gender Spectrum's mission is to create a gender-inclusive world for all children and youth. To accomplish this, we help families, organizations, and institutions increase understandings of gender and consider the implications that evolving views have for each of us."

https://transequality.org/

"The National Center for Transgender Equality advocates to change policies and society to increase understanding and acceptance of transgender people. In the nation's capital and throughout the country, NCTE works to replace disrespect, discrimination, and violence with empathy, opportunity, and justice."

https://www.translatinacoalition.org/

"Members of the TransLatin@ Coalition are TransLatin@ Leaders who reside in different parts of the US who organize and advocate for the issues and needs of Trans Latin@ Individuals who reside in the United States."

ACTIVITIES

She's Not There: A Life in Two Genders by Jennifer Finley Boylan

She's Not There is the story of a person changing genders, the story of a person bearing and finally revealing a complex secret; above all, it is a love story. By turns funny and deeply moving, Jennifer Finney Boylan explores the remarkable territory that lies between men and women, examines changing friendships, and rejoices in the redeeming power of family.

9 Interesting TED Talks on Breaking Bad Habits: blog.hubspot.com/marketing/habit-research-ted-talks

A Simple Way To Break A Bad Habit: Why is it so hard to stop smoking or lose weight when we know these habits are bad for us?

http://www.uky.edu/~eushe2/Bandura/BanEncy.html

Reading on Self-efficacy

http://www.upworthy.com/how-lady-dynamite-hilariously-nails-comedy-about-serious-mental-illness ?c=upw1&u=781e1b682edf6d11d917cd528b9824421641e9e5

This funny TV show helps us all understand mental health better.

http://www.successconsciousness.com/index_000006.htm

This is a website about conscientiousness and self-discipline. For example, it suggests that willpower is not something that exerts us, but rather something that is easy. After a discussion of these topics, the reader is provided with exercises to reinforce and improve one's self-discipline.

www.mindtools.com/

This site provides practical suggestions for problem solving, memory improvement, increasing creativity, and much more.

https://www.upworthy.com/5-things-i-didnt-want-to-hear-when-i-was-grieving-and-1-thing-that-helped

5 things I didn't want to hear when I was grieving and 1 thing that helped.

www.authentichappiness.sas.upenn.edu/testcenter.aspx

This Optimism Test measures optimism about the future.

https://www.translifeline.org/

"**Trans Lifeline** is a national trans-led 501(c)(3) organization dedicated to improving the quality of trans lives by responding to the critical needs of our community with direct service, material support, advocacy, and education. Our vision is to fight the epidemic of trans suicide and improve overall life-outcomes of trans people by facilitating justice-oriented, collective community aid."

https://www.glaad.org/tags/trans-people-color-coalition

Trans People of Color Coalition (TPOCC) was founded in 2010 to connect people and resources on the local, state and national level to make sure trans and gender non-conforming people of color voices were visible, respected and at the table. Trans People of Color Coalition (TPOCC) envisions a world where trans people of color can live and work in safety, where health and economic equity are basic rights, and we are celebrated for our leadership.

http://www.imatyfa.org/index.html

"**TYFA** empowers children and families by partnering with educators, service providers and communities, to develop supportive environments in which gender may be expressed and respected."

What Controls Your Life?

PURPOSE

This is a device to measure your attitudes toward rewards and punishments: Do you feel that they come as a result of your own behavior, or from outside sources? We have reproduced this device below so that you can measure yourself and determine your own beliefs. Read each set of two statements and decide which statement seems to you more accurate and place a check mark (✔) next to it. Read and answer carefully. There are no right or wrong choices. They are based on your personal judgments. Try to respond to each pair of statements independently, apart from your responses to other pairs of statements.

1. _____ a. A great deal that happens to me is probably a matter of chance.
   _____ b. I am the master of my fate.

2. _____ a. It is almost impossible to figure out how to please some people.
   _____ b. Getting along with people is a skill that must be practiced.

3. _____ a. People like me can change the course of world affairs if we make ourselves be heard.
   _____ b. It is only wishful thinking to believe that one can really influence what happens in society at large.

4. _____ a. Most people get the respect they deserve in this world.
   _____ b. An individual's capabilities often pass unrecognized no matter how hard he or she tries.

5. _____ a. The idea that teachers are unfair to students is nonsense.
   _____ b. Most students do not realize the extent to which their grades are influenced by accidental happenings.

6. _____ a. If you do not get the right opportunities, you cannot become a good leader.
   _____ b. Capable people who fail to become leaders have not taken advantage of their opportunities.

7. _____ a. Sometimes I feel that I have little to do with the grades I get.
   _____ b. In my case, the grades I make are the results of my own efforts; luck has little or nothing to do with it.

8. _____ a. Heredity plays the major role in determining one's personality.
   _____ b. It is one's experiences in life that determine what one is like.

9. _____ a. It is silly to think that one can really change another person's basic attitudes.
   _____ b. When I am right, I can convince others.

10. _____ a. In my experience I have noticed that there is usually a direct connection between how hard I study and the grades I get.
    _____ b. Many times the reactions of teachers seem haphazard to me.

11. _____ a. The average citizen can have an influence in government decisions.
    _____ b. This world is run by the few people in power, and there is not much the little guy can do about it.

12. _____ a. When I make plans, I am almost certain that I can make them work.
    _____ b. It is not always wise to plan too far ahead, because many things turn out to be a matter of good or bad fortune anyhow.

13. _____ a. There are certain people who are just no good.
    _____ b. There is some good in everybody.

14. _____ a. In my case, getting what I want has little or nothing to do with luck.
    _____ b. Many times, we might just as well decide what to do by flipping a coin.

15. _____ a. Promotions are earned through hard work and persistence.
    _____ b. Making a lot of money is largely a matter of getting the right breaks.

16. _____ a. Marriage is largely a gamble.
    _____ b. The number of divorces indicates that more and more people are not trying to make their marriages work.

17. _____ a. In our society, a person's future earning power is dependent on their ability.
    _____ b. Getting promoted is really a matter of being a little luckier than the next person.

18. _____ a. Most people do not realize the extent to which their lives are controlled by accidental happenings.
    _____ b. There is really no such thing as luck.

19. _____ a. I have little influence over the way other people behave.
    _____ b. If one knows how to deal with people, they are really quite easily led.

20. _____ a. In the long run, the bad things that happen to us are balanced by the good ones.
    _____ b. Most misfortunes are the result of lack of ability, ignorance, laziness, or all three.

21. _____ a. With enough effort, we can wipe out political corruption.
    _____ b. It is difficult for people to have much control over the things politicians do in office.

22. _____ a. A good leader expects people to decide for themselves what they should do.
    _____ b. A good leader makes it clear to everybody what their jobs are.

23. _____ a. People are lonely because they do not try to be friendly.
    _____ b. There is not much use in trying too hard to please people—if they like you, they like you.

24. _____ a. There is too much emphasis on athletics in high school.
    _____ b. Team sports are an excellent way to build character.

25. _____ a. What happens to me is my own doing.
    _____ b. Sometimes I feel that I do not have enough control over the direction my life is taking.

Scoring Key for Project: For each of the responses below, give yourself 1 point.

ITEM #	RESPONSE				
1	a	10	b	19	a
2	a	11	b	20	a
3	b	12	b	21	b
4	b	13	a	22	b
5	b	14	b	23	b
6	a	15	b	24	a
7	a	16	a	25	b
8	a	17	b		
9	a	18	a		

Total Points _____

Your total number of points indicates the degree to which you view control as external or internal. **The higher the score (above 15), the more you perceive control as external.** Remember, this means that you perceive yourself as not being in control of your own destiny, that outside forces are determining your fate, and whatever effort you put into something, it will not make any difference. **The lower the score (below 15) means the more you perceive control as internal.** This means that you perceive yourself as being in control of your own destiny and your success is dependent upon your efforts and not on others.

DISCUSSION

1. What are the benefits of being an Internal?

2. What are the advantages of being an External?

3. If you decided that you would rather be an Internal than an External, how would you go about changing yourself?

4. What did you learn from this activity?

Name _____ Date _____

Are You an Optimist or a Pessimist?

PURPOSE

The following scale, a version of the Life Orientation Test, can help raise your awareness about whether you are the type of person who tends to see the proverbial glass as half full or half empty.

INSTRUCTIONS

Using numbers 0 to 4, indicate your responses to the following items in the spaces provided. Then check the scoring key.

4 = strongly agree
3 = agree
2 = neutral
1 = disagree
0 = strongly disagree

_____ 1. In the uncertain times, I usually expect the best.

_____ 2. It's easy for me to relax.

_____ 3. If something can go wrong for me, it will.

_____ 4. I'm always optimistic about my future.

_____ 5. I enjoy my friends a lot.

_____ 6. It's important for me to keep busy.

_____ 7. I hardly ever expect things to go my way.

_____ 8. I don't get upset too easily.

_____ 9. I rarely count on good things happening to me.

_____ 10. Overall, I expect more good things to happen to me than bad.

Total Score _____

Scoring Key

The first step is to reverse the scoring for items 3, 7, and 9. In other words, change a 4 to a 0, a 3 to a 1, a 1 to a 3, and a 0 to a 4. A 2 remains a 2. Next, add your score for items 1, 3, 4, 7, 9, and 10 to obtain an overall score. (Do not score items 2, 5, 6, and 8. These items are considered "fillers" and are not scored as part of the test.) Total scores can range from **0 to 24.**

Now, you can compare your score to those of a sample of 2,055 college students. Higher scores indicate greater optimism, while lower scores indicate greater pessimism. The average (mean) score in the college sample was **14.33.** About two-thirds of the sample scored from **10 to 19.** Scores greater than **14** reflect relatively higher levels of optimism. Psychologists believe that people can change their attitudes—that optimism can be learned.

Discussion

1. Do you agree with your score? Why or why not?

2. If you scored low on optimism, what do you think you need to do to change your attitude?

3. Psychologists believe that optimism can be learned. How do you feel about this belief?

Source: Based on Scheier, Carver & Bridges (1994).

Life's Lessons

PURPOSE

To review the messages used by significant others to help you change behavior and learn some important lessons in life.

INSTRUCTIONS

Thinking about individuals who were most beneficial in helping you change some behavior and learn some lessons in life:

1. Parents:

    What did you learn?

2. Friends/friends' parents/ teachers/instructors/the school system:

    What did you learn?

DISCUSSION

1. To whom are you a significant (influential) other? Explain any contributions you think you have made to their life. What did they learn?

2. What did you learn?

What Kind of Reinforcement Do You Use?

PURPOSE

To learn the value of reinforcement.

INSTRUCTIONS

1. You can either answer the following questions individually or with a partner. After you have completed the questions, get into larger groups and answer the discussion questions.
2. Put yourself in the following roles and state how you think each form of reinforcement and/or negative consequences will influence the person involved. Also explore learned helplessness.

   a. Parent—Discuss how or if you would use the following forms of positive reinforcement, negative reinforcement, and negative consequences in the training and education of your child. What impact will it have on your child?

   Money

   Hugs and kisses

   Spanking

   Compliments

   Gifts

   Allowance

"Time-out"

Video games and TV

Encouragement

Special outings—zoo, miniature golf, science museum, movie theater.

b. If you are a teacher, what kind of positive reinforcement, negative reinforcement, and negative consequences would you use? What effect do you think each of these would have on your students? Would it be motivating for the student or would it have a detrimental effect? Explain how or if you would use the following:

Compliments

"Time-out"

Sitting them in the corner

The "star" or "point" system

Taking away recess time

Encouragement

Negative comments

"Student of the Week"

Grades

Sending them to the principal's office

No after school activities

(1) Which of the above would have the greatest effect on your students' motivation, positive and negative? Explain.

c. If you were an employer, what would be the best way to motivate your employees? How would you use the following?

A plaque for accomplishments

A salary increase; how much is needed in order to motivate them? 1%, 5%, 10%, or more?

Positive comments

Larger work area

New job title

Extra time off

Flex-time

Special commendations

Criticism

Feedback on undesirable behavior

Bonus

Commission

Fines

Probation

a. Which of the above do you think would motivate your employees the most? Explain.

b. Which of the above would be most detrimental to your employees' motivation and morale? Explain.

DISCUSSION

1. Considering all of the above situations:
   a. Which forms of reinforcement seem to be most effective? Explain.

   b. Which forms of negative consequences seem to be most effective? Explain.

   c. Which forms of reinforcement do not seem to be very effective? Explain.

2. Can you think of any types of reinforcement and/or negative consequences that could be used in any of the above situations that would be more effective than what has been previously mentioned? Explain what it is and in what situation it would be most effective.

3. Some people say that physical punishment is the best way to control another person's behavior. Other people say that physical punishment should never be used. What do you think? How is this different from negative consequences?

Name _____ Date _____

Self-Change Project

PURPOSE

To understand how learning theory applies to your life.

INSTRUCTIONS

Review the section on Learning Theory, specifically the Self-Change Program. This program will explain how you can apply this to your life.

1. Identify the behavior you would like to change.

   _____

2. Observe the target behavior for 5 to 7 days to get the baseline (operant level). (Make a record every few hours of the behavior you are changing.)

   Day 1 _____

   Day 2 _____

   Day 3 _____

   Day 4 _____

   Day 5 _____

   Day 6 _____

   Day 7 _____

3. What is your goal and the date to be completed?

   _____

   _____

4. Identify your reinforcers, long-term reinforcement, and short-term reinforcement. What will motivate you to change?

_____

_____

_____

_____

_____

5. Make a plan. What are you going to do to change the behavior?

_____

_____

_____

_____

_____

6. Change the behavior. (This can take anywhere from one to six weeks.) Keep records of the daily activity relating to the project. Record the daily activity in a separate notebook.

7. What are the results?

_____

_____

_____

_____

DISCUSSION

1. What kinds of changes would you like to make yourself?

2. What is motivating (reinforcing) enough to get you to change your behavior?

3. What could people use as reinforcers in order to facilitate the behavior change?

4. How could you apply the methods of the Self-Change Project to other aspects of your life (job, children, spouse, mate, and so on)?

Who's in Control?

LEARNING JOURNAL

Select the statement below that best defines your feelings about the personal value or meaning gained from this chapter and respond below the dotted line.

I learned that I . . .	I was surprised that I . . .
I realized that I . . .	I was pleased that I . . .
I discovered that I . . .	I was displeased that I . . .

. . . .

chapter 4
Dealing with Emotions

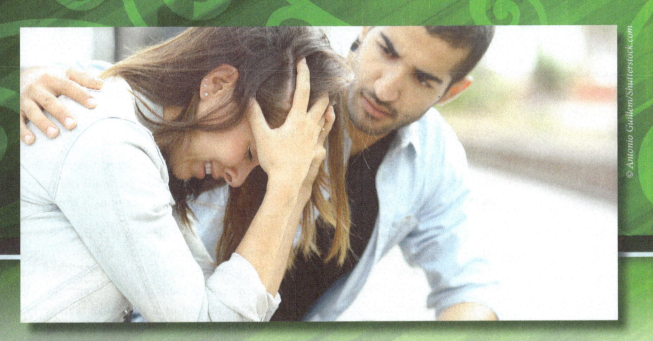

It's unfortunate that we're never really taught how to show emotion in ways that help our relationships. Instead, we are usually told what we should not do. However, too little emotion can make our lives seem empty and boring, while too much emotion, poorly expressed, fills our interpersonal lives with conflict and grief. Within reason, some kind of balance in the expression of emotion seems to be called for. —Gerald Egan, *You and Me*

Think About This...

WHAT EMOTIONS WOULD YOU FEEL IN THESE SITUATIONS?

- You have just turned on the TV and the screen is filled with shootings of police and protestors.
- It has finally happened! You have found that special person, and the two of you are discussing marriage.
- Once again, your boss said some critical, unfair things to you today.
- The telephone rings, and you learn that one of your best friends has been killed in an accident.
- Your spouse has just come in and told you, quite unexpectedly, that he or she wants a divorce.

Becoming Aware of your feelings Think about the preceding questions and include your thoughts in your journal. Would your feelings and emotions be similar to the feelings and emotions that other people have when they are having the same experiences? How do you feel when you are in love? Can you easily verbalize the words: "I love you"? Do you verbally express your anger, or do you save your "bad" feelings and explode at a later date? Could you talk about your feelings if your best friend or someone very close to you died? How would you deal with your feelings if your spouse walked out?

What are the emotions these questions trigger in you?

We know that our emotions play an important part in making our relations with other people pleasant and joyful, or sad and painful. We also know that what we respond to emotionally is learned. Do we learn what triggers the emotions, or do we learn what we are expected (by our culture) to feel?

Because emotional responses and expressions are learned, we can learn how to change emotional patterns that are self-defeating or harmful to our growth toward self-actualization. We can also learn how to develop ways to become more emotionally expressive.

In our society, people often experience alienation. Some actually lack the ability to express emotions. And it sometimes appears that many of us have almost forgotten how to cry or laugh or express genuine feelings for ourselves and others. Therefore, we hope this chapter will help you become a more emotionally mature person and help you better understand the reasons behind some of your own emotional reactions to certain people or situations. And we hope that you will be able to get ideas about ways you can manage emotional patterns that are giving you trouble in living with yourself and others.

What Are Emotions?

If someone asked you to explain *emotions*, what would you say? In all probability, you would say, "They are the different feelings I have." You might even give these feelings a label, such as anger, love, hate, and so on. Now, suppose someone asked you to explain the term *feelings*. Would you be likely to say, "They are the different emotions I have"? And, you might even give these emotions a label, such as anger, love, or hate. The point is, it is quite difficult to separate the two; therefore, we will use the two interchangeably.

Dr. Daniel Goleman (2006), author of *Emotional Intelligence,* defines emotion in this way: "I take emotion to refer to a feeling and its distinctive thoughts, psychological and biological states, and range of propensities to act." In the *New York Times* bestseller, *Don't Sweat the Small Stuff . . . and it's all small stuff,* Carslon says your "feelings act as a barometer, letting you know what your internal weather is like." Therefore, we are going to think of **emotions** as feelings that are experienced.

Without emotions, we would be little more than drab, colorless machines that run the same way day after day. We would not know the happiness of success or the pangs of disappointment. We would not experience joy from the companionship of others and would feel no grief at their loss. We would neither love nor hate. Pride, envy, and anger would be unknown to us. We would not even be able to understand the joys and sorrows of others. The definition of **emotion** is a feeling state that involves certain components: physiological changes, subjective cognitive states, and expressive behaviors.

Fortunately, we are not machines; we are humans. Therefore, each of us, young or old, male or female, is capable of having and expressing many different emotions. Although it is true that individuals experience and express their emotions in many different ways, psychologists generally agree that emotions are very complex experiences, with at least four common characteristics: physiological or internal changes, behavioral expressions, cognitive interpretations, and motivational tendencies (Wood & Wood, 2014). We will now look more closely at these characteristics, as well as briefly discuss the effect our moods have on our emotional reactions.

Becoming Aware of Your Skills: Strategies to Become More Emotional Intelligent
https://www.youtube.com/watch?v=pt74vK9pgIA

Daniel Goleman explains the best strategies to improve our emotional intelligence to create better long-term relationships.

Characteristics of Emotions

We process emotions in many ways.

BECOMING AWARE OF YOUR EMOTIONS

Take a moment to **Become Aware** of this case study on feelings:

Physiological or internal changes. Pretend that you are walking alone at night when suddenly a large object jumps in front of you. Would your neck muscles tighten? Would your stomach possibly feel "funny"? Would you be able to hear the sound of your heartbeat, even when you later discovered that the "large object" was just a box blowing in the wind? Would you still be breathing faster? What would be happening inside of you? How do you feel inside when you are nervous, frightened, or angry?

© Sam Wordley/Shutterstock.com

These are characteristic of emotional states in that they involve physiological changes.

The daily challenge we have of dealing effectively with emotions is critical to the human condition, because our brains are hardwired to give emotions the upper hand, wrote Bradberry and Greaves in *Emotional Intelligence 2.0* (2009).

When our emotions are aroused, there are physiological changes over which we have no control. In strong fear and anger, you do not tell your adrenal glands to pump adrenaline into the bloodstream so that you will have extra energy. These physiological changes in the nervous system are nature's way of preparing you to react faster and more intensely for longer periods of time. In essence, your whole body is mobilized for action—you are physiologically ready to run or fight.

When you experience strong feelings, the internal changes in your body contribute to your feelings. For example, in grief or depression, there is a reduction of pulse rate, breathing, and muscular strength. Consequently, you feel tired (Reidbord, 2016).

Behavioral expressions. Even though emotions are felt internally, they often lead to observable expressions. These expressions may come in the form of a blush, trembling hands, sweating palms, or a tremor in the voice. Behavioral expressions can also include crying, laughing, cursing, kicking a chair, or even hitting another person. Sometimes people will deny they are feeling anything, even though their external and behavioral expressions indicate something else. We will discuss some suggestions for verbally expressing feelings later in the chapter.

Cognitive interpretation. While it is true that there is some connection between physical behavior and emotional states, in most situations, our emotions cannot be separated from our mental lives. Cognitive appraisals are an essential part of the experience. Realistically, individuals are constantly appraising the events they experience for their personal implications: Do I care about what is happening? Is it good or bad for me? Can I do anything about it? Is this matter going to get better or worse? Can I cope? Psychologist Arnold Lazarus (2000a) believes that the cognitions involved in emotion range from your immediate perceptions of a specific event to your general philosophy of life. Is your outlook positive or negative?

Cognitive therapists Albert Ellis and Robert Harper (1998) and Dienes et al. (2019) believe our thoughts, beliefs, and prior experiences will color the way we view an event and, thus, profoundly influence our emotional reaction to that event. Two people confronted with the same situation may interpret it in a different way and, therefore, respond with different feelings.

Actually, we go through life describing the world to ourselves, giving each event or experience some label. We make interpretations of what we see and hear; we predict whether they will bring danger or relative safety. Sometimes, these thoughts are very powerful, and as you will discover in Chapter Eight, they can create most of the major stresses we experience in life.

Motivational tendencies. Emotions themselves may function as motives, directing you toward pleasant situations and away from those that are emotionally unsatisfying, anxiety provoking, or painful. In fact, the root of the word *emotion* means *to move*, indicating the close relationship between motivation and emotion (Kagan, 2009). In essence, when we are feeling a particular way, we are going to do certain things because of that feeling, in spite of that feeling, or to avoid or change that feeling. Another way of saying this would be: We do what makes us feel good, and we avoid what makes us feel bad. UCLA psychologist Gary Emery (2000) explains this further:

> *Nothing can make you frustrated. Nothing can make you depressed. Nothing can make you angry. For that matter, nothing can make you happy, either. All your emotions are produced from your own mental interpretations.*
> —ANDREW BERNSTEIN

- **Pleasure** motivates you to move toward something. Your pleasure feelings, for example, motivate you to move toward a certain crowd of people ("They think my jokes are funny!"); you continue to interact with these people until it no longer feels good ("They made fun of me because I don't drink").
- **Anxiety** motivates you to run or escape from a possible loss ("I had to keep away from those people!").
- **Anger** motivates you to fight against a perceived loss ("I wanted to punch his lights out!"). You yell or you attack someone to get rid of your angry feelings, even though you know your outburst will make matters worse.
- **Sadness** motivates you to shut down and withdraw after a loss. If you lose money in the stock market, your sad feelings motivate you to be much more cautious playing the market and protect the money you have left.

Moods. Before we leave our discussion of the characteristics of emotions, we need to briefly discuss the effect our moods have on how we respond emotionally. Our *moods* are a general feeling tone, and they have a definite influence on your emotions. Stated another way, Gardner (2002) says, "Our mood generally informs about the general state of our being." Even though we do not like to admit it, our moods are often evident to others: For example, "Don't ask Mr. Jones for a day off—he's really grouchy" or "Mrs. Smith is in such a good mood, I bet we can talk her out of the test today."

Think for a moment and try to recall how your moods affect your emotions. In psychology, a mood is an emotional state. In contrast to emotions, feelings, or affects, moods are less specific, less intense, and less likely to be provoked or instantiated by a particular stimulus or event. Moods are typically described as having either a positive or negative valence. In other words, people usually talk about being in a good mood or a bad mood. Often, we do not know what event or events put us in a particular mood.

Now that we have a better idea of what emotions are and how they affect us, we will discuss some of the emotions which cause us the most difficulty.

Are many of us upset by things that we can't control?

Types of Emotions

If you are feeling cranky and snap at your friends ... remember the word HALT ... you might be Hungry, Angry, Lonely, or Tired. Take care of yourself!

How many different emotions exist? We really do not know the answer to this question, because our emotions include many subjective factors and individual differences. Our language is rich with words to describe our emotions. Table 4.1 gives a partial list of some common emotions we may experience.

This list only represents labels we give to our feelings. Perhaps we need to explain these labels further. One way we can do this is to identify emotions or feelings as either primary, mixed, mild, or intense.

Table 4.1 SOME EMOTION WORDS: HOW DO YOU FEEL TODAY?

accepted	envious	insecure	sad
afraid	exhilarated	intimidated	sentimental
aggravated	fearful	isolated	self-reliant
angry	friendly	jealous	shy
annoyed	frightened	joyful	sincere
anxious	glad	lazy	sorry
ashamed	grieving	lonely	supported
bitter	guilt-free	loved	surprised
calm	guilty	loving	tense
cautious	happy	optimistic	terrified
cheerful	helpful	out of control	tired
comfortable	hopeless	overcontrolled	trusting
confident	hostile	pessimistic	uneasy
confused	humiliated	powerful	unsure
contented	hurried	powerless	uptight
defeated	hurt	puzzled	vulnerable
defensive	impatient	regretful	wanted
depressed	inadequate	relieved	weak
embarrassed	incompetent	resentful	worried
energetic	inferior	restless	overwhelmed

Primary and mixed emotions. Psychologists who study emotions have made up lists of certain basic emotions. Robert Plutchik (2003) identified eight *primary emotions*: joy, acceptance, fear, surprise, sadness, disgust, anger, and anticipation. The emotion wheel (see Figure 4.1) illustrates that these *primary emotions* are inside the perimeter of the circle. He suggests that these primary feelings can combine to form other *mixed emotions*, some of which are listed outside the circle: love, submission, awe, disappointment, remorse, contempt, aggressiveness, optimism.

Psychologist Gary Emery (2000), however, indicates that there are only four basic emotions: mad, sad, glad, and scared. He suggests that all the other emotions we experience are just derivatives of these basic four. For example, too much sadness becomes depression, too much gladness becomes mania, too much fear becomes panic, and too much anger becomes rage.

Although you may not agree with the specific primary and secondary emotions just identified, you would probably agree that it is possible to experience several different emotions at the same time.

Intense and mild emotions. We have discussed that it is human to have and express emotions, and that our emotions have a lot to do with how much pleasure and enjoyment we get out of life. There are no negative or positive emotions. Each type of feeling is a normal response to some form of stimulus. Any emotion taken to any unhealthy level can do harm. Even love! Our emotions can have negative effects, however, and cause problems for us. For example, strong emotions such as fear, depression, anger, and hate can disrupt our functioning and ability to relate to other people.

Figure 4.1 **THE EMOTION WHEEL**

PRIMARY AND MIXED EMOTIONS
PLUTCHIK (2003)

CONSIDER THIS

BECOMING AWARE OF YOUR EMOTIONS

You are going to have some friends over for hamburgers. Your date is going to help you get ready for your guests and also act as a host for the evening. An hour before your date is due at your house, you get a call that he has an unexpected guest from out-of-town arriving and will be unable to join you and your friends. Your date tells you that this is just an "old friend" he used to date, and she is only going to be in town for the evening.

Now, would you just be angry?

You would probably be hurt, jealous, and even embarrassed that you are the only one without a date. The point is, an emotional event can create a wide range of feelings. We generally communicate only one feeling, however, usually the most negative one. In this case, it would probably be your anger.

Could your anger become a problem for you?

Now, let us answer the question concerning your date who did not show for dinner:

When could your anger become a problem for you? It would be normal for you to be angry if you were left in this situation. If this anger becomes so bad that you awoke for "nights on end" and "stewed" about your anger, or even tried to harm your date and his "guest," then your intense anger or rage would be a problem for you.

Generally, our emotions begin to have negative effects when they are viewed as being excessive in *intensity* and *duration* (Ellis, 2001). For example, if intense emotions linger, your ability to get enjoyment from life may be decreased. It is perfectly normal to be sad when someone close to you dies. However, if you are still depressed about this three years later, this sustained, intense emotion may be a problem for you. For example, other people may want to avoid being with you, because you are so sad.

Another example is the mild anxiety most of us feel when asked to give a speech in front of a group. A small amount of anxiety before a speech can help us prepare and do a more effective job in its delivery. Total fear, however, will probably cause us to be unable to concentrate on preparing adequately for the speech. In some cases, intense anxiety can cause us to stammer and forget important aspects of our speech.

We say that when mild, emotions can be *facilitative*—they assist us in preparing for the future, solving problems, and in doing what is best for us. However, intense, sustained emotions can be *debilitative*—they disrupt our overall functioning (Ellis, 2001). For example, we may experience difficulty in performing certain tasks, such as passing a test or giving a speech, and in solving problems.

The natural reaction to feeling off is to try our hardest to pump ourselves up and out of it, because these things happen. Sometimes, injecting our understanding of the situation at hand with some context can be a super-effective secret ingredient for restoring our mood to a state of happiness. Yet, even though this does sometimes work, it's essentially an act of emotional suppression that usually leads to a resurfacing of those pushed-down feelings that's only more severe on the second go-around.

But what about just accepting it—accepting that it's going to be a grayer day in the universe, and that we might feel grumpier, sadder, or more peeved than normal. Could this work? Might it even help to dig ourselves out of the bad mood abyss?

> "I think it's very important to recognize a sad or blue mood—even as it's coming on," says clinical psychologist Carla Marie Manly, PhD. For me, the culprit is sometimes PMS, sometimes a symptom of my depression, and sometimes it's genuinely nothing. As human beings, we're all entitled to off days, and it's okay to be in a bad mood for no good reason. Still, being able to acknowledge it is helpful, Dr. Manly says."

> "If you know the cause, it's lovely to just allow space for the sadness. This can be done by making more quiet time, having an extra cup of comforting tea, journaling, or simply honoring that you might need more down time that day," Dr. Manly says. "Thus, one's gray day may be lighter and more likely to pass with ease by respecting that it has its own purpose, which is often to ask us to slow down and be gently reflective."

> That said, leaning into the off days isn't an excuse to be awful to everyone in your line of fire. It's possible to be introspective while also being authentic about your feelings—no matter how negative they may be—without scapegoating others (Manly, 2019).

Essentially, emotions can serve a purpose in one situation, and in other situations may serve as a hindrance.

Becoming Aware of Technology: Your Emotions Are For Sale
https://www.pbssocal.org/programs/braincraft/your-emotions-are-for-sale-pm0zfi/

Moods and manipulation: explore the relationship between AI, voice assistants, and neuroscience through the lens of philosophy.

Coping with Problem Emotions

Humans have evolved over millions of years, and our ancestors who excelled at fighting or fleeing from dangerous situations were more likely to survive. We have inherited their genes, but living in the modern developed world does not typically bring us into constant, life-threatening danger. Our threat systems are vigilant, and they are being bombarded with the 24-hour news cycle, trade wars, robbery and arson, bombings, and facts and fiction from the Internet. We are being bombarded as never before, according to Professor David Sloan from Binghamton University and President of the Evolution Institute (Keemanovic, 2019). Some emotions cause more difficulties than others: fear, anxiety, anger, guilt, grief, and love are such emotions that are experienced often and with mixed reactions.

> *Of all the passions, fear weakens judgment most.*
> —JEAN-FRANÇOIS PAUL DE GONDI, CARDINAL DE RETZ

FEAR

We all experience the emotion of fear. It can take many forms, serve many purposes, and create many different responses. It is important to distinguish *fear* from *anxiety* (Ellis, 2016).

> A specific situation or object elicits *fear*, whereas *anxiety* is objectless. Therefore, we speak of **fear** when we think we know what we're afraid of, and **anxiety** when we're unsure.

Types of fear. We may feel the emotion of fear as a type of warning that danger is near. This warning may take the form of an external "cue," or it may reflect our learning. For example, if you walked into your house and met a burglar carrying a gun in the hallway, you would feel frightened. This feeling of fear was triggered by an external force. Sometimes fear reactions are learned through past associations. You might be afraid of thunderstorms because your father reacted to them as dangerous and had a tendency to believe that lightning could result in a tornado. After all, his mother had been killed in a tornado when he was quite young.

Although most of the above examples reflect physical dangers, we also have fears of being left out of the crowd, of being ridiculed, of being a failure, or of being rejected. For example, if you have ever been rejected in a relationship, you may be afraid of getting involved in another relationship again. Actually, this is a good example of where we are really experiencing *mixed emotions*. Is it fear we are feeling, or is it hurt? Could it be that we want to protect ourselves from getting hurt again? This type of fear

Speaking to a group is a common source of anxiety.

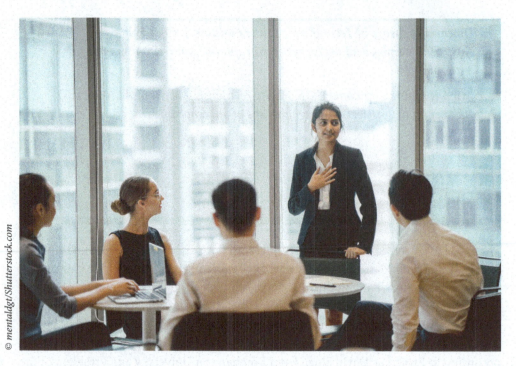

© mentaldgt/Shutterstock.com

or hurt is one that takes time to work through. After all, do we really want our "bad feelings" from one relationship to "rob" us of the opportunity to have a healthy and satisfying relationship with someone else?

Some people have a personal fear of failure. Have you been wanting or at least considering a financial, personal, or scholastic risk? What is the worst that could happen if you did experience a disappointment? Could you cope with that? Remember that even if you do fail, some good can come from it. How did you learn to walk? You did not just jump up from your crib one day and waltz gracefully across the room. You stumbled and fell on your face, and got up and tried again. David M. Burns (2019) writes:

> At what age are you suddenly expected to know everything and never make any more mistakes? If you can love and respect yourself in failure, worlds of adventure and new experiences will open up before you, and your fears will vanish.

Because fear and anxiety are closely related, below are some suggestions for dealing with these emotions. First of all, let us get a clearer picture of the sometimes troublesome emotion of anxiety.

ANXIETY

Serious mental stress is a fact of life for many American teens. In a recent survey, seven-in-ten teens say anxiety and depression are major problems among their peers—a concern that's shared by mental health researchers and clinicians (DeSiver, 2019).

Becoming *Aware*

As we mentioned earlier, when the basis for our feeling of fear is not specific, we are experiencing anxiety. Actually, *anxiety* is an unpleasant, threatening feeling that something bad is about to happen. Rollo May (1973) in his classic book, *Man's Search for Himself,* states:

> Anxiety is the feeling of "gnawing" within, of being "trapped and overwhelmed." Anxiety may take all forms and intensities, for it is the human being's reaction to a danger to his existence, or to some value he identifies with existence. . . . It is the quality of an experience which makes it anxiety rather than the quantity.

Courage is seeing your fear in a realistic perspective, defining it, considering the alternatives and choosing to function in spite of risk.
—LEONARD ZUNIN

How to Face Your Fears and Anxieties

1. **Admit your fears.** It is one thing to mask your anxieties with physical and creative activities; but if these activities become avoidance techniques, anxiety eventually increases.
2. **Take risks.** Fear does not go away unless you take chances to make your dreams come true. You will gain new strength and improved self-esteem with each accomplishment.
3. **Acknowledge the positive.** Anxious people tend to overlook their own strengths. When you are scared, make a conscious effort to remember some past positive experiences instead of focusing on your failures.
4. **Recognize your worst fears.** Ask yourself what the worst possible outcome of the situation could be. Having faced the worst possibility makes it easier to deal with what does come.
5. **Stay in the present.** Much anxiety is the result of projecting yourself into future situations. Stay focused in the present—here and now—because that is all you can control anyway.
6. **Have patience.** If you are overwhelmed by the thought of confronting an anxiety-triggering situation, take it one step at a time. Do not get in a hurry.

Types of anxiety. Many times the basis of our anxiety is so vague it is very difficult to explain what we are really feeling. As Rollo May suggests above, anxiety may occur in slight or great intensity. It may be mild tension before going for an important job interview, or it may be mild apprehension before taking an examination. These are common examples of *preparation anxiety*, which helps us get energized to deliver our best.

The emotional tension that we commonly refer to as anxiety also functions as a signal of potential danger. For example, "I better study for that test, or I will flunk!" However, when the perception of the threatening experience is blown way out of proportion to the actual danger posed, and rises to the level that our anxiety hinders daily functioning, it becomes extreme anxiety, or *"neurotic" anxiety*. A common example of this is when a student loses his "cool" over a test: "I can't do it—I just know I am going to flunk" and *goes totally blank.* Is this normal anxiety or neurotic anxiety?

There is a great difference between worry and concern. A worried person sees a problem, and a concerned person solves a problem.
—HAROLD STEPHENS

Olivia Remes discusses how being kinder to ourselves and to others can help us cope with anxiety.

Worry is a form of anxiety (Leahy, 2011). For example, it is normal for people to worry about future events they are going to be involved in and whose outcome they are uncertain about. However, some people worry and lose sleep over things that never happen. Does this ever happen to you? In recent years, researchers have learned that there is a genetic component to anxiety; some people seem to be born worriers (Gorman, 2002).

The difference in normal and neurotic anxiety may be in one's ability to handle or cope with the anxiety-producing situation. Just ask yourself, "Am I in control of this situation, or is the anxiety controlling how I react to this situation?"

The fears that resulted from the World Trade Center bombing of September, 11, 2001 have been minimal for some individuals, and for others the anxiety has led to extreme overreactions. In the wake of the most horrendous bombing attack in American history, it is healthy to feel some fear and anxiety. Dr. Brad Schmidt (2002), an expert on fear, reminds us, "Just don't allow that fear to defeat you."

ANGER

Be not hasty in thy spirit to be angry: for anger resteth in the bosom of fools.
—ECCLESIASTES 7:9

Anger is a signal that tells us that we do not like what is going on. **Anger** refers to a feeling of extreme displeasure, usually brought about by interference with our needs or desires. Anger is an emotion characterized by antagonism toward someone or something you feel has deliberately wronged you. Anger can be a good thing. It can give you a way to express negative feelings, for example, or motivate you to find solutions to problems. But excessive anger can cause problems. Increased blood pressure and other physical changes associated with anger make it difficult to think clearly and harm your physical and mental health (APA, 2016).

Therefore, anger can range from mild to very strong (Parker Hall, 2008). Carol Tavris (1989) has identified several forms of anger:

Carrying resentment is like taking poison and hoping the other person dies.
—MALACHY MCCOURT

- **Hate** may be thought of as intense anger felt toward a specific person or persons.
- **Annoyance** is used to describe a mild form of anger.
- **Rage** describes intense anger and implies that the anger is expressed through violent physical activity.
- **Hostility** is a mild form of anger/hate directed to a specific person or group; often it is unintentionally conveyed to others, either verbally or nonverbally.
- **Resentment** is chronic anger that may be entirely subjective. It is a combination of the emotions and actions and thought patterns resulting from our unresolved anger at an injustice. *Resentment comes from anger just as smoke comes from fire.*

Remember, anger is a completely normal, usually healthy, human emotion. However, when it gets out of control and turns destructive, it can lead to problems. It can become problematic, leading to fractured or difficult relationships at work, problems at home, and in the overall quality of your life. And, it can lead you to you feel as though you're at the mercy of an unpredictable and powerful emotion (Nay, 2010). It can lead people to treat you with fear and emotional distance, because they feel you will snap at them. It is helpful to remember that when you are angry at someone, you are the one with the problem; therefore, you must be the one to correct the problem. Anger most often begins with a loss or the threat of a loss, such as (Lerner, 2014):

- **Anger** is a very powerful emotion, and one that requires a balance between spontaneous expression and rational control.
- **Loss of self-esteem.** We get angry when we think we have failed or "let ourselves down."
- **Loss of face.** Public exposure of one's failures or inadequacies can be both humiliating and infuriating.
- **Threat of physical harm or violence.** Anger helps activate our instinct for self-preservation.
- **Loss of valued possessions, skills, or abilities.** Regardless of who is to blame, losing something we are proud of can trigger both hurt and anger.
- **Loss of a valued role.** If we lose a part of our life, such as a job, which is important to our identity, we may feel angry at having the role removed.
- **Loss of valued relationships.** Anger is often a response to the loss of an important relationship.

Now stop and think for a moment about the times you have experienced genuine anger. Do you agree that your anger began with some loss, or even the threat of a loss, you incurred? Which type of loss just described were you dealing with?

HOW TO MANAGE YOUR ANGER

Anger Do's and Don'ts

- Do speak up when an issue is important to you.
- Do take time out to think about the problem and clarify your position.
- Do speak in "I" language: "I feel."
- Do try to appreciate the fact that people are different.
- Do recognize that each person is responsible for his or her own behavior.
- Do avoid speaking through a third party.
- Don't strike while the iron is hot. Cool off and then discuss it.
- Don't use "below-the-belt" unethical tactics.
- Don't blame the other person.
- Don't tell another person what she or he thinks or feels or "should" think or feel.
- Don't participate in repetitive arguments that go nowhere.
- Don't expect change to come about from hit-and-run confrontations.   —Lerner (2014)

PHYSICAL SYMPTOMS OF ANGER

One way to learn how to manage your anger is to recognize the physical signs as they occur. This gives you the chance to use different anger management tips when anger first starts.

Anger affects the gastrointestinal, cardiovascular, and musculoskeletal systems.

Some signs are:

- Headache
- Stomachache
- Constipation
- Clenching of the jaw
- Grinding your teeth
- Rapid heartbeat
- Increased blood pressure
- Sweating, especially on the palms
- Feeling warm or flushed, especially around the face or neck
- Shakiness
- Dizziness

Your emotions also start to change when you start getting angry. You may start to feel:

- Irritation
- Sad or depressed
- Resentful
- Guilty
- Anxious
- Like you want to lash out at someone
- Like you want to get away, to escape the situation

There may be other signs that can tip you off to an episode of anger:

- You begin to raise your voice
- You feel on the verge of crying
- You adopt a sarcastic tone
- You lose your sense of humor
- You start pacing back and forth
- You may want a drink or other substance to help relax you

There may be other signs that can tip you off to an episode of anger.

While some of these signs may be subtle, you can learn to change your behavior if you are aware of the symptoms and signs of your anger before they happen.

(https://stress.lovetoknow.com 2019)

There are four *psychological reactions* to anger. They are:

1. seeing yourself as a victim,
2. feeling discounted or ignored,
3. feeling powerless, and
4. looking for justice and revenge.

In dealing with these psychological reactions to anger, it is important to remember the characteristics of anger.

- **Anger can be misdirected.** Everybody gets angry. Haim Ginott (2003) confirms this but provides some limits, too: You have the right to get angry, but you do not have the right to attack vulnerable people or their character traits.
- **You are vulnerable when angry.** Anger is triggered by a sense of loss. Loss, or the absence of a person or quality important to us is a vulnerable place. We often feel less secure and stable when we lose a beloved person in our lives or even a treasured possession. The sudden change creates an instability in our lives that leaves us off balance. You may say or act in ways that are totally uncharacteristic of you.

4 Tips To Diffuse Anger

1. When you're upset, pause, and slowly count to ten.
   To offset the adrenaline surge of anger, train yourself not to lash back impulsively. Wait before you speak. Take a few deep breaths and *very* slowly, silently, count to ten (or to fifty if necessary). Use the lull of these moments to regroup before you decide what to do so you don't say something you regret.
2. Take a cooling-off period.
   To further quiet your neurotransmitters, take an extended time-out; hours or even longer. When you're steaming, retreat to a calm setting to lower your stress level. Reduce external stimulation. Dim the lights. Listen to soothing music. Meditate. Do some aerobic exercise or yoga to expel anger from your system.
3. Don't address anger when you're rushed.
   Make sure you have adequate time to identify what's made you angry. A Princeton study found that even after theology students heard a lecture on the Good Samaritan, they still didn't stop to help a distressed person on the street when they thought they'd be late for their next class. Thus, allotting unhurried time to resolve the conflict lets you tap into your most compassionate response.
4. Don't try to address your anger when you're tired or before sleep.
   Since anger revs up your system, it can interfere with restful sleep and cause insomnia. The mind grinds. Better to examine your anger earlier in the day so your adrenaline can simmer down. Also, being well rested makes you less prone to reacting with irritation, and allows you to stay balanced.

The goal with anger is to own the moment so this emotion doesn't own you. Then you can mindfully respond rather than simply react. You'll have the lucidity to be solution-oriented, and therefore empower how you relate to others. (Orloff, 2011)

Sometimes anger triggers more anger. Uncontrolled anger leads to bitterness, hatred, and even violence. if you read daily police reports, notice the assaults and even murders that occur because people are angry and lose control of their emotions. Sometimes people even strike out at others with aggressive behavior.

If you are patient in one moment of anger, you will escape a hundred days of sorrow.
—CHINESE PROVERB

- **Anger can be expressed in right or wrong ways.** It is important to remember that anger released in inappropriate ways destroys relationships. This most often occurs when we *displace* our anger toward important people onto other relationships. In this way, anger at a boss gets deflected onto our spouse, anger at a spouse onto our child, and so on. Because we trust them to accept us as we are, we often unconsciously choose our strongest relationships as a "dumping ground" for our anger (Simon, 2005). Researchers have found that associating an object with anger actually makes people want the object—a kind of motivation that's normally associated with positive emotions. "People are motivated to do something or obtain a certain object in the world because it's rewarding for them. Usually this means that the object is positive and makes you happy," says Henk Aarts of Utrecht University in the Netherlands (APA, 2010).

- **Anger can be released by taking action to address the perceived loss or injustice.** Such action can take the form of working for change, or it can take the form of physical activity like exercise. It may also devolve into attacks upon systems or individuals perceived as causes of the initial loss or damage. Such attacks are unproductive and frustrating; they may lead to situations of further damage and eventual legal consequences.

Aggression. *Aggression* is any behavior that is intended to hurt someone, either verbally or physically (Weiten, 2016). Curses and insults are much more common than shootings or fistfights, but aggression of any kind can be a real problem. Why do people behave in such fashion? Some psychologists believe that aggression is largely learned in humans. Albert Bandura (2008), a proponent of social learning theory, indicates that aggressive models in subcultures, families, and the media all play a part in increasing the level of aggression in our society. Bandura and other researchers also believe that violence in films, television, video games, and other media not only desensitizes us to violence (that is, makes it less bothersome) but also induces aggressive thoughts, feelings, and behavior in children and adults (Anderson et al., 2007). Research suggests that violent media can cause aggressive behavior in children and that this behavior can be incredibly problematic if violent media includes guns. Indeed, children are incredibly curious about guns, and they can have difficulty understanding the difference between real and toy guns (Benjamin, Kepes, & Bushman, 2017).

There is recent research suggesting that guns don't need to be featured in the media to cause aggression; the mere presence of a gun is enough to elicit aggressive behavior. For example, having a gun sitting on a table makes people behave more aggressively (Berkowitz & LePage, 1967), and recent work shows that having a gun in the car makes people (even non-gun owners) more aggressive drivers (Bushman, Kerwin, Whitlock, & Weisenberger, 2017). These effects even exist in children, whether or not the gun is real or is just a toy (Benjamin Kepes, & Bushman, 2017).

Expressing anger. Anger is a very powerful emotion, and one that requires a balance between spontaneous expression and rational control. Again, it is helpful to remember that when you are angry at someone, you are the one with the problem; therefore, you must be the one to correct the problem. Anger is like fire. Sometimes it can be useful, sometimes it can be destructive, sometimes it can feel that we just can't get a spark started although we feel like we're sitting on a powder keg. We're all human and we all have anger, whether others see us as angry and bitter or smiling and carefree (Howie, 2015). The question now might be: How do we express our anger? Carol Tavris (1989) suggests that we have been told that, if we vent our anger, we will experience the following:

- Improved communication and closeness with the target of our anger,
- Physiological relief and catharsis,
- Resolution of problems instead of brooding about them, and
- We will just feel better, because we addressed the feeling.

Tavris goes on further to say that sometimes we get the benefits of this list, but most frequently, we get exactly the opposite:

- Decreased communication and feelings of closeness with the target of our anger,
- Physiological arousal and even higher blood pressure,
- The problem becomes worse, and
- We frequently just rehearse the anger and get angrier.

The question then is, how can we ensure the benefits and avoid the "exact opposites"? Psychologist Harriet Lerner (2004) feels that the expression of anger provides maximum results when the Do's and Don'ts under How to Manage Your Anger (above) are followed. Also, you will find the discussion dealing with resolving interpersonal conflict through the use of "I" messages in Chapter Seven helpful in dealing with your anger.

How about learning to shift your anger from an emotional level to an intellectual level? It is possible to manage anger by learning to question your anger. Redford Williams, director of the Behavioral Medicine Research Center at Duke University Medical Center in Durham, North Carolina, suggests asking yourself four questions whenever you feel angry: 1) Is this important?, 2) Is my anger appropriate?, 3) Is the situation modifiable, and 4) Is it worth taking action? Such evaluation helps convert your anger into rational thought. The anger is then responsive to you, instead of the other way around. Williams further suggests that if the answers to those questions are all "yes," decide what result you want, make a plan, and follow it. Even one "no" means you need to reevaluate your anger as a response to the situation (Foltz-Gray, 2002).

> *Anyone can become angry. That is easy. But to be angry with the right person to the right degree, at the right time for the right purpose, and in the right way: This is not easy.*
> —ARISTOTLE

> *It hurts to lose something important. It hurts worse to pretend otherwise. To expect more than reality can offer only sets you up to hurt badly and needlessly.*
> —DAVID VISCOTT

Becoming Aware—Study Skills: 8 Things to STOP Doing When You Wake Up in the Morning
https://www.youtube.com/watch?v=sBfng6Jd4Cc

Thomas Frank breaks down eight common habits that you need to remove from your mornings if you're currently doing them.

Cyberbullies Increasingly Target Peers Online

Mary Aiken works in the new field of **cyber psychology.** Anger against friends and others is a concern in cyberbullying. The belief that the cyber environment is safer than real life and connecting to people online is safer than meeting them in person is an illusion. Aiken feels that "people behave differently when they are interacting with technology than they do in the real world" (Aiken, 2016). She observed we are more altruistic online than in giving face to face. She also believes that people are more trusting of others they meet online; they may quickly disclose too much information. She has observed human behavior is often amplified and accelerated online (Aiken, 2016). We can see this with the changing role of selfies, sexting, and flirting on social networks. Bullying and stalking have become quite common as well, most likely because people feel anonymous online.

Sexting means using a phone, computer, or camera to take or send sexy messages or images—usually selfies. But sexts can outlast your crush or even your relationship. Remember, once you click send, there's no way to get your pictures and messages back. PlannedParenthood.org has an informative section on teen bullying, sexting, privacy, and safety at https://www.plannedparenthood.org/learn/teens/bullying-safety-privacy/all-about-sexting (2019).

Bullying is when one person picks on another person again and again. Usually children who are being bullied are either weaker or smaller, are shy, and generally feel helpless. The experience of being bullied is challenging and upsetting. It can negatively impact a person's mental health and can alter the path a person takes, depending on how the situation is handled. The Pew Research Center's survey found that 55% of teens said bullying was a major problem among their peers, while a third called gangs a major problem (Desilver, 2019).

Bullying is used as a strategy to establish and maintain social dominance, and groups are often organized in dominant hierarchies. Dominance is not an end in itself, but a means to get prioritized access to the resources that are valued for the group. Individuals can use aggressive and agonistic strategies as well as prosocial and cooperative strategies in order to position themselves in the dominant hierarchy.

Deiter Wolfe (2019) found that children are more likely to be bullied by a sibling if they have more than one, and firstborn children and older brothers are most likely to bully siblings, a new study finds. Wolfe noted that sibling bullying "does not discriminate. It occurs in wealthy families just as much as lower-income families and it occurs in single-parent households just as much as two-parent households." Wolke said in a journal news release that "Despite our cultural differences, humans are still very biologically driven. A firstborn child will have their resources halved with the birth of a sibling, and even more so as more siblings are added to the family" (Preidt, 2019).

As more of life has become digital and online, bullies have gone there, too. The problem with online bullies is that they are faceless and often harder to identify and stop than bullies who are physically present. The negative effect, though, is no less significant, on children and on adolescents. In fact, online bullying—**cyberbullying**—may be worse; anonymous bullies can make you feel like everyone is against you. It is the most common negative situation that can happen to any of our kids while they are spending time in the online space.

Robert Preidt (2019) found that cyberbullying among teens is highly likely to involve current or former friends and dating partners. Researchers analyzed data from a 2011 survey of nearly 800 students in grades 8 through 12 at a public school in a New York City suburb. About 17% had been involved with cyberbullying in the previous week, the study found. Nearly 6% of those students were victims, about 9% were aggressors; and about 2% were both. Cyberbullying usually occurred through social media or texting, the study author said. "A common concern regarding cyberbullying is that strangers can attack someone, but here we see evidence that there are significant risks associated with close connections," lead author Diane Felmlee said in an American Sociological Association news release. Felmlee called "the large magnitude of the effects of close relationships on the likelihood of cyberbullying" surprising (2016).

Although research has examined the relationship between online bullying and depression, the University of Buffalo NY study is one of few to explore the connection between cyber victimization and sleep quality. The study surveyed more than 800 adolescents for sleep quality, cyber aggression, and depression.

The research was presented by Misol Kwon, first author and doctoral student in the UB School of Nursing, at SLEEP 2019, the 33rd annual meeting of the Associated Professional Sleep Societies in San Antonio, Texas. Nearly 15% of high school students reported being bullied online. "Cyber victimization on the internet and social media is a unique form of peer victimization and an emerging mental health concern among teens who are digital natives," said Kwon. "Understanding these associations supports the need to provide sleep hygiene education and risk prevention and interventions to mistreated kids who show signs and symptoms of depression."

Nearly one third of teens have experienced symptoms of depression, which, in addition to changes in sleep pattern, include persistent irritability, anger, and social withdrawal, according to the U.S. Office of Adolescent Health. And nearly 15% of U.S. high school students report being bullied electronically, says Kwon. At severe levels, depression may lead to disrupted school performance, harmed relationships or suicide.

The risks of allowing depression to worsen highlight the need for researchers and clinicians to understand and target sleep quality and other risk factors that have the potential to exacerbate the disorder (University of Buffalo, 2019).

> We believe that competition for status and esteem represents one reason behind peer cyberbullying. Friends, or former friends, are particularly likely to find themselves in situations in which they are vying for the same school, club, and/or sport positions and social connections.
>
> In terms of dating partners, young people often have resentful and hurt feelings as a result of a breakup, and they may take out these feelings on a former partner via cyber aggression. They might also believe they can win

back a previous boyfriend or girlfriend, or prevent that person from breaking up with them or dating someone else, by embarrassing or harassing him or her. (Felmlee, 2016).

Becoming Aware of Technology—Technology and Bullying: Trolls, Cry Bullyies and Passive Aggressive Bullying in the Attention economics Internet age

The American Psychological Association defines bullying as "a form of aggressive behavior in which someone intentionally and repeatedly causes another person injury or discomfort. Bullying can take the form of physical contact, words, or more subtle actions." A bully can be an aggressive juvenile, an intimidating boss or colleague, a controlling romantic partner, an unruly neighbor, a high pressure sales/business representative, a condescending family member, a shaming social acquaintance, or those in a variety of other types of abusive relationships and it has now moved to the Internet according to Ni (2017).

Passive-aggressive or covert bullying is a less frequently mentioned form of bullying, but in some ways it's the most insidious. With many bullies, we can see them coming because they are quick to make their intimidating presence known. A passive-aggressive or covert bully behaves appropriately on the surface, but takes us down with subtlety, especially online. The attention economy of the INTERNET has been a good thing for passive-aggressive trolls, and some people hide behind the INTERNET.

David Brooks, columnist for the *New York Times*, commented when communication styles change, so do people. In 1982, the scholar Walter Ong described the way, centuries ago, a shift from an oral to a printed culture transformed human consciousness. Once, storytelling was a shared experience, with emphasis on proverb, parable, and myth. With the onset of the printing press it became a more private experience, the content of that storytelling more realistic and linear. New social types emerge in such a communications regime. The most prominent new type of bully is the troll in online technology (2019). Many types of tangible, verbal, and passive-aggressive bullying behavior can be conveyed online via social media, texting, video, email, online discussion, and other digital formats. Think about it; identity theft is also a form of **cyberbullying**.

Becoming Aware of Technology and Cyberbullying: Smartphones Could Be Correlated with Teen Depression: Why We Need to Talk About Kids & Phones
https://www.youtube.com/watch?v=SJXLPShSJTs

A discussion of why we need to talk about kids and phones

Trolls bid for attention by trying to make others feel bad. Studies of people who troll find that they score high on measures of psychopathy, sadism, and narcissism (Brooks, 2019). Online media hasn't made them vicious; they're just vicious. The online platform has given them a platform to use viciousness to full effect. Brooks writes, trolls also score high on cognitive empathy. Intellectually, they understand other people's emotions and how to make them suffer. But they score low on affective empathy. They don't feel others' pain, so when they hurt you, they don't care (Brooks, 2019).

Trolling is a very effective way to generate attention in a competitive, volatile attention economy. It's a way to feel righteous and important, especially if you claim to be trolling on behalf of some marginalized group. Attention economics considers awareness, recognition, and action thereof to be integral to economic decision making (World Atlas, 2019).

Another prominent personality type in this attention economy is the **cry-bully**. This is the person who takes his or her own pain and victimization and uses it to make sure every conversation revolves around himself or herself. The cry-bully starts with a genuine trauma. The terrible thing that happened naturally makes the cry-bully feel unsafe, self-protective, and self-conscious to the point of self-absorption. The trauma makes that person intensely concerned about self-image (Brooks, 2019).

The problem comes from the subsequent need to control any situation, the failure to see the big picture, and the tendency to lash out in fear and anger as a way to fixate attention on oneself and obliterate others. Brooks mentions that cry-bullying is at the heart of many of our campus de-platforming (taking down INTERNET sites) and censorship outrages.

Brooks believes trolling, cry-bullying, and other attention-grabbing tactics emerge out of a feeling of weakness, and create a climate that causes more pain, in which it is not safe to lead with vulnerability, not safe to test out ideas or do the things that create genuine companionship (2019).

The INTERNET has become a place where people communicate out of their competitive ego: I'm more fabulous than you (a lot of **Instagram**). You're dumber than me (much of **Twitter**). It's not a place where people share from their hearts and souls. Of course, people enmeshed in such a climate are more likely to feel depressed, and to suffer from mental health problems.

Disturbing Cyberbullying Statistics

Techjury reports about:

- 38% of cyberbullying victims are willing to admit it to their parents
- 34% of kids in the US have experienced cyberbullying at least once
- Global cyberbullying awareness is at 75%
- 210 out of 1,000 victims of bullying are high school girls with a different skin color
- Over 80% of children own a mobile phone and have multiple social network accounts
- 42% of LGBT youth have experienced cyberbullying
- 33% of young respondents have sent explicit images or text to someone else at least once
- 66% of female victims have feelings of powerlessness because of cyberbullying

The simplest definition of **cyberbullying** is a form of harassment that employs electronic forms of contact. Online bullying statistics encompass a variety of shapes and forms of this aggressive behavior—hate speech, sexual remarks, stalking, trolling, and ridicule. Techjury.net believes if we ignore this toxic behavior, it can easily escalate to criminal levels like impersonation, leaking private images/video, even death threats. (Petrov, February 28, 2019).

Ybarra and Mitchell (2006) found, in earlier research, that cyberbullying among teens and preteens had increased by 50% in the preceding five years as youths increasingly chronicled their lives on Web logs, or "blogs," and socialized online through chat rooms, instant-messaging, and other social media. Examples included receiving unnerving messages relating to their appearance or containing disturbingly personal details or threats of being assaulted at school. Others said harassers threatened to spread rumors about them or post embarrassing photos of them online.

Facebook had many people complaining about **cyberbullying** and the use of **hate speech**. It is one of several types of content that Facebook reviews, in addition to threats and harassment. Facebook defines hate speech as an **attack**, such as a degrading generalization or slur.

Targeting a "**protected category**" of people, including one based on sex, race, ethnicity, religious affiliation, national origin, sexual orientation, gender identity, and serious disability or disease (FACEBOOK HATE SPEECH 2019). They have also created a **Bullying safety hub** at https://www.facebook.com/safety/bullying.

New evidence suggests that adolescent bullying and victimization may have origins in the home. Many bullies have parents who are hostile, punitive, and rejecting. A unique longitudinal study provides a more complete understanding of how parents' belittling and critical interactions with adolescents thwart their ability to maintain positive relationships with peers. Derisive parenting precipitates a cycle of negative affect and anger between parents and children.

The study, published in the *Journal of Youth and Adolescence*, emphasizes the emotional underpinnings of peer difficulties. The researchers followed 1,409 children for three consecutive years from grades 7 to 9 (ages 13–15 years).

Findings show that derisive parenting fosters dysregulated anger in adolescent children. Dysregulated anger is indicative of difficulties regulating emotion, which typically result in negative emotions, verbal and physical aggression, and hostility. Increases in dysregulated anger, in turn, place adolescents at greater risk for bullying and victimization, and for becoming bully-victims (bullies who also are victimized by other bullies).

The latter finding is noteworthy given that past research indicates that bully-victims are at the greatest risk for poor mental health, behavioral difficulties, and suicidal thoughts when compared to "pure" victims, "pure" bullies, or non-victims. Identification of the family-specific origins of bully-victim status may be a key step in limiting or preventing such poor outcomes (Florida Atlantic University (2019).

Being Bullied

Evans and Chapman (2014) suggest a relationship between being called gay, lesbian, and queer and the most extensive experiences of bullying including physical, cyber, and relational victimization. Youth who experience social and emotional bullying, and youth who experience all forms of social and physical bullying (including being bullied by being called gay, lesbian, or queer) are at a high risk of experiencing all forms of bullying behavior, highlighting the importance of increased support for these vulnerable students (2014). This has also been similar to the research of Diane Felmlee and Robert Faris (2016) in the *Social Psychology Journal.* They found approximately 17% of the NY students reported some involvement in cyber aggression within the past week. LGBTQ youth were targeted at a rate over four times that of their heterosexual peers, and females were more frequent victims than males. Rates of cyber aggression were 4.3 times higher between friends than between friends of friends (Felmlee & Faris, 2016).

"Some people try to be tall by cutting off the heads of others."
—PARAMHANSA YOGANANDA

Two interpretations of their survey findings are possible.

First, the victims of bullying may comprise youth who are particularly susceptible to bullying and are bullied in several different ways. In this case, the actual or perceived sexual orientation of the victim does not affect the bullying; homophobic name-calling is one technique in the bullies' arsenal of bullying tactics (Evans and Chapman, 2014).

A second possibility is that the victim openly identifies as LGBTQ or is perceived by others to be LGBTQ, and therefore, the youth is bullied by being called gay, lesbian, or queer due to their actual or perceived sexual orientation. The youth in the 2014 survey (whether they identified as LGBTQ or not) had nearly equal probabilities of reporting that they were bullied (87% and 90%, respectively), indicating that most youth who have experienced the behaviors assessed in the study define those behaviors as bullying. (Evans & Chapman, 2014).

So what do you do when you are bullied? It may be hard to do, but tell someone! Start with your loyal friends, then parents, teachers, caregivers, and administrators.

- **Try not to react to the bully and not give into their demands.** A bully likes scaring others and often tries to get the victim to cry or become visibly upset in other ways. Save all emails, notes, or online notes.
- Form strong friendships for yourself (you need a loyal friend preferably with people you MEET IN PERSON, NOT ONLINE).
- Have your parents talk to the other parents, school staff, and advocates to determine what may have gone on.

A new form of cyberbullying has been started by innocently sending photos or selfies to your latest love. Sexting is sending, receiving, or forwarding sexually explicit messages, photographs, or images, primarily between mobile phones, of oneself to others. It may also include the use of a computer or any digital device. You might think that sexting is just a harmless way to flirt or show your boyfriend or girlfriend that you're into them. But sexts can outlast your crush, or even your relationship (Planned parenthood.org)

Think about it and remember . . . once you click send, there's no way to get your pictures and messages back. Sexting can cause serious problems, whether you send them or share them. The pics might get shared or posted online, where people like your family, teachers, and friends could see them. Sharing these pictures or messages without permission is a serious violation of privacy, and isn't okay. And if the pictures you send or share are of someone under 18 (even if that's you), you could even be arrested for child pornography, which is a serious crime.

For more information, go to https://www.plannedparenthood.org/learn/teens/bullying-safety-privacy/all-about-sexting

Think/Pair/Share Activity

TECHNOLOGY

Take a moment to **Become Aware** of this online issue.

How the Internet turns us into trolls

https://www.youtube.com/watch?v=bRQrk2tbAEA

After watching this online, discuss in your group or friends and share your thoughts and experiences with the class or friends.

The 2016 book *The Cyber Effect,* by Mary Aiken, examines the escalation of cyberstalking, and organized cybercrime in the Deep Web. Aiken provides horrifying statistics and incredible-but-true case studies of hidden trends that are shaping our culture and raising troubling questions about where the digital revolution is taking us. She also covers a wide range of subjects, from the impact of computer screens on the developing child to the explosion of teen sexting, and how rapid addictive behaviors are growing such as online gaming, shopping, and pornography. Dr. Aiken examines the escalation of cyberchondria (which is anxiety produced by self-diagnosing online), cyberstalking, and organized cybercrime in the Deep Web:

> At this moment in time we can describe cyberspace as a place, separate from us, but very soon that distinction will become blurred. By the time we get to 2020, when we are alone and immersed in our smart homes and smarter cars, clad in our wearable technologies, our babies in captivity seats with iPads thrust in their visual field, our kids all wearing face-obscuring helmets, when our sense of self has fractured into a dozen different social-network platforms, when sex is something that requires logging in and a password, when we are competing for our lives with robots for jobs, and dark thoughts and forces have pervaded, syndicated, and colonized cyberspace, we might wish we'd paid more attention. As we set out on this journey, into the first quarter of the twenty-first century, what do we have now that we can't afford to lose? (Aiken, 2016)

246

Of course, they are more likely to see human relationships through the abuser/victim frame, and to be acutely sensitive to any power imbalance. Imagine you're 17 and people you barely know are saying nice or nasty things about your unformed self. It creates existential anxiety, and hence fanaticism (Brooks, 2019).

Name-calling and rumor-spreading have long been an unpleasant and challenging aspect of adolescent life. But the proliferation of smartphones and the rise of social media has transformed where, when and how bullying takes place. A new Pew Research Center survey finds that 59% of U.S. teens have personally experienced at least one of six types of abusive online behaviors (2018 Anderson). At the same time, teens mostly think teachers, social media companies and politicians are failing at addressing this issue.

While similar shares of boys and girls have encountered abuse, such as name-calling or physical threats online, other forms of cyberbullying are more prevalent among girls. Some 39% of girls say someone has spread false rumors about them online, compared with 26% of boys who say this.

Girls also are more likely than boys to report being the recipient of explicit images they did not ask for (29% vs. 20%). And being the target of these types of messages is an especially common experience for older girls: 35% of girls ages 15 to 17 say they have received unwanted explicit images, compared with about one-in-five boys in this age range and younger teens of both genders (Anderson, Rainie, 2018).

Online harassment does not necessarily begin and end with one specific behavior, and 40% of teens have experienced two or more of these actions. Girls are more likely than boys to have experienced several different forms of online bullying. Some 15% of teen girls have been the target of at least four of these online behaviors, compared with 6% of boys. These behaviors are offensive name-calling, spreading false rumors, physical threats, and inquiring who they are with, what are they doing (Anderson, 2018).

In addition to these gender differences, teens from lower-income families are more likely than those from higher-income families to encounter certain forms of online bullying. For example, 24% of teens whose household income is less than $30,000 a year say they have been the target of physical threats online, compared with 12% whose annual household income is $75,000 or more. However, teens' experiences with these issues do not statistically differ by race or ethnicity, or by their parent's level of educational attainment (Anderson, 2018).

Guilt and Shame

Two other powerful emotions that can rule our lives are guilt and shame. **Guilt**, in its simplest form, is the remorse over having done something morally, socially, or ethically wrong. Although shame is an emotion that is closely related to guilt, it is important to understand the difference. **Shame** can be defined as a painful emotion caused by consciousness of guilt, shortcoming, or impropriety. David Burns (2019) indicates that, when we feel guilt, *it is about something we did or did not do.* When we feel shame, *it's about who we are as a person.* Shame is often a much stronger and more profound emotion than guilt. Shame and vulnerability researcher Dr.

Guilt is feeling bad for what you have done or not done, while shame is feeling bad for who you are, measured against some standard of perfection or acceptability.
—HAROLD KUSHNER

Brené Brown has studied the power of these intensely painful feelings. Brown says shame is the most primitive human emotion we all feel—and the one no one wants to talk about (Brown, 2007). "I think shame is lethal," she says. "I think shame is deadly. And I think we are swimming in it deep." Brown explains that feelings of shame can quietly marinate over a lifetime. "Here's the bottom line with shame," she says. "The less you talk about it, the more you got it. Shame needs three things to grow exponentially in our lives: secrecy, silence, and judgment" (2018, pg. 188). By keeping quiet, Brown says, shame will grow exponentially. "It will creep into every corner and crevice of your life," she says. The antidote, Brown says, is **empathy**. She explains that, if you talk about your shame with a friend who expresses empathy, the painful feeling cannot survive. "Shame depends on me buying into the belief that I'm alone," she says. "Shame cannot survive being spoken. It cannot survive empathy" (2018, pg. 68).

You can do it
Sometimes, everyone we have
ever trusted turns their back
on us and we are left
wading in a puddle of
disappointment and self-shame
and we can't tell the difference in
the muddy water and our tears
but they invented rain boots for
a reason and we will overcome
because puddles are not oceans
and we will not let ourselves drown
because despite all the weight we carry
we will rise and rise and rise
until the ocean is just a puddle.

—Colton Snead

Experts in human behavior report that unjustified, excessive guilt and shame can sour our enjoyment of living, disrupt our social and business lives, worry, dishearten, and even humiliate us. They can cause fears and anxieties and even torment a person to the point of suicide. As you can see, tragedy and much human suffering have been triggered by needless feelings of guilt and shame. Guilt and shame are not always bad, however. Andrew Rosenthal (2009), founder of Happier.com and researcher with Martin Seligman, has this to say:

I would not want to enhance one's ability to block out the sense of shame or guilt; these emotions help stabilize society and provide disincentives for destructive behavior. Without shame or guilt, we would fail to learn effectively from mistakes. These fundamental *emotions are at the core of what it means to be human* (Rosenthal, 2009).

Becoming Aware of Feelings-Shame
https://youtu.be/L0ifUM1DYKg

Brené Brown on listening to shame

"Shame [is] highly correlated with addiction, depression, eating disorders, violence, bullying and aggression. Guilt? Inversely correlated with those." Therefore, the ability to change the self-talk—and believe it—can dramatically affect the outcomes of those measures and others (Brown, 2007, p. 13). An extreme to negative self talk, shame, guilt, and body image is body dysmorphic disorder (BDD). It is a distinct mental disorder in which a person is preoccupied with an imagined physical defect or a minor defect that others often cannot see. As a result, people with this disorder see themselves as "ugly" and often avoid social exposure or turn to plastic surgery to try to improve their appearance. If someone has this issue a mental health expert needs to be contacted to discuss the issue. Search: www.webmd.com/ for mental health.

How To Deal With Guilt

- **Examine why you feel guilty.** Take a long inward look, seeking the reason for your feelings. It is important to remember that powerful guilt feelings are sometimes pushed far beneath the layers of our conscious thinking. In such cases, professional help may be needed to help bring them to the surface. The point is to find out exactly why you feel guilty.
- **Determine whether you really need to feel guilty.** Reappraise all the rules that have been set down for you during your lifetime. Take a whole new look at the principles, not created by yourself, but prescribed by parents, friends, society, and others. Are these principles realistic and valid for you at your stage of life and relevant in the society in which you now live and work?
- **Do what is right for you.** Make decisions that sound "good" to you. No one can tell you how you should live your life. You must make your own decisions about what is right and what is wrong. Do not live your life by listening to what other people say you should or should not do. Obviously, you will have to accept the consequences of your choices, but be your own person.
- **Forgive yourself.** Learn to accept the fact that perfection is an unattainable ideal. Mistakes happen. If you have done something morally or ethically wrong, accept it and forget it. Apologize if you can or correct the misdeed in whatever way is proper. Say nothing if you will hurt someone else grievously, recognizing that "telling all" is actually asking for punishment to ease your sense of guilt. It is possible to feel sorry about something without feeling guilty. The point is that you will need to tell yourself and also internalize that you have done something wrong, that it was wrong, and do your best to make amends.

Grief and Bereavement

Coping with losing a loved one is one of life's more difficult, yet inevitable tasks. *Grief and bereavement*, sometimes even referred to as mourning, can be defined as "to be deprived." In *mourning*, we use our memory to recall the deceased and what was great about them, and then try to move on in our own lives (Simonini, 2011). The grief process consists of 1) freeing ourselves emotionally from the loss, 2) readjusting to life without this loss, and 3) resuming ordinary activities and forming new relationships (Dickenson & Leming, 2020).

Grief has long been broken down into stages. One cycle made famous by Elisabeth Kübler-Ross, M.D. (1997) uses stages of denial, anger, bargaining, depression, and acceptance. However, researchers have shown that stages don't always apply. Camille Wortman, Ph.D.

and Roxane Cohen Silver, Ph.D. have found that there are individual patterns of grieving. For example, some people suffer profound grief, some interminable grief, and others show no distress at all. Furthermore, while some people recover in a year, some individuals find the second year to be much worse, and others have difficulty for several years. The response depends on the individual, the relationship of the loss, and the circumstances surrounding the loss (Greenberg, 2003). There is no correct way to grieve (Freeman, 2005). A recent development is that some individuals use a deceased person's Facebook page to express their grief and connect with the person they lost.

Dealing with the loss. While there are individual differences in how people grieve, some common reactions might be sense of shock and disbelief, especially when death occurs unexpectedly. When we've been anticipating a person's death, the initial response may be subdued, often accompanied by a sense of relief. In general, we may experience unexpected memories of the deceased, and feelings of expected sadness to various degrees of depression are very, very common. Emotions, such as anger and guilt, may even surface, particularly if the loss was due to suicide. Regardless of the circumstances surrounding the loss, we may have feelings of guilt over things we said, did, or feel we should have done while the person was still alive. It is not even uncommon to experience *survivor's guilt,* that is, feeling guilty simply because we are still alive and the other person is not.

It is important to emphasize that we never get over the loss of someone to whom we feel especially close. We just learn to adjust to the loss. We get used to the loss, and we "reinvest" in a new reality. *Grief work*, the process of freeing ourselves emotionally from the deceased and readjusting to life without that person, takes time. We will need a strong support system of family and friends to aid us in our progress. (Some of the suggestions below may be helpful in assisting a grieving friend.) People who are fortunate to work through their grief may eventually find it becomes a positive growth experience—sometimes called *good grief* (Welshons & Dyer, 2003).

Granger Westburg (2009), author of *Good Grief*, explains the results of **good grief** as the following:

1. We come out of a grief experience at a slightly higher level of maturity than before.
2. We come out of grief as deeper persons, because we have been down in the depths of despair and we know what it's like.
3. We come out of it stronger, for we have had to learn how to use our spiritual muscles to climb the rugged mountain trails.
4. We come out of it better able to help others. We have walked through the valley of the shadow of grief. We can understand.

> *We cannot become separate people, responsible people, connected people, reflective people without some losing and leaving and letting go.*
> —JUDITH VIORST

HOW TO ASSIST A GRIEVING FRIEND

- Respect what the person wants; do not expect them to react a specific way.
- Each loss is unique to the ones who experience it. Avoid any temptation to minimize the loss. Be patient.
- Be a better listener. Be aware of your feelings; and know you can't solve the problem.
- Be present with the mourner. Things to say:—"I'm sorry about your loss." "I'm here for you."

BECOMING AWARE OF TECHNOLOGY AND GRIEF

Nicola Wright is an Internet Communications graduate from Curtin University of Technology, Western Australia, and has written in the internet journal *First Monday* about "Death and the Internet" and the implications of the digital afterlife. It is clear that in the digital age, our cultural experience of death has changed in various ways. New ways of communicating online through social networks together with access to online news sources that amplify death imagery have brought an end to the modern era of "sequestered death." Online mourning practices and web memorialization have expanded traditional mourning practices and have been largely embraced, allowing for the formation of new rituals around death that extend beyond traditional locally-based rituals of funerals and wakes. Mourning rituals are changed and expanded not only in terms of how we grieve but also in scope due to the global scale of online mourning practices that is afforded by social networks and the architecture of the Internet (Wright, 2014).

HOW TO HELP PEOPLE GRIEVE

In helping others you often find people who need to grieve. Whether it is a loss of a close friend or loss of a parent, knowing how to handle the situation is a simple technique developed by clinical psychologist Susan Silk and negotiator Barry Goldman to help people help others. It works for all kinds of crises: medical, legal, financial, romantic, and even existential. Susan Silk calls it the **Ring Theory**.

Draw a circle. This is the center ring. In it put the name of the person at the *center of the current trauma*. For Katie's aneurysm, that's Katie. Now draw a larger circle around the first one. In that ring put the name of the person <u>next closest</u> *to the trauma*. In the case of Katie's aneurysm, that was Katie's husband, Dan. Repeat the process as many times as you need to. In each *larger ring put the next closest* people. Parents and children before more distant relatives. Intimate friends in smaller rings, less intimate friends in larger ones. When you are done you have a Complaining Order. It looks like a target.

Here are the rules. **The person in the center ring** can say anything they want to anyone, anywhere. They can complain and whine and moan and curse the heavens and say, "Life is unfair" and "Why me?" That's the one payoff for being in the center ring. **We need to give them room to grieve.**

Sometimes it's hard to know which ring is yours. If your spouse's mother is sick, you maybe in the family ring, or your spouse and siblings may unintentionally push you to the next ring. This can be very hard for you. Again, take those feelings outside until after

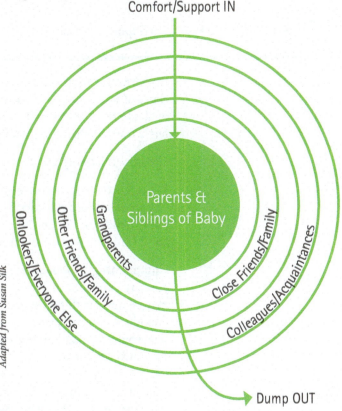

Adapted from Susan Silk

the grief and stress has subsided to a point where you can discuss it with your spouse. This can be especially true with the death of a close relative or old friend.

Everyone else can say those things too, but only to people in **larger rings.** The person in the center will have a hard time processing your complaints, so let them have time to grieve in their own way. And don't lament to them.

When you are talking to a person in a **ring smaller** than yours, someone closer to the center of the crisis, the *goal is to help*. **Listening** is often more helpful than talking. If you are going to say something, ask yourself if what you are about to say is likely to provide comfort and support. If it isn't, don't say it. Don't, for example, give advice. People who are suffering from trauma don't need advice. They need comfort and support. So say, **"I'm sorry"** or **"This must really be hard for you"** or "Can I bring you a pot of soup?" Don't say, "You should hear what happened to me" or "Here's what I would do if I were you." And don't say, "This is really bringing me down."

What to say when your goal is to help to provide comfort and support

Do say: "I'm sorry; this must be hard for you."
"Can I bring you a pot of soup or something?"
Don't Say: "You should hear what happened to my Aunt."
"If I were you, I would DO ..."

Remember: Comfort and Support In, Dump Out.

If you want to scream or cry or complain, if you want to tell someone how shocked you are or how horrible you feel, or whine about how it reminds you of all the terrible things that have happened to you lately, that's fine. It's a perfectly normal response. **Just do it to someone in a bigger ring.**

Comfort **IN**, dump **OUT**.

For example, there would be nothing wrong with Katie's friend saying she was not prepared for how horrible Katie looked, or even that she didn't think she could handle it. The mistake would be if she said those things to Katie's husband Dan. She would be dumping **IN**.

Complaining to someone in a smaller ring than yours doesn't do either of you any good. On the other hand, **being supportive** to her principal caregiver may be the best thing you can do for the patient. Most of us know this. Almost nobody would complain to the patient about how rotten she looks. Almost no one would say that looking at her makes them think of the fragility of life and their own closeness to death. In other words, we know enough not to dump into the center ring! Ring Theory merely expands that intuition and makes it more concrete: Don't just avoid dumping into the center ring; *avoid dumping into any ring smaller than your own.* Remember, you can say whatever you want if you just wait until you're talking to someone in a larger ring than yours. And eventually you'll get your turn in the center ring; we all deal with trauma in our lives (Silk & Goldman, 2016)

Becoming *Aware*

Becoming Aware of Relationship Ending

Something to think about when a relationship ends:

- Sleep more. Take care of yourself.
- Do things you enjoy and surround yourself with special friends.
- Think about it; we all have friends or lovers we loved and lost.
- The best way to deal with it is to enjoy the good memories and try not to repeat the bad ones. Remember: "better loved and lost than never loved before."
- Often relationships and friendships revolve around activities we do like work, school, church. Volunteering is a good way to meet people because you share your common interests.
- If your friendships last for years they are very special: you are special, too.
- Happiness can become your new project.

LOVE

Countless volumes have been written about the subject of love. Yet, do we really understand the true meaning of love? You will have the opportunity to explore love as it relates to more intimate relationships in Chapter Six. Therefore, our discussion in this chapter will be limited to the learned attitudes that interfere with our ability to give and receive love, as well as the use and misuse of love.

Learned attitudes. Certainly, our ideas about love are shaped by childhood experiences. If our parents or family hug us and tell us how great we are, hugs and praises become a part of our vocabulary of love. If they slap us and tell us we are stupid, however, we may conclude that abuse is part of a loving relationship. From a child's perspective: "These people are my family; families love their children; therefore, the way my family loves me is loving behavior." Whatever we learn in our families as children becomes our understanding of "normal."

Our ideas about love are shaped by childhood experiences.

We also grow up assuming that others will find the same things lovable that our parents did. For example, if we are lucky, our families love us unconditionally and continue to love us even when they do not love our behavior, or when we disagree with them. Consequently, we grow up believing that we deserve to be loved just because we are who we are.

If, however, our families love us only when we are compliant and undemanding, we may mistakenly learn that compliance is loving behavior. Therefore, we assume that we should not make demands on those we love. In essence, our parents' loving us only when we please them teaches us that we must always be pleasing, or risk losing love.

Use and misuse of love. There are also problems we encounter through the misuse of the emotion love. Because love is such a powerful and yet complicated emotion, we may even have a tendency to "smother" other people because we "love" them. Do we love them in the appropriate manner?

> You may find yourself feeling confused about the relationship, off balance or like you are "walking on eggshells" all the time. This is the kind of abuse that often sneaks up on you as you become more entrenched in the relationship. I am talking here about psychological abuse, which is also known as mental or emotional abuse. Psychological abuse occurs when a person in the relationship tries to control information available to another person with intent to manipulate that person's sense of reality or their view of what is acceptable and unacceptable (Feuerman, 2018)

Psychiatrist Dr. Foster Cline (2014) writes: "Love becomes a problem when it gets in the way of our allowing individuals the right to experience the consequences of their choices." For example, what about the countless hours spent in enabling a child or spouse who has a drug or alcohol problem? Why do we find it difficult for those we love to suffer the consequences of their choices? The answer is simple: We love them, and we do not like to see those we love suffer—we want to spare them their pain.

Remember, to let go is not to care for, but to care about.

Letting Go

To let go does not mean to stop caring,
It means I can't do it for someone else.

To let go is not to cut myself off,
It's the realization I can't control another.

To let go is not to enable,
But to allow learning from natural consequence.

To let go is to admit powerlessness,
Which means the outcome is not in my hands.

To let go is not to try to change or blame another,
It's to make the most of myself.

To let go is not to care for,
But to care about.

To let go is not to fix,
But to be supportive.

To let go is not to judge,
But to allow another to be a human being.

To let go is not to be in the middle arranging all the outcomes,
But to allow others to affect their own destinies.

Deserved love easily leaves a bitter feeling that one is not loved for oneself, that one is loved only because one pleases, that one is, in the last analysis, not loved but used.
—ERICH FROMM

To let go is not to be protective,
It's to permit another to face reality.

To let go is not to deny,
But to accept.

To let go is not to nag, scold, or argue,
But instead to search out my own shortcomings and correct them.

To let go is not to adjust everything to my desires,
But to take each day as it comes, and cherish myself in it.

To let go is not to criticize and regulate anybody,
But to try to become what I dream I can be.

To let go is not to regret the past,
But grow and live for the future.

To let go is to fear less and love more.   —Author unknown

The reality is that love can mean letting go of the responsibility we sometimes impose on ourselves to "take care" of those we love. It is in the best interest of those we love to let them assume the responsibility for making their choices and experience the consequences of those choices. When we jump in and "protect" them, we take away their choices and their freedom to be self-sufficient human beings. In essence, we do them a major injustice, quite the opposite of what we really believe we are doing. This is extremely difficult for many people to accept, and it takes a great deal of time to work through this emotional understanding of the true meaning of love.

Another misuse of love is when we find ourselves or others using love as a control agent—"If you loved me, you would do this/or you wouldn't do that." This is obviously a strong form of manipulation, and can totally destroy whatever love and caring there may be in a relationship. And if we can't objectively see if/when we're being consumed by our relationship, it's possible our relationship is failing because, in reality, it is a toxic relationship. **Toxic relationships** only ever survive on drama, and as the drama ramps up to keep the relationship going, we become dependent on that drama, or even addicted to it. And then we're really in trouble, because now the meaning we derive from that toxic relationship is skewed and distorted.

A good time to explore who we are is in contexts outside of that relationship. Rushing out to find someone to fill that void without really figuring out what *we* want and what *we* need is a recipe for recurring relationship disaster. Good people and good relationships will offer unconditional support. Toxic friends and family members will look to adopt the drama of our loss and make it theirs as well. This just makes everything worse (Chapman, 2015).

The problem with allowing our identity to be consumed by a romantic relationship is that as we change to be closer to the person we love, we cease to be the person they fell in love with in the first place. It's important to occasionally get some distance from our partners, assert our independence, and maintain some hobbies or interests that are just ours. Have some separate friends. Love is sometimes described as crazy and irrational. And the best love works when our irrationalities complement one another and our flaws enamor one another (Chapman, 2015).

It may be our perfections that attract one another. But it's our imperfections that decide whether we stay together or not. Connecting/reconnecting with people who care about us will start to add meaning back into our lives.

Another way to separate ourselves from our past relationships and move on is to take an objective look at what the relationships were really like. If part of the story we tell ourselves is, "We were so perfect for each other. We should be together forever! Why doesn't he/she see that?" then I'd bet we're falling victim to more than a few biases that we're simply not aware of.

The truth is, our memories are not always right, and we often only remember the things that fit into whatever story we want to believe right now. In this case, we remember the good times most, because that's what we want our reality to be right now (Brown, 2017).

Although there are many definitions of love, in the final analysis, love may truly be the desire to see another individual become all he or she can be as a person—with room to breathe and grow. It may be caring as much about another person's well being as we do our own. This is true whether our love be for a spouse, friend, child, or co-worker.

Expressing love. Certainly, there are many types of love relationships. Depending upon the relationship involved, the true meaning of love will be expressed in various ways. Some people have trouble saying the words, "I love you!" Instead, they show their love by buying presents or doing nice things for those they love. Obviously, for one who says, "I love you" frequently, it is difficult to understand why another person

BECOMING AWARE—HOW TO EXPAND YOUR ABILITY TO LOVE

- **Express yourself.** You have positive feelings, so put them into words: "Our relationship means a lot to me," "I like being with you," "I love you."
- **Love yourself.** Self-love is the **opposite of selfishness**. If you do not love yourself, you cannot love someone else.
- **Be tolerant.** You can love and be loved without sharing exactly the same opinions, values, and personality traits. Do not make constant agreement your main criterion for love. This is unrealistic.
- **Hang in there.** You are vulnerable, and there is always the risk of hurt, but do not give up at the first sign of trouble. Relationships can be difficult but rewarding.
- **Learn to be alone.** You cannot be happy until you can be happy being alone. Do not ask another person to be your "security blanket." If you love someone, give the person room to breathe and grow while you keep your distance.
- **Grow up.** Immature love says, "I love you because I need you"; or "I love because I am loved." Mature love says, "I need you because I love you"; or "I am loved because I love."
- **Practice.** The more you practice developing a loving attitude, the more love you will attract. The more frequently you say, "I really care about you," "I love you," the more comfortable you will become in expressing these loving words.

From *The Art of Loving* (Fromm, 2009) and *Love: What Life Is all About* (Buscaglia, 1996).

cannot say the words. People express their emotions in different ways. Although it is true that adults who did not know love as a child have a greater difficulty learning how to express love, it is never too late to develop or expand our ability to love. As women surpass men on college campuses, the threat felt by thin-skinned males often reveals itself in the relationships where they feel most exposed. "Boys are not only more invested in ongoing romantic relationships but also have less confidence navigating them than do girls," writes the sociologist Robin W. Simon in *The Journal of Health and Social Behavior*. That's problematic, because "romantic partners are their primary sources of intimacy," whereas young women tend to confide in friends and family (Reiner, 2016).

Now that we have a better idea of how some of our more common emotions affect us, we will discuss how we got to be feeling persons. The chapter concludes with a discussion on learning how to express emotions, as well as the benefits to be derived in achieving a balance between emotional expression and emotional control.

Development of Emotions

From early infancy, human beings display tendencies toward responding emotionally. Most authorities agree with Jungian philosophy's classical theory that heredity does predispose us toward fairly specific emotional tendencies (Jung, 2016). For example, one child develops a natural tendency to react calmly to most emotional stimuli, whereas another shows a tendency to react quickly and intensely to all emotional stimuli.

An infant's first emotional expression is crying. For several months, babies will continue to show their excitement by crying when they feel like doing so. After a few weeks, they have learned to distinguish and respond to two basic emotions—*distress* and *delight*. Bodily discomfort (a wet diaper or hunger) brings forth the earliest unpleasant reaction, known as **distress**. **Delight**, the earliest pleasant reaction, appears several weeks after distress, in the form of smiling, gurgling, and other babyish sounds of joy.

Soon, we become more aware of the world within us and the world outside us. Consequently, we learn from others and our own experiences other emotional responses such as love, anger, frustration, fear, jealousy, and so on. We learn which emotions will bring us rewards and those that will bring us punishment.

Through our family, school, and social experiences, we learn various ways of dealing with our emotions. We also receive messages on how to express and deal with some of our emotions. For example, we may hear: "Don't make a scene by crying"; "There is nothing to be afraid of"; "Don't let everybody see how angry you are"; "Cheer up, there is no reason to feel bad"; "Be strong and endure your pain"; or even, "Control yourself; don't let others know how excited you are." It is even possible that you heard the statement, "Big boys don't cry." Consequently, we may grow up thinking that girls and women can cry, but boys and men must not do so. Could these messages have anything to do with the cultural stereotype of the unexpressive male and the more expressive female? See Gender & You, below. Do you agree or disagree with the findings?

This is an example of how sexist behavior is learned and can be unlearned in the same manner. Men can be brought up to learn to show their feelings more and to be more emotionally aware (Rolls, 2010).

With modeling and messages from our parents, society, and our peers, is it any wonder that we grow up confused about *what to do with our feelings?*

Emotional Intelligence

Have you ever wondered why some people with high academic IQs are "poor pilots of their private lives," while those with modest academic IQs may do surprisingly well? Why do some "really bright people" make disastrous choices in business and in their personal lives? Are we either emotional beings or rational beings? Could it be possible to have an intelligent balance of the two, whereby the head and heart are in harmony with each other? Most people understand what academic or intellectual intelligence means, but what does it mean to use emotion intelligently?

Women tend to be more emotionally empathetic than men—that is, better able to pick up the emotions of others. Men tend to be faster than women at returning to normal after experiencing distressing emotions. "Some universities offer counseling services for men of color and gay men, and some sponsor clubs through which male members explore the crisis of sexual violence against women. Only a precious few colleges offer ways for all men to explore their shared struggles. And these don't exist without pushback. But wouldn't encouraging men to embrace the full range of their humanity benefit women? Why do we continue to limit the emotional lives of males when it serves no one?" (Reiner, 2016)

The concept of emotional intelligence was originally developed by John Mayer and Peter Salovey (2004) and Daniel Goleman has made it more popular. ***Emotional intelligence*** consists of the ability to monitor, access, express, and regulate one's own emotions; the capacity to identify, interpret, and understand others' emotions; and the ability to use this information to guide one's thinking and actions. Emotional intelligence includes four essential abilities:

1. *First*, people need to be able to accurately perceive emotions in themselves and others and have the ability to express their own emotions.
2. *Second*, people need to be aware of how their emotions shape their thinking, decisions and coping behavior.
3. *Third*, people need to be able to understand and analyze their emotions, which may have important social implications.
4. *Fourth*, people need to be able to regulate their emotions so they can minimize negative emotions and make effective use of positive emotions (Mayer et al., 2009).

Daniel Goleman, an emotional intelligence writer, writes, "If your emotional abilities aren't in hand, if you don't have self-awareness, if you are not able to manage your distressing emotions, if you can't have empathy and have effective relationships, then no matter how smart you are, you are not going to get very far" (http://cultureofempathy. com/references/Experts/Daniel-Goleman.htm).

Becoming Aware of Feelings: *The Power Paradox: How We Gain and Lose Influence*
https://www.youtube.com/watch?v=HS9VHBlYklc

Celebrated UC Berkeley psychologist Dr. Dacher Keltner argues that compassion and selflessness enable us to have the most influence over others and the result is power as a force for good in the world.

GENDER AND YOU

ARE WOMEN MORE EMOTIONALLY EXPRESSIVE THAN MEN?

In *Scientific American* (August 2017) Dr. Cindi May from the Univerity of Charleston, S.C. had 2,000 participants explore sex differences in facial expressions across different affective states. A unique paradigm was developed for evaluating facial behaviors in response to emotional stimuli. Participants watched advertisements for different, commonly-used products and an automated facial coding system evaluated the facial expressions of the men and women as they watched the ads.

In some ways, the results from this study confirm previous findings of greater emotional expressiveness for women. Women did smile more often than men in response to the ads, and their smiles were longer in duration. They also engaged in more inner brow raises, though the duration of these brow raises did not differ from that of men. This data not only aligns with the belief that women are more likely than men to display emotion, but also suggests that this tendency extends to negative as well as positive emotions, as inner brow raises are thought to be reflective of states of fear and sadness.

In other ways, however, the data suggests a more nuanced account of sex differences in expressiveness. Women were not universally more expressive than men, as men were more likely to demonstrate anger-based facial behaviors than women. Men showed more brow furrowing than women, and their brow furrows were longer than those of women as well. In addition, lip corner depressors were significantly longer in men than in women.

Because the researchers focused on facial behaviors rather than distinct internal emotional states, little is known about sex differences in reactions to specific states like disgust, hope, or gratitude. As scientists further pursue these questions, we can be fairly confident in one thing: Despite Hollywood portrayals, women are not universally expressive and men are not consistently stoic. Instead, the intensity of the reaction is likely to depend not only on the sex of the individual but also on the specific emotional state (May, 2017).

This pattern of findings, with women expressing more happiness and sadness, and men expressing more anger, could reflect social conventions about gender-appropriate behavior. If so, these conventions seem to hold across several different cultures, as the general pattern of findings was consistent across the five countries (US, Germany, UK, China, France) included in the study (May, 2017).

Becoming Aware of Emotional Intelligence
https://youtu.be/Y7m9eNoB3NU

Explores the four domains of emotional intelligence—self-awareness, self-management, social awareness, and relationship management—as defined by psychologist and author Daniel Goleman. The domains build on one another, starting with a greater awareness of self and others, and ending with the management of relationships that are critical to everyone.

Actually, emotional intelligence (EI) has become a popular phrase in homes, schools, and businesses due to Daniel Goleman's book, *Emotional Intelligence: Why It Can Matter More Than IQ* (2006). The author, a Harvard-educated psychologist, believes that emotional intelligence is involved in some of the most important things in our lives, such as managing bad moods, maintaining hope after setbacks, getting along with people, and making important decisions. People who are high in emotional intelligence have the ability to use their emotions wisely, and they appear to have a deeper understanding of their emotional lives (Goleman, 2011).

In fact, emotional intelligence may be a more important contributor to success in life than IQ. (However, more research is needed in this area as well as continued research into the meaning of emotional intelligence. At present, ways to cultivate emotional intelligence are being explored in classrooms and workplaces.) Emotional intelligence is an assortment of mental abilities and skills that can help you to successfully manage both yourself and the demands of working with others.

Developing your own EI enables you to:

1. Know yourself reasonably well.
2. Control your own emotions.
3. Show empathy with the feelings of others.
4. Use social skills in an effective as well as simply a pleasant way (Walton, 2013).

In any case, we are *both* emotional and rational beings, and we need an intelligent balance of the two (Gibbs, 2001; Duffy, 2007/2008).

THE FULLY HUMAN BEING

The fully human being is aware of the vitality of [sic] his senses, emotions, mind, and will; and he is neither a stranger to, nor afraid of, the activities of his body and emotions. He is capable of the whole gamut of emotions: from grief to tenderness. What I mean, is that the fully human being experiences the fullness of his emotional life; he is in touch with, attuned to his emotions, aware of what they are saying to him about his needs and his relationships with others.

—Carl Rogers, *On Becoming a Person*

Social Emotional Learning (SEL) is comprised of the skills we use to recognize and manage our own emotions and being able to recognize emotions in others. This concept arose out of research about Emotional Intelligence Methods for improving social skills. **Social Emotional Learning** emphasize learning personal and social skills and setting personal goals (Ng'andu, 2015). Casel.org has a coordinated framework for educators, families, and communities to promote SEL and academic learning.

FEELING AWE—THE EMOTION TO BALANCE AND BECOME FULLY HUMAN

Awe may be the the secret emotion to help you get your balance and feel better. In fact, Paula Spencer Scott believes that feeling awe may be the secret to health and happiness. It is not a commonly discussed emotion. Awe has been researched by Dacher Keltner, a pioneer in the study of emotions. He consulted on the movie about emotions, *Inside Out,* released in 2015. (That movie did a great job of talking about the "big six" emotions: happiness, sadness, fear, anger, disgust, and surprise.) Keltner started Project Awe in 2013, a three-year research project funded by the Sir John Templeton Foundation. *Awe* is the "take your breath away feeling," or it might be your "spine tingle" that you feel when you see something or experience something that can be new, like a sunset over the Rockies or just a beautiful cluster of butterflies.

Becoming Aware of Feelings: The biological effects of sympathy, gratitude and awe
https://www.youtube.com/watch?v=fmS8L6pQYss

Dacher Keltner explains his research into these emotions at the University of California, Berkeley, and asks how we can create societies which promote them.

The definition of *awe* is 1. an overwhelming feeling of reverence, admiration, fear, etc., produced by that which is grand, sublime, extremely powerful, or the like: in *awe* of God; in *awe* of great political figures. 2. Archaic. power to inspire fear or reverence. (https://www.merriam-webster.com/dictionary/awe)

- Keltner believes **we are wired to feel awe**. Awe binds us together in a collaborative way. It helps us to realize we are a small part of something larger, like the solar system.
- Awe helps us **see things in new ways** and **makes us more receptive to details.**
- Awe can **make us nicer and happier**. It makes us act more generously, ethically, and fairly.
- Awe can **help us fight depression**. Take a walk in nature. Researchers are looking into whether a lack of access to nature and other opportunities for feeling awe might add to the stresses and health damage that come from living in urban blight or poverty (Scott, 2016).

THE COSTS OF DENYING EMOTIONS

We receive all kinds of messages about expressing or controlling emotions. Were we taught to express emotions openly, or did we grow up believing that we should "stop showing" our emotions, even though we continued to experience them? We are humans, not robots or machines. We have two basic choices in dealing with the the emotional aspects of our lives: deny or express. The greatest challenges occur in the many ways we have been taught to deny emotions. We will start with two common forms of control of emotions.

> *When feelings are avoided, their painful effects are often prolonged, and it becomes increasingly difficult to deal with them.*
> —ANDREW SALTER

Repression. The most common form of overcontrol is repression. In *repression*, the self automatically excludes threatening or painful thoughts and feelings from awareness. By pushing them into the subconscious, we are able to manage the anxiety that grows out of uncomfortable situations.

Perhaps the most destructive aspect of repression is that although we realize we are hurting when we have repressed our true feelings, we do not know why. We have hidden the source of pain in the subconscious. Repressed emotions unfortunately do not die. They refuse to be silenced, and continue to influence our whole personality and behavior. For example, when we repress guilt feelings, we continually, though subconsciously, try to punish ourselves. We will not allow ourselves success or enjoyment because we have a feeling that we are so unworthy. For example, rather than accepting compliments, we "qualify" them or quickly give all the credit to someone "more" deserving than us!

Repressed emotions, such as fear, anger or strong passions, may still affect one physically. Symptoms such as headaches, insomnia (which can have additional effects), or other painful manifestations can occur. While medical treatment may be necessary, often a process of learning to accept and express emotions in a healthy way will address the symptoms effectively. Extensions or long-term repression may require both medication and professional support, such a psychotherapy.

In his book *The Language of Feelings*, David Viscott (1990) indicates that feelings always follow a predictable pattern when you suffer one of three major kinds of loss: *1) the loss of someone who loves you or the loss of their love or your sense of lovability; 2) the loss of control; and 3) the loss of self-esteem.*

The predictable pattern then becomes:

- When a loss threatens, you feel anxious.
- When a loss occurs, you feel hurt.
- When hurt is held back, it becomes anger.
- When anger is held back, it creates guilt.
- When guilt is unrelieved, depression occurs.

Viscott goes on to say that if you take care of your fear, hurt, and anger, the guilt and depression will take care of themselves. In other words, they will be nonexistent, just like the sleeplessness, the tension headaches, or ulcers. When a person is especially sensitive to one type of loss, however, they tend to bury the unpleasant feelings associated with the loss.

Suppression. Sometimes people suppress rather than repress their emotions. In *suppression*, people are usually conscious of their emotions, but deliberately control rather than express them. For example, we might say, "I'll never let her know that I'm jealous." Why would we say this? We might be afraid that our emotional admissions could be used against us; maybe she would bring it up later. Then we would probably always wonder if she might distance herself from us because of the feelings we confided. Obviously, these are all threats to our self-esteem, so why take the risk? After all, what we do not say cannot be used against us.

Although suppression of emotions is a healthier way of handling feelings than is repression, habitual suppression may lead to many of the undesirable effects of repression. Furthermore, chronic suppression of feelings interferes with rational problem-solving. When people have unexpressed feelings that are held back within, they cannot think clearly. Consequently, they may have difficulty studying, working, or even socializing with others. More importantly, when people consistently suppress emotions, they may eventually explode and do things or say things totally uncharacteristic and unlike the people they want to be. Obviously, this makes life situations much, much worse. As you can see, chronic suppression can be just as unhealthy as repression (Duffy & Atwater, 2014).

Now we are left with the other choice of dealing with our feelings—expressing them. This may seem difficult when we have been holding them back for a long time.

Getting Out of Emotional Debt

Everybody gets into emotional debt from time to time. Gary Emery (2000) defines *emotional debt* as a condition of imbalance in which feelings are trapped instead of expressed. As stated above, keeping feelings from being naturally expressed employs defenses and drains energy. The more feelings are held in, the less energy you have to be yourself. Obviously, this interferes with your ability to interact with others in healthy ways.

The ability to accept and manage our emotions is a significant mark of maturity. We are feeling beings. In order to fully enjoy the feelings of love, achievements, self-worth, and other more desirable emotions, we must also deal with the difficult feelings of anger, fear, grief, etc.

We must learn to manage our feelings without repressing, suppressing, or in other ways denying our human needs to feel. This ability will also make us more able to tolerate other's upsets, not prompted to run from them (Marino 2016).

> *Buried emotions are like rejected people; they make us pay a high price for having rejected them. Hell hath no fury like that of a scorned emotion.*
> —JOHN POWELL

> *To feel intensely is not a symptom of weakness; it is the trademark of the truly alive and compassionate. There is no shame in expressing your authentic feelings. Those who are at times described as being a "hot mess" or having "too many issues" are the very fabric of what keeps the dream alive for a more caring, humane world. Never be ashamed to let your tears shine a light in this world.*
> —ANTHON ST. MAARTEN

Guidelines for Dealing with Your Emotions

Learning to constructively express and utilize our emotions is a lifelong process: we learn by doing. Emotions are a fact of life, and communicating them certainly is not a simple matter. It is obvious that showing every feeling of anger, frustration, and even love and affection could be unhealthy. The following suggestions can help you to decide when and how to express your emotions (Adler & Proctor, 2016).

- **Listen to your body.** What is happening inside of you? What are those butterflies in your stomach telling you? Why is your heart pounding? Remember, physiological changes are a part of your emotions. Those internal changes speak to you very clearly; do not ignore them.

- **Identify your feelings.** Ask yourself, "What am I really feeling?" Is it fear, anger, frustration? Give your feelings a label if you can. If you have difficulty with an exact label, use the techniques in the next suggestion to help you express your feelings. Remember to name all the feelings you are having. Try to identify your primary feeling and then your secondary feeling. Above all, do not deny or suppress your feelings.

- **Personalize your feelings.** There are times when you can name the feeling: "I'm feeling hurt," "I love you," "I'm angry." There are times, however, when it is easier to describe the *impact* the feelings are having on you: "I feel like I'm being dumped on," "I feel used," "I feel he cares for me." Metaphors with a *colorful description*, such as "I'm sitting on top of the world," "I feel like my world has caved in," "I'm down in the dumps," can be used. Feelings can also be expressed by describing what action you feel like taking: "I feel like giving up," "I feel like telling him off," "I just want to jump for joy."

- **Own your feelings.** Your feelings are yours; no other person can cause or be responsible for your emotions. Of course, we feel better assigning our emotions to other people: "You made me angry," "You frightened me," "You made me jealous." The fact is that another person cannot "make" you feel *anything*. Another person can only stimulate the emotions that are already in you, waiting to be activated. The distinction between *causing* and *stimulating* emotions is not just a play on words. The acceptance of the truth involved is critical. If we think other people can make us angry, we lay the blame and pin the problem on them.

- **Decide what you will do with your feelings.** This is often very difficult, because there are many factors to consider. Careful consideration of the following may be of assistance to you:
  - **Timing and Appropriateness of Place.** We are all familiar with the thought: *there is a time and a place for all things.* This is particularly true when expressing emotions. You also want your message to be heard, and you hope your message is understood. As we will discuss in Chapter Five, your receiver will probably be more receptive to your message if he or she is not distracted by outside stimuli, such as your emotional needs, and if the receiver has the energy and time to listen.

– **How Much Emotion to Express.** Young children may squeal with delight or cry with anguish in the grocery store, at church, or wherever they so please. Adults, however, are expected to exert "control" over their emotional expressions. This does not mean that adults should not express emotion spontaneously. Instead, it means that adults feel an emotion, understand it, and decide how intensely to express it. For example, in some circumstances, such as some religious services or in a public event where quiet is a norm, adults are expected to manage feelings of excitement, amusement, etc. Regardless of how sad you feel that your child is marrying this "certain" person, it might not be a good idea to cry loudly and profusely through the entire wedding. A quiet sob might be much more appropriate.

– **Significance of Relationship.** There is some risk involved in expressing feelings. In an encounter with a store clerk, an acquaintance, or a distant relative, expressing your feelings of frustration may do nothing more than relieve tension. In other words, you might be able to get away with "telling off this person." If you value this person's friendship, however, you may want to carefully consider how you address your feelings, out of consideration for *their* feelings. You may find that this relationship means so much to you, you need to be very careful in expressing feelings. You may choose a softer or more indirect approach. After all, you want the net effect to be a closer, more meaningful relationship. It is important to take into account whether you are going to be interacting with this person in the future.

– **Words and Mannerisms.** You already know some ways to personalize your feelings. You will also want to consider the appropriate verbal and nonverbal techniques to use in expressing yourself. This will be discussed in more detail in Chapter Five. Careful selection of words means that you use tact and deal with facts instead of interpretations, judgments, or accusations.

- **Recognize the Difference between Feeling and Acting.** **Allowing ourselves the freedom to feel and observe our emotions does not necessarily mean that we should act on those emotions.** As a small child, you might punch someone in the nose when you get angry. This is not appropriate, and usually results in corrective discipline ("punishment"). As an adult, however, if physical punishment usually results in more severe outcomes, including jail. To live effectively in our world requires that we be sensitive to situations and adjust our emotional expression accordingly. Note that we used the term *adjust,* not *deny.*

People express their emotions differently and respond to situations differently. Sometimes, however, it is just not possible to openly express what we really feel. In these instances, we need to choose some indirect ways to express our feelings. As we already know, feelings do not just go away. Here are some suggestions for these times:

1. "Vent" or share your feelings with a trusted friend or confidant.
2. Choose some type of physical or creative activity to help release emotions constructively.
3. Work to maintain a positive or realistic perspective of the situation.
4. As much as possible, keep a sense of humor.

> *An emotion without social rules of containment and expression is like an egg without a shell: a gooey mess.*
> —CAROL TAVRIS

You might be thinking to yourself, "I'll never remember all these guidelines." If this is true for you, perhaps the "shorthand technique" developed by Gary Emery (2000) and illustrated below will be a quick way for you to remember the key concepts in expressing your feelings.

CONSIDER THIS

FEEL—THE SHORTHAND TECHNIQUE

F Focus on your feelings.
E Experience them.
E Express them constructively.
L Let them go.

Emery (2000)

UNDERSTANDING CULTURE AND EMOTION

Research shows that certain basic emotions are experienced by people around the world. The ability to feel and recognize happiness, sadness, surprise, anger, disgust, and fear seems to be universal, regardless of a person's background or where they are born (Gudykunst & Young, 2002). Culture plays a key role in moderating our expression of emotion and in helping us cognitively appraise situations in appropriate ways. Paul Eckman found that different cultures have different "display rules": norms about when, where, and how much we should show emotions. The Focus on Diversity on the following page gives examples of some of these cultures' display rules (Adler & Proctor, 2017; King, 2020).

We are emotional human beings. Understanding our emotions, how they affect us, and developing ways of handling them can be beneficial for all of us. Learning how different cultures express emotions can certainly eliminate some potential communication problems. Empathy and sympathy are needed to help others deal with their feelings.

Becoming Aware of Emotions: Brené Brown on Empathy
https://youtu.be/1Evwgu369Jw

Brené Brown explains empathy and sympathy

Benefits of Expressing Your Feelings

Many emotional responses feel good to us. Feelings of love, tenderness, and warmth toward other people give us a sense of well-being. Emotional responses involved in happy or joyful experiences in life are also enhancing to us, as are emotional responses found in humor or laughter that tend to help us feel good about being alive.

However, the real benefit of having good feelings can only be found if one chooses to truly experience emotions and share them with others.

As we have stated several times in this chapter, strong feelings that are not expressed or dealt with rarely go away. Instead, you may begin to collect your feelings and cash them in at a later date for a free mad, temper tantrum, or an angry outburst at someone else. Also, bottled-up anger may "leak out" in the form of a lack of cooperation, silence, coldness, cynicism, or even sarcasm. Obviously, none of us would really want these types of behaviors to occur.

Becoming Aware of Your Anger
https://www.psychologistworld.com/stress/anger-test

Anger test: This test will see how you react in stressful situations.

FOCUS ON DIVERSITY: HAPPINESS

CULTURAL DISPLAY RULES

Display rules are a social group or culture's informal norms that distinguish how one should express themselves. They can be described as culturally prescribed rules that people learn early on in their lives by interactions and socializations with other people.

Americans say, "I Love You" more frequently than members of other cultures (Duffy & Atwater (2014).

Happiness is an emotion that gives you a sense that life is good—a state of well-being that outlasts yesterday's moment of elation, today's buoyant mood, or tomorrow's feeling of sadness, said David Myers in *The Pursuit of Happiness* (1993).

Becoming Aware–Happiness: *There's more to life than being happy*
https://www.youtube.com/watch?v=y9Trdafp83U

Our culture is obsessed with happiness, but what if there's a more fulfilling path? Happiness comes and goes, says writer Emily Esfahani Smith, but having meaning in life—serving something beyond yourself and developing the best within you—gives you something to hold onto. Learn more about the difference between being happy and having meaning as Smith offers four pillars of a meaningful life.

"There's a naive belief out there that maybe we shouldn't be focused on making people happier or increasing their well-being because they won't be motivated to do anything," says lead researcher Kostadin Kushlev. "But our findings suggest the opposite: Being happier links to more action, not less" (Suttie, 2019).

We also bottle up love, happiness and other feelings that we might not be comfortable expressing. These feelings can leak out in ways we didn't expect. Sometimes we also experience resentment about the need to contain them.

Is individual happiness actually bad for society and the world? A common concern—which is referred as the" Pollyanna hypothesis"—is that happy people might be too happy to care enough about important current issues. So they might be less likely to improve society and the world. In three studies, however, the authors found that feeling good predicted more, not less, action on current issues. This pattern was in the context of the 2017 far-right rallies in Charlottesville, VA (Study 1), a wide range of social, political, and environmental issues chosen by participants (Study 2), and environmental action within a nationally representative sample (Study 3). These findings speak against the Pollyanna hypothesis: Happiness does not seem to preclude caring about local and global issues. People were willing to take action to make the world a better place (Kostadin Kushlev, Danielle M. Drummond, Samantha J. Heintzelman & Ed Diener, July 2019).

If you express your feelings, there may be benefits.

> *The things that most clearly differentiate and individuate me from others are my feelings and emotions.*
> —JOHN POWELL

The real benefit of having good feelings can only be found if one chooses to truly experience emotions and share them with others.

1. **You Will Develop Positive Feelings about Yourself.** You cannot possibly understand that part of yourself which you deny or repress. Furthermore, you cannot possibly appreciate yourself when you know you are not being honest with yourself and others. Once you begin to openly and honestly deal with your feelings in a constructive way, you will automatically experience increased feelings of self-esteem. People who feel good about themselves are not afraid of their emotional responses. That is, they trust themselves and their emotions. Obviously, this type of dual trust leads to a sense of inner harmony and freedom—you do not have to *pretend* any longer.

© nd3000/Shutterstock.com

2. **Your Relationships Will Grow Stronger.** The expression of feelings is vital to effectively building meaningful relationships. How can others know what you are feeling if you never tell them? How can another person really get to know you if you only talk about the "weather" or "surface" type issues?

Other people will not experience fears, frustrations, love, and joy in the same way as you do. So, you must tell others how you feel, what your "gut" is saying, if you really want to establish and maintain meaningful relationships.

Often, when you begin expressing your feelings, others will be more likely to express some of their own. Consequently, you each know more about each other. When two people can share their feelings in an open, honest, and caring way, their relationship will deepen, even if these feelings are sometimes negative.

3. **Pressure Is Relieved.** Experts in psychosomatic medicine believe that the most common cause of fatigue and actual sickness is the repression of emotions. We all experience frustrations and anxieties in our daily lives. For example, our goals may be thwarted, our self-esteem and integrity may be threatened, and our abilities to handle situations may seem overwhelmed. As we have seen, our health and our relationships are negatively affected when we deny "what we are really feeling." When we are able to express what we have kept "bottled up" inside us, we normally feel better. Consequently, we naturally reduce some of the stress we are feeling. We will discuss stress and its effects more fully in Chapter Eight.

Sometimes in the process of expressing and dealing with our feelings, we even go through a healing process, known as *forgiveness*. Let us see what this process involves.

Forgiveness—The Healing Process

Almost everyone has been hurt or experienced a painful injustice from one of these sources:

- Parents
- Lovers
- Children
- Spouses (former and present)
- Brothers and sisters
- Grandparents
- Friends
- Co-workers
- Employers
- People of the opposite sex, other races, or religions
- Ourselves
- Whole systems (schools, government, criminal justice system, the media)

We have all experienced some hurts and had some painful past experiences, but many of these no longer influence our life. On the other hand, there may be some hurts that bother us. We have not forgiven the people who hurt us, but more important, we

> There's no "should" or "should-not " when it comes to having feelings. They are part of who we are and their origins are beyond our control. When we can believe that, we may find it easier to make constructive choices about what to do with those feelings.
> —FRED ROGERS

have not let go of the pain. Sidney and Suzanne Simon (2014), authors of the book, *Forgiveness: How to Make Peace with Your Past and Get On with Your Life,* explain that the pain has not let go of us:

> Many of us wake up each morning and fill an enormous suitcase with pain from our pasts. We stuff it with grudges, bitterness, resentment, and self-righteous anger. We toss in some self-pity, envy, jealousy, and regret. We load that suitcase with every injury and injustice that was ever done to us; with every memory of how others failed us and how we ourselves have failed; and with all the reminders of what we have missed out on and what we can never hope to have. Then, we shut that suitcase and drag it with us wherever we go. (Simon & Simon, 2014)

Becoming Aware–Forgiveness test
https://belmontwellness.com/forgiveness-self-test-2/

Throughout our lives, we have all heard the following statements:

- Forgive and forget,
- Let bygones be bygones,
- Turn the other cheek, and
- Kiss and make up.

However, it is often very difficult to forgive the people who have caused us real pain. Instead, we believe that the people who hurt us should pay for the pain they caused—they *deserve to be punished, not forgiven.* Sometimes we may even say, "I'll work at forgiving when they say they are sorry. I will work at forgiveness when somehow they communicate to me that they realize and regret what they have done."

In all probability, the people who hurt us have not made up for what they did to us, and even if they wanted to, they probably could not really do that. Furthermore, no amount of *punishment* they may have endured could relieve our pain or evaporate our resentment. What if they never apologize? What if they are never sorry? What if they are never even capable of knowing what they did to us? Then what? Then what do you do? Do you continue to let them dictate the quality of your life (Larsen, 1992)?

Forgiveness has nothing to do with "them." It's natural and certainly tempting to blame others or unfortunate circumstances for feelings of anger, guilt, depression, anxiety, shame, or insecurity. But look at the word *blame.* It is just a coincidence that the last two letters spell the word *me.* Other people or unfortunate circumstances may have caused us to experience some pain, but only *we control whether we allow that pain to go on.* We may not have had any power or control over what happened to us when we were 5, 10, or 15 years old, but we do have a choice now whether we are going to keep on carrying that hurt and resentment with us (Enright, 2019).

What can you do to make those feelings go away? What can we do to get those people who hurt us off our *blame list*? Forgiveness is not done as a favor to the people who hurt us or because someone once told us that forgiving was the good or right thing to do. Forgiveness is something we do for *ourselves*, for our own health, happiness, and

When you grant forgiveness, you are simply removing yourself from the justice equation.
—CRAIG ETHEREDGE

To forgive is to set the prisoner free and then discover the prisoner was you.
—ELLIS COSE

emotional well-being. We forgive so that we can let go of the pain and finally get rid of the excess emotional baggage that has been weighing us down and holding us back.

Rabbi Harold Kushner, author of *When Bad Things Happen to Good People* (2004) and *Overcoming Life's Disappointments* (2007), explains what is meant by carrying around emotional baggage that has been weighing one down:

> When I would counsel a divorcée still seething about her husband's having left her for another woman years ago and having fallen behind on child support payments, she would ask me, "How can you expect me to forgive him after what he's done to me and the children?" I would answer, "I'm not asking you to forgive him because what he did wasn't so terrible; it was terrible. I'm suggesting that you forgive him because he doesn't deserve to have this power to turn you into a bitter, resentful woman. When he left, he gave up the right to inhabit your life and mind to the degree that you're letting him. Your being angry at him doesn't harm him, but it hurts you. It's turning you into someone you don't really want to be. Release that anger, not for his sake—he probably doesn't deserve it—but for your sake, so that the real you can re-emerge." (2007)

University of Wisconsin's Robert Enright (2019), head of the International Forgiveness Institute, reminds people that forgiving does not mean letting the guilty party off the hook. It is not excusing, forgetting, or even reconciling—it is giving up resentment to which you are entitled and offering compassionate understanding to someone who may not deserve it. The paradox, he says, is that "by giving this gift to the other, it is the gift-giver who becomes psychologically healed."

Benefits of forgiveness. "Holding on to hurts and nursing grudges wears you down physically and emotionally," says Stanford University psychologist Fred Luskin (2007), author of *Forgive for Love*. Luskin, director of the Stanford Forgiveness Project, applied his method to help families in Northern Ireland recover emotionally from the murder of loved ones, some of whom had been killed more than 20 years earlier. Rather than agonizing over the past, his subjects were able to enjoy the present. Feelings of hurt, measured by using psychological tests, had fallen more than half. They were also less likely to feel depressed and angry. Their health also improved. On average, they saw stress-related symptoms like backaches and stomach pain dip by almost 35%.

To heal, some people take fate's raw material and transform it. Judy Keane, 54, whose husband of 31 years, Richard, was killed at the World Trade Center, felt she had to move forward. Despite her anguish, she did not want to become more rigid and hostile. Keane responded by starting a foundation in her husband's name that will open a sports center in her Connecticut town. Her goal is to offer programs built on Richard's philosophy for coaching kids: in true sports, kids learn how to deal with life.

Forgiveness is truly a journey of hard work and an exercise in personal power. Lewis Smedes (2007) reminds us that "you will know that forgiveness has begun when you recall those who hurt you and feel the power to wish them well." If this is difficult for you to imagine, Robert Enright (2019), in his insightful book, *Forgiveness Is a Choice*, says, "forgiveness is feeling free of negative energy." If you remain angry, the hostility

Forgiveness is the fragrance the violet sheds on the heel that has crushed it
—MARK TWAIN

When we forgive, we free ourselves from the bitter ties that bind us to the one who hurt us.
—CLAIRE FRAZIER-YZAGUIRRE

CONSIDER THIS

THE HEALING PROCESS

While a variety of strategies can be used in the forgiveness process, at least some of these important stages will be involved:

- Exploring the anger you have
- Deciding to forgive
- Working on forgiveness
- Discovery and release, whereby one learns a great deal about oneself, the other person, and relationships.

Adapted from Enright (2019); Cose (2005).

Human pain does not let go of its grip at one point in time. Rather it works its way out of our consciousness over time. There is a season of sadness, a season of anger, a season of tranquility, and a season of hope.
—ROBERT VENINGA, GIFT OF HOPE: HOW TO SURVIVE OUR TRAGEDIES

will reverberate through all your relationships. When we're angry, we cannot help but inflict pain on children, spouses, close friends, and coworkers.

Consider the words of columnist Berta Sisemore (2009):

Forgiveness is truly a gift to ourselves. Holding onto resentment and thoughts of revenge keeps us bound to the offense committed against us, whereas forgiveness allows us to live freer and grants one greater peace of mind.

Chapter Review

We would all agree that emotions are a crucial part of being human. Indeed, we experience life's pains and pleasures through our emotions.

- **Emotions** are feelings that are experienced, with at least four common characteristics: physiological or internal changes, behavioral expressions, cognitive interpretations, and motivational tendencies.
- Although authorities do not always agree on the exact number of basic emotions, there appear to be both primary and mixed emotions. Primary and mixed emotions suggest that many feelings need to be described in more than a single term.
- Generally, our emotions begin to have negative effects when they are viewed as being excessive in intensity and duration. When mild, emotions can be facilitative—they increase our functioning. When emotions are intense, or sustained, they are debilitative—they disrupt our overall functioning.
- Some emotions cause us more difficulty than others. Some of these are fear, anxiety, anger, guilt, grief, and love.
- Although there are gender differences with respect to several potential causes of anger, both males and females report physical and verbal aggression as the most anger-provoking behaviors they could encounter.
- **Anger** most often begins with a loss or the threat of something or someone, such as: loss of self-esteem, loss of face, threat of physical harm or violence, loss of valued possessions, skills, or abilities, loss of a valued role, or loss of valued relationships.
- Four psychological reactions to anger are: 1) seeing yourself as a victim, 2) feeling discounted or ignored, 3) feeling powerless, and 4) looking for justice and revenge.
- Three characteristics of anger are: 1) anger is neither right nor wrong, 2) anger can be released in a right or wrong way, and 3) you are vulnerable when angry.
- When we feel **guilt**, it is about something we did or did not do. When we feel **shame**, it's about who we are as a person.
- The **grief process** consists of: 1) freeing ourselves emotionally from the loss, 2) readjusting to life after this loss, 3) resuming ordinary activities and forming new relationships. There are individual patterns of grieving.
- In **mourning**, we use our memory to recall the deceased and what was great about them, and then try to move on in our lives. In helping others you often find people who need to grieve. The **Ring Theory** often helps by buffering the main griever.
- With modeling and messages from our parents, society, and our peers, it is not surprising that we grow up confused about what to do with our feelings.
- We are both emotional and rational beings, and we need an intelligent balance of the two. **Emotional intelligence** consists of the ability to monitor, access, express, and regulate one's own emotions; the capacity to identify, interpret, and understand others' emotions; and the ability to use this information to guide one's thinking and actions.
- Because over-control poses our biggest problem in the expression of emotions, there are two common ways we deny our emotions—repression and suppression.
- **Repression** is a defense mechanism consisting of the exclusion of painful, unwanted, or dangerous thoughts and impulses from the conscious mind. **Suppression** is a defense mechanism by which people are conscious of their emotions, but deliberately control rather than express them.
- It is helpful to remember the following suggestions when deciding when and how to express your emotions: Listen to your body, personalize your feelings, identify your feelings, own your feelings, and decide what you will do with your feelings.

- **Cultural display rules** are a social group or culture's informal norms that distinguish how one should express themselves. They can be described as culturally prescribed rules that people learn early on in their lives by interactions and socializations with other people.
- Different cultures have different **display rules**—norms about when, where, and how much we should show emotions. These differences, if not understood, can lead to communication problems.
- Several long-term, positive benefits can be derived from learning to express emotions: You will develop positive feelings about yourself, your relationships will grow stronger, and pressure is relieved.
- Sometimes in the process of expressing and dealing with our feelings, we may even go through a healing process, known as **forgiveness**. Forgiveness is something you do for yourself, for your own happiness, health and well-being.
- **Social Emotional Learning (SEL)** comprises the skills we use to recognize and manage our own emotions and being able to recognize emotions in others. This concept arose out of research about emotional intelligence. Methods for improving SEL emphasize learning personal and social skills and setting personal goals. **Happiness** is an emotion that gives you a sense that life is good—a state of well-being that outlasts yesterday's moment of elation, today's buoyant mood, or tomorrow's feeling of sadness. (David Myers, *The Pursuit of Happiness*)
- The competition for status and esteem represents one reason behind **peer cyberbullying**. Friends, or former friends, are particularly likely to find themselves in situations in which they are vying for the same school, club, and/or sport positions and social connections,

Important stages involved in the forgiveness process include

- Exploring the anger you have
- Deciding to forgive
- Working on forgiveness
- Discovery and release

As we go through adulthood, we have the opportunity to experiment with a full range of behaviors and full range of emotions. Hopefully, we learn to express our emotions in constructive ways and to control those emotions and expressions that might be destructive to ourselves and others.

Learning Outcomes Review

1. What are emotions? Explain their four characteristics.
2. Describe how cognitive appraisals can be a part of an emotional experience.
3. What are the eight primary emotions? What is the difference in primary and mixed emotions?
4. Differentiate between mild (facilitative) and intense (debilitative) emotions. When do our emotions begin to have negative effects?
5. What is the difference between fear and anxiety? Define preparation anxiety and neurotic anxiety.
6. Anger most often begins with what kinds of losses or threats?
7. What are the four psychological reactions to anger? What are the three characteristics of anger? What are at least six do's and don'ts to remember in the expression of anger?
8. Explain the difference between guilt and shame.
9. What seem to be three causes of aggression in our society?

10. Discuss the common reactions people have in coping with a loss.
11. Define and discuss the mourning process. What is the Ring Theory?
12. Compare and contrast the importance of intellectual IQ and emotional intelligence.
13. Name and define the two common ways we deny our emotions.
14. What is the difference between repression and suppression?
15. List and discuss the five guidelines for dealing with your emotions. What is the shorthand technique for dealing with emotions?
16. Define the term "cultural display rules" and be able to give examples of some ways these rules are expressed in different cultures.
17. What is a toxic relationship?
18. What are the important stages in forgiveness?
19. Discuss the three common benefits of learning to express emotions.
20. Why do we need to consider going through a forgiveness process?
21. What important stages are involved in the forgiveness process?
22. Identify the four questions to ask yourself when attempting to shift your anger from an emotional level to an intellectual level.
23. Discuss cyberbullying, trolls, and what can be done to protect yourself.
24. Is happiness an emotion? Why?
25. How is this different from authentic happiness?
26. What is awe and how can it affect your life? What things do you like to do to produce awe in your life?

Key Terms

Aggression	Emotions	Mild Emotions
Anger	Empathy	Mixed Emotions
Annoyance	Facilitative Emotions	Moods
Anxiety	Fear	Neurotic Anxiety
Authentic happiness	Forgiveness	Preparation Anxiety
Awe	Good Grief	Primary Emotions
Cultural Display Rules	Grief and Bereavement	Rage
Cyberbullying	Grief Work	Repression
Cyberpsychology	Guilt	Resentment
Debilitative Emotions	Happiness	Ring Theory
Delight	Hate	Social Emotional Learning (SEL)
Distress	Hostility	Shame
Emotional Debt	Intense Emotions	Stress
Emotional Intelligence	Love	Suppression

Reflections: Critical Thinking Activity

Answer the following questions and turn them into your instructor for grading. (All questions answered = A; 13 questions answered = B; 8 questions answered = C).

1. Why do our emotions often color our point of view and affect our opinions?
2. How were you taught to express and deal with your emotions?
3. Do you believe that feelings follow a predictable pattern when we suffer a loss? If so, explain the process for you.
4. Of the problem emotions discussed, which one(s) present the greatest problem for you?
5. How do you deal with guilt and shame in your life?
6. When someone close to you dies, what do you want others to do for you?
7. Which part of the Shorthand Technique for expressing your feelings will be the most difficult for you? Why?
8. Which one of the four psychological reactions to anger is the most difficult for you to deal with?
9. What can be done to decrease aggression in our society?
10. Do you believe there is really emotional intelligence?
11. Discuss any "cultural display rules" you have experienced.
12. Do happy people care about social issues? Why or why not?
13. How do you deal with forgiveness in your life?
14. How do we measure social and emotional learning? Why is it important?
15. What is authentic happiness?
16. How is it different from happiness?
17. Why do we need to consider going through a forgiveness process?
18. Why is cyberbullying so prevalent?
19. Explain why you would use the Ring Theory.
20. Why should you pursue experiencing awe? Is this something everyone can do?

Technology Resources and Activities

RESOURCES

Anger Test: https://www.psychologistworld.com/stress/anger-test

This test by Psychologist World will assess how you react in stressful situations, and includes online evaluation after you finish.

Assessment Source: http://www.swin.edu.au/victims/resources/assessment/assessment.html

Devilly, G.J. (2004). Assessment Devices. Retrieved March 24, 2004, from Swinburne University, Clinical & Forensic Psychology

Online gamers Anonymous (olganon.org) is a 12-step program based on the principles of AA, and may be of help for uncontrolled gaming.

ACTIVITIES

www.authentichappiness.sas.upenn.edu/testcenter.aspx

Choose from a number of questionnaires at this site from the University of Pennsylvania. Develop insights into yourself through these questionnaires. The PANAS Questionnaire measures positive and negative effect(s) of different feelings and emotions. The Transgression Motivations Questionnaire measures forgiveness. They are free, but you need to register. Log in, pick one and get started. You do not need to be a student at the university.

http://www.apa.org/topics

Explores various topics on emotions and feelings.

http://www.schooltools.info/resources-1/2016/7/8/how-do-we-measure-social-and-emotional-learning

How do we measure social and emotional learning?

http://www.apa.org/topics/anger/control.aspx

Controlling anger before it controls you.

READINGS & PODCASTS

https://www.npr.org/lifekit

Life Kit, NPR's family of podcasts for making life better—everything from finances to exercise to relationships

For more information, sign up for the newsletter and follow @NPRLifeKit on Twitter.

http://www.varietiescorpus.com/learn

https://www.nytimes.com/2016/04/10/education/edlife/teaching-men-to-be-emotionally-honest.html

"Teaching Men to Be Emotionally Honest" by Andrew Reiner, *The New York Times* (April 4, 2016)

https://uwgreenbay.qualtrics.com/jfe/form/SV_5yTEVZUBBMLzLc9

Online Anger Consequences Questionnaire, a test that measures the common repercussions people experience when they express their anger online.

http://www.eiconsortium.org/reports/technical_report.html

A report issued for research on Emotional Intelligence in Organizations.

http://blog.online.saintleo.edu/degree-programs/10-useful-ted-talks-for-online-psychology-degree-students

Depression: the secrets we share.

https://www.youtube.com/watch?v=y9Trdafp83U

There's more to life than being happy: A TEDTalk by Emily Esfahani Smith (September 26, 2017)

Learn more about the difference between being happy and having meaning as Smith offers four pillars of a meaningful life.

https://www.youtube.com/watch?v=KTvSfeCRxe8

Violence against women: It's a men's issue, by Jackson Katz.

https://www.youtube.com/watch?v=qsEPUth4ovU

Anger, Rage & Relationships, an interview with Sue Parker Hall.

https://www.youtube.com/watch?v=juET61B1P98

The Adventure of Grief, by Dr. Geoff Warburton. Psychologist, writer and innovator Geoff Warburton challenges conventional apathy about grief and loss by offering an approach that evokes curiosity, openness and compassion.

https://youtu.be/PBzEwf1k59Y

Good grief! What I learned from loss | Elaine Mansfield | TEDxChemungRiver

There is power in grieving intentionally and purposefully. Telling her own story of loss, Elaine Mansfield explains the use of ritual as a tool for empowerment for life's most challenging times

https://www.youtube.com/ShotsOfAwe

Jason Silva: Shots of Awe: Technology Empathy and Awe video log (vlog)

https://www.youtube.com/watch?v=HTfYv3IEOqM

Daniel Goleman on "Social Intelligence."

https://www.youtube.com/watch?v=esPRsT-lmw8

The most important lesson from 83,000 brain scans by Daniel Amen.

https://www.youtube.com/watch?v=3aYWvujaT6M

Falling in Love Is the Easy Part, by Mandy Len Catron, TEDTalk.

https://www.youtube.com/watch?v=1Evwgu369Jw&feature=share

Dr. Brené Brown on Boundaries, Empathy, and Compassion

What is the best way to ease someone's pain and suffering? In this beautifully animated RSA Short, Dr Brené Brown reminds us that we can only create a genuine empathic connection if we are brave enough to really get in touch with our own fragilities.

https://www.ted.com/talks/susan_david_the_gift_and_power_of_emotional_courage?utm_source=ted-comshare&utm_medium=email&utm_campaign=tedspread

The gift and power of emotional courage, by Susan David

Psychologist Susan David shares how the way we deal with our emotions shapes everything that matters: our actions, careers, relationships, health, and happiness. In this deeply moving, humorous and potentially life-changing talk, she challenges a culture that prizes positivity over emotional truth and discusses the powerful strategies of emotional agility.

https://www.youtube.com/watch?v=hRCcQZEKVv4

The Fear of Being Fully Alive: Jason Silva (Shots of Awe)

From Wikipedia: The Jonah complex is the fear of success which prevents self-actualization, or the realization of one's potential. It is the fear of one's own greatness, the evasion of one's destiny, or the avoidance of exercising one's talents.

https://www.ted.com/talks/anne_lamott_12_truths_i_learned_from_life_and_writing?utm_campaign=tedspread&utm_medium=referral&utm_source=tedcomshare

12 truths I learned from life and writing, by Anne Lamott

Anne Lamott dives into the nuances of being a human who lives in a confusing, beautiful, emotional world

https://youtu.be/78nsxRxbf4w

How to Be Happy Every Day: It Will Change the World, by Jacqueline Way

The World Happiness Report states "Over 1 billion adults suffer from anxiety and depression." How do we get to happy? Jacqueline Way, Founder of www.365give.ca shares a secret to happiness so simple a three-year-old can do it.

https://www.youtube.com/watch?v=aaXBYcfVYZM

Living without shame: How we can empower ourselves, by Whitney Thore

http://www.ted.com/talks/brene_brown_listening_to_shame

Listening to shame by Brené Brown.

https://www.youtube.com/watch?v=H_8y0WLm78U

The price of shame, by Monica Lewinsky

Monica Lewinsky takes a look at our "culture of humiliation" and why it leads to bullying.

http://www.helpguide.org/articles/depression/dealing-with-depression.htm

Resources for overcoming depression.

https://www.youtube.com/watch?v=An6GJt3KYD4

TEDxTinHauWomen welcomes Jessie Lam to share her story on the importance of talking about mental health, self-care, and use of data and technology in daily lives.

https://www.youtube.com/watch?v=apbSsILLh28

What Really Matters at the End of Life by BJ Miller, TED Talks.

https://www.youtube.com/watch?v=PY9DcIMGxMs

What really causes addiction—to everything from cocaine to smart-phones? And how can we overcome it? Johann Hari has seen our current methods fail firsthand, as he has watched loved ones struggle to manage their addictions. He started to wonder why we treat addicts the way we do—and if there might be a better way. As he shares in this deeply personal talk, his questions took him around the world, and unearthed some surprising and hopeful ways of thinking about an age-old problem.

http://tedxtalks.ted.com/video/Beat-bullying-why-young-people;search%3Abullying

Beat bullying; why young people hold the key, by Alex Holmes.

https://www.youtube.com/watch?v=-FyVetL1MEw

Be The Warrior Not The Worrier: Fighting Anxiety and Fear by Angela Ceberano

http://tedxtalks.ted.com/video/The-Upsides-of-Anger-Dan-Moshav;search%3Aanger%20management

Dan Moshavi, Professor of Management in the Barowsky School of Business at Dominican University of California, explores the upsides of an often misunderstood emotion: Anger.

https://www.youtube.com/watch?v=PTlmho_RovY

Killing Us Softly 4: Image of women

https://www.youtube.com/watch?v=WLMJHdySgE8

Violence—a family tradition by Robbyn Peters Bennett at TEDxBellingham, November 23, 2013. Robbyn Peters Bennett, LMHC, CMHS, is a psychotherapist, educator, and child advocate who specializes in the treatment of trauma-related mental health problems resulting from the effects of early childhood stress, abuse, and neglect.

https://www.apa.org/pi/oema/resources/ethnicity-health/asian-american/bullying-and-victimization

Bullying & Victimization and Asian-American Students

Myths About Asian-American Bullying and Victimization

https://www.apa.org/pi/oema/resources/ethnicity-health/african-american/stress

Ethnicity and Health in America Series: Invisibility in the African-American Community

Becoming *Aware*

Three Coping Exercises and Activities

1. Acceptance with ice cubes

Acceptance is an essential positive coping technique. This exercise will allow you to notice your sensations and accept their existence without trying to control or change them. There are four steps in this exercise, and you can learn more about it from the Ice Cubes Exercise at https://positivepsychology.com/tools/practicing-acceptance-with-ice-cubes/

Step 1—**Take one or two ice cubes and hold them gently on your palm. Try to keep holding them for the next couple of minutes.**

Step 2—After a few seconds, you will start feeling extreme cold on your skin. At this point, you might have thoughts about letting go of the ice cubes to restore warmth and comfort. **Your goal at this stage would be to notice these thoughts without trying to act on them.**

Step 3—**The third stage is about tuning into your emotions.** You may notice feelings such as fear or discomfort. Try to see how you are feeling and what thoughts are popping into your mind while you continue holding the ice cubes.

Step 4—**The fourth step of this exercise is about offering kindness and gratitude to yourself.** While you may continue experiencing extreme sensations, try to comfort and remind yourself that this is not harmful to you.

Step 5—**Finally, release the ice cubes and warm your hands with a dry towel or cloth.**

When you feel the cold sensation fading away, try to recall the experience and ask yourself:

What did I learn from this exercise?

What thoughts and emotions did I experience while I was holding the ice cubes?

How did I react to my emotions? Can I use a similar approach to my life problems?

Adapted from Positive Psychology.com

Name _____ Date _____

Am I Emotionally Intelligent?

PURPOSE

To get a sense of your emotional intelligence.

INSTRUCTIONS

Respond by placing a check mark (☒) next to each of the items below, using the following scale:

1 = very much unlike me 2 = unlike me 3 = neutral 4 = like me 5 = very much like me

	1	2	3	4	5

Emotional Self-Awareness

1. I am good at recognizing my emotions.
2. I am good at understanding the causes of my feelings.
3. I am good at separating my feelings from my actions.

Managing Emotions

4. I am good at tolerating frustration.
5. I am good at managing my anger.
6. I have positive feelings about myself.
7. I am good at coping with stress.
8. My emotions don't interfere with my ability to focus and accomplish my goals.
9. I have good self-control and am not impulsive.

Reading Emotions

10. I am good at taking the perspectives of others (such as students and parents).
11. I show empathy and sensitivity to others' feelings.
12. I am good at listening to what other people say.

Handling Relationships

13. I am good at analyzing and understanding relationships.

14. I am good at solving problems in relationships.   ____ ____ ____ ____ ____
15. I am assertive (rather than passive, manipulative, or
    aggressive) in relationships.   ____ ____ ____ ____ ____
16. I have one or more close friendships.   ____ ____ ____ ____ ____
17. I am good at sharing and cooperating.   ____ ____ ____ ____ ____

SCORING AND INTERPRETATION

Add up your scores for all 17 items. My total emotional intelligence score is _____.

If you scored 75–85, you probably are very emotionally intelligent, someone who is emotionally self-aware, manages emotions effectively, knows how to read emotions, and has positive relationships with others. **If you scored 65–74,** you probably have good emotional intelligence but there probably are some areas on which you still need to work. Look at the items on which you scored 3 or below to see where you need to improve. **If you scored 45–64,** you likely have average emotional intelligence. Give some serious thought to working on your emotional life. Examine your emotional weaknesses and strive to improve them. **If you scored 44 or below,** you likely have below-average emotional intelligence. You might contact the counseling service at your college for some recommendations.

DISCUSSION

1. Do you agree or disagree with your score and the interpretation? Why or why not?

2. What, if anything, do you think you need to do to improve your emotional intelligence?

Adapted from John Santrock, 2006, Human Adjustment. New York: The McGraw-Hill Company.

Emotional Expressivity Scale

PURPOSE

To assess your degree of emotional expression.

INSTRUCTIONS

Using the following scale, place the number on the line that best describes your agreement with the following statements:

5 = Strongly Agree   4 = Agree   3 = Neither Agree nor Disagree   2 = Disagree   1 = Strongly Disagree

_____ 1. I think of myself as emotionally expressive.
_____ 2. People think of me as an unemotional person.*
_____ 3. I keep my feelings to myself.*
_____ 4. I am often considered indifferent by others.*
_____ 5. People can read my emotions.
_____ 6. I display my emotions to other people.
_____ 7. I don't like to let other people see how I am feeling.*
_____ 8. I am able to cry in front of other people.
_____ 9. Even if I am feeling very emotional, I don't let others see my feelings.*
_____ 10. Other people aren't easily able to observe what I am feeling.*
_____ 11. I am not very emotionally expressive.*
_____ 12. Even when I am experiencing strong feelings, I don't express them outwardly.*
_____ 13. I cannot hide the way I am feeling.
_____ 14. Other people believe me to be very emotional.
_____ 15. I don't express my emotions to other people.*
_____ 16. The way I feel is different from how others think I feel.*
_____ 17. I hold my feelings in.*

SCORING

Recode these statements:* 2, 3, 4, 7, 9, 10, 11, 12, 15, 16, and 17 with the following:

5 = 1   4 = 2   3 = 3   2 = 4   1 = 5

After you recode the negative items, sum all the scores together. **My Score: _____**

Range of Emotional Expressivity = 17–85 (17 is the lowest expression of emotions, and 85 is the highest expression of emotions).

DISCUSSION

1. Do you agree with your results? Why or why not?

2. What do you think you need to do to be more emotionally expressive?

Identifying Feelings

PURPOSE

To determine how you deal with various feelings and emotions.

INSTRUCTIONS

Complete the "feelings" survey below by circling the number that expresses how well you deal with each feeling listed.

1. Can express easily and completely in any situation
2. Can express most of the time
3. Can express some of the time—with difficulty
4. Can express rarely—with reservation
5. Cannot express this emotion

Caring	1	2	3	4	5	Love	1	2	3	4	5
Concern	1	2	3	4	5	Sadness	1	2	3	4	5
Depression	1	2	3	4	5	Fear	1	2	3	4	5
Anger	1	2	3	4	5	Tension	1	2	3	4	5
Disappointment	1	2	3	4	5	Hurt	1	2	3	4	5
Excitement	1	2	3	4	5	Pride	1	2	3	4	5

Complete the sentences below:

1. I very much care about _____

2. The thing that depresses me most frequently is _____

3. I feel tense when _____

4. The thing that hurts me most is _____

5. I am excited about _____

6. I take pride in _____

7. I am disappointed with _____

8. The thing that frightens me most is _____

9. I get angry when _____

10. I am concerned about _____

11. I feel sad when _____

12. Love is a feeling _____

DISCUSSION

1. Is there a feeling that you absolutely cannot deal with? If so, what?

2. Which feeling do you think you deal with most successfully? Why?

3. How important are feelings to you in your interactions with others?

4. How can you learn to express your emotions in a positive way?

How I Express My Feelings

PURPOSE

To identify how you personally express a variety of emotions/feelings.

INSTRUCTIONS

Being as spontaneous as possible, complete the following sentences:

1. When I'm angry, I express it by . . .
2. When I'm worried, I express it by . . .
3. When I'm sad, I express it by . . .
4. When I'm happy, I express it by . . .
5. When I feel like a failure, I express it by . . .
6. When I'm afraid, I express it by . . .
7. When I feel successful, I express it by . . .
8. When I feel affectionate, I express it by . . .
9. When I feel guilty, I express it by . . .
10. When I feel lonely, I express it by . . .
11. When I feel hurt, I express it by . . .
12. When I feel rejected, I express it by . . .

DISCUSSION

1. Which of these feelings would you like to be able to express in a different manner?

2. Explain what steps you would take to learn how to express the feelings identified in Question 1.

3. Which of these feelings are the most difficult for you to express?

4. Which of these feelings are the easiest for you to express? Why?

Feeling Connected

A writing exercise to foster connection and kindness. Time Required: 10 minutes.

Try to do this practice at least once per week, selecting a different example each time.

HOW TO DO IT

Try to think of a time when you felt a strong bond with someone in your life. Choose a specific example of an experience you had with this person where you felt especially close and connected to them. This could be a time you had a meaningful conversation, gave or received support, experienced a great loss or success together, or witnessed an historic moment together.

Once you've thought of a specific example, spend a few minutes writing about what happened. In particular, consider the ways in which this experience made you feel close and connected to the other person.

WHY YOU SHOULD TRY IT

Humans have a strong drive to be kind, but that drive is usually stronger when they feel connected to other people. To help foster that feeling of closeness, this exercise asks you to think about a time when you felt a strong connection to another person and to describe the experience in writing. Research suggests that reflecting on feelings of connection can increase people's motivation to help others, whether by helping a friend or stranger in need, volunteering, or donating money. Helping others can, in turn, increase happiness and improve relationships.

WHY IT WORKS

Feeling connected to others is considered to be a fundamental psychological need. When people feel rejected or alone, they may be more likely to focus on themselves and on striving to meet their own unmet needs rather than attending to the needs of others. When people feel connected and cared about, by contrast, they are better able to expend energy on helping and caring for others.

By reflecting on times when you've felt a strong connection with others, and by striving to cultivate more of these experiences, you are fueling your drive to practice kindness and compassion.

EVIDENCE THAT IT WORKS

Pavey, L., Greitemeyer, T., & Sparks, P. (2011). Highlighting relatedness promotes prosocial motives and behavior. *Personality and Social Psychology Bulletin*, 37(7), 905–917.

Some study participants reflected on a time when they felt a strong bond with someone else; other participants wrote about a time when they felt especially competent or autonomous.

Compared with those in the other groups, the participants who reflected on their experience of closeness reported greater feelings of connectedness and concern for others. They also reported a stronger intention to carry out a variety of altruistic behaviors over the next six weeks, including giving money to charity and going out of their way to help a stranger in need.

When they analyzed the data more closely, the researchers found that a greater desire to be kind depended on whether participants experienced greater feelings of connectedness to others after doing the writing exercise.

Adapted from the Greater Good in Action Science Foundation.

Name _____ Date _____

Do Women Express More Emotions than Men?

PURPOSE

Is the cultural stereotype of the unexpressive male and the more expressive female true?

INSTRUCTIONS

Divide the class between the males and the females, with the males on one side, and the females on the other.

Beginning with one of the following statements, have one gender give their views on the following statements, and then have the other gender respond until all statements have been addressed.

1. Is it true that women are more likely than men to express positive emotions like love, liking, joy, and contentment and that women have a hard time expressing anger? Why or why not?

2. Is it true that women are more likely than men to express feelings of vulnerability like fear, sadness, loneliness, and embarrassment, and that men have difficulty expressing sadness? Why or why not?

3. Is it true that men rarely express positive emotions and feelings of vulnerability, especially to their male friends, although they may be more expressive to the woman or man they love? Why or why not?

4. Is it true that men are less bashful about revealing their strengths? Why or why not?

5. Is it true that while men experience emotions much like women, they may tend to mask their emotional inclinations? Why or why not?

6. Is it true that men often express their feelings through actions and activities rather than words? Why or why not?

292

7. Is it true that women are better able to "pick up" (read) the emotions of others? Why or why not?

8. Is it true that men tend to be better than women at returning to normal after experiencing distressing emotions? Why or why not?

9. What is a "Real Man"? Give your definition.

10. Discuss violence in families and against women. What can be done to help men control anger against women?

Post-Activity Discussion Questions:

1. Is there a difference in the way men and women express emotions? If so, how?

2. Is it possible that the real difference in the expression of emotions between men and women is just an individual personality difference?

3. What do you plan to teach your male children and your female children about the expression of emotions?

Name _____ Date _____

Develop a "Wellness Toolbox" to Deal with Mental Health

DEVELOPING A WELLNESS TOOLBOX | MENTALHEALTHRECOVERY

mentalhealthrecovery.com/info-center/developing-a-wellness-toolbox/

Come up with a list of things that you can do for a quick mood boost. The more "tools" for coping with depression, the better. Try to implement a few of these ideas each day, even if you're feeling good.

- Spend some time in nature
- List what you like about yourself
- Read a good book
- Watch a funny movie or TV show
- Take a long, hot bath
- Take care of a few small tasks
- Play with a pet
- Talk to friends or family face-to-face
- Listen to music
- Do something spontaneous

Other information you might find interesting and helpful:

According to the latest statistics from the National Alliance on Mental Illness, 43.8 million Americans, or 18.5% of the national population, experience mental illness every year. Mental illness is a broad term defined by the Mayo Clinic as any disorder that affects one's mood, thinking, or behavior. When mental illness influences family life, work, education, and other aspects day-to-day life, the condition is known as a psychiatric disability.

A recent report from Johns Hopkins University notes that psychiatric disabilities are not caused by singular life events; rather, they are persistent conditions that may have a significant, lifelong impact. Those diagnosed with a psychiatric disability may mitigate the effects of their condition with medication and/or ongoing psychotherapy. Even with treatment, many psychiatric disabilities will persist in some form.

- College students with psychiatric disabilities face unique educational challenges. Dedicated mental health counselors and disability coordinators are available on most campuses, and students can typically seek medical attention. Many students, however, do not know how to get help for their problems. (http://www.bestcolleges.com/resources/college-planning-with-psychiatric-disabilities) Suicide Facts at a Glance 2015 (n.d.). Retrieved October 23, 2015, from http://www.cdc.gov/violenceprevention/pdf/suicide-datasheet-a.pdf—See more at: https://www.nami.org/Learn-More/Mental-Health-By-the-Numbers#sthash.yCoO1hWO.dpuf

  NAMI-Want-to-know-how-to-help-a-friend.pdf at https://www.nami.org/NAMI/media/NAMI-Media/Infographics/NAMI-Want-to-know-how-to-help-a-friend.pdf

KNOW THE TEN COMMON WARNING SIGNS

1. Feeling very sad or withdrawn for more than two weeks
2. Seriously trying to harm or kill oneself or making plans to do so
3. Severe out-of-control, risk-taking behaviors
4. Sudden overwhelming fear for no reason
5. Not eating, throwing up or using laxatives to lose weight; significant weight loss or weight gain
6. Seeing, hearing, or believing things that are not real
7. Repeatedly using drugs or alcohol
8. Drastic changes in mood, behavior, personality, or sleeping habits
9. Extreme difficulty in concentrating or staying still
10. Intense worries or fears that get in the way of daily activities

ADDITIONAL RESOURCES

- National Institute of Mental Health (NIMH): The leading federal agency in the field of mental health research, NIMH is one of 27 branches of the National Institutes of Health. The NIMH website is a compendium of news, published reports, academic journals, data tables, and other academic resources.
- National Alliance on Mental Illness (NAMI): Founded in 1979, NAMI is the nation's largest grassroots organization in the country that supports people living with mental illness. NAMI maintains a toll-free hotline to provide advice and medical referrals. Representatives from the organization also work closely with lawmakers nationwide to ensure fair and equal protection for people with mental health issues.
- Treatment Advocacy Center (TAC): This nonprofit organization has worked to promote mental health treatment and fight social stigma related to mentally ill individuals for nearly 20 years. TAC also collaborates with researchers to publish the latest developments in medication and treatment for mental illnesses.
- MentalHealth.gov: This website maintained by the U.S. Department of Health and Human Services maintains an up-to-date listing of toll-free hotlines accessible to people living with mental illness.
- Shining a Light on Mental Illness: an Invisible Disability: This blog post from the World Bank explores various issues faced by people living with mental illness. Links to other related blogs and websites are included.

Name _____ Date _____

Learning to Forgive

This activity is to do alone and at your own pace.

WHY IT WORKS

Forgiveness is a long and often challenging process. These steps may help along the way by providing concrete guidelines. Specifically, they may help you: to narrow and understand whom to forgive; to name and describe your pain; to understand the difference between forgiving and excusing or reconciling; and by thinking about the person who has caused you pain in a novel way, you may begin to feel some compassion for him or her, facilitating forgiveness and reducing the ill will you hold toward this person. (These steps also attune you to residual pain from your experience, and encourage you to find meaning and some positivity in it. You may want to see a counselor or therapist to help you to forgive someone who deeply harmed you—particularly as a young person or child. The difference between forgiveness and reconciliation is very, very important. In our culture, we often try very hard to be "good," hoping that will right past pains, when just realizing our own feelings are valid and understandable given the circumstances is equally as important in the process. In addition, simply addressing the issue honestly and openly with the person who harmed you may, in fact, cause them pain, particularly if they have been living in denial.)

We suggest that you move through the steps below based on what works for you.

1. Make a list of people who have hurt you deeply enough to warrant the effort to forgive. You can do this by asking yourself, on a 1-to-10 scale, How much pain do I have regarding the way this person treated me?, with 1 involving the least pain (but still significant enough to justify the time to forgive) and 10 involving the most pain. Then, order the people on this list from least painful to most painful. Start with the person lowest on this hierarchy (least painful).

2. Next to the person's name, consider one offense by the first person on your list. Ask yourself: How has this person's offense negatively impacted my life?

    Reflect on the psychological and physical harm it may have caused. Consider how your views of humanity and trust of others may have changed as a result of this offense. Recognize that what happened was not okay, and allow yourself to feel any negative emotions that come up.

3. When you're ready, make a decision to forgive. Deciding to forgive involves coming to terms with what you will be doing as you forgive—extending an act of mercy toward the person who has hurt you. When we offer this mercy, we deliberately try to *reduce* resentment (persistent ill will) toward this person and, instead, offer them kindness, respect, generosity, or even love.

Becoming *Aware*

It is important to emphasize that forgiveness does not involve excusing the person's actions, forgetting what happened, or tossing justice aside. Justice and forgiveness can be practiced together.

Another important caveat: To forgive is not the same as to reconcile. Reconciliation is a negotiation strategy in which two or more people come together again in mutual trust. You may not choose to reconcile with the person you are forgiving.

4. Start with cognitive exercises. Ask yourself these questions about the person who has hurt you: What was life like for this person while growing up? What wounds did they suffer from others that could have made them more likely to hurt you? What kinds of extra pressures or stresses were in this person's life at the time he or she offended you? These questions are not meant to excuse or condone, but rather to better understand the other person's areas of pain, those areas that make them vulnerable and human. Understanding why people commit destructive acts can also help us find more effective ways of preventing further destructive acts from occurring in the future.

5. Be aware of any little movement of your heart through which you begin to feel even slight compassion for the person who offended you. This person may have been confused, mistaken, and misguided. They may deeply regret their actions. As you think about this person, notice if you start to feel softer emotions toward them.

6. Try to consciously bear the pain that they caused you so that you do not end up throwing that pain back onto the one who offended you, or even toward unsuspecting others, such as loved ones who were not the ones who wounded you in the first place. When we are emotionally wounded, we tend to displace our pain onto others. Please be aware of this so that you are not perpetuating a legacy of anger and injuries.

7. Think of a gift of some kind that you can offer to the person you are trying to forgive. Forgiveness is an act of mercy—you are extending mercy toward someone who may not have been merciful toward you. This could be through a smile, a returned phone call, or a good word about him or her to others. Always consider your own safety first when extending kindness and goodwill toward this person. If interacting with this person could put you in danger, find another way to express your feelings, such as by writing in a journal or engaging in a practice such as compassion meditation.

8. Finally, try to find meaning and purpose in what you have experienced. For example, as people suffer from the injustices of others, they often realize that they themselves become more sensitive to others' pain. This, in turn, can give them a sense of purpose toward helping those who are hurting. It may also motivate them to work toward preventing future injustices of a similar kind.

Once you complete the forgiveness process with one person on your list, select the next person in line and move up that list until you are forgiving the person who hurt you the most.

Adapted from Baskin, T.W., & Enright, R. D. (2004). Intervention studies on forgiveness: A meta-analysis. *Journal of Counseling and Development, 82*, 79–90.

Chapter 4 group activity

STRESS

For an interesting discussion on stress, please read this and discuss it in groups of 4.

The Science of Stress and How Our Emotions Affect Our Susceptibility to Burnout and Disease

https://www.brainpickings.org/2015/07/20/esther-sternberg-balance-within-stress-emotion/

Group report notes: turn in to your teacher and include it in your learning journal.

Dealing with Emotions

LEARNING JOURNAL

Select the statement below that best defines your feelings about the personal value or meaning gained from this chapter and respond below the dotted line.

I learned that I . . .   I was surprised that I . . .

I realized that I . . .   I was pleased that I . . .

I discovered that I . . .   I was displeased that I . . .

....

Watch the following Kindness Motiviational Video and write a small critique to turn in.

https://www.youtube.com/watch?v=mTsvSAItPqA&feature=share

How You Treat People Is Who You Are!

chapter 5
Interpersonal Communication

© YAKOBCHUK VIACHESLAV/Shutterstock.com

Communication is the lifeblood of every relationship. When open, clear, sensitive communication takes place, the relationship is nurtured. When communication is guarded, hostile, or ineffective, the relationship falters. When the communication flow is largely obstructed, the relationship quickly deteriorates and ultimately dies. Where communication skills are lacking, there is so much lost love—between spouses, lovers, friends, parents, and children. For satisfying relationships, it is essential to discover methods that will help us to at least partially bridge the interpersonal gaps that separate us from others. —Robert Bolton, *People Skills*

Think About This...

- Friends say, "We can't communicate anymore. We aren't even on the same wavelength."
- Kids say, "I can't talk to my parents. They just don't understand me."
- Parents say, "I can't talk to my kids. They won't even listen to me."
- Marriage partners say, "We can't talk to each other. We just don't have anything meaningful to talk about."
- Students say, "We can't discuss our lack of understanding with Mr. Jones. He thinks he has explained the chapter perfectly well. There is no use in us trying to talk to him."
- An employer learns that her assistant is leaving and just can't believe they didn't say they were so unhappy. She replies, "I've tried to many times in the past, but we just can't communicate."
- You think, "Every time I think we are having a romantic dinner my partner keeps glancing at the cellphone like someone's call is more important than me. I should be the one to focus on!"

Have you ever said to another person, "We just can't communicate"? Has another person ever said that to you? Actually, you were both communicating at some level, but you were not connecting. What, then, is communication?

Mary Kassian (2014) indicates that the Greek word for group communication is *koinonia*, which means sharing; making known; exchanging thoughts, feelings, and information; joining together; having fellowship with; forming a connecting link; and sharing.

Because communication underlies all relationships, and the process of communication is such a complex topic, we want to begin by providing some organizational structure for our discussion. The first half of the chapter deals with the communication process, including the verbal and nonverbal aspects of communication. The remaining part of the chapter is devoted to learning how to improve our listening and responding skills.

Why Do We Need to Communicate?

Without communication, we, as humans, would not be able to survive. We need to find out about the world we live in; we need to know how to interpret the experiences we have; we need to release tension; we need to find out about other people; we need to know how to get information from others; and we need to know how to let others know what is going on inside of us.

Communication has been described as *the process of conveying feelings, attitudes, facts, beliefs, and ideas between individuals, either verbally or non-verbally* in such a way that the message intended is received. On the surface, then, communication appears to be such a simple act. After all, our daily lives are filled with one communication experience after another. When we are with other people who are aware of our presence, it is impossible not to communicate. No matter what we do, we send out messages that say something about ourselves.

This points to the fact that communication is perhaps the most important factor in determining the kinds of relationships we have with others. Furthermore, communication is the way relationships are created, maintained, and destroyed. The ability to send clear messages and to be heard is central to any ongoing relationship—husband and wife, parent and child, employer and employee, friends, siblings. In her classic book *Making Contact*, Virginia Satir (2011) confirms this:

> I see communication as a huge umbrella that covers and affects all that goes on between human beings. Once a human being has arrived on this earth, communication is the largest single factor determining what kinds of relationships [sic] makes with others and what happens to him in the

world about him. How he manages his survival, how he develops intimacy; how productive he is, how he makes sense, how he connects with his own divinity—all are largely dependent on his communication skills. (2011)

However, as much communicating as we do, most of us are not all that efficient in performing this simple act. Perhaps, the trite common statement—*"keep the communication channels open"*—reminds us of the complexity, rather than simplicity, of communication. Be open, honest, and flexible when you communicate (Hannah et al., 2008).

Nonviolent communication (abbreviated NVC, also called compassionate communication or collaborative communication) is a communication process developed by Marshall Rosenberg beginning in the 1960s. Nonviolent communications leads to clearer and less hurtful communications (2019).

Why Is Communication Difficult?

Think about the following statement:

When two people talk, these are some of the messages that can get through:

1. *What you mean to say.*
2. *What you actually say.*
3. *What the other person hears.*
4. *What the other person thinks they hear.*
5. *What the other person says about what you said.*
6. *What you think the other person said about what you said.*

We are all concerned with the ability to communicate real meaning and understanding. Some people think that communication is really the sending and receiving of messages, because both elements must be present for communication to take place. They think that communication originates with the sender, and they believe that the message sent is the one that is received. They expect their listeners to act in accordance with the intentions of their message, and they are often bewildered, hurt, or angry when their listeners do not do so. An additional factor is the use of technology that promises instant access to everyone and everything, along with real-time response.

As we can see, the fundamental transaction of the message sent and received does not guarantee that communication has occurred. In essence, if I speak and you listen, I may be transmitting information, but that is all. If I speak, however, and you listen, and we both understand, then we are communicating more effectively. Effective communication exists between two people when the receiver interprets the sender's message the way the sender intended it (Johnson, 2014).

Effective communication is not just an event, but a process—a process that requires the cooperation and understanding of both parties.

The Communication Process

In any given situation, there are three commonly accepted parts to the communication process. There is always: 1) *a sender of the message,* 2) *a receiver of the message* and 3) *the content of the message.* The message can be either verbal or nonverbal. In practice it is a much more complex process than these three parts suggest.

Let us look at a simple diagram (see Figure 5.1) of what is involved in a communication transaction. Assume that Jill wants to inform John, her husband, that she would like to remodel the house.

Step one: *The idea.* Here the sender creates an idea or chooses a fact to communicate. Jill says to herself, "I think I'll ask John if he agrees we should remodel the house."

Step two: *Encoding.* The sender, in attempting to get their message across, forms a mental picture of that message and then organizes and translates this picture into symbols that will make the sender's idea receivable. Symbols involve such things as the selection of words, tone and pitch of voice, nonverbal methods, or even types of supportive materials. Jill says, "John, there is something I would like to talk to you about after dinner and when the children are in bed." Later, Jill says, "I would like for us to remodel the house this summer."

Step three: *Transmission.* This refers to the means by which the encoded communication is to be made, or the channel through which the message must pass from the sender to the receiver. *Communication channels* can be a face-to-face discussion, something in writing, the telephone, or even radio or television. In this instance, Jill chose to talk to John face to face.

Step four: *Receiving.* John can only receive the message if he is attentive to Jill. He must not be reading the newspaper or watching news or catching up on email and working.

Figure 5.1   COMMUNICATION PROCESS

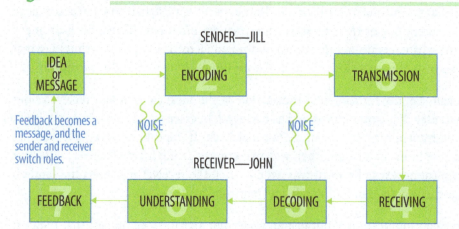

Step five: *Decoding.* This is done by the receiver. The message that has been transmitted by the sender must be interpreted and translated into meaning. By decoding, the listener has now formed his or her own mental picture of what the sender said. In our example, decoding is not complete until John hears the whole message. The opening comment, "John, there is something I would like to talk to you about," is a good way to get John's attention and help him listen for the whole message. There is no guarantee that the listener is as attentive as they seem.

Step six: *Understanding.* If the receiver has decoded accurately, the mental picture they have formed of what the sender said will possibly match. Consequently, the message has been understood correctly. In our example, John does not have any trouble understanding that Jill wants to remodel the house this summer. He may hear his own image of what "remodel" means, or where Jill wants to make changes. So the process should continue with questions and answers until they reach a consensus.

There is always the possibility that the listener may have misinterpreted the speaker's words, however, thus forming a totally different mental picture. This would mean that communication did not properly take place. Too often, this type of communication breakdown occurs, resulting in all sorts of problems, ranging from not knowing what to study for an exam to painful relationship situations.

There is a means of preventing, or at least reducing, this type of communication problem by checking and decoding for accuracy and thus improving the quality of our communication. This method is called feedback.

Step seven: *Feedback.* Feedback, the process by which the sender clarifies how their message is being received and interpreted, is really the only means for determining whether there is mutual understanding between the sender and receiver.

In our example, John understands Jill's request, but he does not agree. He acts, or gives feedback, by telling Jill that she will have to wait six more months until his promotion and salary increase will become effective. Jill understands John's position and tells him, "Okay, but I am counting on us starting November 1." As you can see from this illustration, as well as in Figure 5.1, *feedback* becomes a message, and the sender and receiver switch roles (Reece & Brandt, 2017). There needs to be feedback in every step.

Noise. Before we leave the communication diagram, it is important to note that noise can occur at every stage of the communication process. *Noise* includes anything that interferes with communication and distorts the impact of the message. *External noise* includes such elements in the physical environment as temperature, a show on television, music, email, social media, loud traffic, children or roommates talking, or any other external event or distracting influences. *Internal noise* includes such things as a headache, lack of sleep, daydreaming, preoccupation with other problems, or even a preconceived idea that the message is going to be unimportant or uninteresting (Hamilton, 2017).

Becoming Aware of Technology and Social Media: The Attention Economy Needs to Change. But How?
https://www.pbssocal.org/programs/braincraft/big-techs-battle-for-our-attention-w1fxgb/

We're in the middle of an Attention War—where big tech battle it out to win over our eyeballs. Our attention spans are considered a precious—and scarce—commodity. So what is the price of your attention? This video explores the psychology, design, and impact of tech and social media on both ourselves and society.

Implicit Bias. One of the key aspects of interpersonal communications that can happen in your verbal and nonverbal response is implicit bias. Being diligent in your communications is key to dealing with it. "Implicit bias refers to the attitudes or stereotypes that affect our understanding, actions, and decisions in an unconscious manner. These biases, which encompass both favorable and unfavorable assessments, are activated involuntarily and without an individual's awareness or intentional control" (Kirwan Institute, 2016).

A Few Key Characteristics of Implicit Biases

- Implicit biases are **pervasive**. Everyone possesses them, even people with avowed commitments to impartiality, such as judges.

- Implicit and explicit biases are **related but distinct mental constructs**. They are not mutually exclusive, and may even reinforce each other.

- The implicit associations we hold **do not necessarily align with our declared beliefs** or even reflect stances we would explicitly endorse.

- We generally tend to hold implicit biases that **favor our own in-group**, though research has shown that we can still hold implicit biases against our in-group.

- Implicit biases are **malleable**. Our brains are incredibly complex, and the implicit associations that we have formed can be gradually unlearned through a variety of debiasing techniques (Kirwan Institute for the Study of Race and Ethnicity, 2016).

> *It takes two to make communication.*
> —IRVING LEE

One- and Two-Way Communication

As we have just discussed, since there are so many sources of error or distortion in a message, it is wise for both the sender and receiver to provide adequate feedback to one another in an effort to gain understanding and rapport. This completes the process of *two-way communication*, with the *key element being feedback*. One-way communication frequently results in our making inaccurate inferences or assumptions (Reece & Brandt, 2017).

One-way communication is sometimes referred to as *passive listening*, because there is an *absence of verbal feedback*. Examples of one-way communication might be a class which is *strictly* lecture oriented, or a certain person you know who tends to dominate and control conversations, with little interest shown in your ideas or concerns. Even written messages can become avenues for two-way communication. For example, "I'll follow up with a phone call to you within a week to hear your ideas on this proposal," or "Send me your ideas on this proposal, and then we will get together for lunch and discuss our mutual concerns."

Without a doubt, many of the difficulties that arise in communication stem from the fact that we fail to remember that communication is really a two-way process. Open two-way communication facilitates understanding in communication, which in turn helps such things as developing a fulfilling relationship and being able to work together effectively (Johnson, 2008).

BECOMING AWARE OF NEW SKILLS—CONSTRUCTIVE LISTENING TECHNIQUE

By listening and then repeating back in your own words the essence and feeling of what you have just heard, from the speaker's point of view, you allow a speaker to feel the satisfaction of being understood (a major human need). Listening responsively is always worthwhile as a way of letting people know that you care about them.

After having reviewed the complete communication process, it becomes apparent that "breakdowns" can occur at any step. Sometimes these "breakdowns" are caused by a *communication barrier*—something that stops, blocks, prevents, or hinders. In communication, we may be hindered by a number of barriers that seem to arise from natural human differences and others that are the result of personal habits or attitudes. All or most can be eliminated, changed, or minimized.

Having an unhelpful cheerful attitude is called "dismissive positivity" or "toxic positivity." Instead of acknowledging a friend's anguish, a "chipper" upbeat attitude minimizes their anxiety. Strive to be more compassionate when people share their despair. Instead of saying, "You'll get over it," to someone in distress, say something to impart validation and hope: "This is hard. You've done hard things before and I believe in you."

Review Table 5.1 for a partial listing of barriers to interpersonal communication. Which barriers sometimes prevent you from achieving clear, open communication?

Table 5.1 BARRIERS TO INTERPERSONAL COMMUNICATION

Background and experience	Hidden agendas
Health and physical condition	Stereotyping
Feelings and emotions	Physical environment
Word meaning and usage	Preoccupation—technology?
Listening only for words	Closed mind
Jumping to conclusions	Being self-centered
Making snap judgments	Failure to listen—technology?
Failure to seek clarification	Unclear messages
Disregarding feedback	Highly charged, emotion-laden words
Defensiveness	Talking too fast
Incongruent verbal and nonverbal behavior	Generalizations
Lack of eye contact is determined by culture.	Language level
Toxic positivity	Dismissive Positivity

The remaining sections of this chapter will discuss ways to minimize these barriers and reduce communication "breakdowns." We will begin with a discussion of nonverbal communication.

Nonverbal Communication

Can you tell what his body language is saying?

The science or study of nonverbal communication, called *kinesics*, comprises a great deal of the meanings between people. Most experts on the subject of nonverbal communication agree that between 65 and 70% of our communication is by nonverbal means. Thus, nonverbal communication is an extremely important medium of communication. Actually, nonverbal communication relates to verbal communication in three ways:

1. Nonverbal communication can reinforce the verbal message.
2. Nonverbal communication can replace the verbal message.
3. Nonverbal communication can contradict the verbal message.

When the nonverbal message contradicts the verbal message, a *double bind* exists. Usually, however, the nonverbal message is more accurate and is believed over the verbal message. How does technology impact non-verbal messaging? How about deception? How is this interpreted when you use technology?

Microexpressions, fleeting facial expressions that last only a fraction of a second, can sometimes be helpful signals. These are often caught by only the most astute observers. Many people try hard to control their facial expressions, but deceivers may blink more or smile more in an effort to deceive. Some individuals are so good at monitoring and controlling their faces that their true feelings are difficult to detect. However, while liars can control certain facial expressions when facing scrutiny, they can't suppress them completely or every time; therefore, monitoring inconsistencies becomes key (Burgoon & Levine, 2010).

Signals of deception, often called *body leakage*, where body postures rather than the face leak the truth, can be extremely revealing. Individuals who choose to deceive can sometimes concentrate so much on controlling their words and facial expressions that they pay less attention to their bodies, which actually reveal their true feelings. In the verbal realm, changes in word usage, word flow, or voice pitch may signal the extra cognitive horsepower lying demands (Perina, 2011). The increased use of texting and email has made it extremely difficult to communicate effectively. Deception is also much harder to detect, although overly careful wording may raise red flags.

> Use of texting and other technology can limit communication significantly. Using video chat can help, but there are still limitations. Deception, intentional or otherwise, is a different issue.

© *fizkes/Shutterstock.com*

Conscious Nonverbal Communication

Senders of conscious nonverbal communication are aware that they are sending a message and the general meaning of that message. For example, the individuals extending a hug know that they are embracing someone and that action is normally perceived as indicating affection.

Receivers of conscious nonverbal communication are aware that they received the message and the meaning intended by the sender. The receiver of a hug, for example, generally realizes that the message is a sign of affection.

Becoming Aware of Your Body Language and Nonverbal Communications: Your body language may shape who you are
https://www.ted.com/talks/amy_cuddy_your_body_language_shapes_who_you_are

Amy Cuddy describes how language affects how others see us, but it may also change how we see ourselves.

FOCUS ON DIVERSITY

MICROAGGRESSIONS V. MACROAGGRESSIONS

Macroaggressions occur on a systemic level; for example, unequal pay practices or conditions for a certain group of people. They are often unacknowledged, and casually degrade, demean, or put down someone who is part of a group (for example, a gender, race, or ethnic group). According to research, 64% of women are exposed to this form of discrimination, with non-White women experiencing it more than anyone else.

Microaggressions are the everyday verbal, nonverbal, and environmental slights, snubs, or insults, whether intentional or unintentional, which communicate hostile, derogatory, or negative messages to target persons based solely upon their marginalized group membership (Anderson, 2019; Sue, 2010). Such incidents have become a commonplace experience for many people of color (POC) because they seem to occur constantly in our daily lives (Anderson, 2019; Sue 2010). In reality, these types of incidents inhibit women from doing their best work, being optimally productive, and undermine their success. Women and people of color cite these types of disrespectful, sometimes toxic, behaviors as one of the factors that influence their decisions to leave a job. A steady diet of macroaggressions and microaggressions disconnect and wear people down. People cite these types of behaviors as factors that lead to a reluctant decision to leave a job that they otherwise like.

They are subtle but offensive comments or actions directed at a minority or other nondominant group that unintentionally or unconsciously reinforce a stereotype, such as: "I don't see you as Black" or "you run like a girl." When a White couple (man and woman) passes an Hispanic man on the sidewalk, the woman automatically clutches her purse more tightly, while the man checks for his wallet in the back pocket. (Hidden message: Hispanics are prone to crime and up to no good.) Whether they are meant to be offensive or said to be not hurtful, these actions are offensive to the receiving party and others who may see or hear them. Sometimes the sender does not realize the receiver is offended; sometimes the sender is not aware of sending a message at all.

Infringing on someone's space as a microaggression is about more than inappropriate touching. Women express frustration that their male colleagues often disrespect their space. Examples include "manspreading," leaving belongings on other peoples' desks, and not moving out of the way to make room for others while walking down the hallway (Anderson, 2019).

The term *racial microaggressions* was first coined by psychiatrist Chester Pierce, MD, in the 1970s. But the concept is also rooted in the work of Jack Dovidio, PhD (Yale University) and Samuel Gaertner, PhD (University of Delaware) in their formulation of aversive racism: many well-intentioned Whites consciously believe in and profess equality, but unconsciously act in a racist manner, particularly in ambiguous situations (Sue, 2010).

Subliminal Nonverbal Communications

Subliminal messages are communicated to the *subconscious* mind of the receiver. Receivers of subliminal messages are not consciously aware of the message. Subliminal means "under the boundary," and refers to things we perceive but are not fully aware of perceiving. However, these messages are important.

- Gut reactions are frequently based upon your subconscious reading of subliminal nonverbal communications.
- Police and military uniforms subliminally communicate the authority of those wearing them.
- Well-dressed executives project success and credibility.
- Inappropriate dress transmits messages of failure and a lack of credibility.

Although subliminal messages do not create awareness on a conscious level, depending on social/cultural judgment, they still influence the receiver. In fact, subliminal messages are often more powerful than conscious messages. The advertising world is replete with examples of the value of subliminal nonverbal messages.

- Young, beautiful people are often seen in advertisements to communicate the subconscious message that the advertised product is associated with youth and beauty.
- Companies pay large sums of money to have their products appear in movies. While these appearances are not typical product advertisements, the mere association of the product with the movie transmits subliminal messages that will influence viewers. This is called "product placement," and it is very common in television and videos.

> *Becoming Aware of Technology and Social Media: Google Owns 28% of Your Brain*
> *https://www.pbssocal.org/programs/braincraft/google-owns-28-of-your-brain-xxhpbs/*
>
> *This chapter of a miniseries details how social media giants continue to control our attention.*

Do you know how you communicate nonverbally? Do you know how other cultures communicate nonverbally? Let's look at some possible ways.

Facial expressions and eye contact. More than any other nonverbal factor, facial expressions can communicate more emotional meaning more accurately. For example, the face:

- Communicates evaluative judgment.
- Reveals the level of interest or lack of it.
- Can exhibit the level of intensity of the emotions.
- Reveals the amount of control we have over our expressions.
- Shows whether we understand or not.

© Prostock-studio/Shutterstock.com

Through our facial expressions, we reveal a great deal about our feelings and responses to other people as we nonverbally convey shock, sadness, anger, happiness, worry, and so on. This is confirmed by researcher Paul Eckman (2007):

> The rapid facial signals are the primary system for expression of emotion. It is the face you search to know whether someone is angry, disgusted, afraid, sad, etc. Words cannot always describe the feelings people have; often words are not adequate to express what you see in the look on someone's face at an emotional moment. (2007)

Nonverbal communication can also be controlled by a knowledgeable person.

- A person who knows that people telling falsehoods often blink their eyes can take special care not to blink when telling a falsehood.
- A person who knows that a hug indicates friendship can consciously hug his/her worst enemy as trick to put the person off guard or as part of an effort to improve their relationship.

The eyes, hands, and mouth are the most expressive parts of the face, and have considerable effect on communication. We may use eye contact in a positive way to:

- Invite interaction with another by looking directly at them.
- Show friendship and positive regard by extended mutual eye contact.
- Demonstrate believability or honesty.
- Demonstrate interest by extended eye contact.
- Signal turn-taking in normal conversation.
- In some cultures, direct eye contact is an invitation; in others, it is rude.

Many times we avoid eye contact when we want to hide feelings, when we are tense, when we are interacting with someone we dislike, or when attempting to end social contact. However, it is important to note here that nonverbal expressions have different meanings in various cultures. Therefore, it is wise to be careful about assigning your culture's meanings for eye behavior to all people. See Focus on Diversity—Facial Expressions and Eye Contact.

Vocal qualities. *Paralinguistics* is the study of vocal cues such as pitch, rate, tone, or fluency. Almost everyone distinguishes meanings by noting differences in vocal qualities. For example, the statement "What a vacation I had" can have at least two different meanings, depending on the tone of voice of the speaker. The ambiguous phrase might mean that it was a most enjoyable weekend. With different qualities, however, the listener would assume that it was quite unpleasant (Hamilton, 2018).

The nonverbal messages communicated by the sound of the human voice can provide valuable information during meetings. Look at Table 5.2 and try to accentuate the one word in the sentences which appears in *boldface italics*.

Becoming *Aware*

FOCUS ON DIVERSITY

FACIAL EXPRESSIONS AND EYE CONTACT

Researchers indicate we can move people from culture to culture and they know how to make and read the same basic expressions: anger, fear, sadness, disgust, surprise, and happiness. The six appear to be hardwired in our brains (Matsumoto, 2004).

The mouth is a very expressive part of the face, and not just for the words that come out of it. However, reactions in the eyes are harder to control. So while Americans, big on personal expression, look to the mouth to read each other, the relatively subdued Japanese rely more on those revealing orbs (Perina, 2006).

For example, in the United States we encourage eye contact as an indicator of honesty and interest. People in some other societies believe that they should look down when talking to another person to indicate deference and respect. White Americans consider a reluctance to make eye contact as rude, disrespectful, and hostile, as well as conveying disinterest. However, looking someone in the eye is often perceived as a sign of disrespect or rudeness by people from many Asian, Latin American, African, Native American, and Caribbean cultures (Baruth & Manning, 2016).

Amina Dunn from Pew Research found that four-in-ten Black and Hispanics adults and a third of Whites often or sometimes feel the need to talk differently around different races and ethnic groups, especially Black college graduates under 50 years old. This has been called "code-switching" (2019).

BECOMING AWARE: THINK-PAIR-SHARE ACTIVITY

Using Table 5.2, have each group member say a sentence and listen to how each sounds.

Discuss this with the group:

Read the quote in the side bar by Lois Wyse. Independently take 5–10 minutes and write a response for this quote. What did the speaker mean, how did it make you feel, and how could it be interpreted? Find a partner in class and discuss it. Did you agree? Disagree? How did you both interpret it? Has it been said to you before?

Just put extra emphasis on that one word as you read out loud. Each sentence is exactly the same, but watch what happens when you place emphasis on the different words.

Table 5.2 CAN THE WAY YOU SAY SOMETHING ALTER WHAT YOU MEAN TO SAY?

Accentuate the one word in each sentence that appears in *boldface italics*. What are the different possible meanings?
I didn't say she stole the money.
I *didn't* say she stole the money.
I didn't *say* she stole the money.
I didn't say *she* stole the money.
I didn't say she *stole* the money.
I didn't say she stole the *money*.

With practice, we can all learn to notice the pitch and timbre of a person's voice, the rhythm of speech, and the rapidity of expression. These vocal qualities help us to tune into the mood of the speaker, as well as to understand how different cultures use vocal qualities in their communication.

Gestures and other body movements. Because movements and gestures of other parts of the body are also closely tied to culture, it is extremely misleading to isolate a single body movement (such as crossing the arms) and give it a precise meaning. Regardless of our intentions, however, our gestures and body movements may be given specific meanings by others.

For example, the way a person stands may indicate self-confidence, status, friendliness, or enthusiasm. Various types of gestures may be used to indicate feelings of restlessness, nervousness, pain, or disability or perhaps the need to emphasize a meaning.

I suppose it was something you said that caused me to tighten and pull away. And when you asked, "What is it?" I, of course, said, "Nothing." Whenever I say, "Nothing," You may be very certain there is something. The something is a cold, hard lump of "Nothing."
—LOIS WYSE

FOCUS ON DIVERSITY

GESTURES AND OTHER BODY MOVEMENTS

Gestures are not universal. For example, White Americans view a firm handshake as a sign of strength and power. However, Native Americans view a firm handshake as aggressive and disrespectful (Atkinson, 2004). Furthermore, the sign shown in Figure 5.2, which in our culture usually means "OK," has other meanings in other cultures. In Japan, it can mean "coins." In France and Belgium, it means "worthless" (as in "zero worth"). In Greece and Turkey, it is a vulgar sexual invitation.

Another example of how a simple gesture can be subject to misunderstanding and offense is noted in Figure 5.3. The sign of the University of Texas football team, the Longhorns, is to extend the index finger and the pinkie. In Italy and other parts of Europe, this gesture means a man's wife has been unfaithful to him—a serious insult (Tavris & Wade, 2016)! Without a doubt, tourists should be very careful about their gestures.

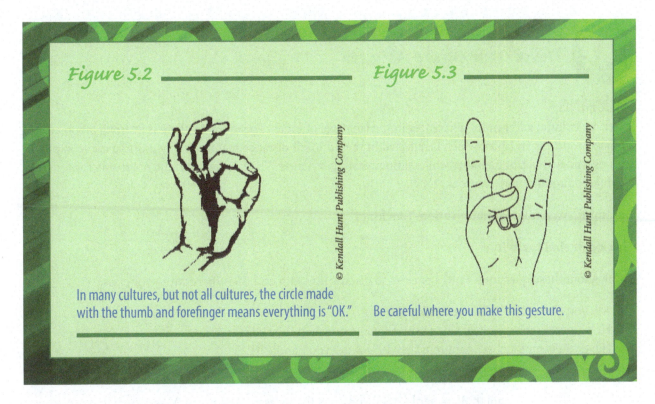

Figure 5.2

In many cultures, but not all cultures, the circle made with the thumb and forefinger means everything is "OK."

© Kendall Hunt Publishing Company

Figure 5.3

Be careful where you make this gesture.

© Kendall Hunt Publishing Company

Frequent hand movements, for example, often communicate a positive, enthusiastic attitude. However, movements such as constantly tapping your pencil or may indicate nervousness and boredom. Even weak or overly strong handshakes will be given some significance by many people. They can communicate enthusiasm, or they can communicate uneasiness.

Touching. *One of the most meaningful methods* of nonverbal communication can be physical contact or touch. There are times in our lives when it is difficult to express our feelings through words. We may use a hug, a pat on the shoulder, or a clasp of the hand to communicate meaning without words. Touching is risky, however, because this form of nonverbal communication may violate the personal space of others. Some people use the language of touch more easily and readily than others. Because there is indeed a complex language of touch, researchers Heslin and Alper (1983) have suggested a number of factors to consider:

© sirtravelalot/Shutterstock.com

What is this touch communicating?

- What part of the body does the touching?
- What part of the body is touched?
- How long does the touch last?
- How much pressure is used?
- Is there movement after contact is made?
- Is anyone else present?
- What is the situation in which the touch occurs?
- What is the relationship between the persons involved?
- In addition, one must also be sure that touch is welcome. The best way to ensure this is to ask, e.g., "May I take your hand?" "May I give you a hug?" If one is unsure, one must ask.

TOUCHING

There are cultural and gender differences in the language of touch. For example, there is a strong taboo against strangers touching in Japan, which is reflected in the sufficient distance maintained by most Japanese in public. Latinos tend to touch one another while communicating, whereas White Americans tend not to touch one another while communicating (Santrock, 2009).

Becoming Aware of Communication-Touching

Think pair share activity

Think about these questions. Find a partner to discuss this with and then share with your class.

- Are you a" toucher" when you talk to others?
- How does it make you feel when others touch you when they talk?
- Have you been touched inappropriately? How did you handle it?

Kenneth Blanchard (2006) confirms the ideas of Heslin and Alper: *There is a very simple rule about touching—when you touch, don't take.*

CONSENT

Touch has, in the recent past, been treated as something that one can engage without verbal interaction as long as one does so carefully. There are so many ideas of what it means to be "careful" of touch. For some, a long friendship opens up possibilities for hugs, an arm around the shoulders, and other forms of companionable contact. For others, only close family members are welcome to touch.

It is important to recognize the social and professional relationality of both parties. A subordinate might be too intimidated to refuse a hug from a supervisor, even if the subordinate felt very uncomfortable with the contact. The supervisor may interpret the absence of obvious resistance as permission to hug freely.

This can lead to dangerous misunderstandings.

It is better to **always seek consent**. Even a close friend who is comfortable with hugging most of the time may have a moment in a stressful time when they don't want to be touched. It's appropriate to offer touch, but not actually touch, until the other shows or clearly indicates consent. In some power dynamics, as with a supervisor and subordinate co-worker, even the offer is problematic. Touch beyond a handshake is not a part of professional life in the United States, although in some nations a ritualized embrace of some sort is normal.

Proxemics is the area in the nonverbal world of body language that is known as spatial relationships. Introduced by Edward T. Hall in 1963, proxemics is the study of measurable distances between people as they interact with one another. *The study of the nature, degree, and effect of the spatial separation individuals naturally maintain (as in various social and interpersonal situations) and of how this separation relates to environmental and cultural factors* is the way Merriam-Webster's dictionary (2019) defines it.

 Think/Pair/Share Activity

BODY LANGUAGE

Take 5 minutes to think about this. Then turn to a partner and share what you thought about before sharing with your group or class.

Think for just a moment and respond to these questions: How do you feel when a friend touches you on the shoulder? How do you feel when your boss touches you on the shoulder? How do you feel when a family member touches you on the shoulder? How do you feel when a stranger touches you on the shoulder? When the balance of power is off, like a boss and employee, touch could be considered a microaggresion or actual sexual assault by the person of less power.

We would guess that you will have many different answers to these questions, which just illustrates that we feel differently and interpret differently the language of touch.

You already pick up on more body language cues than you're consciously aware of. UCLA research has shown that only 7% of communication is based on the actual words we say. As for the rest, 38% comes from tone of voice and the remaining 55% comes from body language (Bradberry, 2016).

Personal space and distance. Our own personal space is an invisible bubble around us that allows us to feel safe. As we said earlier, if this bubble is violated, we are uncomfortable and may become defensive. Usually, only intimates can violate the space without making us uncomfortable. Sometimes, violation of this space by another can demonstrate that person's dominance of the situation.

FOCUS ON DIVERSITY

PERSONAL SPACE AND DISTANCE

French people maintain very small personal space in trains, buses, cafés, and even in their homes, and they increase their involvement with other people by using more direct body postures and eye contact. In consequence, when Americans visit Paris, they are sometimes shocked when strangers approach so closely and stare right into their eyes. Furthermore, when Americans attempt to protect their invaded personal space, Parisians interpret their retreat as a lack of good manners (Dresser, 2005).

Many times you can tell how people feel toward one another by observing the distance between them. Anthropologist Edward T. Hall in 1966 (1992) defined four distances in which most men operate for interactions among good friends or family members that we use in our everyday lives (see Figure 5.4). These are:

- *Intimate distance*, for embracing, touching, or whispering, which begins with skin contact and ranges out to about 18 inches. Close phase—less than 6 inches (15 cm), Far phase—6 to 18 inches (15 to 46 cm). This is reserved for close friends and loved ones, or other people to whom you feel affectionate.
- *Personal distance*, from 18 inches to 4 feet, for interactions among good friends or family members. Close phase—1.5 to 2.5 feet (46 to 76 cm) Far phase—2.5 to 4 feet (76 to 122 cm). This is where you may carry on a friendly conversation or sometimes even a heated argument.
- *Social distance*, from 4 for (close) social and consulting (not as close), which is 5–8 feet to 10 feet. This is reserved for social interactions that are businesslike or impersonal.
- *Public distance*, ranging out from 10–20 feet. This is reserved for speaking to a large audience.

Hall is careful to note that these distances pertain to **Americans** only and may be quite different for people raised in other cultures. For example, Americans are quite comfortable conducting business at a distance of approximately three to four feet, but people from the Middle East, Italy, Greece, and other southern European cultures stand much closer. Therefore, it is easy to see how feelings of uneasiness can occur without either individual possibly knowing why depending on their culture (Hall, 1968, 1992).

Physical environment and territory. What characteristics in a physical environment make you feel comfortable or uncomfortable? What do you think your room, house, or car communicates to others? Do you prefer a neat and "tidy" room, house, or car, or do you prefer the more "lived-in" look? What meaning do you give to a spotless house or to a friend's constantly clean car? How about your desk at home or work? Physical

Figure 5.4 ZONE AND DISTANCE

Zone 1	Zone 2	Zone 3	Zone 4
Intimate distance	Personal distance	Social distance	Public distance
0"–18"	18"–36'	Social 36"–48" Consulting 5'–8'	10–20'

Appropriate people and situations			
Parents and children, lovers, spouses/partners	Close friends	Co-workers, social gatherings, friends, work situations	Speaking to groups

Hall (1992) and Weiten et al. (2012).

Becoming *Aware*

environments not only reveal characteristics of the owner of the territory, but also actually affect how a person communicates.

Clothing and personal appearance. What we wear and how we groom ourselves are also important means of nonverbal communication. We send messages about our economic level, level of success, social position, educational background, moral character, and sometimes just our personal preferences. We also may send messages that suggest, "Notice me." For example, there is a tremendous amount of pressure in schools to wear the "in" brand of jeans, shoes, dress, and so on.

Although it is natural to make assumptions about clothing and personal appearances, it is equally important to note that this area of nonverbal communication is filled with ambiguity. A stranger, wearing worn, ill-fitting clothes, might equally be a stylish person or even a millionaire. Maybe today he or she is on vacation, going to do some "dirty" work, just wants to be comfortable, or is wearing what is considered stylish in their community. This points to the fact that as we get to know others better, the importance of clothing and personal appearance decreases.

Silence. Silence is *communication.* Silence may convey relaxation, contentment, fatigue, anxiety, frustration, uncertainty, shyness, avoidance, or thoughtful analyses. Sometimes, what we do not say has more impact than what we do say. For example,

Whom do you allow within your intimate distance?

WEARING IT WELL

What kind of messages do you send with your clothing and grooming choices? Choose a partner. What is their opinion? Discuss what you thought, then share with your group or class.

What kind of messages do you think you send about the clothing you wear and the manner in which you groom yourself?

silence can be used to convey negative messages such as "I'm angry with you," or "I'm not OK," or positive messages of "It is nice just to be alone," "I understand."

Nonverbal communication, Everything we do, excluding the actual words being uttered, is nonverbal. In the Arabic world a click sound means *no*; it is not derisive, but a shortcutting communication. If an Indian person is shaking their head, it could mean one of several emotions, one of which conveys happiness with the situation.

It is important to remember that nonverbal signals are the largest part of our personal communication. In face-to-face interaction we may convey over 90% of the information we process, while the words carry the rest. When verbal and nonverbal signals do not match, it creates distrust, unclear messages, misunderstandings and confusion. Nonverbal communication can be more impactful than verbal communication (Bajrachary, 2018). At times nonverbal communication can be difficult to decipher. Mark Knapp and Judith Hall (2009), authors of *Nonverbal Communication in Human Interaction*, remind us that as we become aware of nonverbal messages in our everyday lives, we need to think of them not as facts, but as clues that need to be examined. Furthermore, we can be more effective in communicating messages if we support words with appropriate forms of nonverbal communication.

Becoming Aware of Nonverbal Communication: Why Is Nonverbal Communication Important?
https://www.businesstopia.net/communication/why-non-verbal-communication-important

Shraddha Bajrachary on how actions are not always so parallel to words spoken.

HOW TO IMPROVE NONVERBAL COMMUNICATION

The following actions can dilute the most compelling words; avoid them.

- Pointing a finger
- Pounding your fist
- Placing hands on hips
- Repeatedly adjusting your glasses
- Assuming a stern facial expression
- Repeatedly touching your hair

Many of these may also be personal management techniques used to keep an even temper or contain unexpected energy.

- Licking your lips
- Looking at the floor
- Playing with pocket change
- Playing with rubber bands or paper clips
- Twirling your mustache
- Clicking pens

Pachter (2006).

Verbal Communication

Verbal communication—words and language—is generally considered the primary means of communication. We gather, share, give, and receive information through words, and establish, continue, or terminate relationships through words. Words can us feel good or miserable; they can lead us to lose our tempers or remind us to keep our cool; they can persuade us to take action or convince us not to move; they can be clear and concise or ambiguous and confusing. Most importantly, *they cannot be unsaid once they are said.*

Actually, the way we use words may communicate much more than the actual words used. As already discussed, tone of voice and the emphasis placed on words may reveal far more than the choice of words. The meaning and understanding behind words is the essence of communication. And, *meanings are in people*—not in words. Let us look at some barriers or ways that meanings can go astray.

Semantics. *Semantics* is the study of meaning and changes of meanings in words. It is virtually impossible to communicate effectively if the people conversing do not understand the same terminology, or if they hold different meanings for the same word. For example, consider the common expressions:

> I'll be back in a little while.
> I'll be back in a few minutes.
> I'll be back about 5:00 p.m.

What or when is *a little while* or *a few minutes*? Do we mean a little late, or do we mean 5, 10, or 30 minutes? Does "about 5:00 p.m." mean exactly 5:00 p.m., or does the expression mean between 5:00 and 6:00 p.m.? What do you mean when you use these expressions?

> [
> *Our language is funny—a fat chance and a slim chance are the same thing.*
> —J. GUSTAV WHITE
>]

FOCUS ON DIVERSITY

SEMANTICS

Two first-time visitors to Montréal, Quebec (the French-Canadian province), entered a restaurant for dinner. After looking over the menu, the husband suggested they order the shrimp cocktail entrée. He said to his wife, "A whole shrimp dinner for $11.95 Canadian is quite a deal. I guess it's because Montréal is a seaport." When the entrée arrived, the visitors were sadly disappointed because they were the size of an *appetizer*.

The husband asked the server why the entrées were so small in Montréal. With a smile, the server replied, "You folks must be Americans. In French-speaking countries, the word *entrée* is just the beginning of the meal, like the word *enter*. In the United States, it's just the reverse—the entrée is the main meal. Are you now ready to order your main meal?"

Certain occupations have their own jargon; realtors talk about going after "leads" and "listings"; individuals working in finance and credit talk about a "class 2-A credit rating." Any profession, avocation, or field of specialization will develop such word usages or even slang words. This often splits persons inside the group from those outside the group in that they will use the same terms to mean different things. Sometimes this difference is used deliberately to separate "us" from "them"

Even English-speaking countries have different meanings for the same word. For example, in the United States, "Let us *table* that motion" means: "Let us put it aside." In England, the same phrase means: "Let us bring it up for discussion."

Often such differences can lead a speaker to assume that their conversation partner hears the same meaning as the speaker intends, while the listener is either misled or confused. Use of professional terminology should always be cleared, or checked out, with a new person. Some people will find this patronizing if it is not handled well; we must be sure not to suggest that our concern reflects anything other than a desire to be clear in our own communication. Often misunderstanding happens when the listener has to guess what the sender is implying or assuming in communications. Mutual misunderstandings are often a result.

Often we have needs that we do not express to each other and, if that happens, someone gets their feelings hurt. If we can actually provide our need and our feeling to the other person, they can better understand us. "The following list of needs is neither exhaustive nor definitive. It is meant as a starting place to support anyone who wishes to engage in a process of deepening self-discovery and to facilitate greater understanding and connection between people," according to its source, the Center for Non-Violent Communication (https://www.cnvc.org/Training/needs-inventory).

> The following are words we use when we want to express a combination of emotional states and physical sensations. There are two parts to this list: feelings we may have when our needs are being met and feelings we may have when our needs are not being met. (Use them in your communications—it might help.) These are **words about feelings,** not to be confused with feelings themselves.

That words are powerful may seem obvious, but the fact is that most of us, most of the time, use them lightly. We choose our clothes more carefully than we choose our words, though what we say about and to others can define them indelibly.
— JOSEPH TELUSHKIN

322

Becoming *Aware*

FEELING WORDS WHEN YOUR NEEDS ARE SATISFIED

AFFECTIONATE
compassionate
friendly
loving
open hearted
sympathetic
tender
warm

ENGAGED
absorbed
alert
curious
engrossed
enchanted
entranced
fascinated
interested
intrigued
involved
spellbound
stimulated

HOPEFUL
expectant
encouraged
optimistic

CONFIDENT
empowered
open
proud
safe
secure

EXCITED
amazed
animated
ardent
aroused
astonished
dazzled
eager
energetic
enthusiastic
giddy
invigorated
lively
passionate
surprised
vibrant

GRATEFUL
appreciative
moved
thankful
touched

INSPIRED
amazed
awed
wonder

JOYFUL
amused
delighted
glad
happy
jubilant
pleased
tickled

EXHILARATED
blissful
ecstatic
elated
enthralled
exuberant
radiant
rapturous
thrilled

PEACEFUL
calm
clear headed
comfortable
centered
content
equanimous
fulfilled
mellow
quiet
relaxed
relieved
satisfied
serene
still
tranquil
trusting

REFRESHED
enlivened
rejuvenated
renewed
rested
restored
revived

FEELINGS WORDS WHEN YOUR NEEDS ARE NOT SATISFIED

AFRAID
apprehensive
dread
foreboding
frightened
mistrustful
panicked
petrified
scared
suspicious
terrified
wary
worried

ANGRY
enraged
furious
incensed
indignant
irate
livid
outraged
resentful

ANNOYED
aggravated
dismayed
disgruntled
displeased
exasperated
frustrated
impatient
irritated
irked

AVERSION
animosity
appalled
contempt
disgusted
dislike
hate
horrified
hostile
repulsed

CONFUSED
ambivalent
baffled
bewildered
dazed
hesitant
lost
mystified
perplexed
puzzled
torn

DISCONNECTED
alienated
aloof
apathetic
bored
cold
detached
distant
distracted
indifferent
numb
removed
uninterested
withdrawn

DISQUIET
agitated
alarmed
discombobulated
disconcerted
disturbed
perturbed
rattled
restless
shocked
startled
surprised
troubled
turbulent
turmoil
uncomfortable
uneasy
unnerved
unsettled
upset

EMBARRASSED
ashamed
chagrined
flustered
guilty
mortified
self-conscious

FATIGUE
beat
burnt out
depleted
exhausted
lethargic
listless
sleepy
tired
weary
worn out

PAIN
agony
anguished
bereaved
devastated
grief
heartbroken
hurt
lonely
miserable
regretful
remorseful

SAD
depressed
dejected
despair
despondent
disappointed
discouraged
disheartened
forlorn
gloomy
heavy hearted
hopeless
melancholy
unhappy
wretched

TENSE
anxious
cranky
distressed
distraught
edgy
fidgety
frazzled
irritable
jittery
nervous
overwhelmed
restless
stressed out

VULNERABLE
fragile
guarded
helpless
insecure
leery
reserved
sensitive
shaky

YEARNING
envious
jealous
longing
nostalgic
pining
wistful

Source: Center for
Nonviolent Communication

https:www.cnvc.org/Train-
ing/needs-inventory

"Everyone has a Story"

I used to get bored with people
so easily and
so quickly.
Then I began seeing them
as more than people—
as beautiful
and interesting.
As worth more than my judgments.
As people with a story to tell.
I began seeing them.
I began listening.

— COLTON SNEAD, 2016

HOW TO IMPROVE VERBAL COMMUNICATION

- Speak with enthusiasm
- Enunciate
- Use inflection
- Avoid antagonistic words
- Use short, simple sentences
- Adjust the volume of your voice to the situation
- Adjust your speaking rate to the situation
- Keep the door open for feedback

Technology. Digital culture expert and MIT professor Sherry Turkle (2017) reports on the various ways humans have adapted their sense of self and relationships to the digital age. In her opinion, this period has seen a decline in the face-to-face communication needed for self-reflection, empathy, and intimacy. Turkle has done extensive research to examine what is lost and gained as digital communication becomes more pervasive (2017). There are intersections between emotion and technology, such as apps for computers and phones designed to find romantic partners and algorithms that assess psychological states. Turkle believes that technology communication encourages a "friction-free" style of communication, defined by self-editing and the immediate gratification of a "like" on social media. She suggests that this approach degrades the quality of performance at work and school, and that democracy is undermined as citizens accept the surveillance provided by social media as a new way of life (2016). Teens now enjoy more than five and a half hours of leisure a day (5 hours, 44 minutes). The biggest chunk of teens' daily leisure time is spent on screens: 3 hours and 4 minutes on average. This figure, which can include time spent gaming, surfing the web, watching videos and watching TV, has held steady over the past decade. On weekends, screen time increases to almost four hours a day (3 hours, 53 minutes), and on weekdays teens are spending 2 hours and 44 minutes on screens (Livingston, 2019).

Becoming Aware of Technology: Reclaiming Conversation: The Power of Talk in a Digital Age
https://www.youtube.com/watch?v=DyvJ6mqfJ6o

Sherry Turkle presents some of her findings on social media and relationships.

Facebook—which celebrated its 15th anniversary in 2019—remains one of the most widely used social media sites among adults in the U.S. Roughly seven-in-ten adults (69%) say they use the platform. (A separate 2018 Pew Research Center survey showed Facebook use among U.S. teens had dropped in recent years.) YouTube—which contains many social elements, even if it is not a traditional social media platform—is the only other online platform measured that matches Facebook's reach: 73% of adults and 94% of 18- to 24-year olds report using the video sharing site. But certain online platforms, most notably Instagram and Snapchat, have an especially strong following among young adults. Some 78% of 18- to 24-year-olds use Snapchat, and a sizeable majority of these users (71%) visit the platform multiple times per day. Similarly, 71% of Americans in this age group now use Instagram and close to half (45%) are Twitter users. The typical (median) American reports that they use three of the eight major platforms that the Center measured in this survey (Smith & Anderson, 2019).

These findings also highlight the public's sometimes conflicting attitudes toward social media. For example, the share of social media users who say these platforms would be hard to give up has increased by 12 percentage points compared with a survey conducted in early 2014. But by the same token, a majority of users (59%) say it would not be hard to stop using these sites, including 29% who say it would not be hard at all to give up social media (Smith & Anderson, 2019).

The cellphones or cybermedia carried put social media on a 24-hour cycle. It is known that with cell phones, the amount of time spent on them increases when bored or lonely. Navigate your cyber landscapes, and learn how to evaluate those spaces and differentiate potentially damaging content from potentially enlightening content. Search Twitter for people who use that platform to speak on Human Relations topics like justice and equity. Check out videos, apps, and blogs that present ideas you are learning in this class and push beyond snarky tweets.

It is important to think before we type and to engage respectfully on digital media. Our cellphones and any digital media can promote thought and meaning rather than mindless destruction and negativity. There are several links to Marshall Davis Jones reading his poem "Touchscreen," and considering how social media can affect personal communication and interpersonal relationships. "Lost Voices" by Darius Simpson and Scout Bostley opens up our thoughts to serious topics of racial and gender equality in this country. Slam poetry as a genre is both entertaining and socially conscious.

> *The real art of conversation is not only to say the right thing in the right place but to leave unsaid the wrong thing at the tempting moment.*
> —LADY DOROTHY NEVILL

Becoming Aware of Technology & Art: Slam Poetry
https://www.youtube.com/watch?v=070-xKeZYps

Marshall Davis Jones reading "Touchscreen"
https://www.youtube.com/watch?v=lpPASWlnZIA

"Lost Voices" by Darius Simpson and Scout Bostley
https://www.youtube.com/watch?v=-6PRIGW6pqA

Digital Nation: a multiplatform project exploring what it means to be human in a 21st century digital world.

 Think/Pair/Share Activity

SOCIAL MEDIA AND SOCIAL JUSTICE

Research and find three (3) tweets/social media each day that are pro-social justice or just Human Relations-positive.

Find two (2) Facebook posts that are about pro-social justice or HR issues.

Find one news source each day that is well documented about an HR issue for the next week.

Share them with your classroom or group.

Assumptions. To *assume* is to accept as fact without any evidence of proof (Milliken, 2017). Often, we make the mistake of assuming that others will understand more than we actually say to them. "If it is clear to me, it must be clear to you, also." This assumption is one of the most difficult barriers to successful human communication. In personal relationships, for example, we may expect our intimates to be able to read our minds because they know us so well. "She ought to know how I feel," you may say to yourself, even though you have said nothing about your feelings.

A story is told of a family ruckus that occurred when the father sent his son to the lumberyard for a *longer* board. The young man thought he knew what his father wanted—but the longer board he brought back was still three feet too short. His father became angry and accused the boy of being stupid and not listening. The father had simply assumed that since he knew what he meant by *longer*, his son would also know. Could it be possible that Dad had not bothered to make himself clear or to check his meaning with his son?

Self-concept. The most important single factor affecting our communication with others is our self-concept. Chapter Two showed that a strong self-concept is necessary for healthy and satisfying interactions. On the other hand, if we have a weak self-concept, we may feel inadequate and lack the confidence to converse with others. As a result, we feel our ideas are not worth communicating, and we become guarded in our communication attempts.

In circumstances where we feel insecure or unsafe, it is extremely easy for us to feel that our self-image is being threatened. As a result, our defenses are immediately aroused. It is so easy to take an innocent remark and reply with, "What did you mean by that?" We may distort questions into accusations. Our replies become immediate justifications.

For example, a person may ask their partner, "Did you happen to get my blue shirt from the cleaners?" Their intention may be informational. If their partner feels insecure, they may respond as if the issue was that partner's inability to meet their needs. Their partner may say, "No, I didn't. I can't think of everything, you know, when I've got the kids with me and time is getting short, and I can't even find a decent roast that we can afford. I suppose you think my getting your shirt is more important than preparing a good meal." The partner assumes an accusation is made. This accusation may be seen as an "intended putdown." Does one partner really mean to cut the other partner down, or does the other partner just feel insecure?

Deception. It is a difficult task to identify deception in others, with the ability to judge whether someone is lying around 50% (Burgoon & Levine, 2010). There is no bulls-eye that "tells" that a person is lying. A lack of eye contact, quavering voice, and descriptive vagueness are all signs of lying, but they can also be signs of anxiety or personal quirks. The most reliable signals of deception pertain to the cognitive effort and emotion that surround the lie itself. A person who lies may exhibit discomfort (Perina, 2011).

Technology and Communication

There has been a tremendous increase in electronic and wireless communication technology. Communicating by email, text messaging, blogs, instant messaging, chat rooms, videoconferencing, or using the latest communication device have reduced traditional memos, letters, phone calls, and face-to-face conversations. Text messaging is a global phenomenon and is increasing dramatically as more people own smartphones. Most states have addressed the issue of using cellphones for talking and texting. According to the Insurance Institute for Highway Safety, as of June 2019, talking on a hand-held cellphone while driving is banned in 20 states and the District of Columbia (Minnesota's law becomes effective on August 1, 2019; Arizona will issue warnings until 2021, when it will issue tickets). Text messaging is banned for all drivers in 48 states and the District of Columbia. Laws for novice drivers are even more restrictive: the use of all cellphones by novice drivers is restricted in 38 states and the District of Columbia, and novice drivers are banned from texting in Missouri. Some states do allow hands-free use of phones while driving, and newer vehicles have cellular capability (2019). Texting and looking up information and maps while driving have caused numerous accidents and near misses from distracted drivers.

BECOMING AWARE OF TECHNOLOGY AND DISTRACTION

Dr. Larry Rosen and Adam Gazzaley have explored our brains and technology and how distracted we are becoming. We "think" we can do it all, everyday, every hour, around the clock! Never mind the errors in the email, the near-miss on the road, and the unheard conversation at the table. And this constant connection drives our brain chemistry to be in a constant state of high alert which disrupts our work, our interactions, and our all-important night's sleep. Our brains aren't built for multitasking, and stress and anxiety can be prevalent if we let our technology control our life. There are better ways to live in a high-tech world without giving up our modern technology.

Take the free online "Am I Addicted to My Smartphone? Quiz at https://www.itstimetologo .com/ wp_quiz/am-i-addicted-to-my-smartphone-quiz/ by Time to Log Off. There you can access resources to help you do a Digital Detox.

Digital connectivity offers many potential benefits, from connecting with peers to accessing educational content, but we need to be careful not to abuse and overuse it. Parents have voiced concerns about the behaviors teens engage in online, the people with whom they interact, and the personal information they make available. Indeed, these concerns are not limited to parents. Some lawmakers have raised concerns about issues such as online safety; many people use mobile apps or Internet sites and do not see what harm it can be doing to others. More mobile applications are created every day for finding people to date or to "hook up with" (have sex) or for "catfishing" (to fabricate an online dating identity) or for cyberbullying (such as sharing personal photos to others without the consent of those in the photo).

In a 2019 survey, the Pew Research Center found that:

By providing ways to meet others that they wouldn't bump into in their day-to-day lives, online dating made its users more likely to choose a partner who is different from them in race or ethnicity, education, political party or income. (Pew, 2019)

A 2019 Pew Research Center analysis of recently released survey data from Stanford University finds that couples who meet online are, in fact, more likely to be diverse in some of these dimensions. But this can be explained by the fact that online daters tend to be younger than those who meet offline, and younger people are more likely to be in relationships with people who are different from them, regardless of how they meet.

In the Stanford study (which included 3,394 U.S. adults who are currently married, in a relationship, or who have ever previously been in a relationship), the median age of people who met their partners online was 36, compared with 51 among those who met their partners in another way. Previous research suggests that populations with small pools of potential partners—such as people seeking a same-sex partner—are most likely to meet a partner online. The Pew Research Center analysis bears this out. Roughly four-in-ten people in same-sex relationships (37%) report meeting their partner online, compared with only 11% of opposite-sex couples. These differences remain after taking age into account (Brown, 2019).

Roughly four-in-ten people in same-sex relationships (37%) report meeting their partner online, compared with only 11% of opposite-sex couples. These differences remain after taking age into account.

People who met their partner online are more likely than those who met offline to identify as lesbian, gay, or bisexual (13% of those who met their partner online say they are LGB, vs. 4% of those who met their partner offline). This difference is similar among those younger than 40 (Brown, 2019).

https://www.pewresearch.org/fact-tank/2019/01/17/where-millennials-end-and-generation-z-begins/ft_19-01-17_generations_2019/

https://www.pewresearch.org/wp-content/uploads/2019/06/FT_19.06.24_OnlineDating_Couples-who-meet-online-more-likely-different-races-thnicities.png?resize=1024,658

https://www.pewresearch.org/fact-tank/2019/06/24/couples-who-meet-online-are-more-diverse-than-those-who-meet-in-other-ways-largely-because-theyre-younger/

As online dating has increased in popularity and lost much of its stigma over the past few decades, researchers have speculated that it could change the landscape of dating—and perhaps marriage—in big ways. According to the *Economist* (2018), the Internet is the second-most-popular way for Americans to meet people of the opposite sex, and is fast catching up with real-world "friend of a friend" introductions.

BECOMING AWARE OF TECHNOLOGY-INTERPERSONAL COMMUNICATION-"TECHNOFERENCE"

Technology is taking its toll on relationships according to research by psychologist Sarah Coyne, PhD, psychology professor at Brigham Young University, and Brandon McDaniel, a psychology graduate student at Pennsylvania State University. They found that "*technoference*," (technology-interference) or the everyday intrusions or interruptions in couple interactions or time spent together that occur due to technology, is hurting relationships. Coyne and McDaniel surveyed 143 women in committed relationships about how often smartphones, tablets, and computers interrupted daily interactions with their husbands or partners. About 70% of the women said that technology interfered in their relationship with their partner at least sometimes or often, and about a quarter said their partners actively texted others during the couple's face-to-face conversations.

Moreover, women who reported more technoference in their couple relationship also reported more conflict over technology use, lower relationship satisfaction, more depressive symptoms, and lower life satisfaction.

"Many of these interruptions are likely unintentional or unconsciously done, but can still send a message that the technology device is more important in that moment than one's romantic partner," McDaniel says. "If this happens frequently, the relationship can really suffer" (Coyne, 2016).

Another study by Coyne et al. (2016) found younger individuals reported using all forms of media (except for email) more frequently than older participants. Relationship satisfaction did not predict specific use of media, but predicted several reasons for media use. Additional analyses revealed that text messaging had the strongest association with individuals' positive and negative communication within their relationships. Specifically, text messaging to express affection, broach potentially confrontational subjects, and to hurt partners were associated with individuals' view of positive and negative communication within their relationship.

WANT TO MINIMIZE THE PITFALLS OF SMARTPHONE USE? RESEARCH SUGGESTS SEVEN GOOD PLACES TO START.

1. Make choices. The more we rely on smartphones, the harder it is to disconnect. Consider which functions are optional. Could you keep lists in a paper notebook? Use a standalone alarm clock? Make conscious choices about what you really need your phone for, and what you don't.

2. Retrain yourself. Larry Rosen (2016) advises users not to check their phone first thing in the morning. During the day, gradually check in less often—maybe every 15 minutes at first, then every 20, then 30. Over time, you'll start to see notifications as suggestions rather than demands, he says, and you'll feel less anxious about staying connected.

3. Set expectations. In many ways, our culture demands constant connection. That sense of responsibility to be on call 24 hours a day comes with a greater psychological burden than many of us realize, according to Karla Klein Murdock, PhD. Try to establish expectations among family and friends so they don't worry or feel slighted if you don't reply to their texts or emails immediately. While it can be harder to ignore messages from your boss, it can be worthwhile to have a frank discussion about what his or her expectations are for staying connected after hours.

4. Silence notifications. It's tempting to go with your phone's default settings, but making the effort to turn off unnecessary notifications can reduce distractions and stress.

5. Protect sleep. Avoid using your phone late at night. If you must use it, turn down the brightness. When it's time for bed, turn your phone off and place it in another room. Murdoch found that students who were more attuned to their nighttime phone notifications had poorer subjective sleep quality and greater self-reported sleep problems (Murdock, 2016).

6. Be active. When interacting with social media sites, don't just absorb other people's posts. Actively posting ideas or photos, creating content, and commenting on others' posts is associated with better subjective well-being.

7. And, of course, don't text/email/call and drive. According to the National Safety Council, cell phone use while driving leads to 1.6 million crashes annually. Texting while driving is 6 times more likely to cause an accident than driving under the influence of alcohol is. One out of every 4 traffic crashes that occur in the U.S. are caused by cell phone usage (National Safety Council, April, 2018). When you're driving, turn off notifications, and if you need to use your phone, pull over in a safe spot to answer a call or text.

There have been concerns regarding the overuse of technology and its impact on face-to-face communication, so much so that Emily Drago in her Strategic Communications class at Elon University created a survey to observe students' technology use and habits while in the company of others as well. She found that 38 of 100 students (38%) while with others used no technology; the other 62% were either texting, talking on the phone, or using a computer or tablet.

In an effort to determine what impacts technology has on face-to-face communication, the survey asked students to rank the following statement on a scale from strongly agree to strongly disagree: "It bothers me when my friends or family use technology while spending time with me." Seventy-four percent of respondents said that they either agreed or strongly agreed with this statement, while only 6% disagreed. Among respondents, 20% neither agreed nor disagreed.

Another survey question asked students whether they believed the presence of technology, while spending time with others, affects face-to-face interpersonal communication negatively. "An overwhelming 92% of respondents believed technology negatively affects face-to-face communication, and only 1% did not. Only 7% of respondents neither agreed nor disagreed" (Drago, Spring 2015).

Becoming Aware of Technology: Conversation on Modern Romance
https://www.youtube.com/watch?v=69FXjBPG7F4

MIT Professor Sherry Turkle in conversation with Logan Ury. They discuss themes from her book Reclaiming Conversation, *including the importance of solitude and the power of boredom. They also discuss "Turkle's Tips" for modern romantic relationships.*

MIT psychologist Sherry Turkle observes in her book *Reclaiming Conversation: The Power of Talk in a Digital Age* (2016) that face-to-face conversation is the most human and humanizing thing we do. Think about it—body language, facial expressions, and tone of voice and empathy that might be lost on media, makes a huge difference in understanding a conversation: "The Net teaches us to need it." She found that couples need to reclaim life's unstructured moments of reflection and openness to each other and not fill the time with digital intrusion. Turkle also discusses "phubbing," which is phone snubbing by being able to keep eye contact with someone who is texting and only act like they are listening. According to the Pew Research Survey cited above, 42% of cell phone-owning 18- to 29-year-olds in a serious relationship say their partner has been distracted by mobile devices while they were together, which is more than the 25% of all couples reporting such problems. The survey reported 18% of young adults argue over the amount of time spent online (Marano, 2016).

 Think/Pair/Share Activity ————————————

GENDER AND COMMUNICATIONS

Complete the quick questionnaire and then **pair** up with a classmate and discussion your responses to the questions.

Then **share and discuss** the questions and what you thought about the questions with the class.

REMEMBER, BEFORE YOU SAY OR WRITE SOMETHING YOU MIGHT REGRET, THINK ABOUT IT. DON'T REGRET NOT THINKING

Read your messages again before you send them. If they do not fit the reminders of THINKING, you might need to adjust what you are saying.

T... Is it **True?**
H... Is it **Helpful?**
I... Is it **Inspiring?**
N... Is it **Necessary?**
K... Is it **Kind?**
I... Is it **Not Inappropriate?**
N... Is it **Needed?**
G... Is it **Good?**

If your answer is yes, go ahead, but if your answer is no, **stop.**
(adapted from Alan Redpath)

GENDER AND COMMUNICATION

For just a moment respond to the following questions with either T or F.

_____ 1. Women are better at interpreting nonverbal cues while listening.
_____ 2. Men generally do most of the talking in mixed-gender groups.
_____ 3. Women are more willing to ask for help than men.
_____ 4. Men are more likely to interrupt more often.
_____ 5. Women are more likely to initiate confrontations in relationships than men.
_____ 6. Men are less likely to be verbally expressive.

> "We've begun to raise daughters more like sons... but few have the courage to raise our sons more like our daughters."
> —GLORIA STEINEM

According to research, if you answered true to all of these statements, you were correct (Hamilton, 2018; Wood, 2018).

Actually, these are just some of the possible differences in communication styles between males and females. Also, men often talk about sports, money, facts, business, and events, while doing something else, and often without looking at each other. Women, on the other hand, talk about feelings, relationships, and people face to face, sitting down. See Gender & You—Communication: Different Languages, for more differences in the way men and women communicate.

GENDER AND YOU

COMMUNICATION: DIFFERENT LANGUAGES

In the national best-seller *You Just Don't Understand: Women and Men in Conversation*, Deborah Tannen (2001) contends that males and females are typically socialized in different "cultures." That is, males are likely to speak and hear a language of "status and independence" while females are likely to speak and hear a language of "connection and intimacy." Stated in another way, men use language to challenge others, to achieve status in a group, to convey information, and to keep from getting pushed around. On the other hand, women use language to achieve and share intimacy with others, to promote closeness and equality in a group, and to prevent others from pushing them away. It is not so much that men want to dominate women as that they simply have different ways of communicating. She states that "communication between men and women can be like cross cultural communication, prey to a clash of conversational styles." The influence of gender differences begins very early in childhood and can shape the communication style of the adult (Tannen, 2001). Research by Dr, Erina MacGeorge, a professor from Penn State, shows there are small differences between men's and women's comforting skills, but not enough to claim the sexes are their own cultures or come from different planets, and strongly prefer the same ways of comforting others—listening, sympathizing, and giving thoughtful advice. Yet books like John Gray's *Men are From Mars and Women are From Venus* and Deborah Tannen's *You Just Don't Understand* tell men that being masculine means dismissing feelings and downplaying problems. That isn't what most men do, and it isn't good for either men or women."

MacGeorge's study in 2004, "The Myth of Gender Cultures: Similarities Outweigh Differences in Men's and Women's Provision of and Responses to Supportive Communication," appeared in *Sex Roles: A Journal of Research*. MacGeorge's article includes three studies. Unlike the anecdotes used to support the gender myth of extreme cultural differences between men and women, MacGeorge's research is based on questionnaires and interviews. At any rate, it is important to be cautious about putting all men and all women into some type of category. America's multiracial population has grown at three times the rate of the general population since the beginning of the millennium (Pew Research, 2019). Differences in communication among other races and multiracial families are another area to examine. Watch the following video from Pew research to learn more about communication.

Becoming Aware of Diversity-Multiracial Americans
http://www.pewresearch.org/multiracial-voices/

Listen to the Pew research on multi-racial Americans sharing their views, experiences and perspectives. What do you think?

Listening (What Did You Say?)

Sometimes, our communication attempts go astray because we fail to listen. We will now discuss the skills of listening and the qualities essential for improving person-to-person communication.

It is not uncommon to be in a meeting or class or conversation and suddenly realize we have not actually heard what is being said. Effective listening is not waiting for others to finish speaking so you can make your point. Effective listening is suspending judgment so you can truly understand what others are trying to tell you. **Listening** is a form of *paying attention,* which is an active process involving much more than hearing and seeing.

According to Stephen Covey (2013), when another person speaks, we are usually "listening" at one of four levels. We may be *ignoring* another person, not really listening at all. We may practice *pretending*. "Yeah. Uh-huh. Right." We may practice *selective listening*, hearing only certain parts of the conversation. Or we may even practice *attentive listening*, paying attention and focusing energy on the words that are being said. Very few of us ever practice the fifth level, however, the highest form of listening, *empathetic listening*—listening with the intent to *understand*. We will discuss listening with the intent to understand in greater detail later in the chapter.

Communication experts describe listening as our primary communication activity. One study explored how college students spend their time communicating and what impact, if any, communications devices may be having on how that time is spent. Undergraduates (N=696) at four southeastern colleges were surveyed. Results revealed that listening comprises 55.4% of the total average communication day, followed by reading (17.1%), speaking (16.1%), and writing (11.4%). Each of these communication behaviors includes some aspect of Internet use. College students spend as much time listening to media as they do engaged in interpersonal interactions. They feel

© Motortion Films/Shutterstock.com

Have you ever had a conversation with someone who wasn't paying attention?

new technology is changing the way mediated communication activities are perceived (Emanuel et, al, 2008). It is interesting to note that while universities often require classes that evaluate competence in writing and speaking, few highlight listening as an important communication skill.

Unfortunately, few people are good listeners. Few realize that 80% of communication is not by words, but by body language (Dejaresco, 2015). It just seems that the speaker's words go *in one ear and out the other.* Yet, the quality of our friendships, the closeness of our family relationships, and our effectiveness at work depend to a great extent on our ability to listen (O'Neill & Chapman, 2008).

Is there really a difference between hearing and listening? *Hearing* is a word used to describe the physiological sensory process by which auditory sensations are received by the ears and translated to the brain. *Listening*, on the other hand, is an intellectual and emotional process that integrates physical, emotional, and intellectual inputs in a search for meaning and understanding (Barker & Watson, 2000).

In fact, Cheryl Hamilton (2018), author of *Communicating for Results*, says there are Five Stages of Listening, where listeners …

1. Sense   Hear what is important to them
2. Interpret   Assign meaning to what is seen, heard, and felt
3. Evaluate   Determine speaker credibility and message importance
4. Respond   React to speech, usually through nonverbal cues
5. Remember Retain parts of message in memory

Is it possible to hear what another person is saying without really listening to them?

> *We have been given two ears but a single mouth, in order that we may hear more and talk less.*
> —ZENO OF CITIUM

Barriers to Listening

We all have habits, attitudes, or interests that may screen out what is being said. Sometimes we are too busy to really listen. Let us examine some of the possible barriers to listening, such as irrational feelings, internal psychological filters, hidden agendas, and preoccupation and lack of interest.

> *Eyes see only light, ears hear only sound, but a listening heart perceives meaning.*
> —DAVID STEINDL-RAST

Listen

When I ask you to listen to me and you start giving advice, you have not done what I asked.

When I ask you to listen to me and you begin to tell me why I shouldn't feel that way, you are trampling on my feelings.

When I ask you to listen to me and you feel you have to do something to solve my problems, you have failed me, strange as that may seem.

Listen! All I asked was that you listen, not talk or do—just hear me. And I can do for myself; I'm not helpless.

When you do something for me that I can and need to do for myself, you contribute to my fear and weakness.

But when you accept as simple fact that I do feel what I feel, no matter how irrational, then I quit trying to convince you and can get about the business of understanding what's behind this irrational feeling.

And when that's clear the answers are obvious and I don't need advice.

Irrational feelings make sense when we understand what's behind them. So, please listen and just hear me, and if you want to talk, wait a minute for your turn, and I'll listen to you.

–Author Unknown

Becoming Aware-Habits
https://www.charlesduhigg.com/the-power-of-habit/

Charles Duhigg believes a habit has a routine of behavior repeated regularly and tends to subconscious. Check out this video from The Power of Habit to learn more about your habit cues and how to change them.

Internal psychological filter. Each of us has an internal psychological filter, a barrier through which we process all the information we receive. This filter consists of prejudices, past experiences, expectations, and anxieties. Everything that we hear, see, or read is interpreted through this filter. For example, the style of a speaker's clothing, facial expressions, posture, accent, color of skin or hair, mannerisms, or age can cause you to make prejudgments and tune him or her out—all because of what is in your filter.

The further we go through life, the more clogged that filter can get. Regardless of what we intend to say, what is ultimately heard depends on what is in the filter of the listener. If your filter contains memories of many painful past experiences, then you may perceive hurt where none is intended. If your filter contains a reservoir of unexpressed anger from the past, then you may hear anger in what others say, regardless of their intent. In *Principle-Centered Leadership*, Stephen Covey summarizes the *root* of most communication problems as being *perception problems*:

> None of us see the world as it is but as we are, as our frames of reference or "maps" define the territory. And our experience-induced perceptions greatly influence our feelings, beliefs, and behavior. (2005)

Hidden agenda. Sometimes we enter a conversation or situation with a special interest in mind, a grudge which we want to bring into the open, or even a "chip on our shoulder." Consequently, we may hear the message in accordance with our own needs. Either consciously or unconsciously, we may sabotage a meeting or direct a conversation in such a way as to further our own needs and motives.

The word listen *contains the same letters as the word* silent.
—ALFRED BRENDEL

Listening is a magnetic and strange thing, a creative force. The friends who listen to us are the ones we move toward, and we want to sit in their radius. When we are listened to, it creates us, makes us unfold and expand.
—KARL MENNINGER

Preoccupation and lack of interest. The communication failures arising from the gap between what the senders meant and the receivers understood does not usually arise from word usage or lack of verbal ability. Many times we are so preoccupied that we just do not listen to what others are saying. We may allow our mind to wander while we are waiting for the speaker to make his or her next point. Perhaps we need to remember that the *rate of speech* is about 100–150 words per minute and the *rate of thought* is about 400–600 words per minute. Also, we may be so preoccupied with what we have to say that we listen to others only to find an opening to get the floor to say what we want to say. Sometimes, our fast-paced lifestyle contributes to our not taking the time to really listen to others. We may not even be interested or care enough to listen.

A story is told of a very busy business executive who every morning rushed through the office and asked his secretary, "How are you?" She always said, "Fine, thank you." After all, is that not what we expect others to say to such a question? Rushing through the office, the executive replied, "That is great." One day, the secretary decided to really "test" the executive's ear. When the usual question came the next morning, the secretary said, "Terrible, terrible, thank you." The executive, still rushing into his office replied, "That is great." The executive's ear had really been tested.

It may seem as though the capacity to listen effectively is a "natural gift" for some people. However, the ability to listen can be cultivated by anyone who wants to develop this capacity. It requires a conscious alertness that can become a *habit* with practice.

How to Improve Your Listening Skills

- Be receptive and attentive
- Allow the speaker to speak freely; limit your lip
- Focus on the speaker and ignore distractions
- Avoid preoccupation with your own thoughts and what you want to say next
- Use verbal following or minimal encourages (minimal encourages are brief indicators to the speaker that you are following their thoughts; e.g., "mm-hmm," nods, or repeating one or two of the speaker's words)
- Avoid all judgments, initially
- Try to listen for more than just the spoken words
- Use feedback and reflect on what the speaker said

Adapted from Hamilton (2018) and Fisher-Sykes (2005).

Styles of Responding

Often we respond with reluctance or on the other hand, with judgment, when we are asked to be part of a deep or intense conversation. Our styles of response can change the entire conversation.

Noted psychologist Carl Rogers (1995) indicates that a major barrier to building close relationships is the very natural tendency we have to *judge and evaluate the statements made by others.*

Sometimes we overuse one style, rely on the style too early in the conversation, or fail to know when and how to use a style that will be of most benefit to the sender and thereby create a better relationship. Let us discuss six of the more common styles of responding: 1) Evaluative or Judging, 2) Advising, 3) Interpretative, 4) Supportive, 5) Questioning, and 6) Understanding (Adler, et al., 2015).

Evaluative or judging. This type of response shows that the receiver is making a judgment about the motive, personality, or reasoning of the sender. The evaluation indicates the sender's statement is either "right" or "wrong." The response may be positive, "You're right on target," or unfavorable, "You shouldn't feel that way." In both cases, the receiver appears to be qualified to suggest to the sender what they might or ought to do.

Since evaluative or judgmental responses often lead to defensiveness, it is best to begin our responses with "I feel …," rather than "You are …" Evaluative or judgmental responses are best accepted when we have been specifically asked to make a value judgment and when we want to disclose our own values and attitudes. In the early stages of relationships, it is generally best to avoid evaluative or judgmental responses.

Criticizing. Even though criticizing is often a part of the evaluative or judging response, it is also a commonly used and even misunderstood response pattern. Therefore, we have decided to discuss it separately. Sometimes, we may want to give someone some constructive feedback, but we are afraid they will perceive it as criticism. After all, haven't we all perceived feedback as really just criticism? Criticism often has a negative connotation and may not be pleasant, but it can be helpful when it leads to productive changes. If we want to give constructive criticism or feedback, rather than destructive criticism or feedback, it is wise to remember these points (Groder, 2017)

- **Emphasize Behavior Rather than Personalities.** Concentrate on what a person does or says rather than who you think the person is. The use of choice adjectives oftentimes leads to labeling the person rather than the behavior. This causes defensiveness. There is a big difference between saying, "John is lazy" and in "John works slowly."
- **Refrain from Using "You" Messages.** The use of "You" messages creates a feeling of blame and accusation. It is more appropriate to say, "I felt hurt today when …" rather than use, "You were cruel today when …"
- **Focus on Actual Observations Rather than Judgments.** Reporting what actually occurred is giving objective feedback. However, reporting on what we think about what actually occurred is giving subjective, value-laden feedback. It is one thing to say, "I really liked the house better the way it was decorated," and quite another to say, "The house looks terrible now."
- **Don't Offer Critical Feedback When Angry or Upset.** Other people will hear only anger and not the message. We may need to cool ourselves down emotionally before engaging in a critical response. It is acceptable to say, "I need to think this through and get back with you later."

Chapter 5: Interpersonal Communication

Don't judge any person until you have walked two moons in their moccasins.
—NATIVE AMERICAN PROVERB

I've learned that people will forget what you said, people will forget what you did, but people will never forget how you made them feel.
—MAYA ANGELOU

- **Concentrate on Sharing Ideas Rather than on Giving Advice.** It is less threatening to say, "Here are some ideas for you to think about …" rather than, "Well, you would be wise to do …" Sharing ideas gives options to others; advising implies, "My solution is the best way."

Criticism that is sought and welcomed is different from unexpected critique. When others respond with criticism, it is easier to handle if we can learn to deal with it *intellectually* and not *emotionally*. *Remember to respond rather than react.* Rather than hearing criticism as a personal attack, it might be helpful to remember some suggestions from Harriet Lerner (2014):

- **Listen.** Do not panic and get defensive when someone offers criticism, Calm listening helps us think clearly.
- **Analyze.** Is the criticism factually correct, or is the critic mostly venting anger? If the critic is really just venting, we can sympathize with their feelings without accepting the content of what they say.
- **Decide What to Do.** If the criticism is accurate, what can we do to remedy the situation and prevent recurrences? We might decide to change our behavior as a result of the criticism.
- **Practice.** Make an honest effort to consistently practice new routines or behaviors until they feel natural or become a habit.

Advising. Advising is responding to others by offering a solution. Advising is criticism that is sought and welcomed. That is different from an unexpected critique. Sometimes this type of response is helpful, and sometimes it is not. For example, we may have the tendency to tell others how we would behave in their place. They may not want to hear what we would do; they may just want us to listen to their thoughts. Giving advice also means that we may be blamed if the advice is followed and *does not work*. Remember to be sure: 1) the advice is correct, 2) the other person really wants advice, 3) the other person is willing to accept the responsibility for choosing to follow the advice.

Foster Cline (Cline & Fay, 2006), a nationally known psychiatrist, frequently suggests two magic sentences that will keep you from appearing dogmatic when offering advice:

I wonder if it would be helpful to … rather than, *if I were you, I would …*

Do you think it would be beneficial to … rather than, *you really should …*

When giving advice, it is important to consider the point from Paula Englander-Golden and Virginia Satir:

> We maximize our chances of being heard when we express our caring friendship and support while expressing our hopes, wishes, and a specific suggestion that our friend can consider. (1995)

Interpretative. In this response, the receiver tries to convey understanding of the sender's problem or issue by offering the alternative wordings:

Would it be fair to describe the main issue as …

It sounds to me that what bothers you most is … If

If I'm hearing you right, the most troublesome part is …

An interpretive response can give the sender another way of seeing the situation, which may lead to greater or even merely different insights. Interpretive responses are best received when they are made as suggestions, or even asked as questions, rather than offered as absolutes or, worse, corrections.

There is a danger of being unintentionally prescriptive—telling the sender what they "ought to" or "should" be feeling—rather than descriptive—describing what the receiver understands about the situation. Interpretive responses are best received when they are offered with integrity and empathy.

Supportive. This type of response shows the receiver's intent to reassure, or comfort the intense feelings of the sender. The receiver must be careful to avoid implications that the sender should or should not feel as they do. Supportive statements take the form of acknowledging the situation and the feelings without attempting to solve or change them.

Supportive statements are like: *That sounds so difficult. I'm sorry you have to deal with this. How uncomfortable for you!*

Supportive statements are best received when they are sincere and help others to feel accepted. Statements that appear to dismiss or minimize the sender's experience should be avoided, as should jokes or attempts to "fix" the feeling.

Questioning. This response indicates that the receiver is interested and needs to know more to respond effectively. Example questions might be as follows:

What is your understanding of why your husband lost his job?

How do you feel about that?

Questioning is a way to get additional information so that the receiver can understand the situation in more detail. It can be extremely important that the receiver ask questions for clarification before responding fully.

There are two types of questions: *closed questions and open questions. Closed questions* often result in *yes, no,* or a very short response. *Open questions,* on the other hand, provide space for the speaker to explore his or her thoughts in greater detail.

Let us look at a typical example between a boss and an employee who have been having conflict with a valued customer. The employee enters the boss's office, and the boss asks:

Closed question: Do you want to see me about the Smith account?

Open question: What's on your mind, Linda?

In short, closed questions are like multiple choice or true/false test questions, whereas open questions are like essay questions.

> *Some people are born more Tigger-ish, and others are born more Eeyore-ish.*
> —GRETCHEN RUBIN

It is also important to ask questions about the issue raised, rather than asking questions about irrelevant issues. Do not distract the sender from the original issue, which might imply lack of interest.

Another important aspect of questioning is to remember to avoid *interrogating and manipulating* the other person. Too many questions do precisely that. Ask one question and wait for the sender to formulate a response.

Often, starting with a supportive response will settle a sender enough to be able to respond well to questions and other types of dialogue.

Understanding. This response indicates that the receiver is seeking to fully understand what the sender is actually saying. Stephen Covey (2013), author of *The 7 Habits of Highly Effective People,* believes that understanding is the key to achieving effective interpersonal communication. Covey makes a profound point about understanding:

> If I were to summarize in one sentence the single most important principle I have learned in the field of interpersonal relations, it would be this: Seek first to understand, then to be understood. (2013)

Because this is the most effective way of responding to others and requires the specific skills of active listening, sometimes referred to as empathetic listening, we will now discuss the meaning and development of these skills.

Games people play

When we want attention, we behave in ways that we believe will produce desired reactions in others. But when such behavior goes too far, the desired result often is not just attention but also manipulation. When people repeatedly manipulate others, they eventually are met with resistance and other negative reactions.

Psychologists refer to these behavior patterns as the games people play. Once we understand the reasons behind the games, we can take steps to avoid them in ourselves and others.

Psychiatrist Eric Berne, MD first reported on this "game" behavior in 1964, in his best-selling book *Games People Play*. He explained that people play games to get attention and fill up time if intimacy or productivity is not available. Even stirring up negative attention—anger, outrage, and hurt—is more gratifying than being ignored or feeling bored or useless, he pointed out.

Martin Groder's 2017 research explored the very important role that games play in the workplace, where people use them to exercise power, deal with risk, and manage interpersonal relations.

In Berne's definition, one can think of a game as a series of interactions (words, body language, facial expressions, etc.) between two or more people that follow a predictable pattern. The interactions ultimately progress to an outcome in which one individual obtains a "payoff" or "goal." In most cases, the participants of the games are unaware that they are "playing."

Becoming Aware of Interactions-Examples of Games

"See what you made me do." In this game, a person becomes irritated at being interrupted while performing a task, such as cooking or balancing the checkbook. Then, when a mistake is made, the other person blows up at the person who made them slip up.

Why the game is played: Feeling victimized puts the player in a morally superior position of power—as opposed to having to recognize the failure.

What you can do to stop it: Instead of falling into the trap, firmly refuse to provide suggestions unless you are empowered to act on them.

"Now I've got you" is played by someone who seems engaged in a meaningful activity, but whose real aim is to trap others when they slip up. The player often is heard to proclaim that "no one does anything right around here."

Why the game is played: It allows the player to feel justified. The player can "righteously" vent his anger.

What you can do to stop it: Make rules and obligations explicit—who is responsible for what and by when—and strictly adhere to them.

"Kick me." In this game, the player behaves in a way that others find obnoxious, irritating, and arrogant. The negative response by others always arouses a hostile reaction by the player, often followed by an injured wail of "Why does this always happen to me?" The player is like a person wearing a sign that reads "Kick Me."

Why the game is played: The player enjoys watching others lose control while he remains calm. He likes being victimized while feeling superior.

What you can do to stop it: Don't rise to the bait. Instead, point out the unnecessary provocation. (Berne, 1996)

Active Listening—Empathetic Listening

In *active listening*, the receiver tries to see the expressed idea, attitude, or problem from the other person's, the sender's, point of view, to sense how it feels to the sender, and to achieve the sender's frame of reference in regard to the thing they are talking about. This really means to listen with the whole body and to pay careful attention to the person who is talking. How is this achieved?

> *The reality of the other person is not in what he reveals to you, but in what he cannot reveal to you. Therefore, if you would understand him, listen not to what he says but rather to what he does not say.*
> —KAHLIL GIBRAN

As a vehicle of communication, listening must focus on the whole person, not just on what the sender is saying. This has been referred to as *listening with the third ear*. The third ear hears what is said between the lines and without words, what is expressed soundlessly, and what the speaker feels and thinks. It is listening in such a way that it creates an atmosphere of communication; others will be able to hear us because they feel we have heard them, that we are in touch with them and not just what they are saying.

Robert Bolton (1986) and Thomas Gordon (2000) have written extensively about the requirements of active listening. Four of these are: 1) develop a posture of involvement, 2) make use of door openers, 3) keep the other person talking with minimal encouragement, and 4) respond reflectively.

Develop a posture of involvement. **Practice** the habit of inclining your body toward the speaker rather than leaning back in the chair or slouching around on the floor or on the sofa. **Position** yourself at a comfortable distance from the speaker so that you can have close eye contact. Usually, about three feet is a comfortable distance in our society. Effective eye contact expresses interest and a desire to listen. Turn off or set aside any electronic devices, including TV, phone, etc. Remove any environmental distractions.

Use door openers. These encouraging phrases are invitations for the sender to say more. These responses do not communicate any of the receiver's own ideas or judgments or feelings; they merely invite the sender to share their own ideas, judgments, or feelings. Here are some examples

> *Tell me more about that …*
>
> *Let's talk about it …*
>
> *Go ahead, I'm listening …*
>
> *Sounds like you have a lot of feelings about that …*

Are you an effective listener?

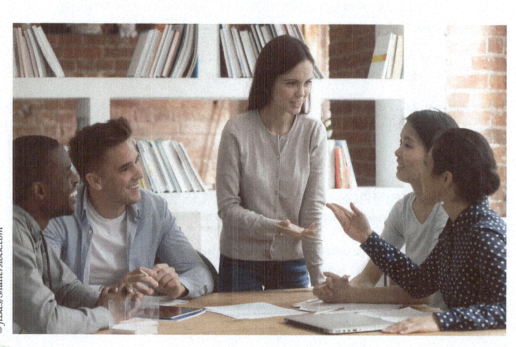

© fizkes/Shutterstock.com

Becoming *Aware*

This seems like something that is important to you …

I'd like to hear some more about that …

Can you tell me what's going on …?

Sounds like this is difficult for you to talk about …

Most people feel encouraged to talk with the use of door openers. More importantly, people feel worthy, respected, significant, and accepted when we invite them to share their feelings and ideas.

Keep the other person talking with minimal encouragement. Minimal encouragement (Bolton used the term "minimal encourages") are brief indicators to the other person that you are still listening. Here are some examples

- "Mm-hmmm"
- "Really?"
- "You did, huh."
- "How about that!"
- "Go on."
- "I see."
- "Oh."
- "And?"
- "Interesting."
- "I hear you."

Another way to use minimal encourages is to repeat the last word or two of the speaker's comment. When the speaker says, "I just don't know what to do; I guess I'm confused," the listener may respond, "Confused?" Generally, the speaker will then express more about his or her confusion.

Respond reflectively. Thomas Gordon explains responding reflectively in this way:

> In active listening, the receiver tries to understand what the sender is feeling or what the message means. Then, he puts his understanding into his own words and feeds it back for the sender's verification. The receiver does not send a message of his own—such as an evaluation, opinion, advice, logic, analysis, or question. He feeds back only what he feels the sender's message meant—nothing more, nothing less. (2000)

As you can probably see, when you use active listening, you really respond reflectively in two ways. **First, the receiver paraphrases or states the essence of the sender's content in their own words, focusing on facts and ideas, rather than the emotions the sender is expressing.**

Paraphrased responses usually begin with of these phrases, or something like them:

What I hear you saying is …

Correct me if I'm wrong …

Do I understand you correctly that …

Let us look at this exchange:

> **Sender:** "My psychology professor is really piling the assignments on, and I'll never get caught up. Does she think psychology is the only course I am taking?"

> **Receiver:** "Do I understand you correctly that she is giving you too much work and doesn't realize you have three other college courses?"

> **Sender:** "Oh, she knows I have other courses, but it is just the end of the semester, and she is shoving it all in at the last minute."

> **Receiver:** "It doesn't seem fair, is that it?"

> **Sender:** "It really isn't, but I'll just have to buckle down and get the work done. I need this course on my degree plan."

Sometimes people confuse paraphrasing with *parroting*. However, *parroting* means to repeat exactly the speaker's words. This can be heard as mocking, and should be avoided.

Secondly, when possible, mirror back to the speaker the emotions they are communicating. The most difficult part of learning to respond reflectively is to listen for the feeling of the other person. The format is simple when you learn to listen for feeling words. For example:

"You sound _____ about _____."

- Angry
- Frustrated
- Worried
- Upset
- Excited
- This
- That
- The other thing
- All of this
- These

Let us look at some examples:

> **Sender:** "I could die here, and no one would even notice."

> **Receiver:** "You sound really frustrated."

> **Sender:** "Oh, I just get to thinking that no one really cares about me."

> **Receiver:** "So, maybe you aren't frustrated, but just a little angry?" It is not a statement (don't tell people what they feel).

> **Sender:** "Yeah, I suppose I am a little angry. I just wish I knew whether my family really cares about me."

Note that in both of these examples, the receiver actively demonstrates that they genuinely want to understand the sender and to hear more of the problem. The receiver does not make evaluative or judgmental responses regarding either the sender or the content. Instead, the receiver paraphrases or mirrors what the sender has said. By maintaining an objective stance, the active listener encourages a sharing of ideas and paves the way for a freer exchange of other points of view. Something to remember is that you don't tell people what they are feeling. You are asking a question about how they feel.

Active listening is an excellent tool to use when emotions are running at high intensity.

> *Next to physical survival, the greatest need of a human being is psychological survival—to be understood, to be affirmed, to be validated, to be appreciated.*
> —STEPHEN COVEY

 Think/Pair/Share Activity

ACTIVE LISTENING IN COMMUNICATION

Form groups of 4. Take a few minutes and find a topic to discuss from the previous chapters. Pair up and try to use the Rogers "communication rule."

When you know an upcoming conversation will be emotionally difficult, ask if your discussion partner or partners will use this communication rule by Carl Rogers:

Each person can speak up only after he or she has restated the ideas and feelings of the previous speaker accurately and to that speaker's satisfaction. This is the heart of active listening.

This rule asks that each sender practice receiving first. Each speaker agrees to try to summarize the perspective of the previous speaker first. Be aware that this is a very difficult thing to attempt. For one thing, once you have been able to state a sender's point of view, your own perspective will reflect that. You will also find that when all parties agree to use this type of listening and response, an attitude of open, two-way communication tends to develop.

WHICH STYLE OF RESPONDING DO YOU USE?

Of the styles of responding we have discussed in this chapter, how often do people use each response? Carl Rogers (1995), a noted psychologist, conducted a series of studies on how individuals communicate with each other in face-to-face situations. *(You will note that Rogers studied five styles, whereas we included six in our discussion. That is because Rogers considered the advising response style to be closely related to the evaluative or judging style.)* He found that the categories of evaluative or judging, interpretative, supportive, questioning, and understanding statements encompass 80% of all the messages sent between individuals. The other 20% of the statements are incidental and of no real importance. From his observations of individuals in all sorts of different settings—business, home, people at parties and conventions, and so on—he found that the responses were used by individuals in the following frequency: 1) *evaluative or judging* was most used, 2) *interpretative* was next, 3) *supportive* was the third most common response, 4) *ques-*

tioning the fourth, and 5) *understanding* was the least-used style in human communication. Finally, he found that if a person uses one category of response as much as 40% of the time, then other people see that person as *always* responding that way.

This last statement may seem like a serious misjudgment, but it is a very normal human response. So it's useful to self-monitor our own responses.

Person-to-Person Communication

We have the task of integrating all that we have discussed in this chapter to improve our communication with those with whom we live and work. In the late 1950s, psychologist Carl Rogers (1957) hypothesized that there were three qualities essential to constructive communication: 1) *genuineness, or authenticity,* 2) *acceptance and respect of others,* and 3) *empathy.* Since then, numerous research studies have been conducted that support Rogers's theory.

Genuineness. This term is from Rogers's original work, and is another word for authenticity. The concept is to be one's truest self without artificial masks. This means being honest and open about one's feelings, needs, and ideas. The authentic person experiences feelings and is able to express those feelings when appropriate. A genuine person can spontaneously be themselves with another so they come to know the person as they truly are: "What you see is what you get." Being a genuine person involves constant attention to self-awareness, self-acceptance, and self-expression. Robert Bolton, a human performance and communication skills consultant in New York, summarizes genuineness in this way:

> Genuineness is essential to all vital relationships. To the degree that I lack authenticity, I am unable to relate significantly to any other person. I must dare to be me to be able to relate to you. (2009)

Acceptance of and respect for others. Acceptance of others means to take them as we find them—to choose not to judge them or demand that they change. Respect for others overlaps acceptance; we respect others when we recognize that they have agency, the capability to make their own choices and decisions. We choose to acknowledge that others do not require our guidance. Note that acceptance and respect are not the same as approval or agreement. We can accept another person's feelings. Menninger and Holzman (2010) of the Menninger Clinic in Topeka, Kansas, speak of this quality in the following way:

> Acceptance is not an easy thing to do, but it's something you must conquer if you want to make the most out of your life. It will help you recover from the painful things that happened to you, and it can help you look forward to the positive things that are about to come your way.
>
> I believe this quality is demonstrated by a person's patience, fairness, consistency, rationality, and kindliness for the other person—accepting the other person as he or she is.

To be persuasive, we must be believable; to be believable, we must be credible; to be credible, we must be truthful.
—EDWARD R. MURROW, JOURNALIST

FOCUS ON DIVERSITY

THE LANGUAGE OF RACE

For much of the nation's history, America has discussed race in the singular form. But the language of race is changing. With the rise of interracial couples, combined with a more accepting society, America's multiracial population has grown at three times the rate of the general population since the beginning of the millennium. The U.S. Census Bureau says 2.1% of American adults check more than one race. Using a broader definition that factors in the racial backgrounds of parents and grandparents, a Pew Research Center report finds that 6.9% of U.S. adults, or nearly 17 million, could be considered multiracial today. Intermarriage and the children of such marriages—particularly White and Black—haven't always been accepted by society. It was less than 50 years ago that the U.S. Supreme Court, in the case bearing the evocative title *Loving v. Virginia*, struck down laws prohibiting mixed-race marriages that had been in place in 16 states, all in the South. And about one-in-five intermarried couples in the U.S. include a Hispanic husband and a White wife. Among both Gen Zers and Millennials, 53% say people of different races marrying each other is a good thing for our society, compared with 41% of Gen Xers, 30% of Baby Boomers and 20% of those in the Silent Generation, according to the Center's 2019 report.

Large majorities of Generation Zers, Millennials, Generation Xers, and Baby Boomers say couples living together without being married doesn't make a difference for our society, according to a 2019 Pew Research Center report.

Multiracial Americans are no longer rare in number. They're front and center in our culture—represented on television, in professional sports, in music and politics (Pew Research Center, 2015). Americans see advantages and challenges in this country's growing racial and ethnic diversity, and most value workplace diversity, but few want employers to consider race or ethnicity in hiring and promotion decisions (Pew Research Center 2019).

Listen to some multi-racial people tell their stories at https://www.pewresearch.org/multiracial-voices/

Empathy. You will recall, when we were discussing the tremendous benefits of the understanding response style, we referred to specific methods that foster empathetic listening. You may also recall that in Chapter Four we referred to *empathy* as one of the key qualities of emotional intelligence. In fact, Carl Rogers (1995) indicates that empathy is the most effective agent we know for fostering personal growth and improving a person's relationships and communications with others. What, then, is this quality, *empathy*?

Empathy refers to the ability to understand how another person feels and how he or she perceives the situation. To see things from the other person's point of view, Sam

> *Anger is one letter short of Danger.*
> —ANONYMOUS

Horn (1997), author of the communication book, *Tongue Fu! How to Deflect, Disarm and Defuse Any Verbal Conflict*, recommends using the Empathy Phrases:

How would I feel?

How would I feel if I were in their shoes?

How would I feel if this were happening to me?

It is important to note that empathy is not sympathy (Ciaramicoli and Ketchen, 2001). *Sympathy* is an involuntary feeling—the passive experience of sharing another person's fear, grief, anger, or joy. *Empathy* is an active process in which we try to learn all we can about another person, rather than having only a superficial awareness. With sympathy, we view the other person's situation from our point of view. With empathy, we view it from the other person's perspective (Adler & Proctor, 2015). Milton Mayeroff describes what it means to *learn all you can about another person*:

> To care for another person, I must be able to understand him and his world as if I were inside it. I must be able to see, as it were, with his eyes what his world is like to him and how he sees himself. Instead of merely looking at him in a detached way from outside, as if he were a specimen, I must be able to be with him in his world, "going" into his world in order to sense from "inside" what life is like for him, what he is striving to be, and what he requires to grow. (1990)

As we have discussed, genuineness, acceptance and respect of others, and empathy are actually attitudes that foster improved relationships with people. The dictionary defines an *attitude* as a "mental or emotional orientation to some object." When these three attitudes are missing, a person's relationships are diminished. When these attitudes are present, the relationships can flourish. However, they have little or no effect on a relationship until they are communicated, usually by practicing them, to the other party. These three attitudes are strengthened and nourished every time they are expressed. Plan to start practicing the art and skills of genuineness, acceptance and respect of others, and empathy at every opportunity.

Being authentic is the summary of all the traits we have discussed. Meeting someone living a uniquely made life is a breath of fresh air. These people are rare—it takes courage and self-confidence to be who you really are despite reactions from skeptics and attempts to bring you back to conformity and a false exterior. If you're ready to show to the world the real you, it might just be the beginning of your journey to authenticity. Dale Carnegie, author of *How to Win Friends and Influence People*, has these words of wisdom:

Six Ways to Make People Like You

1. **Become genuinely interested in other people.** "You can make more friends in two months by being interested in them, than in two years by making them interested in you." The only way to make quality, lasting friendships is to learn to be genuinely interested in them and their interests.

2. **Smile.** Happiness does not depend on outside circumstances, but rather on inward attitudes. Smiles are free to give and have an amazing ability to make others feel wonderful. Smile in everything that you do.

3. **Remember that a person's name is, to that person, the sweetest and most important sound in any language.** "The average person is more interested in their own name than in all the other names in the world put together." People love their names so much that they will often donate large amounts of money just to have a building named after them. We can make people feel extremely valued and important by remembering their name.

4. **Be a good listener. Encourage others to talk about themselves.** The easiest way to become a good conversationalist is to become a good listener. To be a good listener, we must actually care about what people have to say. Many times people don't want an entertaining conversation partner; they just want someone who will listen to them.

5. **Talk in terms of the other person's interest.** The royal road to a person's heart is to talk about the things he or she treasures most. If we talk to people about what they are interested in, they will feel valued and value us in return.

6. **Make the other person feel important—and do it sincerely.** The golden rule is to treat other people how we would like to be treated. We love to feel important and so does everyone else. People will talk to us for hours if we allow them to talk about themselves. If we can make people feel important in a sincere and appreciative way, then we will win all the friends we could ever dream of. (2012)

> *All the mistakes I have made, all the follies I have witnessed, all the errors I have committed have been the result of action without thought.*
> —ANONYMOUS

BECOMING AWARE—TECHNOLOGY, COMMUNICATION, AND FRIENDSHIPS.

Have you heard of the phrase "You need to be a good friend to have friends"? This was my mother's mantra when I would come home from school upset by something a friend said to me. Also, have you heard the song "Make new friends but keep the old, one is silver and the other is gold"? Think about all the things that you have been told about friendship. Write them down and share with your friends. Are they the same as yours?

"Friendship" is becoming an increasingly complex and confusing topic. What does it mean to be a good friend? What does being a good friend look like in a world of constant connection?

We can actually try to make our friendships better using technology.

1. Remember people's names, important aspects of them, and even birthdays.
2. Write heartfelt and humorous letters or notes to people throughout the years.

3. Make sure you have all information about your friends in your contacts and even have birthdays in your calendar. There are great apps or websites to send birthday cards, "I miss you" notes, or "get well soon" cards. Get the birthday card reminders in your calendar so you can call or send friends a note on their special day .

4. You can also use audio or text messaging to send personal notes to your friends, to your mentors/teachers, and to family.

Audio notes or texting is easy and appreciated. It allows you to be "as close to in-person" as you can. Of course, you can send a video text if you'd like. However, audio is powerful because a person can listen to your words, in your voice, and be able to remember what you sounded like last time they were with you.

Chapter Review

We all share the common problem of trying to combat communication breakdowns. When we stop to think of how many ways we can misunderstand each other, it seems a wonder that any effective communication can take place.

- **Communication** is the process of conveying feelings, attitudes, facts, beliefs, and ideas between individuals, either verbally or nonverbally. Communication is effective when the message we intend to convey is the message that is actually received.

- In any given situation, there are three commonly accepted parts to the communication process. There is always: 1) a sender of the message, 2) a receiver of the message, and 3) the content of the message. There are several elements involved in a communication transaction: the idea, encoding, transmission, receiving, decoding, understanding, and feedback.

- **Feedback** is really the only means for determining whether there is mutual understanding between the sender and receiver. Feedback completes the process of two-way communication. In one-way communication, there is an absence of active verbal feedback.

- A large percentage of our communication is by **nonverbal** means. This can include facial expressions and eye contact, vocal cues, gestures and other body movements, touching, personal space and distance, physical environment and territory, clothing and personal appearance, and silence.

- Nonverbal communication can relate to verbal communication in three ways: it can reinforce, replace, and contradict the verbal message. When the nonverbal message contradicts the verbal message, the nonverbal message is generally more accurate.

- The ability to identify deception in others is around 50%. **Microexpressions**, fleeting facial expressions that last only a fraction of a second, are oftentimes helpful. Signals of deception are often called **body leakage**, where body postures rather than the face leak the truth.

- **Microagressions** are the everyday verbal, nonverbal, and environmental slights, snubs, or insults, whether intentional or unintentional, which communicate hostile, derogatory, or negative messages that target persons based solely upon their marginalized group membership.

- The meanings of various kinds of nonverbal communication can vary from culture to culture. Communication can be enhanced when these meanings are understood.

- We share, give, and receive information through words and establish, continue, or terminate relationships through words—verbal communication. The meaning and understanding behind words are the essences of communication.

- There are several barriers or ways that meanings can go astray: semantics, assumptions, self-concept, and emotion-packed phrases.

- Authentic Self is true to one's own personality, spirit, or character. The authentic self is the you that can be found at your absolute core. It is the composite of all your skills, talents, and wisdom. It is all of the things that are uniquely yours and need expression, rather than what you believe you are supposed to be and do. Being authentic is defined as not being false or copied; being genuine; real: representing one's true nature or beliefs and being true to oneself.

- Men and women often use different styles in communication. That is, males are likely to speak and hear a language of "status and independence," while females are likely to speak and hear a language of "connection and intimacy."

- **Listening** is a form of paying attention, which is an active process involving much more than hearing and seeing. When another person speaks, we are usually listening at one of four levels: ignoring, pretending, selective listening, and attentive listening. Very few of us listen with the intent to understand—**empathetic listening**. Some of the barriers to listening include: internal psychological filter, hidden agenda, preoccupation, and lack of interest. **Noise** can occur while sending and receiving a message.

- There are five stages of listening: to sense, interpret, evaluate, respond, and remember.
- There are at least six common styles of responding to others: 1) Evaluating or judging, 2) advising, 3) interpreting, 4) supporting, 5) questioning, and 6) understanding.
- The most common form of responding to others is evaluating or judging, and the least-used style in human communication is the understanding style.
- Criticizing is often a part of the evaluating or judging response. It is extremely important to remember to give and receive criticism intellectually, rather than emotionally.
- The understanding style requires the specific skills of active listening, sometimes called empathetic listening—seeing the expressed idea, attitude, or problem from the other person's point of view. The requirements of active listening or empathetic listening are to develop a posture of involvement, make use of door openers, keep the other person talking with "minimal encouragement," and respond reflectively.
- Researchers and theorists in the behavioral sciences have identified three qualities or attitudes that, when communicated to others, foster improved relationships with people. These qualities are genuineness, acceptance and respect of others, and empathy.
- **Implicit bias** refers to the attitudes or stereotypes that affect our understanding, actions, and decisions in an unconscious manner. These biases, which encompass both favorable and unfavorable assessments, are activated involuntarily and without an individual's awareness or intentional control.
- Acceptance is not an easy thing to do but it's something you must conquer if you want to make the most out of your life. It will help you recover from the painful things that happened to you and it can help you look forward to the positive things that are about to come your way.

Learning Outcomes Review

1. Define communication. Why do we need to communicate?
2. What are the three commonly accepted parts to the communication process? What is involved in a communication transaction?
3. Define feedback and explain why it is so important. Describe the difference in feedback in one-way and two-way communication.
4. What are the three ways nonverbal communication relates to verbal communication? When the nonverbal message contradicts the verbal message, which message is usually more accurate?
5. How likely is it that deception can be detected in others? Define microexpressions, microaggressions, and body leakage.
6. What are at least five different types of nonverbal communication? Which form of nonverbal communication communicates more emotional meaning more accurately? Define paralinguistics and give at least two examples in sentence form. Define the four distances Edward T. Hall discovered in his research.
7. Give at least five examples of cultural differences in nonverbal communication.
8. Explain at least four barriers or ways that meanings can go astray in verbal communication.
9. What are some examples of emotion-packed phrases? What is the key to remember in dealing with these phrases?
10. Compare and contrast at least six differences in the communication styles of men and women.

11. What is the difference between listening and hearing? List and discuss the five different levels of listening we may employ when another person speaks.

12. Name and describe the five stages of listening.

13. What are the barriers to listening? What is the difference between external and internal noise?

14. Give at least four techniques for improving nonverbal communication, verbal communication, and listening skills.

15. Define and give examples of the six common styles of responding to others. What is the most used responding style in human communication? What is the least-used responding style in human communication?

16. What are the suggestions to remember when giving and receiving criticism?

17. Give examples of the four requirements for active listening or empathetic listening.

18. What are the three qualities or attitudes, when communicated to others, that improve relationships with people?

19. Explain the empathy phrases. What is the difference between empathy and sympathy?

20. What is acceptance?

Key Terms

Acceptance
Active Listening
Advising Response
Assume (Assumptions)
Attentive Listening
Authentic self
Body Leakage
Closed Questions
Communication
Communication Barriers
Communication Channels
Communication Process
Decoding
Door Openers
Emotion-Packed Phrases
Empathetic Listening
Empathy
Encoding
External Noise
Feedback
Genuineness

Hearing
Hidden Agenda
Ignoring while Listening
Implicit Bias
Internal Noise
Internal Psychological Filter
Interpretative Response
Intimate Distance
Judging Response
Kinesics
Listening
Listening with the Third Ear
Microaggressions
Microexpressions
Minimal Encourages
Noise
Nonverbal Communication
One-Way Communication
Open Questions
Paralinguistics
Paraphrase

Parroting
Parts of a Communication
    Transaction
Passive Listening
Personal Distance
Pretending while Listening
Public Distance
Questioning Response
Reacting to Others
Responding Reflectively
Responding to Others
Selective Listening
Semantics
Social Distance
Supportive Response
Symbols in Communication
Sympathy
Two-Way Communication
Understanding Response
Verbal Communication
"You" Messages

Reflections: Critical Thinking Activity

Answer the following questions and turn them into your instructor for grading. (All questions answered = A; 13 questions answered = B; 8 questions answered = C).

1. Discuss the causes for communication breakdown. In your opinion, what presents the biggest problem?
2. Many times nonverbal messages are more honest and revealing than what is verbally expressed. Why? Give examples of nonverbal communication to support your answer.
3. Discuss the signals you rely on to try to detect deception in others.
4. Discuss some examples of semantics in your field of work—occupational jargon.
5. Is it possible to give constructive criticism without causing the other person to become defensive? How?
6. Of the techniques discussed for improving listening skills, which technique will be most difficult for you to use?
7. Of the six common styles of responding to others, which style of responding is the most difficult for you to use? Why?
8. Discuss any examples of cultural differences you have experienced in verbal or nonverbal communication.
9. Is it possible that the differences in communication styles of men and women, as discussed in this chapter, have more to do with basic personality styles, rather than gender?
10. What are the key qualities in the communication skills of others that impress you the most?
11. Which part of the empathy phrase is more helpful for you and why?
12. Have you ever felt you were not chosen for a job or a team because of implicit bias?
13. Explain implicit bias.
14. How has technology impacted your life? What about your friends and family?
15. Discuss how you avoid the pitfalls of cell phones?

Technology Resources and Activities

TECHNOLOGY

http://www.tolerance.org/youth-united

> Teaching Tolerance website: Teaching Tolerance, Diversity, and Justice.

http://www.kirwaninstitute.osu.edu/research/understanding-implicit-bias/

> Understanding Implicit Bias: Kirwan Institute for Bias Free Communication. 7 day Race and Gender Bias cleanse activity

http://www.pewresearch.org/multiracial-voices/

> Multiracial Voices in America.

https://www.youtube.com/watch?v=Of3FL4X7mLoCouples

> Share the Happiness and Heartache of Interracial Marriage | National Geographic

https://www.ted.com/talks/julian_treasure_5_ways_to_listen_better?language=en

Julian Treasure: 5 Ways to Listen Better.

https://www.youtube.com/watch?v=CWry8xRTwpo

TED Talk: How Body Language and Micro Expressions Predict Success

www.youtube.com/watch?v=xAIFGBlEsbQ

Microagressions in Everyday Life, by Derald Wing Sue

https://www.youtube.com/watch?v=WDbxqM4Oy1Y

How To Skip the Small Talk and Connect With Anyone, by Kalina Silverman

https://www.youtube.com/watch?v=GAx845QaOck

Marshall Davis Jones: "Touchscreen." National slam poetry contest winner.

https://www.youtube.com/watch?v=lpPASWlnZIA

Darius Simpson and Scout Bostley, "Lost Voices"

https://www.ted.com/talks/amy_cuddy_your_body_language_may_shape_who_you_are

Amy Cuddy: Your body language shapes who you are, a TED Talk

https://www.youtube.com/watch?v=PnDgZuGIhHs

Love has no Labels.

ACTIVITIES:

www.authentichappiness.sas.upenn.edu/testcenter.aspx

Brief Strengths Test or VIA Survey of Character Strengths. A self-test that measures 24 character strengths.

https://www.tbytmedia.com/

Think Before You Type Media Group is a media outlet affiliated with Think Before You Type, Inc. (TBYT), an anti-cyberbullying and positive self-esteem non-profit organization.

https://www.implicit.harvard.edu/implicit/takeatest.html

Take the Implicit Bias test from Harvard University.

http://www.greatergood.berkeley.edu/quizzes

Quizzes, all based on scientific research, to learn more about yourself, your emotional makeup, and how you relate to others. Quiz and resource topics include awe, empathy, social capital, altruism, anxiety and many more.

http://www.nonverbal.ucsc.edu/

This website gives you a chance to learn more about nonverbal communication. You can even test your own ability to "read" samples of real nonverbal communication.

Beginning activities are free, and prices for the University of California video series on Nonverbal Communication start at $50.

http://www.mindtools.com/CommSkll/ActiveListening.htm

Learning how becoming a better listener can increase your productivity and improve your relationships. (First 2 publications are free.)

http://www.newconversations.net

A free guide to better communication skills for work, family, and friendships.

Connected: The Surprising Power of Our Social Networks and How They Shape Our Lives

by James H. Fowler and Nicholas A. Christakis

https://www.ctb.ku.edu/en/table-of-contents/culture/cultural-competence/culture-and-diversity/main

The Community Tool Box is a service of the Center for Community Health and Development at the University of Kansas.

Chapter 5 Interpersonal Communications

LET'S EXPLORE—RACE

https://www.brainpickings.org/2015/01/06/albert-einstein-w-e-b-du-bois-racism/

For an interesting discussion on race please read the Brainpickings link above and discuss it in groups of 4

Make sure you use your best interpersonal communications skills. Plan to report to the full class after you have finished 20 minutes of discussion. Groups should assign a moderator who will report back to the class.

Group Moderator_____

Member _____

Member _____

Member _____

Member _____

Group report notes:

Name _____ Date _____

Personal Communication Concerns

PURPOSE

To review individual communication concerns and problems.

INSTRUCTIONS

Following is a list of 15 problems many individuals have as they try to communicate effectively. Read the list and rank your top five individual concerns from 1 to 5, with 1 being your top choice.

_____ A. I often speak before I really think.
_____ B. I usually speak rather than really listen to others.
_____ C. I feel that I am shy.
_____ D. I let others do most of the talking.
_____ E. I would rather communicate in writing rather than speaking face-to-face.
_____ F. People tell me that I speak too fast.
_____ G. I often misunderstand what people say to me.
_____ H. People often misinterpret what I say.
_____ I. When talking, I gesture more than others.
_____ J. I often interrupt others while they are talking.
_____ K. I feel uncomfortable looking into someone's eyes when talking.
_____ L. When meeting others, I tend to get very nervous.
_____ M. I have trouble when speaking to people in authority positions.
_____ N. I feel that others lose interest in what I am saying.
_____ O. I often find myself playing games with others instead of expressing how I really feel.

DISCUSSION

1. List your top 5 communication concerns and share them with a small group of 4 or 5 classmates.

Becoming *Aware*

2. What steps can you take to begin working on these concerns?

3. What suggestions can the group give you for working on your personal concerns?

Adapted from Communication Research Associates (2016). *Communicate! A Workbook for Interpersonal Communication*. Dubuque, IA: Kendall Hunt Publishing Company.

One-Way/Two-Way

PURPOSE

To demonstrate how descriptive communication can be interpreted differently by other people and also to show the superior functioning of two-way communication.

INSTRUCTIONS

1. A sender is selected to give information to the class.
2. The sender is given a drawing, made up of designs of geometric figures. The participants are given a blank sheet of paper; they are instructed to label one side Diagram I and the other side Diagram II.
3. The sender turns his or her back to the rest of the group and tries to describe verbally how to reproduce the geometric model. This is Diagram I.
4. Participants may neither ask questions nor give audible responses; participants may not talk or compare sketches with the other group members.
5. After 10 or 15 minutes, repeat the exercise with the sender facing his group, and giving directions for Diagram II. Participants should use the other side of their paper, designated as Diagram II.
6. Participants may ask any questions they desire. Senders may respond verbally, but no gestures, please.
7. When Diagram II has been completed, the sender shows the participants the two diagrams, and they are to tell how many figures they drew correctly.

NOTE: Instead of selecting one sender for the entire group, triads may be formed, with one student being the sender, one student being the receiver, and one student being the observer. The sender and receiver will place their desks or chairs back to back, with the observer nearby. The observer should record the length of time required for completing Diagram I and Diagram II. The observer will also give feedback to the sender and receiver when the diagrams are complete. For example, what contributed to the diagrams being accurate or inaccurate? Were there any unusual terms used by the sender? How long did it take to complete each diagram?

DISCUSSION

1. What assumptions might you make about one- and two-way communications? Which takes longer? Which is more accurate?

2. Explain which is more frustrating for the sender. Explain which is more frustrating for the receiver.

3. What parallels does this exercise have in your everyday life? Does this exercise tell you anything about the way you listen?

Name _____ Date _____

Gender and Communication

Purpose

To question if the gender differences in language and communication style make a difference in communication styles so we can be more effective.

Instructions

1. Individually respond to the questions below, being as specific as possible.
2. Divide into groups of five. Select a spokesperson for the group. Each group member will share their responses to the questions below, with the spokesperson taking notes to present to the entire class.

Questions

1. List three differences in how men and women communicate and how other genders listen and understand various types of communication issues. (Women and men complete both responses.)

Women

Example: *They (We) just want to talk about feelings and relationships.*

Men

They (We) just want to talk about sports and business events.

2. What would you suggest the "other sex" do to facilitate their communication with you?

Example: *I would like them to express their feelings more.*

I would like them to become more interested in sports and cars.

3. What would you like others to learn and understand about the way you communicate? Are there cultural differences?

Women

Example: *I just want them to listen— not try to solve my problems.*

Men

I don't like to feel pressured into talking about my feelings and problems.

DISCUSSION

1. What have you learned most about the communication style of others? What are the stereotypes?

2. Is there a difference in all gender communication? Do you think it is because of the parenting, culture or society? Is there stereotyping? others? Is it from the 1970–80s research and literature of Tannen and Gray?

3. What do you think you need to do to communicate more effectively with the "other sexes"? How does technology (i.e., cellphones, online chats etc.) change gender communications? Can you always tell the gender of the person you are chatting with?

Name _____ Date _____

Empathetic Listening

PURPOSE

To develop an understanding of the importance of active listening.

INSTRUCTIONS

1. Find a partner, and then move to a place where you can talk comfortably. Designate one person as **A** and the other **B**.

2. Find a subject on the list below on which you and your partner apparently disagree, or you may select a current events topic, a philosophical or moral issue, or perhaps simply a matter of personal taste.
   A. Abortion
   B. Death Penalty
   C. Single Parenting
   D. Teenage Pregnancy
   E. Homosexuality
   F. Euthanasia
   G. Education Standards
   H. Drug/Alcohol Abuse—How to Prevent Their Use
   I. Internet Regulation
   J. Cohabitation
   K. Divorce/Children
   L. Prison Reform
   M. Other …

3. **A** begins by making a statement on the subject. **B**'s job is then to paraphrase the idea back, beginning by saying something like, "What I hear you saying is …" It is very important that in this step **B** feeds back only what they heard **A** say *without adding any judgment or interpretation*. **B**'s job is simply to understand here, and doing so in no way should signify agreement or disagreement with **A**'s remarks.

4. **A** then responds by telling **B** whether or not their response was accurate. If there was some misunderstanding, **A** should make the correction and **B** should feed back their new understanding of the statement. Continue this process until both partners are sure that **B** understands **A**'s statement.

5. Now it is **B**'s turn to respond to **A**'s statement, and for **A** to help the process of understanding by correcting **B**.

6. Continue this process until each partner is satisfied that they explained themselves fully and have been understood by the other person.

Discussion

1. As a listener, how accurate was your first understanding of the speaker's statements?

2. How did your understanding of the speaker's position change after you used active listening?

3. Did you find that the gap between your position and that of your partner narrowed as a result of your both using active listening?

4. How did you feel at the end of your conversation? How does this feeling compare to your usual emotional state after discussing controversial issues with others?

5. How might your life change if you used active listening at home, at work, or with friends?

Name _____ Date _____

Are You an Active Listener?

PURPOSE

To assess your active listening skills and establish goals for improvement.

INSTRUCTIONS

1. Before responding to the statements below, make a copy and have a person with whom you talk regularly answer these questions about you.
2. Select the response that best describes the frequency of your actual behavior. Place the letters A, U, F, O, or S on the line before each of the 15 statements.

Almost Always	Usually	Frequently	Occasionally	Seldom
A	U	F	O	S

_____ **1.** I like to listen to people talk. I encourage them to talk by showing interest, by smiling and nodding, and so on.

_____ **2.** I pay closer attention to speakers who are more interesting or similar to me.

_____ **3.** I evaluate the speaker's words and nonverbal communication ability as they talk.

_____ **4.** I avoid distractions; if it is too noisy, I suggest moving to a quiet spot, turning off the TV, and so on.

_____ **5.** When people interrupt me to talk, I put what I was doing out of sight and mind and give them my complete attention.

_____ **6.** When people are talking, I allow them time to finish. I do not interrupt, anticipate what they are going to say, or jump to conclusions.

_____ **7.** I tune people out who do not agree with my views.

_____ **8.** While the other person is talking or the professor is lecturing, my mind wanders to personal topics.

_____ **9.** While the other person is talking, I pay close attention to the nonverbal communications to help me fully understand what the sender is trying to get across.

_____ **10.** I tune out and pretend I understand when the topic is difficult.

_____ **11.** When the other person is talking, I think about what I am going to say in reply.

_____ **12.** When I feel there is something missing or contradictory, I ask direct questions to get the person to explain the idea more fully.

_____ **13.** When I do not understand something, I let the sender know.

_____ **14.** When listening to other people, I try to put myself in their position and see things from their perspective.

_____ **15.** During conversations I repeat back to the sender what has been said in my own words (paraphrase) to be sure I understand correctly what has been said.

KEY FOR SCORING

For items 1, 4, 5, 6, 9, 12, 13, 14, and 15, give yourself: 5 points for each A, 4 for each U, 3 for each F, 2 for each O, and 1 for each S statement. Place the numbers on the line to your response letter. For items, 2, 3, 7, 8, 10, and 11 the score reverses: 5 points for each S, 4 for each O, 3 for each F, 2 for each U, and 1 for each A. Place these score numbers on the lines next to the response letters. Now add your total number of points. Your score should be between 15 and 75. Place your score on the continuum below.

Poor Listener 15 _____ 25 _____ 35 _____ 45 _____ 55 _____ 65 _____ 75 _____ Good Listener

Generally, the higher your score, the better your listening skills.

Note: To improve active listening, items 1, 4, 5, 6, 9, 12, 13, 14, and 15 should be implemented, whereas items 2, 3, 7, 8, 10, and 11 should be avoided.

DISCUSSION

1. Explain how you did on the items to be implemented for improved active listening.

2. Explain how you did on the items to be avoided for improved active listening.

3. How did your perception of your listening skills compare to those of the individual who rated you? Do you agree or disagree?

4. After comparing your perception of your listening skills with those of the individual who rated you, in what areas do you feel you could improve to become a more effective active listener?

Name _____ Date _____

Activity: Are you too connected to technology?

PURPOSE

To make you more aware of how technology effects your interpersonal relationship skills.

INSTRUCTIONS

Read one of the following books about technology (or something about how interpersonal relations and technology are in your life). You need to read it in book form; that is, not on your computer or phone. You will need to cut yourself off from technology while you are reading your book.

In a 1-page paper, you will write a review about turning yourself off from technology and how it felt to read a book without using any technology.

Some suggested books you might read are:

Andrew Keen's *The Internet Is Not the Answer*

Danah Boyd's *It's Complicated: The Social Lives of Networked Teens*

Jonathan Haidt's *The Happiness Hypothesis*

Sherry Turkle's *Alone Together: Why We Expect More From Technology and Less From Each Other*

Sherry Turkle's *The Second Self*

Nicholas Negroponte's *Being Digital*

Alan B. Albarran's *The Social Media Industries*

James Barrat's *Our Final Invention: Artificial Intelligence and the End of the Human Era*

John Seabrook's *Nobrow: The Culture of Marketing, the Marketing of Culture*

Simon Head's *Mindless: Why Smarter Machines Are Making Dumber Humans*

Nicholas Carr's *The Glass Cage*

Name _____ Date _____

Interpersonal Communication

LEARNING JOURNAL

Select the statement below that best defines your feelings about the personal value or meaning gained from this chapter and respond below the dotted line.

I learned that I …   I was surprised that I …

I realized that I …   I was pleased that I …

I discovered that I …   I was displeased that I …

···

Chapter 6

Developing Relationships

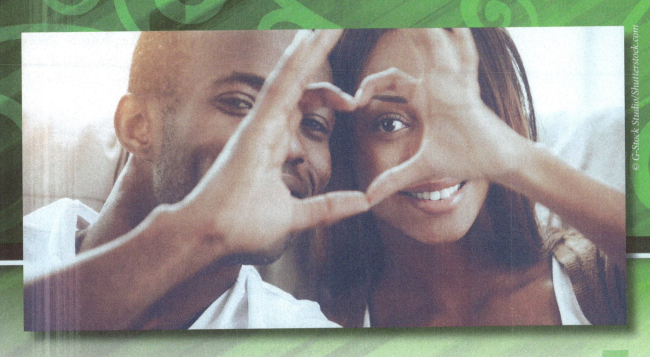

© G-Stock Studio/Shutterstock.com

The 10 Most Important Words in Any Loving Relationship
1. Trust   2. Intimacy   3. Communication   4. Commitment   5. Love
6. Friendship   7. Patience   8. Humor   9. Flexibility   10. Forgiveness
— Gregory J. P. Godek

Think About This...

Relationships mean many things to all of us. We have relationships with our community, our neighbors, our families, our friends and our lovers. A positive healthy relationship with a variety of people is the best way to lead a healthy life. Studying Human Relations can help make the experience of "relating" to others a fun and memorable experience. The more knowledge learned about humans and healthy relationships, the wider your circle of friends/ lovers will be. Widening a circle of friends will gives a healthy support system. Dating and developing an intimate relationship is a goal for many, and is often encouraged by the media and advertising. (Both positively and negatively). Taking your time and enjoying your life—meeting and dating a variety of friends before committing to an intimate relationship—will lead to a happy, fulfilling experience.

The Development of Relationships

In this chapter, the focus is on intimate relationships, which usually involve mutual physical and sexual contact. Relationships require the commitment of *time* and *effort* and there is no guarantee that the work will have the result we seek. The first step in a relationship is *becoming aware* of the other person—*first impressions*. At this time we evaluate the person, using our past experience, prejudices, and stereotyping to make a judgment about whether or not to take the next step. Now that a person has *become aware* it is time to make a decision or take the next step, that is, *making contact,* or getting acquainted with other person. This is a difficult step for many individuals.

How do we do it? The *mere exposure phenomenon* may work in this situation (Wood et al., 2014). The more familiar we are with someone or something, the greater the chance of liking them. The more another person sees us, the greater the chance of us interacting and liking each other. We could improve the odds of *making contact* by sitting in the chair next to them *(proximity)* or standing by the door before they enter the classroom *(exposure).* We should not be too aggressive in this process, or the other person may feel threatened.

The third step is *disclosure.* As we become friends, we are more willing to disclose more about our personal lives—our hopes, dreams, and fears. As we begin to disclose information about ourselves, we are demonstrating to our partner that we trust them, and they in turn will disclose to us. Thus, the relationship will become stronger and more personal. We can ask questions about classes, then talk about school-related subjects, ask about hobbies and interests, and talk about our interests, making sure not to take over the conversation. As people continue disclosing information about themselves to each other, their interest in one another will continue to grow.

Do all the terms and concepts mentioned so far sound familiar? They should; we discussed all of them thoroughly in Chapter One. That was a review of how a relationship develops over a period of time, and now we will discover how the relationship will continue to evolve into a more personal relationship.

> *Be slow in choosing a friend, slower in changing.*
> —BENJAMIN FRANKLIN

Becoming Friends

Friends provide us with the *emotional support* and *social ties* that are vital to our well-being. A good friend will always be there when they are needed. We can rely on their support, no matter what happens to us. They also provide us with a feeling of belonging and a feeling that we are part of a group. We need an identity, and our friends help us in the development of finding out who we are. Good friends satisfy these needs. Relationships rely on mutual interactions. It is important to examine our own contribution to the dynamics of a friendship. It is only our own behavior that we can change, and there are certain personal characteristics that are essential to cultivate in order to build healthy, lasting friendships.

Texting is the most common and frequent way that teens communicate with all types of friends, from the ones they've just met to more established relationships. But teens haven't abandoned phone calling yet. A 2015 research study by the Pew Research Center surveyed teens about technology and friendship and found that phone calls are an important way that teens connect, particularly with their closest friends. Teens with close friends said they reach their friends by text messaging, with 80% of teens nam-

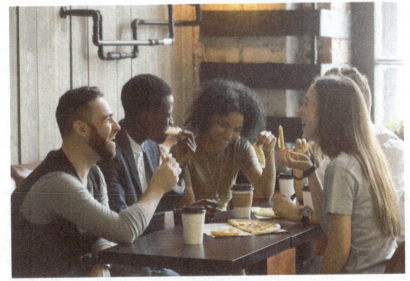

© fizkes/Shutterstock.com

Who are your good friends?

Think/Pair/Share Activity

THE 13 ESSENTIAL FRIENDSHIP TRAITS

After thinking about the list below, mark the statements you agree with. Pair up with someone you usually do not sit by (making a new friend).

Note which items you need to work on, and with your partner, come up with ideas to help you make changes.

How much do you agree with each statement?

1   I am trustworthy.
2   I am honest with others.
3   I am generally very dependable.
4   I am loyal to the people I care about.
5   I am easily able to trust others.
6   I experience and express empathy for others.
7   I am able to be non-judgmental.
8   I am a good listener.
9   I am supportive of others in their good times.
10   I am supportive of others in their bad times.
11   I am self-confident.
12   I am usually able to see the humor in life.
13   I am fun to be around.

These traits fall into three general categories, each representing an essential aspect of relational behavior. If you find that you disagree with many of the statements, you may struggle to develop meaningful, lasting friendships (Degges-White, 2015).

ing it as one of their top three choices and 49% saying it is the *most common* way they keep in touch. Phone calls are second, with 69% of teens saying that this is the favored way to keep in touch with their best friends, and only 13% used it just for keeping in touch occasionally. Pew Research Center focusgroups reinforce the notion that teens use different channels of communication depending on the closeness of a friendship. Phone calls are reserved for more intimate relationships. Anderson found teens saying, "if they are just friends, not best friends, you don't really have anything to talk about (Anderson 2015).

According to evolutionary biologists, dependence on others for survival made our friendships stronger. We cherish our friends, but we don't realize the importance they are in our lives.

We all need to make good friends. The scientific research recently gathered has insights about the ways friendships influence us. This has been called "friendfluence." Many people are marrying later—or not at all—and more families are having just one child, so friendships are becoming "family relationships," and are gaining in importance. The research suggests that friends have a greater hand in our development and well-being than do our romantic partners and relatives (Flora, 2013).

According to Dr. Degges-White (2015), there are three categories of friendship traits:

Traits of Integrity

These qualities, represented by the first five traits on the list of Essential Friendship Traits above, are related to core values held by most cultures—**trustworthiness**, **honesty**, **dependability**, **loyalty**, and, as an interrelated quality, **the ability to trust others**.

Traits of Caring

These qualities, represented by the traits listed as numbers 6 to 10 above, include **empathy**, **the ability to withhold judgment**, effective **listening skills**, and **the ability to offer support** in good times and bad. These traits require personal insight, self-discipline, and unconditional positive regard for our friends.

Traits of Congeniality

This group, representing by the final three traits listed above, includes **self-confidence, the ability to see the humor in life**, and **being fun to be around**. This trio of traits has also been associated with overall well-being and happiness in life.

BEFORE YOU CAN INCREASE YOUR FRIENDSHIP QUOTIENT, YOU MUST ADMIT THAT THE NEED EXISTS

Remember: Everyone brings a different level of the 13 traits to their relationships. However, the very best friends offer a generous helping of this baker's dozen.

Remember from Chapter Two that Carl Rogers believed in the importance of unconditional acceptance from a friend: *Accept me as I am—not how you want me to be.*

In my own relationships, I know that I should break up with someone who doesn't encourage me to be strong and make my own choices and do what's best in my life, so if you're dating someone who doesn't want you to be the best person you can be, you shouldn't be dating them.
—VERONICA ROTH

Becoming *Aware*

How long does it take to make a friend? Why do we make friends with some people and not others? In 2018 professor Jeffrey Hall from the University of Kansas wrote in the *Journal of Social and Personal Relationships* a study on how to make friends in school—or in any situation. It's all about time. Using Dunbar's social brain hypothesis and Communicate Bond Belong theory, friendship status was examined as a function of *hours together, shared activities, and everyday talk.*

Professor Hall showed how much time people need in order to become friends. He, surveyed 112 freshmen at the University of Kansas by them how many people they had met since starting school two weeks before.

Next, he followed up with the participants four and seven weeks later to see how their relationships had developed. As a result, he found that it takes 50 hours of time together to move from acquaintance to casual friend, 90 hours to go from casual friend to friend, and more than 200 hours before you can consider someone your close friend (Hall, 2018).

> *Try to be a rainbow in someone's cloud.*
> —MAYA ANGELOU

CONSIDER THIS

FRIENDSHIP

Can you trust your friends? If not, are they friends? Keeping confidence and trust are almost synonymous. Trust and respect are things people need to earn, and should not be given away lightly. There are three questions that need to be answered that will help us make decisions about whether to trust someone or not:

1. **How predictable is the individual?** A predictable person is someone whose behavior is consistent—consistently good or bad. An unpredictable person keeps us guessing about what might happen next. Such volatile people may make life interesting, but they do not inspire much in the way of confidence.
2. **Can I depend upon them?** A dependable person can be relied upon when it counts. One way to tell is to see how a partner behaves in situations where it is possible to care or not to care.
3. **Do I have faith in that person?** Through "thick and thin" you know you can rely on this person. They make us feel "safe."

Similarities. Is it true that "opposites attract"? Or is it true that "birds of a feather flock together"? Look around. Do most of your friends have different interests, beliefs, and political preferences from you, or are they similar? Research indicates that similarities attract. We tend to select friends who are similar to us in many different aspects, including ethnic background, social status, interests, income level, occupation, status, educational level, and political preferences (Myers, 2017). Similarities are also important in the selection of a mate. There is a correlation between length of marriage and the similarities between the two people. The more similarities there are between the two spouses, the longer the marriage tends to last.

> *Friends are the family you can choose.*

What would it be like if our friends always disagreed with us? We are Republicans and they are Democrats; we are pro-life and they are pro-choice; we are religious and they are not; we are conservative and they are liberal; we smoke and they do not; they like rock music and we like classical music; we like to participate in sports and they would rather hang out. Are we going to have fun together, or is there going to be a lot of conflict? Research studies have found that there are two critical similarities that are important within a relationship: they are *similar beliefs* and *similar attitudes* (Taylor & Peplau, 2009). When considering a long-term commitment between yourself and another person, ask yourself, what do we have in common? Are our beliefs and attitudes similar? If they are not, you may discover that over a period of time, conflict is more apt to develop between the two of you.

So, similarity breeds content. *Birds of a feather do flock together* (Hyde & DeLamater, 2019). Surely you have noticed this upon discovering a special someone who shares your ideas, values, and desires—a soul mate who likes the same music, the same activities, even the same foods you do. So, how do we find someone who has something in common with ourselves?

Male and female friends. Chatterjee (2016) believes that male-female friendship can be tricky, but both benefit from cross-sex buddyhood. "The belief that men and women can't be friends comes from another era in which women were at home and men were in the **workplace,** and the only way they could get together was for romance," explained Linda Sapadin, a psychologist in Valley Stream, New York. "Now they work together and share **sports,** interests, and **socialize** together" (*Psychology Today,* 2016)." This cultural shift has encouraged psychologists, sociologists, and communications experts to put forth a new message: Though it may be tricky, men and women can successfully become close friends (Chatterjee, 2016).

The media supports the confusion, with movies and television implying that sex always comes between friends, making true friendship, whether supportive or confused, a "precursor" to romance. Don O'Meara, Ph.D., at the University of Cincinnati-Raymond Walters College, published a landmark study in the journal *Sex Roles* on the top impediments to cross-sex friendship. "I started my research because one of my best friends is a woman," said O'Meara. "She said, 'Do you think anyone else has the incredible friendship we do?'" He decided to find out, and after reviewing the scant existing research, O'Meara identified the following challenges to male-female friendship: defining it, dealing with sexual attraction, seeing each other as equals, facing people's responses, and social expectations of sex that color all relationships unfairly. These expectations have tended to target the men, to the relationship, and meeting in the first place.

CHALLENGE # 1: Defining the Relationship: Friends or Lovers?
Platonic love does exist, O'Meara asserted, and a study of 20 pairs of friends published in the *Journal of Social and Personal Relationships* (Sapadin, 2014) lends credence to the notion. Distinguishing between romantic, sexual, and friendly feelings, however, can be exceedingly difficult, but needs to be discussed.

CHALLENGE # 2: Overcoming Attraction: Let's Talk About Sex

A study published in the *Journal of Social and Personal Relationships* (Sapadin, 2014) asked more than 150 professional men and women what they liked and disliked about their cross-sex friendships. Topping women's list of dislikes: sexual tension. Men, on the other hand, more frequently replied that sexual attraction was a prime reason for initiating a friendship, and that it could even deepen a friendship. Either way, 62% of all subjects reported that sexual tension was present in their cross-sex friendships.

CHALLENGE #3: Establishing Equality: The Power Play

Friendship should be a pairing of equals, like all healthy, stable relationships of all kinds.

CHALLENGE #4: The Public Eye: Dealing with Doubters

Society is entirely ready for friendships between men and women that have no sexual subtext.

CHALLENGE #5: The Meeting Place: Finding Friends

These obstacles may seem numerous and formidable, but male-female friendship is becoming not only a possibility, but also a necessity.

We find friends in places where we find other people who have similar interests and needs. *Proximity*, or physical nearness, is a major factor in the development of friendships. When you were young, most of your friends came from the local neighborhood where you lived, then from the local school you attended. This is what we mean when we say proximity—you get to know the people you are near or close to in regards to location. Rather than picking our friends based on intentional choice and common values and interests, our friendships may be based on more superficial factors like proximity or group assignments (Science Daily, 2008).

Do opposites attract? Or is it birds of a feather flock together?

© Dean Drobot/Shutterstock.com

PROXIMITY.

Discuss these questions in triads.

So, where do you go to meet people? Where have you met most of your friends? Should you go to church? What about bars and sports bars? What about political events, if you are interested in politics? Should you consider the Internet?

© Jacob Lund/Shutterstock.com

Where do you go to find friends?

Do opposites attract? This is an old saying that is really not true. For a period of time, until the novelty wears off, people who are really different may enjoy the explorations. When a relationship seeks stability, these dissimilar beliefs, interests, and attitudes cause more conflict than attraction. We may find someone from a different value system exciting and interesting, but over time we may discover that we do not have enough in common, and the excitement and interest is likely to wane.

Another interesting phenomenon is the fact that some people are initially and spontaneously repulsed by strangers who are very dissimilar to themselves (Bordens, 2013). This is referred to as the *repulsion hypothesis*. Attitudes and values that contradict our own are physiologically arousing in either direction. Just as we implicitly assume that people who are similar to us will probably like us and treat us well, so we implicitly assume that people who are very different from us will probably dislike us and treat us poorly. Thus, initial dissimilarities can cut a relationship short.

Think/Pair/Share Activity

DISSIMILARITIES

Discuss these questions with a partner

Can you think of some examples where you have experienced this?

But, what about people we know who have been married for years and seem to be to be totally different and seem to be happy together? Even though they seem to be opposites, they are very compatible. Why?

In the article "Love and Power," Gottman says, "In 200 years, heterosexual relationships will be where gay and lesbian relationships are today." That's a long time to wait for change, but it reflects his findings that couple interactions are far more direct and kind with same-sex relationships than the power struggles that arise with heterosexual ones. Rather than rely on cultural assignment of gender roles, gay men and women must come up with their own ways to divide labor and share decisions. Having to actively decide who does what pulls for greater consciousness of fairness and equality, even after children arrive. Lesbian parents—family responsibilities among gay men are too new to have undergone similar study—are "dramatically more equal in sharing of child-care tasks and decision making than heterosexual parents," researchers report (Marano, 2016).

Do they complement each other? People with *complementary needs* seem to be drawn to each other. We might notice that one of our friends is very outgoing, and their boyfriend is very shy. This does not seem consistent with the idea that similarities attract. Why do they get along so well? We discover that differences in which one person's strengths compensate for the other person's weaknesses may lead to mutual attraction (Strong et al., 2020). The personalities seem to complement each other. In most relationships, each person supplies certain qualities that the other partner is lacking. Does your partner supply these missing characteristics? "A relationship has to feel fair. And that requires flexibility and responsiveness to emotions. People try to get their partner's attention or interest, or open a conversation or share humor or affection. We look at what proportion of the time a partner turns toward such a bid or a need. The turning towards needs to be at a very high level." Fairness has one critical element, says University of Washington sociologist Pepper Schwartz—respect. In interviewing thousands of couples around the world, she found that the American definition of a good relationship is "best friend." (Europeans prefer "passionate lover." Europeans do not expect to find both in one relationship.) Best friends are egalitarian, and what most characterizes good friendship is respect—equal dignity (Marano, 2014).

Social exchange theory. According to *social exchange theory*, **we measure our actions and relationships on a cost-benefit basis.** People maximize their rewards and minimize their costs by employing their resources to gain the most favorable outcome (Strong et al., 2020). Americans generally think of rewards and costs as tangible objects, like money. However, in personal relationships, resources, rewards, and costs are more likely to be things such as love, companionship, status, power, fear, loneliness, and so on. As people enter into relationships, they have certain resources—either tangible or intangible—that others consider valuable, such as intelligence, warmth, good looks, or high social status. Individuals consciously or unconsciously use their various resources to obtain what they want, as when they "turn on" the charm. Have you ever wondered what a friend of yours sees in their partner? Your friend is so much better looking and more intelligent than their partner. (Attractiveness and intelligence are typical resources in American society.) However, it turns out that their partner has a good sense of humor, is considerate, and is an accomplished artist, all of which your friend values highly.

Reciprocity. "Flattery will get you . . . everything or nowhere." Which is true? What have you heard? The evidence on **reciprocity indicates that we tend to like those who show that they like us, and that we tend to see others as liking us more if we like them** (Baron et al., 2017). Thus, there does seem to be an interactive process in which liking leads to liking, and loving leads to loving.

Chapter 6: Developing Relationships

> *A real friend is one who walks in when the rest of the world walks out.*
> —WALTER WINCHELL

> *If you like me, you must have excellent judgment.*
> —S. A. RUTHUS

Something to Think About

REFLECT IN YOUR JOURNAL:

If our self-esteem is low, we are more susceptible to flattery, especially if the compliment is from someone of higher status. A person of high self-esteem may not be so easily swayed by positive treatment. Do you like to receive compliments? How do you feel about the person who is giving the compliments? Do they have a positive or negative influence on you? Do you now understand why some people seem to be greatly influenced by people who are nice to them, especially if that person is perceived as important to them?

We have discovered the importance of a friend, and now we will see how the relationship evolves into a more intimate level as we begin the process of dating and mate selection.

 Think/Pair/Share Activity

THE THREE PEOPLE WE MARRY.
Discuss this statement in triads.

You don't marry one person, you marry three: the person you think they are, the person they are, and the person they are going to become as a result of being married to you.

Dating and Mate Selection

The changing roles of men and women, economic pressures, and the fragility of the environment have caused relationships to be stress tested on a daily basis. Even within this stressful context, however, relationship development and mate selection continue to thrive. Many people desire and seek out "mating," also called sexual reproduction, in some capacity. It can include anything from a brief encounter to a romantic courtship of a spouse. Regardless of what an individual is looking for, the process of meeting a potential partner and forming a romantic or sexual connection can be a challenge. *Psychology Today* writers believe the rise of online dating has increased the number of potential mates ("Science of Mating," *Psychology Today*, 2019) The basis of mate selection is courtship—the interesting processes in which two people get together and hopefully stay together. So, what makes someone desirable to us? What are the traits we find attractive in potential dates and mates?

Internet dating/Social Networking. There was a time when online dating or the posting of personal ads in newspapers was seen as a crutch used only by those desperate for a date. Times have changed.

According to the August 2019 issue of *The Economist*, "smart-phones have put virtual bars in people's pockets, where singles can mingle free from the constraints of social or physical geography and worldwide about 200 million people use digital dating services every month." They also said that in America, more than a third of marriages now start with an online match-up, and online is the second-most-popular way for Americans to meet people of the opposite sex.

> 12% of American adults have ever used an *online dating site*; up slightly from 9% in early 2013, and 9% of American adults have ever used a *dating app on their cellphone*. The share of Americans who use dating apps has increased threefold since early 2013—at that point just 3% of Americans had used these apps. The share of 18- to 24-year-olds who report having used online dating has nearly tripled in the last two years. Today 27% of these young adults report that they have done so, up from just 10% in early 2013. Also, the share of 55- to 64-year-olds who use online dating has doubled over the same time period (from 6% in 2013 to 12% in 2015). (https://www.economist.com/leaders/2018/08/18/modern-love)

As was the case in previous Pew Research Center surveys of online dating, college graduates and the relatively affluent are especially likely to know people who use online dating or to know people who have entered into a relationship that began online. Nearly six-in-ten college graduates (58%) know someone who uses online dating, and nearly half (46%) know someone who has entered into a marriage or long-term partnership with someone they met via online dating. By comparison, just 25% of those with a high school diploma or less know someone who uses online dating—and just 18% know someone who has entered into a long-term relationship with someone they met this way.

Online Dating Guidelines

Sameer Chaudhry, MD, an internist at the University of North Texas in Dallas, coauthored a 2015 BMJ Evidence-Based Medicine paper for which he and his coauthor considered nearly 4,000 studies across psychology, sociology, neurocognitive science, and other disciplines to come up with a series of guidelines for how to set up a profile, how to select matches, and how to approach online interactions.

Setting up a dating profile a certain way is by no means a guarantee for meeting the love of your life. But Chaudhry's findings do offer some pointers on how to share information about yourself and how decide who to take a chance on. "There are small subtleties that can help," he says. Here are a few tips:

1. Pick your apps wisely

Online dating isn't one of those see-all-of-your-options-and-then-make-a-decision games. Be selective. Some apps have a reputation for being hookup apps; others are designed to connect users of the same religion or some other shared hobby or attribute. "Use apps according to your partner preferences," Hallam says.

2. Be honest

Research shows that people tend to fall for people similar to themselves when it comes to things like relationship history, desire for children, pet preferences, and religion. Being honest about what you want and who you are makes it more likely that the people you end up talking to and meeting are people things might work out with, Hallam says.

3. Choose a photo that puts your best foot forward (or at least the one you want to show off)

Photos should accurately depict your physical appearance—but they should be photos you generally like, Hallam says.

Having never met this person before, photos can have a big bearing on likeability and someone's initial attitude toward you, Chaudhry says. Specific attributes that generally increase attractiveness and likeability, according to his research, were: a genuine smile (one that makes your eyes start to crinkle up) and a slight head tilt.

4. Get to the point—and *do* include what makes you interesting in your profile

Nobody's going to read a six-paragraph essay, Reis says. People swipe through profiles quickly. State things that are really important to you and be done with it.

5. Be open-minded

Just because someone isn't a runner or has a hobby you're not so sure about, don't give up on them, Reis says. "Try to be as open minded as possible to the idea that you could actually grow in new ways from someone you might meet online."

6. Keep conversations (somewhat) short and non-generic

There are certain aspects of a relationship you're never going to be able to gather from online interactions alone, Reis says. He suggests not drawing out the pre-face-to-face meeting for too long.

Chaudhry says his research suggests keeping online, pre-meeting exchanges to two weeks or shorter. And actually make an effort to get to know someone. Ask about a specific part of someone's profile or about likes and dislikes.

7. Have fun

"Using dating apps should be fun," Holmes says. It shouldn't feel like work.

Holmes suggests checking in with yourself regularly. "If it's feeling like a chore, you're not enjoying yourself, or you are feeling bad about yourself, then take a break and try something else."

Those who have tried online dating offer mixed opinions about the experience—most have a positive outlook, even as they recognize certain downsides. But despite these reservations, those who have personally used online dating themselves—or know someone who does—tend to have much more positive attitudes compared to those with little direct exposure to online dating or online daters. For instance, just 55% of non-users agree that online dating is a good way to meet people, while six-in-ten agree that online dating is more dangerous than other ways of meeting people (Pew, 2018).

Overall, men and women who have used online dating tend to have similar views of the pros and cons—with one major exception relating to personal safety. Some 53% of women who have used online dating agree that it is more dangerous than other ways of meeting people, substantially higher than the 38% of male online daters who agree with this statement (Pew Research Center, 2018).

Also, online matchmaking sites in the U.S. are eyeing millions of singles in China, India, and beyond. Since it is true that some of these sites focus on helping people find suitable marriage partners, other sites focus on less committed involvements, and some even focus on specific populations—people over 50, parents without partners, Christian and single, and so on (Overstreet, 2018). So, be sure to research thoroughly and think carefully about how different sites work before you decide to join a site. And, be quite cautious of what personal information you post, as well as specific arrangements for meeting in person.

In 2018 Elizabeth Overstreet provided online dating tips that offer wisdom to people getting ready to try online dating.

1. Don't give too many details: Your description gives an overview of who you are, what you enjoy, and your sense of adventure. It makes the person looking at your profile want to know more about you.
2. Show your personality: Show that you enjoy life outside of your work. Having a sense of humor, and being open to trying new adventures or activities is extremely attractive. Showing who you are as a person makes you stand out more than others who talk themselves up and create a false impression.
3. Make your photos look interesting: Show pictures of you being silly, engaging in an activity you enjoy, or on a trip you may have recently made. The key in pictures is giving a person a sense of your personality, spirit, and interests.
4. Think from the perspective of a partner: Some research is needed to figure out what works. Look at profiles of others who are popular on the dating sites, take notes, and integrate some of their practices when creating your profile. When something works for others, there is no harm in making it work for you!

5. Be flexible with your search criteria: Getting over your usual habits and trying something different in dating is going to garner better dating results for you.

6. Analyze your past dates: If you meet some people you don't click with, that is okay. Try to analyze your past dates. Think about what went well, what didn't, and what you would like to do differently. Once you do, you'll become even better at weeding out the non-starters.

7. Make the first move: Some people have snagged some great dates just by approaching them and starting a friendly conversation. If you see someone who catches your eye online, and they haven't reached out to you, send them a friendly message with something that might get their interest.

8. Be responsive, but play it cool: When someone reaches out, and you are interested, make sure you are responsive. You don't have to respond in 2 minutes, but 24 hours is an excellent time window to show interest.

WHAT ARE THE MOST IMPORTANT QUALITIES FOR A HAPPY RELATIONSHIP?

Decades of research went into 4 relationship satisfaction and longevity points to several key qualities you may be able to spot early on:

1. Kindness, loyalty, and understanding (not looks, status, and excitement).
2. Similarity. Research has shown that couples who share tastes, interests, and expectations tend to encounter fewer conflicts.
3. Conscientiousness is about being reliable, practical, rule-following, and organized. This may not sound like the sexiest set of traits, but it's a good package for a long-term mate. People who are conscientious tend to bring that trait into their relationships, and are more dependable and trustworthy.
4. Emotional stability is the personality trait that affects our relationships most. Those who lack it tend to be moody, touchy, anxious, and quicker to anger—all traits that make someone more difficult to live with.

Gwendolyn Seidman, Ph.D. is an associate professor of psychology at Albright College who studies relationships and cyberpsychology. She believes you can get a sense of how hard you will work to maintain a happy relationship and resolve conflicts. How? You need to understand a person's general philosophy about relationships.

Researchers have identified two primary sets of beliefs about relationships—growth beliefs and destiny beliefs. Those with destiny beliefs think that relationships are either "meant to be" or not. They believe that once two soul mates unite, everything will be perfect—when a relationship is meant to be, everything will just work out. But if there are problems, that's just a sign that you're with the wrong person.

In contrast, those with growth beliefs think that relationships take hard work and that a strong relationship is something that you develop over time. They believe that all relationships inevitably encounter problems, and that having a stronger relationship means working hard to cope with difficulties that arise.

These different attitudes toward relationships have major implications for how people cope with relationship difficulties. When people with destiny beliefs hit a bump, they assume it's a sign that their relationship is doomed. So they tend to avoid conflicts and become angry if they must acknowledge their partner's faults—because that would mean the relationship is not meant to be. And when the going gets tough, they give up, rather than working to repair the damage.

In contrast, those with growth beliefs are more open to discussing problems, and respond positively to challenges in the relationship by working to resolve them. What type are you?

Attraction What attracts a person to their potential mate? In part, romantic attraction is a mystery. Scientists may not know everything about why people are drawn to the people that they are, but they know something. Every culture has standards for courtship and marriage. Without really thinking about it, most of us dutifully follow our cultural dictates. As we discussed the development of friendships and relationships in the previous pages of this chapter and in Chapter One, we will discover that the same characteristics that are important in finding friends are also very important in date and mate selection. As Brené Brown (2014) writes, "Our imperfections are what connect us to each other and to our humanity. Our vulnerabilities are not weaknesses; they are powerful reminders to keep our hearts and minds open to the reality that we're all in this together."

Most of us are looking for dates, mates, and friends who are similar to us (similarities). We seek out others who are about our own age, who are from the same socioeconomic class, religion, and educational level. They cannot be too tall or too short, too fat or too thin in comparison to us. Such preliminary screening cuts out a surprising number of potential partners. But most of us want more. Generally, we want someone who we perceive as good looking (physical attractiveness), personable, warm, has a good sense of humor, is someone we can trust, and is intelligent. We also want someone whose views match our own. Other important variables that most of us also consider are reciprocity, personality fit, and most important, our own self-concept (self-confidence).

Dating, sexual attraction, and mate selection exist for many different people. Friendships evolve in to more intimate relationships. Love and romance is a human feeling for all people, no matter sexual orientation, race, or religion. We all belong equally in the human race, we all love, we all have caring and nurturing capabilities. Labels currently exist to describe sexual orientation along the continuum, in addition to the larger categories of straight, homosexual, heterosexual, and bisexual. The term *gay* refers to men who are attracted to other men, and *lesbian* refers to women who are attracted to other women. *Pansexuality* encompasses attraction to persons of any gender or sex. *Asexuality* applies to those who do not experience sexual attraction, although that doesn't preclude them from feeling romantic or emotional attraction. *Demisexual* refers to an individual, perhaps on a spectrum of asexuality, who experiences sexual attraction only once a strong emotional bond has formed with a partner. Similarly, *demiromantic* refers to someone who feels romantic attraction only after establishing a sexual connection. This list isn't a comprehensive catalogue of terms, and understanding of sexual orientation—and the language used to describe it—continues to evolve.

GENDER & YOU

Think about this question and write down some of your ideas.

What characteristics do I desire in a potential mate?

Then work with a partner or in triads. Compare your lists of characteristics and decide how you would rate them in order of importance. Are there any other gender mate preferences?

Every year, more women than men become college-educated. The disparity is already prevalent across North America and Europe, and the trend is beginning to spread across the world more widely. Many causes can be considered, like gradual gender discrimination barriers lifted, or it could be more women have better grades and college application qualifications; the disparity is creating an unintended mating crisis among educated women. Buss (2019) believes that women and men both have evolved multiple mating strategies: some of each gender are having casual hook-ups and some committed relationships. Most educated women are unwilling to settle for men who are less educated, less intelligent, and less professionally successful than they are. The flip side is that men are less exacting on precisely these dimensions, choosing to prioritize, for better or worse, other evolved criteria such as youth and appearance. The good news for those who succeed is that marriages among the educated tend to be more stable, freer of conflict, less plagued by infidelity, and less likely to end in divorce. Educated couples enjoy a higher standard of living with dual professional earnings.

Research is still focused on binary gender understanding, although this is changing. A study of males and females showed both similarities and differences in what they look for in a marital partner:

- In the *Journal of Relationships Research*, Eletra Gilchrist-Petty, an associate professor of communication arts at the University of Alabama in Huntsville, and Lance Kyle Bennett, a doctoral-degree student at the University of Iowa, recruited 346 people, ranging in age from 18 to 64, who were or had been in a heterosexual relationship with someone who had a different-sex best friend. When they surveyed participants' attitudes toward cross-sex best friendships, they found that people who are engaged to be married looked more negatively on those friendships than married, single, or dating people. Those who were skeptical of cross-sex best friendships in general are more likely to be angry at their partner when they feel threatened by the partner's best friend instead of constructively communicating with their partner, or with the friend, about the situation.

- According to prior studies, sexual attraction between cross-sex friends seems to decrease the overall quality of the friendship—and is also extremely common.) True platonic friendships between men and women of compatible sexualities have, of course, been common for what researchers believe to be a few generations now. Gilchrist-Petty and Bennett's study suggests that nothing is inherently wrong with privately feeling jealousy toward a partner's best friend of a different sex—but that there are healthy and unhealthy ways to act on it (Fetters, 2019).

A 2020 Pew research report found that three-in-ten U.S. adults say they have ever used a dating site or app, but this varies significantly by age and sexual orientation. While 48% of 18- to 29-year-olds say they have ever used a dating site or app, the share is 38% among those ages 30 to 49 and even lower for those 50 and older (16%).

- At the same time, personal experiences with online dating greatly differ by sexual orientation. Lesbian, gay, or bisexual (LGB) adults are roughly twice as likely as those who are straight to say they have ever used a dating platform (55% vs. 28%).
- A small share of Americans say they have been in a committed relationship with or married someone they met through a dating site or app.
- About one-in-ten U.S. adults say this (12%), though these shares are higher among LGB adults, as well as those ages 18 to 49.
- Americans who have used a dating site or app in the past year say their recent experience left them feeling more frustrated (45%) than hopeful (28%).
- More than half of Americans (54%) say relationships that begin on a dating site or app are just as successful as those that begin in person.
- A smaller share of U.S. adults—though still about four-in-ten—say online relationships are less successful than relationships that begin in person.
- In the more than two decades since the launch of commercial dating sites such as Match.com, online dating has evolved into a multi-billion-dollar industry serving customers around the world (Vogels, 2020).

Pew research found in 2020, six-in-ten women under the age of 35 who have used online dating sites or apps say someone continued to contact them after they said they were not interested, compared with 27% of men in this age range. Younger female users are also about twice as likely as their male counterparts to say someone on a dating site or app has called them an offensive name (44% vs. 23%) or threatened to physically harm them (19% vs. 9%).

According to Pew research, among those who have used an online dating platform—as well as among Americans overall—women are less likely than men to view meeting someone through a dating site or app as safe. Around a third of women who have online dated (36%) believe these platforms are not too or not at all safe for meeting people, compared with 22% of men. Still, majorities of online daters view these platforms as a safe way to meet others (Anderson & Vogels, 2020).

- Women tend to place a higher value than men on potential partners' socio-economic status, intelligence, ambition, and financial prospects (Buss, 2019). Women tend to prefer men who are taller than they are, with symmetrical features (Alkon, 2010).
- Men consistently show more interest than women in potential partners' youthfulness, good health, and physical attractiveness (Buss, 2019).

- Men prefer wives who are somewhat younger than they are, and women prefer husbands that are somewhat older. However, we are noticing a new trend—as women become more economically independent, they are becoming more interested in selecting younger men as dates and sometimes mates.

Mate selection throughout the world. Do people from different countries and different cultures look for the same traits when selecting a mate? The traits that people look for in a marriage vary around the world. In one large-scale study from thirty-seven countries and five islands, people varied in what they considered important in selecting a mate (Buss et al., 2019). Chastity was the most important factor in marital selection in China, India, Indonesia, Iran, Taiwan, and the Palestinian Arab culture. Adults from Japan and Ireland placed moderate importance on chastity. In contrast, adults in Sweden, Finland, Norway, the Netherlands, and Germany generally said that chastity was not important in selecting a marital partner. Researchers were surprised that men and women in the Netherlands, for example, do not care about chastity at all. Neither is virginity valued much in the Scandinavian countries such as Norway and Sweden. In China, however, virginity is indispensable in a mate—marrying a non-virgin is virtually out of the question. The Chinese also possess less permissive views toward dating and sexuality. Tang and Zuo's (2013) cross-cultural study found that Chinese college students generally possess less open-minded attitudes toward dating, date less frequently, tend to date at an later age, and are less likely to have sex in their encounters than do their American counterparts. Thus, people in cultures in which more conservative norms regarding sexuality are held are less likely to discuss their own sexuality freely. Otherwise they may be seen as promiscuous or dirty (Buss, 2019).

Adults from the Zulu culture in South Africa, Estonia, and Colombia placed a high value on housekeeping skills in their marital preference. By contrast, adults in all Western and Western European countries (except Spain, Canada, and the United States) said that housekeeping was not an important trait in their partner (Buss, 2019).

What about religion? It plays an important role in marital preferences in many cultures. For example, Islam stresses the honor of the male and the purity of the female. It also emphasizes the woman's role in childbearing, childrearing, educating children, and instilling the Islamic faith in their children (Buss, 2019).

Whether we are drawn to people by familiarity, similarity, beauty, or some other quality, mutual attraction sometimes progresses from friendship to the more intense, complex, and mysterious feeling of love.

BECOMING LOVERS

Love is what's left in a relationship when all the selfishness has been removed. —CULLEN HIGHTOWER

There is a great similarity between romantic relationships and friendship relationships. In both of these are high levels of trust, mutual respect, and acceptance. Further, the interactions between the people involved are characterized by high levels of understanding, nurturing, and confiding. Nonetheless, the love relationship with its greater depth of caring and exclusiveness typically generates greater emotion and power. As a result, it can affect individuals more, having the potential to meet a broader sweep of human needs or to cause greater frustration and distress.

Becoming *Aware*

What is "love"? Have you ever looked at someone for the first time and said to yourself, "I think I'm in love"? Is there such a thing as *love at first sight*? Research has found that we do not fall in love—we grow into love. Then, what is love? This is a question people have been asking for years. Mass media, romantic novels, soap operas, and songs have all been attempting to answer this question.

BECOMING AWARE—LOVE ACTIVITY JOURNAL

Our lives seem to revolve around this subject. But, does anyone know what love is? Everyone seems to have their own definition of love. When your date says that he or she loves you, what does your date mean? Is it the same as when your mother or father says it to you? What is your definition of love? Before you continue, take a few minutes and write down your definition of love. Share your definition of love with your friends and loved ones. Compare your definition with theirs.

> *Love is not finding someone you can live with; it's finding someone you can't live without.*
> —RAFAEL ORTIZ

We have found a definition of *love* that we would like to share with you. **When the satisfaction, security, and development of another person is as important to you as your own satisfaction, security, and development, love exists** (Barton, 1996).

 Think/Pair/Share Activity

MEASUREMENTS OF LOVE
Discuss this statement and question with a partner.

Using the above definition of love, you will find that you can measure your love not only for your significant other, but your mother, father, siblings, friends, animals, and even inanimate objects. What do you think?

MYTHS ABOUT LOVE

True or False

T   F   1. True love lasts forever.
T   F   2. Love can conquer all.
T   F   3. Love is a purely positive experience.
T   F   4. When you fall in love, you'll know it.
T   F   5. When love strikes, you have no control over your behavior.

What are your answers to the above questions? These are some interesting myths about love that many of us have been agonizing over for years. Let us take a look at these myths and dispel some of the confusion regarding them (Weiten et al., 2017).

1. *Does true love last forever?* It would be nice if love would last forever, but most of us have found that it does not. People who believe this myth may pursue love forever, looking for the ideal one that will bring complete happiness. This person will experience a lifetime of frustration. Would we have divorce if love lasted forever? It would be more realistic to view love as a wonderful experience that might be encountered on several occasions throughout life.

2. *Does love conquer all?* Many people believe that love and marriage will allow them to overcome (conquer) all their frustrations and problems in life. A supportive partner will help you solve many of your problems, but it does not guarantee success. Many people jump into relationships for this purpose, only to discover that the relationship creates additional problems.

3. *Is love a purely positive experience?* Mass media, television, movies, and romance novels are creating an unrealistic expectation that love is such a positive experience. In reality it can be a peak experience, but love can also bring intense negative emotions and great pain. As many of you know, a lover is capable of taking us to emotional peaks in either direction.

4. *Do you know when you are in love?* There is no physiological cue to tell us we are in love. So the emotional feeling and the cognitive interpretation is different for each of us. It is a state of confusion that many of us agonize over. It is normal to question our feelings toward another person. Remember, we grow to love someone gradually and usually do not fall in love.

5. *Do you behave irrationally when you fall in love?* Does love take control of your behavior? Some people stop eating, quit studying, are unable to concentrate on their job, and avoid taking responsibility for their actions because they are in love. If you allow your heart to take control of your behavior, you may become vulnerable to irrational decisions about sexual involvement or long-term commitments.

Love is? Love is complex! Love is confusing! Most of you are aware of this. Love is difficult to measure and perplexing. People are yearning for it, will die for it, and even kill for it. But for some reason we have avoided studying it until the last few years. Psychologists are now doing research attempting to discover what love is.

The **triangular theory of love** is a theory of love developed by psychologist Robert Sternberg. In the context of interpersonal relationships, "the three components of love, according to the triangular theory, are an intimacy component, a passion component, and a decision/commitment component":

1. **Intimacy** – Which encompasses feelings of **attachment**, closeness, connectedness, and bondedness.
2. **Passion** – Which encompasses drives connected to both **limerence** [infatuation] and **sexual attraction**.
3. **Commitment** – Which encompasses, in the short term, the decision to remain with another, and in the long term, plans made with that other (Sternberg, 2004).

"The amount of love one experiences depends on the absolute strength of these three components, and the type of love one experiences depends on their strengths relative to each other" (Sternberg, 2007). Robert Sternberg (2007) has developed a theory of love that includes three distinct components: 1) *passion*, an intense physiological desire for another person; 2) *intimacy*, the feeling that one can share all one's thoughts and actions with another; 3) *commitment*, the willingness to stay with a person through thick and thin, or for better or worse, or in sickness or health. Ideally, marriage is characterized by a healthy amount of all three components. Various combinations of these components result in quite different types of love. Figure 6.1 will demonstrate some of these. For example, Sternberg suggests that romantic love involves a high degree of *passion and intimacy*, yet lacks substantial *commitment* to the other person. The passion component of love peaks early in a relationship, and then declines. Intimacy and commitment components build gradually over time. Growth in intimacy and commitment occurs as passion grows weaker, and can sustain a relationship as difficulties arise once passion fades. *Companionate love* is marked by a great deal of intimacy and commitment but little passion. *Consummate love* is the most complete because it includes a high level of all three components. It is the most satisfying because the relationship is likely to fulfill many of the needs of each partner.

> *Love is the word used to label the sexual excitement of the young, the habituation of the middle aged, and the mutual dependence of the old.*
> —JOHN CIARDI

Learn the qualities that make a person an ideal partner. They may not be what you expected:

Seven Qualities of an Ideal Partner:

1. An ideal partner has grown up.

2. An ideal partner is open and non-defensive.

3. An ideal partner is honest and lives with integrity

4. An ideal partner is respectful of and sensitive to the other, having uniquely individual goals and priorities.

5. An ideal partner has empathy for and understanding of their partner.

6. An ideal partner is physically affectionate and sexually responsive.

7. An ideal partner has a sense of humor!

Lisa Firestone, Ph.D., Director of Research and Education at The Glendon Association.

© StockImageFactory.com/Shutterstock.com

Does true love last forever?

What things can you do to maintain the components of love?

© Ruslan Huzau/Shutterstock.com

FOCUS ON DIVERSITY

IS THERE A CULTURAL INFLUENCE ON LOVE?

Cultural factors have a strong influence on the value of love. In the United States, love is crucial to a satisfying marriage. In the former Soviet Union, however, only 40 percent of the people say that they married for love; most did so because of loneliness, shared interests, or an unplanned pregnancy (Baron et al., 2017). In research including two individualistic societies (Canada and the United States) and three collectivist societies (China, India, and Japan), romantic love is more likely to be considered an important basis for marriage in individualistic societies than in collectivistic ones. In many Asian societies, the persons getting married are supposed to take into account the wishes of others, especially of parents and other family members. It is not unusual for marriages to be arranged by the respective families on the basis of such factors as occupation and status, not on the basis of love and the lovers' free choice. The intense feelings of passionate love and the self-absorption of two lovers would be disruptive to the functioning of the group. In collectivist cultures, such as India and Japan, love is considered less important to a successful marriage than is the ability to resolve family conflicts (Matsumoto, 2016; Dresser, 2005).

A TRIANGULAR MODEL OF LOVE

Sternberg conceptualized love in the form of a triangle with three basic components: intimacy, passion, and decision/commitment. Love may be based primarily on one of these components, on a combination of two of them, or on all three. As shown in the figure, seven different types of relationships are possible, depending on how the components are combined.

Figure 6.1   IS THIS WHAT LOVE IS MADE OF?

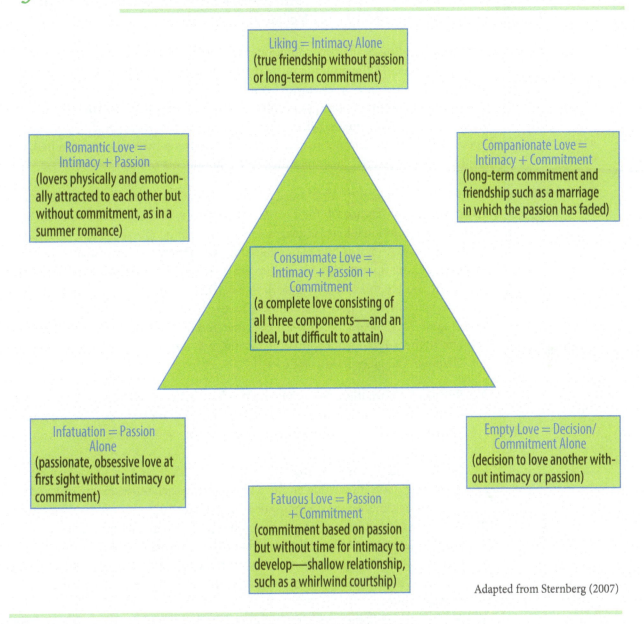

Liking = Intimacy Alone
(true friendship without passion
or long-term commitment)

Romantic Love =
Intimacy + Passion
(lovers physically and emotionally attracted to each other but
without commitment, as in a
summer romance)

Companionate Love =
Intimacy + Commitment
(long-term commitment and
friendship such as a marriage
in which the passion has faded)

Consummate Love =
Intimacy + Passion +
Commitment
(a complete love consisting of
all three components—and an
ideal, but difficult to attain)

Infatuation = Passion
Alone
(passionate, obsessive love at
first sight without intimacy or
commitment)

Fatuous Love = Passion
+ Commitment
(commitment based on passion
but without time for intimacy to
develop—shallow relationship,
such as a whirlwind courtship)

Empty Love = Decision/
Commitment Alone
(decision to love another without intimacy or passion)

Adapted from Sternberg (2007)

The development of love. Early in a relationship, passion is usually high, which may be one reason new love relationships and affairs are most intense. Intimacy, however, is not as high because the partners have not spent enough time together or shared enough experiences and emotions to be able to understand each other completely. Passionate love without intimacy creates a risk of misunderstanding and jealousy about any other person or activity that seems to interfere with the relationship.

Over time, passion seems to fade while intimacy and commitment grow stronger. According to Sternberg, passion is like an addiction: in the beginning a touch of the hand, a smile, even a mere glance will produce excitement. Gradually, however, one needs a greater dose of stimulation to get the same feeling. We habituate to the passion, and thus to continue this intense feeling for one another, *novel and significant stimuli* must be provided by each of the two individuals.

An understanding of the three components of love and the developmental process will help couples in the building of their relationship. A couple may want to schedule specific times each week, away from children and family, for a period of intimate sharing—a time to discuss problems as well as happy times. You may want to keep the passion burning by scheduling a weekend at the beach, buying your mate a special gift, taking them out to a special dinner, serving them breakfast in bed, etc. What else can you do to maintain the three components of love?

The five love languages. After more than 30 years of marriage counseling, Dr. Gary Chapman (2015), author of *The Five Love Languages*, has concluded that there are basically five emotional love languages—five ways that people speak and understand emotional love. And, it is highly possible that your emotional love language and the language of your spouse may be as different as Chinese is from English. No matter how hard you try to express your love in English, if your spouse understands only Chinese, you will never understand how to love each other. Dr. Chapman believes that love is something you do for someone else; therefore, it is critical to learn to express or respond to the needs of your spouse. Realizing that none of these are gender specific, Dr. Chapman's languages are as follows:

1. **Words of Affirmation.** Some people need verbal appreciation and encouragement in order to feel loved. This may be nothing more than "You look great in that suit," or "You are the best yard guy we've ever had," or "I know you will finish your degree."
2. **Quality Time.** This is more than mere proximity. It's about focusing all your energy on your mate. It's turning off the TV and giving each other quality time—quality listening time, or just doing something together.
3. **Receiving Gifts.** It is one thing to remember birthdays and anniversaries; it's quite more to learn how to give "little" gifts of thoughtfulness throughout the week. Free, frequent, expensive, or rare, if your mate relates to the language of giving gifts, any visible sign of your love will leave them feeling happy and secure in your relationship.
4. **Acts of Service.** Sometimes simple chores or tasks around the house that are helpful to another person can be an undeniable expression of love. The task may be to discover what acts performed out of the kindness of your heart—not obligation—will show your love for your partner.
5. **Physical Touch.** Many mates feel the most loved when they receive physical contact from their partner—a hand on the shoulder, a hug, a kiss, holding hands, a touch on the cheek. Remember, also, that sexual contact, although extremely important, is only one dialect of physical touch.

Perhaps the greatest task is to determine which love language means the most to your partner, but it is well worth it for a satisfying life together.

GENDER AND YOU

EMOTIONAL LABOR IN RELATIONSHIPS

If you are female and you think you do a lot more of the work when it comes to making your relationship run smoothly—you are right. Researchers say that women have more relationship skills.

- Women are better communicators. They are more comfortable in sharing their feelings and being psychologically intimate (Elder, 2016).
- On the communication score, most men are still playing catch-up with women. For men, actual physical proximity is often as good as intimacy ("I'm here, aren't I?") (Elder, 2016).
- Women feel more committed and get more involved in their relationships than men, and women make greater efforts to maintain these relationships (Canary & Wahba, 2006).

Male and Female Socialization. On the whole, men tend to think they are compatible with their partner before women do. One reason may be that men and women tend to have different attitudes about love. Men are more likely to be "romantics." For example, they are inclined to believe in love at first sight, and to regard true love as magical, impossible to explain or understand.

Women are more likely to be "pragmatists," believing that financial security is as important as passion in nourishing a close relationship and that there are many possible individuals that a person could learn to love. Women tend to be more cautious than men before deciding to take the final step. Researchers say that women seem to do a lot more work when it comes to making a relationship work. What is the next step? Is it marriage or some alternative?

> *Marriage is not a noun; it's a verb. It isn't something you get. It's something you do. It's the way you love your partner every day.*
> —BARBARA DE ANGELIS

Becoming Committed

It is not entirely clear how and when commitment begins. At some time and in some way, people in a relationship decide that their satisfaction or happiness with each other is significantly enough to decide to commit to a level of "exclusivity"—to agree to confine their intimate time to only one another. They agree to begin a relatively long-lasting, more intimate relationship that to some extent excludes other close relationships. The couple agrees to depend on each other for the satisfaction of important needs, including companionship, love, and sex. The commitment may or may not include the decision to live together.

Is Love a Feeling or a Decision?

One neglects to see an important factor in love, that of will.

To love somebody is not just a strong feeling—it is a decision, it is a judgment, it is a promise.

If love were only a feeling, there would be no basis for the promise to love each other forever.

A feeling comes and it may go.

How can I judge that it will stay forever, if my actions do not involve judgment and decision?

—ERICH FROMM, PSYCHOANALYST

> *Important as it is to choose the right partner, it's probably more important to be the right partner. We focus on changing the wrong person.*
> —PATRICIA LOVE

Making an agreement with another person to enter into a deeper, more exclusive, and lasting relationship is a crucially important life decision that must be made freely and with careful thought. Many individuals, consciously or unconsciously, feel pressured to enter into a relationship that they are not sure is good for them. Many people are not happy in their existing relationship or social situation, be it a bad home environment, an abusive mate, getting too old, being lonely, having or being an an alcoholic or addicted mate, etc., so they feel pressured to commit themselves to a new relationship as a means to escape the bad situation. A person who is pushed or pressured into a relationship will discover that their commitment is weaker and less enduring. If the commitment is made in defiance of pressure from parents or peers, the commitment may be very strong. *Psychological reactance* is the tendency to protect or restore one's sense of freedom or social control, often by doing the opposite of what has been demanded. This is also known as the *Romeo and Juliet effect*, where their love was intensified, not weakened, by their families' opposition. In summation, a commitment is likely to be strongest when it is arrived at freely and when it is cemented by taking action as a result of the commitment.

Gadoua and Larson (2014) believe we need to focus first on what our *authentic truth* is, and what needs have to be met for us to feel fulfilled before we enter a relationship.

Instead of trying to manipulate ourselves or the situation to get an outcome that we're comfortable with, consider what our *authentic truth* is. There's no one right direction for our relationships to go, but consider what's healthiest and happiest for both people involved.

Should I remain single? Sociologists note that Americans have a rate of marriage—and of remarriage—among the highest in the Western world (Cherlin, 2010). Demographic trends in the 2000s showed the continuing separation of family and household due to factors such as childbearing among single parents. In addition, demographers demonstrated during the decade that trends such as marriage and divorce were diverging according to education. Moreover, demographic trends in the age structure of the population showed that a large increase in the elderly population will occur in the 2010s. Overall, demographic trends produced an increased complexity of family life and a more ambiguous and fluid set of categories than demographers are accustomed to measuring. Despite the emphasis on flexibility and freedom in relationships, most emerging adults—at least 90%—wish to fall in love, commit, and marry someday. They are just not in a rush to do so (Regnerus & Uecker, 2011). The average age of marriage has risen steadily. According to Census Bureau data (2019), the average age women marry is 27.5 years, and for men 29 years. Furthermore, the proportion of people ages 30 to 34 who have never married continues to increase (Note: These are close to the ages in Puritan New England in the 1600s).

Remaining single is becoming a more viable lifestyle. More and more people are remaining single. Furthermore, the negative stereotype of people who remain single, which pictures them as lonely, frustrated, depressed, odd, and unchosen, is disappearing.

Studies have shown that married people live longer and are healthier throughout those extra years. Marriage does seem to help both spouses cope better with stress, though men benefit more than women. However, the stress of a bad marriage can undo much of the good that comes along with a happy one (Strong et al., 2020).

It is interesting to note that most studies find that single women are more satisfied with their lives and less distressed than comparable single men, and various lines of evidence suggest that women get along without men better than men get along without women (Stack & Eshleman, 1998; Weiten et al., 2017).

Becoming Aware: The Generations Defined
https://www.pewresearch.org/fact-tank/2019/01/17/where-millennials-end-and-generation-z-begins/˅ _19-01-17_generations_2019/

Where Millennials end and Generation Z begins

In a 2018 article in the *Washington Post*, Tara Bahrampour cites research from the Council on Contemporary Families (CCF) and studies from the Centers for Disease Control (CDC) that seems to show a decline in sexual activity in Gen Z young adults (those born after 1995).

According to the studies, people in this generation, while they tend to be more open about a variety of forms of consensual sex, are also more discerning about what consent looks like and are unlikely to respond well to anything that appears to be undue pressure to have sex (2018).

The effect appears most significant among Gen Z—the first generation to come of age in the smartphone environment. The lead author of the CDC studies, Jean Twenge, suggests that the use of screens to communicate, and the decline of in-person contact, may be a contributing factor. The fact that people can judge each other by a small photo before ever meeting may increase the importance of appearance (Barampour, 2018).

Bahrampur reports that the question "Which is more important for a good match? Same politics or good sex?" is one of questions that the dating site OKCupid poses to members to help narrow down their search for a partner. The results of the admittedly unscientific study make a slight U-curve with a long right-hand tail, with just 17% of Baby Boomers (born before 1965) and 15% of Gen X-ers (born between 1965 and 1980) choosing politics over sex. But among Millennials, which the company defines as born between 1981 and 1997, 38% choose politics over sex, and for Generation Z, born in 1998 or later, it's nearly half and half, with 48% preferring political rather than sexual compatibility.

Barampour's contacts among college-age people indicate a comfort with letting things develop and not seeking physical contact; some students report that parents are concerned about the delay. On the other hand, some also express concern about a casual, one-night stand or "hookup" culture on campuses, and colleges are looking for ways to counteract binge drinking and hookup parties while emphasizing consent (Barampour, 2018).

The prevalence of screens also appears to fuel concerns about cyberbullying and posting intimate photos without consent. Laws are on the books in several states and more are being written; whether the ability to punish a perpetrator will have a long-term effect when cyberbullies have so many ways to hide is still uncertain (Barampour, 2016).

According to Lisa Wade, author of *The Rise of Hookup Sexual Culture on American College Campuses* (2017, scholars.org), about a quarter of students thrive in hookup culture, at least at first. They enjoy hooking up and adapt well to hookup culture's rules calling for only fun and casual, short-term encounters. At the same time, about a third of students opt out altogether; they find hookup culture unappealing and would rather not have sex at all than have it the way this culture mandates. The remaining students are ambivalent, dabbling in hookups with mixed results. Overall, about one in three students say that their intimate relationships have been "traumatic" or "very difficult to handle." Many of them experience a persistent malaise, a deep, indefinable disappointment. And one in ten say that they have been sexually coerced or assaulted in the past year (Wade, 2017).

Wade believes that changing the power structures and destructive sexual norms is what society today needs. Understanding that the forces shaping sexual relationships on campuses are cultural, and problems lie not so much in particular encounters but hookup culture overall is the first step toward clarifying what needs to change. Wade believes because culture is a type of shared consciousness, and many people need to work together to make changes happen. And they can, because of the strong ties in student bodies, campuses can transform themselves faster than one might suspect (2017). Research shows that today's young people are more open, permissive, earnest, hopeful for the future, and welcoming of diversity than any other generation in memory (Wade, 2017).

The call for safe spaces on college campuses has fueled a different debate; emotional safety is a new concern for generations who have only recently come to terms with the need to provide ways to find physical safety.

By and large, the decline in sexual activity among the Gen Z population does not seem likely to prevent eventual intimate relationships. While the lack of easy access to sex may frustrate some in Gen Z, researchers remind us that the sex drive is a powerful element of species survival. Some believe that eventual marriages among this generation may be stronger for the delay.

I am not a book

I am not a book.
You cannot read me,
enjoy me,
at your convenience.
You cannot pick me
up and sit me down
when you want.
You cannot underline
the parts of me you like
and ignore the parts
you don't.
You cannot bend my edges
to mark the spot
you stopped being interested, so
you'll remember
when you're bored.
I am not a book.
You cannot break my spine
so you can hold me
better.
You cannot throw me
around when you're
angry with me.
You cannot blame me because
I am not what you
imagined me to be—
because I am different
than you planned.
You cannot put me
on a shelf between the others
and forget about me.
I am worth far
more than that.

Colton Snead
2019

> *Marriage perhaps represents the ideal of human relationships— the setting in which each partner, while acknowledging the need of the other, feels free to be what he or she by nature is, a relationship in which giving and taking are equal, in which each accepts the other, and I confronts Thou.*
> —ERICH FROMM

Cohabitation, or living together in an intimate relationship. There was a time when living together without being married was not viewed in a positive light. Today, this is called *cohabitation,* meaning two partners living together as if married, and it's no longer negatively viewed by much of the population. Cohabitation has undergone considerable changes in recent years (Stepler, 2017; Cherlin, 2004; Oppenheimer, 2003; Seltzer, 2004). 7.3 million Americans live in unmarried-partner households in 2015. Of this number, 433,539 were same-sex households (US Census, 2017). R. Stepler from the Pew Research Center found that the number of U.S. adults cohabiting with a partner has risen 75% among those 50 and older since 2007 (2017). When it comes to couples living together without being married, roughly two-thirds of each generation (with the exception of Silents) say this doesn't make much of a difference for society. About one-in-five Gen Zers and Millennials say cohabitation is a good thing for society—higher than the shares for older generations.

Large majorities of Generation Zers, Millennials, Generation Xers, and Baby Boomers say couples living together without being married doesn't make a difference for our society, according to a 2019 Pew Research Center report. While 54% of those in the Silent Generation say cohabitation doesn't make a difference in society, about four-in-ten (41%) say it is a bad thing, compared with much smaller shares among younger generations (Geiger, Livingston, 2019).

Cohabitation has become increasingly common not only in the United States, but also in other industrialized countries. For example, rates are high in Great Britain, Australia, Denmark, Finland, France, and Sweden. In fact, more children in Sweden are born to cohabitating couples than to married couples.

In 2017, for the first time in more than 130 years, adults ages 18 to 34 were slightly more likely to be living in their parents' home than they were to be living with a spouse or partner in their own household (U.S. Census Bureau, 2019). Among young adults, living arrangements differ significantly by gender. For men ages 18 to 34, living at home with a parent or parents has been the dominant living arrangement since 2009. In 2014, 28% of young men were living with a spouse or partner in their own home, while 35% were living in the home of their parent(s). For their part, young women are on the cusp of crossing over this threshold: They are still more likely to be living with a spouse or romantic partner (35%) than they are to be living with their parent(s) (29%) (Pew Research Center, 2016). It has increased all across socioeconomic, age, and racial groups (Strong, 2020).

Becoming Aware of Relationships: Relationship DUI—are you sure you're in love?
https://www.youtube.com/watch?v=CwlLyhebmro

A four-minute illustrated lecture, based in part on the research by Drs Scott Stanley, Galena Rhoades, and Howard Markman, that outlines why so many of us slide into bad relationships, and choose the wrong partners and hang on long a er we know it should end. Share this video with anyone you think might be settling for the wrong person or the wrong reasons.

Not only do many couples consider cohabitation a prelude to marriage—a form of trial marriage—they also believe that cohabitation improves the chances of marital success (Wartik, 2005). However, researchers have found an association between pre-marital cohabitation and increased marital discord and divorce rates (Coontz, 2006). Among both men and women aged 15–44 who had ever cohabited and/or married, the largest proportion cohabited before their first marriage. Approximately 28% of men and women cohabited before their first marriage, whereas 23% of women and 18% of men married without ever cohabiting. About 15% of men and women had only cohabited (without ever marrying), and less than 7% of men and women first co-habited after their first marriages ended (Centers for Disease Control and Prevention, 2010). If cohabitation is preceded by an engagement, no previous cohabitation, and no children, the negative effect on a marriage's chances can be less (Luscombe, 2010).

We do not know all the reasons for the higher divorce rate among couples who co-habit. Researchers believe that couples who decide to cohabit are already at a higher risk of divorce than couples who do not, since they tend to be more liberal, sexually experienced, have less traditional attitudes toward marriage, family, and divorce, have slightly lower incomes, and are slightly less religious than non-cohabitants (Smock, 2002; Cherlin, 2010). A lot depends on the individual couple—especially their values.

As more and more people across different backgrounds enter cohabitation relation-ships, we will learn more concerning whether the *experiences of cohabitation or characteristics of those who cohabit* have greater impact on later marriage.

Becoming Aware - Types of relationships

Monogamous relationships tend to be the first ones people learn about, as they are the most traditional, and usually the easiest for children, who often see it exhibited by their parents, to understand. Those in *monogamous relationships only have one sexual/romantic partner at a time.* Most people who enter into "traditional" relationships and marriages do so because they want to be monogamous, though they don't always stay that way.

That's why some choose to enter into **polyamorous relationships** instead. When someone is *polyamorous, that means they have more than one romantic relationship at a time. Often, polyamorous couples have a primary partner, a secondary partner, etc.* with the understanding that these "rankings" can change as their individual needs do. Others treat every simultaneous relationship they are engaging in as perfectly equal. The key to any successful relationship, but especially polyamorous ones, is honest and effective communication between all parties involved.

In a way, **open relationships** are a hybrid of monogamous and polyamorous relation-ships. While an *open relationship allows both partners to share physical intimacy with anyone they want, they reserve their emotional intimacy for each other.* So each person can have as many sexual partners as they want, but only one romantic partner.

A **long-distance relationship** is pretty self-explanatory, as they only occur when *partners have a long amount of distance separating them*. Due to the lack of physical intimacy caused by the couple's physical separation, some choose to open their relationship while they live far apart. While the "long-distance" part of this relationship type is often temporary, some couples choose to live happily ever apart indefinitely.

Hook-up relationships According to Lisa Wade (2017), author of *The Rise of Hookup Sexual Culture on American College Campuses*, "hookup culture" refers to the idea that casual sexual encounters are the best or only way to engage sexually; and the concept also refers to rules of social interactions that support these casual "one night stands."

Reasons to marry People tend to marry out of mixed motives—many of them unclear even to themselves. Now that marriage is no longer necessary for economic survival or the satisfaction of sexual needs, love has become the major rationale for getting married and staying married. Psychologist Harry Stack Sullivan has given us an excellent definition of love: "When the satisfaction, security, and development of another person is as important to you as your own satisfaction, security, and development, love exists" (2019).

Unfortunately, people sometimes marry for the wrong reasons: to become respectable, for money, for a regular sexual outlet, for status, or to make their parents happy. Even cohabiting couples may marry for the wrong reason. Just when the relationship begins to falter, marriage may be sought to save the relationship. It's a temporary "fix," because it does not solve the underlying conflicts.

Ted Huston, Ph.D., a professor of human ecology and psychology at the University of Texas at Austin, conducted a long-term study of married couples. His 2009 article "What's love got to do with it? Why some marriages succeed and others fail" (https://onlinelibrary.wiley.com/doi/abs/10.1111/j.1475-6811.2009.01225.x) is reported by K. Perina in her *Psychology Today* article, "The Success of Marriage" (2016). Huston's research, as reported by Perina in 2016, indicated that the rhythm and pacing of the courtship had some effect on the durability of the marriage. In his study of mixed gender couples, Huston found that men in a dating relationship who were not committed to the idea of marriage, tended to have rockier experiences in marriage. Women were less likely to mention these concerns, however; Huston theorized that women who were committed to the idea of marriage would be reluctant to bring up concerns that might disrupt the courtship, and the combination of the two attitudes tended to create an unstable marriage (Perina, 2003). So if your new romance starts to resemble a movie script, try to remember: The audience never sees what happens after the credits roll.

On June 26, 2015, the U.S. Supreme Court issued a landmark ruling that granted same-sex couples a constitutional right to marry. The 5-4 decision in *Obergefell v. Hodges* legalized gay marriage nationwide, including in the 14 states that did not previously allow gays and lesbians to wed. The decision rested in part on the court's interpretation of the 14th Amendment; the justices ruled that limiting marriage to heterosexual couples violates the amendment's guarantee of equal protection under the law.

Becoming *Aware*

Around four-in-ten U.S. adults (37%) favored allowing gays and lesbians to wed in 2009, a share that rose to 62% in 2017. But views are largely unchanged over the last few years. About six-in-ten Americans (61%) support same-sex marriage in the most recent Pew Research Center survey on the issue, conducted in March 2019. 79% of Americans who are religiously unaffiliated favor same-sex marriage, as do 66% of White mainline Protestants and 61% of Catholics. Among White evangelical Protestants, however, only 29% favor same-sex marriage. Still, this is roughly double the level (15%) in 2009.

The U.S. is among 29 countries and jurisdictions that allow gay and lesbian couples to wed. The first nation to legalize gay marriage was the Netherlands, which did so in 2000. Since then, several other European countries—including England and Wales, France, Ireland, all of Scandinavia, Spain and, most recently, Austria, Germany and Malta—have legalized gay marriage.

Support for same-sex marriage has steadily grown over the past 15 years. And today, support for same-sex marriage remains near its highest point since Pew Research Center began polling on this issue. Based on polling in 2019, a majority of Americans (61%) support same-sex marriage, while 31% oppose it. Today, 66% of women and 57% of men support same-sex marriage. Today, 62% of Whites support same-sex marriage, as do 58% of Hispanics and 51% of Blacks. The increase in the share of adults who favor same-sex marriage over the past 15 years is due in part to generational change. Younger generations express higher levels of support for same-sex marriage (https://www.pewforum.org/fact-sheet/changing-attitudes-on-gay-marriage/).

In *Are You the One for Me?*, Barbara De Angelis (2012) reminds readers of some potentially bad love and marriage choices:

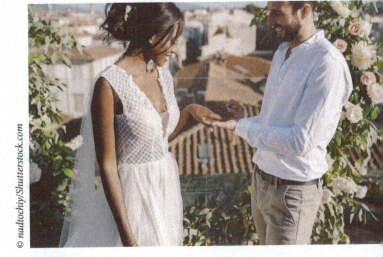

- You care more about your partner than he or she does about you.
- Your partner cares more about you than you care about him or her.
- You are in love with your partner's potential.
- You are on a rescue mission.
- You look up to your partner as a role model.
- You are infatuated with your partner for external reasons.
- You have partial compatibility—a lot in common in one area—but you ignore the rest of the relationship.
- You choose a partner to be rebellious.
- You choose a partner as a reaction to your previous partner.
- Your partner is unavailable (married or living with someone).

© nadtochiy/Shutterstock.com

What can this couple do to make their marriage last?

Marriage is a risky proposition. In deciding to get married, people make a long-range projection about the future of their relationship. Obviously, it is difficult to predict 30, 40, or even 50 years of commitment on the basis of one or two years of premarital interaction.

Author Brittany Wong (2016) gathered qualities happy relationships have in common from marriage therapists to share the one quality they believe couples needed to develop in order to stay together for life.

1. Compassion
2. Compromise
3. A sense of humor
4. Trust
5. Positivity
6. Intimacy
7. Mutual Respect
8. Presence
9. Love
10. Understanding
11. Friendship

In a classic study done by Robert and Jeanette Lauer, the most frequently given reason for a lasting marriage is *having a positive attitude toward one's partner*. These individuals see their spouse as their best friend, and they like him or her as a person. They are aware that their partner has faults, but their likable qualities more than offset their shortcomings. Many people stated that the present generation takes the marriage vows too lightly and are not willing to work at solving their problems. Marriage is a commitment and takes a lot of work. Both partners have to work at solving their problems. Another key ingredient to a lasting marriage is a mutual agreement about aims and goals of life, such as the desire to make the marriage last. A satisfying sex life is important, but this is not what makes the marriage last. In his *New York Times* best-seller, *The Seven Principles for Making Marriage Work*, John Gottman (Gottman & Silver, 2015) believes that the determining factor in whether wives feel satisfied with the sex, romance, and passion in their marriage is, by 70%, the quality of the couple's friendship. For men, the determining factor is, by 70% the quality of the couple's friendship.

> *Marry your best friend as well as your lover. Don't keep secrets or harbor grudges.*
> —JUDITH LIPTON

Marital Adjustment

During courtship, many of us wear *rose-colored glasses* a metaphor for seeing everything as positive, whether it is or not. We tend to ignore or not notice our partner's faults. We tend to focus mostly on pleasurable activities and our partner's positive characteristics. But when people marry, they must face reality and the problems that they will encounter within this new relationship. Suddenly, marriage brings duties and obligations. One is no longer responsible for only oneself, but now shares responsibility for two people, and perhaps more if children arrive.

Furthermore, one's identity is changed with marriage. No longer are you simply you— you are now Ashley's husband, or David's wife, or Jon's mother or father. You become interdependent with others in your family, and not independent. For some people this loss of independence may become a crisis, but for others, this new identity may give them a new lease on life.

The changing nature of male and female roles creates problems for all types of couples as they settle down to live together. Even the most mundane tasks may become a problem. Who pays the bills? Who takes out the trash? Who cooks? Who will stay home and take care of the family? There is no such thing as a problem-free marriage. Successful marriages depend on the couples' ability to handle their problems.

Role expectations. What is the woman's role in married life? Is it different from a man's role? Should gay partners' roles be different? When a couple marry, they assume new roles, that of traditional "husband and wife." We all have developed our own expectations of how a couple should behave in society. These expectations may vary greatly from one person to another. This is sometimes determined by family of origin and even media portrayal. What happens if our expectations are different from our partner's? Sometimes serious problems may occur. The more the two partners work to agree about marital roles, the more likely the marriage will last over a longer period of time.

Where did you learn what the role of a partner should be? Most of us learned this from watching our parents through the process called *modeling* (see Chapter Three). But times are changing, and other social forces are having an effect on our roles within a relationship. Careers are changing the timing of marriage and caretaking roles of the family. The women's movement has given women more options and has changed their perception of what their role is in a relationship. Marriage seems to be in a state of transition, and, consequently, most of us are in a state of confusion as to what role we should be playing.

It is imperative that couples discuss role expectations in depth before marriage. If they discover that their views are very different, they need to take seriously the potential for problems. Many people ignore gender-role disagreements, thinking they can "straighten out" their partners later on. But as we have all discovered, it is difficult to change our own behavior and more difficult to change someone else's behavior—especially their attitude.

While we are dating, and during the *honeymoon period*, which can be any time from the wedding day to a year or so from that day, many people do not see the people they love as they really are, but rather as they wish (expect) them to be. *We see what we expect to see, we hear what we want to hear—this is a psychological phenomenon of perception that can interfere with the way we perceive the world. We tend to perceive only the positive characteristics of our partners and ignore the negative*

> *A happy home is one in which each spouse grants the possibility that the other may be right, though neither believes it.*
> —DON FRASHER

What are your expectations of what married life will be?

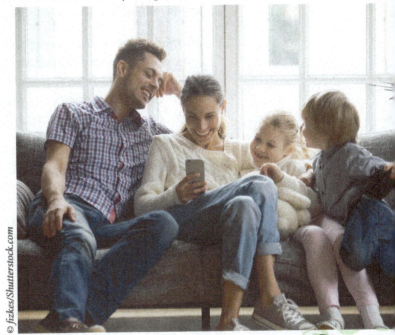
© fizkes/Shutterstock.com

characteristics. In essence, a person is in love with their own dreams and ideals, and not with the person they marry. Living together day in and day out makes it only a matter of time until each partner is forced to compare ideals with reality.

This stage is very important in most marriages. It usually indicates that the unrealistic, overly high expectations about marriage and one's mate created by "love" are being reexamined. No one can live up to the perfection that is often portrayed in the media, or what they think "should" happen in a marriage. Often couples will consult a therapist or take marriage encounter classes to work out some of the issues they have problems with.

In a successful relationship, it means that subjective perceptions are becoming more realistic and more objective. It also means that we are at last coming to know our mate as a real human being, rather than as a projection of our expectations. Realizing the humanness of our partner allows us to relax, to be human as well and not feel that we have to live up to our partner's expectations. If our partner can make mistakes and be less than perfect, so can we, thank goodness.

After the *honeymoon period,* intensity diminishes and satisfaction with marriage generally dips, especially for wives. The most commonly cited reason for this change is the arrival of children. For most couples, the time and effort spent on parenting usually takes time away from the partner relationship. Within the past two decades, there does appear to be an increase in married couples making the choice not to have children, or at least delay having or adopting children (U.S. Census Bureau, 2019). Some of the reasons often cited are the great costs involved in raising children, the possible conflicts involved with preparation for college and/or career improvements/advancements, loss of autonomy, and the great responsibility of raising children (Belsky, 2018).

What are some of the other issues and problems that a couple may encounter as they begin to face the reality of being married and functioning as a "twosome" rather than an individual? Yes, so many decisions to make!

Marriage, career, and parenthood. As birth control of various kinds has become more common, many individuals choose when they will have children and how many children they will raise. Currently, there is a tendency in the United States to have fewer children; the number of one-child families is increasing. People are not only marrying later, but also having children later (Grolnick & Gurland, 2001).

What are some of the advantages of having children early or late? Some of the advantages of having or adopting children early (in one's twenties) are as follows:

- the parents are likely to have more physical energy
- they can cope better with getting up in the middle of the night with infants
- they can cope better with waiting up until adolescents come home at night
- the birth mother is likely to have fewer medical problems with pregnancy and childbirth

- the parents may be less likely to build up expectations for their children, as do many couples who have waited many years to have children

There are also advantages to having children later (in their thirties):

- Parents will have had more time to consider their goals in life, have traveled or saved more money for a family, will be more mature, and will be able to benefit from their experiences to engage in more competent parenting.
- The parents are likely to be better established in their careers and have more income for childrearing expenses, which can impact the issue of who gives up their job or cuts back on work to care for children.

Paid Parental leave or *family leave (FMLA)* is an employee benefit available in almost all countries except the U.S. (NY Daily News 2011). The **Family and Medical Law Act of 1993** protects a job by requiring employers to give workers time off for family changes (care of a child or relative) or for medical emergencies, but employers are not required to pay employees for this time away from work. Hopefully this will be changed in the near future, because, while dual-career couples are the norm today, finances often make the decision regarding childcare. However, resentments and mixed feelings can occur for many couples.

Americans are making major strides toward gender equality. Women have surpassed men in obtaining college degrees. Women have flocked to many formerly male-dominated occupations, such as law and medicine. In 2018, a record number of women candidates were elected to Congress. But research found that men do fewer chores, according to an analysis by Dan Cassino, a professor at Fairleigh Dickinson University, and his wife Yasemin Besen-Cassino, from Montclair State University, which relied on the American Time Use Study. They found that overall in the U.S., women clean more than men do. American men did an average of 15 minutes of housework each day, while women did 45 minutes (Cassinos, 2016). Most men (77 %) did no housework on any given day, while most women (55%) did at least some.

That women should take on the bulk of domestic responsibilities is still a widespread belief in America. Married American mothers spend almost twice as much time on housework and child care than do married fathers. Although American mothers—including those with young children—are far more likely to be working now than in past decades, they spend more time on child care today than did moms in the 1960s (Rao, 2019). About 29% of married women in the United States out-earn their husbands. Without policies allowing them to pursue an egalitarian family life, men and women tend to fall back on unequal family arrangements that prioritize a male breadwinner and female homemaker. But individuals can play a role in changing their own behavior within families. This gendered division of housework will not be made equal by women doing less, but by men doing more.

If a woman has to work to help provide for a family, she may feel guilty because she is not at home taking care of the kids. What if she doesn't have to work, but prefers to work rather than staying home with the kids? Should she feel guilty for this when this is clearly what makes her happy? What if the woman has the more lucrative career and the decision is made for the man to stay home with the kids? Will he resent his breadwinning wife? Will he maintain his feelings of masculinity when he is not the person who provides money for the family?

Whatever arrangements couples make, Dr. Deborah Siegel (2007) indicates that psychologist Barry McCarthy urges couples to talk about their arrangements in terms of two-year timeframes, agreeing to make a point to check in every six months to see how well the arrangements are working for each individual. Are there other issues to consider? For many working parents, balancing their jobs and their family obligations can be a challenge for the family, "with 14% saying this is very difficult and 42% say it's somewhat difficult. Working mothers (60%) are somewhat more likely than fathers (52%) to say it's difficult for them to balance work and family, and this is particularly the case for mothers who work full time. In fact, one-in-five full-time working moms say balancing the two is *very* difficult for them, compared with 12% of dads who work full time and 11% of moms who work part time" (Pew Research Center, 2015).

The Bureau of Labor statistics for 2018 show that, while the pressures on men to be breadwinners and women to be housewives have been on their way out over the years, they're still far from gone. According to the 2018 American Time Use Study by the U.S. Bureau of Labor Statistics, employed men work an average of 50 minutes per day more than their female counterparts. And, while that's partially due to more women working part-time jobs than men, even among full-time employees men worked 8.2 hours per day compared to women's 7.8 hours. Additionally, 50% of women said they did some housework, such as cleaning or laundry, every day, while only 22% of men said the same. And 70% of women said they prepped or cleaned up food in an average day, while 43% of men said the same. Men were slightly more likely than women to participate in yard work—12% to 8%. On an average day, 85% of women and 67% of men spent some time doing household activities such as housework, cooking, lawn care, or financial and other household management.

Home or career or both? The question is often a struggle.

Men's contribution to housework and childcare has almost tripled since 1965, but studies indicate that wives are still doing the bulk of the household chores in America, even when they work outside of the home (Coontz, 2006; Konigsberg, 2011). Employed mothers may very well feel exhausted, so they frequently ask their husbands to help out more with housework and children; this may cause conflicts in the marriage. In a July 2011 report called, tellingly, "The New Male Mystique," the Families and Work Institute surveyed 1,298 men and concluded that 60% of fathers said they were having a hard time managing the responsibilities of work and family, compared with only 47% of mothers in dual-earner couples (Konigsberg, 2011). As you might expect, men who are better educated or younger tend to be more helpful around the house.

© Sellwell/Shutterstock.com

Increasingly, gay and lesbian couples are creating families that include children. Researchers have found that children growing up in gay or lesbian families are just as popular with their peers, and there are no differences in the adjustment and mental health of children living in these families when they are compared with children in heterosexual families (Hyde & DeLamater, 2019). Also, the overwhelming majority of children growing up in a gay or lesbian family have heterosexual orientation

 Think/Pair/Share Activity

SUCCESS IN MARRIAGE
Work in small groups or triads to answer the question.

What other issues and concerns do married couples encounter as they strive to succeed in their marriage? You may need to do a little research.

Marital Conflict

Most couples argue about many things: sex, money, children, power, roles and responsibilities, jealousy, or extra-marital affairs. However *money* ranks as the single most common cause of conflict in marriage. Money not only influences a couple's lifestyle but also their feelings of security, self-esteem, confidence, and acceptance by others. Without money, families live in a constant state of stress, fearing the loss of jobs, illness, or household emergencies. Partners may tend to view themselves as poor providers, and their self-esteem may crumble as a result. Dr. Karen Horney (1885–1952) developed an approach to spychology that examined the ways people try to attain and maintain a favorable self-image. The clinical writings of Horney, and other psychotherapists as well, document the ways in which people attempt to defend and enhance self-esteem; they also suggest that difficulty maintaining self-esteem, and maladaptive efforts to do so, may be central to a variety of mental health problems.

Neither financial stability nor wealth can ensure marital satisfaction. Even when financial resources are plentiful, money can be a source of marital strain. Quarrels about how to spend money are common and potentially damaging at all income levels. Money is freedom, money is power, and sometimes men and women even lie about it. In fact, Louise Lague (2001) reported, in a poll of 1,000 married people ages 18 and over, half of them men and half women said that the least openly discussed issue was how much the respondents paid for something they bought. Couples that tend to be more satisfied with their marriage engage in more joint decisions regarding their finances in comparison to couples who eventually divorce.

Think/Pair/Share Activity

DECISIONS IN MARRIAGE
Work in small groups or triads for this discussion.

Examine the last sentence, and decide what underlies most problems in relationships—be it a marriage, a business relationship, or wherever two or more people interact. Reflect on the questions and make a list. How are finances in your household handled? What would you do differently?

Psychologist John Gottman has been studying love and marriage for over 30 years. A concentrated 10-year study has provided valuable research data behind his theories. He believes that some negative emotions used in arguments are more toxic than others: criticism, contempt, defensiveness and stonewalling. *Criticism* involves constantly expressing negative evaluations of one's partner. *Contempt* involves communication of insulting feelings that one's spouse is inferior. *Defensiveness* involves responding to criticism and contempt with obstructive communication that escalates marital conflict. *Stonewalling* involves withdrawing from a discussion, most frequently seen among men. Gottman further indicates that he has learned at least two things from the couples he has studied: *First* is the importance of building and maintaining a friendship in your marriage so that you give your partner the benefit of the doubt when times are tough. **This takes constant work.** *Second,* there is always a choice every time you say something to your partner. He feels you can say something that will either nurture the relationship or tear it down. In other words, you may win a particular fight with your spouse, but you could damage or lose the marriage in the long run (Gottman & Silver,2004, Gottman & Declaire, 2007).

In some cases, there is no one necessarily to blame for the toxicity; rather, the toxicity is caused by the inability to communicate with each other. It can be difficult to establish healthy boundaries, conversations, and communication in relationships.

Not all *toxic relationships* are caused by two unhealthy people. Remember, toxic relationships survive on drama, and as the drama ramps up to keep the relationship going, we become dependent on that drama, or even addicted to it. The meaning we derive from that toxic relationship is skewed and distorted. Take time to explore who you are outside of a relationship. Rushing out to find someone to fill that void without really figuring out who you are, what you want, and what you need is a recipe for recurring relationship disaster.

Good people and good relationships will offer unconditional support.

Toxic friends and family members will look to adopt the drama of your loss and make it theirs as well, and this just makes everything worse (Gottman, 2015).

Becoming *Aware*

Gottman calculates that 69% of all marital problems are immutable, arising from basic personality differences between partners. Since behaviors rarely change, what we can change is our perspective (Dixit, 2009). Through all of this, Gottman recommends that both partners need to create an *emotional bank account* by continuing to make small, everyday sacrifices and by making efforts to notice and appreciate the kindnesses of our partner. He suggests this *emotional bank account* will help sustain couples through more demanding times in which these efforts may fall a bit short (Gottman, 2007).

Gottman contends that many aspects of marriage, often considered critical to long-term success, for example, how intensely people fight; whether they face conflict or avoid it; how well they solve problems; how compatible they are socially, financially, even sexually, are less important than people and professionals once thought. Gottman believes that none of these things matter to a marriage's longevity as much as maintaining a crucial ratio of five-to-one.

The five-to-one ratio: This is the difference between divorce and a positive long-term relationship according to Gottman, and it is mind-boggling in its simplicity. Satisfied couples maintain a five-to-one ratio of positive interactions to negative interactions in their relationship. In other words, the longevity of your relationship depends primarily on you being five times as nice to your partner as you are nasty to them (Gottman, 1995; Gottman & Silver, 2015).

The five-to-one ration may be a very important concept to learn. Gottman found that:

- Wildly explosive relationships that vacillate between heated arguments and passionate reconciliations can be as happy—and long lasting—as those that seem more emotionally stable. They may even be more exciting and intimate.
- Couples who start out complaining about each other have some of the most stable marriages over time, while those who do not fight early on are more likely to face the road to divorce.
- Fighting, whether rare or frequent, is sometimes the healthiest thing a couple can do for the relationship. In fact, blunt anger, appropriately expressed, "seems to immunize marriages against deterioration" (Gottman, 1996).
- Emotionally inexpressive marriages, which may seem like repressed volcanoes destined to explode, are actually very successful—so long as the couple maintains the five-to-one ratio in what they do express to each other. In fact, too much emotional catharsis among such couples can "scare the hell out of them," says Gottman.

> *What counts in making a happy marriage is not so much how compatible you are, but how you deal with incompatibility.*
> —GEORGE LEVINGER

 Think/Pair/Share Activity

Think, individually about the question. Pair, into small groups or get a partner. Share, with each other and discuss in the larger group. What do you think about the five-to-one ratio? Should we be teaching couples how to apply this to their relationship?

- How warmly you remember the story of your relationship foretells your chances of staying together. In one study that involved couples telling about how their relationship evolved, psychologists were able to predict—with an astonishing 94% accuracy—which couples would be divorced within three years.
- Men who do housework are likely to have happier marriages, greater physical health, and even better sex lives than men who do not.
- In happy marriages, there are no discernible gender differences in terms of the quantity and quality of emotional expression. In fact, men in happy marriages are more likely to reveal intimate personal information about themselves than women.

Think/Pair/Share Activity

Think, individually about the question. Pair, into small groups or get a partner. Share, with each other and discuss in the larger group. What do you think about the five-to-one ratio? Should we be teaching couples how to apply this to their relationship?

COMMUNICATION PROBLEMS

Successful communication is the cornerstone of any relationship. Such communication must be open, realistic, tactful, caring, and valued. Maintaining this kind of communication is not always easy unless all the people involved are committed to the belief that good communication is important to life and marital satisfaction. This sounds simple, yet couples in marital trouble almost always list failure to communicate as one of their major problems. Communication failures tend to occur because one or perhaps both partners choose not to communicate or because one or both lack communication skills. Refer back to Chapter Five to review and apply the material discussed in that chapter to improve communication skills.

"The ability of couples to withstand stress, respond to change, and enhance each other's health and well-being depends on their having a relatively equal power balance," reports Carmen Knudson-Martin of Loma Linda University. Equality, psychologists agree, is the world's best antidote to isolation; however, it is not easy to attain or to sustain (Marano, 2016). Many couples get so involved in the activities of everyday life—their career, their family activities, and their outside interests—that they forget about the needs and interests of their spouse. Even though they spend time with their spouse, they really do not communicate. If this seems to be true of your relationship, you may want to change this by *scheduling a time to communicate.* Tell your mate that you would like to take them out to dinner every Thursday night, even if it is to a fast food restaurant, so you have a time to sit down and talk. This is your time; do not take the kids or anyone else. You may want to write down things you want to talk about during the week so you won't forget about them. Many times a person will get to the scheduled session and say, "There's something I want to talk about, but I forgot what it was." You may want to schedule a weekend away from the family every few months so you can talk and plan for the future. See "Consider This: Making Up versus Breaking Up" further in the chapter to see the importance of communication in a relationship.

Becoming *Aware*

HOW TO HAVE A HAPPY RELATIONSHIP

- **Learn to Calm Down**—Do not let emotions take control of you. Do not over-react; wait, relax, take a walk, remove yourself from the stress event for a period of time until you have time to be calm and respond thoughtfully. Be sure you are ready to not bring up past faults, mistakes, and problems. Once you are ready emotionally, you can work on the other basic "keys" to improving your relationship.

- **Validate Your Partner**—Validation involves "putting yourself in your partner's shoes and imagining his or her emotional state." Let your partner know that you understand how he or she feels and why, even if you do not agree. You can also show validation by acknowledging your partner's point of view, accepting appropriate responsibility, and apologizing when you are clearly wrong. If this still seems too much of a stretch, at least let your partner know that you are trying to understand, even if you're finding it hard.

- **Learn to Speak and Listen Non-Defensively**—This is tough, Gottman admits, but defensiveness is a very dangerous response to one's partner, and it takes real effort to identify and manage. One of the most powerful things you can do—in addition to working toward the ideal of listening with empathy and speaking without blame—is to "begin to apply praise and admiration into your relationship." A little positive reinforcement (appreciation) goes a long way toward changing the chemistry between couples.

- **Practice, Practice, Practice**—Gottman calls this "overlearning," doing something so many times that it becomes second nature. The goal is to be able to calm yourself communicate non-defensively, and validate your partner automatically—even in the heat of an argument.

(Gottman & Declaire, 2007)

FAMILY AND DOMESTIC VIOLENCE

Physical violence is most apt to erupt in families lacking communication skills (Strong et al., 2020). Family violence is difficult to measure and document because most of it occurs in the privacy of the home, away from public view, and much of it goes unreported. Family violence includes child abuse, violence between spouses, sibling abuse, sexual abuse, and parental abuse by children, especially elderly parents (Duffy & Atwater, 2013).

What Is Domestic Violence?

Domestic violence can be physical or psychological, and it can affect anyone of any age, gender, race, or sexual orientation. It may include behaviors meant to scare, physically harm, or control a partner. While every relationship is different, domestic violence generally involves an unequal power dynamic in which one partner tries to assert control over the other in a variety of ways.

Insults, threats, emotional abuse and sexual coercion all constitute domestic violence. Some perpetrators may even use children, pets, or other family members as emotional leverage to get the victim to do what they want. Victims experience diminished self-esteem, self-worth, anxiety, depression and a general sense of helplessness that can take time and often professional help to overcome. A clinician who works with

Intimacy is often followed by disillusion in domestic violent homes

Per information gathered from all over the United States in September 2018, the Domestic Violence National Summary answered 19,459 hotline calls.

In 2018, statistics show 74,823 Victims were served in one day. 42,494 adult and child victims of domestic violence found refuge in emergency shelters, transitional housing, or other housing provided by local domestic violence programs. 32,329 adult and child victims received non-residential assistance and services, including counseling, legal advocacy, children's support groups, and more.

Domestic violence hotlines are a lifeline for victims in danger, providing support, information, safety planning, and resources. During the 24-hour survey period, Local and State Hotline staff answered 18,473 calls and National Domestic Violence Hotline staff answered 986 calls. This averages more than 13 calls every minute. 25,479 attended Prevention and Education trainings on Census Day. Local domestic violence programs educated 25,479 individuals in communities across the US.

Abusers are experts at zeroing in and preying on vulnerability (Cohan 2019). 1-(800) CDC-INFO | www.cdc.gov/violenceprevention/nisvs/

victims of domestic violence may be able to help an individual extract themselves from the situation, as well as offer psychological support.

Women are most often the battered party in a relationship, though men are frequently victimized too in both heterosexual and same-sex relationships. More than 38 million American women have been victims of domestic violence (Cohen, 2019). The technological revolution has opened up new ways for abusers to dominate, intimidate, and control the people in their lives through manipulation, cyber-stalking, and emotional blackmail.

But the #MeToo movement and new research have exposed ways for abuse victims to fight back and free themselves from the fear and control of dangerous, narcissistic abusers. A real narcissist may also have a tendency to disregard other people's feelings and take advantage of others to get what they want.

© BlurryMe/Shutterstock.com

SEXUAL ASSAULT AND THE LGBTQ COMMUNITY

June is unofficially recognized as Pride month, a time to celebrate the Lesbian, Gay, Bisexual, Transgender, and Queer (LGBTQ) communities. It is held in June to commemorate the anniversary of the Stonewall Rebellion in New York City on June 28, 1969, which is widely considered the birth of the modern LGBTQ movement. At the time, it was common for police to raid bars that catered to LGBTQ patrons. On that night, patrons of the Stonewall Inn fought back, igniting a wave of activism that brought nationwide visibility to the struggle for equality (https://www.psychologytoday.com/us/basics/domestic-violence, 2019).

Pride is a time to celebrate. It also is a way for LGBTQ people to take a stand against discrimination and violence, and to promote dignity, equality, and increased visibility. Individuals can attend Pride events throughout the country .

As we participate in Pride, it is vital to consider all aspects of the LGBTQ experience in the United States. Sexual violence is a common challenge faced by LGBTQ individuals, one that is often overlooked in the face of more sensational issues such as homophobia and transphobia. However, according to the Centers for Disease Control and Prevention (CDC), lesbian, gay and bisexual people experience sexual violence at rates that are the same or higher than heterosexual people (2019).

The Center for Disease Control National Intimate Partner and Sexual Violence Survey found that for lesbian, gay, and bisexual people, sexual violence is far too common.

- 44% of lesbians and 61% of bisexual women experience rape, physical violence, or stalking by an intimate partner.
- 46% of bisexual women have been raped.
- 22% of bisexual women have been raped by an intimate partner.
- 40% of gay men and 47% of bisexual men have experienced sexual violence other than rape.
- 26% of gay men and 37% of bisexual men experience rape, physical violence, or stalking by an intimate partner.
- 48% of bisexual women who are rape survivors experienced their first rape between the ages of 11 and 17 (2019).

Berastain (2016) states that partner abuse also manifests itself in the LGBT community, which experiences domestic violence at equal rates—and sometimes higher—than those of the rest of the population (25 to 33% of the LGBT population experiences domestic violence in their lifetime). Intimate partner abuse in the LGBT population can manifest itself differently from the cisgender pattern, thus presenting specific challenges to recognizing partner abuse and to accessing services. These include: the threat of outing, identity theft, withholding or selling medication, child-custody issues, and the lack of screening to distinguish between abuser and victim and lack of resources, since most shelters are set up for women only. There is also LGBTQ phobia among officials of the court and lack of community awareness, and, finally, LGBT abuse survivors who are closeted might not have friends, family members, faith communities, or other social circles to provide help and support.

Becoming Aware of Intimate Abuse: Intimate Partner Violence
https://www.youtube.com/watch?reload=9&v=vK3RhRwMwIg

Intimate partner violence, which you may have heard called "teen dating violence" or "domestic violence," is when a person behaves in a way to control another person in an intimate relationship. Intimate relationships exists between boyfriends and girlfriends, romantic partners, lovers or husbands and wives.

If you are in an abusive relationship, it is important to get support. An abuser is usually very good at isolating their partner, keeping them and away from their family and friends. As a result, victims often begin to feel ashamed and alone and believe that no one would understand. Many survivors have even described feeling as if they did not know who they were anymore. This makes it even more difficult to survive the abuse, to sort through the feelings, and to make decisions that will be best for you and your children. If you find that you don't have anyone to talk to, consider calling the National Domestic Violence Hotline or a domestic violence program in your area.

Recent research shows that in most relationships where violence has occurred, some form of abuse began during the *dating period*. If a person is abusive while the couple is dating, they are almost certain to continue that behavior unless they have gotten therapy or treatment. A person does not change overnight, nor does a marriage license make a difference in personality. To the contrary, some people feel that the marriage license is a sign of ownership, and they can now do whatever they want to their partner. If you are in an abusive relationship before marriage you may want to "think twice" before making a serious commitment to that person. Abuse is gender nuetral, and it can come from either partner.

 Check this out

Becoming Aware of Violence

Go to www.jacksonkatz.com

Ten Things Men Can Do to Prevent Gender Violence

Tough Guise: Violence, Media & the Crisis in Masculinity

Violence against women is a men's issue

CODEPENDENCE

Codependency is many things. It is a dependency on people—on their moods, behavior, sickness or well-being, and their love. It is a paradoxical dependency. Codependents appear to be depended upon, but they are dependent. They look strong but feel helpless. They appear controlling but in reality are controlled themselves, sometimes by a disorder or illness such as alcoholism.

> *Love creates an "us" without destroying a "me."*
> —BITS & PIECES
> (Cohen, 2019)

You may feel you can help that person, They need your help and your love them and you feel you can help them change. Perhaps you feel that if you can get them to marry you, it will be easier to help them change. This is the beginning of a *codependent relationship*—where person A has allowed person B's behavior (abuse, chemical addiction, etc.) to affect person A, and where A is obsessed with controlling B's behavior (Beattie, 2011). If, like so many others, you've lost sight of your own life in the drama of tending to someone else's, you may be codependent. It is natural to want to protect and help the people we care about. It is also natural to be affected by and react to the problems of people around us. As the problems become more and remain unresolved, we become more affected and react more intensely to them. We can allow ourselves to become lost in those issues, to result in damage to ourselves.

Are you codependent?   If you see yourself in the description above, you may be codependent. Codependency involves a habitual system of thinking, feeling, and behaving toward ourselves and others that can cause us pain. Codependent behaviors or habits are self-destructive, not only to the individual, but also to all of their relationships. Most codependent people have been so busy responding to the problems of others that they have not had time to identify, much less take care of, their own issues.

Codependent people can change. As we have however already learned, change is not easy—it takes a lot of work and effort on everyone's part. The first step toward change is awareness of the problem, and the second step is acceptance. In order to become aware of what codependence is, we need to know what the characteristics of a codependent are.

Codependency can be a destructive relationship in which you and your partner emotionally hurt each other. The behaviors that can be self-destructive only belong to the person who is hurting themselves and others that care about them. A codependent usually started these habits out of necessity to protect themselves or meet unfulfilled needs. If you find yourself in a codependent relationship, you may want to read some of the new literature and self-help books available at your local bookstores or seek professional help through the counseling office or mental health center near you.

> *I didn't realize it then, but my "perfect" friendship was actually causing small pockets of loneliness in my life.*
>
> *When my best friend told me he was having trouble getting out of bed, completing regular tasks, and finishing his residency applications, the first thing I did was look up flights. It wasn't even a debate on my end.*
>
> *At the time, I was living in Karachi, Pakistan. He was in medical school in San Antonio. I was a freelance writer with ample flexibility. He needed me. And I had the time.*
>
> *Three days later, I was on a 14-hour flight, and opening my journal to record a phrase from the book I'd been reading. That's when I noticed a sentence I'd written less than a year before.*
>
> *This wasn't the first time I'd dropped everything to help him out. As I flipped through the pages of my journal, I began to notice this reflection wasn't a second or third time thing. While I was giving my whole self to him, I somehow always got left behind once his life recovered from being in shambles.*

CONSIDER THIS

BECOMING AWARE – CONCEPTS A CODEPENDENT LIVES

- My good feelings about who I am stem from being liked by you.
- My good feelings about who I am stem from receiving approval from you.
- Your struggles affect my serenity. My mental attitude focuses on solving your problems or relieving your pain.
- My mental attention is focused on pleasing you.
- My mental attention is focused on protecting you.
- My mental attention is focused on manipulating you "to do it my way."
- My self-esteem is bolstered by solving your problems.
- My self-esteem is bolstered by relieving your pain.
- My own hobbies and interests are put aside. My time is spent sharing your interest and hobbies.
- Your clothing and personal appearance is dictated by my desires, because I feel you are a reflection of me.
- I am not aware of how I feel. I am aware of how you feel. I am not aware of what I want. I ask you what you want. If I am not aware, I assume.
- The dreams I have for my future are linked to you.
- My fear of rejection by you determines what I say and do by you.
- My fear of your anger determines what I say and do.
- I use giving as a way of feeling safe in our relationship.
- My social circle diminishes as I involve myself with you.
- I put my values aside in order to connect with you.
- I value your opinion and way of doing things more than my own.
- The quality of my life is in relation to the quality of yours.

THESE QUESTIONS THAT CAN HELP YOU IDENTIFY CODEPENDENCE.
- Have you become so absorbed in other people's problems that you do not have time to identify or solve your own?
- Do you care so deeply about other people that you have forgotten how to care for yourself?
- Do you need to control events and people around you because you feel everything around and inside you is out of control?
- Do you feel responsible for so much because the people around you feel responsible for so little?

I don't remember when I first realized that our relationship wasn't healthy. What I can remember, though, is learning that there was a name for what we were: codependent.

According to Sharon Martin, a psychotherapist in San Jose, California who specializes in codependency, codependent relationships are not a diagnosis. It's a dysfunctional relationship where one person loses themselves in their attempt to take care of someone else. Somewhere down the line, or from the beginning, one person becomes the "codependent" and ignores their own needs and feelings. They also feel guilty and responsible for tackling the other person's problems and solving their concerns.

Enabling is often accidental, but often, instead of allowing their partners to learn from their mistakes, they swoop in and "fix" everything, never allowing the other person to truly experience rock bottom.

During the courtship period and continuing throughout married life, there is an insecure feeling in many individuals when they fear the loss of affection of their partner, especially when they feel threatened by an outside source. That outside source may be a new baby, a new friend, or a new career.

"THE GREEN-EYED MONSTER"

In his play *Othello*, Shakespeare calls jealously "the green-eyed monster" which eventually leads the main character to an extremely violent rage. *Jealousy* is an emotion familiar to most of us, if not from direct experience, at least through the experience of friends, from novels, television, and movies. *Romantic jealousy* carries the additional stress associated with the threat of losing an important relationship and often involves feelings of having been betrayed and perhaps deceived. Thus, this feeling of *romantic jealousy* provokes a host of negative feelings focused on the lover, the self, and the perceived rival. And it can be very destructive in relationships (Anderson, 2003).

Gender differences characterize jealousy. Men tend to show strong feelings of sexual jealousy and are especially upset about sexual infidelity. This can motivate them to be very concerned about their partner's faithfulness (Myers, 2017). However, women are often more upset by their partner's emotional infidelity (Buss, 2019).

Is it Jealousy vs. Envy? *Jealousy* is defined as the thoughts and feelings that arise when an actual or desired relationship is threatened. *Envy* is defined as the thoughts and feelings that arise when our personal qualities, possessions, or achievements do not measure up to those of someone relevant to us. In general, society is more accepting of jealousy than envy, understanding the desire to protect lovers from rivals but not the begrudging of a friend's good fortune.

Researchers have suggested that jealousy and envy are rooted in a weak sense of self, low self-esteem, or insecurities about self-worth (Marano, 2006). People with poor self-concepts are more likely to fear that the existing relationship is vulnerable to threat. Jealousy is also more likely to occur when people believe they are putting more into a relationship than their partner is; they have serious doubts about their partner's commitment. Men seem to respond differently to jealousy than women. Males seem less likely to admit they feel jealous but are more likely to express anger with themselves or toward the perceived rival; females are more likely to react with depression and with attempts to make themselves more attractive to the partner (Buss, 2016).

Overcoming jealousy is not easy. Anything we can do toward becoming confident, secure individuals will help us cope with our own jealousy. We can try to learn what is making us jealous. What exactly are we feeling, and why are we feeling that way? We can try to keep our jealous feelings in perspective. We can also negotiate with our partner to change certain behaviors that seem to trigger our jealousy. Negotiations assume that we too are working to reduce our own unwarranted jealousy. Choosing partners who are reassuring and loving will also help reduce our irrational jealousies.

Jealousy is not a barometer by which the depth of love may be read. It merely records the degree of insecurity. It is a negative, miserable state of feeling, having its origin in a sense of insecurity and inferiority.
—MARGARET MEAD

Unfortunately, it is not as easy as it sounds to follow this advice, because jealousy is so often irrational, emotional, and unreasonable. Jealousy remains one of the puzzling components of love relationships (Myers, 2017).

GROWING APART

Is there a point at which you have to admit that it is just not going to work? In *Relationship Rescue*, Dr. Phil McGraw (2007) offers two suggestions: First, never make a major decision when you are emotional and in a hurry. And second, if you did everything you could to save your relationship and it could not be done, let it go (2001).

When considering what it takes to make relationships work, it is useful to look at those who have tried and succeeded as well as those who have tried and failed. Research shows that a few crucial compatibilities make the difference between making up and breaking up. See Consider This: Making Up versus Breaking Up.

Who divorces? At a time when divorce is becoming less common for younger adults, "gray divorce" is on the rise: Among U.S. adults ages 50 and older, the divorce rate has roughly doubled since the 1990s (Stepler, 2017). Stepler also found the divorce rate for adults ages 25 to 39 has fallen from 30 persons per 1,000 married persons in 1990 to 24 in 2015. This decline is attributed at least in part to younger generations putting off marriage until later ages (Stepler, 2017).

The median age at first marriage in the United States has continued to rise in recent years from 27.1 and 25.3 years in 2003 for males and females, respectively, to 29.8 and 27.8 years in 2018. Divorces in 2017 were at 11% (US Census, 2018). Those who do end up marrying are more likely to be college-educated, and research shows that **college-educated adults have a lower rate of divorce** (Stepler, 2017).

CONSIDER THIS

DIVORCE STATS

2019 Countries with Highest Divorce Rates (Abayomi Jegede, 2019, Trendr.net)

10. USA 53% (highest states are Oklahoma, Nevada, & Arkansas)
9. France 55%
8. Cuba 56%
7. Estonia 58%
6. Luxembourg 60%
5. Spain 63%
4. Czech Republic 66%
3. Hungary 67%
2. Portugal 68%
1. Belguim 71%

Marriage and divorce are both common experiences. In Western cultures, more than 90% of people marry by age 50. Healthy marriages are good for couples' mental and physical health. They are also good for children; growing up in a happy home protects children from mental, physical, educational and social problems. However, about *40 to 50% of married couples in the United States divorce* (Adapted from the Encyclopedia of Psychology; apa.org, 2019).

In addition, divorce rates in the United States are higher than rates elsewhere in the industrialized world (Strong et al., 2017). In *The 7 Principles for Making Marriage Work*, Dr. John Gottman & Silver (2015) lists the seven things that predict divorce. His ability to predict divorce is based in part on his analysis of the 130 newlywed couples who were observed at his "Love Lab" apartment at the University of Washington.

1. **Harsh Startup**. When a discussion leads off with criticism and/or sarcasm (a form of contempt).
2. **Four Horsemen**. Use of criticism, contempt, defensiveness, and stonewalling.
3. **Flooding**. When a partner's negativity is so overwhelming, and so sudden, that it leaves you shell-shocked.
4. **Body Language.** Bodily changes during a conflict discussion (racing heart, hormonal levels).
5. **Failed Repair Attempts.** Analyzing the disagreement pattern they follow .
6. **Bad Memories.** Don't remember the early days of the relationship as positive. (Fulwiler, 2014; Gottman, 2015).

What predicts divorce? Amato and Previti (2003) found that communication problems, sexual infidelity, jealousy, foolish spending, and substance abuse were the most consistent predictors of divorce.

Your marriage will have a greater chance of lasting if:

- You marry after the age of 22;
- You grew up in a stable, two-parent home;
- You dated for a long time prior to marriage;
- You are well and similarly educated;
- You have a stable income from a job you enjoy;
- You do not cohabit or become pregnant before marriage;
- You are religiously committed;
- You share similar value systems and have mutual life goals;
- You do not have emotional and/or psychological disorders;
- You enjoy spending time together;
- You have "affective affirmation" of each other;
- You are able to communicate and solve problems together (Strong et al., 2010; Parker-Pope, 2011).

None of these predictors, by themselves, is essential to a stable marriage, but the more you have, the greater the chance the marriage will last.

Do you fight fair? Take a look at how you are feeling and when you're the one who has been putting up with a behavior or something about your partner that you don't

> *A good marriage is not so much finding the right person as being the right person.*
> —SCOTT ROWLEY

> *What makes your marriage work: Maybe it's the ability to say you're sorry. I know that sounds so simple. If you're willing to tell somebody that you love them, are you also willing to say you're sorry? You need to, even when you think you're in the right.*
> —KEVIN COSTNER

CONSIDER THIS

MAKING UP VERSUS BREAKING UP

Pepper Schwartz (2016), professor of sociology at the University of Washington, analyzed data from the Enrich Couple Inventory involving questions administered to 21,501 couples throughout the country. The researchers compared the answers of the happiest couples to those of the most unhappy and found that the differences between their answers to a few key questions tell a lot about what makes relationships work:

My partner is a very good listener
Unhappy couples 18%   Happy couples   83%

My partner does not understand how I feel
Unhappy couples 79%   Happy couples   13%

We have a good balance of leisure time spent together and separately
Unhappy couples 17%   Happy couples   71%

We find it easy to think of things to do together
Unhappy couples 28%   Happy couples   86%

I am very satisfied with how we talk to each other
Unhappy couples 15%   Happy couples   90%

We are creative in how we handle our differences
Unhappy couples 15%   Happy couples   78%

Making financial decisions is not difficult
Unhappy couples 32%   Happy couples   80%

Our sexual relationship is satisfying and fulfilling
Unhappy couples 29%   Happy couples   85%

We are both equally willing to make adjustments in the relationship
Unhappy couples 46%   Happy couples   87%

I can share feelings and ideas with my partner during disagreements
Unhappy couples 22%   Happy couples   85%

My partner understands my opinions and ideas
Unhappy couples 19%   Happy couples   87%

What do you think about these findings?

like. We start to expect that same behavior again from them, and when it's repeated, we bring up the issue to our partner. In discussing it so often starts with something like one of these:

"I hate how you …"

"You always …"

"It's so frustrating how you …"

"Why do you have to …"

"I feel hurt that you …"

"I'm disappointed that you …"

These kinds of phrases are an automatic "button that gets pushed," and the other person is left grasping to defend themselves rather than opening up for understanding (Gottman & Silver 2015).

Today, marriage partners have a much more flexible view of marriage roles and responsibilities and are likely to expect each other to be a friend, lover, and confidant, as well as wage-earner and care-giver.

Gottman, a University of Washington psychology professor, believe "the simple truth that happy marriages are based on deep friendship. By this I mean a mutual respect for each other's company," plus an intimate knowledge of each other's quirks, likes, and dislikes (Chatterje, 2016).

The impact of divorce. The dissolution of a marriage tends to be a very traumatic event for most people. Divorced men suffer primarily from loss of *emotional support* and disrupted *social ties* to friends and relatives and sometimes even children (Belsky, 2018). In comparison, divorced women suffer most from *reduced income*.

Men and women differ in how they cope with a failed relationship: women tend to confide in their friends, whereas men tend to start a new relationship as quickly as possible. Some individuals appear to adapt in the early stages of divorce, but show effects later (Hetherington et al., 1998). It takes most people at least two to three years to recover fully from the distress of a divorce, and some have more difficulty than others (Lucas, 2005).

Table 6.1 indicates the steps many people experience as they go through the divorce process.

Table 6.1 DIVORCE GRIEF

■ Relief—Moment of no more fussing.
■ Shock and surprise—I can't believe this is happening to me.
■ Emotional release—How much should I let people see my feelings, and how long will I keep crying?
■ Physical distress and anxiety—Will I lose my friends?
■ Panic—There is something wrong with me; I cannot eat or I eat all the time.
■ Two basic emotions in divorce:

> a. Guilt—What did I do wrong?
>
> b. Rejection—I am not capable of being loved.
>
> ■ Hostility and projection—I know we are both angry, but we are going to end this divorce in a friendly manner.
>
> ■ Lassitude—Suffering in silence, hard to get anything done.
>
> ■ Healing—Gradual overcoming of grief and getting on with reality.

For some, divorce can be enhancing. In a healthy divorce, ex-spouses must accomplish three tasks: let go, develop new social ties, and, when children are involved, redefine parental roles (Lucas, 2005).

The first emotional impact of divorce is often that the former spouses become even more angry and more bitter with each other than they were in the marriage. This increased hostility is often followed by and interspersed with periods of depression, disequilibrium, altered patterns of eating and sleeping, drug and alcohol use, along with work and residence change (Kelly, 2004). It is most likely to be the wife who first finds fault with the marriage and files for divorce. In fact, many men are surprised and shocked by the breakup, and in the short term, divorce is more devastating to the man than the woman. Over the long term, however, women are more affected, primarily because they are likely to have less money and fewer marriage prospects than divorced men. If they are mothers with custody, the impact of divorce is particularly strong (Duffy & Atwater, 2011).

Effects on the children Divorce may have more of an impact on children than anyone else. The children have no control in this relationship; they are helpless in this situation. Whatever they kids say or do will not help or change the situation. Generally, no one will listen anyway. Amato and Booth offer that this has received limited support solely as a financial variable. However, research has shown that children living in their father's custody were financially better off than those living in their mother's custody. This is often because fathers maintain the same or a similar financial picture, while mothers, earning less as women and often neglecting their careers to care for their children, make less money. Thus, financial loss, as it relates to family stress, is more likely important than simple decrease in the mother's monthly income. Evidence suggests that in the long run it is less damaging to the children if unhappy parents divorce than if the children grow up in a home with "intact" marriage that is filled with dissent and anger (Booth & Amato, 2004).

Parents' Relationship quality, Parental Divorce and Children's Well-being

For children's well-being, having both kinds of problems (parental divorce and parents' relationship quality) is worse than having only one. In fact, children who experience parental divorce/separation have more psychological problems than those that had experienced poor parents' relationship quality. Also, children who experienced poor relationship quality have more psychological problems than those whose parents divorced (2012).

And in a 2005 research project, Amato shows that children growing up with two continuously married parents are less likely to experience a wide range of cognitive, emotional, and social problems into adulthood. Although it is not possible to demonstrate that family structure causes these differences, studies suggest it (Ama-

© *Photographee.eu/Shutterstock.com*

to, 2005). For internalizing and externalizing problems, there is little evidence in favor of the interaction hypothesis.

Though divorce can be hard on the children, psychologists often advise that parents can protect their children and minimize the impact of divorce by taking steps such as the following (Nevid & Rathus, 2019):

- Try, in spite of differences, to agree on how to handle the children.
- Help each other maintain important roles in the children's lives.
- Do not criticize or disparage each other in front of the children.

New research on divorce focuses on the number of family transitions rather than on divorce as a single event (Amato, 2010).

Remarriage. Between 70 and 80% of divorced people remarry, on the average within *three to four years* of being divorced (men tend to marry sooner than women after a divorce). Remarriage is more likely to occur if the divorced person is relatively young, since there are likely to be more potential partners available. There is no guarantee that marriage will be better the second time around; the divorce rate for remarriages is about 65% higher than that for first marriages. However, the average duration for second marriages is about the same as for first, about eight to nine years (Kreider, 2009). It may be that some lonely, divorced people remarry too quickly. Stepchildren can also be a disruptive factor.

Blended families. An increasing number of remarriages now involve children. Remarriages involving children place special demands on all of the adults as well as the children. In addition to learning how to live with one new person, which can be difficult enough for most people, one or both partners must also become accustomed to a ready-made family. When the children are young, the stepparent has more opportunity to develop rapport and trust with the children. This often involves some contact with the stepchildren's other parent, which can be a personal source of personal stress

But when there are adolescents involved, it is more difficult for everyone involved. Both parents must make allowances for their stepchildren's initial suspicion, jealousy, and resistance. When both parents develop a good working relationship, talking things out and cooperating on discipline and household chores, the blended family may do at least as well as intact families.

As we have previously noted, the traditional model of marriage has changed within our culture. More and more people are selecting alternatives to marriage; earlier in the chapter we discussed two alternatives: single life and cohabitation. Another alternative should be mentioned.

Gay/lesbian relationships. The dynamics of a gay/lesbian relationship do not seem to be any different than those in a heterosexual relationship. They are similar in terms of the forces that bring couples together, the factors that predict satisfaction with the relationship, and the problems couples face (Weiten et al., 2017). An increasing number of same-gender couples are rearing children.

The major problem that most gays/lesbians encounter is the negative attitude about homosexuality in our society. Most gay men and nearly all gay women prefer stable, long-term relationships. Promiscuity among gay men is clearly on the decline. Lesbian relationships are generally sexually exclusive. Gay/lesbian relationships are characterized by great diversity. It is not true that gays/lesbians always assume traditional masculine and feminine roles. Both gays/lesbians and heterosexual cohabitants may face some opposition to their relationship from their families, and society in general, and now universally enjoy the legal and social access to marriage in the United States. This also means that LGBTQ people are now facing issues that go with divorce, including legal costs and custody issues.

Chapter Review

We are motivated not only to seek the company of others, but also to form close and lasting relationships. The relationships you have are your greatest assets.

- Relationships evolve, they do not just happen. They take time and effort.
- The three steps involved in a relationship are: 1) **Becoming aware** of the other person—first impression; 2) **Making contact** or getting acquainted; and 3) **Disclosure**.
- Friends play a significant role in our lives. They provide us with *emotional support* and *social ties*. Without friends we experience loneliness.
- We are drawn to people who are similar to us. Research studies have found that similar beliefs and attitudes are the most important aspects of a relationship in order to keep a relationship together over a long period of time.
- In order to find friends, you must go to those places (proximity) where you will find other people who have similar interests and needs.
- The **repulsion hypothesis** indicates that many of us are repulsed by people whom we do not know, and we perceive them as dissimilar to us.
- The **social exchange theory** states that we measure our actions and relationships on a cost-benefit basis. People maximize their rewards and minimize their costs by employing their resources, either tangible or intangible, to gain the most favorable outcome.
- We tend to like people who like us—reciprocity.
- During the last decade, online matchmaking sites have evolved as a huge industry.
- The most important factor people want in marital selection in China, India, Indonesia, Iran, Taiwan, and the Palestinian Arab culture is chastity. People from the Zulu culture in South Africa, Estonia, and Colombia placed a high value on housekeeping skills.
- Both men and women of many cultures want a mate who possesses qualities of mutual attraction/love, dependable character, and emotional stability/maturity, respectively the highest.
- Men prefer wives who are younger than they are. Women prefer husbands who are somewhat older—but there is an increase in women seeking younger dates and mates.
- Harry Stack Sullivan has given us an excellent definition of love—"When the satisfaction, security, and development of another person is as important to you as your own satisfaction, security, and development, love exists."
- Robert Sternberg has developed a theory of love that includes three components: **passion**—an intense physiological desire for another person; **intimacy**—the feeling that one can share all one's thoughts and actions with another; **commitment**—the willingness to stay with a person through thick and thin.
- According to Sternberg, there are at last seven types of love relationships: liking, romantic, companionate, consummate, infatuation, empty, and fatuous.
- **Psychological reactance** is the tendency to protect or restore one's sense of freedom or social control, often doing the opposite of what has been demanded. This is also known as the Romeo and Juliet effect.
- Although alternatives to marriage are more viable than ever, at least 90% of us will marry at least once. Individuals are waiting longer to get married.

- **Cohabitation** has become increasingly more common throughout the world. Couples who do decide to cohabit are at a higher risk of divorce than couples who do not.

- The dynamics of a gay/lesbian relationship do not seem to be any different than those in a heterosexual relationship. The main problem is the lack of support/negative support they may get if their community does not believe in gay marriage.

- Men and women differ in how they cope with a failed relationship: women tend to confide in their friends, whereas men tend to start a new relationship as quickly as possible. Some individuals appear to adapt in the early stages of divorce, but show effects later.

- Gadoua and Larson (2014) believe you need to focus first on what your *authentic truth* is, and what needs have to be met. Authentic Truth is what's healthiest and happiest for both people involved in a marriage or relationship.

- The more two partners agree about marital roles, the more likely the marriage will last over a longer period of time. It is imperative that couples discuss role expectations in depth before marriage.

- Dr. Gary Chapman indicates there are five love languages: words of affirmation, quality time, receiving gifts, acts of service, and physical touch.

- Successful communication is the cornerstone of any relationship. Such communication must be open, realistic, tactful, caring, and valued. Physical violence is most apt to erupt in families lacking communication skills.

- John Gottman's research indicates that most relationships will be successful as long as the couple maintain the five-to-one ratio of positive responses to negative responses. Gottman also feels that some negative emotions used in arguments are more toxic than others (the "Four Horsemen"): criticism, contempt, defensiveness, and stonewalling.

- Gottman believes 69% of all marital problems arise from basic personality differences. He does not feel behavior changes that much, so changing one's perspective is the best advice. He suggests creating an emotional bank account in marriage, meaning to continue to make small, everyday sacrifices, as well as making efforts to notice and appreciate the kindness of your partner.

- A **codependent relationship** is where one person has allowed another person's behavior (abuse, chemical addiction, etc.) to affect them, and is obsessed with controlling that person's behavior.

- **Jealousy** is defined as the thoughts and feelings that arise when an actual or desired relationship is threatened, and **envy** as the thoughts and feelings that arise when our personal qualities, possessions, or achievements do not measure up to those of someone relevant to us.

- The prevailing estimate from the American Psychological Association (2019) is that somewhere between 40 and 50% of U.S. marriages will end in divorce.

- Divorce affects all individuals—parents and children. Parents can help minimize the effect on children by trying to agree on how to handle the children, helping each other to maintain important roles in the children's lives, and not criticizing or making disparaging remarks about each other in front of the children.

- According to Amato in 2004, new research on divorce focuses on the number of family transitions rather than on divorce as a single event.

Test Review Questions: Learning Outcomes

1. Discuss what is involved in the three steps in the development of a relationship.
2. What are the qualities of a good friend?
3. Explain the importance of similarities, proximity, complementarity, social exchange theory, and reciprocity in the development of friendships.

4. What are the top three mate preferences shared by men and women in Buss's cross-cultural research?
5. Discuss the effective strategies for meeting dates and mates.
6. Discuss the difference between love and infatuation.
7. What is the current estimate of how many marriages will end in divorce?
8. Describe Sternberg's theory of love.
9. Explain the phenomenon known as psychological reactance (the Romeo and Juliet effect).
10. Describe the positive and negative aspects of cohabitation.
11. What makes a happy and successful marriage?
12. Discuss Dr. Gary Chapman's Five Love Languages.
13. What do most couples argue about? Why? What does Gottman say most marital problems arise from?
14. Explain the five-to-one ratio.
15. Explain the four negative emotions John Gottman feels are more toxic than others.
16. What is a codependent relationship?
17. Describe the difference between jealousy and envy.
18. Explain the impact of divorce on the individuals involved, including children. What do psychologists recommend parents can do to minimize the effect on the children?
19. Explain the emotional bank account in marriage. How can it be helpful?
20. Discuss how role expectancies—child care, career, and housework—responsibilities can impact a relationship.
21. Discuss the Traits of Friendship categories: Traits of Caring, Traits of Congeniality, and Traits of Integrity, each representing an essential aspect to relational behavior.
22. What is social capital? Why does it matter?
23. What is authentic truth?
24. Discuss Gottman's belief that "the simple truth is that happy marriages are based on deep friendship. By this I mean a mutual respect for each other's company." Agree or disagree? Explain.

Key Terms

5-to-1 Ratio
Authentic Truth
Blended Families
Codependent Relationship
Cohabitation
Commitment
Communication
Companionate Love
Complementary Needs
Confidant
Consummate Love
Divorce
Emotional Bank Account
Empathy
Empty Love

Envy
Fatuous Love
Friend
Gay/Lesbian Relationships
Honeymoon Period
Infatuation
Intimacy
Jealousy
Liking
Love
Love languages
Marriage
Mere Exposure Phenomenon
Parenthood
Passion

Psychological Reactance
Reciprocity
Remarriage
Repulsion Hypothesis
Role Expectations
Romantic Love
Romeo and Juliet Effect
Similarities
Singlehood
Social Exchange Theory
Traits of Caring
Traits of Congeniality
Traits of Integrity

Reflections: Critical Thinking

Answer the following questions and turn them into your instructor for grading. (All questions answered = A; 13 questions answered = B; 8 questions answered = C).

1. Explain why we need friends.
2. What is your definition of a good friend? Explain what a good friend is.
3. If you knew someone who was new to town, what would you recommend they do to find new friends?
4. Friendships satisfy needs. Study three relationships (friendships) that you currently have. What needs are they satisfying for you? Explain.
5. How have you used the social exchange theory in your relationships?
6. What is your definition of love? How do you know when you are in love?
7. What are the pros and cons of cohabitation vs. marriage? Explain.
8. What are your experiences with jealousy? How should a person deal with a jealous lover?
9. Explain the role of the male and the role of the female in a heterosexual married relationship. Thinking about heterosexual relationships in your family, are these roles different from how your older-generation relatives viewed their roles within their marriages? Explain.
10. What direct or indirect impact has divorce had on your life?
11. Explain codependence. Have you ever been in a codependent relationship? Discuss the relationship and explain how you could change the situation.
12. Which of the "Five Love Languages" is most important to you?
13. Explain your definition of an Emotional Bank Account in marriage.
14. Which type of lifestyle are you living today? What do you think are its advantages and disadvantages for you? If you could have a different lifestyle, which one would it be? Why?
15. Describe authentic truth. What is your authentic truth?

Technology Resources and Activities

National Network to End Domestic Violence

1325 Massachusetts Ave NW 7th Floor Washington, DC 20005-4188 T: 202.543.5566 | F: 202.543.5626

http://www.artofpeoplebook.com/quiz

Self Assessment Quiz from the book *The Art of People*.

www.gottman.com

Numerous articles related to Gottman's extensive research on making marriage work.

http://www.marriagebuilders.com/

Insightful answers to questions about infidelity, marriage counseling, and divorce.

http://hughson.com/

Named one of the top five websites in relation to divorce information, this is an address for individuals contemplating or involved in a divorce.

https://www.5lovelanguages.com/quizzes/

The Chapman Love languages website

http://marriage.about.com/cs/communicationkeys/a/lovelanguage.htm

Discussion of five love languages, etc.

Activity: www.authentichappiness.sas.upenn.edu/testcenter.aspx

Close Relationship Questionnaire that measures attachment.

http://www.themachoparadox.com/images/10%20Things%20Flyer.pdf

10 things men can do to Prevent Gender Violence handout.

https://www.usaid.gov/sites/default/files/Violence_in_Womens_Lives.pdf

Information on violence toward women in the United States.

https://www.ted.com/talks/helen_fisher_studies_the_brain_in_love

Why do we crave love so much, even to the point that we would die for it? To learn more about our very real, very physical need for romantic love, Helen Fisher and her research team took MRIs of people in love—and people who had just been dumped.

http://wapo.st/2aOz3em

The sex lives of Millenials.

http://www.centredaily.com/news/local/article93227647.html

Talking to your doctor about your sexual health.

https://www.youtube.com/watch?v=Ql0Q5uf-AbA

The changing American family (2014) before the 2015 ruling on gay marriages.

https://www.pewforum.org/fact-sheet/gay-marriage-around-the-world/

Gay Marriage around the World

https://www.ted.com/talks/helen_fisher_tells_us_why_we_love_cheat

Why we love, why we cheat by Helen Fisher.

https://www.hrc.org/videos/doctors-speak-out-for-trans-youth

Doctors Speak Out for Trans Youth.

https://youtu.be/P3fIZuW9P_M

The person you really need to marry, by Tracy McMillan. McMillan answers the question: "Who is the one person you need to marry in order to have a successful relationship? (Yourself)."

http://tedxtalks.ted.com/video/Arranged-Marriages-American-Sty

Arranged Marriages: American Style by Pepper Schwartz, TEDxGatewayArch.

https://www.youtube.com/watch?v=_UoMXF73j0c

The price of invulnerability: Brené Brown at TEDxKC.

https://www.ted.com/talks/mandy_len_catron_falling_in_love_is_the_easy_part

Did you know you can fall in love with anyone just by asking them 36 questions? But … is that real love? Did it last? And what's the difference between falling in love and staying in love?

https://www.youtube.com/watch?v=7vhOAk5T3qA

Can abuse feel good? Kristin Carmichael at TEDxABQWomen.

https://www.ted.com/talks/helen_fisher_studies_the_brain_in_love

Why do we crave love so much, even to the point that we would die for it?

https://www.5lovelanguages.com/podcasts/

Chapman Love Languages website

Roles and Expectations

PURPOSE

To discover the roles and expectations people have of themselves and other people in specific categories such as a spouse, parent, student, breadwinner, male, and female.

INSTRUCTIONS

1. Select one of the three alternatives:
   a. Ask four to five married students—may or may not be from the class—to be on a panel. Have the class members ask questions regarding roles and expectations in a marriage.
   b. Divide into groups of approximately four individuals (two females and two males would be ideal).
   c. Each student interviews four or more individuals, from different careers, from different socioeconomic income levels, and/or different ethnic groups.
2. The class may want to create their own questions or ask the questions listed below and then answer the discussion questions.
   a. What career have each of you chosen for yourself? What type of career is selected by the females; by the males? Are the careers sex-role oriented?
   b. What roles do you expect to play at home? Specify the tasks you are willing or not willing to do.
   c. What roles will you take as a parent (full-time parent, half-time, change diapers, and so on)?
   d. What roles will you take as a breadwinner and in the financial management of your marriage?
   e. What role expectations did you have of your spouse before marriage?

DISCUSSION

1. Do you see evidence that today's college students subscribe to traditional sex roles, or that they are free of such barriers to independent choice? Give examples.

2. What messages did you receive as you were growing up regarding specific expectations or behaviors appropriate to your gender?

3. How do you feel that your life would be different, if at all, if you were a member of the opposite sex? (Imagine, when you wake up tomorrow morning, you are the opposite sex.) What would you do? How would you act? Would others relate to you differently? What would your expectations of yourself be? How would they change?

Name _____ Date _____

Are You Compatible?

PURPOSE

To discover whether you and your prospective mate or date are compatible.

INSTRUCTIONS

1. Make a copy and give to your mate.
2. Answer the following questions with the appropriate number.

   1 = Strongly agree   4 = Disagree

   2 = Agree   5 = Strongly disagree

   3 = Neither agree nor disagree
3. Compare, contrast, and discuss responses with your mate.

   1. We have similar religious beliefs and values. _____
   2. We enjoy the same type of leisure activities. _____
   3. We like each other's friends. _____
   4. We enjoy each other's sense of humor. _____
   5. We like to be with each other as much as we can. _____
   6. We are willing to share whatever we have with each other. _____
   7. We share our thoughts and feelings about even the most private topics. _____
   8. We have similar political values and beliefs. _____
   9. We are willing to listen to each other's problems and help resolve each other's problems. _____
   10. We tend to agree on how to spend money and how to save money. _____
   11. We support our partner's interest and activities even if they differ from our own. _____
   12. Our personal lives, work schedules, sleep habits, outside interests and activities, fit together harmoniously. _____
   13. We work well together in making decisions. _____
   14. We are able to resolve conflict situations without getting too emotional or aggressive toward one another. _____
   15. Our efforts to work out differences usually bring us closer together. _____
   16. We desire the same level of openness. _____
   17. We are able to work out a division of tasks and who is responsible for specific responsibilities. _____
   18. We are both neat or disorderly, etc. _____
   19. We enjoy the same type of vacations and travel. _____
   20. We share pleasant feelings and unpleasant feelings about each other and our relationship. _____

SCORING

Add up your total score. The higher the score, the less compatible you seem to be: between 60–80. The lower the score the more compatible you seem to be: between 20–40.

DISCUSSION

After you have completed the rating scale, answer the following questions:

1. Why is it important to have a lot in common with your mate?

2. How can you improve your relationship with your mate to make your relationship more compatible?

3. Do you think that two people who score high on this test could still be compatible? Explain.

RELATIONSHIP CONFLICT RESOLUTION ACTIVITY

Why You Should Try It

All couples experience conflict, but researchers have found that how partners deal with this conflict has major implications for the longevity of their relationship. In particular, leading couples researcher John Gottman and his colleagues have identified four specific behaviors, which they call the "four horsemen of the apocalypse," that spell doom for couples.

To help you guard against these "four horsemen," this exercise teaches you to recognize them and consider more constructive alternatives.

Understanding the signs of these toxic behaviors is a vital step toward avoiding them and having a healthier response to conflict.

Why It Works

Most couples experience conflict in their relationship from time to time, and although occasional conflict is not necessarily harmful to a relationship (some research suggests it can even be helpful), conflict can sometimes elicit destructive behaviors that undermine relationship satisfaction. Identifying destructive behaviors is an important first step toward reducing them and replacing them with more constructive behaviors, which can in turn improve communication and increase satisfaction. This process takes time and practice, and in some cases couples may benefit from seeking the support of a relationship counselor.

Evidence That It Works

Carrere, S., Buehlman, K.T., Coan, J.A., Gottman, J.M., Coan, J.A., and Ruckstuhl, L., (2000). Predicting Marital Stability and Divorce in Newlywed Couples, Journal of Family Psychology, 14(1), 42-58.

A long-term study of 95 newlywed couples found that how they handled conflict between them in a single, brief interaction, recorded in a laboratory, predicted the stability of their relationship four to six years later with 87.5 percent accuracy, and seven to nine years later with 81% accuracy. Couples who displayed the "four horsemen" behaviors were significantly more likely to have broken up when the researchers followed up with them years later.

Sources

John Gottman, Ph.D., The Gottman Institute

Why Marriages Succeed or Fail … and How You Can Make Yours Last, by John Gottman, Ph.D.

Name _____ Date _____

Reflective Questions for Journaling

Self-exploration activities and journaling exercises specific to each assessment to enhance self-discovery, learning, and healing.

HOW TO DO IT

Read the descriptions of the "four horsemen" below and consider whether you and/or your close friend or partner ever engage in any of these behaviors during conflicts.

Read the descriptions of the constructive alternatives that can be used in place of the "four horsemen" and consider how you might put these behaviors into practice, if you have not already.

The next time you find yourself in a conflict with your partner, make an active effort to avoid the "four horsemen" and engage in more constructive behaviors instead. Don't be too hard on yourself if you slip up—it can be challenging to stay focused during the heat of an argument, and these habits can take time to change.

After the conflict, make a note of how things went. Did you or your partner engage in any of the "four horsemen" behaviors, and if so, did you catch yourself and try to take a different approach during the conflict? What went well, and what could you improve for next time?

THE FOUR HORSEMEN

1. Criticism. Some forms of criticism are constructive, but in this case criticism refers to making negative judgments or proclamations about your partner in extreme, absolute terms. A sign that you may be engaging in this more harmful form of criticism is if you catch yourself using terms like "never" and always"—for example, "You never think about anyone but yourself!" or, "You are always so stubborn!"

Note that criticism itself is not necessarily a recipe for relationship failure—the problem with criticism is that excessive or extreme criticism can, over time, lead to the more destructive "horsemen."

Constructive alternative: There's nothing wrong with voicing concerns and complaints in a relationship, but try to do so in a way that focuses on your own feelings (and how your partner's behavior affects you)—for instance, by making "I" statements, like "I feel lonely when you come home late for dinner"—and mentions specific negative behaviors rather than making global attacks on his or her entire personality ("I feel neglected when you make plans without me" rather than "You are so inconsiderate!").

440

2. Contempt. Contempt is a more destructive form of criticism that involves treating your partner with disrespect, disgust, condescension, or ridicule. It may involve mean-spirited sarcasm, mockery, eye-rolling, sneering, or name-calling. Contempt can grow over time when a person focuses on the qualities they dislike in their partner and builds up these qualities in their mind.

Constructive alternative: Instead of keeping score of all of your partner's flaws, consider their positive qualities and the things you appreciate most about them. In fact, it may help to write a list of these qualities and return to it when you need a reminder.

3. Defensiveness. Defensiveness tends to arise when people feel criticized or attacked; it involves making excuses to avoid taking responsibility, or even deflecting blame onto your partner. If you hear yourself saying "I didn't do anything wrong," or blaming your partner for something else after he or she has leveled a complaint against you, ask yourself whether this is really the case. Even if your partner made some mistakes, that doesn't free you from responsibility for things you could have done differently as well.

Constructive alternative: Instead of keeping score of all of your partner's flaws, consider their positive qualities and the things you appreciate most about them.

4. Stonewalling. Stonewalling involves putting up a (metaphorical) wall between you and your partner by withdrawing, shutting down, and physically and emotionally distancing yourself from your partner. An example of stonewalling is to give your partner the "silent treatment" or to abruptly leave without telling your partner where you're going. Stonewalling can sometimes result when the first three "horsemen" accumulate and become overwhelming. Stonewalling is especially destructive to relationships because it can make one's partner feel abandoned and rejected.

Constructive alternative: If you need time out to take a few deep breaths and collect your thoughts, let your partner know, and then return to the conversation when you're ready. This way, your partner will understand that you are taking care of yourself, not trying to reject him.

Activity adapted from https://ggia.berkeley.edu/

What Do You Think of These Trends?

PURPOSE

Pew Research Center, in conjunction with *Time* magazine, conducted a nationwide survey of 2,691 adults ages 18 and older to get their opinions on attitudes about the changing American family. See how your judgments compare with those in the survey.

INSTRUCTIONS

1. For each trend, simply place an X in the appropriate column, indicating whether you think the trend is a good thing for society, a bad thing for society, or does not make much difference. Then, compare your attitudes with the responses given in the nationwide survey.
2. Divide into groups of four or five and have small group discussions or have a large class discussion on the discussion questions.

	Good Thing for Society	Bad Thing for Society	Doesn't Make Much Difference
1. More women not ever having children.	_____	_____	_____
2. More unmarried couples raising children.	_____	_____	_____
3. More gay and lesbian couples raising children.	_____	_____	_____
4. More single women having children without a male partner to help raise them.	_____	_____	_____
5. More people living together without getting married.	_____	_____	_____
6. More mothers of young children working outside the home.	_____	_____	_____

SURVEY RESULTS

These were the results calculated as appearing more frequently.

1. 29% bad for society   11% good for society
2. 43% bad for society   10% good for society
3. 43% bad for society   12% good for society
4. 69% bad for society   4% good for society
5. 43% bad for society   9% good for society
6. 37% bad for society   21% good for society

Note: Percentages may not add up to 100% because not all possible response categories are shown. The category of Doesn't Make Much Difference, for example, was added for consideration by the author.

DISCUSSION

1. Why did you mark each trend as you did—good thing, bad thing, or doesn't make much difference?

2. What other trends do you feel should have been included in the survey? Why do you feel this way?

3. Were you surprised by any of the survey results? Why or why not?

4. Do you think the results would have changed in the current year? Why or why not?

Rate-A-Mate

PURPOSE

To discover what is important to you and others in selecting a partner. What is important to you in selecting a prospective partner? What is important for other individuals in selecting a partner? How do you think people from other cultures would respond to this survey?

INSTRUCTIONS

1. Make 3 copies of the survey. Then, take the survey individually to see what is important to you in a prospective partner.
2. Give the survey to one of your parents, or someone at least 20 years older than you.
3. As a group or individually, you may want to select individuals from other cultures or different socio-economic groups, or both.
4. If you are involved in a relationship presently, give this survey to your partner.
5. Take the survey again, but this time, circle the number as you see it relating to you. For example, give yourself a 4 if you feel your health is excellent, a 1 if you are not a good cook or housekeeper, etc.

Circle the number indicating the importance to you.

	INDISPENSABLE OR EXTREMELY IMPORTANT	VERY HIGHLY DESIRED	DESIRED, BUT NOT TERRIBLY IMPORTANT	IRRELEVANT OR UNIMPORTANT
Good health	4	3	2	1
Good cook and housekeeper	4	3	2	1
Attractiveness	4	3	2	1
Pleasing disposition	4	3	2	1
Dependable character	4	3	2	1
Emotional stability and maturity	4	3	2	1
Desire for home and children	4	3	2	1
Refinement	4	3	2	1
Good financial prospect	4	3	2	1
Similar religious background	4	3	2	1
Ambition and industriousness	4	3	2	1
Chastity—No sexual intercourse before marriage	4	3	2	1

Sociable (friendly)	4	3	2	1
Favorable social status	4	3	2	1
Mutual interests	4	3	2	1
Similar educational background	4	3	2	1
Intelligence	4	3	2	1
Complementarity	4	3	2	1

SCORING

Add up your total score. If your score is within 15 points of another individual who took the survey, there is a high probability that you will get along well. But, the important aspect to consider is that your score on each individual value is similar to the individuals who are important to you.

DISCUSSION

1. How important is it for partners to have similar values? Can a couple be compatible with many dissimilar values?

2. Are your values different from a person 20 years older than you? What are the differences? Why do you think they have different values?

3. How do your values differ with people from different cultures and different socioeconomic groups? Explain.

4. Do you think it should be important to have a partner whose score is similar to your score as you took the survey the second time (as #5 in the instructions stated)? Explain.

5. What did you learn from this experience?

Name _____ Date _____

Divorce Panel

PURPOSE

To develop an understanding of some key issues to consider when divorce involves children.

INSTRUCTIONS

1. Use class members who are from divorced families as the panel members.
2. Assume the remaining members of the class are all married with children. However, some have already filed for divorce, and some are considering divorce.
3. Therefore, what advice/wisdom from experience would the panel members give to the following questions?

QUESTIONS FOR PANEL MEMBERS

1. What general advice would you suggest for dealing with the children?

2. Should parents stay together for the kids? Why or why not?

3. Did the divorce of your parents have any impact on your personal views of marriage? If so, please explain.

4. Did the divorce have any impact on your dating relationships? If so, please explain.

5. As you think of important events in your life; weddings, for example, how will the divorce impact that event in your life?

6. Did any of you feel that you lost a parent as a result of the divorce? Why or why not?

7. Did any of you feel that you gained a parent figure as a result of a stepparent relationship? Please explain, if possible.

8. Did your relationship with your biological mother or father change as a result of having gained a stepparent?

DISCUSSION

1. What is the reaction from the class members to the Divorce Panel experience?

Why People Get Divorced—Why People Get Married

PURPOSE

- To better understand why people divorce and what it requires to choose to remain married.
- To get a better understanding of why people stay married.
- To discover if unmarried individuals perceive the reasons for divorce differently than divorced individuals.
- To discover whether unmarried, married, and divorced individuals have similar perceptions of why people stay married.

INSTRUCTIONS

1. Interview four to six people who have been divorced, 4 to 6 people who have never been married, and 4 to 6 people who are married to find out why they feel divorce generally occurs. As a group you may want to create a form for all to use with questions.
2. Ask them what they would consider the major reason (in order of importance) for the high divorce rate in this country. (Ask the divorced individuals to make this judgment based on their own experiences.)
3. Ask them what they would consider the major reasons (in order of importance) for staying married.
4. Divide into small groups or have a large class discussion.

DISCUSSION

1. Do any individuals consider unrealistic romantic expectations to be a contributing factor for getting divorced? If so, what are they?

2. Do the divorced and the never-married people respond differently? If so, how would you characterize these differences? If not, why do you think people agree on the basic causes even when they have had very different experiences?

3. What seem to be the major reasons for divorce?

4. What seem to be the major reasons for staying married?

5. What could we do to prevent the high number of divorces in our society?

6. Did the exercise stimulate your thinking about yourself, your interpersonal style, and your relation-ships to your fellow group members? Why or why not?

Developing Close Relationships

LEARNING JOURNAL

Select the statement below that best defines your feelings about the personal value or meaning gained from this chapter and respond below the dotted line.

I learned that I . . .   I was surprised that I . . .

I realized that I . . .   I was pleased that I . . .

I discovered that I . . .   I was displeased that I . . .

....

chapter 7
Resolving Interpersonal Conflict

The quality of our lives depends not on whether or not we have conflicts but how we respond to them.
—Thom Crum

Think About This...

Have you ever found yourself in one of the following situations?
- Your parents have really been yelling at you. They do not understand you, and you do not understand them.
- You and your roommate cannot seem to divide the chores equally. Is there any hope for this living arrangement?
- You and your best friend had a major argument. You left mad and hurt.
- You and your co-workers have been squabbling, and productivity is down. The boss is really angry.

Actually, the list could go on and on, but the fact is clear: when two or more people live or work closely together, for any length of time, a degree of conflict will be generated (O'Neill & Chapman, 2007). Furthermore, the greater the emotional involvement and day-to-day sharing, the greater the potential for conflict. Although it is impossible to eliminate conflict, there are ways to manage it effectively. There is hope for healthier, stronger, and more satisfying relationships.

What Is Conflict?

The word *conflict* comes from the Latin roots *com,* meaning "together," and *figere,* meaning to "strike." Common synonyms of conflict emphasize words like "struggle," "fight," "clash," and "sharp disagreements." Using these thoughts, Joyce Hocker and William Wilmot (2010) provide an interesting definition of conflict. Their idea is that **conflict** is an expressed struggle between at least two people who perceive the situation differently and are experiencing interference from the other person in achieving their goals.

> *Everything that irritates us about others can lead us to an understanding of ourselves.*
> —CARL JUNG

What Causes Conflict?

Conflicts occur between people because people are different, think differently, and have different needs and wants. In fact, social psychologist Morton Deutsch (Deutsch et al., 2006) believes that conflicts usually involve any of six basic types of issues: 1) control over resources, 2) preferences and nuisances, 3) values, 4) beliefs, 5) goals, and 6) the nature of the relationship between the partners.

Perhaps the key word is *differentness,* because this is what causes conflict in human relationships. Differentness is a reality to reckon with, and the reality is that people enter relationships with differences in socioeconomic and cultural backgrounds, sex-role expectations, levels of self-esteem, ability to tolerate stress, tastes and preferences, beliefs and values, interests, social and family networks, and capacity to change and grow. And, add to these differences that many people are deficient in communication and conflict resolution skills and frequently have misunderstood styles of conflict management (Tannen, 2001). Therefore, it is easy to understand why *differentness* leads to disagreement and conflict.

Becoming *Aware*

The Realities of Conflict

Even though conflict is inevitable, it can have positive as well as negative effects. Thomas Gordon, noted author and psychologist, explains this clearly:

> A conflict is the moment of truth in a relationship—a test of its health, a crisis that can weaken or strengthen it, a critical event that may bring lasting resentment, smoldering hostility, psychological scars. Conflicts can push people away from each other or pull them into a closer and more intimate union; they contain the seeds of destruction and the seeds of greater unity; they may bring about armed warfare or deeper mutual understanding (2000).

In our society, conflict is often viewed negatively: It is "bad" to show anger, to disagree, or to fight. Some people look at conflict as something to avoid at all costs; but conflict is not necessarily bad—it exists as a reality of any relationship. It would truly be a rare relationship if over a period of time one person's needs did not conflict with the other's needs. In school and in the workplace clashes can happen. Since conflict is inevitable, coping with confrontations is one of the most critical of social skills. It's not the degree of conflict that sinks relationships, but the ways people resolve it. We must remember that conflict needs to be viewed from a problem-solving perspective. Often, solutions bring about change, and changes in a relationship should not be feared. Human relationships are dynamic, and reflect the changes that accompany personal growth. Disagreements, if handled well, can help people know themselves better, improve language skills, gain valuable information, and cement their relationships (Marano, 2000).

Constructive ways for resolving conflict will be discussed later in the chapter.

We will now discuss in more detail three common benefits of constructive conflict resolution (Dubrin, 2016).

> *A quarrel between friends, when made up, adds a new tie to friendship, as experience shows that the callosity formed round a broken bone makes it stronger than before.*
> —ST. FRANCIS DE SALES

POSITIVE EFFECTS OF CONFLICT

Promotes growth in a relationship. People who work through their conflicts can develop a stronger and more intimate relationship. They take the time to learn about each other's needs and how they can be satisfied. They take the time to clarify their feelings. They take the time to share, and in so doing, realize that dealing with problems can be an opportunity to know each other better.

Allows for healthy release of feelings. When conflicts are resolved in constructive ways, both parties are able to air their feelings and leave the situation free of anger and hostility. For example, in a family conflict, unresolved anger and hostility can affect a person's performance at work or school. Likewise, unresolved anger and hostility in a work-related conflict is frequently brought home, and may interfere with family and even social relationships. Talking things out and sharing what is going on are marvelous ways to relieve tension and anxiety (Weiten et al., 2014, Weiten, 2017).

Increases motivation and self-esteem. When a personal conflict is resolved constructively, both parties tend to feel stronger and more motivated to tackle other struggles and difficult aspects of life. There is a real sense of pride and freedom when joining others and showing respect for personal rights and the rights of others. As a result, self-esteem is enhanced, and we are more motivated to take other interpersonal risks.

Conflicts can be turned into creative opportunities for more positive relationships.

D.W. Johnson found that research shows that, a conflict positive person, you can be enriched:

First, conflicts can focus attention on problems that need to be solved.

Second, conflicts generate the energy, focus, and motivation needed to solve the problems.

Third, conflicts stimulate curiosity, interest, and a search for information.

Fourth, conflicts facilitate the understanding of other people's perspectives on the problems.

Fifth, conflicts can clarify your identify (who you are and what you stand for), what you care about and are committed to, and values.

Sixth, conflicts provide an arena for the full and active use of your skills and abilities, allowing you to test yourself and assess your abilities.

Not everything that is faced can be changed, but nothing can be changed until it is faced.
—JAMES BALDWIN

Seventh, conflicts may promote cognitive, social, moral and even physical development. Conflicts can stimulate change and growth. It is through conflicts, for example, that dysfunctional patterns of behavior that need to be changed can be identified.

Eighth, conflicts can release anger, anxiety, insecurity, and sadness that, if kept inside, make us mentally and physically sick.

Ninth, conflicts may keep our relationships clear of irritations and resentments and strengthen our confidence that we and our friends can resolve conflicts constructively (Johnson, 2015).

NEGATIVE EFFECTS OF CONFLICT

How we view conflicts and how we manage them can cause destructive outcomes. DeCenzo and Silhanek (2002) outline two negative effects:

The manner in which we approach interpersonal conflict. People generally view conflict with a belief that there must be a winner and a loser. It is human nature to want to win, just like it is human nature to not want to lose. When people approach a conflict situation with attitudes of winning and losing, the issues often take second place to the personal motivation to "win." The net result is often one of disaster.

Larger problems and deeper personal resentments may occur. Just because we avoid a conflict or fail to resolve a conflict does not mean the conflict is forever gone. It is likely to return again with much greater intensity. We may be less willing to cooperate if we have leftover anger or "bad" feelings from a previous confrontation. Failure to deal with conflict constructively can even "rob" us of a potentially satisfying relationship.

So far, we have been discussing the positive and negative realities of conflict. The question now is: when faced with a conflict, how do we handle it?

What Is Your Style of Conflict Management?

How did your parents manage conflicts?

You are probably thinking that your style of conflict management depends on the conflict and who is involved. Although that is probably true, most people develop a characteristic style of managing conflicts. This style emerges from our unique personality traits, as well as from what we learned growing up.

© 4 PM production/Shutterstock.com

Think for a moment about how your parents managed conflicts. If your mother cried, sulked, or avoided confrontations, you may find yourself imitating her behavior. If your father yelled, intimidated, and dominated others with his anger, you may see some of these traits in your own pattern of conflict management. The question then is: How is your style of conflict management like and unlike those of your parents?

Actually, most of us go through life responding to conflict in a natural way that feels good to us. We may be unaware of our particular style and of even what methods we use to resolve interpersonal conflict. We may continue to use our approach whether it is appropriate or not.

Before we discuss different styles of responding to conflict, it might be beneficial to identify some rights that each person has in interpersonal interactions, whether conflictual or not. Based on the writings of Smith (2000), and Davis et al. (2008), the "Consider This" below lists a sample of these Basic Human Rights.

CONSIDER THIS

BASIC HUMAN RIGHTS

1. The right to say no to a request without feeling guilty
2. The right not to give people reasons for every action you take
3. The right to ask other people to listen to your point of view
4. The right to ask others to correct errors they made that affect you
5. The right to change your mind
6. The right to ask other people to compromise rather than get only what they want
7. The right to ask others to do things for you
8. The right to persist in making a request if people will not respond the first time
9. The right to be alone if you wish
10. The right to maintain your dignity in relationships
11. The right to evaluate your own behavior and not just listen to evaluations that others offer
12. The right to make mistakes and accept responsibility for them
13. The right to avoid manipulation by other people
14. The right to have and express your own feelings and opinions
15. The right to get what you pay for
16. The right to ask for information from professionals
17. The right to choose not to assert yourself
18. The right to set your own priorities
19. The right to be *successful*
20. The right to be treated with respect

Smith (2000); Davis et al. (2008).

Now that you know some rights that each person has in interpersonal interactions, what would your answers be to these questions: Is it difficult for you to make your wishes known to others? Are you sometimes pushed around by others because of your own inability to stand up for yourself? Do you ever push others to get what you want? Do you speak your thoughts and feelings in a clear, direct manner, without judging or dictating to others? Can you recognize your idea of "successful" may be very different from the other person's? The answers to these questions characterize your behavior style in responding to conflict.

Cellphones have become ubiquitous, in part because they are a great way to keep in touch with others. But they've also turned into a source of strain in our relationships.

A common complaint among relationship partners is that they're being ignored by a partner who can't tear themselves away from their cellphone. We often shake our heads in disapproval when we're dining out and see a couple at the next table more interested in their phones than each other. The term *phubbing* (for phone snubbing) has been used to describe the act of interrupting or ignoring an in-person conversation in order to attend to one's phone, and several studies have shown that phubbing is a fairly common behavior among couples (McDaniel & Coyne 2014).

There is good reason to believe that cellphone interruptions could make partners feel disconnected and less present in interactions with one another. Recently, James Roberts and Meredith David at Baylor University designed a scale to measure how often people phub their romantic partners, in the process coining the term Pphubbing ("partner phubbing") (Roberts & David, 2016). The scale asks people to rate how much they agree with nine statements, including "My partner keeps his or her cellphone in their hand when he or she is with me" and "My partner glances at his/her cellphone when talking to me."

In one study, 308 adults completed an online survey containing the Pphubbing scale, as well as measures of cellphone-related conflict and relationship satisfaction. In a second study, 145 adults completed the same measures, plus a measure of attachment anxiety. See the following links:

https://www.psychologytoday.com/us/blog/compassion-matters/201307/how-your-attachment-style-impacts-your-relationship

https://www.psychologytoday.com/us/blog/compassion-matters/201307/how-your-attachment-style-impacts-your-relationship

Two elements underlie romantic attachment: abandonment anxiety (fears that your partner doesn't love you and will leave you) and intimacy avoidance (avoiding closeness with others). These represent two different elements of insecure attachment that may or may not co-exist in the same person. Both of these factors were measured by the researchers, but abandonment anxiety was the trait the researchers expected to play a role in reactions to phubbing.

In both studies, high levels of phubbing were associated with less satisfying relationships and more cellphone-related conflict.

It is likely the case that phubbing is both a cause and a consequence of unsatisfying relationships. The next time you catch yourself glancing at your phone when you're with your partner, ask yourself why: Are you bored or angry with your partner? If so, you should figure out why you're feeling that way, and work on improving the relationship and your communication with your partner—or consider ending it if things are really going poorly. Or are you just being carelessly distracted by the beeping, flashing urgency of the phone? If that's the case, you should keep it out of sight and focus on your partner. They probably need your attention more than whoever just posted a status update.

Behavior Styles

Now, we will return to our earlier question: How do we respond to conflict? Elizabeth Scott (2019), an authority on conflict resolution and communication skills, has indicated that poor communication can weaken bonds, creating mistrust and even contempt. George Bach (1989) felt that dirty fighting techniques can weaken relationships and cause much pain, resentment, and hostility.

In *The Beauty of Conflict for Couples*, from Mango Media, C. Campbell & S. Clarke discuss a 5-5-5 method that is simple, according to Clarke. When a disagreement comes up, each partner will take 5 minutes to speak while the other simply listens, and then they use the final five minutes to talk it through.

"My job is to just listen, and then she'll listen and I'll talk for 5 minutes, and then we dialogue about it for the last five minutes," Clarke says. "And it's important to keep it a 5-5-5, not a 5-5-45." Campbell says the beauty of 5-5-5 is that it only takes 15 minutes, and gives each partner the opportunity to say how they feel, and then discuss it without the conflict spiraling out of control.

"You'll be solving a whole different problem," she says, "because you're solving more around the core values or what's out of alignment versus you're just not the person for me."

Couples who are not used to talking through conflict this way may have a rough time getting started. To make it easier in the beginning, Clarke and Campbell recommend beginning with only three minutes each (3-3-3), and then building the discussion to 5-5-5 as you get more comfortable. During your 5-5-5, do not interrupt your partner. Often, when we interrupt, it's because our partner is saying something that makes us uncomfortable. In these situations, the interrupting partner will usually interject with apologies or solutions, but they are really trying to "manage the tension instead of just listening," says Clarke. She says you need to fight through your own discomfort and allow your partner to say what they need to say (Clarke & Campbell, 2019).

While you are doing this, note whether you are assertive, nonassertive (passive), or aggressive in your response to the conflict.

There are basically **three behavior styles** we use in handling opposition and responding to conflict. These have been classified as *passive* (also known as nonassertive), *aggressive*, and *assertive*.

Assertive behavior style is the most positive of the styles for many reasons (Scott 2016). We will discuss the behaviors, belief systems, advantages, disadvantages, and when it might be appropriate to use each style.

Becoming Aware of Conflict: Use It, Don't Defuse It
https://www.youtube.com/watch?v=o97fVGTjE4w

Authors CrisMarie Campbell and Susan Clarke share about their journey with finding the beauty in conflict, and why getting past being polite was so powerful for their relationship.

MISTAKES TO AVOID

Elizabeth Scott (2019) believes that communication is the best way to avoid conflict. This is her list of mistakes to avoid by dealing with issues as they occur.

1. **Avoid Conflict Altogether.** Rather than discussing building frustrations in a calm, respectful manner, some people just don't say anything to their partner until they're ready to explode, and then blurt their frustrations out in an angry, hurtful way.

2. **Being Defensive-often the result of seeing the disagreement as a personal attack.** Denying responsibility may seem to alleviate stress in the short run, but it creates long-term problems when partners don't feel listened to and unresolved conflicts continue to grow.

3. **Overgeneralizing.** Avoid starting sentences with "You always" and "You never," as in, "You always come home late!" or "You never do what I want to do!" Stop and think about whether or not this is really true.

4. **Being Right.** It's damaging to decide that there's a "right" way to look at things and a "wrong" way to look at things, and that your way or anyone's way of seeing things is right.

5. **Mind-Reading or "Psychoanalyzing" (making assumptions about anyone else's viewpoint).** This creates hostility and misunderstandings. It's important to keep in mind that we all come from a unique perspective and work hard to assume nothing; really listen to the other person and let them explain where they are coming from.

6. **Forgetting to Listen.** Never underestimate the importance of really listening and empathizing with the other person. These listening skills are important to bear in mind.

7. **Playing the Blame Game.** Some people handle conflict by criticizing and blaming. When you blame someone else, you have put yourself in the role of the victim and see yourself as helpless. But if you take responsibility, you become empowered to change whatever is not working. Owning the problem and being willing to look at your part in it doesn't mean you need to spend time blaming yourself; it's rarely helpful and it's a waste of your energy. Instead, try to view conflict as an opportunity to analyze the situation objectively, assess the needs of both parties, and come up with a solution that helps you both.

8. **Trying to "Win" the Argument.** The goal of a relationship discussion should be mutual understanding and coming to an agreement or resolution that respects everyone's needs.

9. **Making Character Attacks.** Sometimes people take any negative action from a partner and blow it up into a personality flaw. Remember to respect the person, even if you don't like the behavior.

10. **Stonewalling.** When one partner wants to discuss troubling issues in the relationship, sometimes people defensively stonewall, or refuse to talk or listen to their partner. This is an indication that the person feels attacked or defensive. If you are told you are a "stonewall," examine yourself about this. If someone really needs to "win" or be "right," the conflict is really about something else.

Passive/Nonassertive Style of Conflict Resolution

We may respond to conflict situations by **avoidance**. That is, we may remove ourselves from the situation by leaving, shutting up, placating, concealing our feelings, or postponing a confrontation until a better time (Hocker & Wilmot, 2010).

Behavior description: When we behave passively, sometimes referred to as *submissively*, we are usually emotionally dishonest, indirect, and self-denying. We are likely to listen to what has been said and respond very little. Because we do not express our honest feelings, needs, values, and concerns, we actually allow others to violate our space, deny our rights, and ignore our needs. More importantly, we actually demonstrate a lack of respect for our own needs and rights.

Belief system: The message of a passive/nonassertive person is, "I should never make anyone uncomfortable or displeased except myself. I'll put up with just about anything from you; my needs and my feelings don't matter, and you can take advantage of me."

Advantage: They usually do not experience direct rejection or get blamed for anything. Others may view them as nice, selfless, and easy to get along with. This approval from others is extremely important to them.

Disadvantage: They are taken advantage of and may *store up a heavy load of resentment and anger*. They do not get their needs met and other people do not know what they want or need. Consequently, passive people lack deep and enduring friendships. They frequently lose the love and respect of the people they were busy making sacrifices for.

Aggressive Style of Conflict Resolution

We may respond to conflicting situations by *fighting*. That is, we **move against** another with the intent to hurt or control them, personally or professionally. In his book *Human Aggression*, Green (2001) refers to the aggressive style as **domination**.

Behavior description: We may literally or verbally attack another person. Typical examples of aggressive behavior can be verbal abuse, physical fighting, blaming, accusing, threatening, and generally stepping on people without regard for their feelings, needs, or ideas. We may be loud, abusive, rude, and sarcastic. We are in this world to intimidate and to overpower other people.

Belief system: The inner message of an aggressive person is, "I have to put others down in order to protect myself; I must exert my power and control over others. This is what I want; what you want is of lesser importance or of no importance at all." Often, others see aggressive people as controlling, hostile, unfriendly, or meanspirited. These responses tend to reinforce the aggressive person's inner monologue of fear.

Advantage: Other people do not push the aggressive person around, so they seem to wind up getting what they want. They tend to be able to protect themselves and their own space. They *appear* to be in control of their own life and even the lives of others.

Disadvantage: In the process of their gaining control, the other person in the interaction frequently feels humiliated, defensive, resentful, and usually hurt. Others do not want to be around aggressive people, and they wind up with an accumulation of enemies. This causes them to become more vulnerable and fearful of losing what they are fighting for: power and control over others. In the worst case, one aggressive person meets another. Therefore, they may create their own destruction.

WORDS AND PHRASES THAT ARE TRANSPHOBIC, AND WHY

Transphobia is the fear of hatred of transgender people or people who do not meet society's gender role expectations. Transphobia is closely linked to homophobia and biphobia.

Calling someone "It or "He/She" is demeaning, and does not validate their identity or respect them as a person.
"What are you really? Have you had sex change surgery? If not, then you are not really a man/woman."
Asking anyone personal questions about their bodies and surgeries is invasive and inappropriate. We don't ask non-transgender (cisgender) people what is under their clothes; nor should we ask trans people.

What does a man or woman really look like?
There is no one way to look like a man or a woman. It should also not be assumed that all transmen want or have to strive to be masculine, or that transwomen should be feminine. Gender presentation is fluid, and we should support all the ways people choose to present their gender.

"Why would you transition if you are going to be gay?"
Gender identity and sexual orientation are two separate aspects of one's identity. This question demonstrates how heterosexual identity is more valued in our society, and reinforces homophobia and heterosexism.

It is important to honor everyone's gender identity and not question their validity.

For more information, contact the UC Davis LGBT Resource Center: 530-752-2452

Assertive Style of Conflict Resolution

We may respond to conflicting situations by *moving toward*. That is, we move toward our opposition until we are either closer together or on the same side. In *Changeable: How Collaborative Problem Solving Changes Lives at Home, at School, and at Work* by J. Stuart Ablon (2018), the author indicates this style is used in **cooperative (collaborative) problem solving**, with some negotiation and compromise along the way.

Behavior description: We behave assertively when we stand up for ourselves, express our true feelings, and do not let others take advantage of us; in addition, we also consider others' feelings. Actually, assertion is a manner of acting and reacting in an appropriately honest manner that is direct, self-respecting, self-expressing, and straightforward. We defend our rights and personal space without abusing or dominating other people. Joseph Telushkin, in the revised edition of his powerful book *Words That Hurt, Words That Heal*, expresses these thoughts:

> In a dispute with someone, you have the right to state your case, express your opinion, explain why you think the other party is wrong, even make clear how passionately you feel about the subject at hand. But these are the only rights you have. You do not have a moral right to undercut your adversary's position by invalidating him or her personally. It is unethical to dredge up past information about the person—information with which you're most likely familiar because of your formerly close association—and use it against that person (2019).

Belief system: The message of the assertive person is, "I respect myself, and I have equal respect for others, too. I am not in this world to conform to others' expectations of me, and likewise, they are not in this world to conform to my expectations."

The Great Dishwashing Controversy

Two roommates had a problem: One of them (A) often left dirty dishes in the sink rather than cleaning them up at once. This infuriated B, who felt disrespected. For a long time, B suffered in silence.

Eventually, however, B confronted A. B was astounded when A stoutly maintained that it was B's refusal to let A do the dishes on A's own schedule that was rude and disrespectful.

Now that A and B were talking, however, they discovered they both had unstated beliefs about when dishes should be done—beliefs they had simply assumed the other person knew and had chosen to ignore. They were finally able to work out a compromise, though, when they realized that expectations are useless (and even detrimental) until you communicate them.

SITUATION	ASSERTIVE	AGGRESSIVE	NONASSERTIVE
In conflict situations	Communicates directly	Dominates	Avoids the conflict
In decision-making situations	Chooses for self	Chooses for self and others	Allows others to choose
In situations expressing feelings	Is open, direct, honest, while allowing others to express their feelings	Expresses feelings in a threatening manner; puts down, inhibits others	Holds true feelings inside
In group meeting situations	Uses direct, clear "I" statements: "I believe that . . ."	Uses clear but demeaning "you" statements: "You should have known better . . ."	Uses indirect unclear statements: "Would you mind if ...?"

Adapted from Reece & Brandt (2017).

Advantage: They generally get more of what they want without making other people mad. They do not have to feel wrong or guilty because they vented their feelings—they left the door to communication open. Consequently, effective confrontation is mutually acceptable. From this, they develop more fulfilling relationships. Also, because they exercise the power of choice over their actions, they are in a much better position to feel good about themselves. In *Asserting Yourself,* Sharon and Gordon Bower (2004) remind readers: "The extent to which you assert yourself determines the degree of your confidence and self-esteem."

Disadvantage: As they become more open, honest, and direct, they also take some real risks in how others will perceive them. Some people have difficulty with these kinds of exchanges; therefore, they may experience some hurts and disappointments in some of their relationships.

Now that we have discussed the three styles, it might be helpful to note the behaviors exhibited by the three styles in various situations. Table 7.1 lists these behaviors. Then, we will look at the three styles in action. The *passive/nonassertive, aggressive,* and *assertive* styles are illustrated in the following examples of a woman who wants help with the house.

> *Sarcasm is dirty fighting.*
> —GEORGE BACH

The Styles in Action

Passive/nonassertive style:

> **Margret:** Excuse me, but would you be a sweetie and pick up your clothes in the bathroom?
>
> **Charles:** I'm reading the paper.
>
> **Margret:** Oh, well, all right.

> *Cutting comments create hostility.*
> —HAIM GINOTT

Analysis: The statement "Oh, well, all right" only rewards Charles for postponing Margret's request. Margret certainly does not get what she wants. She probably feels sorry for herself and may pay him back by giving him the "silent treatment" over dinner.

Aggressive style:

Margret: I've got another thing to tell you. I've had it with picking up after you and trying to keep this house straight. You either pitch in or help me, or I'm quitting this nonsense.

Charles: Now, calm down, I'm reading the paper.

Margret: Did your mother just "wait" on you and treat you like a king? You don't give a flip about anything around this house, as long as you get to read the daily news whenever you want.

Charles: Now, don't start in on me about my mother.

Margret: All you do is come home and relax in the easy chair and grab the paper.

Charles: Shut up! What's wrong with you?

Analysis: The opening statement is an attack, and Margret "relives" hostilities of earlier annoyances. Interactions such as this clearly have no winner, because aggressive behavior hurts another person, creates resentment, and guarantees resistance to change.

Assertive style:

Margret: I would like for you to pick up your clothes in the bathroom.

Charles: I'm reading the paper.

Margret: I am doing a load of clothes. If you want your clothes washed with this load, you need to get them in now.

Charles: I'm almost finished with the sports section.

Margret: Well, I can start the wash. Will you help me when you are through reading the sports section?

Charles: Sure!

Analysis: Assertive behavior's first goal is to address an interpersonal problem. Assertive requests include a specific goal and the willingness to negotiate a mutually agreeable plan to solve the problem. Assertive behavior does not have hurting others or controlling others as a goal.

It would be unreasonable to expect people to use assertive behavior exclusively. There are times when it is wise to be passive and just give in to others; there are times when it is necessary to aggressively defend our rights; there are times when being assertive does not succeed in obtaining its goal.

Jay Heinrichs (2013) asserts that whether we believe it or not, arguments surround us and play with our emotions, change our decisions, and are attitude changers.

We do not have to always win, and being assertive lets us get our way more often than not without arguing and hurting others.

Learning to Be Assertive

The main goal of assertiveness training is to help people express their thoughts, feelings, and rights in a way that respects those of others. An assertive person uses negotiation to smooth the way through life without imposing on others or allowing them to impose on themselves. Becoming assertive is not about taking over and insisting you have what you want.

It's about resisting being controlled or to be put down, or our self-confidence being shaky. Assertiveness skills are particularly useful to help us reassess our self-image and raise our self-esteem. It is clear, calm, frank communications as a means of establishing relationships in which everybody knows where they stand and no one feels ill used.

As we learn to do this, it is important that we become aware of the different types of assertive expressions (Hayman, 2014; Atwater & Duffy, 2013).

Basic assertion is learning to stand up for our rights or express our feelings, such as saying, "Pardon me, I'd like to finish what I was saying."

A useful formula to use is to say:

When… Describe the situation or behavior that is troubling you.

Next, **I feel …** Say how it makes you feel, and what it is about the situation or behavior that upset you.

Explain what you would like to be different: "What I would like …"

Another type of assertiveness is *learning to express positive feelings*, such as, "I really liked the way you cleaned the car." Do you have difficulty in giving compliments, as well as receiving them? Some people do.

We may have to use an *escalating type of assertion when people fail to respond to your earlier request*. An example here would be, "This is the third time I'm going to tell you. I don't want to change insurance companies."

In communication studies, the broken-record response is the conversational strategy of forestalling further discussion by repeating the same phrase or sentence over and over. Depending on the circumstances, the broken-record response may be a negative politeness strategy or a comparatively tactful way of avoiding an argument or a power struggle.

> *I'm going to let what you just said season a bit before responding.*
> —KATHLEEN REARDON

"With the broken-record technique," says Suzie Hayman in *Be More Assertive*, "it is important to use some of the same words over and over again in different sentences. This reinforces the main part of your message and prevents others raising red herrings or diverting you from your central message" (Hayman, 2014).

Then, there are occasions when we need to express *negative feelings*. The *"I" message*, frequently referred to as the focal point of learning to be assertive, is a way of expressing ourselves effectively before we become angry and act in self-defeating ways.

Probably the most important strategy we need to learn to become assertive is to use "**I**" statements. We make **you** statements for several reasons...

- "How could **you** do to that to me?"
- "**You** make me so angry!"
- **You** statements often let **you** off the hook. (Hayman 2014)

The "I" message. According to Thomas Gordon (2000), an "I" message has four parts: 1) an objective, nonjudgmental description of the person's behavior in specific terms, 2) how I feel about this, 3) the concrete effects on me, and 4) a request and an invitation to respond. Let us look at each part.

1. **An objective, nonjudgmental description of the person's behavior in specific terms.** There are four guidelines to help you deliver an effective behavior description.

   First, describe the person's behavior in specific terms, rather than fuzzy, unclear words. For example,

Specific	Fuzzy
When you frequently call after 11 o'clock at night . . .	When you frequently call me late at night . . .

   The person you are angry with may have a different idea of what *late* means. Therefore, if you want your needs to be met, you will need to give the exact time you consider too late to receive a phone call.

   Second, keep your thoughts and perceptions about the other person's possible motives, attitudes, character, and so on to yourself. It is human nature to describe another person's behavior by stating what you think the other person intended. This causes defensiveness, whereas describing what a person actually did creates an atmosphere for further communication.

   Third, make your behavior description an objective statement, rather than a judgment. Assertion messages avoid character assassinations, blame, sarcasm, and profanity.
   Fourth, behavioral descriptions should be as brief as possible. The longer your message is, the more likely you will not be heard and understood. Also, there are fewer tendencies for others to judge and evaluate when you keep your message simple. One sentence is ample.

2. **How I feel about this.** Once you have identified what your feelings are, you must take the responsibility for your own feelings. This means you say about the issue "I feel angry or disappointed," rather than "You made me feel angry or disappointed." Continuing with the late-night calls as an example, we now have the following:

When you call me after 11:00 o'clock at night, I feel angry.

3. **The concrete effects on me.** People may not be aware of how their behavior is affecting you. In most instances, they are not deliberately trying to annoy or frustrate you. Once they become aware of how their behavior affects you, they are usually more considerate. Our example now becomes:

When you call me after 11:00 o'clock at night, I feel angry, because I am awakened by your calls at least twice a week.

4. **A request and an invitation to respond.** Simply stated, this means that you use "I" messages and tell others what behavior you would like for them to substitute the next time a similar exchange occurs. Be sure to express your request in one or two simple sentences. It is important to be firm, specific, and kind. Then, give the person an invitation to respond to your request. Also, where possible, give a positive response for the agreement. Some examples might be: "We'll have more time together . . ."; "We'll have a neater house . . ."; "We'll save money . . ."; "I'll be able to get my work in on time . . ."; "I'll be less tired and more fun to be with . . ."; and so on. Our example now looks like this:

When you call me after 11:00 o'clock at night, I feel angry, because I am awakened by your calls at least twice a week. I'd like you to call before 10:00 o'clock, except in an emergency. Will you agree to that? Then, we can have a much more pleasant conversation.

To be sure that you understand each part of the "I" message, review the examples in Table 7.2. **You will notice that these "I" messages do not attack or blame the other person.**

Suggestions for Delivering an Assertive "I" Message

Alberti and Emmons (2008) offer three suggestions for improving the success of assertive "I" messages.

Write and practice your message before delivering it. This will give you an opportunity to review two important questions: 1) Is it likely to arouse defensiveness in the other person? 2) Are you likely to get your needs met with this assertion?

Table 7.2 **EXAMPLES OF "I" MESSAGES**

NONJUDGMENTAL DESCRIPTION OF PERSON'S BEHAVIOR	MY FEELINGS ABOUT IT	CONCRETE EFFECTS ON ME	A REQUEST AND AN INVITATION TO RESPOND
1. When you call me after 11:00 o'clock at night . . .	I feel angry . . .	because I am awakened by your calls at least twice a week.	I would like you to call before 10:00 o'clock, except in an emergency. Will you agree to that? If so . . .
2. When you are late picking me up from work. . .	I feel frustrated . . .	because I waste a lot of time waiting for you.	I would like to be picked up on time. Will you agree? If so . . .
3. When you do not put your dirty clothes in the hamper . . .	I feel irritated . . .	because it makes extra work for me when I do the wash.	I would like you to put your dirty clothes in the hamper each day. Will you agree to that? Then . . .
4. When you borrow my car and bring it home on "empty" . . .	I feel annoyed . . .	because I have to get gas before I can go to work.	I would like you to refill the tank with as much gas as you use. Will you? If so . . .

Remember: You can arrange the four parts of the "I" message in a way that is natural and fits your personal style. For example, *I feel irritated when you do not put your dirty clothes in the hamper because it makes extra work for me when I do the wash. I would like you to put your dirty clothes in the hamper each day. Will you agree to that? Then, we will have more time together.*

Develop assertive body language with your "I" message. In order to assure that your verbal message is congruent with your nonverbal behavior, you will need to (review Chapter Five for more details):

- Maintain direct eye contact
- Maintain an erect body posture
- Speak clearly, firmly, and with sufficient volume to be heard
- Emphasize your message with appropriate gestures and facial expressions
- Do not whine or have an apologetic tone to your voice

> *Peace cannot be kept by force. It can only be achieved by understanding.*
> —ALBERT EINSTEIN

Don't be sidetracked by the defensiveness or manipulation of others. This can be accomplished by calmly repeating your point without getting sidetracked by irrelevant issues. Some examples might be:

- Yes, but . . .;
- Yes, I know, but my point is . . .;
- I agree, but . . .;
- Yes, but I was saying . . .;
- Right, but I'm still not interested.

Remember, persistence is one of the keys to effective assertion. One of the main reasons why people do not get their needs met when they assert is because they give up or give in after the first defensive or manipulative response of the other person (Communication Research Associates, 2012).

How to Say No without Feeling Guilty

There is a rampant myth in our culture that to be considered nice, we have to say *yes* all the time. Perhaps we don't want to hurt someone's feelings or we don't want another person to be upset with us. When we keep saying *yes*, resentment and anger build. It is possible to develop the skills to say *no* with confidence, kindness, and peace of mind. And, we can have more time, more space, more efficiency, and control over our lives. In *How to Say No without Feeling Guilty: And Say Yes to More Time, More Joy, and What Matters Most to You*, Patti Breitman et al. (2001) give these pointers:

- **Start small.** Practice saying *no* in nonthreatening encounters, where little is at stake and success is almost assured.
  Examples: Tell your best friend you don't want to go to her favorite restaurant . . . then suggest another. Tell your son he can't have more ice cream before bedtime.
- **Keep it simple.** The most effective *"nos"* are the least complicated. The more details you supply, the more likely the other person will try to change your mind. Furthermore, if you supply too many details, the other person may feel your "excuse" isn't good enough.
  Examples: Say *no* to requests for money in simple language, without offering a reason—"I wish I could, but I can't." Say *no* to someone who wants to change shifts with you by simply saying, "I have plans."
- **Buy time** when responding to requests. It relieves pressure when you're not sure how to say *no* diplomatically, or simply need more time to make a decision.
  Examples: "I'll check my calendar and get back to you." "Let me ask my wife, husband, friend, etc., about their plans for that day."
- **Remain generous.** Saying *no* without guilt is much easier when it is done in the context of generosity. This means being helpful and available to family, friends, and co-workers whenever you can—as long as it doesn't cause you significant stress or inconvenience.
  Examples: "I'm sorry I can't go shopping with you this weekend. Give me a call again." "I can't help you with the fundraiser this time, but perhaps I can next time."
- **Understand your *Yes*.** You will feel most confident saying *no* if you have a strong vision of what to say *yes* to. Why are you saying *no* to a particular request? What obligation or priority are you trying to make room for?

Remember, once we stop investing the better part of ourselves doing things we don't want to do or being with people we don't want to see, we can focus our actions on our core beliefs, priorities, and passions. Margo Maine (2005), co-author of *The Body Myth*, has a thought-provoking comment: *I finally found a way to be nice: by saying yes—to myself.* Remember, *No* is a complete sentence. And, saying *no* is a powerful form of assertive behavior.

So far, we have discussed the passive, aggressive, and assertive behavior styles used in interpersonal conflict. Added to these different behavior styles are two powerful variables that affect the way people manage conflict: gender and culture. We will now discuss each of these factors.

Gender and Conflict Management

A look at the entire body of research on gender and conflict suggests that the differences in how the two sexes handle conflict are actually rather small. Although men and women may have characteristically different conflict styles, the individual style of each communicator—regardless of gender—and the nature of the relationship are more important than gender in shaping the way he or she handles conflict (Adler & Proctor, 2014).

You will recall that in Chapter Five, we discussed the different communication styles that men and women use. We indicated that males are likely to speak and understand a language of "status and independence," while females are likely to speak and understand a language of "connection and intimacy." These different communication styles obviously lead to different approaches in dealing with conflict.

Gender differences. Actually, these differences can be seen in childhood. For example, males are more likely to be aggressive, demanding, and competitive, while females are more cooperative. Boys try to get their way by ordering each other around. In contrast, girls like to make proposals for action: "Let's go ask her" or "What do you think?"

Male children make light of aggressive demands and are competitive, while females are more cooperative as children from preschool through early adolescence. In later years, adolescent men are described as being concerned with power and more interested in content than relational issues. Teenage boys often engage in verbal showdowns, and many engage in physical fights. Adolescent girls also use aggression and conflicts, but their methods are usually more indirect than boys'.

Teenage girls more often use gossip, backbiting, and social inclusion to fight.

Phrases that people use to describe male conflict include "men don't worry about feelings"; they think men are more direct. Phrases used about women's conflict styles include: "women are better listeners," "women try to solve problems without controlling the other person," and "females are more concerned with others' feelings" (Weitan et al., 2014). Deborah Tannen (2001) views this difference in childhood language as reflecting the different social structures of girls and boys, and women and men.

> *We meet naturally on the basis of our sameness and grow on the basis of our differentness.*
> —VIRGINIA SATIR

Gender differences start at a young age—females tend to be more cooperative.

© Johnstocker Production/Shutterstock.com

In the hierarchical order that boys and men find or feel themselves in, status is indeed gained by telling others what to do and resisting being told what to do. But girls and women find or feel themselves in a community that is threatened by conflict, so they formulate requests as proposals rather than orders, to make it easy for others to express other preferences without provoking a confrontation. If a man struggles to be strong, a woman struggles to keep the community strong.

GENDER AND YOU

WHO MAKES THE DECISIONS AT HOME?

- Of the 1,260 individuals surveyed in 2008—either married or living together—women wielded more decision-making power at home.
- In 43% of the couples, women made more decisions—almost twice as many as men—in the four areas Pew surveyed: planning weekend activities, household finances, major home purchases, and TV watching.
- The survey also found that 43% of men don't have the final say in any of those decisions; they either share the decision making or defer to their partners.
- As for household finances, the Pew study found that couples disagree on who has the greater influence. About 45% of women surveyed said they manage the family's money; 37% of the men say they manage it.
- Older couples are more likely than younger couples to make a decision together, the study found. More than a third of those 65 or older said they share in the decision making in at least three or four areas.

Pew Research Center (2008).

These differences often persist into adulthood. M. J. Collier's (1991) survey of college students revealed that, regardless of cultural background, men and women view conflicts in contrasting ways. From this study, female students described men as being concerned with power and more interested in content than relational issues. By contrast, women were described as being more concerned with maintaining the relationship during a conflict. Do you agree or disagree with what the college students said?

Benjamin Seider (2010), conducted did a laboratory study of 154 couples and noted that couples who use the pronoun *we* behave in more positive ways during disagreements. Couples who regularly talk about their conflicts by saying *we*, *our*, and *us* show more affection and less anger during arguments. Couples who tend to use pronouns that express separateness—such as *I*, *you*, and *me*—have lower levels of marital satisfaction. Using the word *we* during arguments may help couples align themselves on the same team or it may indicate a healthier relationship.

> *We find comfort among those who agree with us—growth among those who don't.*
> —FRANK CLARK

Learning flexibility. Tannen (2001) suggests that when one's habitual style is not working, trying harder by doing more of the same will not solve problems. She advises men and women to adopt some flexibility in their styles. For example, women who avoid conflict at all costs would be better off if they learned that a little conflict can be healthy, and men who habitually take oppositional stances would be better off if they broke their addiction to conflict. After all, people are different, not only in gender but in cultural background. Therefore, differences in attitudes toward verbal opposition will persist among friends, lovers, and fellow workers. Frustration can be reduced by simply realizing that what seems like unfair or irrational behavior may just be the result of a different style in approaching conflict.

Culture and Conflict Management

Different cultures often define and deal with conflict in different ways. When individuals from different cultures face a conflict, their normal, habitual communication patterns may not blend smoothly. An example of the challenge faced by an American husband and his Chinese wife is illustrated on the following page (Fontaine, 1999).

Ting-Toomey and Oetzel (2002) suggest that the way in which people manage conflict varies depending on their cultural background. That is, high-context and low-context cultures manage conflict quite differently.

Think/Pair/Share Activity

CULTURAL CONFLICT

Work in triads to discuss the cultural conflict described. Answer the questions, and prepare to share your answers with the class.

An American husband would typically confront his Asian wife verbally and directly (as is typical in the United States), leading her to generally withdraw completely from the discussion. She, on the other hand, would indicate her displeasure by changes in her mood and eye content (typical for Asian culture) that were either not noticed or uninterpretable by her husband. Thus neither "his way" nor "her way" was working, and they could not see any realistic way to "compromise" (Fontaine, 2005).

What do you think this couple can do to more effectively deal with conflict? With their cultural differences, will they be able to find a conflict style that is comfortable for them both?

FOCUS ON DIVERSITY

CROSS CULTURAL RELATIONSHIPS

The loyalty we often feel toward our own culture and traditions can sometimes mean we find it difficult to understand another's cultural signals. In a relationship situation where two people have differing beliefs, it is these feelings that can be pushed to the forefront, overwhelming the individual feelings they have for one another. Making families mesh and understand one another when they come from two completely different backgrounds isn't always the easiest thing. **But having conversations about the topic of culture and how it plays into your relationship and how to deal with others prejudices is something you need to do together.** One way to appreciate each other's culture is to learn how to express love (and other stuff) in different languages (Kruschewsky, 2014).

High-context cultures. These cultures value self-restraint, avoid confrontation, rely heavily on nonverbal systems, and give a great deal of meaning to the relationships between communicators. Preserving and honoring the "face" or public reputation or appearance of the other person is a prime goal, and communicators go to great lengths to avoid any communication that might risk embarrassing a conversational partner. The Japanese, Chinese, other East Asian, and Latin American cultures are examples of high-context cultures. Japanese people, for example, are reluctant to say "no" to a request. They will probably respond with, "Let me think about it for a while," which someone familiar with Japanese culture would recognize as a refusal (Adler & Proctor, 2014).

Low-context cultures. These cultures use more explicit language, are more direct in their meanings, rely less on nonverbal systems, and stress goals and outcomes more than relationships. Examples include the German, Swedish, American, and English cultures. Individuals in low-context cultures manage conflict more directly. They are more confrontational and more goal oriented rather than being relationally focused, and they are less concerned about "saving face." Therefore, conflict in low-context cultures is more open, volatile, and threatening than high-context conflict (Gudykunst, 2005).

Let's get back to our example of the American husband and the Chinese wife. The husband from a low-context culture and the wife from a high-context culture were simply responding to their cultural learning of how to deal with conflict. For example, when indirect communication (as used by the wife) is a cultural norm, it is unreasonable to expect more straightforward approaches to succeed (as used by the husband). Will either of them notice? Can the husband learn to be cautious in his straightforward approach and more attuned to his wife's nonverbal signals? Can the wife be more verbally direct without relying so much on her nonverbal signals to express her real feelings?

A mutual understanding about their cultural attitudes toward verbal conflict may result in less frustration in the future. Conflicts will still arise, but they will be able to address the issue rather than fight each other's style of conflict.

STRATEGIES FOR HANDLING CONFLICT

When you approach a conflict situation, you can choose to *avoid* the situation, *fight* with use of power and force, or *move toward,* using negotiation skills (Adler & Rodman, 2011). Most research indicates that in deciding how to handle conflict, two distinct factors come into play: **assertiveness,** which is the degree to which you want to have your own way or satisfy your own interest, and **cooperativeness,** the degree to which you are concerned about maintaining the relationship or satisfying the concerns of others (Alberti & Emmons, 2017; Cloud and Townsend, 2017; Rahim, A., Magner, N., and Shapiro, D., 2000).

Therefore, depending on the levels of assertiveness and cooperativeness, there are five general strategies for handling conflict: avoiding, accommodating, competing/forcing, compromising, and collaborating (Hocker & Wilmot, 2010). See Table 7.3.

Avoiding (lose-lose). In this approach, individuals attempt to passively ignore the conflict rather than resolve it. They may avoid the conflict by refusing to take a stance, physically leaving it, or escaping the conflict by mentally leaving the conflict. Often, people who use this strategy hope that ignoring the problem will make it go away. If the relationship is not very important or the conflict is very minor, it may just be wise to avoid the confrontation. However, if the relationship is important or the conflict is much greater, avoiding the conflict generally results in greater misunderstandings, resentments, hurt feelings, and more conflicts. Unfortunately, avoiders have a low concern for self and others, and a lose-lose situation is created because the conflict is not resolved.

Accommodating (lose-win). When using this strategy, individuals attempt to resolve the conflict by passively giving in to the other party. The accommodating approach is unassertive and cooperative. Individuals who use this strategy prefer harmony to conflict, desire to be liked, and believe that conflict is damaging to relationships. If they don't have strong preferences or feelings about a particular situation or issue, occasional accommodating is appropriate. However, if they often find themselves "giving in" just to please the other person, they will probably have feelings of resentment and be increasingly taken advantage of by the other person. This approach represents a low concern for self and a high concern for others, thus resulting in a lose-win situation.

Competitive/Forcing (win-lose or maybe even lose-lose). This strategy is characterized by the use of aggressive behavior, an uncooperative attitude, and an autocratic attempt to satisfy one's own needs at the expense of others, if necessary. When maintaining close supportive relationships is not critical, this strategy is sometimes used. And, there are times when a legitimate authority figure has to make a difficult decision, knowing others will not like it. Since this win-lose approach to conflict involves a high concern for self and low concern for others, deep feelings of resentment and hostility often result. In some instances, feelings of wanting to get even and compete on a deeper level may even result in a lose-lose situation. This may also be called Passive/Aggressive.

Compromising (partial lose-lose). This approach is used with attempts to resolve the conflict through assertive give-and-take concessions or cooperation. Compromisers value harmony as well as individual satisfaction, and often will try to work out the situation so nobody gets all they want, but everyone gets something. Compromising is a constructive way to resolve conflicts because neither side experiences a total loss and both sides experience some sense of winning, thereby resulting in a partial lose-lose outcome. The advantage of this strategy is that the conflict is resolved, and relationships are maintained.

Collaborating strategy (win-win). Using this strategy, parties attempt to jointly resolve the conflict with the best solution agreeable to all parties. Since collaborating involves a high degree of assertiveness and a high degree of cooperation from all parties involved, it is also called the problem-solving strategy. Collaborating encourages openness and honesty and stresses the importance of criticizing or critiquing **ideas** rather than the persons involved. Because there is a high concern for self and others, collaborating tends to produce a climate of trust and respect in a win-win situation. Research shows if you participate in coming up with a solution, you are much more likely to comply with it (Harrison, 2019).

Behavior is a mirror in which everyone shows his image.
—GOETHE

If you want to go fast, go alone, but if you want to go far, go together.
—MANDINKA PROVERB

Table 7.3 THE THOMAS-KILMAN CONFLICT MODEL

These are the five conflict strategies or styles of conflict management. Each has a different level of assertiveness and cooperation.

COMPETING/FORCING (Win-Lose)	COLLABORATING (Win-Win)
Confrontational aggressive. Must win at any cost. Also called Passive-Aggressive.	Needs of both parties are legitimate and important. High respect for mutual support. Assertive and cooperative.

COMPROMISING (Partial Lose-Lose)	
Important all parties achieve some goals and maintain good relationships. Assertive but cooperative.	

AVOIDING (Lose-Lose)	ACCOMMODATING (Lose-Win)
Nonconfrontational. Ignores or passes over issues.	Agreeable, non-assertive behavior.
Denies issues are a problem.	Cooperative even at the expense of personal goals.

Adapted from Lamberton & Minor (2018).

Mastering Interpersonal Conflict

As we have noticed, it is highly possible to resolve conflict constructively. Here are a few general suggestions and guidelines to remember (Lerner, 2014; Verderber et al., 2009):

- Choose your battles carefully. Is this a minor, moderate, or major conflict? Think about the nature and impact of the conflict before you react.
- Be calm: no yelling or speaking in harsh, loud tones. Avoid loaded words that may hurt or harm others—no "put downs."
- Don't blame the other person or make accusations. Remember "I feel ... when ... happens." Tell the other party how you feel. Rather than, "You make me mad ...", or "It's all your fault ..." say, "I am angry ...", or "I like it when we cook dinner together."
- Remember to request. Do not demand. Rather than, "You should ..." or "You ought to ..." say, "I would appreciate your watering the yard."
- Do not bring up the past. Doing so will only kindle old resentments and get in your way of dealing with the current problem.
- Avoid categorical statements like "You *always* ..." or "You *never* ..." These statements will only put the other person on the defensive.
- Take responsibility for your actions. Do not be afraid to say, "I made a mistake. I am sorry. Please forgive me." It is often amazing how many hours are often spent avoiding the words "I was wrong."
- Listen without judging by showing respect for the other person and their position. Try to emphasize and understand their frame of reference.
- Learn to say you are sorry.

Cooperation is the thorough conviction that nobody can get there unless everybody gets there.
—VIRGINIA BURDEN

Becoming *Aware*

The pillow method. When it seems impossible to gain empathy and understand another's position and frame of reference, it might be helpful to remember the *pillow method*. The pillow method is a five-step process used to resolve a disagreement or enable two people to gain understanding from a disagreement. The process involves each individual to look at the problem through five different perspectives (Adler and Proctor, 2014). Author and poet Paul Reps describes how a group of Japanese school children created it to remind people that a problem can be viewed from four different angles (*like the four corners of a pillow*). And, it just might be possible to form a new conclusion based on your new view of the issue, which is the *middle* of the pillow. This technique is now taught in business schools throughout the world (Punches, 2010). Here are the angles or positions to consider:

Position 1: "I am right, and you are wrong." This position is easy and comfortable, since we generally see the strengths in our position and find fault with anyone who disagrees with us.

Position 2: "You are right, and I am wrong." This is the hard part. Now, think about the other person's frame of reference. Put yourself in the other person's shoes and imagine how the person feels about the situation. What justification does this person have to feel the way he or she feels?

Position 3: "We're both right, and we're both wrong." In this position, you try to identify common ground. What are the strengths and weaknesses of each side? There is merit in both views. Be fair and even-handed as you evaluate both sides.

Position 4: "The issue is not as big as I was making it." In this position you consider that when compared to everything else you could be concerned about, you may be blowing the issue out of proportion. You may want to ask yourself, "Is this really where I want to focus my time and attention? Is the issue really as important as I had originally thought?"

Conclusion: There is truth in all perspectives. How do you think and feel about the issue now? What will you do about it? After you have looked at an issue from these different perspectives, you may not change your mind or even solve the problem. However, you will definitely gain new insights, increase your tolerance for the other person's position, and improve the overall communication climate with this individual. By looking at the problem from multiple perspectives, each person gets the chance to enhance their cognitive complexity (Alder & Proctor, p. 104).

BECOMING AWARE- GUIDELINES FOR "GETTING TO YES"

These six integrative negotiation skills and steps by Katie Shonk from Harvard Law School can help you on your journey of getting to "yes" in negotiations (2019).

Bargainers can and should look for negotiation strategies that can help both sides get more of what they want. By listening closely to each other, treating each other fairly, and jointly exploring options to increase value, negotiators can find ways of getting to yes that reduce the need to rely on hard-bargaining tactics and unnecessary concessions.

> *To discover needs, we try to find out why the person wants the solution he/she initially proposed. Once we understand the advantages that a solution has for them, we have discovered their need.*
> —ROBERT BOLTON

1. **Separate the people from the problem.** Exploring each side's perceptions openly and avoiding the tendency to blame are key negotiation skills.

2. **Focus on interests, not positions.** By identifying what interests are motivating the other party, and sharing your own interests, you can open up opportunities to explore tradeoffs across issues and increase your odds of getting to yes. When you are angry, overly upset, or in a hurry this frequently causes you to say things you really do not mean. Making a date to discuss what is bothering you increases the likelihood of a positive outcome. You might say, "Something's been bothering me. When would be a convenient time for us to talk about it?"

   Second, *be sure to use "I" messages and the assertive techniques* you have already learned in this chapter. You will remember that the most important part of the "I" message is to describe how your partner's behavior affects you—not attach blame or labels.

   The final part of this step is to confirm your partner's understanding of what he or she heard.

3. **Learn to manage emotions.** When you know that you will have your turn to express how you're feeling, it will be easier for you to listen when your counterpart has their turn.

4. **Express appreciation.** In their book *Beyond Reason* (Penguin, 2005), Fisher and Dan Shapiro advised negotiators to express appreciation by working to understand the other's perspective, seeking merit in that perspective, and communicating understanding through words and actions—all critical negotiation skills.

5. **Put a positive spin on your message.** Communicating in a positive way is a much more effective means of getting to "yes" than blaming and criticizing. Instead of speaking on behalf of your group, speak only for yourself.

6. **Escape the cycle of action and reaction.** Channel your resistance and avoid escalation by refusing to react. Your solution will be effective only if you mutually agree *on who does what and by when.* If changes need to be made, now is the time to discuss what is on your mind.

Personal problem solving. It is important to note here that a modification of the win-win approach to interpersonal conflict resolution can also be used in personal problem solving. Hammond (2002) and his colleagues provide these steps:

- Identify and define the conflict-problem.
- Generate a number of possible solutions.
- Evaluate the alternative solutions.
- Decide on the best solution.
- Reevaluate the solution at a later date.

> Consider how hard it is to change yourself and you'll understand what little chance you have of trying to change others.
> —JACOB M. BRAUDE

Ken Watanabe (2009), author of *Problem Solving 101*, summarizes personal problem solving by saying, "Problem solving is easy when you know how to set a clear goal, figure out how to reach it, and follow through while reviewing your progress and making changes to your plan as necessary."

When people join together and take the time to find a solution acceptable to both, most problems that occur between them can be resolved with a high degree of success. However, the win-win approach to conflict resolution is not a panacea for all life's problems. There are some occasions when this method will not work, or when another approach is more fitting.

When Conflicts Cannot Be Resolved

Sometimes, the most well-thought-out plans do not always work. Despite your best intentions and most dedicated efforts, not all conflicts can be worked through. In *Beyond Blame*, Jeffrey Kottler, author of *On Being a Therapist* (2003), a professor of counseling and educational psychology, describes three occasions when conflicts may not be resolved: differences in basic beliefs, values, and past issues; struggles where there is no solution; and situations out of our control. The author would like to add one more—when things have to be a certain way. Let's look more closely at these.

Differences in basic beliefs, values, and past issues. There are times when two people are so different in their basic beliefs and values, and in the ways they perceive the world, that conflict between them is unavoidable, no matter what they do. There may be a person in your life with whom you have to work or associate frequently who has completely different political or religious orientations from you. Some people have unresolved family issues with a relative from the past that can not really be laid to rest completely. Perhaps you have tried and tried to see each other's point of view, but you still disagree, and each party leaves feeling angry or hurt. You may have to face a reality of life: agree to disagree when you discuss certain topics.

Struggles where there is no solution. The reality of life is that there is no guarantee that any particular human struggle has a solution, and certainly not a "best" one that can be determined easily. People must endure the situation in such a way that they minimize its effect on their relationship.

Situations out of your control. Have you ever had to deal with a situation in which you believed that if only you worked harder, if you knew more, or were more highly skilled, you could make things better?

In life, it is critical to recognize realistically what is within your power to change and what is not. Accept that not everyone really wants to change, no matter what they might say. Sometimes the payoffs of a person's dysfunction and behavior are

Maturity begins when we're content to feel we're right about something, without feeling the necessity to prove someone else is wrong.
—SIDNEY J. HARRIS

too unattractive, or they just do not want to do the hard work that is involved. Rather than blaming someone for the situation, take inventory of all the things that have been tried that have not worked, and rather than repeating them, try something else. Perhaps George may need to separate from Jenny for a period of time and let Jenny decide what she wishes to do for herself. George can choose to take up a new hobby, or interest, with friends who can be supportive of him during this time. He can build a new life for himself; someone cannot "fix" someone else's problem—only Jenny can.

When things have to be a certain way. Have you ever wanted someone to change to meet wants or expectations you believe are important? "If only they would . . . things around here would be so much better." Consider the following situation, assuming you are the roommate who wants "things around here to be better."

> *The reality of the world is that some relationships don't work out; there are supposed to be disagreements and disappointments. If you feel responsible for fixing every problem, you will pay a high price because that's an impossible task.*
> *—ELISABETH KÜBLER-ROSS AND DAVID KESSLER*

There is growing tension between you and your roommate. She has an 8:00 class and gets up before you do and eats a breakfast muffin and orange juice at your kitchen table. Your roommate continues to leave her dirty plate, glass, and crumbs on the table. You clean your side of the table and put your dishes in the dishwasher when you leave for school. This is just essential—the way it is supposed to be! You are irritated and decide to discuss this with your roommate, knowing that she is quite good about cleaning her side of the table when she gets in from class and sharing in the other chores around the apartment. Your roommate listens to your concerns and indicates a willingness to change. However, the problem continues, and you become more and more irritated.

What are your options? You can clean up her side and run the risk of having to do more of the cleaning chores around the apartment, you can get another roommate, you can decide to live by yourself, or you can decide to not let the dirty dishes bother you so much.

When you live and work with other people, it is only natural that differences in the way some things should be done can create problems. The reality of life is, however, that if you want some things to be a "certain" way, then it is unrealistic to think that other people will necessarily do what you believe is essential. Thinking otherwise is a guarantee for conflict and stress to exist. In our example, the problem is yours—your roommate is happy and just trying to get to class on time. In other words, the person who is bothered by the problem is the person who needs to correct the problem. This could be considered perfectionism.

Review the options discussed above and decide what to do, but remember—*when you believe something must be done a certain way and at a certain time, these beliefs may create some unnecessary stress in your life.* Sometimes, we all need to learn to live with less than what we want! Chapter Eight will discuss in more detail the stress involved in placing unrealistic demands and expectations on other people.

Conflict with Technology and the Digital Divide

Anderson and Kumar found that thirty years after the start of the World Wide Web, Internet use and smartphone ownership have grown rapidly for all Americans, including those who are less well-off financially. Even as many aspects of the digital divide have narrowed over time, the digital lives of lower and higher-income Americans are different (Pew Research Center, May 2019).

Roughly three-in-ten adults with household incomes below $30,000 a year are "smartphone-dependent" Internet users—meaning they own a smart phone but do not have broadband Internet at home. They use the library or public Wifi for access to the Internet. At home, more than four-in-ten (44%) don't have access to the Internet or a traditional computer. The majority of lower-income Americans are not tablet owners, and a total of 29% do not own smartphones (Pew Research Center, 2019). By comparison, each of these technologies is ever present among adults in households earning $100,000 or more a year.

In 2019, 26% of adults living in households earning less than $30,000 a year but only 5% of those living in households earning $100,000 or more fell into this category (Pew Research Center, 2019).

Becoming Aware of Technology– Technoconferencing

Psychologists' research shows how smartphones are affecting our health and well-being, and points the way toward taking back control. University of Arizona psychology professor David Sbarra and his collaborators at Wayne State University in Detroit have examined existing research on technoferencing. They propose an explanation for why humans are so drawn to their smartphones, even when the devices take us out of the moment in our close relationships. It's because of our evolutionary history, they say.

Sbarra and his colleagues argue that humans are hard-wired to connect with others. In the course of evolutionary history, we have relied on close relationships with small networks of family and friends for survival as individuals and as a species. These relationships were based on trust and cooperation, which is built when people disclose personal information about themselves and are responsive to others.

Smartphones, and the constant access they provide to text messaging and social media, make it easier than ever for people to disclose personal information and respond to others in their social networks. These networks are much larger and more far-flung than those of our ancestors.

"Between 2000 and 2018, we've seen the largest technological advances, arguably, at any point in the last 100 years," he said. "We are interested in understanding the role of social relationships in human well-being. We can understand this from the level of what individuals do in relationships, but we can also understand it at the level of societal changes and societal forces that may push on relationships" (Sbarra, 2019).

Chapter Review

When any two people live or work closely together, conflict is bound to occur just because people are different, think differently, and have different needs and wants that sometimes do not match.

- **Conflict** is an expressed struggle between at least two people who perceive the situation differently and are experiencing interference from the other person in achieving their goals.
- Conflicts usually involve any of six basic types of issues: 1) control over resources, 2) preferences and nuisances, 3) values, 4) beliefs, 5) goals, and 6) the nature of the relationship between the partners.
- Constructive resolution of conflicts can promote growth in a relationship, allow for a healthy release of feelings, and increase motivation and self-esteem.
- Two negative effects of conflict can be: the manner in which we approach interpersonal conflict (believing there must be a winner and a loser), and larger problems with deeper personal resentments may occur.
- The three behavior styles used in handling opposition and responding to conflict are: 1) **passive**—also known as nonassertive, 2) **aggressive**, and 3) **assertive**. The assertive approach is generally the most appropriate, effective, and constructive way of responding to conflict.
- There are several types of assertive expressions: basic assertion, learning to express positive feelings, and an escalating type of assertion when people fail to respond to our earlier request.
- The **"I" message** is frequently referred to as the focal point of learning to be assertive—expressing ourselves effectively before we become angry and act in self-defeating ways. The four parts of the "I" message are: 1) an objective, nonjudgmental description of the person's behavior in specific terms; 2) how I feel about this; 3) the concrete effects on me; and 4) a request and an invitation to respond, with positive consequence.
- When delivering an assertive "I" message, it is helpful to remember these suggestions: Write and practice your message before delivering it, develop assertive body language with your "I" message (I feel___ when ___ happens), and do not be sidetracked by the defensiveness or manipulation of others.
- When we keep saying yes, resentment and anger build. Some pointers in learning to say no are: start small, keep it simple, buy time, remain generous, and understand your yes.
- Making families mesh and understand one another when they come from two completely different backgrounds isn't always the easiest thing
- Added to the different behavior styles used in interpersonal conflict are two powerful variables that affect the way people manage conflict: gender and culture. Regardless of cultural background, men and women view conflicts in contrasting ways. Likewise, high- and low-context cultures manage conflict quite differently.
- According to Sbarra (2019), relationships are based on trust and cooperation, which is built when people disclose personal information about themselves. Technology makes it easier to disclose personal information and respond to others and this may be changing our way of developing relationships. How can this be a benefit and a problem?
- Research shows that couples who use *we, our,* and *us* show more affection and less anger during arguments. And, couples who use *I, you,* and *me* during disagreements have lower levels of marital satisfaction.

- Most research indicates that in deciding how to handle conflict, two distinct factors come into play: assertiveness and cooperativeness.
- The **pillow method** helps a person view a conflict from **four different angles** and possibly reach a new conclusion.
- **Win-win problem solving** works best when it follows a seven-step approach: 1) define the problem in terms of needs, not solutions; 2) share your problem and unmet needs; 3) listen to the other person's needs; 4) brainstorm possible solutions; 5) evaluate the possible solutions and choose the best one—check possible consequences; 6) implement the solution; and 7) evaluate the solution at a later date.
- Personal problem solving can be facilitated with the following steps: 1) identify and define the conflict, 2) generate a number of possible solutions, 3) evaluate the alternative solutions, 4) decide on the best solution, and 5) evaluate the solution at a later date.
- There are some occasions when the win-win approach to conflict resolution may not work. Possible occasions can include: differences in basic beliefs, values, and past issues; struggles where there is no solution; situations out of our control; and when things have to be a certain way.
- The list of mistakes in conflict: 1) Avoiding Conflict Altogether, 2) Being Defensive, 3) Overgeneralizing, 4) Being Right, 5) Mind-Reading, 6) Forgetting to Listen, 7) Playing the Blame Game, 8) Trying to "Win" the Argument, 9) Making Character Attacks, and 10) Stonewalling

How you resolve your interpersonal conflicts is the single most important factor in determining whether your relationships will be healthy or unhealthy, mutually satisfying or unsatisfying, friendly or unfriendly, deep or shallow, or intimate or cold.

Learning Outcomes Review

1. Define conflict and what causes conflict.
2. Why is conflict generally viewed negatively?
3. What are the positive and negative effects of conflict?
4. What are the three behavior styles used in handling opposition and responding to conflict? Explain the behavior description, belief system, advantages, and disadvantages of each style.
5. What are at least five suggestions given for mastering interpersonal conflict?
6. List at least ten Basic Human Rights.
7. Explain the behaviors exhibited by the assertive, aggressive, and nonassertive person in conflict situations and in situations expressing feelings.
8. What is the focal point of learning to be assertive? List and write an example of each of the four parts of an "I" message.
9. When delivering an "I" message, what three suggestions should you remember?
10. Explain the pointers given for learning to say *no*. Is *no* a complete sentence?
11. What are at least three different ways in which men and women view and deal with conflict?
12. Explain the different approaches high- and low-context cultures use in conflict resolution.
13. What two factors come into play when deciding how to handle a conflict?
14. List and give examples of the three methods you can use in conflict resolution.
15. Explain the pillow method. What different positions are involved?
16. What are the seven steps to use in win-win conflict resolution? What does research show about the level of commitment often demonstrated when one participates in coming up with a solution to a problem?

17. What are the steps to be used in personal problem solving?
18. Explain possible occasions when conflict may not be resolved.
19. Explain the differences between genders regarding conflict resolution.
20. What do laboratory studies reveal about couples who use the pronouns *we, our, us, I, you,* and *me* during disagreements?
21. Can all conflicts be resolved? Explain.
22. How is technology impacting interpersonal relationships?

Key Terms

Accommodating Strategy	Competing/Forcing Strategy	"I" Message
Aggressive	Compromising Strategy	Low-Context Culture
Assertiveness	Conflict Management	Partial Lose-Lose
Avoidance	Cooperativeness	Passive/Nonassertive
Avoiding Strategy	Domination	Pillow Method
Broken-Record Technique	Forgiveness	Stonewalling
Collaborating Strategy	Gender Differences	Win-Lose
Collaborative Problem Solving	High-Context Culture	Win-Win

Reflections in Critical Thinking Activity

Answer the following questions and turn them into your instructor for grading. (All questions answered = A; 11 questions answered = B; 8 questions answered = C).

1. What kinds of differentness in others cause you the greatest interpersonal conflict?
2. What situations do you find most difficult to respond to with assertive behavior?
3. Generally speaking, have your conflicts made your relationships stronger or weaker? Why?
4. Which one of the parts of the "I" message is most difficult for you to remember to use?
5. Discuss any personal experiences you have had with the different approaches high- and low-context cultures use in conflict resolution.
6. Do you agree that men and women view and deal with conflict differently? Why or why not?
7. Do you disagree with any of the Basic Human Rights? If so, explain.
8. Is the win-win approach to conflict resolution too good to be true?
9. With whom is it most difficult for you to say *no*? With whom is it most difficult for you to be assertive?
10. What is your preferred strategy for resolving conflict?
11. Do you think it is possible to resolve conflict with the pillow method? Why?
12. Discuss gender differences in interpersonal conflict.
13. Why do you think many low income families do not have income? What do you think society needs to do or not worry about it? With technology as the example can the conflict between the "haves" and "have-nots" be easily solved? Discuss.
14. How would you define the digital divide?

Technology Resources and Activities

http://stress.about.com/od/relationships/a/conflict_res.htm

Conflict skills for healthy relationships.

http://www.crinfo.org/

Links to Internet resources and information about publications and organizations on conflict resolution.

http://helpguide.org/mental/eq8-conflict-resolution.htm

Learn how to manage and resolve conflict in your work and family relationships.

www.communicationandconflict.com/skills.html

Reviews the skills involved in practicing both effective communication and effective conflict resolution.

http://www.peacemakers.ca/bibliography/bib50resolution.html

Conflict transformation and peacebuilding: A selected bibliography.

https://www.verywell.com/conflict-resolution-

Conflict resolution mistakes to avoid.

https://www.mindtools.com/pages/article/Assertiveness.htm

Mindtools: Essential skills for an excellent career: Assertiveness training.

http://ggia.berkeley.edu/

Greater good in action: Science-based practices for a meaningful life.

https://www.ted.com/talks/luvvie_ajayi_get_comfortable_with_being_uncomfortable?utm_campaign=tedspread&utm_medium=referral&utm_source=tedcomshare

Luvvie Ajayi isn't afraid to speak her mind or to be the one dissenting voice in a crowd, and neither should you. "Your silence serves no one," says the writer, activist and self-proclaimed professional troublemaker. In this bright, uplifting talk, Ajayi shares three questions to ask yourself if you're teetering on the edge of speaking up or quieting down, and encourages all of us to get a little more comfortable with being uncomfortable.

https://www.ted.com/talks/julian_treasure_how_to_speak_so_that_people_want_to_listen?language=enn

How to speak so that people want to listen.

https://www.youtube.com/watch?v=V5MIUGjyC-M

Leo Buscaglia: Born for Love.

https://www.youtube.com/watch?v=xBp1hkxz_Ow

Rejection on Social Media: It Hurts! by Guy Winch, PhD.

https://www.youtube.com/watch?v=KY5TWVz5ZDU

Conflict resolution.

https://www.youtube.com/watch?v=o97fVGTjE4w

Conflict – Use It, Don't Defuse It, by CrisMarie Campbell and Susan Clarke, TEDxWhitefish

https://www.youtube.com/watch?v=_l5GowKNXpU

The Pillow Method: A Tool for Building Empathy.

https://www.youtube.com/watch?v=ibmqUz6g8PU

Shifting Perspectives: Pillow method planning wedding.

https://www.ted.com/talks/amy_cuddy_your_body_language_shapes_who_you_are?language=en

Body language affects how others see us, but it may also change how we see ourselves, by social psychologist Amy Cuddy.

http://www.ted.com/talks/william_ury

The walk from "no" to "yes" by William Ury, a mediator, writer, and speaker who works with conflicts ranging from family feuds to boardroom battles to ethnic wars. He's the author of *Getting to Yes*.

https://www.youtube.com/watch?v=cFdCzN7RYbw

Reciprocity as one of the factors of the science of persuasion.

The Assertiveness Inventory

PURPOSE

To assess your strengths and weaknesses in being assertive and to establish goals for improvement.

INSTRUCTIONS

1. Respond to the following questions by drawing a circle around the number that describes you best.
    For some questions, the assertive end of the scale is at 0, for others at 4.
    Key:
    0   means no or never
    1   means somewhat or sometimes
    2   means average
    3   means usually or a good deal
    4   means practically always or entirely

    1. When a person is highly unfair, do you call it to their attention?   0   1   2   3   4
    2. Do you find it difficult to make decisions?   0   1   2   3   4
    3. Are you openly critical of others' ideas, opinions, behavior?   0   1   2   3   4
    4. Do you speak out in protest when someone takes your place in line?   0   1   2   3   4
    5. Do you often avoid people or situations for fear of embarrassment?   0   1   2   3   4
    6. Do you usually have confidence in your own judgment?   0   1   2   3   4
    7. Do you insist that your spouse or roommate take on a fair share of
       household chores?   0   1   2   3   4
    8. Are you prone to "fly off the handle"?   0   1   2   3   4
    9. When a salesperson makes an effort, do you find it hard to say "No"
       even though the merchandise is not really what you want?   0   1   2   3   4
    10. When a latecomer is waited on before you are, do you call attention to
        the situation?   0   1   2   3   4
    11. Are you reluctant to speak up in a discussion or debate?   0   1   2   3   4
    12. If a person has borrowed money (or a book, garment, thing of value)
        and is overdue in returning it, do you mention it?   0   1   2   3   4
    13. Do you continue to pursue an argument after the other person has
        had enough?   0   1   2   3   4
    14. Do you generally express what you feel?   0   1   2   3   4
    15. Are you disturbed if someone watches you at work?   0   1   2   3   4
    16. If someone keeps kicking or bumping your chair in a movie or a
        lecture, do you ask the person to stop?   0   1   2   3   4
    17. Do you find it difficult to keep eye contact when you are talking to
        another person?   0   1   2   3   4

18. In a good restaurant, when your meal is improperly prepared or served, do you ask the waiter/waitress to correct the situation? 0 1 2 3 4

19. When you discover merchandise is faulty, do you return it for an adjustment? 0 1 2 3 4

20. Do you show your anger by name calling or obscenities? 0 1 2 3 4

21. Do you try to be a wallflower or a piece of the furniture in social situations? 0 1 2 3 4

22. Do you insist that your property manager (mechanic, repairman, janitor) make repairs, adjustments, or replacements which are his or her responsibility? 0 1 2 3 4

23. Do you often step in and make decisions for others? 0 1 2 3 4

24. Are you able openly to express love and affection? 0 1 2 3 4

25. Are you able to ask your friends for small favors or help? 0 1 2 3 4

26. Do you think you always have the right answer? 0 1 2 3 4

27. When you differ with a person you respect, are you able to speak up for your own viewpoint? 0 1 2 3 4

28. Are you able to refuse unreasonable requests made by friends? 0 1 2 3 4

29. Do you have difficulty complimenting or praising others? 0 1 2 3 4

30. If you are disturbed by someone smoking near you, can you say so? 0 1 2 3 4

31. Do you shout or use bullying tactics to get others to do as you wish? 0 1 2 3 4

32. Do you finish other people's sentences for them? 0 1 2 3 4

33. Do you get into physical fights with others, especially with strangers? 0 1 2 3 4

34. At family meals, do you control the conversation? 0 1 2 3 4

35. When you meet a stranger, are you the first to introduce yourself and begin a conversation? 0 1 2 3 4

2. **Analyzing Your Results:** When you complete the Inventory, you'll probably be tempted to add up your total score. Don't! It really has no meaning, since there is no such thing as a general quality of assertiveness. The authors of the inventory suggest the following steps for analysis of your responses to the Assertiveness Inventory:

   a. Look at individual events in your life, involving particular people or groups, and consider strengths and shortcomings accordingly.

   b. Look at your responses to questions 1, 2, 4, 5, 6, 7, 9, 10, 11, 12, 14, 15, 16, 17, 18, 19, 21, 22, 24, 25, 27, 28, 30, and 35. These questions are oriented toward nonassertive behavior. Respond to these questions: Do your answers to these items tell you that you are rarely speaking up for yourself? How do you feel about what you have learned about yourself?

   c. Look at your responses to questions 3, 8, 13, 20, 23, 26, 29, 31, 32, 33, and 34. These questions are oriented toward aggressive behavior. Respond to these questions: Do your answers to these questions suggest you are pushing others around more than you realized? How do you feel about what you have learned about yourself?

DISCUSSION

Most people confirm from completing these three steps that assertiveness is situational in their lives. No one is nonassertive all the time, aggressive all the time, assertive all the time! Each person behaves in each of the three ways at various times, depending upon the situation. It is possible that you have a characteristic style that leans heavily in one direction. Reread each question on the Inventory and carefully analyze your answers. Look specifically at four aspects (situations, attitudes, obstacles, and behavior skills) of the information and respond to the questions below:

1. What *situations* give you trouble? Which can you handle easily?

2. What are your *attitudes* about expressing yourself? For example, do you feel you have a "right" to be assertive? Why or why not?

3. What *obstacles* are in the way of your assertions? For example, are you frightened of the consequences, or do other people in your life make being assertive especially difficult? Who?

4. Are your *behavior skills* (eye contact, facial expression, body posture) intact? Can you be expressive when you need to?

5. What specific goals do you need to set for yourself in learning to be more assertive?

Name _____ Date _____

Becoming Aware–Resolve Conflict at Work

Key steps for discussing issues collaboratively.

PURPOSE

Try this exercise any time a conflict arises at work. The duration of the exercise will vary depending on the conflict at hand.

HOW TO DO IT

Consider a conflict, big or small, that you are facing with another person at work. Perhaps you disagree on the direction of an upcoming project, or maybe you feel your colleague isn't pulling their weight on your team.

THEN, FOLLOW THESE STEPS:

1. Choose to actively resolve this conflict rather than ignoring it. When your boss makes a decision you disagree with, or a colleague isn't respecting your time, your instinct may be to accommodate their wishes, and ignore your thoughts and feelings on the matter.
    Instead of avoiding the conflict and allowing suppressed emotions to build inside, we can decide to take an active approach and address the conflict head-on.
2. Embrace a mindset of collaboration. If you have an instinct to avoid conflict, it may be the result of a workplace culture where it's normal to keep doubts and disagreements quiet for the sake of reducing tension. Or maybe the norm at your workplace is to aggressively hold your ground until one person "wins" the debate. Instead, the best way to resolve conflict is somewhere in the middle: choosing a collaborative mindset.
    Collaboration means that individuals feel safe to share opposing opinions and strive for a compromise.
3. Practice active listening. In order to have an effective discussion, it is important to demonstrate mutual respect for one another. One critical way to do this is to actively listen when someone is speaking, as opposed to preparing your rebuttal. When both parties feel heard, they can more effectively come to a cooperative solution.
4. Talk a walk. If possible, suggest discussing the matter on a walk indoors or outdoors. As you walk side by side, adjust the pace of your gait to synchronize with your colleague's. Consider this walk together to be a constructive opportunity to exchange ideas.

DISCUSSION–WHY YOU SHOULD TRY IT

Solving conflict at work can be difficult, and there are often deadlines to come to an agreement. In this high-pressure environment, strategies to promote collaboration, listening, and cooperation are vital. Research suggests that neglecting to advocate for our point of view can increase feelings of distress at work.

Adapted from https://ggia.berkeley.edu/

Name _____ Date _____

Understanding the Passive, Aggressive, and Assertive Styles

PURPOSE

To practice composing passive, aggressive, and assertive responses to real-life situations.

INSTRUCTIONS

1. After each situation, compose a passive, aggressive, and assertive response.
2. Then, share your responses in an open class discussion or divide into small groups of four students.
   a. You have just paid for your dinner at one of your favorite restaurants. However, you suddenly realize that your change is a dollar short.

   Passive Response:

   Aggressive Response:

   Assertive Response:

   b. You are relaxing with the paper after a long day. Your partner rushes in and hands you a list of food items and says, "I never thought you would get here. Quick, pick these up from the store."

   Passive Response:

   Aggressive Response:

   Assertive Response:

Becoming *Aware*

c. Your teacher lost the test you handed in and says you must take the test again.

   Passive Response:

   Aggressive Response:

   Assertive Response:

d. Your roommate has not been doing their share of chores around the apartment.

   Passive Response:

   Aggressive Response:

   Assertive Response:

e. While you wait patiently for the clerk to finish with the customer ahead of you, another customer comes in and the clerk waits on him before you.

   Passive Response:

   Aggressive Response:

   Assertive Response:

DISCUSSION

1. Which responses were the most difficult for you to compose: the passive, aggressive, or assertive?

2. Would others who know you well say you are more passive, aggressive, or assertive in dealing with conflicts and problem solving? Explain.

3. Do you think there are gender differences in certain styles?

Say It with "I" Messages

PURPOSE

To learn how to construct an assertive "I" message in order to express your feelings and get your needs met.

INSTRUCTIONS

1. Respond to each of the following situations by writing an appropriate "I" message. Each "I" message should include the following five key phrases: Remember, you can rearrange the phrases in a way that is natural and fits your personal style.

When you . . .

I feel . . .

Because . . .

I'd prefer or like . . . Will you . . .?

So that . . . or, If so . . . or Then . . .

Sample Situation

Your sister, brother, or friend borrowed your new coat and returned it dirty.

"I" message: **When you** borrow my coat and return it dirty,

I feel angry,

because now I will have to take it to the cleaners before I can wear it.

I'd like you to return my coat clean the next time you borrow it. Will you agree to that?

If so, you can borrow it again.

a. **Situation:** Your co-worker has been asking you to change shifts with him/her. You only have two or three hours' notice of the desired shift change.

"I" message:

b. **Situation:** Your best friend is to meet you at the movie, and they are late *again*. This time they show up 40 minutes late.

"I" message:

c. **Situation:** Your group is working on a class project. Other people in the room are talking so loudly that you can't hear what your group is saying.
   "I" message:

d. **Situation:** The teacher had promised to return your test on Monday. It is now Friday and you still don't know how you did.
   "I" message:

e. **Situation:** A friend borrows your English book and promises to return it the next day. She doesn't bring it back.
   "I" message:

f. Make up a situation and make an "I" Message to go with it.
   Situation:

   "I" message:

2. Now, divide into groups of four and share your assertive messages. Members of the group will give each person feedback on his or her assertive messages.
3. Correct any errors in your assertive messages and try to practice giving "I" messages during the next week.

DISCUSSION

1. What errors, if any, did you find in your assertive messages?

2. Do you think you will be able to practice any of these assertive messages in the next week? Explain how.

3. What will your biggest problem be in learning to be assertive?

4. How do you plan to overcome this problem?

Name _____ Date _____

The Pillow Method—Developing Empathy

OBJECTIVE

To gain a greater understanding and empathy for another person's perspective on a situation when it is different from your own and is causing problems in your relationship with that person.

INSTRUCTIONS

1. Identify a situation in which you and someone important to you have different conflicting viewpoints. This might be a husband-wife issue, a friend-friend issue, a parent-child issue, a teacher-student issue, a brother-sister issue, an employer-employee issue, etc. Describe the issue and why the issue has evolved into such a great disagreement.

2. Review the discussion of the Pillow Method. Then, identify the reasons, facts or examples that support each position.
   a. I am right, and you are wrong.

   b. You are right, and I am wrong.

Becoming *Aware*

c. We're both right, and we're both wrong.

d. This issue is not as big as I am making it.

e. Conclusion: There is truth in all four positions.

DISCUSSION

1. What new insights about the conflict or areas of disagreement have you gained?

2. How do you think and feel about the issue now, and what will you do about it?

Name _____ Date _____

A Critical Decision

PURPOSE

To give students an opportunity to participate in a critical family decision.

INSTRUCTIONS

1. Participants will read the following case history and arrive at an individual decision.
2. Small groups of five members will be formed and will be asked to arrive at a group (family) decision.
3. A spokesman from each group will be selected to reveal the group's decision to the entire class.
4. While reading the following case history, bear in mind that you are a member of Mr. Smith's family.

Mr. Smith, age 63, has been physically disabled for almost 13 years. This disability has been due to 8 major surgeries, 2 of which were the successful removal of malignant tumors. Furthermore, Mr. Smith has a very severe case of emphysema, which has caused tremendous damage to his lungs. However, for the last 3 years, Mr. Smith has been experiencing excellent health—considering his known difficulties. Nevertheless, Mr. Smith enters the hospital today for an endoscopic exam of his esophagus. This was due to the passing of blood during the past week.

The exam revealed a large tumor toward the bottom of the esophagus. The chest specialist stated the tumor was definitely malignant and that the cancer had probably spread into the lymph glands. She advised that surgery be done immediately. However, she did state that there was probably only a 5% chance that the tumor could be removed and that—at most—Mr. Smith would have only one year to live. If surgery was not done, Mr. Smith would choke to death. However, if surgery was done, Mr. Smith's chances of tolerating the 5-hour surgery and anesthesia, due to his severe emphysema and damaged lungs, would be "nip and tuck." In other words, his chances of dying on the operating table were very great.

Mr. Smith, not knowing all of the above details, stated that if surgery had to be done, it had to be done—but he would like to wait a week or two. However, he would do whatever the family members thought best.

5. Now, consider that you are a member of Mr. Smith's family and you and the other family members will make this critical decision. (Your instructor will reveal what actually happened.)

6. Questions to consider:
   a. What is the problem involved?

   b. What are the alternatives?

   c. What are the consequences and responsibilities involved for each alternative?

   d. What is the preferred solution of each family member, and why?

   e. What emotional or logical factors contributed to your solution?

   f. Was there any interpersonal conflict with the family members?

DISCUSSION

1. Have any of you ever been involved in a decision such as this? How did you feel?

Becoming Aware–Interpersonal conflict

LET'S EXPLORE—RACE

For an interesting discussion on race, please read the Brainpickings link and discuss it with class members.

Assign a moderator and work in your groups for 20 minutes. Make sure you use your best interpersonal communications and conflict resolution skills. Plan to report to the full class. Turn in your group notes and list of people you talked with to the teacher if you are in an online class.

Resolving Interpersonal Conflict

LEARNING JOURNAL

Select the statement below that best defines your feelings about the personal value or meaning gained from this chapter and respond below the dotted line.

I learned that I . . .   I was surprised that I . . .

I realized that I . . .   I was pleased that I . . .

I discovered that I . . .   I was displeased that I . . .

. . . .

Chapter 8
Managing Stress and Wellness

© kurhan/Shutterstock.com

We are never presented with lessons until we are ready to learn them. So, life always gives exactly the teacher we need at every moment. This includes every mosquito, every misfortune, every red light, every traffic jam, every obnoxious supervisor (or employee), every illness, every loss, every moment of joy or depression, every addiction, every piece of garbage, every breath.

—Charlotte Joko Beck,
Zen teacher and author

I try to take one day at a time, but sometimes several days attack me at once.

—Jennifer Yane

Think About This...

Dr. Norman Vincent Peale (1898-1993), champion of Positive Thinking, "put life into perspective":

One day I was walking down the street when I saw my friend George approaching. It was evident from his downtrodden look that he wasn't overflowing with the ecstasy and exuberance of human existence, which is a high-class way of saying George was dragging bottom.

Naturally, I asked him, "How are you, George?" While that was meant to be a routine inquiry, George took me very seriously and for 15 minutes he enlightened me on how bad he felt. And the more he talked, the worse I felt.

Finally I said to him, "Well, George, I'm sorry to see you in such a depressed state. How did you get this way?" That really set him off.

"It's my problems," he said. "Problems—nothing but problems. I'm fed up with problems. If you could get rid of all my problems, I would contribute $5,000 to your favorite charity."

Well now, I am never one to turn a deaf ear to such an offer, and so I meditated, ruminated, and cogitated on the proposition and came up with an answer that I thought was pretty good.

I said, "Yesterday I went to a place where thousands of people reside. As far as I could determine, not one of them has any problems. Would you like to go there?"

"When can we leave? That sounds like my kind of place," answered George.

"If that's the case, George," I said, "I'll be happy to take you tomorrow to Woodlawn Cemetery because the only people I know who don't have problems are dead." (Peale, 2003)

Becoming Aware-Positive Thinking: You Can if You Think You Can
https://www.youtube.com/results?search_query=%23PositiveThinking
Rev. Norman Vincent Peale presents a reminder to stay positive, no matter what you're going through

---

Did this story "put life into perspective" for you? Certainly it is true that fewer health, financial, family, work, or social problems would make life more secure and satisfying. However, not having any problems or any stress would leave you with no choices in life, which would be dull and uninteresting. A certain number of problems and stresses can be stimulating. While some stress is good and necessary, excessive stress can create physical problems and/or behavioral changes.

Most people have the power to modify both the amount of stress in their lives and their reactions to it. Some may need to make only a few minor adjustments in their daily lives for stress to become more constructive and manageable. Some will have to make more radical external changes (for example, change jobs) or internal changes (such as change some social requirements and/or attitudes).

Most people, who with courage and support undertake such changes, have only one regret: that they did not make the changes sooner. We encourage you to begin considering what adjustments you may need to make in your daily life for stress to become more constructive and manageable.

Let's begin by discussing what stress is, and what causes it.

What Is Stress?

Stress has become such an ingrained part of our vocabulary and daily existence that it is difficult to believe that our current use of the term originated only a little more than 50 years ago, when it was essentially "coined" by Hans Selye (Rosch, 2016). Even though there is no widely accepted definition of stress, the following viewpoints are worthy of consideration. Hans Selye studied stress for over 50 years. He considered stress to be the <u>demand</u> made on an organism to adapt, cope, or adjust. Selye defines **stress** as the rate of wear and tear (the demand) within the body. Stress has also been defined as the anxious or threatening feeling that comes when we interpret or appraise a situation as being more than our psychological resources can adequately handle (Lazarus, 2006).

Which of the following would you call stressful?

1. Building a new home
2. Being audited by the IRS
3. Getting a promotion
4. Sitting in a dentist's chair
5. Getting married
6. Taking an exam

All of these six life events are stressful because they require us to adapt and change in response to them, which taxes our mental and physical adaptive mechanisms. Because positive or pleasurable events, such as getting a new home, can require as much adaptation on our part as negative or painful events, like being audited by the IRS, they can all be stressful. Living a stress-free life is not a reality.

TYPES OF STRESS

Hans Selye, in his classic book (1974) *Stress without Distress*, has described and labeled four basic types of stress:

1. *Eustress* is defined as moderate or normal psychological stress. This type of stress strengthens us for immediate physical activity, creativity, and enthusiasm. It is characterized as short-lived, easily identified, externalized, and positive. Two examples would be an individual who experiences short-term stress by psyching up

Stress is like spice—in the right proportion it enhances the flavor of a dish. Too little produces a bland, dull meal; too much may choke you. The trick is to find the right amount for you.
—DONALD TUBESING

Successful activity, no matter how intense, leaves you with comparatively few "scars." It causes stress but little distress.
—HANS SELYE

Even positive or pleasurable events can be very stressful.

© *michaeljung/Shutterstock.com*

for the hundred-yard dash and an individual who is really excited about beginning a new project at work. The secret of positive stress is a sense of control. When we can make choices and influence the outcome of a situation, we meet the challenge successfully and return to a normal level of functioning relatively quickly. This is the happy feeling of "I did it!"

2. *Distress* is negative or harmful stress that causes us to constantly readjust or adapt. Distress occurs when we feel no control over outcomes; we see few or no choices; the source of stress is not clear; the stress is prolonged over a period of time; or several sources of stress exist simultaneously. However, not all negative events cause psychological distress. According to Richard Lazarus (2000), distress arises only when the stressor makes demands on the individual that exceed the individual's ability to cope. Therefore, distress is accompanied by feelings of tension, pressure, and anxiety rather than the concerted energy of eustress.

3. *Hyperstress* or overload occurs when stressful events pile up and stretch the limits of our adaptability. Examples for an individual might include someone who goes through a marriage or a divorce, relocates to a new home, starts a new job, or loses a parent; stress can be positive or negative stress. It is when we have to cope with too many changes at once or adapt to radical changes for which we are not prepared that stress can become a serious problem.

4. *Hypostress* or underload occurs when we are bored, lacking stimulation, or unchallenged. This type of stress frustrates our need for variety and new experiences. For example, having a job that does not have new challenges can cause constant frustration. This is considered negative stress. Hans Selye believes that people who enjoy their work, regardless of how demanding it may be, will be less stress-ridden than people who are bored with a job that makes few demands or is too repetitive. The excitement or stimulation of the anticipated rewards balances the demands of the work. If you are involved in something you like, you are much more likely to handle frustration, pressure, or conflict effectively (Rosch, 2016).

We have seen that some stress is necessary to give our lives variety and to challenge us to grow and expand our abilities. Too much stress, or the wrong kind, or at the wrong time, becomes debilitating.

As important as it is to understand what stress is, it is even more important to understand where the stress originates. When we determine what stress means for us, we have a choice of dealing with it more effectively or eliminating it completely. The key to reducing stress is to prevent it. Getting enough sleep, eating a proper diet, avoiding excess caffeine and other stimulants, and taking time out to relax may be helpful in this regard. We will be discussing prevention later in the chapter.

CAUSES OF STRESS

Is it other people, your job, too many things to do, your financial situation, pressure, illness? **Stress** consists of an event, called a *stressor*, plus how we feel about it, how we interpret it, and what we do to cope with it.

Common stressors include:

- The setting in which we live
- Other people
- Places we go
- Our daily routine
- Family members
- Our job
- Time—too little, too much
- Money
- School
- Dating
- Our given health condition
- A spoken word
- A certain event
- A simple thought

Any age can be stressed. Young Americans between 18 and 33 years old are more stressed than the rest of the population, according to a new report from the American Psychological Association. The 2019 Stress in America™ survey was conducted online within the United States by The Harris Poll on behalf of the American Psychological Association between August 1 and September 3, 2019 (3,617 adults age 18+ who reside in the U.S. were surveyed).

What gives you the most stress? The daily routine or an unbalanced routine?

The survey found at least three in five members of every generation express that they feel hopeful about their future. Gen Z adults (62%) are the least likely to feel this way. Comparatively, 81% of older adults and around three in four Boomers (74%), Millennials (74%), and Gen Xers (73%) feel hopeful about their future. Individuals who do not identify as LGBT are significantly more likely than those who are members of the LGBT community to report that they feel hopeful for their future.(13th annual Stress in America™ survey by the Harris Poll 2020).

© G-Stock Studio/Shutterstock.com

"Clearly there are a number of pressures facing young people that might account for this increase in stress," said Norman Anderson, CEO of the American Psychological Association. "These individuals are growing up in an era of unprecedented economic upheaval. This coincides with the time they are finishing school and trying to establish themselves in society." What's stressing them out? "Jobs and money mostly," said Anderson (APA, 2016).

Life events. Two words best relate to the actual cause of stress: *change* and *threat*. Either or both can disturb the psyche. When workers lose their jobs, that job loss is a significant change and usually a threat to their ego, self-esteem, and even the material aspects of their life. Similarly, the loss of a spouse is a major change and may pose many different threats.

On the other hand, there are positive events such as marriage, starting a job, and retirement, which can also create changes and threats that must be faced. The changes that result from positive events, however, are generally not as difficult to cope with as the changes that result from negative ones.

Changes and threats often fall into three possible categories:

1. **Anticipated Life Events.** Examples might be graduation from high school and entering college, a job promotion, marriage, birth, and retirement.
2. **Unexpected Life Events.** Some examples might be a serious accident, separation from a spouse or someone we love, sudden death of a loved one, divorce, and financial problems.
3. **Accumulating Life Events.** This would include a dead-end job, traffic, deadlines and pressures, and ongoing conflict with friends or family members (Taylor & McGee, 2000).

As you can see, some of the changes and threats above are major, and some may be described as just the everyday circumstances of life. What about the daily hassles of living?

Daily hassles. Some health psychologists believe information about daily problems provides a better clue to the effects of stress than that of major life events (Bottos & Dewey, 2004). Richard Lazarus (2006), a leading psychologist who studies emotions and stress, calls these irritating and frustrating incidents that occur in our everyday transactions with the environment ***daily hassles***.

What about your own life? What are the biggest hassles? Are any of the following everyday problems or nuisances stressful for you: misplacing or losing things, having too many tasks to do, wasting time, or worrying about meeting high achievement standards?

While traumatic life events, such as the death of a loved one or the loss of one's job, are stressful and exert adverse effects on health, the minor hassles of daily life—perhaps because of their frequent, repetitive nature—may sometimes pile up until they overwhelm us (Almeida, 2005). Whatever their relative importance, both traumatic life events and daily hassles are important sources of stress for many individuals. Remember, stress eventually adds up.

Now, consider this question: What causes some people to be devastated and others motivated by the same event? After all, change by itself does not necessarily lead to stress reactions in all individuals (Nairne, 2013).

> *Have you ever felt that it's the little things in life that get you down? Daily hassles may have a greater effect on our moods and health than do the major misfortunes of life.*
> —RICHARD LAZARUS

Cognitive appraisal. Modern stress theory agrees that what causes us stress is not what happens, but how we perceive or *appraise* the situation. To feel stress, it is necessary to: 1) perceive there is some kind of demand or threat present, and 2) conclude that you may not have adequate resources available to deal with that threat (Lazarus, 2006). For example, our first reaction to potentially stressful situations, such as waiting in line, dealing with a sloppy roommate, making a public speech, taking an exam, seeing a vicious animal, or being in a car accident, is to appraise the situation in terms of whether it harms, threatens, or challenges our physical or psychological well-being. The secret lies in knowing that we have choices about how we look at external events, how we define them, how we attribute meaning to them, and how we react to them mentally and emotionally (Gallwey et al., 2009).

Remember, identical environmental events can lead to two very different stress reactions, depending on how the event is interpreted. Consider an upcoming exam: everyone in the class receives the same test, but not everyone will feel the same amount of stress. Those people who are prepared for the exam are likely to feel less stress. They perceive the threat, and have adequate resources to deal with it.

 Think/Pair/Share Activity

BECOMING AWARE OF YOUR DAILY HASSLES

Consider this question: What causes some people to be devastated and others motivated by the same event?

Create your list and share with a classmate.

1. Anxiety over tests and grades
2. Troubling thoughts about the future
3. Difficulty relaxing
4. Concern about health
5. Not getting enough sleep
6. Concern about physical appearance
7. Misplacing or losing things
8. Not enough time to do the things you need to do
9. Being lonely
10. Interpersonal relationship problems
11. Traffic delays
12. Financial status
13. Home maintenance chores, shopping, and preparing meals
14. Job dissatisfaction and/or concerns about job security
15. Wasting time in lines at the store, restaurant, or for appointments

Which ones are hassles for you? What else represents a hassle for you?

Often, our greatest source of stress is the tremendous pressure and anxiety that we create internally with our thoughts and feelings.

Trying to control things that are outside our control is enormously stressful, yet many of us unwittingly do this. When you feel stressed, consider . . . *What don't I control here? What am I trying to control here? What could I control here that I'm not currently controlling?* Confronting these questions can help us focus on things that we can accomplish and reduce our stress over things that we cannot (Gallwey et al., 2009).

Since the way we interpret and label our experiences can serve either to relax or stress us, we will learn how to deal with stressful thoughts and feelings later in this chapter. However, one helpful technique seems appropriate to discuss at this time.

We can control our thoughts, so we would be wise to practice *thought-stopping* techniques in stressful situations. **Thought stopping**, developed by Joseph Wolpe, a noted behavior therapist, involves concentrating on the unwanted thoughts and, after a short time, suddenly stopping and emptying your mind. The command *stop* is generally used to interrupt the unpleasant thoughts. Negative thoughts are sometimes so strong that they sap our energy and drain our motivation, making us feel physically tired and even sickly. However, with a little practice at thought-changing, anyone can break free of negative thought patterns for good (Seguin, 2015). Then, it is time to substitute thoughts that are reassuring and self-accepting. This technique, called **cognitive restructuring**, can turn off some of the negative chatter (Jacobs, 2004). For example, you say, "I know I am going to survive this divorce," rather than, "I will never make it without Joe." One positive thought at a time can gradually shift the balance of our thinking from negative to positive.

Now, let's see what happens to the body when stressful events and thoughts arise.

I Am Your Master

I can make you rise or fall. I can work for you or against you.

I can make you a success or failure.

I control the way that you feel and the way that you act.

I can make you laugh . . . work . . . love. I can make your heart sing with joy . . . achievement . . . elation. . . .

Or I can make you wretched . . . dejected . . . morbid . . .

I can make you sick . . . listless. . . .

I can be as a shackle . . . heavy . . . attached . . . burdensome . . . lost forever unless captured by pen or purpose.

I can be nurtured and grown to be great and beautiful . . . seen by the eyes of others through action in you.

I can never be removed . . . only replaced.

I am a THOUGHT

Why not know me better?   —Robert Conklin

BECOMING AWARE ACTIVITY—INTERNALLY-CREATED PRESSURES

Answer the questions and be prepared to discuss it with a small class group.

- Do you expect problem-free living?
- Are you pessimistic and expect the worst from life?
- Do you compare your achievements, or lack of them, to those of others?
- Do you worry about situations you cannot control?
- Are you a perfectionist? Do you expect too much of yourself or others?
- Are you competitive and seem to turn every encounter into a win/lose situation?
- Are you a victim of "hurry sickness" and constantly expect yourself to perform better and faster?
- Are you self-critical? Do you focus on your faults, rather than your strengths?
- Do you expect others, rather than yourself, to provide your emotional security?
- Do you assume you know how others feel and what they want from you, instead of asking them?
- Do you feel powerless and fail to see your available choices?
- Do any of these sound familiar to you?

THE EFFECTS OF STRESS

Dr. Hans Selye, in his years as a stress researcher, found that the body has a three-stage reaction to stress. He termed this chain of stress reaction the *general adaptation syndrome* (Rosch, 2016):

Stage 1—Alarm,
Stage 2—Resistance, and
Stage 3—Exhaustion

We will discuss each of these reactions.

The alarm stage. Our bodies recognize the stressor and prepares for fight or flight, which is done by a release of hormones from the endocrine glands. These hormones cause an increase in the heartbeat and respiration, elevation in the blood sugar level, increase in perspiration, dilated pupils, and slowed digestion. According to Dr. Walter B. Cannon of the Harvard Medical School, we then choose whether to use this burst of energy for fight or flight.

The resistance stage. This is a period of recovery and stabilization, during which the individual adapts to the stress. Consequently, the individual does what they can to meet the threat. Although it is true that the level of bodily arousal is not as high as it was in the alarm stage, it does remain higher than usual. This is nature's way of giving us greater protection against the original stressor. Coping responses are often strongest at this point. Because the individual attempts to do what is necessary to meet the threat, the most effective behavior of which the person is capable often comes forth. Often, people are so overwhelmed in the alarm stage that they simply cannot function. However, if there is effective functioning, it occurs in the resistance stage.

The exhaustion stage. Stress is a natural and unavoidable part of our lives, but it becomes a problem when it persists and becomes long term. Continuous stress will not enable the important *resistance* step to take place, and we will go from step one, *alarm*, directly to step three, **exhaustion**. When we remain exhausted because of continual exposure to stress, we become more receptive to physiological reactions and behavioral changes.

The immune system. The *immune system* is the body's defense and surveillance network of cells and chemicals that fight off bacteria, viruses, and other foreign or toxic substances (Plotnik, 2014). Have you ever gotten a cold, strep throat, or some other bacterial or viral infection after a stressful period, such as when final exams are over? This rather common experience of "coming down with something" illustrates how prolonged stressful experiences can decrease the effectiveness of our immune systems. The primary weapons of the immune system are *lymphocytes*, which are specialized white blood cells that attack and destroy most of these foreign invaders. Stress can lower the immune response by either decreasing the number of lymphocytes in the bloodstream or by somehow suppressing the response of the lymphocytes to foreign substances that have invaded the body.

It is important to note that short-term stress, under most circumstances, actually boosts the immune system, functioning as an adaptive response for injury or infection. "It's extreme, constant stress over a long period of time that impairs the immune system," explains Monika Fleshner, a neuroimmunopsychologist at the University of Colorado in Boulder (Raeburn, 2006).

Physical Effects of Stress

In various ways, stress takes a heavy toll on our well-being. For example, more than three out of every five doctor's office visits are for stress-related problems, and up to 90% of reported illness and disease is stress-related (Duffy & Atwater, 2014).

Increasingly, medical research links stress, including work-related forms such as job strain, to a range of serious health effects, such as obesity, diabetes, certain types of cancers, and heart disease. One of the main hormones released in response to stress is cortisol (Rudolph et al., 2016). Chronic stress can contribute to higher risks for heart disease, increased progress of cancer and increased speed at which cancer may return, more susceptibility to develop a prediabetic condition, memory problems and Alzheimer's, irritable bowel syndrome, peptic ulcers, and more (Hall, 2008).

In *The Sharp Solution: A Brain-Based Approach for Optimal Performance* (Wiley Press)

Heidi Hanna introduces a brain-based approach to realistic, sustainable energy management that supports a healthier brain. She believes that by engaging our brain, we can strategically re-wire how we operate, creating more energy and improving productivity while simultaneously reducing stress (Hanna, 2013).

According to Heidi Hanna in *Stressaholic, 5 Steps to Transform Your Relationship with Stress* (2014), chronic multitasking and increasing demands on our time and energy have caused a neurochemically based dependence on sources of stress and stimulation. As a result, modern society is tired and wired, suffering from physical exhaustion while mentally amped up, and unable to get adequate rest (Hanna, 2014). Hanna has developed a strategy called the Sharp solution to help make changes to your bad stress habits. Addiction to stress is one of the results of not balancing our brain with rest and we need to take the time to recharge it. By engaging our brain, we can strategically re-wire how we operate, become more focused and productive, flexible and resilient.

Yet, before these more serious health problems can develop, our bodies have a natural way of telling us there is too much stress and tension in our lives. Furthermore, most of us have a special physical organ or target area that lets us know when the stress is too great. Do you know what your special target is? Once you have learned to tune into your own signals, you will be able to recognize stress when it starts, before it takes a toll on your body. Review Table 8.1 for some of the physical effects of stress.

BEHAVIORAL EFFECTS OF STRESS

Another measuring tool for us to help recognize excessive stress in ourselves and others is through behavioral changes. Review these changes in Table 8.1, Effects of Stress.

Evaluate this list in relationship to your own life and add any other physical or behavioral changes you may experience that are not included here. This list can help you recognize imbalance and disharmony within and without, and that recognition is necessary if you are to effect a positive change for yourself.

How do I cope with stress? I clean and organize.
—SANDRA LEE

Table 8.1   EFFECTS OF STRESS

PHYSICAL		
Headaches	Rapid heart rate	Excessive sweating
Dermatitis	Impotence	Dizziness
Ulcers	Indigestion	Muscle spasms
Asthma	Diarrhea	Hypertension
Colitis	Stomach aches	Blurry vision
Common colds	Fatigue	Burning stomach
Skin rashes	Aching back and limbs	Vomiting
Allergies	Neck and shoulder tension	Delayed menstruation
Hyperventilation		
BEHAVIORAL		
Nervous tics	Clammy skin	Nail biting
Door slamming	Withdrawal	Grinding of teeth
Fist clenching	Depression	Temper tantrums
Insomnia	Irritability	Apathy
Tears	Acts of violence	Changed smoking habits
Frowning	Impatience	Worry
Hair twisting	Changed eating habits	Boredom
Jaw tightening	Changed drinking habits	Visible fears

Davis et al. (2008).

Knowing how to recognize physiological and behavioral effects of stress is only the beginning. The next step or steps involving change. Albert Ellis found that change is hard for most people; they do not want to do what is difficult, even if it is in their best interest (Ellis, 2002).

PERSONALITY TYPES

Research has indicated that there are basically three personality types in relation to stress, with each type differing in their abilities to handle stress effectively. These types are *Type A, Type B,* and a combination of *Type A* and *Type B.*

Type A.   There has been a tremendous amount of research directed toward determining the correlation between heart disease and emotional stress. Among the findings is evidence that there is an association between coronary artery and heart disease and a complex of emotional reactions, which have been designated as the **Type A behavioral pattern** by Friedman and Rosenman (1982). Because the study used an all-male sample, it is unknown if the results could be generalized to a female population (McLeod, 2014). These researchers found that almost all of their cardiac patients had in common a competitive, aggressive, ambitious, and stressful lifestyle (McLeod, 2014).

Research on the link between Type A personality behavior and coronary disease indicates that the lethal core of the Type A personality is not time urgency. Attention is focusing on *hostility and anger-prone tendencies*, which fuel an aggressive, reactive temperament (Smith & Ruiz, 2002; Rayl, 2007; McLeod, 2014). The Type A personality type's behavior makes them more prone to **stress-related illnesses** such as raised blood pressure. Such people are more likely to have their "flight or fight" response set off by things in their environment. As a result, they are more likely to have the stress hormones present, which over a long period of time leads to a range of stress-related illnesses. Researchers found that more than twice as many Type A people as Type B people developed coronary heart disease. When the figures were adjusted for smoking, lifestyle, etc. it still emerged that Type A people were nearly twice as likely to develop heart disease as Type B people.

Here are some other characteristics of the ***Type A*** behavioral pattern (Kleinke, 2002):

- A drive to succeed, coupled with impatience, irritability, and aggressiveness
- Trouble relaxing and restlessness
- Perfectionist and seeks results *now*
- Feelings of pressure even when relaxed
- A constant clock watcher
- Ignores fatigue while doing strenuous work
- Thrives on stress; his or her work is never done
- Only happy with a vigorous, fast-paced lifestyle
- Time pressures frequently create frustration and sometimes hostility
- May appear nervous, scattered, and hyper
- Eats fast, walks fast, and talks fast

Type B. This behavior pattern is the opposite of the Type A (Friedman & Rosenman, 1982). People with ***Type B behavioral pattern*** tend to be more tolerant of others, are more relaxed than Type A individuals, more reflective, experience lower levels of anxiety. and display higher levels of imagination and creativity (McLeod, 2014). Type B people are seldom harried by the need to be involved in an ever-increasing series of

> *The greatest weapon against stress is our ability to choose one thought over another.*
> —WILLIAM JAMES

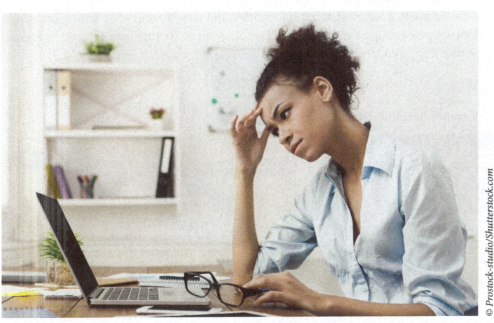

How do you perform under pressure?

© Prostock-studio/Shutterstock.com

activities in a continually decreasing amount of time. Here are some other characteristics of Type B people (Kleinke, 2002):

- Serious and easy going
- Patient and relaxed
- Enjoy leisure and opportunities to experiment and reflect
- Prefer a peaceful, steady, quiet, and generally tranquil lifestyle
- Not easily irritated
- Are less competitive than Type A
- Slower paced; feel no need to hurry
- May appear lethargic, sluggish, and bored
- Are stress avoiders; may avoid new challenges
- Speak slowly, walk slowly, eat slowly
- Sometimes lack the excitement, enthusiasm, and dynamism needed to perform at peak levels under pressure

Type B people may have a tremendous drive, but they may not take the risks necessary for big rewards. When they do take risks, their drive is coupled with time to ponder leisurely and weigh alternatives. It may sound like Type B people do not have a lot of stressors. However, if they are in a Type A environment that requires a great deal of structure, this can be very stressful to them. Studies carried out on women have not shown such a major difference between Type A and Type B and subsequent health. This may suggest that different coping strategies are just as important as personality. The study was able to control for other important variables, such as smoking and lifestyle. This is good, as it makes it less likely that such extraneous variables could confound the results of the study (McLeod, 2014).

Which type are you? Most of us are either Type A or Type B, with varying degrees of Type A and B. It is estimated that about 40% of the population is Type A and 60% is Type B (Paulus et al., 2000).

You will be given an opportunity to complete a personality type inventory at the end of this chapter. Like most stress inventories, this one is somewhat flawed because it does not give enough weight to individual differences. Be sure to take this into consideration when you look at your scores.

Are you …

or somewhere in between?

a racehorse

a turtle

LIFESTYLES AND STRESS LEVELS

Consider this question in triads or small groups:

What kind of lifestyle do you prefer to live: rushed, relaxed, or a balance between the two?

Actually, each of us is really the best judge of ourselves, and we can gradually develop an instinctive feeling that tells us whether we are running above or below the stress level that suits us best. Do you know what your normal stress endurance level is? The key to effective stress management is recognizing when stress becomes more debilitating than stimulating.

NEGATIVE AND DEFENSIVE COPING AND PTSD

Coping refers to active efforts to master, reduce, or tolerate the demands created by stress (Weiten et al., 2014). When we cope, we consciously think and make a decision to deal with the problems we face. However, we may cope in negative ways. We may drink too much, eat too much, worry too much, or even abuse medication and drugs.

Sometimes the stress, frustration, and conflict of dealing with these problems interferes with our ability to maintain a healthy self-concept. We become extremely sensitive to threats to our ego. We will do almost anything to avoid, escape, or shield ourselves from the anxieties elicited by these threats.

In order to protect our feelings of self-esteem and self-respect, we may unconsciously resort to various distortions of reality, frequently referred to as *defense mechanisms* (Freud, 1936).

Defense mechanisms do not eliminate the problems that are the cause of anxiety, but they help us to hide or disguise our feelings and temporarily deal with anxiety or stress. Defense mechanisms have two primary characteristics.

- *First, they distort and deny reality.*
- *Second, they operate unconsciously, so that we are unaware that we are using them.*

See Table 8.2 for some examples of commonly used defense mechanisms.

Defense mechanisms are designed to help us escape the pain of anxiety in stressful situations. Most of us would have difficulty maintaining our mental health without resorting to such defenses. However, the trouble is that these defenses can become common patterns of behavior for reacting to problems and stress.

The more aware we are of the defense mechanisms we use and why we use them, the more likely will be our attempts to face our stressful situations in an open and honest manner. It is important for us to remember that, although defense mechanisms offer us short-term relief, our discomfort quickly returns, because the problem has not been solved.

> The best years of your life are the ones in which you decide your problems are your own. You do not blame them on your mother, the ecology, or the president. You realize that you control your own destiny.
> —ALBERT ELLIS

> Life is not what it's supposed to be. It's what it is. The way you cope with it is what makes the difference.
> —VIRGINIA SATIR

Table 8.2   EXAMPLES OF COMMONLY USED DEFENSE MECHANISMS

DEFENSE MECHANISM	DEFINITION
Rationalization	When the explanations offered are reasonable, rational, and convincing, but not real reasons.
Projection	When we attribute our own feelings, shortcomings, or unacceptable impulses to others.
Reaction Formation	When impulses are not only repressed, they are also controlled by emphasizing the opposite behavior.
Denial	When we refuse to recognize or acknowledge a threatening situation.
Repression	When we exclude painful, unwanted, or dangerous thoughts and impulses from our conscious mind.
Sublimation	When we direct our basic responses to the situation into some other socially acceptable or valued behavior.
Regression	When we psychologically return to a form of behavior characteristic of an earlier stage of development.
Displacement	When we redirect strong feelings from one person or object to another that seems more acceptable and less threatening.

Adapted from Pastorino & Doyle-Portillo (2011); Nairne (2010).

How people behave under stress depends to some extent on the level of stress experienced. For example, survivors of traumatic events such as rape, military combat, medical emergencies, witnessing a death or near-death, major accidents, and terrorist attacks may cope well at the time of the trauma, but months later experience a delayed emotional reaction known as *post-traumatic stress disorder (PTSD)*. Post-traumatic stress disorder is a severe anxiety disorder characterized by symptoms of intense fear, anxiety, and avoidance behavior, resulting from an unusually distressing event (Duffy & Atwater, 2014). Furthermore, PTSD is a prolonged maladaptive reaction to a traumatic event, and it may last for years or even decades afterward.

Women have a two to three times higher risk of developing post-traumatic stress disorder, compared to men. Several factors are involved in explaining this difference. Men and women experience different types of trauma, both in private life and at work (e.g., police officers). Women are exposed to more high-impact trauma (e.g., sexual trauma) than men, and at a younger age. Trauma early in life has more impact, especially when it involves type II trauma interfering with neurobiological development and personality. Traumatic stress affects different areas of the brains of boys and girls at different ages (Christiansen & Hansen, 2015).

GENDER, CULTURE, AND STRESS

As we have already discussed, individuals have different levels of tolerance for stress. Some seem to thrive in situations in which others feel uncomfortably stressed. Also, some individuals actually seem to seek out stressful situations. As a result of these differences, methods of coping with stress vary accordingly.

Gender and stress. One of the major differences between men and women is how they cope with stress. Researchers have found that while men are more likely to fight or flee when stressed, women show a different response to stress, called *tend* and *befriend*, which involves nurturing and seeking social support (Taylor, 2004). Also, men tend to become increasingly focused and withdrawn, while women tend to become increasingly overwhelmed and emotionally involved. These differences in coping styles can lead to friction in relationships.

A wellness issue that might start out looking like a stress or body image issue that turns into an extreme body issue that effects males and females will need help from a counselor or doctor. This is called **body dysmorphic disorder,** and is a mental disorder in which an individual can't stop thinking about one or more perceived defects or flaws in their appearance—a flaw that, to others, is either minor or not observable. But the individual may feel so ashamed and anxious that they may avoid many social situations.

Body dysmorphic disorder typically starts in the early teenage years, and it affects both males and females. An obsession that body build is too small or not muscular enough (muscle dysmorphia) occurs almost exclusively in males.

Body dysmorphic disorder usually doesn't get better on its own, and if untreated, it may get worse over time, leading to severe depression, anxiety, and extensive medical bills, and may lead to suicidal thoughts and behaviors (Mayo Clinic, 2019).

In *You Just Don't Understand*, Deborah Tannen (2001) suggests that men should just listen to women's problems, without giving advice. Remember, talking is a woman's natural and healthy way of reacting to stress, and if she feels she is being heard, her stress will seem much less. On the other hand, women need to let men disengage and ponder their own problems, and when they have discovered the solution for themselves, they will then share some of "what has been going on with them" and possibly even report their personal solution(s). Remember, quiet concentration, without an immediate need to talk, is often a man's natural and healthy way of reacting to stress.

If women resent men's tendency to offer solutions to problems, men complain about women's refusal to take action to solve the problems they complain about.
—DEBORAH TANNEN

Culture and stress. Who you are is a factor in what you may find stressful and how stressed you feel. For example, in 1995, Judith Pliner and Duane Brown surveyed 229 students (123 females and 106 males) from four ethnic groups (Caucasian, African American, Hispanic, and Asian American) who were asked to estimate how stressful they would expect to find events in three different domains: academic, financial, and personal (Rosch, 2016). Responses to the survey, summarized in Focus on Diversity, indicate that an individual's ethnic background is associated with what that person appraises as stressful.

Does ethnicity-related stress have harmful effects on individuals' mental and physical health? Researchers are showing increased interest in exploring the stress experienced by members of various ethnic groups in at least the following areas: 1) discrimination or perceived discrimination, 2) concern that their behavior might be interpreted as characteristic of derogatory stereotypes, and 3) pressure to not abandon their cultural heritage (Weiten et al., 2014).

A pleasure a day keeps stress away.
—ETHEL ROSKIES

FOCUS ON DIVERSITY

Four ethnic groups—Caucasian, African American, Hispanic, and Asian American—estimate how stressful they would expect to find events in three different domains:

Academic Domain: Older African Americans and Hispanics perceived more academic stress than older Asian Americans. Older Hispanics perceived significantly more academic stress than older Caucasians.

Financial Domain: Both African American and Hispanic individuals felt more stress in meeting financial events than did either Caucasian or Asian American individuals.

Personal Domain: African American men perceived greater stress in the personal domain than did African American women. Young Caucasian women perceived more stress in this domain than did older Caucasian women.

(Rosch, 2016)

WHAT AFFECTS THE WAY INDIVIDUALS COPE WITH STRESS?

It seems that some individuals are stress resistant and others are more susceptible to the harmful effects of stress. What accounts for the difference in the way different individuals cope with stress? Dr. Lyle Miller and Dr. Alma Smith (1994) give an interesting view in their book, *The Stress Solution*:

> People are quite different from one another in their susceptibility to stress. Some are like horses, and some are like butterflies. The horses tolerate great amounts of stress without faltering or breaking stride; the butterflies fall apart under the slightest demand or pressure. Whether you're a horse or a butterfly depends on several ingredients: your physical constitution, how well you take care of yourself, and your resources for coping with stress. The tougher you are, the more you can take. If you have a stress-prone constitution, are lazy about exercise, eat poorly, abuse stimulants, don't get enough sleep, or don't use your coping resources, you don't stand much chance against stress (Miller & Smith, 1994).

Hardiness. One characteristic that seems to distinguish stress-resistant people from those who are more susceptible to its harmful effects is known as **hardiness**. Actually, this term refers to a cluster of characteristics rather than just one. Stress researcher S. R. Maddi's (2006) findings suggest that hardy people seem to differ in attitudes from others in three respects:

- **Commitment** (rather than alienation)—they have deeper involvement in their jobs and other life activities.

© ayelet-keshet/Shutterstock.com

- **Control** (rather than powerlessness)—they believe that they can, in fact, influence important events in their lives and the outcomes they experience.
- **Challenge** (rather than threats)—they perceive change as a challenge and an opportunity to grow rather than as a threat to their security.

One thing seems fairly certain: stress-hardy people manage their lives by managing themselves—they control their own attitudes and coping tendencies. Without a doubt, there are resilient individuals who bounce back from stressful experiences quickly and effectively. As a matter of fact, they use humor, positive emotions, cognitive flexibility, cognitive reappraisal, social support, and optimism to cope with adversity (Southwick et al., 2005). It is important to remember that individuals can and do experience personal growth during adverse times (Duffy & Atwater, 2014).

Some of these findings point to the role of an optimistic outlook in stress tolerance (Nairne, 2010).

Afterward: If I Could Live It Over

If I had to live my life over again, I'd dare to make more mistakes next time.

I'd relax.

I would limber up.

I would be sillier than I have been this trip.

I would take more chances.

I would take more trips. I would climb more mountains, swim more rivers.

I would eat more ice cream and less beans.

I would perhaps have more actual troubles, but I'd have fewer imaginary ones.

You see, I'm one of those people who live seriously and sanely hour after hour, day after day.

Oh, I've had my moments. And if I had it to do over again, I'd have more of them.

In fact, I'd try to have nothing else, just moments, each after another, instead of living so many years ahead of each day.

I've been one of those persons who never goes anywhere without a thermometer, a hot water bottle, a raincoat and a parachute.

If I had it to do over again, I would travel lighter than I have.

If I had to live my life over, I would start barefoot earlier in the spring and stay that way later in the fall.

I would go to more dances.

I would ride more merry-go-rounds.

I would pick more daisies.

—NADINE STAIR

(This delightful perspective of life was written at age 85.)

Optimism or pessimism. *Optimism* is defined as a general tendency to envision the future as favorable. In contrast, *pessimism* may be defined as a general tendency to envision the future as unfavorable. Research suggests that optimists cope with stress in more adaptive ways than pessimists (Bernstein, 2010). For example, optimists are more likely to engage in action-oriented, problem-focused coping. They are more willing than pessimists to seek social support, and they are more likely to emphasize the positive in their appraisals of stressful events. David Armor, an assistant professor of psychology at Yale, notes, "Positive assumptions about the future may allow us to tolerate stressful situations that would otherwise be unbearable" (Paul, 2011). For the person who expects to achieve success, stress may be viewed as an obstacle to be overcome rather than as an obstacle that cannot be hurdled. Consequently, pessimists are more likely to deal with stress by giving up or engaging in denial. Studies show that optimists are better at coping with the distress associated with *everything*, from menopause to heart surgery (Newman, 2000).

Are you a horse or a butterfly? . . .

Think/Pair/Share Activity

CHOICES AND CHALLENGES

Consider these questions with a partner.

Are you a horse or a butterfly? Do you believe you can influence important events in your life and the outcomes you experience? Do you perceive change as a challenge or a threat to your security? What choices do you have when confronted with stressful events and situations?

Three coping options. Actually, we have three different options when we are confronted with stressful events and situations. According to Taylor and McGee (2000), we can:

1. **Change Environments.** We might choose to move to another city, change jobs, separate from our spouse, and so on.
2. **Change the Environment.** We can often work to improve the situation that is causing us so much stress.
3. **Change Me (Improve My Coping Skills).** William James once said, "The greatest discovery of our generation is that men can alter their lives by altering the attitudes of their mind." This is especially important to remember in relation to stress because, as we stated earlier, *it is not really the event that causes stress, it is our reaction to it—our attitude.*

Cognitive reappraisal Alex Korb, a neuroscientist and author of *The Upward Spiral: Using Neuroscience to Reverse the Course of Depression, One Small Change at a Time*, believes that many of us—whether due to genetics, brain chemistry, our experiences or coping skills—tell ourselves way too many negative thoughts. We ruminate, thinking the same negative, unproductive thoughts over and over. Each thought is made up of a complex pattern of activity between proteins and other chemicals, gene expressions, and neural connections in our brain. The more we have a thought, the stronger this circuit grows. A well-developed thought "is like a ski track in the snow. The more you ski down a path, the easier it is to go down that path and not another." By practicing with intent you can create another path. Psychologists call the technique *cognitive reappraisal*. The result will be stronger neural networks devoted to positive thoughts, or a happier brain. People who do this have better mental health and more life satisfaction, and even better-functioning hearts, research shows (Korb & Seigel, 2015).

Cognitive reappraisal is at the heart of **Cognitive Behavioral Therapy** practiced by many psychologists. The goal is to reframe your thoughts constructively, so they are based in reality. Hooria Jazaieri, a licensed marriage and family therapist in San Jose, California, and researcher in the psychology department at the University of California, Berkeley, who studies emotion regulation believes that stopping the *ruminations* (going over an issue again and again) can be done with cognitive behavioral techniques.

Another goal is to see yourself more accurately, says Steve Orma, a clinical psychologist in San Francisco, and author of *Stop Worrying and Go to Sleep*. Orma uses Cognitive Behavioral Therapy (CBT), a collaborative, supportive approach to help an individual manage and resolve personal challenges. The process is active, focused, and goal-oriented, with the aim of helping an individual achieve their highest potential. He has the following steps to follow:

Be Aware
You need to know your thoughts to change them. Learn to notice when you are ruminating. Remind yourself that this is a waste of time. Write down the thoughts. Identify what triggered them. Be specific!

Look for Supporting Evidence
A lot of the things people tell themselves when they ruminate are untrue. You need to challenge your beliefs and turn the negative thoughts into questions.

Practice, Practice, Practice
You can turn your new thoughts into a habit in a relatively short time. Keep writing down your negative thoughts every time you have them—and challenging them.

Create an Imaginary Friend
We're often nicer to our friends than we are to ourselves. If a friend told you he was telling himself the same irrational things you tell yourself, you'd have no trouble telling him he is wrong.

Exaggerate the Thought
Follow your negative thought to its extreme conclusion. You are such a big loser that even your dog ignores you. Turn it in to something humorous.

Shift Lanes
If a huge truck pulled in front of you dangerously on the highway, you'd switch lanes quickly. You need to do this when negative thoughts arise. Imagine your favorite vacation spot! You can't keep two thoughts and the same time. (Orma 2016)

Elizabeth Bernstein (2016) also commented on a November 2014 study in the journal *Behaviour Research and Therapy* that people who practiced Cognitive Reappraisals as part of Cognitive Behavioral Therapy were able to significantly reduce their negative emotions in 16 weeks. The study was led by Philippe R. Goldin, a research scientist at Stanford University (Bernstein, 2016).

Our reaction to any event, stressful or not, depends on our thoughts and feelings about what happened or what should have happened. Earlier in this chapter, we stated that, most often, the greatest source of stress is the tremendous pressure and anxiety we create internally with our own thoughts and feelings. We also indicated that we would discuss how to deal with stressful thoughts and feelings. We are now ready to do this.

In the following section, we will discuss some negative and debilitating techniques of coping with stress, including Negative or Defensive Coping Mechanisms like body dysmorphia and Bingeing/Purging, and PTSD.

DEALING WITH STRESSFUL THOUGHTS AND FEELINGS

Have you ever said, "I can't help the way I feel"? You want to feel calm when taking tests, but you still get butterflies in your stomach. You want to feel confident when talking to your teacher about a "bad" grade, but you still feel nervous. You do not want to be afraid of heights, but you cannot keep yourself from feeling scared. It is almost like you have no control over your feelings. These feelings are just automatic responses to certain stressful events and people in your life.

Consequently, you may say that these events or people cause you to feel the way you do. After all, touching your hand to a hot burner causes pain, so why can't people and certain events cause you stress? Let us diagram two events and see what is happening.

Activating Event	•	Causes	•	Consequences or Feelings
Touching your hand to a hot burner		•		Physical pain
Talking to your teacher		•		Stressful, tense feelings

By now, you are still convinced that certain events and other people cause you to feel the way you do. The author will not argue with you that touching your hand to a hot burner really does cause pain. However, I cannot agree that talking to a teacher really causes us to have tense, stressful feelings. Here's why!

THE POWER OF SELF-TALK

Rational emotive therapist Albert Ellis (2001), who died at the age of 93 in 2007, indicated that the event of talking to a teacher does not cause us to feel tense and stressed. Instead it is our beliefs, or what we say to ourselves *(self-talk)* about talking to a teacher that causes us to feel tense, nervous, and stressed.

Ellis (2001) believed that a great deal of our stress is unnecessary, and that it really comes from faulty conclusions we have made about the world. It is really our interpretations, *what we say to ourselves about our experiences,* which creates the debilitating emotions of anxiety, anger, and depression, as discussed in Chapter Four.

The Chinese word for crisis means opportunity with danger. In the middle of every difficulty lies opportunity.
—ALBERT EINSTEIN

In a real sense, through our own self-talk, we are either in the construction business or the wrecking business.
—DOROTHY CORKVILLE

Let us examine the theory of Dr. Ellis by looking at an example he frequently gave at the Institute for Rational-Emotive Therapy in New York:

> Assume you walk by your friend's house, and he sticks his head out the window and calls you a bunch of nasty names. You would probably become angry and upset with your friend.

> Now let's imagine that you were walking by a mental hospital, rather than your friend's house, and your friend is a patient in the hospital. This time, he yells at you, calling you the same ugly names. What would your feelings be? Would you be as angry and upset now that you know he is not normal and does not live in his house? Probably not!

Actually, the activating event (being called nasty names) was identical in both cases, but our feelings were very different because we are saying something very different to ourselves.

In the first example, we were probably saying things like, "He shouldn't call me those nasty names! That's really awful! I'll pay him back!"

However, in the second example, we might be telling ourselves something like, "Poor sick John. He can't help what he is doing." Instead of feeling angry, we were probably feeling a degree of sympathy for our friend.

It is easy to see that our *different beliefs (interpretations and thoughts)* about the events determined our feelings. Let us look at the diagram of our two emotional experiences: A + B = C.

> *People feel disturbed not by things, but by the views they take of them.*
> —EPICTETUS

A	+	B	=	C
ACTIVATING EVENT	+	THOUGHTS OR BELIEFS	=	CONSEQUENCES OR FEELINGS
Being called names		My friend shouldn't do this		Angry, upset
Being called names		My friend must be sick		Pity, sympathy

Ellis (2003) and cognitive therapist Aaron Beck (Beck et al., 2006) stress that our extreme, debilitative, and stressful emotions are due largely to our *irrational beliefs*—what we say to ourselves. This is also called **cognitive reappraisal**. Remember that cognitive reappraisal is an emotion response strategy that involves changing the way we respond to stress by reinterpreting the meaning of the emotional stimulus. Have you ever failed a series of tests and thought negatively about yourself? If you did, your self-talk might be defeating. Or, you could be positive and not engage in defeating self-talk.

Self-talk is one of the most simple and powerful ways we can change our attitudes. Think about it: what we think determines how we feel, which in turn determines what we do, which is what defines us. So short circuit the negative self-talk and learn how to be your own hero. Mary Mueller (2001), author of *Taking Care of Me*, suggests we work on replacing some of our negative self-talk with the following:

- "I should" with "I want . . ."
- "I can't" with "I haven't yet . . ."
- "I'll try" with "I'll do my best . . ."
- "He/she makes me . . ." with "I feel _____ when . . ."

What Is the Difference between Irrational and Rational Beliefs—Self-Talk?

Sometimes, *self-talk*, what we say to ourselves about an event or situation, is irrational. It does not even make sense, but we believe that it is true. *The ingredient that makes a belief irrational is that it cannot be scientifically verified. There is no empirical evidence or proof to support the belief.*

Irrational beliefs (self-talk) result in inappropriate emotions, behaviors, and more stress. Inappropriate emotions and behaviors are those that are likely to thwart an individual's desired goals. Consequently, the individual feels stressed. An example of this cycle is **must**urbation, a term coined by Albert Ellis to refer to demandingness about the self, others, or the world. "**I must do …**"

On the other hand, *rational beliefs (self-talk)* are those beliefs that result in appropriate emotions and behaviors. Appropriate emotions and behaviors are those that are likely to help an individual attain desired goals. Consequently, the individual feels less stress. It is important to remember that even negative emotions (such as disappointment, concern, etc.) can be appropriate. *The ingredient that makes a belief rational is that it can be scientifically verified. There is empirical evidence or proof to support the belief.*

We will now examine the characteristics of irrational and rational self-talk: What makes sense and what doesn't? What objective evidence can be provided to support your self-talk—your beliefs?

> *Your most important irrational pathway is musturbation—or you're devoutly following the tyranny of the shoulds.*
> —ALBERT ELLIS

Characteristics of Irrational and Rational Self-Talk

Almost all irrational self-verbalizations include Should Statements, Awfulizing Statements, and Overgeneralizations. David Burns (2006) refers to these irrational self-verbalizations *as a twisted form of absolutist thinking.* We will now look at these individually.

Should statements. These are absolutistic demands or moral imperatives that the individual believes must occur. Individuals tend to express their shoulds in three areas: *I should, you should,* and *the world should.* Should statements also contain words such as *ought, have to,* and *must.*

Have you ever made statements similar to the ones below?

Helen **should not** be so inconsiderate.

John **should** be a better teacher.

People **ought** to be at meetings on time.

I **have to (must)** make an "A" on the next test.

Do not "should" on yourself.

These statements all imply that other people and things in your world need to be as you want them to be. This is really unreasonable.

True, it would be more pleasant if Helen were more considerate; it would be helpful if John were a better teacher; it would be beneficial if people were at meetings on time; it would be nice to make an "A" on the exam.

Think about it like this: Does it really make sense that a person *should* or *should not* do something? Where can you find objective proof that a person *should* or *should not* do something? Is it not reasonable that people can actually do or choose not to do whatever they want? What evidence or proof can you provide that you *must* make an A on the test? Are you going to die if you do not make an A?

It is perfectly rational for us to wish that people would behave differently and that things in our world would be as we want them to be. It is even okay to change what can be changed and accept those things that cannot be altered. It is unreasonable, however, for us to expect that other people or the world will ever meet our unrealistic expectations. Reality is reality! Failure to accept this reality can result in our lives being filled with disappointments and *more stress.* Albert Ellis (2003), author of *How to Stubbornly Refuse to Make Yourself Miserable about Anything—Yes, Anything,* has an interesting insight:

> "You mainly make yourself needlessly and neurotically miserable by strongly holding absolutist irrational beliefs, especially by rigidly believing unconditional shoulds, oughts, and musts, and ruminating them over and over again ..." (Ellis, 2003)

Awfulizing statements. Generally, when we say that the world, ourselves, or someone *should* be different, we imply that it is *awful* or *terrible* when they are not different. Have you ever made any of the following statements? If so, ask yourself, "Where can I find the proof or evidence to support these beliefs?"

What she did to me is just **awful!**

It is just **terrible.**

I just can't **stand it.**

I can't **bear it.**

It is true that things in our world could be improved and that events that happen to us are unfortunate. However, when you consistently talk about how *terrible* or *awful* something is, you will eventually convince yourself that what you are thinking and saying is right. This kind of *self-talk* causes you to feel angry, depressed, and, therefore, stressed.

In some instances, something is so *terrible* or *awful* that you convince yourself that *you can't stand it* or *you can't bear it.* As cold and callous as it may sound, if you are alive and conscious, you are *standing it,* you are *bearing it.*

Would it not be far less stressful and certainly more rational for your self-talk to be:

"This situation is going to be difficult for me, but I will work hard and use my positive attitude and abilities to be as successful as I can be."

Overgeneralizations. We often make overgeneralizations based on a single incident or piece of evidence, and we ignore everything else that we know about ourselves and others. Cue words that indicate you may be overgeneralizing are: *all, every, none, never, always, everybody,* and *nobody.* Overgeneralizations frequently lead to human worth statements about ourselves and other people. And, these statements do not even make sense. Think about these statements!

You Were Fired: I'll never get another job—I'm a complete failure.

Your Spouse Left You: No one will ever want to marry me now—I must be unlovable.

First of all, *never* and *ever* mean a long time. Just because you lost your job, does that prove that no one else will ever hire you and that you are a *complete* failure? To be a *complete* failure, you would have to fail 100% of the time. This is unrealistic. Oh yes, have you forgotten that you have had other jobs besides the one you just lost? Just because your spouse left you, does that *prove* that you are unlovable? Think about it: Who else in your life cares about you? Surely, someone else does.

Sometimes we use overgeneralizations when we exaggerate shortcomings of others. For example:

You **never** listen to me.

You **never** do anything for me.

The chances are highly probable that "they" can remember and prove to you at least one time they listened, and at least one time they did something for you.

Statements such as these lead to anger, resentment, alienation from other people, and more stress. Would it not be more accurate to say:

Sometimes you do not listen to me.

You have done some nice things for me.

Remember, the real question for you to answer is: What did you think to feel that?
—DAN TAYLOR

Our real blessings often appear to us in the shapes of pains, losses and disappointments; but let us have patience, and we soon shall see them in their proper figures.
—JOSEPH ADDISON

Disputing Irrational Beliefs

How do you avoid these irrational beliefs that create feelings of stress? Ellis and MacLaren (2005) recommend these steps:

1. **Monitor Your Emotional Reactions.** Try to describe what you are *feeling* as accurately as possible. Say, "I feel angry, depressed, fearful, hurt, jealous, sad, worried." Because it is possible to experience more than one negative emotion at the same time, be sure to write down all the unpleasant feelings that you are having.

2. **Describe the Activating Event.** Write down your perception of the event or whatever seemed to trigger the events that led to your unpleasant feelings and your present stressful condition. It may be something that someone did; it may be something you need to do but are afraid of doing; it may be a series of several small unpleasant happenings, and you have just had too much!

3. **Record Your Self-Talk.** What are you saying to yourself that is causing you to feel angry, depressed, and so on? What are you thinking or what is going through your head? What are you worried about? When you think about … (the activating event), how do you make yourself depressed or angry? Becoming aware of your self-talk may be difficult at first, but with practice, you can learn to do so.

4. **Dispute Your Irrational Beliefs.** It is now necessary for you to go back to step 3 and do three things: 1) decide whether each statement is a rational or an irrational belief, 2) explain why the belief does or does not make sense, and 3) write some different statements that you can say to yourself in the future to prevent yourself from having such debilitative emotions and experiencing such stress. For example, let us say that you are the type of person who over-generalizes about the consequences of failing a test. You think such irrational thoughts as:

> *A man is hurt not so much by what happens, as by his opinion of what happens.*
> —MONTAIGNE

"Why do I always mess up?"

"This is going to be terrible."

Some effective coping statements might include:

"I'm not going to think about failing."

"I'm going to concentrate on being successful; that's better than getting nervous."

"I'm going to take three deep breaths, relax, calm down, and practice positive thinking; then I'll start to work on the exam."

Now that you know how to identify and dispute the irrational beliefs that have been causing you stress, we will now discuss some additional ways of managing stress.

Tips for Managing Stress

LEARNING TO REACT TO STRESS IN A HEALTHY WAY

Stressful events are facts of life. And you may not be able to change your current situation. But you can take steps to manage the impact these events have on you. You can learn to identify what stresses you and how to take care of yourself physically and emotionally in the face of stressful situations. The reward for learning to manage stress is peace of mind and perhaps a longer, healthier life.

Following is a list of several suggestions that may help you live with stress, whether it is an occasional mild upset, which most of us experience, or one that is more lasting and severe.

- **Identify Your Causes of Stress.** Monitor your state of mind throughout the day. If you feel stressed, write down the cause, your thoughts, and your mood. Once you know what's bothering you, develop a plan for addressing it. That might mean setting more reasonable expectations for you and others or asking for help with household responsibilities, job assignments, or other tasks. List all your commitments, assess your priorities, and then eliminate any tasks that are not absolutely essential.

- **Build strong relationships.** Relationships can be a source of stress if they are not healthy. But strong, mutually supportive relationships can reduce stress.

- **Work Off Stress.** If you are angry or upset, try to do something physical such as running, gardening, playing tennis, or cleaning out the garage. Working the stress out of your system will leave you much better prepared to handle your problems.

- **Have Fun.** Do something each day that you really enjoy, whether it is reading your favorite book or magazine, having lunch with a friend, watching your favorite TV program, taking a walk, playing a musical instrument, or having fun with some kiddie-toy collection. Authorities agree that people who preserve their sense of fun are better equipped to solve problems, think creatively, and manage stress.

- **Talk It Out.** When something is bothering you, talk it out with someone you trust and respect, such as a friend, family member, clergyman, teacher, or counselor. Sometimes another person can help you see a new side to your problem and, thus, a new solution.

- **Focus on Gratitude.** It is physiologically impossible to be stressed and thankful at the same time. Two thoughts cannot occupy our mind at the same time. If you are focusing on gratitude, you can't be negative (Brown, 2012). Gratitude is a way for people to appreciate what they have instead of always reaching for something new in the hopes it will make them happier, or thinking they can't feel satisfied until every physical and material need is met. Gratitude helps people refocus on what they have instead of what they lack. And, although it may feel contrived at first, this mental state grows stronger with use and practice (Emmons, 2019).

- **Do Something for Others.** If you find that you are worrying about yourself all the time, try doing something for somebody else. This helps get your mind off yourself and can give you a sense of well-being.

> *I have been sustained throughout my life by three saving graces—my family, my friends and a faith in the power of resilience and hope.*
> —ELIZABETH EDWARDS

Work off your stress with some physical activity!

© Goran Bogicevic/Shutterstock.com

- **Have Some Real Close Friends.** Having true friends that you do not need to fear criticism from, and whom you can talk freely to, is important. Friends who are accepting are not a threat to your ego. Without at least one such friend, a person is forced into emotional isolation, which in itself is a stress, and one that usually produces adverse responses.
- **Eat Sensibly.** Try to have balanced meals and pay close attention to the habit of eating "junk foods." Do not starve yourself to lose weight. Watch excessive sugar and caffeine. Think of your body as a car. If you do not put oil, gas, and water in your car frequently, it will quit running. So will your body if you abuse it with improper eating habits.
- **Get Organized.** Plan, schedule, take notes, and keep good files. Organizing the daily nitty-gritty of life reduces stress. Save your memory for more creative and pleasurable things (Dembling, 2006).
- **Rehearse.** When you are facing a situation that you know will be stressful to you, rehearse it. Either mentally or with a friend, anticipate what might occur and plan your response. Being prepared reduces stress.
- **Overcome Procrastination.** One of the simplest and most effective solutions is to just get started—anywhere on a task. The moment you think "I'll feel more like doing this later" or "I work better under pressure," recognize that you're just about to procrastinate—to give in to feel good (Pychyl, 2011). Tim Pychyl believes procrastination is an emotional problem. If you stop treating procrastination like a time-management issue, it becomes easier to manage. As for what procrastination is (and isn't): "Procrastination is a voluntary delay of an intended act despite the knowledge that this delay may harm us," Pychyl explains in his book *Solving the Procrastination Puzzle.* That is, procrastination is by definition an irrational behavior because it runs counter to our own idea of what will make us happy (Kemmis-Zapier, 2019).

- **Learn to Say "No."** Say no when your schedule is full, to activities you do not enjoy, to responsibilities that are not really yours, to emotional demands that leave you feeling drained, to other people's problems that you cannot solve.

- **Learn to Accept What You Cannot Change.** Remember the words of the philosopher, Epictetus: "Happiness and freedom begin with a clear understanding of one principle: Some things are within your control, and some things are not. It is only after you have faced up to this fundamental role and learned to distinguish between what you can and cannot control that inner tranquility and outer effectiveness become possible."

- **Understand Worry.** You can think about your problems or you can worry about them, and there is a vast difference between the two. Worry is thinking that turned *toxic*. Thinking works its way through problems to conclusions and decisions.

- **Avoid Self-Medication.** There are many chemicals such as alcohol and other drugs that can mask stress symptoms, but they do not help you adjust to stress itself. Also, many are habit-forming and can cause more stress than they solve; consult your doctor before you decide to use them. It is important, too, that the ability to handle stress comes from within you, not from externals.

- **Live a Balanced Life.** Make time for what is important to you. Work and school are important, but they are not the only important areas in your life. What about time with your family and friends? What about time for a hobby? Stop and ask yourself, "Am I spending too much time on one important area of my life and forgetting the others?"

- **Get Enough Sleep and Rest.** Lack of sleep can lessen your ability to deal with stress by making you more irritable. If stress continually prevents you from sleeping, you should inform your doctor.

- **Write in a Journal or Diary.** Studies confirm the value of expressing stressful thoughts to others or getting them down on paper—even if you never tell anyone (Stone et al., 2000).

- **Shun the "Perfect" Urge.** Some people expect too much from themselves and are in a constant state of worry and anxiety because they think they are not achieving as much as they should.

- **Develop a Regular Exercise Program.** A sensible exercise program can begin with a short daily walk that is gradually increased. To avoid excess physical stress, you need to develop your own program gradually and then maintain it constantly. There is increasing evidence that regular, sensible exercise causes a number of important chemical changes in the body. It helps to eliminate depression. It helps to alleviate anxiety. Sensible, enjoyable exercise is nature's antistress reaction remedy. Experts consider aerobics to be an excellent release.

- **Take Care of Yourself.** If you do not, no one else will. Don't say, "I don't have time." You have got all the time there is—24 hours a day—so begin today by choosing some stress reduction techniques that will divert your attention from whatever is causing you stress. Take a leisurely day off from your routine.

- **Learn to Relax.** You can learn to counteract your habitual reaction to stress by learning to relax. Relaxation gives you more energy and normalizes your physical, mental, and emotional processes. Consequently, you are more equipped to handle the stresses in your life (Underwood, 2005). Consider having a relaxing massage.

> *Positive attitudes—optimism, high self-esteem, an outgoing nature, joyousness, and the ability to cope with stress—may be the most important bases for continued good health.*
> —HELEN HAYES

Play

Play is a critical element of holistic wellness. What better way to beat stress! Dr. Stuart Brown is a psychiatrist, clinical researcher, and founder of the National Institute for Play. Dr. Brown is also the author of *Play: How it Shapes the Brain, Opens the Imagination and Invigorates the Soul* (2010). He has found that play shapes our brain, helps us foster empathy, helps us navigate complex social groups, and is at the core of creativity and innovation. Dr. Brown argues that play is not optional. He writes, "The opposite of play is not work—the opposite of play is depression." He explains, "Respecting our biologically programmed need for play can transform work. It can bring back excitement and newness to our job. Play helps us deal with difficulties, fights stress, provides a sense of expansiveness, promotes mastery of our craft, and is an essential part of the creative process. Most important, true play that comes from our inner needs and desires is the only path to finding lasting joy and satisfaction in our work. In the long run, 'work does not work without play.'"

Becoming Aware of the Need for Play: The Power of Play
https://www.youtube.com/watch?v=n34IjfcF1Yg&t=408s

This is an exploration of play and the importance as we become adults. Play is key to enjoyment and can be beneficial in many different ways. Mallory Nezam (Founder of STL Improv Anywhere) instigates unexpected creative interactions in public spaces. Nezam chooses to place art and play in the context of public space to disrupt routine and reconnect passerby with the magic of being alive. Interested in the experiential and bodily, her work does not point at the thing but becomes the thing and invites the audience to take an active part. Nezam believes that collectively performing creative expressions in public, builds a sense of connection between citizens and ownership of place.

The Relaxation Response

Would you like to try a deep breathing and relaxation exercise now? One of the best studied stress relievers is the relaxation response, first described by Harvard's Herbert Benson close to 20 years ago (Benson, 2001). Its great advantage is that it requires no special posture or place. You can use this relaxation response even if you are stuck in traffic, or when you're expected at a meeting. Or, you can use this response if you are having trouble falling asleep because your mind keeps replaying over the events of the day. Are you ready?

- Sit or recline comfortably. Close your eyes if you can, and relax your muscles.
- Breathe deeply. To make sure that you are breathing deeply, place one hand on your abdomen, the other on your chest. Breathe in slowly through your nose, and as you do, you should feel your abdomen (not your chest) rise.

- Slowly exhale. As you do, focus on your breathing. Some people do better if they silently repeat the word *one* as they exhale; it helps clear the mind.
- If thoughts intrude, do not dwell on them; allow them to pass on and return to focusing on your breathing. Although you can turn to this exercise any time you feel stressed, doing it regularly for 10 to 20 minutes at least once a day can put you in a generally calm mode that can see you through otherwise stressful situations. Was Dr. Benson correct? Do you feel more relaxed?

Obviously, not all of these coping strategies and stress-management techniques are applicable to everyone. So take a long, hard look at your own personal lifestyle, and try to make a good evaluation as to what factors are adding stresses to your life, particularly negative stress. Perhaps you will even find yourself falling into the category of Type A behavior. Then, select the specific strategies that fit your personal situation and make a commitment to do whatever is necessary to reduce the negative stress in your life or at least learn to cope with it more effectively.

> *For fast-acting relief, try slowing down.*
> —LILY TOMLIN

When life gets to hard—Things you need to know!

KNOW THE RISK FACTORS OF SUICIDE

Risk factors are characteristics that make it more likely that someone will consider, attempt, or die by suicide. They can't cause or predict a suicide attempt, but they're important to be aware of.

- Mental disorders
- particularly mood disorders
- schizophrenia
- anxiety disorders, and certain personality disorders
- Alcohol and other substance use disorders
- Hopelessness
- Impulsive and/or aggressive tendencies
- History of trauma or abuse
- Major physical illnesses
- Previous suicide attempt(s)
- Family history of suicide
- Job or financial loss
- Loss of relationship(s)
- Easy access to lethal means
- Local clusters of suicide
- Lack of social support and sense of isolation
- Stigma associated with asking for help
- Lack of healthcare, especially mental health and substance abuse treatment

- Cultural and religious beliefs, such as the belief that suicide is a noble resolution of a personal dilemma
- Exposure to others who have died by suicide (in real life or via the media and Internet)

Understanding the issues concerning suicide and mental health is an important way to take part in suicide prevention, help others in crisis, and change the conversation around suicide.

We Can All Take Action

Evidence shows that providing support services, talking about suicide, reducing access to means of self-harm, and following up with loved ones are just some of the actions we can all take to help others.

Becoming Aware of Suicide Prevention: Swimming, a Short Film
https://swimmingshortfilm.com/

This video is about suicide prevention. It was written and developed by a young woman who felt this story needs to be seen by all.

We Believe Hope Can Happen

Suicide is not inevitable for anyone. By starting the conversation, providing support, and directing help to those who need it, we can prevent suicides and save lives.

Know the Warning Signs

Some warning signs may help you determine if a loved one is at risk for suicide, especially if the behavior is new, has increased, or seems related to a painful event, loss, or change. If you or someone you know exhibits any of these signs, seek help by calling the Lifeline.

- Talking about wanting to die or to kill themselves
- Looking for a way to kill themselves, like searching online or buying a gun
- Talking about feeling hopeless or having no reason to live
- Talking about feeling trapped or in unbearable pain
- Talking about being a burden to others
- Increasing the use of alcohol or drugs
- Acting anxious or agitated; behaving recklessly
- Sleeping too little or too much
- Withdrawing or isolating themselves
- Showing rage or talking about seeking revenge
- Extreme mood swings

If you or a friend are having problems and need someone to help, contact these resources.

1-800-273-TALK
https://ok2talk.org/

Call the Lifeline Anytime, 24/7
1-800-273-8255

https://suicidepreventionlifeline.org/how-we-can-all-prevent-suicide/

Becoming Aware of Technology

TECHNOLOGY AND WELLNESS

Pew Research and Elon University's Imagining the Internet Center conducted a large-scale canvassing of technology experts, scholars, corporate and public practitioners and other leaders in 2018, called the Digital Life and Well-being Study. Many of the experts say digital life will continue to expand people's boundaries and opportunities in the coming decade, and that the world to come will produce more help than harm in people's lives. Janna Anderson found that nearly a third say they expect digital life will be mostly harmful to people's health, mental fitness, and happiness (2018).

The Digital Life and Wellbeing Study focused on the following themes:

Connection Digital life links people to people, knowledge, education, and entertainment anywhere globally at any time in a nearly frictionless manner.

Commerce, Government, and Society Digital life revolutionizes civic, business, consumer and personal logistics, opening a world of opportunity and options.

Crucial Intelligence Digital life is essential to tapping into an ever-widening array of health, safety, and science resources, tools and services in real time.

Contentment Digital life empowers people to improve, advance or reinvent their lives, allowing them to self-actualize, meet soulmates, and make a difference.

Continuation Toward Quality Emerging tools will continue to expand the quality and focus of digital life; the big-picture results will continue to be a plus overall for humanity. They felt these digital life topics were MORE HELP THAN HARM.

Digital Deficits People's cognitive capabilities will be challenged in multiple ways, including their capacity for analytical thinking, memory, and focus. They felt that these digital life topics were MORE HARM THAN HELP (Anderson, 2018).

Managing in the Age of the Smartphone

We struggle to imagine how mobile devices will change our social, emotional, physical, and future work lives for better or worse. Growing up in today's Digital Age, we cannot imagine a world without those devices.

How to reconcile this growing divide has become an increasingly important topic for researchers. Yet studies cannot keep up with the pace of accelerating changes in technology, according to the report. In many ways, researchers are swimming upstream, attempting to adapt without enough information on the prevailing currents.

Most researchers agree there are benefits and pitfalls of smartphone usage, but there is not global agreement on just how technology will change the lives of future generations. While there is much uncertainty on how technology and smartphones will impact human development there are intelligent ways to stay healthy in the Digital Age:

1. Manage screen time.
   Create a balance between interacting with technology and developing real-life relationships with humans.
2. Promote physical activity.
   A growing body of research shows that excessive screen time contributes to inactivity and obesity. Nature fosters happiness, as does being physically active.
3. Researchers have associated the growth of social media and technology use with rising rates of depression, anxiety and mental illness.
4. Practice stress-reduction.
   The Global Wellness report says, "the biggest challenges to mental wellness appear to come, not from the technology itself, but from the added pressures and pace of life in the digital age." We are always accessible, responsive to peers, and use social media to compare ourselves to others. Explore mindfulness meditation and various techniques for stress reduction and relaxation, and health and wellbeing.
5. Foster peer friendships.
   It is easy to imagine that social media increases connectivity and friendships. However, there is a growing sense of loneliness. It is important to have social interaction in real time.
6. Use online health resources.
   There is now a wealth of health information available online to investigate health symptoms and learn about prevention.
7. Explore wellness apps.
   Wellness and exercise apps help promote healthier lifestyles for children and parents. Many can be shared, making fitness fun and more challenging.
8. Set a bedtime and try to keep it.
   Turn off social media at night or have it in the other room (Sbarra, 2019).

Chapter Review

Even if it were possible to go through life without stress, we really would not want to, because stress is what prepares us to handle things we are unfamiliar with, or things that appear to threaten us. Without a doubt, some stress challenges us to think creatively and to find innovative solutions to problems.

- **Stress** is the rate of wear and tear within the body.
- There are four basic types of stress: **eustress** (good or short-term stress), **distress** (negative or harmful stress), **hyperstress** (overload), and **hypostress** (underload).
- Stress consists of an event, called a **stressor**, plus how we feel about it, how we interpret it, and what we do to cope with it.
- Two words best relate to the actual cause of stress: **change** and **threat**. Changes and threats often fall into three possible categories: 1) anticipated life events, 2) unexpected life events, and 3) accumulating life events.
- **Daily hassles**—irritating and frustrating incidents that occur in our everyday transactions with the environment—may sometimes pile up until they eventually overwhelm us.
- Modern stress theory agrees that what causes us stress is not what happens to us, but how we perceive what happens to us.
- When you feel stress because of control issues, three questions you can ask yourself are: What don't I control here?, What am I trying to control here?, and What could I control here that I'm not currently controlling?
- The opposite of play is not work—the opposite of play is depression.
- Relaxation done regularly helps you feel less stressed.
- Irrational self-verbalizations include should statements, awfulizing statements, and overgeneralizations.
- Prolonged stressful experiences can decrease the effectiveness of your immune system. Various illnesses can result. Short-term stress generally boosts the immune system.
- The body has a three-stage reaction to stress: alarm, resistance, and exhaustion. These stages of a chain reaction to stress are called the **general adaptation syndrome**.
- Stress can be a problem because it is linked to a number of illnesses. There are both physical and behavioral effects of stress.
- Research has indicated that there are basically three personality types in relation to stress—**Type A**, **Type B**, and a **combination** of Type A and Type B.
- How people behave under stress depends to some extent on the level of stress experienced. Some individuals who have experienced severe cases of trauma may later experience a delayed emotional reaction known as **post-traumatic stress disorder**—PTSD.
- Body dysmorphic disorder is thinking about one or more perceived defects or flaws in our appearance—a flaw that, to others, is either minor or not observable. Stress may be a factor. But we may feel so ashamed and anxious that we may avoid many social situations or undergo surgeries to fix it.
- There are both negative and defensive techniques of coping with stress. Some commonly used defense mechanisms in coping with stress are: rationalization, repression, projection, reaction formation, sublimation, displacement, regression, and denial.
- Although some events are inherently stressful for everyone, many other events are appraised as stressful or not according to an individual's culture, gender, and conditioning.

- **Play** shapes our brain, helps us foster empathy, helps us navigate complex social groups, is at the core of creativity and innovation, and helps reduce stress. Albert Einstein said that "Play is the highest form of research."
- Hardy people seem to deal more effectively with stress. They are more likely to demonstrate the attitudes of commitment, control, and challenge when dealing with stressful situations. Optimistic people are more likely to cope with stress in more adaptive ways than pessimists.
- Three options, when confronted with stressful events and situations, are: 1) change environments, 2) change the environment, and 3) change me—improve my coping skills.
- One of the most effective ways of dealing with stressful thoughts and feelings is to watch or change our **self-talk**—what we say to ourselves about our experiences or what is happening to us.
- Our extreme, debilitative, and stressful emotions are due largely to our **irrational beliefs**—what we say to ourselves.
- If you are focusing on gratitude, you can't be negative.
- **Self-talk** can be irrational, resulting in inappropriate emotions, behaviors, and more stress. Self-talk can also be rational, resulting in appropriate emotions, behaviors, and less stress.
- Many of us—whether due to genetics, brain chemistry, our experiences or coping skills—tell ourselves way too many negative thoughts. We **ruminate**, thinking the same negative, *unproductive thoughts over and over*. Each thought is made up of a complex pattern of activity between proteins and other chemicals, gene expressions and neural connections in our brain. The more we have a thought, the stronger this circuit grows. Alex Korb, a neuroscientist and author of "The Upward Spiral: Using Neuroscience to Reverse the Course" said a well-developed thought "is like a ski track in the snow. The more you ski down a path, the easier it is to go down that path and not another."
- Almost all irrational self-verbalizations contain should statements, awfulizing statements, and overgeneralizations.
- **Irrational beliefs** that create feelings of stress can be improved by using a four-step process: 1) monitoring your emotional reactions, 2) describing the activating event, 3) recording your self-talk, and 4) disputing the beliefs which are irrational.
- There are numerous strategies for learning to live with stress. It is important to select the specific strategies that fit your personal situation and to which you can make a commitment for coping and dealing with the stress in your life.

Handled well, stress is a positive force that strengthens us for future situations. But handled poorly, or allowed to get out of hand, stress becomes harmful and can lead to physical, mental, or emotional problems.

Therefore, it is extremely important not only that we recognize stress, but that we learn how to handle it, live with it, and make it work for us.

Learning Outcomes Review

1. What is stress? Give examples of the four basic types of stress.
2. Define the term stressor, and explain what else stress consists of.
3. What two words best relate to the actual cause of stress? Explain the three categories that changes and threats often fall into.

4. What is the difference between irrational and rational beliefs—self-talk?

5. What is cognitive reappraisal? What are ruminations?

6. In relation to the power of our thoughts, what causes some people to be devastated and others to be motivated by the same event?

7. When you feel stressed over issues about personal control, what three questions would be good for you to ask yourself?

8. Explain the three-stage reaction to stress.

9. Explain the relationship between the immune system and prolonged stressful experiences.

10. How does stress affect you physically as well as behaviorally?

11. Why do these cue words indicate that you may be overgeneralizing: *all, every, none, never, always, everybody,* and *nobody*?

12. Explain the characteristics of the Type A and Type B personality behavior patterns. Which personality type are you?

13. List and define some of the more commonly used defense mechanisms. What are the two primary characteristics of defense mechanisms? What is PTSD?

14. In relation to stress, explain the different coping styles of men and women.

15. Explain the extent that Caucasian, African American, Hispanic, and Asian American cultures perceive stressful events which might be in the academic, financial, and personal domains.

16. List and explain the three characteristics of hardy people. How do optimistic and pessimistic people differ in their reaction to stressful events? Explain resilience (hardiness) in relation to stress.

17. Explain the three options possible when confronted with stressful events and situations.

18. Name and give examples of the three self-verbalizations frequently found in irrational beliefs—self-talk. How could these same examples be worded into rational beliefs—self-talk?

19. How could you rephrase the following negative self-talk statements to make them more positive? "I should," "I can't," "I'll try," "He/she makes me . . ."

20. Identify and explain the four-step process for disputing irrational beliefs.

21. List at least 10 tips for managing stress.

22. According to Albert Ellis, what is the correct equation in relation to the cause of stressful feelings and emotions?

23. What has caused a neurochemically based dependence on sources of stress and stimulation to provide fuel for our chaotic lifestyles?

24. What is gratitude, and how does it help you?

25. Why does ruminating, thinking the same negative, unproductive thoughts over and over, exacerbate depression?

Key Terms

Alarm Stage
Awfulizing Statements
Body dysmorphic disorder
Cognitive Reappraisal
Cognitive Restructuring
Coping
Daily Hassles
Defense Mechanisms
Denial
Depression
Displacement
Distress
Eustress
Exhaustion Stage

General Adaptation Syndrome
Gratitude
Hardiness
Hyperstress
Hypostress
Immune System
Irrational Beliefs
Optimism
Overgeneralizations
Pessimism
Post-traumatic Stress Disorder
    (PTSD)
Projection
Rational Beliefs

Rationalization
Reaction Formation
Regression
Relaxation Response
Repression
Resistance Stage
Rumination
Self-Talk
Stressor
Sublimation
Suicide prevention
Thought Stopping
Type A Behavioral Pattern
Type B Behavioral Pattern

Reflections: Critical Thinking Activity

Individually answer these questions or get into groups of 3 and share answers with a discussion of your findings.

1. What is your personal definition of stress?
2. Discuss the types of situations that are most stressful to you.
3. What are some examples of daily hassles in your environment?
4. What can you do to alleviate some of the stress, as well as daily hassles, in your life?
5. Have you ever gotten a cold, strep throat, or some other bacterial or viral infection after a stressful period? What do you think contributed to your getting sick?
6. How does stress affect you physically, as well as behaviorally?
7. Discuss this statement: Modern stress theory agrees that what causes stress is not what happens to us, but how we perceive what happens to us.
8. In relation to stress, how do Type A and Type B personalities create difficulties in relationships with others?
9. Discuss the differences in the way men and women cope with stress.
10. What techniques do you personally use to manage stress?
11. How do optimistic and pessimistic people differ in their reaction to stressful events?
12. Which defense mechanism do you more commonly use? Why?
13. Explain PTSD from the viewpoint of anyone you have personally known who may have struggled with this diagnosis.
14. Discuss any areas of personal control you currently struggle with.
15. Describe the relaxation response. Does it work for you?
16. Why does gratitude help your stress and wellness?
17. What are suicide risk factors?
18. What are you grateful for?

Technology Resources and Activities

www.youmeworks.com/optimisminterview.html

> Information on a healthy balance between optimism and pessimism.

http://stress.about.com/

> Various links on dealing with stress.

http://www.stress.org

> The site for the American Institute for Stress.

http://cogbtherapy.com/cbt-blog/2014/5/4/hhy104os08dekc537dlw7nvopzyi44

> Improve your cognitive reappraisal.

www.authentichappiness.sas.upenn.edu/testcenter.aspx

> The Gratitude Survey measures appreciation about the past.

https://suicidepreventionlifeline.org/talk-to-someone-now/

https://suicidepreventionlifeline.org/how-we-can-all-prevent-suicide/

> Helpful resources and information from the Suicide Prevention Lifeline

GRATITUDE

https://www.youtube.com/watch?v=y9Trdafp83U

> There's more to life than being happy | Emily Esfahani Smith

https://youtu.be/aRV8AhCntXc

> What Good Is Gratitude? | Robert Emmons

TECHNOLOGY

https://www.ted.com/talks/brene_brown_on_vulnerability?utm_campaign=tedspread&utm_medium=referral&utm_source=tedcomshare

> Brené Brown studies human connection—our ability to empathize, belong, love. In a poignant, funny talk, she shares a deep insight from her research, one that sent her on a personal quest to know herself as well as to understand humanity.

https://youtu.be/AkesEzSn1zI

> The Distracted Mind, by Adam Gazzaley and Larry D. Rosen

https://www.youtube.com/watch?v=Iw3sDgaoBeA

> 21 Ways to Stop Worrying, by Albert Ellis, PhD

https://www.youtube.com/watch?v=_rwkU8BfVgk

How to Deal with Difficult People, by Albert Ellis, PhD

https://www.youtube.com/watch?v=KuWKWjVXcwo

Brené Brown on Fear: A culture of not enough.

https://www.youtube.com/watch?v=_UoMXF73j0c&t=15s

The price of invulnerability: Brené Brown at TEDxKC.

https://www.youtube.com/watch?v=7XFLTDQ4JMk

Getting stuck in the negatives (and how to get unstuck), by Alison Ledgerwood, TEDxUCDavis.

https://www.youtube.com/watch?v=v-t1Z5-oPtU

How stress affects your body, by Sharon Horesh Bergquist.

https://www.youtube.com/watch?v=RcGyVTAoXEU

Kelly McGonigal on How to make stress your friend.

https://www.youtube.com/watch?v=yEh3JG74C6s

What causes wellness, by Sir Harry Burns, TEDxGlasgow.

https://www.youtube.com/watch?v=wmdp7tr8UFc

A journey of a worrier to a warrior, by Colleen Lightbody, TEDxHyderabad.

https://www.youtube.com/watch?v=Awd0kgxcZws

Settle Down, Pay Attention, Say Thank You: A How-To, by Kristen Race at TEDxMileHighWomen.

www.mentalhelp.net/psyhelp/chap4

This site examines aspects of behavior such as procrastination, self-control, and managing loss of control or relapse.

https://www.ted.com/talks/stuart_brown_says_play_is_more_than_fun_it_s_vital/discussion

Stuart Brown discusses play and how it effects relationships.

https://www.youtube.com/watch?v=Bg-GEzM7iTk&feature=youtu.be

The decline of play | Peter Gray | TEDxNavesink (2014)

https://www.youtube.com/watch?v=E4sdVE0Q9Lk&t=97s

Play helps us grow at any age: Dr. Lois Holzman at TEDxNavesink

Wellness Activity

AFFIRMATION LETTER

For an interesting activity and discussion on *affirmation and positivity,* please read this information and **write a letter** to someone that has been a positive person in your life.

Why you are doing this activity: The letter affirms positive things in your life and reminds you how others have cared for you—life seems less bleak and lonely if someone has taken such a supportive interest in us.

If possible, take the letter to the person you are writing about. (Visiting the giver allows you to strengthen your connection with them and remember how others value you as an individual.)

EVIDENCE THAT IT WORKS

When researchers tested five different exercises, the gratitude visit showed the greatest positive effect on participants' happiness one month later. However, six months after the visit, their happiness had dropped back down to where it was before. This is why some researchers suggest doing this exercise once every six weeks or so.

Also, 2009 research led by Jeffrey Froh found that adolescents who don't generally experience positive emotions showed a significant boost in positive emotions two months after doing a gratitude visit.

Research suggests that while there are benefits simply to writing the letter, you reap significantly greater benefits from delivering and reading it in person.

Discuss what ever you want to about your letter and how it felt writing it in a small groups.

Group Moderator?_____

Members _____

Members _____

Members _____

Members _____

SOURCES

Sonja Lyubomirsky, Ph.D., University of California, Riverside

Kristin Layous, Ph.D., Stanford University

Martin Seligman, Ph.D., University of Pennsylvania

Wellness Activity

STRESS AND WELLNESS ACTIVITY

For an interesting discussion on stress please read the article and discuss it in groups of at least 4.

The Science of Stress and How Our Emotions Affect Our Susceptibility to Burnout and Disease

https://www.brainpickings.org/2015/07/20/esther-sternberg-balance-within-stress-emotion/

How your memories impact your immune system, why moving is one of the most stressful life-events, and what your parents have to do with your predisposition to PTSD.

Which member was chosen to be Group Moderator?_____

Members _____

Members _____

Members _____

Members _____

Group report notes:

Where Does the Stress Come from in Your Life?

PURPOSE

To discover where the sources of stress are in your life.

INSTRUCTIONS

1. You need to keep track of any stressful event that occurs in your life for a one-week period of time. Each day at approximately 10:00 a.m., 6:00 p.m., and 10:00 p.m. write down each of the stressful events that occurred to you during the previous period of time.

2. Use the following form:

DAY	TIME	STRESSFUL EVENT	TYPE OF STRESS (INDICATE WHETHER THE EVENT INVOLVES CONFLICT, HASSLE, CHANGE, FRUSTRATION, OR SOME COMBINATION.)	YOUR REACTION

3. Complete the following questions at the end of the week:

   a. Is there a specific type of stress that is most frequent in your life? Explain.

   b. Is there a specific location or set of circumstances that produce a great deal of stress for you? Explain.

   c. What specific reaction to the stressful events did you display? Give examples.

   d. What could you do to reduce the amount of stress in your life?

Gratitude Activity

GRATITUDE JOURNAL

Count your blessings and enjoy better health and happiness.

Write 15 minutes per day, at least once per week for at least two weeks.

Studies suggest that writing in a gratitude journal three times per week might actually have a greater impact on our happiness than journaling every day.

HOW TO DO IT

There's no wrong way to keep a gratitude journal, but here are some general instructions as you get started.

Write down up to five things for which you feel grateful.

The physical record is important—don't just do this exercise in your head. The things you list can be relatively small in importance ("The tasty sandwich I had for lunch today.") or relatively large ("My sister gave birth to a healthy baby boy."). The goal of the exercise is to remember a good event, experience, person, or thing in your life—then enjoy the good emotions that come with it.

AS YOU WRITE, HERE ARE NINE IMPORTANT TIPS

1. **Be as specific as possible**—specificity is key to fostering gratitude. "I'm grateful that my co-workers brought me soup when I was sick on Tuesday" will be more effective than "I'm grateful for my co-workers."
2. **Go for depth over breadth.** Elaborating in detail about a particular person or thing for which you're grateful carries more benefits than a superficial list of many things.
3. **Get personal.** Focusing on people to whom you are grateful has more of an impact than focusing on things for which you are grateful.
4. **Try subtraction, not just addition.** Consider what your life would be like without certain people or things, rather than just tallying up all the good stuff. Be grateful for the negative outcomes you avoided, escaped, prevented, or turned into something positive—try not to take that good fortune for granted.
5. **See good things as "gifts."** Thinking of the good things in your life as gifts guards against taking them for granted. Try to relish and savor the gifts you've received.
6. **Savor surprises.** Try to record events that were unexpected or surprising, as these tend to elicit stronger levels of gratitude.
7. **Revise if you repeat.** Writing about some of the same people and things is OK, but zero in on a different aspect in the details.
8. **Write regularly.** Whether you write every other day or once a week, commit to a regular time to journal, then honor that commitment. But …
9. **Don't overdo it.** Evidence suggests writing occasionally (1–3 times per week) is more beneficial than daily journaling. That might be because we adapt to positive events and can soon become numb to them—that's why it helps to savor surprises.

Adapted from **The Greater Good Science Center**

Why You Should Try It

It's easy to take the good things and people in our lives for granted, but research suggests that consciously giving thanks for them can have profound effects on our well-being and relationships. This exercise helps you develop a greater appreciation for the good in your life. In fact, people who routinely express gratitude enjoy better health and greater happiness.

Why It Works

While it's important to analyze and learn from bad events, sometimes we can think too much about what goes wrong and not enough about what goes right in our lives. A gratitude journal forces us to pay attention to the good things in life we might otherwise take for granted. In that way, we start to become more attuned to the everyday sources of pleasure around us—and the emotional tone of our life can shift in profound ways. What's more, actually writing about these events is key: Research suggests translating thoughts into concrete language makes us more aware of them, deepening their emotional impact.

Evidence That It Works

Emmons, R. A., & McCullough, M. E. (2003). Counting blessings versus burdens: An experimental investigation of gratitude and subjective well-being in daily life. Journal of Personality and Social Psychology, 84(2), 377–389.

Participants who kept a gratitude journal weekly for 10 weeks or daily for two weeks experienced more gratitude, positive moods, optimism about the future, and better sleep.

Sources

Robert Emmons, Ph.D., University of California, Davis

Sonja Lyubomirsky, Ph.D., University of California, Riverside

Practice Gratitude

GRATITUDE QUIZ

Are you truly grateful for the good things in your life—or do you take them for granted?

Grateful people are happy people, research shows. But how grateful are you? To find out—and discover steps for promoting even more gratitude in your life—take this quiz, which is based on a scale developed by psychologists Mitchel Adler and Nancy Fagley.

Please indicate how frequently you experience each of the items listed in the first seven questions; for the final eight questions, indicate how much you agree or disagree with each statement. The last five questions are about you, and they'll be used by our research team to better understand how gratitude relates to factors like age and gender.

When you're done, you'll get your gratitude score, learn more about the benefits of gratitude, and find resources for cultivating more gratitude in your life.

TAKE THE QUIZ

	MORE THAN ONCE A WEEK	ONCE A WEEK	A FEW TIMES A MONTH	ONCE A MONTH	A FEW TIMES A YEAR	ONCE A YEAR	NEVER
1. I feel very thankful for my degree of physical health.	7	6	5	4	3	2	1
2. I count my blessings for what I have in this world.	7	6	5	4	3	2	1
3. I reflect on the worst times in my life to help me realize how fortunate I am now.	7	6	5	4	3	2	1
4. I think of people who are less fortunate than I am to help me feel more satisfied with my circumstances.	7	6	5	4	3	2	1
5. I remind myself how fortunate I am to have the privileges and opportunities I have encountered in life.	7	6	5	4	3	2	1
6. I reflect on how fortunate I am to have basic things in life like food, clothing, and shelter.	7	6	5	4	3	2	1
7. I really notice and acknowledge the good things I get in life.	7	6	5	4	3	2	1

	STRONGLY AGREE	AGREE	SOMEWHAT AGREE	NEITHER AGREE NOR DISAGREE	SOMEWHAT DISAGREE	DISAGREE	STRONGLY DISAGREE
8. When I swerve to avoid a car accident, I feel relieved that I am ok.	7	6	5	4	3	2	1
9. I am content with what I have.	7	6	5	4	3	2	1
10. When I drive by the scene of a car accident, it reminds me to feel thankful that I am safe.	7	6	5	4	3	2	1
11. It is important to appreciate things such as health, family, and friends.	7	6	5	4	3	2	1
12. Although I don't have everything I want, I am thankful for what I have.	7	6	5	4	3	2	1
13. I remind myself to think about the good things I have in my life.	7	6	5	4	3	2	1
14. I appreciate my degree of success in life so far.	7	6	5	4	3	2	1
15. When I see someone less fortunate than myself, I realize how lucky I am.	7	6	5	4	3	2	1

16. What is your age?
    a. Under 18
    b. 18–29
    c. 30–39
    d. 40–49
    e. 50–59
    f. 60–69
    g. 70 or Over

17. In terms of your gender identity, do you see yourself as:
    a. Female/Woman
    b. Male/Man
    c. Gender non-binary
    d. I prefer to self-identify

18. What describes your highest level of education?
    a. Did not finish high school
    b. High school diploma
    c. Associate degree or certificate program
    d. Bachelor's degree
    e. Did some graduate study
    f. Graduate or professional degree

19. What best describes your current employment status?
    a. Employed
    b. Self-employed
    c. Stay-at-home parent
    d. Unemployed
    e. Student
    f. Retired
    g. Unable to work

20. How spiritual are you?
    a. Not at all
    b. Slightly
    c. Somewhat
    d. Very
    e. Extremely

Source: Adler, M. G., & Fagley, N. S. (2005). "Appreciation: Individual Differences in Finding Value and Meaning as a Unique Predictor of Subjective Well-Being." Journal of Personality, 73 (1), 79–114.

Name _____ Date _____

How Much Can You Take?

PURPOSE

To help you become more aware of stress-producing events in your life, whether negative or positive, and to demonstrate the correlation between cumulative stress and possible major health changes.

INSTRUCTIONS

1. Each participant is to individually fill out the Social Readjustment Rating Scale by transferring to the "Your Event" column, the EXACT NUMBER assigned for each stressful event you have experienced in the past 12 months. For example, if you have been fired from your job, you would place 47 in "Your Event" column. Then, total "Your Event" column.
2. In evaluating your scores, pay very close attention to Discussion Questions 3 and 4.
3. Become aware of what your chances are of experiencing a major health change in the next two years:

0–150 points	=	1 in 3 chance
150–300 points	=	50–50 chance
Over 300 points	=	almost 90% chance

4. Divide into groups of four or five to discuss the results of each individual's scale.

SOCIAL READJUSTMENT RATING SCALE

LIFE CHANGES	VALUE	YOUR EVENT
FAMILY:		
Death of a spouse	100	_____
Divorce	73	_____
Marital separation	65	_____
Death of a close family member	63	_____
Marriage	50	_____
Marital reconciliation	45	_____
Major change in health of family member	44	_____
Pregnancy	40	_____
Addition of new family member	39	_____
Major change in arguments with spouse	35	_____
Son or daughter leaving home	29	_____
Trouble with in-laws	29	_____
Spouse starting or ending work	26	_____
Major change in family get-togethers	15	_____

PERSONAL:

Detention in jail	63	_____
Major personal injury or illness	53	_____
Sexual difficulties	39	_____
Death of a close friend	37	_____
Outstanding personal achievement	28	_____
Start or end of formal schooling	26	_____
Major change in living conditions	25	_____
Major change in personal habits	24	_____
Changing to new school	20	_____
Change in residence	20	_____
Major change in social activities	19	_____
Major change in church activities	19	_____
Major change in sleeping habits	16	_____
Major change in eating habits	15	_____
Vacation	13	_____
Christmas	12	_____
Minor violations of the law	11	_____

WORK:

Being fired from work	47	_____
Retirement from work	45	_____
Major business adjustment	39	_____
Changing to a different line of work	36	_____
Major change in work responsibilities	29	_____
Trouble with boss	23	_____
Major change in working conditions	20	_____

FINANCIAL:

Major change in financial state	38	_____
Mortgage or loan for major purchase (home, etc.)	31	_____
Mortgage foreclosure	30	_____
Credit card dept. or loan of more than $5,000	17	_____
	Total Points	_____

DISCUSSION

1. Did you already have an awareness of the amount of stress in your life, or were you surprised? Which area (family, personal, work, or financial) presented more stress-producing events?

2. What are some things you could do to lessen or control stress-producing events in your life?

3. Remember, positive changes may be stressful, but they are less of a hassle than negative changes. Have most of the changes and threats you experienced (listed) been more positive or negative? Why?

4. Hans Selye has said that "all the stress inventories are flawed because they fail to give enough weight to individual differences" (Epstein, 1999). Also, stress inventories often do not take into account how individuals perceive a given change, much less how they cope with it. How do you feel about these statements as you evaluate your score?

Type A and Type B Behavior

PURPOSE

To help you identify individual personality characteristics that would indicate Type A or Type B behavior.

INSTRUCTIONS

1. Rate yourself as to how you typically react in each of the situations listed below by circling one response for each question.
2. Find your total score by adding together the circled number response of each question.
3. Determine whether your behavior is primarily Type A or Type B according to the following scale:

1–47	Extreme Type B
48–94	Type B
95–141	Both Type A and Type B
142–188	Type A
189–235	Extreme Type A

    In general, a score greater than 120 is Type A and a score less than 120 is Type B.

	ALWAYS	FREQUENTLY	SOMETIMES	SELDOM	NEVER
1. Are you punctual?	5	4	3	2	1
2. Do you work under constant deadlines?	5	4	3	2	1
3. Do you indulge in competitive hobbies?	5	4	3	2	1
4. Do you like routine household chores?	5	4	3	2	1
5. Do you prefer to do a task yourself because others are too slow or can't do it as well?	5	4	3	2	1
6. Do you work while you are eating, in the bathroom, etc.?	5	4	3	2	1
7. Do you walk fast?	5	4	3	2	1
8. Do you eat hurriedly?	5	4	3	2	1
9. Are you patient and understanding?	5	4	3	2	1
10. Do you carry on several lines of thought at the same time?	5	4	3	2	1

	ALWAYS	FREQUENTLY	SOMETIMES	SELDOM	NEVER
11. Do you interrupt others when they talk about subjects that don't interest you?	5	4	3	2	1
12. Do you pretend to listen to others when they talk about subjects that don't interest you?	5	4	3	2	1
13. How often does time seem to pass rapidly for you?	5	4	3	2	1
14. How often do you look at your watch?	5	4	3	2	1
15. Do you feel vaguely guilty when you relax and do absolutely nothing for several hours/days?	5	4	3	2	1
16. How often do you become exasperated when standing in line at movies, restaurants, etc.?	5	4	3	2	1
17. Do you ever find that you cannot recall details of the surroundings after you left a place?	5	4	3	2	1
18. How often are you preoccupied with getting materialistic things?	5	4	3	2	1
19. Do you use a relaxed, laid back speech pattern?	5	4	3	2	1
20. How often do you attempt to schedule more and more in less and less time?	5	4	3	2	1
21. How often do you feel aggressive, hostile, and compelled to challenge people who make you feel uncomfortable?	5	4	3	2	1
22. Do you accentuate your speech, talk fast?	5	4	3	2	1
23. How often do you gesture by clenching your fists, banging your hand on the table, pounding one fist into the palm of the other hand, clenching your jaw, grinding your teeth, etc.?	5	4	3	2	1
24. Do you prefer respect and admiration to affection?	5	4	3	2	1
25. Do you listen well and attentively?	5	4	3	2	1
26. Do you evaluate the activities of yourself and others in terms of numbers (e.g., minutes, hours, days, dollars, age)?	5	4	3	2	1
27. How often do you play to win?	5	4	3	2	1

	ALWAYS	FREQUENTLY	SOMETIMES	SELDOM	NEVER
28. How often do you stay up late to socialize?	5	4	3	2	1
29. How often are you angry?	5	4	3	2	1
30. Do you go out of your way to conceal your anger?	5	4	3	2	1
31. How often are you dissatisfied you're your present position or promotional progress?	5	4	3	2	1
32. Do you daydream a lot?	5	4	3	2	1
33. Do you participate in numerous organizations?	5	4	3	2	1
34. Did you ever attend night school?	5	4	3	2	1
35. How often do you go to a doctor?	5	4	3	2	1
36. Do you ever "sigh" faintly between words?	5	4	3	2	1
37. How often do you come to work even when you are sick?	5	4	3	2	1
38. How often is your laughter a grim, forced chuckle?	5	4	3	2	1
39. Do/would you avoid firing people?	5	4	3	2	1
40. How often are you genuinely open and responsive to people?	5	4	3	2	1
41. How often do you go to bed early?	5	4	3	2	1
42. If you smoke, do you prefer cigarettes as opposed to a pipe or cigar?	5	4	3	2	1
43. How often do you salt your meal before tasting it?	5	4	3	2	1
44. How often do you exercise?	5	4	3	2	1
45. Do you ever combine vacations with business?	5	4	3	2	1
46. How often do you work late?	5	4	3	2	1
47. How often do you hum, fidget, or drum your fingers while not involved in an activity?	5	4	3	2	1

Total Points _____

Mirabal, Thomas E. "Identifying Individual Personality Characteristics." Reproduced by permission from Synergistic Training Systems, Inc., Dallas, TX.

DISCUSSION

1. Did the results of this exercise make you aware of any Type A behavior patterns in your own personality? Were you surprised?

2. What are some of the dangers of Type A behavior?

3. Is it possible to change from Type A to Type B? How?

4. Would you want to change your behavior patterns if you could?

Irrational and Rational Self-Talk

PURPOSE

To focus on how irrational and rational self-talk can be used in common, practical events and situations.

INSTRUCTIONS

1. For each situation below, consider how you would feel and what you might say to yourself. Then, write an irrational and a rational belief about each situation.
2. Be prepared to share your responses in a class discussion or in small groups of 4 or 5 students.

SITUATION	IRRATIONAL SELF-TALK	RATIONAL SELF-TALK
1. You have to give a 5-minute speech in your college class (Example)	1. This is terrible. I just can't bear having to give this speech.	1. This is going to be difficult. I will work hard and be as successful as I can be.
2. You didn't meet a very important work deadline.	2.	2.
3. A friend cancelled a date with you.	3.	3.
4. You are criticized publicly in class or at work.	4.	4.
5. You're having a final exam in your most difficult class.	5.	5.
6. You have just had a major "blow-up" with your fiancé/fiancée.	6.	6.
7. You were laid off from your job.	7.	7.
8. Write your own situation.	8.	8.

Discussion

1. Was it easier for you to write the irrational or the rational self-talk and beliefs? Why?

2. How many times did you use *should, should not, must, ought, have to?*

3. How many times did you write awfulizing statements?

4. How many times did you make overgeneralizations?

5. How do you think irrational self-talk contributes to a common situation becoming more stressful?

Name _____ Date _____

Coping with Stress Inventory

PURPOSE

To analyze how you currently manage your stress.

INSTRUCTIONS

Listed below are some common ways of coping with stressful events. Mark ones that are characteristic of your behavior or that you use frequently.

_____	1. I ignore my own needs and just work harder and faster.
_____	2. I seek out friends for conversation and support.
_____	3. I eat more than usual.
_____	4. I engage in some type of physical exercise.
_____	5. I get irritable and take it out on those around me.
_____	6. I take a little time to relax, breathe, and unwind.
_____	7. I smoke a cigarette or drink a caffeinated beverage.
_____	8. I confront my source of stress and work to change it.
_____	9. I withdraw emotionally and just go through the motions of my day.
_____	10. I change my outlook on the problem and put it in a better perspective.
_____	11. I sleep more than I really need to.
_____	12. I take some time off and get away from my working life.
_____	13. I go out shopping and buy something to make myself feel good.
_____	14. I joke with my friends and use humor to take the edge off.
_____	15. I drink more alcohol than usual.
_____	16. I get involved in a hobby or interest that helps me unwind and enjoy myself.
_____	17. I take medicine to help me relax or sleep better.
_____	18. I maintain a healthy diet.
_____	19. I just ignore the problem and hope it will go away.
_____	20. I pray, meditate, or enhance my spiritual life.
_____	21. I worry about the problem and am afraid to do something about it.
_____	22. I try to focus on the things I can control and accept the things I can't.

Evaluate your results: The **even-numbered** items tend to be constructive tactics and the **odd-numbered** items tend to be less constructive tactics for coping with stress.

Congratulate yourself for the even-numbered items you checked. Summarize or list those below.

Think about whether you need to make some changes in your thinking or behavior if you checked any odd-numbered items. Summarize or list below.

DISCUSSION

1. Of the even-numbered items you haven't tried before, which ones do you think might be options for you to try?

2. What other positive ways of coping with stress do you think might be an option for you?

From *Relaxation & Stress Reduction Workbook*, 6th edition. Reprinted by permission of New Harbinger Publications.

Practice laughter techniques and exercises

LAUGHTER EXERCISES

- **Humming Laughter Sounds:** Laugh as you hum, mouth closed. Play with the pitch, up and down the scale, feeling the vibrations resonate through your body. As you get more adept at feeling the resonation, try to move it deliberately, through your chest, your jaw, your nose, your sinus cavities, your forehead, the top of your head, then back down again.
- **Laughter Breath:** Inhale deeply, then exhale in a combination of first quick bursts of air coming out and finishing with vocal laughter. Repeat 5-7 times.

From the Laughter University online, where they have many more…http://www.laughteronlineuniversity.com/exercises/

Becoming *Aware*

Managing Stress and Wellness

LEARNING JOURNAL

Select the statement below that best defines your feelings about the personal value or meaning gained from this chapter and respond below the dotted line.

I learned that I . . .   I was surprised that I . . .

I realized that I . . .   I was pleased that I . . .

I discovered that I . . .   I was displeased that I . . .

. . . .

chapter 9
Values, Ethics, and Choices

© L Julia/Shutterstock.com

[

Make your commitments to enduring values and institutions—honesty, integrity, trust, confidence, family, and other matters of the heart. Go ahead and challenge the status quo, but you must also decide what lasts—what really counts—what no one can take away from you. These are your values, and they will accompany you wherever you work and wherever you live.

—Jack D. Rehm, Business leader

]

Think About This...

At many colleges, professors are asked to give a hypothetical final talk called "The Last Lecture." In this talk, they ruminate on what matters most to them. In 2007, Randy Pausch, a professor in the computer science department at Carnegie Mellon University, agreed to give a last lecture. He learned that he had only months to live—he was dying of pancreatic cancer.

A month after learning that his cancer was terminal, Randy Pausch gave his 76-minute speech, "Really Achieving Your Childhood Dreams." He talked about what his childhood dreams had taught him about life and the lessons he had learned along the way, such as to show gratitude, don't complain, and don't give up when faced by challenges, which he calls "brick walls." He also discussed enabling the dreams of others, having fun, asking for what you want, daring to take a risk, looking for the best in everybody, dreaming big, making time for what matters, and living with integrity and joy. At the end, Pausch tells the audience that his talk isn't for them—it's for his kids. The lecture isn't about dying—it's about living. Ten months after giving the lecture, Randy died at the age of 47.

Randy Pausch's last lecture has become an Internet sensation, a bestselling book, and inspiration to others who are going through cancer or other tough situations. As Randy said, "We cannot change the cards we are dealt, just how we play the hand."

Becoming Aware-Choices
https://www.youtube.com/watch?v=mIysXLiA5s0

In a conversation called "A Final Farewell," Professor Randy Pausch sits down with Jeff Zaslow and discusses his turmoil with death and how he's leaving his family.

So, if you had to vanish tomorrow, what would you want to leave as your legacy?

Randy Pausch (2008)

We face a rapidly changing world, in which old values give way to new ones or to none at all. People are trying to make sense of the world in which we find ourselves. Many who are fortunate enough to achieve power, fame, success, and material comfort nevertheless experience a sense of emptiness. It is no surprise that people are asking more value questions: What is the good life for me? What is really important to me? What is life all about? What are my personal ethics? How can I find meaning and purpose in life? In order to begin to find answers to these questions, we need first of all to be able to identify what values are.

What Are Values?

The Merriam-Webster dictionary has two definitions **of value** we might want to consider:

> 1. the regard that something is held to deserve; the importance, worth, or usefulness of something. Such as "your support is of great value."
> 2. a person's principles or standards of behavior; one's judgment of what is important in life. Such as "they internalize their parents' rules and values."

(Merriam-Webster, Retrieved March 4, 2020, https://www.merriam-webster.com/dictionary/value)

Or we could roll them both together and say "A value is the degree of importance we attach to various beliefs, ideas, objects, or things and our personal goals" (Mynatt & Doherty, 2013).

For just a few minutes, consider the following analogy: If you were going to build a new home, one of the first considerations would be to decide upon your house plan. After having carefully studied your house plan and having made the necessary adjustments, you would have your house plan converted into a blueprint. This blueprint would serve as a guide for the construction of your new home. For example, the choices and decisions concerning the layout of the kitchen, the placement of doors and windows, the design of electrical outlets, and so on, would be in accordance with this blueprint—the plan or guide for your new home.

Authors have written extensively about the meaning of the term *value(s)*. Hunter Lewis (2007) defines *values* in this way:

> Although the term value(s) is often used loosely, it should be synonymous with personal beliefs about the "good," the "just," and the "beautiful," personal beliefs that propel us to action, to a particular kind of behavior and life.

We could conclude, then, that our values give rise to our personal goals and tend to place limits on the means we shall use to reach them (Rathus & Nevid, 2013).

Because we have many values, it is therefore appropriate to speak of our set of values or our value system. A set of values is more than just a set of rules and regulations. Instead, it is the underlying system of beliefs about what is important in life to a person. Our value system represents the blueprint or guideline for the choices and decisions we make throughout our life. Using the language of his time, Kluckhohn (1956) explains these choices and decisions:

> Every individual operates according to a system of values, whether it is verbalized and consistently worked out or not. Although everyone's value system is in some degree unique, an individual's values are usually grounded in the core values of his culture ... Depending on his conception of what is desirable and good in human life, he selects certain goals over others and patterns his behavior according to standards of what he believes to be right and worthwhile.

What is a value system? First of all, it is yours, and it is unique because you are one-of-a-kind. It is your code of ethics by which to live. It is your "behavior-bible." It is what guides your life.
—HELEN JOHNSON

TYPES OF VALUE SYSTEMS

In 1928, Eduard Spranger, a German philosopher and psychologist, defined six different types of people based on their types of value systems, or their frameworks for developing their own beliefs (Lamberton & Minor, 2014). Spranger's Six Values Systems are defined as follows:

1. **The Theoretical Person.** This individual seeks to discover truth.
2. **The Economic Person.** Personal needs, production, marketing, credit, and wealth are more important to this type of person than are social or artistic values.
3. **The Aesthetic Person.** Beauty, form, and harmony are most important to this type of individual.

4. **The Social Person.** Loves other people. Kindness and unselfishness are very important values.
5. **The Political Animal.** This type is very power motivated. Their values center on influence, fame, and power.
6. **The Religious Person.** Believes that the highest value is unity. They try to understand the universe as a whole and relate to it meaningfully.

Most people don't identify with just one single type, since a combination of two or more is often more accurate and descriptive.

BECOMING AWARE OF YOUR VALUES ACTIVITY

Using Spranger's Six Value Systems, evaluate your own life. Which value system(s) do you think are more closely related to your own personal value system?

Include it in your journal for possible class discussion.

HOW DO VALUES DEVELOP?

Throughout your life, you have, in all probability, heard many *life messages:* "Life is …" "Success is …" "The most important thing is …" transmitted to you by parents, peers, and society in general.

We are not born with values, but we are born into cultures and societies that promote, teach, and impart their values to us. We learn to be who we are.

Shoulds and should nots. During the first few years of our life, we lack the knowledge and maturity to evaluate our value orientation (Freiberg, 2009/2010). Most psychologists concur that we first acquire the cognitive understanding of right and wrong by observing the behavior of the people most important to us, usually our parents and caregivers (Begley & Kalb, 2000). Actually, our first goals and ambitions will be drawn from this frame of reference.

> *Do not follow where the path may lead. Go, instead, where there is no path and leave a trail.*
> —RALPH WALDO EMERSON

As we enter school, home influence is combined with the influence of peers, teachers, and public media. We have one set of *shoulds* and *should nots* from our parents. Depending on our experiences, a church or other religious association often suggests a second. Our friends and peer group offer a third view of values. Recent research indicating that many young people spend 30 to 40 hours a week in front of social media screens, which has fueled continuing great concern about the influence of television, the Internet, social media, and advertising claims on values formation (Reece & Brandt, 2017). Close to half of U.S. teens ages 13 to 17 say they are on the Internet "almost constantly," and more than nine-in-ten are social media users. These highly plugged-in youth, however, are just as likely as their less-connected peers to socialize regularly with their friends in person, according to a new analysis of Pew Research Center survey data (Jiang, 2018). "Will this next generation not be as social face to face and value social media relationships more? This is troubling because research has found that we can get physically and psychologically ill without real meaningful human contact" (Lenhart, 2015). It seems the Internet generation, or Igeneration, values technology. Kardasras stated "We now know that those iPads, smartphones and Xboxes are a form of digital drug" (2016).

© fizkes/Shutterstock.com

In 2019, roughly half (51%) of U.S. teens ages 13 to 17 said they use Facebook, notably lower than others who use YouTube, Instagram, or Snapchat.

Most notably, smartphone ownership is an important element of teen life: 95% of teens now report they have a smartphone or access to one. These mobile connections are in turn fueling more-persistent online activities: 45% of teens now say they are online on a near-constant basis (Pew Research, 2019). Also in 2019 teens said they often or sometimes use their devices to connect with other people (85% vs. 83%), just to pass the time (both 90%), or to learn new things (79% vs. 87%) (Pew Research, 2019).

Were your parents the biggest influence on your value system?

With all of this additional information, we begin to question and reevaluate our original value orientation. Much of this questioning was revealed through testing the *shoulds* and *should nots*. Therefore, actual experience becomes very real in the forming of our value system. For some people, this reevaluation period occurs during adolescence, early adulthood, and for some even later.

Individuation. Regardless of the exact time, examining and acquiring your personal set of values was, or is, the birth of your own individuality. In fact, Carl Jung (1923), one of the early psychoanalysts, called the process of becoming an individual "individuation."

Individuation refers to the separation from our family system and the establishing of our identity based on our own experiences, rather than merely following our parents' dreams. Although individuals may accept many of their parents' values, to genuinely individuate they must choose these values freely rather than automatically incorporating them into their personality because they "should."

Life is not measured by the number of breaths we take, but by the moments that take our breath away.
—MAYA ANGELOU

The values we place upon different aspects of our environment have an effect upon how we view things and how we function. In other words, an act viewed as right or wrong, moral or immoral, will depend upon the frame of reference of the perceiver. As a result, something that one person considers worthwhile and desirable may appear exactly the opposite to another person. We therefore tend to judge other people's actions by our own standards—our own values. Sometimes this works, because many of the people around us share some of these values. Sometimes, we may be imposing our own sense of right and wrong on others unjustly—we may be "shoulding" them.

Becoming Aware of Values, Ethics, and Choices: Kindness
https://www.youtube.com/watch?v=mTsvSAItPqA&feature=share

How You Treat People Is Who You Are!

"No matter how educated, talented, rich or cool you believe you are, how you treat people ultimately tells all. Integrity is everything."

The Influence of Other Factors

Other important factors are influential in the formation of our value system. Some of these are religious beliefs, attitudes, prejudices, and stereotypes.

Religious beliefs. What is a belief? A *belief* is the acceptance of some thought, supposition, or idea that a statement is true or that something exists. This belief may be in a God, or in Gods, or even in some form of spirituality. Studies show that most Americans want spirituality, but perhaps not in religious form. Lifeway Christian Resources did a survey in 2010 of 1,200 18- to 29-year-olds and found that 72% say they're really more spiritual than religious (Grossman, 2010). In the United States, for example, women are more likely than men to say religion is "very important" in their lives (60% vs. 47%), according to a 2014 Pew Research Center survey. And by many measures, Millennials are much less likely than their elders to be religious. Data on religious beliefs and practices come from international Pew Research Center surveys of the general population in 84 countries conducted between 2008 and 2015. Based on these wide-ranging and comprehensive datasets, Pew researchers found that, "globally, women *are* more devout than men by several standard measures of religious commitment. An estimated 83.4% of women around the world identify with a faith group, compared with 79.9% of men" (Pew Research Center, Religion and Public Life, March, 2016).

Christians remained the largest religious group in the world in 2015, making up nearly a third (31%) of Earth's 7.3 billion people, according to a new Pew Research Center demographic analysis. But the report also shows that the number of Christians in what many consider the religion's heartland, the continent of Europe, is in decline.

For more information on religions, take this interactive Pew Research Questionaire which provides interesting information on your choices as compared with the facts and others choices:

https://www.pewresearch.org/quiz/u-s-religious-knowledge-quiz/

The short quiz includes some questions recently asked in the nationally representative survey that forms the basis of this report. After completing the quiz, you can see how you did in comparison with the general public and with people like yourself.

For nearly 40 years, Dr. Vern Bengtson, Professor of Sociology and Gerontology at the University of Southern California, has overseen the Longitudinal Study of Generations, which has become the largest study of religion and family life conducted across several generational cohorts in the United States. When Bengtson noticed the growth of nonreligious Americans becoming increasingly pronounced, he decided in 2013 to add secular families to his study in an attempt to understand how family life and intergenerational influences play out among those without religion. He was surprised by what he found: High levels of family solidarity and emotional closeness between parents and nonreligious youth, and strong ethical standards and moral values that had been clearly articulated as they were imparted to the next generation. "Many nonreligious parents were more coherent and passionate about their ethical principles than some of the 're-ligious' parents in our study," Bengston told me. "The vast majority appeared to live goal-filled lives characterized by moral direction and sense of life having a purpose" (Zuckerman, 2016).

Wherever I go meeting the public ... spreading a message of human values, spreading a message of harmony, is the most important thing.
—DALAI LAMA

Roughly three-quarters of Millennials feel a strong sense of gratitude or thankfulness at least weekly (76%). And 51% say they feel a deep sense of spiritual peace and well-being at least once a week (Alper, 2015). In fact, M. Scott Peck (2003), in *The Road Less Traveled,* notes that he likes to speak of *spirituality* rather than *religiosity.* Peck goes on to indicate that every major religion of the world has similar ideas of love, the same goal of benefiting humanity through spiritual practice, and the same effect of making their followers into better human beings. However, in an interview with Robert Epstein (2002) for *Psychology Today*, Peck reminded readers that one person's experience with spirituality would be different from another person's experience.

In some form or another, religion and established moral codes are found in all cultures and societies. A commitment to a chosen moral code helps individuals gain a sense of meaning and purpose in their lives, and thus, plays an integral part in shaping their value system (Compton, 2005).

Altruism David Brooks in his 2016 book *The Power of Altruism*, explains that there are two lenses people use to look at the world: the moral lens and the economic lens. When someone offers money to do something "instead of following their natural bias toward reciprocity, service and cooperation, you encourage people to do a selfish cost-benefit calculation. They begin to ask, 'What's in this for me?'" (Brooks, 2016). Ricard (2016) feels "there's an altruism revolution underway, and it just may be the saving grace for the 21st century."

If someone dropped something, would you pick it up and hand it back to them?

This helpful behavior can be seen in young chimpanzees, but not nearly as readily or as consistently as in human babies. This suggests that altruism is a more human trait. But it's not just a cool part of being human—our inclination to be kind and selfless often benefits us directly in return.

Values

Values come from many sources.

What source has had the greatest influence in the development of your value system?

And that's not only according to one little study—evidence of the mental and physical benefits of altruism have been seen across a wide spectrum of scientific disciplines.

Science educator and creator of the PBS series *BrainCraft*, Vanessa Hill, said "I was always fascinated with why people act the way that they do."

Before becoming a science show host, Hill studied psychology and biology at the University of South Wales in Sydney, Australia. She also worked in science education and outreach at Australia's national science agency. She decided to start making her own science education videos because she wanted to help a wider audience "understand things about themselves that they never realized before."

Having done her own deep dive into the science of altruism, Hill found that we actually have a system built into our brain that recognizes when we do something selfless.

"Neuroscientists have identified circuits in the brain that underlie altruistic behavior," she explains. "When we're kind, we have a brain circuitry that rewards that." So the more we perform altruistic acts, the more often we get a boost of happiness—or oxytocin as scientists might call it—and the better we feel in both mind and body.

What's more, kids will likely stick with kind behavior if it's encouraged from an early age. However, their unique personalities will dictate how it manifests in them.

Believe it or not, there are actually several different types of altruism that humans exhibit.

There's pure altruism, which is giving solely for the benefit of others without expecting anything in return. There's pseudo-altruism, which is giving with the expectation of getting something back (even if you're not doing it consciously). There's egoism, which is doing good things for yourself (like self-care). And there's nurturing altruism, which means doing kind things with the goal of inspiring others to pay it forward.

Becoming Aware of Values, Ethics, and Choices: Altruism
https://www.pbs.org/wnet/religionandethics/2006/03/24/march-24-2006-altruism/12398/

Discussing altruism in and outside of a religious context.

Attitudes. *Attitudes* are positive or negative orientations toward a certain target. For example, you have attitudes toward specific persons (parents, children, teachers), as well as toward groups of people (Blacks, Whites, male ministers, female ministers). You also have attitudes toward things or targets such as food, movies, holidays, or marriage.

The attitudes you have today have been acquired throughout your life. How did you acquire them? You may have acquired some of your attitudes by hearing parents, family, friends, and teachers express positive or negative attitudes toward certain issues or people. The mass media, including advertising, may also be responsible for shaping some of your attitudes. The attitudes you have formed through your own direct experience are strongest, however, and they are also more resistant to change (Compton, 2005). You can learn to make choices that create happiness and decrease suffering by learning to pay more attention to your goals, attitudes, and feelings of self, and spending less time attempting to rescue, control, and manage others (Hetherington, 2008). Brooks (2016) said that to be a good worker or citizen, you often make an altruistic commitment.

More than likely, your positive attitudes are a result of positive experiences, and your negative attitudes are a result of negative experiences. Whatever you learned in these experiences is likely to take the form of *expectations* later in life. It is just natural to expect the same or similar results from similar situations. Consider these statements:

I'm not going to get married again; if I did, it would just probably end in another divorce.

Tom's mother is so different from Frank's mother—certainly not what I expected from a mother-in-law.

> *The meaning of things lies not in the things themselves, but in our attitude towards them.*
> —ANTOINE DE SAINT-EXUPÉRY

I'm sure I can work for Mrs. Jones; I've worked for another female, and we got along just great.

As you can see in these examples, the attitudes were formed from prior *experiences* and *expectations.* Your prior experiences and expectations are shaping the attitudes and values you hold right now, including your attitude toward this text. Often we may need to reevaluate these attitudes and values. The stronger an attitude is, the more difficult it is to change, because your emotions are involved.

We discussed prejudice and stereotypes in Chapter One as they relate to meeting people and forming perceptions about people; we want now to briefly review prejudice and stereotypes as they relate to how we form and act on our beliefs/values.

- **Groups/labels/prejudices.** A *prejudice* is a **preconceived opinion, feeling, or attitude,** either positive or negative, that is formed without adequate information. For example, you may have a negative prejudice toward the African American English teacher who is going to teach your class next semester. Although you have not had this teacher before, you have heard statements made by other students, and you have already formed your opinion. It is only when you are actually in this teacher's class that you can make a justified opinion. Prejudices are often unjustified attitudes; sometimes these attitudes extend to entire groups of people. The word "prejudice" can literally be broken down into "pre-" and "judgment." Aptly, much of prejudice stems from our pre-judging other people's habits, customs, clothes, ways of speaking, and values. We often do this with no basis for the judgment other than the fact that they (the customs, values, food, etc.) are different from our own (Rodolfo Mendoza-Denton, 2011).

> *Reject and condemn prejudice based on race, gender, religion, or age.*
> —MARTIN LUTHER KING, JR.

Actually, there are three components to a positive or negative **prejudice** (Myers, 2013). They are as follows:

- To hold **certain** *beliefs* **about members of a group**—*American Indians are mostly alcoholics.*
- To *feel* **negatively or positively toward them**—*I despise Jews. I adore teachers.*
- To be inclined **to** *act* **negatively or positively** toward them—*I wouldn't hire a Mexican. I really like working with women ...*

Becoming Aware of Prejudice, Discrimination, and Implicit Bias
https://www.youtube.com/watch?v=ruKrqgPMiis

Social psychology research reveals prejudices we don't know we have.

It is interesting to note that our strongest negative emotions are often reserved for groups rather than individuals. As Gordon W. Allport (1979) commented in his classic book *The Nature of Prejudice,* "anger is customarily felt toward individuals only, whereas hatred may be felt toward whole classes of people." If we included multiculturalism early in life so children can learn about others and make friends of many cultures, we would not have as much hatred and misinformation about others. Starting Small, a program produced by the Teaching Tolerance Project of the Southern Poverty

> *The very ink with which history is written is merely fluid prejudice.*
> —MARK TWAIN

Law Center, has many ideas and resources for others to use (2008). Many examples of prejudice involve in-group and out-group processes and often includes the belief that the members of "the other group" are taking too much of whatever is valuable (e.g., good jobs, land, clean water) for their less-deserving group. One hope is that by learning about the psychological processes that underlie prejudice in general and the specific nature of any particular prejudice in a context, we can better understand and more effectively reduce prejudice. Even a small reduction will make this a worthwhile option. Reducing prejudice and stereotyping will take time so that prejudice against specific groups, such as women and girls, the elderly, gays and lesbians, people with disabilities, and other groups will be helped also (Dovidio, Glick, & Rudman, 2005).

Becoming Aware of Prejudice, Discrimination, and Implicit Bias
https://www.khanacademy.org/test-prep/mcat/individuals-and-society/perception-prejudice-and-bias/v/ethnocentrism-and-cultural-relativism-in-group-and-out-group

Ethnocentrism and cultural relativism in individuals and society.

Stereotypes. When we allow our prejudiced attitudes to make *generalizations* by categorizing an object, person, or situation, we are guilty of **stereotyping**. As psychologist Jack Dovidio of Yale University notes in 2014: "we create stereotypes to explain why things are the way they are and stereotypes don't have to be true to serve a purpose." For example:

Women are emotional.

Latinx are a hot-headed race.

Mothers-in-law are bossy and interfering people.

There are just a bunch of hypocrites at that church.

According to these examples, if you are a woman, a Latinx, a mother-in-law, or if you go to *that* church, you have now been given a label. You are not thought of as an individual—you are a member of the group and, of course, you have *their* similar characteristics.

Pause for a minute and just ask yourself these questions: *What prejudices and stereotypes do I have? What are they based on? Do I really want to have these values?* Understanding and trying to not be prejudiced is a very hard thing to change, but is worth doing. Recognizing implicit bias and negative stereotypes are just the beginning.

At this point, you may find it helpful to review Focus on Diversity—Breaking Down Barriers, for some suggestions on dealing with prejudices, bias, and stereotypes.

Live your beliefs and you can turn the world around.
—HENRY DAVID THOREAU

All I've ever tried to tell anyone is that I'm not a black man or a white man or anything else. All I've been was American.
—GEORGE FOREMAN

Becoming *Aware*

FOCUS ON DIVERSITY

BREAKING DOWN BARRIERS

To reduce your prejudices and use of stereotypes, these steps may be helpful:

1. Admit your prejudices and biases and try to understand them.
2. Identify the stereotypes that reflect your prejudices and attempt to modify them.
3. Identify the actions that reflect your prejudices and modify them.
4. Avoid judging differences; view diversity as a strength.
5. Attempt to learn about cultures that differ from your own. Try to understand their values.
6. Accept that we need to recognize and battle our own bias, racism, and privilege.
7. Think about White privilege and how you can discuss it and confront it without hurting others; it can be hard to hear and understand another's point of view.
8. By demonstrating that you respect and care about others, you increase the chances that you can open the door to relationships in which you learn from others, just as they learn from you.

Johnson (2008); Corey & Corey (2008); Henslin (2015); Coleman (2016); Johnson (2014)

Are you willing to test, adapt, and change your perceptions? Take the Harvard Diversity Test, and do the readings, quizzes, and watch the videos at the end of the chapter for further insight.

Think About This

Becoming Aware of your values Activity

Catalog your values
At the present time, what things are most important to you in your life? Is your career of primary importance? How about your school work and/or the training for your future career? How about the time you spend with your family? Do you have outside leisure interests, community activities, or volunteer work?

WHAT ARE MY VALUES?

What you value most determines how you will spend your time. When you decide to work late on a repeated basis rather than go home to dinner, this is a value decision. If you gave up a movie in order to study for a test, this is also a value decision. When you decide to go out with some friends rather than attend your son's baseball game, this is another value decision.

You are always making value decisions, and an awareness of what values are most important to you can help you to live a more harmonious and less stressful life. When you know which values have a higher priority, you can more easily make life's major and minor decisions.

The most interesting thing about any human being is the values by which they live. Unfortunately, most of us never take the time to sit down and really think through the moral precepts that consciously or unconsciously guide our lives.

> I could not, at any age, be content to take my place by the fireside and simply look on. Life was meant to be lived. Curiosity must be kept alive. One must never, for whatever reason, turn his back on life.
> —ELEANOR ROOSEVELT

GENDER—THE SPACE BETWEEN

The gender identity terms you need to know—values, ethics, and choices By Cydney Adams MARCH 24, 2017

https://www.cbsnews.com/video/gender-the-space-between/

Do values change? Your values do change as you go through the various life stages. As children, your highest value might have been play and having fun; as adolescents, perhaps it was peer relationships; as young adults, it may be relationships with the opposite sex; and as adults, your highest value may be your family and the work you do. For many older people, service to others and enjoying leisure time are often the highest values.

GENDER AND YOU

TOP SIX PERSONAL VALUES

In 2013, students taking human relations/psychology of adjustment classes at Tarrant County College, Northeast Campus, revealed their top personal values (1,151 students—51% females and 49% males):

Males
1. Close family and friends
2. Happiness
3. Stable marriage
4. A fulfilling career
5. Financially stable
6. Good health

Females
1. Close family and friends
2. Stable marriage
3. Happiness
4. Good health
5. Financially stable
6. A fulfilling career

What are your top values? How do your top six values compare with what the male and female students said? From the more commonly mentioned values, the final results reveal the top six prioritized values. You will also be given an opportunity to complete this activity, and you might want to compare your results with these findings.

Do you see any changes in your personal set of values over the past five or ten years? Has there been any change in the kinds of values you consider to be important in your life? You will be given several opportunities in the activities at the end of this chapter to review your values—past and present.

If you are currently seeking some change in your career or lifestyle, it may be due in part to the fact that some of your values may have changed. This is called *values clarification* and it is discussed below. What was important to you in the past may be less important now. You may want to devote greater attention in your life to new things or to some of the things you did not have as much time for in the past.

We are unique individuals, and something that one person considers a value might not be a value to another person. For example, we all want a feeling of security. However, your idea of what makes you feel secure may differ remarkably from that of other people. Some people may equate security primarily with money; others may equate security with education, religion, or close family relationships. Sometimes combinations of all these types of security are desired. The order of importance then becomes a matter of value (Coontz, 2016).

> *It's not hard to make decisions when you know what your values are.*
> —ROY DISNEY

CONSIDER THIS

BECOMING AWARE OF YOUR VALUES: SOME HARD QUESTIONS

You probably do not have the answers to these questions on the tip of your tongue. They require some thought and discussion. They will lead you to a better understanding of your values. Answer the following questions in your journal and be prepared to discuss them in class.

1. If you were independently wealthy, what would you do with your life?
2. What issues are of deep concern to you regarding your home, campus, community, church, state, country, or world?
3. If you were independently wealthy, to what causes would you contribute?
4. After your death, what would you like people to say about you? How would you like to be remembered?
5. Have you seen any changes in your personal set of values over the past five or ten years?
6. Has there been any change in the kinds of values you consider to be important in your life?

Clarifying Your Personal Values

© ASDF_MEDIA/Shutterstock.comstock.com

Clarifying our values is a crucial aspect of self-development (Rathus & Nevid, 2012). Sometimes important choices in life are made on the basis of peer pressure, unthinking submission to authority, or the power of propaganda. We may even guide our lives by what others expect of us, instead of what we truly believe is right. At times, we may allow the thoughts and expectations of society and others to influence our value system. Thus, our value orientation can become other-directed rather than self-directed. The obvious result is a feeling of being very insecure and easily threatened in our valuing process.

By assuming that people are selfish, by prioritizing arrangements based on selfishness, we have encouraged selfish frames of mind. Maybe it's time to upend classical economics and political science. Maybe it's time to build institutions that harness people's natural longing to do good.

(David Brooks, 2016)

Values clarification is a process that helps individuals discover their true values. The process of clarifying values involves choosing freely from alternatives, prizing or affirming the choice publicly, and acting repeatedly in some pattern of life. When we become conscious of our own personal value system and how it functions, we can begin to manage our own value system rather than allowing others to manage it for us. Hunter Lewis (2007), in his thought-provoking book *A Question of Values,* emphasizes the importance of managing our own value system:

> People need to think about their own values, think hard about them, think for themselves. Personal values really do matter. Without functioning values, we can hardly live at all, much less lead a purposeful and satisfying life.

How do we discover what our true values are?

Values clarification is a process that helps people arrive at an answer. Howard (2016) shares this thought:

> It is not concerned with an ultimate set of values (that is for you to decide), but it does stress a method to help you determine the content and power of your own set of values. It is a self-audit, and an inventory of soul and spirit. It is a tool to help you freely decide between alternatives or among varied choices. It is a methodology to help you make a decision, to act, to determine what has meaning for you.

It's good to have money and the things money can buy, but it's good to check once in a while and make sure you haven't lost the things that money can't buy.
—GEORGE HORACE LORIMER

According to Howard (2016), the process of clarifying values involves choosing, prizing, and acting, as seen in the How To Clarify Values section below.

Before something can be a *full,* true value, it must meet all seven of the following criteria. Howard (2016) suggests that there are three levels involved in the criteria: *choosing* relies mainly on the cognitive or thinking area; *prizing* relies on the affective or feeling area; and *acting* relies on the behavioral areas. When we have a *full value,* our thoughts, feelings, and actions are in agreement; what we think, say, feel, and do are in agreement and are evident in our lives.

Let us look at the seven criteria a little more closely.

- *Choosing freely* means we consciously and deliberately make the choice ourselves. There is no pressure to believe what our parents taught us. An example of choosing freely would be when you have been raised and taught that there is only one religion worthy of your belief, and you later decide that your beliefs are more in line with another religious faith. Even if you end up choosing the same religious faith which your parents hold, that becomes a full value for you because you make the personal choice to follow that faith.
- *Choosing from alternatives* means there are options. If there are no alternatives, there is no freedom of choice. For example, you really cannot value breathing, of itself, because there is no choice involved; a person must breathe to live. However, you can value mountain air, or a special breathing technique, such as yoga.
- *Choosing after considering* the consequences means you ask yourself, "What would be the result of the alternatives to my choice?" This gives you the opportunity to choose with thoughtful consideration, and not on impulse. Many of the problems which we have are the result of impulsive, poorly thought-out decisions, or action taken without regard for ourselves or others. For example, sometimes people impulsively decide to get a divorce and then later realize they are not happy with their "quick" decision.

> *It is our choices ... that show what we truly are, far more than our abilities.*
> —J. K. ROWLING

Think About This

How To Clarify Values

Choosing:
Freely; from alternatives; after thoughtful consideration of the consequences of each alternative.

Prizing:
Cherishing, prizing, and being happy with the choice; willing to affirm the choice publicly.

Acting:
Doing something with the choice, taking action; acting repeatedly, in some pattern of life.

- *Prizing: Cherishing and feeling happy about the choice* means that it influences your behavior in some way, and you do not mind spending your time on this value. For example, if you value being thrifty and you need to buy a new multimedia device, you will spend a considerable amount of time researching and comparing prices. When you finally get your multimedia device, you will be satisfied and content that you got the best buy.
- *Publicly affirming a value* means you are willing to tell others about it. Some people even crusade for their values. For example, if you value a particular political ideology, you may be seen campaigning for the politician who holds the same value. Remember, you have the right to publicly affirm your values, but you do not have the right to impose your values on others. This interferes with their freedom of choice.

- *Acting: Doing something about a value* means taking action. Full values are those things which we work for, do something about, and take action on. Thus, what a person does reflects his or her values. For example, you will read literature that supports your values; you will join clubs or organizations whose members share your values and whose goals correspond to your values.
- *Acting repeatedly* means there is a life pattern that is evident, and the stronger the value, the more it influences your life. There is a consistency of action which manifests itself in all aspects of your life: in dress, in friends selected, in the place you live, in leisure time, in what you read, in your career, in the selection of your spouse, and in how you spend your time and money.

In summary, a value that is freely chosen from alternatives whose consequences have been thoughtfully considered, of which we are proud and happy to the point that we publicly take a stand, and that we act upon with repetition and consistency, is a full value.

VALUE INDICATORS

If you can bring your actions and the time you spend in your life more into harmony with your values, you will feel more in control of your life and more satisfied with the decisions you make.
—FRED HECKLINGER

Most of us have partial values that are in the process of being formed. Partial values, or *value indicators*, include desires, thoughts not acted on, opinions, interests, aspirations, goals, beliefs, attitudes, feelings, convictions, activities, and daydreams (Rokeach, 2000). For example, we may say that we have a certain goal, but we are not working toward it. Also, we may say that we have an interest in learning to play bridge, but we have never taken the time to act on that interest.

As discussed earlier, the word *should* tends to indicate a standard we or others are *not* meeting. The difference between what we think *should be* true and what *is* true in our lives is an important clue to our values.

We have already stated that the way we use our money and time is a strong value indicator. For example, John may say he values very highly the importance of reading and keeping up in "his thinking." However, if you asked him how much time he spends reading each week or when he last bought a good book, you may be surprised to discover that he does not even remember. A simple process to determine the strength of a value is to ask a person or family to describe how they spend their money. Generally speaking, the more money they spend on something, the greater the value is to people.

Becoming Aware

Life is a series of choices!

What should be. What is.

Establishing your real values involves balancing "what is" with "what should be" in your life.

It is easy to see that we can find out what our real values are by examining our *actual behaviors—the way in which we invest our time, money, energies, and resources.* Consequently, in order to better understand your real values, you might want to apply the following four tests to your value orientation (Rokeach, 2000):

1. **The Choice Test.** What do I do in situations involving a choice?
2. **The Time Test.** How much time and energy am I willing to spend on the value?
3. **The Sacrificial Test.** What satisfaction am I willing to forego on behalf of the value?
4. **The Emotion Test.** How much satisfaction or guilt do I experience when I am true to my value or when I violate it?

POTENTIAL REMEDIES

Reimagine Systems Societies can revise both tech arrangements and the structure of human institutions, including their composition, design, goals and processes.

Reinvent Tech Things can change by reconfiguring hardware and software to improve their human-centered performance and by exploiting tools like artificial intelligence (AI), virtual reality (VR), augmented reality (AR), and mixed reality (MR).

Regulate Governments and/or industries should create reforms through agreement on standards, guidelines, codes of conduct, and passage of laws and rules.

Redesign Media Literacy Formally educate people of all ages about the impacts of digital life on well-being and the way tech systems function, as well as encourage appropriate, healthy uses.

Recalibrate Expectations Human-technology coevolution comes at a price; digital life in the 2000s is no different. People must gradually evolve and adjust to these changes.

Fated to Fail A share of respondents say all this may help somewhat, but—mostly due to human nature—it is unlikely that these responses will be effective enough.

These findings do not represent all the points of view that are possible to a question like this, but they need to be considered (Elon University's Imagining the Internet Center, 2018).

Think about it: never have we been so connected yet mobile, having so much information at our disposal. While technology can enhance your life, it can also paralyze it. There is no doubt about the fact that technology can encourage some very compulsive behavior. It is not about how often we access the digital world, but rather when and why we do so. Always question your intent and understand the cause-effect relationships between the submersion of technology in our daily lives and its impact on being human. Can you put down or put away technology so you can interact face-to-face with others?

Society moved into a techno-economic era in the 1990s with the start of the Internet, and this caused a shift from a stable and slow-paced world to an unstable and fast-paced world, and also a shift from information scarcity to information abundance, according to Rosling & Rosling-Ronnlund (2018). This is called a paradigm shift. It is defined by Merriam-Webster (2019) as an important change that happens when the usual way of thinking about or doing something is replaced by a new and different way. Moving to a more technical world has been a paradigm shift for your teachers and parents, too. As they embrace this new paradigm shift in their life and work principles, they might help you feel more at ease in this new world, too.

While the previous generations were taught to aim for stability and status early in their career, it is much more crucial for your generation. Technology opens new doors of possibility, so you need to look—first—for your purpose. Knowing yourself is essential. This unstable and fast-paced world also requires you to embrace a lifelong learning mentality because changes will be coming quickly. With new technology and knowledge you are constantly bombarded with information, and you will need to learn the fundamentals, the ability to make sense of that information, and the power to learn. Work on something that matters to you more than money. Remember advances in technologies that impact the lives of people (and their data) should be accompanied by morally compassionate conduct that reduces the risk of abuse and protects the abused. Technology, applied with an upright intent, can help governments uncover new insights about their people to showcase their potential and raise their social mobility. But applied with devious intent, technology can discriminate, marginalize, and undermine the well-being of a society.

Applied with compassion, technology can provide hope and opportunities for people looking to break free from their disadvantageous background. But applied without compassion, technology can cause people to be judged permanently on their mistakes for life, creating a culture of anxiety and monotonous social norms.

Currently, personal information is being mined and monetized by organizations. Being clear about the types of data is being collected and how it is being used should be mandatory. Similarly, allowing users to control and edit how much information they are willing to share is crucial. As consumers of technology, it is our role to persuade companies to take responsibility in protecting and respecting privacy.

Seeing users as human challenges companies to build products from the perspective of the person using them. This is why data collection transparency becomes necessary to build more authentic relationships. In a nutshell, as technology improves, it becomes more and more human. Take chat-bots for example—they can be programmed to answer questions from customers, and often in such a way that you forget you've just had your query answered by a piece of AI.

Do We Learn to Value What We Suffer For?

Why does a child who has to work to earn money value his or her bicycle more than the child who is given a bicycle? Why are members of cults so dedicated to their organizations? These questions and many others may be answered by taking a look at cognitive dissonance, the mental pain of inconsistency, and justifying a sacrifice.

Cognitive dissonance. The Merriam—Webster dictionary defines cognitive dissonance as the state of having inconsistent thoughts, beliefs, or attitudes, especially as relating to behavioral decisions and attitude change. We are all motivated to maintain consistency within ourselves. We do not normally hold values, beliefs, or attitudes that are mutually incompatible or dissonant with each other, nor do we behave in ways contradictory to our values or attitudes. Although people differ in the amount of inconsistency they can tolerate, a basic assumption of *cognitive dissonance theory* is that inconsistency is intolerable to an individual.

The concept of cognitive dissonance was introduced by Leon Festinger in 1957 as a way to account for reactions to inconsistencies in attitudes and beliefs. According to this theory, when two or more cognitions (such as beliefs, opinions, and the things we know about various types of behavior, people, objects, or circumstances) are in disagreement (dissonance), a state of tension results. This inconsistency (dissonance) motivates the individual to adjust these cognitions so as to reduce the dissonance and thereby reduce the tension (Aronson et al., 2015).

The mental pain of inconsistency. When there is dissonance between attitudes and behavior, the individual may modify attitudes rather than behavior.

To illustrate these points, suppose that a cigarette smoker is aware of the dangers of smoking to their health, but continues to smoke. The individual is faced with two dissonant cognitions: "I enjoy smoking, or smoking is harmful." The *dissonance theory* predicts that such an inconsistency would produce an uncomfortable state that would motivate the individual either to give up smoking or change their ideas about the risks involved in continuing to smoke. In cases such as this, we typically find the individual expressing one of the following ideas:

- "I enjoy smoking, and it is worth it."
- "No one in our family has ever had cancer."
- "A person can't always avoid every possible dangerous situation and still continue to live an enjoyable life."
- "Perhaps if I stopped smoking I would put on weight, which is equally as bad for one's health."

Thus, Festinger suggests that continuing to smoke is consistent with the person's ideas about smoking.

Although the individual may have stated that they would like to give up smoking, the person's inability to do so resulted in rationalizing some facts to support their belief system and to match the person's behavior. Now the tension is somewhat relieved. However, it has been suggested by some authorities that the individual may have to deal with their true feelings and behavior again.

Justifying a sacrifice. As we have observed through cognitive dissonance, an individual is motivated to justify his or her behavior. A child who has to work to earn money to buy a bicycle will value it more because they put more effort into getting it. Members of cults, and sometimes other members of groups and organizations, will generally experience some type of initiation process that will take a lot of effort on the individual's part. After putting in all this effort, the individual has to justify why they suffered or worked so hard in order to be a member of the organization. As a result of all this, the individual will generally become a very dedicated member of this group as a means of justifying why they went through this process.

Most students would admit they value a class they succeeded in that took more effort than a class they succeeded in that was considered "easy." As you can see from these examples, *we learn to value what we suffer for* (Aronson, 2015). Again, a value that is

---

BECOMING AWARE OF GENERATIONS—THINK ABOUT THIS

Boomers and Silents were born between 1928–1945.

Gen X was born between 1965–1979.

Gen Y, or **Millennials**, were born between 1980–1994.

Generation Z—born from 1995–present—are diverse and on track to be the most well-educated generation yet, moving toward adulthood with a liberal set of attitudes and an openness to emerging social trends, according to the Pew Research Center (2019).

When it comes to views on race, the two younger generations are more likely than older generations to say that Blacks are treated less fairly than Whites in the United States today. And they are much more likely than their elders to approve of NFL players kneeling during the national anthem as a sign of protest.

The younger generations are also more accepting of some of the ways in which American society is changing. Majorities among Gen Z and the Millennial generation say increasing racial and ethnic diversity in the U.S. is a good thing for society, while older generations are less convinced of this. And they're more likely to have a positive view of interracial and same-sex marriage than their older counterparts.

Recent Pew research reports that **Gen Z is the most racially and ethnically diverse generation** we have seen, but this isn't all that's driving the attitudes of this generation when it comes to issues surrounding race and diversity. There are significant generational differences on these issues even among non-Hispanic Whites.

While **Generation Z**'s views resemble those of Millennials in many areas, Gen Zers are distinct from Millennials and older generations in at least two ways, both of which reflect the cultural context in which they are coming of age. Gen Zers are more likely than Millennials to say they know someone who prefers that others use gender-neutral pronouns to refer to them: 35% say this is the case, compared with a quarter of Millennials. Among each older generation, the share saying this drops: 16% of Gen Xers, and 12% of Boomers (Pew Research Center, 2019).

Becoming *Aware*

freely chosen from alternatives whose consequences have been thoughtfully considered, of which we are proud and happy to the point that we publicly take a stand, and that we act upon with repetition and consistency, is a full value.

Making Ethical Choices

This is a confusing world to live in. At every turn, we are forced to make choices about how to live our lives. Many of these choices are not obvious; some are almost automatic. These choices are often coming from our internal ethical compass or system of personal ethics. Consider these questions: **What is your philosophy of life?** What would be included in your system of **personal ethics**? What do you do when you are confronted with confusion and conflicts regarding your **values and ethics**? How do your decisions affect your **character and integrity**? As you think about these questions, one thing is certain; your personal system of ethics is based on the values and attitudes you practice in your daily living. Actually, your system of **personal ethics** becomes an attempt to reconcile what *ought to be* with *what is*. Each of us, relying on our set of personal ethics, must decide what is *right or wrong* for us. There are many alternatives, but each of us can *choose* our direction in life

Character and ethics. Stephen Covey (2004), in his highly popular book, *The 7 Habits of Highly Effective People*, is concerned about some of the choices currently being made. He indicates that prior to World War I, people governed their lives by values like "integrity, humility, fidelity, temperance, courage, justice, patience, industry, simplicity, modesty, and the Golden Rule." He calls these attributes the *character ethic* because they are basic principles of effective living, and true success depends on integrating these principles into one's character. Covey is concerned that we have made a distinct shift away from the character ethic toward the *personality ethic*, where success is based more on image, personality, technique, appearance, and having a positive mental attitude. Covey says:

> We have become so focused on building ourselves up we have forgotten the foundation that holds it up is that of **character** and **integrity**. Many are focused on reaping the goods without the need to sow the fields. And, if there is no **integrity**, the challenges of life will reveal one's true **character**. (2006)

Former U. S. senator Al Simpson said, "If you have character, that's all that matters; and if you don't have character, that's all that matters, too." So what is character? *Character* is composed of personal standards of behavior, including honesty, integrity, and moral strength (Reece & Brandt, 2014). Can this be learned?

The *Six Pillars of Character* is a framework for teaching good character to help instill a positive learning environment for students and a "culture of kindness," making schools a safer environment for students to learn. The Six Pillars of Character values are not political, religious, or culturally biased. In fact, every year for over 20 years the *Character Counts!* program has been officially recognized and endorsed by the

Character is a by-product; it is produced in the great manufacture of daily duty.
—WOODROW WILSON

U.S. Senate and the president of the United States. Ethics educator Michael Josephson (1994) of the Character Counts Coalition has developed the *Character Counts!* model for educational institutions and organizations throughout the country to teach the six pillars of character: 1) trustworthiness, 2) respect, 3) responsibility, 4) fairness, 5) caring, and 6) citizenship. The Character Counts coalition has developed the following list of 10 key guidelines as a foundation for character development (you will have an opportunity to evaluate your own standing on these character traits in an exercise at the end of the chapter—see Guidelines for Character Development):

- **Be honest.** Tell the truth; be sincere; do not mislead or withhold information in relationships of trust; do not steal.
- **Demonstrate integrity.** Stand up for your beliefs about right and wrong; be your best self; resist social pressure to do wrong.
- **Keep promises.** Keep your word and honor your commitments; pay your debts and return what you borrow.
- **Be loyal.** Stand by family, friends, employers, community, and country; do not talk about people behind their backs.
- **Be responsible.** Think before you act; consider consequences; be accountable and "take your medicine."
- **Pursue excellence.** Do your best with what you have; do not give up easily.
- **Be kind and caring.** Show you care through generosity and compassion; do not be selfish or mean.
- **Treat all people with respect.** Be courteous and polite; judge all people on their merits; be tolerant, appreciative, and accepting of individual differences.
- **Be fair.** Treat all people fairly; be open minded; listen to others and try to understand what they are saying and feeling.
- **Be a good citizen.** Obey the law and respect authority; vote; volunteer your efforts; protect the environment.

Andrew Dubrin (2016) defines **character trait** as an enduring characteristic of a person that is related to moral and ethical behavior and that shows up consistently. For example, if an individual has the character trait of being untruthful, he or she will lie or behave deceptively in many situations. However, the character trait of honesty leads to behaving honestly in most situations. Dubrin believes that if you develop, or already have, the ten character traits, it will be easy for you to behave ethically in your dealings with others. Ken Wert (2016) has a similar list of character traits necessary for a happy life:

Ethics and the professions. Many businesses have a code of ethics for their employees to follow in dealing with customers and clients. Likewise, many professions have ethical training and a code of ethics required for continued licensure and/or certification. For example, accounting classes may describe ethical ways to track and document finances, and public relations classes could examine how students would feel about promoting a client with an unhealthful product. See Figure 9.1 for the Gallup survey on honesty and ethics in professions.

Becoming *Aware*

TEN ESSENTIAL CHARACTER TRAITS FOR A HAPPIER LIFE

1. Be Humble
2. Be Courageous
3. Be Grateful
4. Be Tolerant
5. Be Loving
6. Be Forgiving
7. Be Selfless
8. Be Honest
9. Be Persistent
10. Be Expectantly Patient

Ken Wert, *Meant to be Happy* (2020)

Integrity and ethics. If you are ever in doubt when trying to understand the ethics of a situation and find the proper solution, it might be helpful to review and consider your responses to the following questions (Vandeveer & Menefee, 2009):

1. Is it legal?
2. How do I feel about this? Am I feeling unusually anxious? Am I fearful?
3. Will any rules, policies, or regulations be violated?
4. Is the proposed action consistent with past practice?
5. Does my conscience bother me?
6. How would I feel if the details of this situation appeared on the front page of the local newspaper?
7. Does the situation require that I lie about the process or the results?
8. Do I consider this to be an extraordinary situation that demands an unusual response?
9. Am I acting fairly? Would I want to be treated this way?
10. Would I be able to discuss the proposed situation or action with my immediate supervisor, my family, my minister, my closest friends, my company's clients, or the president of the company?
11. What would I tell my child, sibling, young relative, or close, valued friend to do in this situation?
12. Will I have to hide or keep my actions secret? Has someone warned me not to disclose my actions to anyone?

While you may not need to ask yourself all 12 questions in every situation, your honest answers to perhaps even half of the questions may give you guidance in difficult situations.

> You are born with three things: intelligence, endurance, and the opportunity to build integrity. You decide how much intelligence and endurance you are going to use. You build integrity every single day with the choices you make.
> —BOB KERREY

Classic psychologist Lawrence Kohlberg, best known for his theory of stages of moral development, reminds us that "the highest level of moral functioning requires us to use ethical principles to define our own moral standards and then to live in accord with them." Ideally, our choices will be made on the basis of our values and ethics—our standards of conduct or behavior—(DeCenzo & Silhanek, 2002). In short, ethics determines where you draw the line between right and wrong.

Figure 9.1 HONESTY/ETHICS IN PROFESSIONS

How would you would rate the honesty and ethical standards of people in these different fields:
very high   high   average
low   very low

■ % Very high/High
■ % Avergae
■ % Low/Very low

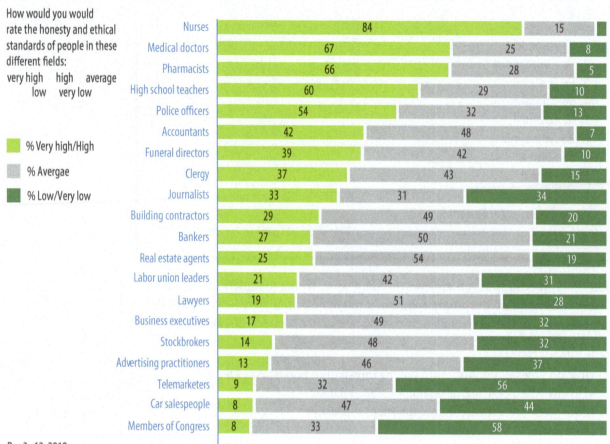

Profession	% Very high/High	% Average	% Low/Very low
Nurses	84	15	
Medical doctors	67	25	8
Pharmacists	66	28	5
High school teachers	60	29	10
Police officers	54	32	13
Accountants	42	48	7
Funeral directors	39	42	10
Clergy	37	43	15
Journalists	33	31	34
Building contractors	29	49	20
Bankers	27	50	21
Real estate agents	25	54	19
Labor union leaders	21	42	31
Lawyers	19	51	28
Business executives	17	49	32
Stockbrokers	14	48	32
Advertising practitioners	13	46	37
Telemarketers	9	32	56
Car salespeople	8	47	44
Members of Congress	8	33	58

Dec 3–12, 2018

Source: Gallup poll, https://news.gallup.com/poll/245597/nurses-again-outpace-professions-honesty-ethics.aspx

It is important to note that *integrity* is exhibited when you achieve congruence between what you know, what you say, and what you do. When your behavior exhibits your beliefs, you have integrity. When you say one thing but do something else, you lack integrity. When your behavior is in tune with your professed standards and values—when you practice what you believe in—you have integrity (Reece & Brandt, 2014).

Moral development. Morality includes a set of principles or ideals that help a person distinguish right from wrong and act on this distinction. Even when we do the "wrong thing," we usually know what the "right thing" is. For many years, Kohlberg (1981) studied how individuals make moral judgments. He was interested in the process by which people arrive at moral choices—what kind of reasoning makes something right or wrong. He proposed three levels of moral development—the knowledge of right and wrong behavior at different stages of life. See Table 9.1 for a summary of these levels and examples of each type of thinking.

Becoming Aware

Table 9.1 KOHLBERG'S THREE LEVELS OF MORAL DEVELOPMENT

LEVEL OF MORALITY	HOW RULES ARE UNDERSTOOD	EXAMPLE
Preconvention morality (typically very young children)	The consequences determine morality; behavior that is rewarded is right; that which is punished is wrong.	A child who steals a toy from another child and does not get caught does not see that action as wrong.
Conventional morality (older children, adolescents, and most adults)	Conformity to social norm is right; nonconformity is wrong.	A child criticizes his or her parent for speeding because speeding is against the stated laws.
Postconventional morality (about 20% of the adult population)	Moral principles determined by the person are used to determine right and wrong and may disagree with societal norms.	A reporter who wrote a controversial story goes to jail rather than reveal the source's identity.

Adapted from Ciccarelli & Noland (2014); Kohlberg (1981).

Confusion and conflict. Being human, sometimes we may experience confusion and conflict. We may even have a value conflict, a clash between values that encourage opposing actions (Wyer, 2004).

Perhaps one of the most difficult things to do is to establish for ourselves a consistent set of values (Pojman, 2012). If we go against a value, we feel bad. Inconsistencies in our values make us unhappy; they make us feel guilty. If we usually live up to our values, we are happy, satisfied people with consistent value systems.

It is true that we cannot always satisfy our values; many compromises must be made, because value conflicts are likely to appear when two or more people get together. Therefore, we need to learn when we can afford to give up and compromise values and when we cannot. It is best not to compromise values of high priority. Values that are not so important may be compromised without destroying our self-concept, as well as our personal ethics. Actually, satisfied, happy people are people who do not compromise their most important values, but are willing to compromise their less important values.

Perhaps the question is really—*What is most important to me?* In making value compromises, therefore, it is very important that we understand our priorities. It is this understanding that helps us define our purpose and gives meaning to our life. Controversial radio icon Dr. Laura Schlessinger (2016) puts it quite simply: "Ultimately, we decide the course of our lives by the ethical decisions we make" (*Psychology Today*, 2016).

Conflicts in values are also seen with social media use today. So many issues arise with social media that everyone has to contemplate how they feel about them and educate themselves. Around four-in-ten U.S. adults (43%) get news from Facebook, according to a survey conducted in July and August 2018, and many adult Facebook users have altered their use of the platform. A little over half of adult Facebook users in the U.S. (54%) have adjusted their privacy settings in the past 12 months, according to a separate Center survey conducted in May-June 2018. The survey followed revelations that former consulting firm Cambridge Analytica had collected data on tens of millions of Facebook users without their knowledge or permission (Pew Research fact tank. 2019). In 2014 78% of Americans felt that, in many ways, U.S. social media had "opened doors and minds" on issues that often people are afraid to discuss. The Pew Research Center Survey from August 2016 shows that Americans are increasingly turning to social media for news and political information. Digital strategist Dr. Dave Chaffey found the number of Internet users worldwide in 2019 is 4.388 billion, up 9.1% year-on-year. The number of social media users worldwide in 2019 is 3.484 billion, up 9% year-on-year, and the number of mobile phone users in 2019 is 5.112 billion, up 2% year-on-year (Chaffey, 2019). In the 1960s and 70s, when integration and women's equal rights were being discussed, protested, and values were changing, television was the medium that spread information. According to Pew Research, in summer social media also served as important valid venues, where groups with common interests came together to share ideas and information. Today, however, you must check the validity of social media news. Many adult Facebook users in the U.S. lack a clear understanding of how the platform's news feed works, according to the May-June 2018 survey. Around half of these users (53%) say they do not understand why certain posts are included in their news feed and others are not, including 20% who say they do not understand this at all. In the 2016 presidential election, "news" was created by foreign news that was not true: Sources it may have affected the results of the 2016 presidential race (CBS News, Nov, 2018). Instagram, Twitter, Facebook, and other social media sites can help users bring greater attention to issues through their collective voice if we monitor and verify sources. Some researchers and activists credit social media with propelling racially focused issues to greater national attention (Anderson & Hitlin, 2016).

Other factors influencing the formation of our value system include religious beliefs, attitudes, prejudices, and stereotypes. Recall that the three components to negative prejudice are: to hold certain beliefs against members of a group, to feel negatively toward them, and to be inclined to act negatively toward them. Because we live and work in a multicultural world, it is extremely important that we be willing to view diversity as a strength and to test, adapt, and change our perceptions as we interact with others (Tolerance.org).

> *Character is what you are in the dark.*
> —DWIGHT MOODY

People share a common social understanding of the stereotypes that are pervasive in their culture, and this knowledge can foster implicit bias even if a person does not necessarily endorse the cultural stereotype (Devine, 1989; Fazio, Jackson, Dunton, & Williams, 1995). One explanation is that people implicitly make associations and evaluations based on cultural knowledge in a way that "may not be available to introspection and may not be wanted or endorsed but is still attitudinal because of its potential to influence individual perception, judgment, or action" (Nosek, 2007).

In other words, the historical and traditional modes of interaction are deeply ingrained- so much so that we may find ourselves acting in biased ways without awareness. This is the basis for implicit bias. That is why you need to take the Harvard Implicit Bias Test, so you know what your biases are.

SELFLOVE

There is no self love with your partner included. If your partner is included, you are identifying yourself with somebody else, feeding your ego, and will face massive destruction if that person spontaneously leaves your life.

We cannot rely on anybody else but ourselves to pick us up when we're down. The support of friends, family, and significant others are great—but we have to do the heavy lifting. We have to self reflect on why we're low.

We have to ask ourselves, how do I make myself feel better?

We have to create the plan of action that changes our life.

Not your parents. Not your best friend. Not your spouse.

The significant other that tells you they require you to be the best version of yourself, is the one that truly loves you. They're the one who sees potential inside of you and want to make sure it always shines. They're the person who will refuse to entertain you if you decide that you want to be negative and angry for six months. They're the person who will push you to find the light because they're not going to put up with your darkness.

Eva Gutierrez, *The Ascent*

The Importance of Meaning and Purpose

Viktor Frankl, a European psychiatrist, dedicated much of his professional life to the study of meaning in life. According to Frankl (1997), what distinguishes us as humans is our **search for purpose**. The striving to find meaning in our lives is a primary motivational force. Humans are able to live and even die for the sake of their ideals and values. Frankl (1997) is fond of pointing out the wisdom of Nietzsche's words: *"He who has a why to live for can bear with almost any how."* Drawing on his experiences in the death camp at Auschwitz, Frankl asserts that inmates who had purpose or a meaningful task in life had a much greater chance of surviving than those who had no sense of mission (Corey & Corey, 2008).

Someone might reasonably ask what having a sense of meaning and purpose gives to a person. Crystal Park (2013) defines *meaning* as simply "perceptions of significance." She argues that meaning gives life significance. Irwin Yalom (2000) reviewed a number of studies of the role of meaning in people's lives and described the following results:

- A person's lack of a sense of meaning in life is related to the existence of emotional and behavioral disorders; the less the sense of meaning, the greater the degree of personal disturbances.
- A positive sense of meaning in life is associated with having a set of religious beliefs.

Gratitude is the single most important ingredient to living a successful and fulfilled life.
—JACK CANFIELD

- A positive sense of meaning is associated with possessing values relating to the betterment of humanity and an interest in the welfare of others.
- A positive sense of meaning is associated with a dedication to some cause and with having a clear set of life goals.
- Meaning in life is not to be seen as a static entity but should be viewed in a developmental perspective. The sources of meaning differ at various stages in life, and other developmental tasks must precede the development of meaning.

In *Tuesdays with Morrie* (Albom, 2002), the dying Morrie shared a thought worth reflecting upon: "Learn how to die, and you learn how to live." Morrie makes some perceptive comments that go to the heart of finding purpose and meaning in life:

> So many people walk around with a meaningless life. They seem half-asleep, even when they're doing things they think are important. This is because they're chasing the wrong things. The way you get meaning into your life is to devote yourself to loving others, devote yourself to your community around you, and devote yourself to creating something that gives you purpose and meaning.

Dr. Barry Schwartz (2000), professor of psychology at Swarthmore College, in his review of social psychologist David G. Myers's book, *The American Paradox: Spiritual Hunger in an Age of Plenty*, discusses additional insights about the importance of meaning and purpose. He notes that in some respects freedom and opportunity have simply made us more miserable than ever. For example, even though wealth is at an all-time high, we have less happiness, more depression, more fragile marital relationships, less communal contentment, more crime and more demoralized children. It seems that we walk aimlessly through life—searching, searching, searching for "what's the meaning" (Madigan, 2012). More research on happiness will be discussed in the next chapter.

Corey and Corey (2013) summarize the importance of meaning and purpose:

> Humans apparently have a need for some absolutes in the form of clear ideals to which they can aspire and guidelines by which they can direct their actions.

It is important to regularly examine our beliefs, ideals, ethics, and personal guidelines. We must also pursue the process of finding and maintaining meaning in our lives. Alex Pattakos (2010) reflects on the work of Victor Frankl and writes about not being a prisoner of our thoughts, and believes that we need to exercise the ***freedom to choose our attitude.***

As human beings, it is our challenge and our task to create our own meaning and attitude. No one can do this for us.

Becoming Aware of Technology: How Technology Impacts Your Life

What do you think about being a child of the digital age? Many of your teachers grew up with less technology than you have, or maybe not any at all. Probably you have often helped your teachers or parents with technology issues.

The reality of our times is that unless you try hard to communicate face to face with your friends and relatives, technology can dominate our communications. We can be maneuvered by technology, marketing, corporations, society, and media.

Some can say we consume everything but rarely listen. We are permanently connected to our devices but rarely to ourselves. That is why you need to practice your human relations techniques discussed in this textbook. We strive to be better versions of ourselves, to be all we can be, but we may never really allow ourselves to savor idle time and just be.

It seems to be in this day and age, we are overwhelmed with information and our own very overwhelming choices: to quit or try to change, keep or let go, shop or save, sleep or get up. We have all the tools to be who we are, look, and eat better, but many are more anxious and depressed than ever before.

How much of your attention do you grant to eye versus screen contact? Some believe that over the past 40 years, technology has had a major impact on most areas of life. Besides the obvious advantages of being able to share our current plate of food with the rest of the world, technology is literally changing the way we meet, work, travel, research, and perform countless other activities.

Technology supports all major aspects of life. The danger that comes with it is the fact that it can be very distracting, and it occupies a lot of our lives. Having big ideas does not require any technology—their implementation or verification, on the other hand, usually does.

Think about it, using Einstein as an example; he came up with the most mind-boggling ideas, yet did not have any access to advanced technology (at least based on current understanding). It took armies of researchers another 100 plus years (and counting) to simulate his ideas. And that's where technology played a crucial part. So, how do you stay curious in today's digital world?

The main point is to build a healthy relationship with technology. In the near future (and even in the present), it will be a skill to know when to use technology and when to access your very own curiosity. We should not forget that although technology simplifies a lot of work, it does not provide new ideas (yet). That's our job as humans!

From driverless vehicles to algorithms controlling your dating life, to simply Google finishing your sentences, it can seem hard to know where free will and the authentic self are. Some believe that it all started with the dream of machines doing what we can't do, like exploring the heights and the depths of our planet, followed by inviting technology into our daily lives so we can improve what we've been doing for centuries: agriculture, war, art, sports, etc. Today we are seeing competition every step of the way, but this kind of competition comes with a twist: who can do everything faster?

> I fought all my life for women to make their own choices, in their personal and professional lives. I made mine.
> —HILLARY CLINTON

Pew Research and Elon University's Imagining the Internet Center conducted a large-scale canvassing of technology experts, scholars, corporate and public practitioners and other leaders in 2018. Many of the experts say digital life will continue to expand people's boundaries and opportunities in the coming decade, and that the world to come will produce more help than harm in people's lives. Still, nearly a third say they expect digital life will be mostly harmful to people's health, mental fitness, and happiness. But some say there are solutions (Anderson, 2018).

"We are how we read," says Maryanne Wolf, a developmental psychologist at Tufts University and the author of *Proust and the Squid: The Story and Science of the Reading Brain.* Wolf worries that the style of reading promoted by the Internet, a style that puts "efficiency" and "immediacy" above all else, may be weakening our capacity for the kind of deep reading that emerged when an earlier technology, the printing press, made long and complex works of prose commonplace. When we read online, she says, we tend to become "mere decoders of information." Our ability to interpret text, to make the rich mental connections that form when we read deeply and without distraction, remains largely disengaged. This can be a worry when research is needed (Wolf, 2018).

Chapter Review

A well-defined value system is basic to personal motivation, self-determination, and a life with meaning. Actually, our value system should be the control point of our life, helping us to choose the direction and course we will take.

- A **value** is the degree of importance we attach to various beliefs, ideas, objects, or things.
- Eduard Spranger, a German psychologist, defined six different types of people based on their types of values systems: the theoretical, economic, aesthetic, social, religious, and political.
- We are not born with values, but we are born into cultures and societies that promote, teach, and impart their values to us. We first gain our value orientation from the "significant others" in our lives, with the years of adolescence being extremely important for the learning and development of values. During this time, we test the shoulds and should nots coming from peers, school, media, and advertising influences.
- As part of Becoming Aware as an individual, **individuation** is the separation from our family system and the establishment of our own identity based on our own experiences and values.
- Other factors influencing the formation of our value system include religious beliefs, attitudes, prejudices, and stereotypes. The three components of a negative **prejudice** are: to hold certain beliefs against members of a group, to feel negatively toward them, and to be inclined to act negatively toward them.
- Because we live and work in a multicultural world, it is extremely important that we be willing to view diversity as a strength and to test, adapt, and change our perceptions as we interact with others.
- Our values do change as we go through various stages of our lives.
- **Values clarification** is a process that helps individuals discover their true values. The process of clarifying values involves choosing freely from alternatives, **prizing** or affirming the choice publicly, and acting repeatedly in some pattern of life.
- Since many Americans value social media, there is potential for social media to increase worker productivity and connect to many other places in the world, but workplaces are realizing that they need to make rules for all workers—not just younger users—about inappropriate social media use at the office.
- **Value indicators** or partial values are values still in the process of being formed. How we use our time and money are often strong value indicators. Four tests to apply to our value orientations include: 1) the choice test, 2) the time test, 3) the sacrificial test, and 4) the emotion test.
- According to the **cognitive dissonance theory**, when two or more cognitions such as beliefs, opinions, and the things we know about various types of behavior, people, or circumstances are in disagreement (dissonance), a state of tension results. This inconsistency (dissonance) motivates the individual to adjust these cognitions so as to reduce the dissonance and thereby reduce the tension. Often, attitudes, rather than behavior, are modified. Quite simply, we are motivated to justify our behavior. We frequently learn to value what we suffer to obtain.
- A person's lack of a sense of meaning in life is related to the existence of emotional and behavioral disorders; the less the sense of meaning, the greater the degree of personal disturbances.
- One of the most difficult tasks we face is living with our values—there are so many choices to make. Since World War I, there has been a focus on behavior and personality—the **personality ethic**—having the right kind of personality defined by the right techniques. Prior to World War I, there was a focus on the **character ethic**—a style of living based first and foremost on prioritized principles and values.
- The six pillars of character are trustworthiness, respect, responsibility, fairness, caring, and citizenship.
- According to Pew Research (2016) social media also can serve as an important venue where groups with common interests come together to share ideas and information.

- Character is composed of personal standards of behavior, including honesty, integrity, and moral strength.
- A **character trait** is an enduring characteristic of a person that is related to moral and ethical behavior that shows up consistently.
- Ten essential character traits for a happier life are: 1) Be Humble, 2) Be Courageous, 3) Be Grateful, 4) Be Tolerant, 5) Be Loving, 6) Be Forgiving, 7) Be Selfless, 8) Be Honest, 9) Be Persistent, 10) Be Expectantly Patient.
- Some guidelines for character development are to be honest, demonstrate integrity, keep promises, be loyal, be responsible, pursue excellence, be kind and caring, treat all people with respect, be fair, and be a good citizen.
- Humans apparently have a need for some absolutes in the form of clear ideals to which they can aspire and guidelines by which they can direct their actions.
- Nurses continue to outrank other professions in Gallup's annual honesty and ethics survey.
- **Ethics** is our standards of conduct or behavior—what we do.
- **Integrity** is exhibited when you achieve congruence between what you know, what you say, and what you do.
- **Morality** includes a set of principles or ideals that help a person distinguish right from wrong and act on this distinction.
- Psychologist Lawrence Kohlberg proposed three levels of moral development—preconventional morality, conventional morality, and postconventional morality.
- In making value compromises, it is extremely important that we remember our priorities.
- Rogers (2005) believes that, even though wealth is at an all-time high, we have less happiness, more depression, more fragile marital relationships, less communal contentment, more crime (even after the recent decline), and more demoralized children. It seems that we walk aimlessly through life—searching, searching, searching for "what's the meaning."
- Pattakos (2010) reflects on the work of Victor Frankl and writes about not being a prisoner of our thoughts, and believes that we need to exercise the *freedom to choose our attitude*.

Learning Outcomes Review

1. Explain what the term value means.
2. Name and explain Spranger's six value systems.
3. Explain how we develop values. Define the term *individuation* and explain its significance in the development of our value system.
4. List and give examples of the three components of a negative prejudice.
5. Explain at least three things you can do to break down barriers in dealing with prejudices and stereotypes.
6. Define *character*.
7. Name and discuss character traits for a happier life.
8. Define *values clarification*, and explain the process of clarifying values.
9. List and give examples of the four tests to apply to your value orientations. Explain at least two strong value indicators.
10. Define *character trait* and discuss the 10 guidelines for character development.
11. What are the 12 questions to ask yourself when trying to understand the ethics in difficult situations?
12. Explain the cognitive dissonance theory, using a personal example, if possible. How does justifying a sacrifice relate to the concept of cognitive dissonance?

13. Distinguish between the personality ethic and the character ethic.

14. What are the six pillars of character?

15. Define and discuss what contributes to a person having integrity.

16. What profession continues to outrank other professions in Gallup's annual honesty and ethics survey?

18. Name and explain Kohlberg's three levels of moral development.

19. What is the most important thing to remember when considering whether to make value compromises?

20. Explain the role and significance of meaning in an individual's life.

21. What are your values?

22. Why do individuals have a need for absolutes in the form of clear ideals to which they can aspire and guidelines by which they can direct their actions?

23. Social media influences and permeates many aspects of daily life for Americans today, and the workforce is no exception. What are positive and negative effects of this fact?

24. Conflicts in values are also seen with social media use today. There are so many issues, in fact, that everyone has to contemplate how they feel about them and educate themselves. In 2014, 78% of Americans felt that, in many ways, the U.S. social media has "opened doors and minds" on issues that often people are afraid to discuss.

25. Do you feel racism, White privilege, and tolerance are issues that impact your generation or just that of your parents? Why?

26. Do you think these issues (racism, White privilege, and tolerance) are "urgent" to deal with, or can they be put aside for a later confrontation? Explain.

Key Terms

Acting	Individuation	The Aesthetic Person
Attitudes	Integrity	The Economic Person
Belief	Morality	The Political Animal
Character	Nurturing Altruism	The Religious Person
Character Ethic	Personality Ethic	The Social Person
Character Trait	Prejudice	The Theoretical Person
Choice	Prizing	Value
Choosing Freely	Racism	Value Indicators
Cognitive Dissonance Theory	Spranger's Six Value Systems	Value System
Ethics	Stereotyping	Values Clarification
Full Value	Tolerance	White privilege
Hate	Tribalism	

Reflections: Critical Thinking Activity

1. What have been some of the factors that have influenced the development of your value system? Which factor has been of the greatest significance?
2. What are some differences between your value system of today and that of 5 or 10 years ago?
3. Two strong value indicators were discussed: how we spend our money and how we spend our time. Which one is a greater indicator?
4. Discuss any prejudices and stereotypes you have personally experienced.
5. How can we minimize prejudice and stereotyping in our society? How would you compare prejudicial attitudes today compared to 10–20 years ago?
6. What is your perception of the value assessment survey of college students discussed in this chapter? Take the test at the following link: https://implicit.harvard.edu/implicit/takeatest.html. What did you learn about yourself with this test?
7. What are some of your partial values or value indicators which are in the process of being formed?
8. Have you ever applied the cognitive dissonance theory to one of your stated values? If so, explain how you changed your belief system to "match" your behavior.
9. How would you describe your personal ethics? How would you describe your philosophy of life?
10. Some social observers believe that our nation is in moral decline. How do you feel about this?
11. What are your thoughts about the six pillars of character being taught in schools?
12. Can you think of other questions to consider when contemplating the ethics of difficult situations?
13. How would you personally define morality?
14. What are the top three ethical professions in the U.S., according to the survey?

Technology Resources and Activities

www.josephsoninstitute.org

Various links on creating a world where decisions and behaviors are guided by ethics.

www.character.org

Numerous articles on developing character education in companies and schools.

https://www.globethics.net

Dedicated to promoting ethical action in a global context.

http://www.globaldialoguecenter.com/collections/frankl/index.shtml

Numerous articles on Viktor Frankl and the importance of meaning and purpose.

www.authentichappiness.sas.upenn.edu/testcenter.aspx

The Meaning in Life Questionnaire measures meaningfulness.

Optimism, Happiness, Grit, and other tests available here also.

http://www.beliefnet.org

What do you believe?

http://www.coe.uga.edu/workethic/

Work ethic: Where do you stand?

http://greatergood.berkeley.edu/ei_quiz/

How well do you read other people?

https://implicit.harvard.edu/implicit/takeatest.html

Project Implicit (The IAT) measures the strength of associations between concepts (e.g., Black people, gay people, disabilities) and evaluations (e.g., good, bad) or stereotypes (e.g., athletic, clumsy). The main idea is that making a response is easier when closely related items share the same response key. When doing an IAT you are asked to quickly sort words into the left and right hand side of the computer screen by pressing the "e" key if the word belongs to the category on the left and the "i" key if the word belongs to the category on the right. The IAT has five main parts.

https://serendipstudio.org/playground/pd.html

This is an interactive site that illustrates the classic prisoner's dilemma negotiation strategy. Go to the site and play the game. What did you learn? How does this relate to human relations?

http://www-popexpo.ined.fr/english.html

Information on world population.

http://ethicsed.org

Resources for ethics and values activities from the School for Ethical Education.

https://www.scu.edu/ethics/ethics-resources/

Resources from the Markkula Center for Applied Ethics.

https://education.wm.edu/centers/ttac/documents/articles/statementofbeliefactivity.pdf

A statement of belief activity to work on with a partner.

http://www.tolerance.org/module/anti-bias-framework-unpacking-identity

A presentation and learning plan from the Anti-Bias Framework: Unpacking Identity.

https://www.cnbc.com/video/2018/10/31/suze-orman-dont-let-your-money-define-you.html

Don't let money define your life!

https://www.tolerance.org/magazine/fall-2018/what-is-white-privilege-really

On racism and recognizing White privilege.

https://greatergood.berkeley.edu/article/item/how_to_avoid_picking_up_prejudice_from_media

How to Avoid Picking Up Prejudice from the Media

https://greatergood.berkeley.edu/article/item/top_10_strategies_for_reducing_prejudice

The Top 10 Strategies for Reducing Prejudice

https://greatergood.berkeley.edu/article/item/the_chauffers_dilemma

The Chauffeur's Dilemma

The rich are getting richer and the poor are getting left behind. Why don't more people stick up for fellow citizens facing hard times? Because, argues Arlie Hochschild, empathy is being squeezed from the American way of life.

http://greatergood.berkeley.edu/article/item/why_you_should_share_your_struggles_on_facebook

Why You Should Share Your Struggles on Facebook

VIDEOS

https://www.discovery.com/shows/why-we-hate

Why We Hate is a six-part documentary television series which is an "exploration into the human condition of hatred and how we can overcome it." It is directed by Geeta Gandbhir and Sam Pollard and will be produced by Steven Spielberg's Amblin Television and Alex Gibney's Jigsaw Productions.

https://www.ted.com/talks/rutger_bregman_poverty_isn_t_a_lack_of_character_it_s_a_lack_of_cash

"Ideas can and do change the world," says historian Rutger Bregman, sharing his case for a provocative one: guaranteed basic income. Learn more about the idea's 500-year history and a forgotten modern experiment where it actually worked—and imagine how much energy and talent we would unleash if we got rid of poverty once and for all.

https://www.ted.com/talks/brene_brown_the_power_of_vulnerability

Brené Brown studies human connection—our ability to empathize, belong, love. In a poignant, funny talk, she shares a deep insight from her research, one that sent her on a personal quest to know herself.

https://www.youtube.com/watch?v=3_t4obUc51A

Introduction to Ethics from the Academy of Ideas.

https://www.youtube.com/watch?v=ji5_MqicxSo

Randy Pausch's (2008) Last Lecture: Achieving Your Childhood Dreams.

https://www.youtube.com/watch?v=MIeAnU7_7TA

The Way We Never Were: American Families and the Nostalgia Trap

https://www.youtube.com/watch?v=Gd7RqwgDUDg

A Date With Your Family: 1950s American Family Values.

https://www.youtube.com/watch?v=n5Q5FQfXZag

Implicit Association Test.

https://www.youtube.com/watch?v=-8H7eeMNfLw

How I Learned to Love Unconscious Bias, by Kristin Maschka, TEDxPasadenaWomen.

https://www.youtube.com/watch?v=Fr8G7MtRNlk

Implicit Bias: How it affects us and how we push through by Melanie Funchess, TEDxFlourCity.

https://www.latimes.com/82917695-132.html

Can kids be good without God? Watch a video chat with columnist Patt Morrison and Phil Zuckerman, author of "Living the Secular Life."

Positive Portfolio Activities

The positive portfolio is a collection of good things about our lives so far. It can include a list of achievements, photos of loved ones, or something that evoke positive emotions in us.

The positive portfolio is an excellent self-help tool and a unique coping intervention, where we choose a positive feeling and commit to focus on it for the next few days.

ACTIVITY

Dealing with Guilt Through Writing Activity

Coping with guilt through writing is helpful. Writing is one of the most favorite methods of self-expression and emotional catharsis. Pennebaker and Beall (1986) developed expressive writing as a method of adaptive coping. Their findings suggest that if we engage in journaling about the things that we are ashamed of and open up about unpleasant thoughts and actions, we can confront stressors and adapt to them more efficiently.

You can find the complete information about dealing with guilt through writing exercises from the toolkit, and below is a summary of how it looks.

Step 1 – Reflect on your thoughts

ASK YOURSELF:

What incidents or actions am I ashamed of? _____

How do I feel about them? _____

What emotions and thoughts are associated with these incidents? _____

Step 2 – Restructure your story

Recall the incidents you noted in step 1 and take a few moments to imagine other possible and more positive ways they could have ended. Consider how you would have advised a friend to deal with the same situation or how you will face similar circumstances in the future.

_____

Step 3 – Self-evaluation

Note down everything that this exercise helped you learn. Summarize your key takeaway points from the activity and jot down how you can use these lessons in your real life. _____

Becoming *Aware*

ACTIVITY

Work in teams of 4-5 people.

Use the following video to spark discussion:

https://www.youtube.com/watch?v=QbTWxFwuQtM

Rutger Bregman on "Utopia for Realists" and Big Ideas for an Equitable Economy, *The Daily Show*, Mar 16, 2019

After watching the video, groups should discuss ideas that would benefit society. Each team should note values, ethics, and choices that would have to be made with the ideas formed. Report your group's conclusion and note your conclusion before and after the group processed it.

Name _____ Date _____

Self-Inventory

PURPOSE

To understand and evaluate your value system for personal goal setting.

INSTRUCTIONS

1. For each statement below, indicate the response that most closely identifies your beliefs and attitudes. Use this code:
    5 = Strongly agree
    4 = Agree in most respects
    3 = Undecided
    2 = Disagree in most respects
    1 = Strongly disagree

    _____   1.   Because of the demands and expectations of others, it is difficult for me to maintain a true grasp of my own identity.

    _____   2.   At this particular time, I have a sense of purpose and meaning that gives me direction.

    _____   3.   I have evaluated and questioned most of the values I now hold.

    _____   4.   Religion gives a source of meaning and purpose to my life.

    _____   5.   I generally live by and proclaim the values I hold.

    _____   6.   I have a close idea of who I am and what I want to become.

    _____   7.   I let others influence my values more than I'd like to admit.

    _____   8.   The majority of my values are similar to those of my parents.

    _____   9.   Generally, I feel clear about what I value.

    _____   10.   My values and my views about the meaning of life have changed a great deal during my lifetime.

    _____   11.   The way I use my time right now reflects my personal values.

    _____   12.   I have a clear picture of "my philosophy of life."

    _____   13.   I must admit that I have some prejudices and stereotypes that are currently part of my value system.

    _____   14.   The way I spend my money right now reflects my personal values.

    _____   15.   The values that I presently believe in are the ones I want to continue to live by.

2. Responses may be shared in small groups or just viewed as a personal inventory.

Discussion

1. Would you like to change your responses to any of the questions? Which ones, and to what numerical degree?

2. What goals would you like to set to ensure that the desired responses occur?

Name _____ Date _____

Guidelines for Character Development

PURPOSE

To determine how you rate on guidelines suggested by Michael Josephson of the Character Counts Coalition as a foundation for character development (1994).

After finishing this form bring to class and form teams to Think/Pair/Share with the class.

What is a character trait you would include that is not listed?

How can society today help young people build character?

Discuss the questions that you answered from this form in your group.

INSTRUCTIONS (REFER TO THE CHAPTER SECTION MAKING ETHICAL CHOICES: SIX PILLARS OF CHARACTER FOR IDEAS).

1. Rate yourself with a check mark (✔) as either completely satisfied, moderately satisfied, or needs improvement on the following character traits:

    1. **Be honest.** Tell the truth, be sincere, do not mislead or withhold information in relationships of trust, do not steal.
        Completely satisfied _____   Moderately satisfied _____   Needs improvement _____

    2. **Demonstrate integrity.** Stand up for your beliefs about right and wrong, be your best self, resist social pressure to do wrong.
        Completely satisfied _____   Moderately satisfied _____   Needs improvement _____

    3. **Keep promises.** Keep your word and honor your commitments, pay your debts, and return what you borrow.
        Completely satisfied _____   Moderately satisfied _____   Needs improvement _____

    4. **Be loyal.** Stand by family, friends, employers, community, and country; do not talk about people behind their backs.
        Completely satisfied _____   Moderately satisfied _____   Needs improvement _____

    5. **Be responsible.** Think before you act, consider consequences, be accountable and "take your medicine."
        Completely satisfied _____   Moderately satisfied _____   Needs improvement _____

6. **Pursue excellence.** Do your best with what you have, and do not give up easily.
   Completely satisfied _____   Moderately satisfied _____   Needs improvement _____

7. **Be kind and caring.** Show you care through generosity and compassion; do not be selfish or mean.
   Completely satisfied _____   Moderately satisfied _____   Needs improvement _____

8. **Treat all people with respect.** Be courteous and polite; judge all people on their merits; be tolerant, appreciative, and accepting of individual differences.
   Completely satisfied _____   Moderately satisfied _____   Needs improvement _____

9. **Be fair.** Treat all people fairly, be open-minded, listen to others, and try to understand what they are saying and feeling.
   Completely satisfied _____   Moderately satisfied _____   Needs improvement _____

10. **Be a good citizen.** Obey the law and respect authority, vote, volunteer your efforts, and protect the environment.
    Completely satisfied _____   Moderately satisfied _____   Needs improvement _____

2. Now make a list of those traits where you feel improvement is needed.

DISCUSSION

1. What do you think you can do to improve the traits you checked as needing improvement?

2. Do you agree that if you have developed all of the above character traits it will be easy for you to behave ethically in your dealings with others? Why or why not?

Name _____ Date _____

Moral Dilemma

PURPOSE

To review your moral reasoning in a situation that pits two opposing moral values against each other.

INSTRUCTIONS

1. Read the following scenario, adapted from a classic ethics test developed by psychologist Lawrence Kohlberg over 50 years ago (1956).
2. Then individually answer the discussion questions below.
3. Your instructor may choose to divide the class into small groups or have a large class discussion after the discussion questions have been individually answered by the class members. (This was the moral dilemma that Kohlberg originally used with Chicago kids to determine the six stages of morality. Kohlberg was not really interested in whether the subject says "yes" or "no" to this dilemma but in the reasoning behind the answer—so in your groups, think about that as you discuss.)

In Europe, a woman was near death from a special kind of cancer. There was one drug that the doctors thought might save her. It was a form of radium that a druggist in the same town had recently discovered. The drug was expensive to make, but the druggist was charging ten times what the drug cost him to make. He paid $400 for the radium and charged $4,000 for a small dose of the drug. The sick woman's husband, Heinz, went to everyone he knew to borrow the money and tried every legal means, but he could only get together about $2,000, which is half of what it cost. He told the druggist that his wife was dying, and asked him to sell it cheaper or let him pay later. But the druggist said, "No, I discovered the drug and I'm going to make money from it." So, having tried every legal means, Heinz gets desperate and considers breaking into the man's store to steal the drug for his wife.

Individual questions to prepare for the group discussion

1. Should Heinz steal the drug?

   1a. Why or why not?

2. Is it actually right or wrong for him to steal the drug?

   2a. Why is it right or wrong?

614

3. Does Heinz have a duty or obligation to steal the drug?

   3a. Why or why not?

4. If Heinz doesn't love his wife, should he steal the drug for her? Does it make a difference in what Heinz should do whether or not he loves his wife?

   4a. Why or why not?

5. Suppose the person dying is not his wife, but a stranger. Should Heinz steal the drug for the stranger?

   5a. Why or why not?

6. Suppose it's a pet animal he loves. Should Heinz steal to save the pet animal?

   6a. Why or why not?

7. Is it important for people to do everything they can to save another's life?

   7a. Why or why not?

8. It is against the law for Heinz to steal. Does that make it morally wrong?

   8a. Why or why not?

9. In general, should people try to do everything they can to obey the law?

   9a. Why or why not?

   9b. How does this apply to what Heinz should do?

10. In thinking back over the dilemma, what would you say is the most responsible thing for Heinz to do?

    10a. Why?

GROUP DISCUSSION

1. Do you agree that the husband's behavior was excusable under the circumstances? Why or why not?

2. Should Heinz have been arrested for theft? Why or why not?

3. If you were Heinz, would you have stolen the drug? Why or why not?

4. If you were Heinz, what would you have done instead of stealing the drug?

Think/Pair/Share Activity

BECOMING AWARE-VALUES REFLECTION ACTIVITY

Read and think about the following statements and note your opinion of the statements in writing. Do you agree? Disagree? With all or part of the statement?

Pair up and discuss:

1. Values are those inner standards from which you receive the motivation to act as you do and by which you judge behavior (both yours and others). **DISCUSS. AGREE? DISAGREE?**
2. Values signify what is important and worthwhile. They serve as the basis for moral codes and ethical reflection. **DISCUSS. AGREE? DISAGREE?**
3. Individuals have their own values based on many aspects including family, religion, peers, culture, race, social background, gender, etc. Do you believe your values are guided by other individuals, professions, communities, and institutions? **DISCUSS. AGREE? DISAGREE?**
4. A value must be chosen freely. If you don't cheat because someone tells you not to, or because you know you will get into trouble with some authority figure, you are not freely acting on your values of honesty and integrity. **DISCUSS. AGREE? DISAGREE?**
5. A value is always chosen from among alternatives. If you don't cheat because you are taking a test in an empty room without any resources, you cannot say you chose not to cheat. There must always be an alternative in choosing your value. **DISCUSS. AGREE? DISAGREE?**
6. If you cheat thoughtlessly or carelessly after considering alternatives and consequences, is your value reflected in that decision? Why? **DISCUSS. AGREE? DISAGREE?**
7. Your honesty and integrity are something to be proud of, and you like these qualities in yourself. Why? **DISCUSS. AGREE? DISAGREE?**
8. Standing up in public to stand by your values and speaking about your position and even trying to convince others not to do something declares in your actions and your words what you value. **DISCUSS. AGREE? DISAGREE?**
9. Do you think when a person has a value, it shows up in every aspect of their life? **DISCUSS. AGREE? DISAGREE?**
10. Do you think values show up in your actions, as in, not cheating on one thing means you hold a value? **DISCUSS. AGREE? DISAGREE?**

Pair up with a partner and develop 2 or 3 statements that the other groups can discuss about values and agree or disagree with.

Report to the class your findings or reflect on your activity in your class journal.

REFLECTION ACTIVITY

Answer questions and put them in your learning journal for later grading, or your instructor might want to have a class discussion first.

Please write a brief reflection about your values based on reflection from the chapter readings and activities.

Use the following questions to guide your reflection:

- Where do your values come from? (Family, religion, friends, media, self, etc.)
- How do these values influence your role as a student ?
- Do your peers share your values?
- How does this make you feel?
- Are you satisfied with where you are headed in school, work, family, etc.?
- Does your race/ethnicity/economic background affect your values?
- How do you believe your values influence your leadership style?

Personal Values Assessment

PURPOSE

To identify your values through priority ranking.

INSTRUCTIONS

1. The following is a list of personal values. Go through this list and rate the personal values in terms of their importance to you. Place a check (✓) mark in the category that best represents your feelings about how important the personal value is to you. (Exercise continues through the next 3 pages.)

PERSONAL VALUE	VERY IMPORTANT	MODERATELY IMPORTANT	SOMEWHAT IMPORTANT	NOT IMPORTANT
Good health				
Having close friendships				
Having a close family				
A fulfilling career				
A long life				
A stable marriage				
A financially comfortable life				
Independence				
Being creative				
Participating in an organized religion				
Intimacy with another				
Having children				
A variety of interests and activities				
Freedom to create my own lifestyle				
Having a house				
A happy love relationship				
Fulfilling careers for me and my spouse				
Contributing to my community				
Abundance of leisure time				
Happiness				
Ability to move from place to place				
A life without stress				

Strong religious values				
A chance to make social changes				
To be remembered for my accomplishments				
Helping those in distress				
Freedom to live where I wish				
A stable life				
Time to myself				
Enjoyment of arts, entertainment, and cultural activities				
A life without children				
A life with many challenges				
Opportunity to be a leader				
Opportunity to fight for my country				
A chance to make a major discovery that would save lives				
A good physical appearance				
Opportunity to establish roots in one place				
Opportunity for physical activities				
An exciting life				
A chance to get into politics				
To live according to strong moral values				
Opportunity to teach others				
To write something memorable				
A chance to become famous				
To help others solve problems				
To make lots of money				

Others:

Fred Hecklinger and Bernadette Black, *Training for Life* (Dubuque, IA: Kendall Hunt Publishing Company, 2012). Used with permission.

2. In the space below, list at least 10 of your most important personal values from your Personal Values Assessment.

1. _____

2. _____

3. _____

4. _____

5. _____

6. _____

7. _____

8. _____

9. _____

10. _____

3. In the space below, list your top 5 personal values in order of priority, with number one as the most important.

1. _____ first priority

2. _____ second priority

3. _____ third priority

4. _____ fourth priority

5. _____ fifth priority

DISCUSSION

1. Does your life right now reflect your values? Is the time you spend consistent with your priorities?

2. If the time you spend in your life right now does not reflect your personal values, how can you change your life so that the time you spend is more in keeping with your values?

3. Are there some parts of your life that you would like to change but that you cannot right now? If so, what is your timetable for bringing your lifestyle more into harmony with your values?

Values in Eight Broad Areas of Life

PURPOSE

To help you identify your values in eight broad areas of life.

INSTRUCTIONS

Below are 16 items. Rate how important each one is to you on a scale of 0 (not important) to 100 (very important). Write the number 0–100 on the line to the left of each item.

Not Important				Somewhat Important					Very Important	
0	10	20	30	40	50	60	70	80	90	100

_____   1. An enjoyable, satisfying job.

_____   2. A high-paying job.

_____   3. A good marriage.

_____   4. Meeting new people, social events.

_____   5. Involvement in community activities.

_____   6. My relationship with God/my religion.

_____   7. Exercising, playing sports.

_____   8. Intellectual development.

_____   9. A career with challenging opportunities.

_____ 10. Nice cars, clothes, home, technological resources, etc.

_____ 11. Spending time with family.

_____ 12. Having several close friends.

_____ 13. Volunteer work for not-for-profit organizations like the cancer society.

_____ 14. Meditation, quiet time to think, pray, etc.

_____ 15. A healthy, balanced diet.

_____ 16. Educational reading, TV, self-improvement programs, etc.

Below, transfer the numbers for each of the 16 items to the appropriate column, then add the two numbers in each column.

	Professional	Financial	Family	Social
	1. _____	2. _____	3. _____	4. _____
	9. _____	10. _____	11. _____	12. _____
Totals	_____	_____	_____	_____

	Community	Spiritual	Physical	Intellectual
	5. _____	6. _____	7. _____	8. _____
	13. _____	14. _____	15. _____	16. _____
Totals	_____	_____	_____	_____

The higher the total in any area, the higher the value you place on that particular area. The closer the numbers are in all eight areas, the more well-rounded you are.

DISCUSSION

1. Think about the time and effort you put forth in your top three values. Is it sufficient to allow you to achieve the level of success you want in each area? If not, what can you do to change?

2. Is there any area in which you feel you should have a higher value total? If yes, which, and what can you do to change?

Multicultural Panel Discussion

PURPOSE

To learn to value and respect fundamental differences among cultures and ethnic groups.

INSTRUCTIONS

Using the diverse populations within your classroom, your instructor will select multicultural, ethnic, and gender-mixed members from the class to participate in a panel discussion of the topics below. Instructors are encouraged to allow time for questions from the class members.

TOPICS

1. Attitudes, beliefs, and values concerning:
   Dating/personal relationships
   Marriage (within culture, outside of culture, interracial marriage)
   Divorce
   Family life (including extended families)
   The purpose and meaning of life
   Education
   Work/careers
   Social involvement
   Religion, worship, spirituality, moral codes
   Death and funerals
   Government enforced laws
   Leisure time
   Male roles/female roles
   Technology and how it impacts your life and culture

2. Customs and practices about:
   Holiday celebrations (religious and other)
   Weddings and funerals
   Appearance (clothing, shoes, or other attire)
   Gift giving and charity
   Food, alcohol, or drugs (differences in types, use or misuse of)

3. Miscellaneous concerns:
   What would you like the class members to understand most about your culture or ethnic group?

DISCUSSION

1. What did you learn as a result of this panel discussion?

2. Explain any prejudices or stereotypes you may have previously held that you perceive differently as a result of this panel discussion.

3. Are there any questions that you would have liked to ask, but didn't feel comfortable asking? If so, what are those questions?

Values and Ethics

LEARNING JOURNAL

Select the statement below that best defines your feelings about the personal value or meaning gained from this chapter and respond below the dotted line.

I learned that I . . .	I was surprised that I . . .
I realized that I . . .	I was pleased that I . . .
I discovered that I . . .	I was displeased that I . .

....

chapter 10
Life Planning

© Harbucks/Shutterstock.com

Advice for Graduates

If you're sitting out there now with a nice, neat little outline for the next ten years, you'd better be careful. Life may have other plans. Life will present you with unexpected opportunities, and it will be up to you take a chance, to be bold, to have faith and go for it.

—JOHN GRISHAM, Writer

Think About This...

Compare your journey through life to a train trip. You are constantly moving ahead, with stops along the way. With every mile and every new passenger, the train changes just a small amount. For every new person you meet or new experience you have, you change a bit. Just as the train will take on new passengers, employees, and supplies, and will eventually let them go, so will you take on new interests, friends, and skills. Some of them you will choose to keep, and others you will let go. But just as the train keeps going, remaining basically the same, so do you keep going. You are changed by your experiences, but you always come back to you, and you must make the decisions that significantly alter your journey through life.

Imagine your life as a journey. You are traveling from where you are to somewhere new. You don't know exactly where it is, and you don't know exactly what it looks like, but you think you have a pretty good idea of both. You don't know how long it will take, but again, you think you have a reasonably solid idea of the time involved.

As you move through your life, each minute involves new things. You may have many different modes of travel in your journey. You meet new people, learn new things, learn new ways to understand things you already know, find new barriers—hills, rivers, canyons, deserts and highways, railway lines, fences, cities—and new ways to cross them. Therefore, each stage of the journey is affected by the world around you, and you are affected by the world and each moment of time.

You cannot always manage the circumstances, but how you react to those circumstances is up to you. You will sometimes be required to make choices. Because you are changing and developing attitudes and goals as you move onward, your decisions will reflect that growth. Most of those choices will entail risks. At any given crossroads or decision point, you must weigh and examine consequences. Imagine that you face a choice represented by three colors. If you choose green, you might be physically safer but lose certain connections and resources. If you choose red, you might get to the next stage more quickly but in a bad condition. If you choose purple, you may acquire resources but at the risk of going nowhere in particular. Any one of these choices may lead to wonderful or terrible—or perfectly ordinary—destinations. Any of them might not lead you where you were planning to go, yet it might lead to a place that is as good or better. Or not.

You must assume the responsibility for the journey and to a great extent for the outcomes along the way. You must invest time and effort on the journey. Eventually, the rewards should be worth the investment (Hecklinger & Black, 2012).

Y ou are now on your journey and have already been through many stations or experiences on the way. You must decide whether to take charge of your trip and be the engineer or simply be a passenger on your train, letting others make the critical decisions for you. Be in the present and be mindful.

You are the person who makes the decisions for your life. This process can be frightening, as well as fun and rewarding. The authors believe that you are more than capable of making the choices you will face in your life, now and in the future. To make these choices, you need to know how to recognize and evaluate risks, how to set goals, and how to identify and maintain your own sense of well-being. This chapter is about those things.

Nobody can go back and start a new beginning, but anyone can start today and make a new ending.
—MARIA ROBINSON

Making Risky Choices

Risk always involves failure or loss. To be serious about life planning, we have to take risks. There is simply no way to grow without taking chances, because everything in life involves taking a risk. To live a creative, interesting, challenging, and successful life, we have to gamble, take some risks, and experiment (Johnson, 2008).

Becoming *Aware*

Psychiatrist David Viscott (2003) defines *risk* in this way:

> To risk is to loosen your grip on the known and the certain and to reach for something you are not entirely sure of but believe is better than what you now have, or is at least necessary to survive.

Basic law of life. One-half of knowing what you want in life is knowing what you are willing to give up to have what you want. This translates into a basic law of life:

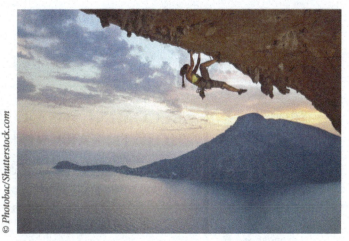

Take a risk!

For everything you get in life, you also have to give up something (Figler, 2013). The risk is to make a choice with the awareness that there is no guarantee of getting the result we want. However, if we plan our choices well, we can minimize the risk.

CHOICES COME WITH RISKS

Think about the truth of this. For example, if you choose to go to college to further your education and career opportunities, you have to give up some time for study and going to class, and you may have to accrue a large amount of debt, if you have no college savings, scholarship, or job; if you take a job promotion in another state, you have to give up the security of your friends and familiar places; if you get married, you have to give up some of your independence; if you decide to have children, you have to give up some of your personal time; if you decide to lose some weight, you have to give up some of your high-calorie snack foods; and if you decide to retire from the world of work, you have to give up a higher paycheck.

As you can see, in every choice, there is some unavoidable loss, something that has to be given up to move ahead. However, life is full of many risks and changes. Dr. Spencer Johnson (2002), author of the best-seller *Who Moved My Cheese?* reminds readers: "Change isn't everything; it's the only thing. Embrace change, don't fight it."

Many people are terrified by any possible loss and try to avoid all risks. However, this is really the surest way of losing.

Dr. David Viscott (2003) explains:

> If you do not risk, risk eventually comes to you. If a person postpones taking risks, the time eventually comes when he will either be forced to accept a situation that he doesn't like or to take a **risk** unprepared. ... If you continually shun any risk, you become comfortable with fewer and fewer experiences. ... Your world shrinks and you become rigid. ... Your life has no direction but is only a reaction to what the world presents to you.

Therefore, the purpose of life planning is not to eliminate risks, but to be certain that the risks you take are the right ones, based on careful thought (Boles, 2011). The question then becomes, how can I find direction for my life? ***Intelligent risk-taking*** means having a process for making good risk decisions.

What do you love? What inspires and motivates you? What are you passionate about? The more you fill your life with what's important to you, the more happiness you will experience.
—KEN WERT, FOUNDER OF M2BH

BECOMING AWARE ACTIVITY
HOW TO TAKE RISKS AND SET GOALS

- **Know your motivations.** What do you really want to achieve? Why? Don't take major chances on something you're not enthusiastic about. You'll work harder on goals that are important to you. Failure at something trivial may make you reluctant to try something really important to you.
- **Define success at the start.** Figure out what you want to achieve in specific, measurable terms. You don't have to account for every variable, but you should have a solid idea of the results you're looking for.
- **Look at the best and worst outcomes.** To evaluate risks and rewards, try to determine what the worst-case scenario would look like, whether the payoff is worth that risk, and how you could prevent it from happening. Consider the best-case scenario as well: How will you recognize success? What will you do next? This helps you prepare for contingencies.
- **Consider your timetable.** Do you have to take this risk right now? How quickly do you need results? Don't rush if you don't have to. Breaking your plan down into individual segments can help you minimize risks and learn what's needed to succeed.
- **Focus on benefits, not dangers.** Keep the hazards in mind, but don't let them overwhelm you. Think about the potential outcome, and you'll be able to stay the course even when the road gets rocky.
- **Get started.** You can make all the plans you want, but ultimately you have to take the leap. Don't turn preparation into a full-time activity. You'll feel more energized when you're in the midst of the struggle than when you're just getting ready.
- **Do what matters most to you.** Taking a risk to please or impress someone else will not produce the gratification or results that you had hoped for (MacKay, 2015).

MacKay's Moral: No risk, no success. Know risk, know success.

1. **Belief.** The first step to goal setting is to have absolute belief and faith in the process. If you don't believe you can absolutely transform your life and get what you want, then you might as well forget about goal setting and do something else. If you are in doubt, look around you. Everything you can see began as a thought. Make your thoughts turn into reality.
2. **Visualize what you want.** Think of what you deeply desire in your life or where you want to be a year from now. What changes have to take place? What do you need to know or learn? What spiritual, emotional, personal,

financial, social, or physical properties need to be addressed? Clarity in each of these dimensions will bring your vision into sharp focus. The clearer you are, the easier it will be to focus on making it happen.

3. **Get it down!** Writing down your goals is key to success. By writing down your goals, you become a creator. Failure to write down your goals often means you will forget them or won't focus on them. Have them written down where you can see them every day.

4. **Purpose.** Knowing why you want to achieve your goals is powerful. Identifying the purpose of your goal helps you instantly recognize why you want that particular goal and whether it's worth working toward. Knowing why you want something furnishes powerful motivation to see it through to the finish. After all, if the purpose of earning a million dollars is to put it in the bank for a rainy day, you probably won't be as motivated as you will if you need it to pay for your child's cancer treatment.

5. **Commit.** This might sound obvious to you, but it's a step that has disastrous consequences when it's taken lightly. Write a few pages about why and how you are committing to each goal; why it's important to you, what it means to you, why the outcome is necessary, and what you are going to do to make it happen. Without strong commitment, you aren't likely to follow through.

6. **Stay focused.** By focusing on your goals, you manifest. You may not know how you'll reach your goals, but when you make a daily practice of focus, they become easier to reach. Having your goals written down somewhere where you will see them each day is a good idea. Your mind will notice that there is a discrepancy between where you are now and where you want to be, which will create pressure to change. If you lose focus you can always bring it back. Without a regular practice of focusing on your goals, you may be distracted by something.

7. **Plan of action.** Being really clear about what you want, knowing your purpose, writing your goals down, committing to them, and staying focused gives you the power of clarity to write down a list of action steps. You may not know all the steps ahead of time but you will know the next steps that take you in that direction. Having goals without a plan of action is like trying to complete a complex project without a project plan. There is too much going on, it's too disorganized, you miss deadlines and you don't have priorities. Eventually you get frustrated and the project/goal fails or collapses under its own weight.

8. **No time like the present.** To show how committed you are to your goals, think of something you can do right now that will get you moving toward fulfilling those goals. Even if it's just making a phone call, do it now. You will be surprised how this simple step reinforces all the previous steps and gets you motivated and moving toward what you desire. If you are not motivated to do something right now, how are you going to get motivated tomorrow?

9. **Accountability.** To push through when things get tough, you have to hold yourself accountable, unless you bring in outside help like a coach who provides it for you. It makes sense to have someone besides yourself who can provide valuable feedback at critical junctures, like a friend or a mentor. Telling your friends and family about your goals may give you the accountability you need.

10. **Review.** Make it part of your day to review your goals and take action. This keeps your goals alive and top of mind. It's a good time to convert the overall plan into discrete action steps that you can take throughout the week. It will also help you be aware if one goal feels stuck and you are over-compensating on another goal.

By following these steps and practicing your goals each day, you have all the elements you need to succeed and achieve your goals. It isn't always easy to push through. Some days will be easier than others, but if you keep focused on your goals you will be amazed at the progress you will make. Remember, almost everything begins as a thought. You can be what you imagine if you follow these simple steps (Foster, 2015).

What Motivates You?

> *Motivation is not a matter of will-power; it's a matter of want-power.*
> —PAUL KARASIK

There's so much pressure—especially in today's hyper-competitive and hyper-informed society—for people to be something they're not. You get it from parents, from friends, from teachers, from television, from the Internet, from magazines, from advertisements you pass in the street, from nearly everything you see and do in any given day. The old saying "Where there's a will, there's a way" means that if you want—really want—to do something, you will find a way to do it. In other words, you must be **motivated** to act. The stronger your motivation, the more likely you are to accomplish your purpose. The weaker your motivation, the less likely you are to reach your goal.

> *Something to do, someone to love, and something to hope for, are the true essentials of a happy and meaningful life. No matter how rich you are, if you lack one of these essentials, life's true fulfillment will not be yours. No matter how poor you are, if you possess all three of these, you can build a satisfying existence for yourself.*
> —DAVID GOODMAN

Needs and drives. A *need* is a condition that exists when we are deprived of something we want or require. When a need exists, it creates a *drive* that pushes (motivates) us to satisfy the need. Therefore, it is appropriate to say that when you're motivated, you are in a state of tension. To relieve this tension, you engage in activity. The greater your tension, the greater your drive to bring about relief (Drafke & Kossen, 2018).

If all the air were suddenly sucked out of the room you are in right now, what would happen to your interest in reading the remaining pages of this chapter for your final exam? You would not care about reading and studying for a final exam and getting a credit in your last college course; you would not care about anything except getting air. Survival would be your only motivation.

But now that you have air, it does not motivate you. Stephen Covey (2016) calls this one of the greatest insights in the field of human motivation: *Satisfied needs do not motivate. It's only the unsatisfied need that motivates.*

Psychologists have said that there is a reason for everything a person does. Therefore, what are some of the needs that lead people to different types of action?

Fundamental human needs. In *First Things First*, Covey and the Merrills (2015) discuss the essence of human needs being captured in this phrase: *to live, to love, to learn, and to leave a legacy.* Specifically, these four human needs are:

1. *To live* is our *physical* need for such things as food, clothing, shelter, economic well-being, and health.
2. *To love* is our *social* need to relate to other people, to belong, to love, to be loved.
3. *To learn* is our *mental* need to develop and to grow.

4. *To leave a legacy* is our *spiritual* need to have a sense of meaning, purpose, personal congruence, and contribution.

Although we will refer to these needs again when we discuss goals and the drive to accomplish, these needs are believed to be fundamental to human fulfillment. If these basic needs are not met, we feel empty and incomplete.

Maslow's Hierarchy of Needs

With all of the pressure that exists in today's hyper-competitive, hyper-informed society, it can be difficult to truly accept oneself holistically. As classic psychologist Abraham Maslow (1998) recognized, we all follow our own paths; it matters only how completely we dedicate ourselves to achieving personal and psychological wholeness. At the top of the self-acceptance ladder lies the concept of self-actualization. It might help us to understand Maslow's theory of human motivation by referring to how we reach the top of a ladder—*one step at a time*. With self-actualization, we achieve the comfort of managing creativity, spontaneity, and problem-solving skills. We find a comfortable and sensible morality; we operate with the ability to separate fact from fiction, while identifying and eliminating prejudice. It is, in its own way, the clearest definition of what it means to be enlightened as a person. Maslow feels that before we can "blossom" and grow toward self-actualization, the top of the ladder, we progress through certain steps. The problem is that self-actualization doesn't have anything to do with the people around you. Notice the "self" part of the term. The only thing that matters is **our** progress, not the progress of others. If we hope to self-actualize—or at least get on the path to self-actualization—we must stop measuring ourselves against other people's accomplishments.

Maslow believes that certain needs must be met before we can become concerned with the satisfaction of other needs. His theory of the stepladder, better known as *Maslow's Hierarchy of Needs,* is represented in Figure 10.1.

Physiological needs. These biological needs include food, water, and air, which are essential to our physical well-being. Hence, they are often referred to as our *primary needs,* because they keep us alive.

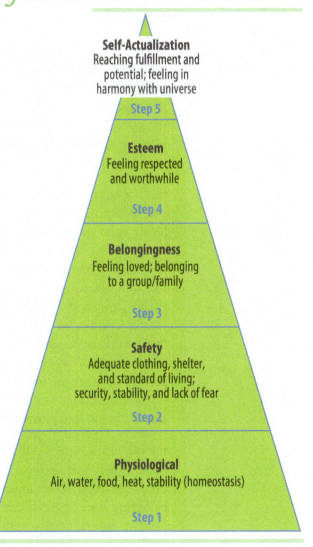

Figure 10.1 MASLOW'S HIERARCHY OF NEEDS

Self-Actualization
Reaching fulfillment and potential; feeling in harmony with universe

Step 5

Esteem
Feeling respected and worthwhile

Step 4

Belongingness
Feeling loved; belonging to a group/family

Step 3

Safety
Adequate clothing, shelter, and standard of living; security, stability, and lack of fear

Step 2

Physiological
Air, water, food, heat, stability (homeostasis)

Step 1

Love and belonging needs drive us to seek meaningful relationships with others.

Safety and security needs. When our physiological needs have been satisfied, the safety needs are the next most important step on the hierarchy. Safety and security needs include a reasonably orderly and predictable way of life which includes safe shelter and dependable income. For Americans this may also include a savings account, insurance policies, etc.

Love and belonging needs. If our physiological needs are satisfied and our safety needs have been reasonably fulfilled, needs for love, affection, and belonging are the next step on the hierarchy. Love and belonging needs drive us to seek meaningful relationships with others. We seek acceptance, approval, and a feeling of belonging in our social relationships. Companionship and friendship are very important in satisfying this need to love and be loved.

Esteem needs. Maslow believes that if people have their survival, safety, and affection needs met, they will develop a sense of appreciation for themselves. This sense of appreciation may be nothing more than the development of self-confidence, which strengthens our self-esteem—our self-worth. We need to experience some degree of success to feel that we have achieved something worthwhile. This may also include some awareness of the respect of others.

Self-actualization needs. The last step on the hierarchy represents the fullest development of our potentialities. Some writers believe that *self-actualization* is the need for self-fulfillment—to fulfill oneself as a creative, unique individual according to their own innate potentialities. Self-actualization does not require any tricks or tools. To reach the next rung, we need only to accept who we are and then take the steps necessary to become the best version of ourselves that we can be. Once we are totally comfortable with who we are, and who we've surrounded ourselves with, we may complete our journey toward self-actualization. As we see who we are becoming, we may find that we stop adapting to societal ideals and start being fully ourselves. The empowerment that results can be astonishing. Note, however, that there are degrees of achievement of self-actualization. One person might feel that complete fulfillment is being the ideal partner. Another person might satisfy this need by setting a career goal and reaching it. Self-actualization is a matter of interpretation, and we have the right to decide what constitutes our own satisfaction.

It is important to realize that this stepladder of needs is somewhat flexible. All people do not fulfill their needs in the same order that Maslow gives; there are some exceptions. For example, some people may feel that self-esteem is more important than belonging and love. Furthermore, many of us move around on the ladder, as we strive to satisfy several needs together.

The following four steps outlined by Green in her article "4 Steps to Self-Actualization and Becoming the Best Version of You" (2013) are another way of describing the process of self-actualization. Note that #4 clearly states that there is no end to the process.

Becoming *Aware*

1. **Stop measuring yourself against others.**
2. **Learn to accept yourself holistically.**
3. **Understand that *you* are in control.**
4. **Don't stop growing.**

Plan Your Life Like You Would a Vacation

In his workshops on life planning, Richard Boles (2019) frequently refers to our lives being divided into three periods. The first period is that of *getting an education;* the second period is that of *going to work and earning a living or working in the home and community;* and the third and last period is that of *living in retirement.*

One of Boles's concerns is that these periods have become more and more isolated from each other. He makes a statement you may find somewhat surprising:

> Life in each period seems to be conducted by those in charge without much consciousness of ... never mind, preparation for ... life in the next period.

Setting goals gives you long-term vision and short-term motivation. It focuses your acquisition of knowledge, and helps you to organize your time and your resources so that you can make the very most of your life. The dictionary says a ***goal*** is an aim or purpose—the first step of a plan. Trying to play the game of life without goals by moving through different periods of your life without any plans or any direction

In short, we might say that goals give purpose and meaning to our lives; they give us something to aim for, something to achieve.

Zig Ziglar (2019) believes that life has so many choices, and if you don't have goals you will not know how to move forward. Goals are what take us forward in life; it is very important that we realize the significance and importance of goal-setting, and apply this knowledge to our lives.

WHAT IS A GOAL?

According to the Merriam-Webster Dictionary (2020), the exact definition of a goal is the:

> desired result a person or a system envisions, plans, and commits to achieve. A personal or organizational desired end-point in some sort of assumed development. Many people endeavor to reach goals within a finite time by setting deadlines.

In other words, any planning you do for the future, regardless of what it is, **a goal**. So the next time you plan on doing the weekly chores or decide on watching that really cool action movie after work, always keep in mind that these small tasks count as smaller goals, and, while they may seemingly insignificant, you are taking steps toward a larger goal.

5 Reasons Why Goal Setting Is Important

1. Goals Give You Focus

Imagine having to shoot an arrow without being given a target. Where would you aim? And say you did aim at some random thing (out of sheer perplexity). Why would you aim there? And what would the purpose be? You get the idea. This is a literal example of what life is like without a goal or target in mind.

> If you aim at nothing, you will hit it every time.
> —ZIG ZIGLAR

You can have all the potential in the world, but *without focus,* your abilities and talent will not rise to that potential. Sunlight can't burn through anything without a magnifying glass to focus it; you can't achieve anything unless a goal is focusing your effort. Goals are what give you direction in life. By setting goals for yourself, you give yourself a target to aim for. This sense of direction is what allows your mind to focus and, rather than waste energy with aimlessness, allows you to hit your target and reach your goal.

2. Goals Allow You To Measure Progress

> I long to accomplish a great and noble task, but it is my chief duty to accomplish small tasks as if they were great and noble.
> —HELEN KELLER

Set concrete and specific goals, and they will provide a **benchmark** with which to measure progress. An author writing a book, for example, might set a goal of 10 pages of writing a day; they would know if they had achieved that goal. A number, like 10 pages, is measurable. A goal of 60 pages per week allows the writer to decide to skip a day if they know they can make it up the next day—or if they got ahead the previous day.

Beware of goal setting in terms of time, however. Setting a goal of studying for 20 minutes a day only works if we have a solid understanding of what "studying" is. Setting a timer and staring at the words in a book for 20 minutes may not help us learn anything at all; on the other hand, spending 20 minutes writing key phrases in a notebook may mean getting through fewer pages but may result in a deeper understanding of the material. There is significant data to support that writing by hand results in a better understanding and a better memory of information than reading, watching, or listening alone.

Remember that time is often fluid; goals should be as concrete as possible to be measurable.

3. Goals Keep You On Track And Undistracted

> One half of knowing what you want is knowing what you must give up before you get it.
> —SIDNEY HOWARD

By setting goals you give yourself mental boundaries. When you have a certain endpoint in mind you automatically stay away from certain distractions and stay focused toward the goal. This process happens automatically and subtly, but according to research, does happen.

To get a better idea, imagine this. Your best friend is moving to Switzerland and the flight takes off at 9:00 p.m. You leave right after work at 8:30 p.m. and you know it's a 20-minute walk to get to the airport. So you make it a goal to reach the airport in 15 minutes by jogging so that you can have more time to say your goodbyes. Would you get distracted by anything along the way? Would you stop for a break or a snack? Would you stop by your house before going to the airport?

4. Goals Help You Overcome Procrastination

When you set a goal for yourself, you make yourself accountable to finish the task. This is in complete contrast with when you do things based on a lark and it doesn't matter whether you complete those things or not. Goals tend to stick in your mind, and if not completed, they give you a reminder. These reminders in the back of your head help you to overcome procrastination and distraction.

Keep in mind that long-term goals can promote procrastination. Most people aren't good with deadlines further than 30-60 days away. When you are facing a long-term goal, break it down into a several short-term goals so you can complete a chunk of the larger, long-term goal every week or even every day.

5. Goals Give You Motivation

The root of all the **motivation or inspiration** you have ever felt in your entire life is goals. Goal setting provides you with the foundation for your drive. By making a goal, you give yourself a concrete endpoint to aim for and get excited about. It gives you something to focus on and put 100% of your effort into; this focus is what develops motivation (Abraham, 2017).

The responsibility is yours. Psychologist Angela Duckworth, in her 2016 book *Grit*, found in her research that passion and perseverance allowed high achievers to get what they wanted in life. They often had a determination that made them resilient and hardworking. They also knew passionately what and where (a direction) they were going. **It is your responsibility to build the road to your own enrichment; you must lay the foundation.** David Campbell (2007), in his thought-provoking book *If You Don't Know Where You're Going, You'll Probably End Up Somewhere Else,* likens life to a never-ending pathway, which has many side roads or paths in the form of options which confront us along that road; these side roads or paths have gates which are open or closed to us. When we come to each new option, there are two factors that determine whether we continue on the same path or take a new direction: one is *credentials,* and the second is *motivation.*

© fizkes/Shutterstock.com

Prepare yourself so you have the tools needed to reach your goals.

If you have credentials (such as education, training, skills), you have an option available to you and may choose or not choose to take a new path. If you do not have credentials, the gate may remain closed at that point, even if you are extremely motivated. In other words, no matter how much you may want that option, if you have not prepared for it, it is not going to be available to you. Motivation is what will propel you to get the credentials or skills you need.

Planning today will help you to get where you want to go, You may not know where you want to be in five years or a decade, but you almost certainly have dreams and ideas. Remember, keep your options open.

Without a doubt, goals help us control the direction of change in our lives. We may have to ask ourselves quite often, "Where am I now? What are my goals? What are my plans for reaching these goals?"

Setting Your Goals: What Do You Want?

It is important that you get to the "heart of yourself" and answer this question: What do you want to achieve? Whatever is satisfying and worthy can be a goal for you to accomplish. Therefore, no goal is too insignificant if it contributes to your sense of achievement. Living each day fully is an important goal of its own; it should not be measured against other goals which can also be important. At any rate, you, not anyone else, must be impressed with the goals you set for your life. Richard Boles (2019) confirms this statement:

> You have got to know what it is you want, or someone is going to sell you a bill of goods somewhere along the line that can do irreparable damage to your self-esteem, your sense of worth, and your stewardship of the talents that God gave you.

Authors Covey (2013), Roger-John and P. McWilliams (2004), and Ziglar (2000) write of at least seven different kinds of goals:

- physical
- financial
- spiritual
- career
- family
- mental
- social

Do you have any needs, wants, or desires that could be worked on in any of the seven goal areas? Think about some of these possibilities:

1. Would you like to start a personal physical fitness program?
2. Would you like to do some volunteer work for nonprofit organizations or become more involved in your community?
2. Is your financial management what it needs to be to provide for necessities and some of your wants? How can you save for a large purchase such as a new car next year?
3. Are you satisfied with your spiritual life? If not, what could you do to improve that element in your life?

4. Would you like an enjoyable, satisfying job? Have you thought of planning to make an appointment with a counselor at your school and begin some serious career counseling?

5. Do you want to spend more time with your family? Do you want to reestablish a relationship with a distant family member?

6. Have you been thinking of further developing your skills and capacities? What would you like to accomplish?

7. Would you like to meet some new people?

Independence

The idea of what it means to become "independent" has evolved significantly in recent generations, and new research from North Carolina State University finds that the concept of being either dependent or independent doesn't apply to almost half of young adults in the United States. Dr. Anna Manzoni (2016) found that young people fell into one of four groups—only one of which had all of the indicators of independence. That "independent" group accounted for 28% of young people. At the other extreme was the "dependent" group, which included people who received financial support from parents and were least likely to live on their own or think of themselves as independent. The dependent group made up 23% of young people. A third group, the "independent non-adults," was made up of people who were independent in terms of the objective residential and financial indicators, but who did not think of themselves as independent adults. Independent non-adults made up 24% of young people. The last group, called "residential dependents," were financially independent and thought of themselves as independent adults, but still lived with their parents, often because of high living expenses. Residential dependents made up 25% of young people (Manzoni, 2016). In further research, Manzoni (2018) found that the graduates receiving monetary transfers graduated and found particularly high occupational status jobs; however, the students living with their parents had found lower occupational status jobs. Manzoni believed different types of parental support may equally act as safety nets, but their divergent implications for youths' occupational attainment raise concerns about the reproduction and possible intensification of inequality during this developmental stage.

> Time = Life. Therefore, waste your time and waste your life, or master your time and master your life.
> —ALLEN LAKEIN

Becoming Aware of Life Advantages: One in Four
https://www.pewresearch.org/fact-tank/2020/03/11/about-one-in-four-americans-say-theyve-had-fewer-advantages-in-life-than-others-their-age/

About one-in-four Americans say they've had fewer advantages in life than others their age.

Contributors to Success

There are countless definitions of what success really is. *Success* has often been referred to as the progressive realization of a worthwhile, predetermined personal goal (McCullough, 2005). For example, some people define success in terms of money and material possessions. Others may feel success is found in personal relationships. Then, there are some people who believe that developing their potential in work or some particular interest defines success. We might conclude that *success* is setting a goal and achieving that goal, whatever that goal may be.

What actually contributes to success?

A sense of direction. Our first step is accepting our true selves, but the second part understands that the journey has no end point. To *self-actualize,* we must continually strive to expand our horizons as human beings. To achieve success, we must always seek it. If we do not know where we are going, we will certainly end up elsewhere. There will, no doubt, be conflicting wants and needs (Green, 2013). However, we need to establish priorities and make choices. *A philosophy of life*—as discussed in chapter 9, or rules for living and values in life—is basic to the direction we choose. Successful people know the direction in which they are moving, and why they are going there.

A feeling of self-confidence. If we want to be successful, a belief in our abilities and our worth as human beings is extremely essential. Most of our actions, feelings, behavior, and even our abilities are consistent with the degree of self-confidence we have. We have all experienced failures as well as successes in life. However, if we allow our failures to rule our life, we will never be able to realize our full potential. We are all imperfect. To be successful, we must learn to accept that our blunders, as well as our successes, are a part of us. Our mistakes are important guides to learning. Johnson (2012) makes this profound statement:

> A basic tenet of all individuals who wish to succeed in any endeavor is "I have to be willing to fail." You cannot learn, you cannot improve your interpersonal effectiveness, you cannot build better relationships, and you cannot try new procedures and approaches unless you are willing to accept your mistakes. You need the ability to fail. Tolerance for failure and the ability to learn from it are very specific characteristics of any highly successful person.

Feelings of successful achievement are a great motivation for continued success. We have all heard the statement that we can do whatever we think we can. We will never experience success unless we have confidence in ourselves. Because our performance is directly tied to the way we see ourselves, real confidence in ourselves is always demonstrated by action.

A healthy mental attitude. Attitude influences our lives more than any other factor. Attitude controls our response to our environment and our entire world. Life is what our thoughts make it.

Certainly, a healthy mental attitude does not imply an artificially cheerful approach toward all our problems. It simply means that we approach our problems and goals with a positive attitude. A negative attitude defeats us before we even start to work on our goals. On the other hand, a positive attitude enables us to take action toward facing our problems and obtaining our goals. Mamie McCullough (2005), author and motivational speaker, defines a positive and a negative attitude in this way: "A positive attitude says, *I can;* a negative attitude says, *I can't* or *I won't.*"

A belief in perseverance. In the game of life, you have to put something in before you can take anything out. After all, is not this what you also have to do with your checking account? Successful people may want a lot in life; they are willing to focus their goals and work hard to be obtain them. Therefore, we must determine how much time we are willing to give and what sacrifices we are willing to make toward the attainment of our goals. The magic word to success has been referred to as *work*—working hard and long to accomplish goals (Doskoch, 2005).

We need to remember that to give up is to invite complete defeat. Some people *quit* before they have given themselves a chance to succeed. People with a true belief in perseverance work toward their goals when encouraged and work harder when discouraged. It is very easy to give up, but much harder to continue, especially when "the going gets rough." However, nothing worthwhile has ever been accomplished the easy way.

© carballo/Shutterstock.com

Do you have a positive mental attitude?

An understanding of others. No one achieves success alone. Others are always a part of the process. More than likely our goals will involve other people. As a matter of fact, it is dangerous to make goals without carefully considering the effects they could have on your family. Remember, you do have to work around and with these folks. Furthermore, you want to take them with you down the road to your successes.

CONSIDER THIS

The value of courage, persistence, and perseverance has rarely been illustrated more convincingly than in the life story of this man (his age appears in the column on the right):

Opened a business which failed	22
Ran for Legislature—defeated	23
Again failed in business	24
Elected to Legislature	25
Sweetheart died	26
Had a nervous breakdown	27
Defeated for Speaker	29
Defeated for Elector	31
Defeated for Congress	34
Elected to Congress	37
Defeated for Congress	39
Defeated for Senate	46
Defeated for Vice President	47
Defeated for Senate	49
Elected to President of the United States	51

That's the record of Abraham Lincoln!

It is important, therefore, that we learn to understand what their needs are, how they feel, and how to interact with them. Learning the art of human communication is vitally important to achieving success. Successful people never make it completely on their own; they have generally been encouraged by others, and have been part of their company; others have contributed in many ways.

Learn the lesson. What did you do right, and what could you have done better? Take the time to review and assess the obstacles you overcame and the goals you accomplished on your journey.

In essence, people who are successful in reaching their goals have *direction, dedication, discipline, and a super-positive attitude, tempered by realism.*

Remember these qualities develop over time.

The Time in Your Life

Time presents a problem to all of us. Alec Mackenzie (2009), a time-management expert, offers some interesting insights on time:

You can't save it and use it later.
You can't elect not to spend it.
You can't borrow it.
You can't leave it. Nor can you retrieve it.
You can't take it with you, either.

For example, we have been told that to be successful we must *learn to manage our time.* This is impossible. We cannot *manage time.* It is frustrating to think we can manage something over which we have absolutely no control. But we can learn to manage *ourselves.*

Another false assumption is saying, "I don't have time to do that." That is probably not so. We have the time. We just do not choose to spend it in that manner. It is probably an unpleasant task that we would rather not do.

We might say, "She has more time than I do." This is not really true. Everybody has the same amount of time. We all spend it doing different things by choice or habit. David Allen, in his 2015 book *Getting Things Done: The Art of Stress-Free Productivity,* believes "a new paradox has emerged in this new millennium: people have enhanced quality of life, but at the same time they are adding to their stress levels by taking on more than they have resources to handle" (2015).

Time management is really self-management. There are several ways of looking at exactly how much time we have. For example, each of us has *twenty-four hours—1,440 minutes a day, 10,080 minutes a week, or 8,760 hours a year* to spend, invest, or fritter away. We spend time doing the maintenance tasks of life—working, eating, sleeping, and so on. We invest time in learning, creating, or loving. These time "investments" continue to pay dividends in personal satisfaction, career advancement, or fond memories. Sometimes we fritter away valuable time in activities we do not really enjoy and soon forget. Often, this is caused by our inability to say "No!" (Lakein, 2008).

Remember, you should be the master of time and not let it master you. Discovering your *time wasters* is the key to managing yourself in relation to time. The word **time waster** can be defined to mean anything preventing you from achieving your objectives most effectively. Most time wasters are self-generated. For example, do you ever procrastinate—put things off until it's too late or no longer matters? You might be surprised to learn that *procrastination* is one of the most common time management problems, or time wasters.

Establishing priorities. Take a moment and reflect on this question: What one thing could you do in your personal and professional life that, if you did it on a regular basis, would make a tremendous positive difference in your life? Now, reflect on this question: How much time are you spending in this area or on this activity?

People who accomplish the most do so not because they have more time, but because they use their time more wisely. They know that planning and goal setting are the keys to successful time management.

Stephen Covey (2013), author of the best-seller *The 7 Habits of Highly Effective People*, teaches participants in personal leadership training groups that the essence of effective time and life management is to organize and execute around *balanced priorities*. Covey then asks his participants to consider the following: If you were to fault yourself in one of three areas, which would it be:

1. The inability to *prioritize*
2. The inability or desire to *organize* around those priorities
3. The lack of *discipline* to execute around them, to stay with your priorities and organization

Covey says that most people believe that their main fault is *discipline*. However, Covey believes the basic problem is that people's *priorities have not become deeply planted in their hearts and minds*. In *First Things First*, Covey (1994) summarizes the importance of priorities with these words:

> Putting first things first is an issue at the very heart of life. Almost all of us feel torn by the things we want to do, by the demands placed on us, by the many responsibilities we have. We all feel challenged by the day-to-day and moment-by-moment decisions we must make regarding the best use of our time.

> Decisions are easier when it's a question of "good" or "bad." We can easily see how some ways we spend our time are wasteful, mind-numbing, even destructive. But for most of us, the issue is not between the "good" and the "bad," but between the "good" and the "best." So often, the enemy of the best is the good (Covey, 1994).

The 80–20 principle. People who effectively manage their time have learned to structure their lives so that they focus most of their time and energy on what is most important to them and minimize the time they spend on activities that they do not val-

$86,400

If you had a bank that credited your account each morning with $86,400, carried over no balance from day to day, allowing you to keep no cash in your account, canceling all unused funds at the end of each day, what would you do?

You have such a bank. It's called time.

Every morning, each person's account is credited with 86,400 seconds. Every night, each second not put toward a good purpose is canceled. Time carries no balance forward. Nor does time allow us to borrow against future allocations.

We can only live on today's deposit and invest our time toward the utmost health, happiness, and success (Covey, 2013).

ue. They realize that the quality of their lives is enhanced when they are able to do a few things well, instead of trying to find time to do a little of everything.

You may be thinking to yourself: "All of my responsibilities are important; I can't simply drop some of them to do what I please." Have you heard of the **80–20 principle**? Vilfredo Pareto, an Italian economist, noted that 20% of what we do yields 80% of the results. Conversely, 80% of what we do yields 20% of the results. This principle can be applied to many areas of life. For example, about 20% of the newspaper is worth your while to read. You are better off just skimming the rest of it. A good 80% of most people's mail is junk and best not read at all. Just about 80% of your housework can wait almost indefinitely, while 20% of it, if not done, would soon make your home uninhabitable (Covey, 2013).

© SG SHOT/Shutterstock.com

What are your time wasters?

Using time effectively is dependent on *your daily identification of priorities of the important things you have to do or want to do* (Lakein, 2008). You must decide what the

HOW TO WASTE TIME

- Procrastination
- Personal disorganization
- Lack of planning
- Poor communication
- Commuting and/or traffic delays
- Lack of self-discipline
- Not setting deadlines
- Inability to say no!
- Playing video games
- Meetings
- Excessive errands
- Watching TV
- Talking on the telephone or cell phone
- Attempting too much at once
- Leaving tasks unfinished
- Drop-in visitors
- Texting
- Internet

Which of these time wasters create a problem for you? Which do you have control over?

important objectives are in your life and then establish priorities every day in relation to these objectives.

Culture and the Organization of Time

Let us assume that you have arranged to meet one of your friends for lunch at 12:30 p.m. The friend has not arrived at 12:45, 1:00, or even 1:15. Now, answer these questions: What time did you arrive? Were you "on time"? How long would you wait for your friend before you started to feel worried or annoyed?

In most parts of the United States and Canada, you would have been there pretty close to 12:30 and not waited much past 1:00. That is because these countries, along with northern European nations, are what Edward T. Hall calls **monochronic cultures**: Time is organized into linear segments in which people do one thing "at a time." Actually, the day is divided into appointments, schedules, and routines, and because time is a precious commodity, people do not like to "waste" time. In such cultures, therefore, it is considered the height of rudeness (or status) to keep someone waiting (Hall, ET, 1959, Fleming & Koppleman, 2005).

However, the farther south you go in Europe, South America, South Asia, and Africa, the more likely you are to find **polychronic cultures**. In these cultures, time is organized along parallel lines. People do many things *at* once, and the demands of friends and family supersede those of the appointment book. As a matter of fact, people in Latin America and the Middle East think nothing of waiting all day, or even a week, to see someone. The idea of having to be somewhere "on time," as if time were more important than a person, is unthinkable. Cohen notes that "Traditional societies have all the time in the world. The arbitrary divisions of the clock face have little saliency in cultures grounded in the cycle of the seasons, the invariant pattern of rural life, community life, and the calendar of religious festivities" (Cohen, 1997; Fleming & Koppleman, 2005).

The differences in time orientation between the two cultural styles is summarized in Focus on Diversity—Time Orientation.

FOCUS ON DIVERSITY

TIME ORIENTATION

Monochronic People	Polychronic People
Do *one* thing at a time	Do *many* things at once
Take time commitments seriously	*Consider time* commitments an objective to be achieved, if possible
Give the *job* first priority	Give *people* first priority
Adhere religiously to plans and schedules	*Change* plans and schedules often and easily
Emphasize promptness	*Care less* about own promptness than other people's needs; are almost never "on time"
Saving time *is* good	"Saving" time *not as* important; it is not even a concept

Which time orientation do you prefer? Does your time orientation change on vacation?
(Hall, 1959)

Creating Balance in Your Life

Stephen R. Covey, son of the late Stephen Covey, recently published a book of writings and thoughts of his father, *The 12 Levers of Success* (2016). He explains that his dad believed there were only two ways to experience life: as primary greatness or secondary greatness. The intrinsic rewards of primary greatness are integrity, responsibility, and contribution. His father felt that primary greatness far outweighed the extrinsic rewards of secondary greatness: money; popularity; and the self-absorbed, pleasure-ridden life that some people consider "success" (Covey, 2016). He discusses the "12 Levers of Success" that you need to work on starting with integrity (2016).

Your chair of life. Someone once said that each individual has a ***chair of life***. This chair contains four legs, each representing an extremely valuable part of our life. For example, the four legs might be: 1) Vocation, 2) Family and friends, 3) Avocation—interests and hobbies, and 4) Spirituality.

If we are experiencing contentment in each of these areas, we must be contributing some quality time to each of these areas. In short, *our chair of life is in balance*—there is a harmonious melody in our life. However, if one of the legs becomes longer or shorter than the others because of too much time or too little time, we feel uncomfortable, stressed, and oftentimes dissatisfied. In short, *our chair of life is out of balance*.

Find a chair with four legs and sit down for just a moment. Label each leg of the chair with the important areas of your life. For this example, we can use 1) Work, 2) Family, 3) School, 4) Playing tennis with friends. Let's assume that by the time you go to school and work and spend some time with your family, you are finding little time for your favorite

> *Believe you have inner strength enough to overcome whatever confronts you, to do what life requires of you, to rise to the best that's inside you, to move forward, in kindness and decency and self-respect, to construct a life worthy of the title.*
> —KEN WERT

stress-relieving hobby—playing tennis with your friends. As a result, you are beginning to feel a little cheated. Put a book under the leg of the chair representing this very important leisure activity. Now, sit down in the chair. How do you feel? Off-balance, right? Are you afraid you are going to fall over?

This is the true picture of what goes on in our life when we direct either too little or too much time to the important areas in our life. Something is "out of synch." You notice yourself getting really irritated or even depressed.

This illustration can even be used to describe a person who is so committed to work that there is little time for family life or anything else. Is the pursuit of a career worth losing the respect and admiration of your family? You will have to decide that, but here is a view from Mary Kay Ash, the founder of Mary Kay Cosmetics:

> It's most fulfilling to build a successful career, but if you lose your spouse and family in the process, then, I think you have failed. Success is so much more wonderful when you have others to share it with. It's no fun to come home and count your money by yourself (Ash, 2008).

The important thing is to learn to recognize when your chair of life is getting out of balance and take immediate action to balance your time and energy on all the important aspects of your life. Otherwise, your whole life is out of balance. M. Scott Peck (2003) makes a thought-provoking statement:

> Mature mental health demands an extraordinary capacity to flexibly strike and continually restrike a delicate balance between conflicting needs, goals,

What would your chair of life look like?

Would it be in balance or out of balance?

duties, responsibilities, etc. The essence of this discipline of balancing is "giving up." ... As we negotiate the curves and corners of our lives, we must continually give up parts of ourselves since the loss of balance is ultimately more painful than the giving up required to maintain balance (Peck, 2003).

In essence, in life there are tradeoffs. There is a price to pay for what is important to you. You and you alone must decide what your trade-offs will be.

RECIPE FOR SUCCESSFUL LIFE PLANNING

- Know what you want.
- Know what you are willing to give up to have what you want.
- Have a game plan.
- Go to work consistently each day on your game plan.

Effective Life Planning: It's All Up to You!

The key to successful life planning is the *willingness to take responsibility for ourselves*. It is indeed possible for us to take control of our lives in the midst of the forces around us. In a life situation, we have three choices: *change it, accept it, or leave it*. To *change it*, we must change our behavior, goals, or circumstances. If we choose to *accept it*, we must recognize that it is our choice to stay with it, for whatever set of reasons. Then, if we choose to *leave our life situation*, we must find another environment for our energies. We must remember that feeling forced to stay with our life situation and hating it is not a viable or productive alternative.

There are many opportunities for us to grow, to find interesting work, and to vary our lives. Actually, the freedom and opportunity to realize our potential are relatively rich and available to a relatively large proportion of people. However, we must choose to actively pursue the possibilities we do have. We cannot wait for "good things" to happen to us; we have to make them happen.

> *Fear is a question. What are you afraid of and why? Our fears are a treasure house of self-knowledge if we explore them.*
> —MARILYN FRENCH

Because goals give direction and purpose to our life, goal setting should be a continuous activity throughout our lifetime. What happens in life planning is that we pause frequently to reevaluate ourselves, our goals, and our performance. As we improve in the understanding of ourselves, our wants, needs, and goals may change.

With this thought in mind, there are some questions you may want to ask yourself about the arena of life and work planning: *Who Am I? What Am I Up To Right Now? Where Am I Going? And What Difference Does It Make Anyhow?* (Corey & Corey, 2013). If we, from time to time, apply these questions to our personal objectives, our lives will be more effective, satisfying, and of course, more in balance.

But, what exactly makes a person feel satisfied and fulfilled? We will conclude this chapter with a discussion of happiness and well-being.

Happiness and Well-Being

The question of what makes a person happy has been the subject of much speculation and increasingly more research studies. Americans have a peculiar relationship to happiness. On the one hand, we consider happiness a right, and we do everything in our power to try to possess it, most particularly in materialistic form. On the other hand, materialistic comforts by themselves have not led to lasting happiness. Having reached that conclusion, often do not see another way and retreat into our comforts, barricading ourselves from what appears to be a hostile and threatening world. And, we continue to crave a happiness that seems both deserved and yet out of reach.

What is happiness to you?

© Exgeny Atamanenko/Shutterstock.com

What is happiness? Psychiatrist Dr. Mark Epstein (2016) believes that one reason we have so much trouble attaining happiness is that we do not know what it is. For example, the ways in which we seek happiness actually block us from finding it. Our first mistake is in trying to wipe out all the sources of discomfort in our lives. Actually, pleasure and displeasure are two sides of the same coin. We cannot have one without the other, and trying to split them off from each other only mires us more deeply in our own dissatisfaction (Kaplin, 2010). Furthermore, Harvard psychologist Daniel Gilbert discovered a deep truth about happiness: Things are almost never as bad—or as good—as we expect them to be (Flora, 2016).

Perhaps we need a neutral midpoint of emotional health. Andrew Weil, MD, the founder and director of the Arizona Center for Integrative Medicine at the University of Arizona, defines contentment as an internal state of well-being that's relatively impervious to life's transient ups and downs, and is independent of what you have or don't have (Weil, 2011). For example, if you hitch your moods to something external—getting a raise, a new car, a new lover—then what happens if that goes away? Contentment, on the other hand, is an inner feeling of calm; it's not dependent on external circumstances, possessions, or an episode of good fortune. Dr. Mark Epstein believes the cultivation of mindfulness or contemplative practice is not done as much as we need to pursue happiness because "We have the illusion there is never enough time for contemplative practice, there are always more pressing things to attend to. The concerns of daily life are like the waves in the ocean; there are an infinite number of them, wherever you are" (Epstein, 2016).

If your definition of happiness only covers moments of giddy and ecstatic joy, be aware that these moments are rare and fleeting for a reason. They involve high levels of adrenaline and other biochemicals, and they are also high energy. Such moments are almost always followed by periods of much lower energy; these afterglow moments can be very positive, but they are not the same as the high energy moments that precede them. Perhaps happiness is both; perhaps it can be a more sustained feeling of

We tend to forget that happiness does not come as a result of getting something we don't have; but rather of recognizing and appreciating what we do have.
—FREDERICK KEONIG

contented satisfaction with life. Most of the research on happiness struggles with these definitions; for this book, we are focusing on the ability to create and sustain a feeling of pervasive contentment.

BECOMING AWARE ACTIVITY—HOW HAPPY ARE YOU?

The Satisfaction with Life Scale was devised by University of Illinois psychologist Edward Diener, a founding father of happiness research. Since then, the scale has been used by researchers around the world (Pavot & Diener, 2008).

Indicate your agreement with each item using the following 1 to 7 scale. Total your score.

7—Strongly agree; 6—Agree; 5—Slightly agree; 4—Neither agree nor disagree; 3—Slightly disagree; 2—Disagree; 1—Strongly disagree.

_____ In most ways, my life is close to my ideal.
_____ The conditions of my life are excellent.
_____ I am satisfied with my life.
_____ So far I have gotten the important things in life.
_____ If I could live my life over, I would change almost nothing.

_____ Total Score

Scoring
31–35—Extremely satisfied; 26–30—Very satisfied; 21–25—Slightly satisfied; 20—Neutral; 15–19—Slightly dissatisfied; 10–14—Dissatisfied; 5–9—Extremely dissatisfied

Most Americans score in the 21–25 range. A score above 25 indicates that you are more satisfied than most Americans are.

Social psychologist David G. Myers (1993) reviews thousands of recent studies conducted worldwide in search of the key to happiness in his book *The Pursuit of Happiness*. Dr. Myers (2018) and Pavot (2008) define **happiness** in this way: "It is a 'pervasive' sense that life is good—a state of well-being that outlasts yesterday's moment of elation, today's buoyant mood, or tomorrow's feeling of sadness." This is about the same as Dr. Weil's definition of "happiness". Happiness is contentment.

Psychologists have defined happiness as a combination of life satisfaction and the relative frequency of positive and negative affect (Myers, 2018). They frequently refer to happiness as subjective well-being (SWB) and are exploring it in their labs. **Subjective well-being (SWB)** refers to how people experience the quality of their lives and includes both a person's emotional reactions and cognitive judgments and affective evaluations of their life (Deiner et al., 2018). One discovery is that happy people show more electrical activity in the left frontal lobe of the brain, while those who tend toward sadness or depression show more right frontal lobe activity (Myers, 2018). University of Minnesota researchers Lyken and Csikszentmihalyi (2001) indicate that about half of one's satisfaction with life comes from genetic programming.

Always live your life with one dream to fulfill. No matter how many of your dreams you have realized in the past, always have a dream to go. Because when you stop dreaming, life becomes a mundane existence.
—SARA HENDERSON

Myths and Truths about Happiness

Additional work needs to be done in refining and redefining studies of who has a sufficient level of SWB, who does not, and why, and how to help those who do not have enough. In the process, researchers are overturning many cherished myths and coming up with surprising new findings:

- **Happiness is not an illusion or a delusion.** SWB can be measured on finite scales and is as real as its opposite, depression. People who define themselves as satisfied are supported in their belief by friends and family who concur. Happiness is evident in practically everything they do.
- **Happiness and marriage may go together.** Some people are happier married than divorced or single, says Dr. Ed Diener (2018), researcher from the University of Illinois. Married people appear to be happier because they generally are less lonely and have roles as spouse and parent that enhance self-esteem and happiness.
- **Happiness knows no gender.** An analysis of 146 SWB studies showed a less than one percent difference in happiness between the sexes (Myers, 2018). This contradicts the popular belief that women are sadder than men. Although it is true that women are twice as likely as men to suffer from depression and anxiety, men have five times their rate of alcoholism and antisocial personalities; this tends to even out the happiness equation.
- **Happiness doesn't depend on age.** No particular stage of life is less happy than any other—not the tumultuous teenage years, not the "midlife crisis" period, not even the waning decades of old age. However, from face-to-face interviews with around 28,000 people ages 18 to 88, Yang (2008), a University of Chicago sociologist, indicates that it does appear that people are most content between ages 60 and 86—a time when most are focusing less on achievements and more on enjoying life and relationships. Researchers from the University of Basel examined the

GENDER AND YOU

QUALITY-OF-LIFE ENHANCERS

In a survey of the *Forbes* 100 wealthiest, Dr. Diener found that the privileged are not much happier, overall, than working-class folk. Money may become an avenue for something bigger and better—a way to keep score and compare. For example, you may have a lovely home, but if it sits next door to a neighbor's mansion, it may be more a source of dissatisfaction than of happiness. Even striking it rich does not seem to have the effect of boosting a person's happiness. Studies of lottery winners reveal that the sudden euphoria experienced upon winning quickly wears off, and many people want your money. What is important, though, is having enough money to buy life's necessities (Diener, 2003).

self-reported emotions of thousands of 13- to 89-year-olds and discovered trends in how we evaluate ourselves over our lifespan. The overall results suggest that the older, the happier (Schreiber, 2011).

- **Wealth does not beget happiness.** Money does buy happiness, but only up to the point where it enables you to live comfortably. Beyond that, more cash doesn't boost your well-being (Kashdan, 2016).

Who Is Happiest?

Diener, E., Lucas, R. E., & Oishi, S. (2018), Myers (2014), and their fellow SWB researchers have pinpointed a number of traits that seem to be shared by happy people:

- **Self-Esteem.** Happy people like themselves. A healthy self-esteem is positive yet realistic and provides a less fragile foundation for enduring joy. Hand in hand with self-esteem go personal identity and having a sense of purpose, accomplishment, and achievement.

- **Optimism.** Happy people are hope-filled and are confident they can make things better, even when they have failed or experienced rejection in some endeavor. People who expect the best are the happiest, and they are also healthier and less vulnerable to illness.

- **People-oriented/Extroversion.** Happy people are more outgoing, more cheerful, and high-spirited. They are more involved with people, have a larger circle of friends, engage in rewarding social activities, experience more affection, and enjoy greater social support.

- **Personal Control.** Happy people believe that they choose their own destinies. You will recall from our discussion in Chapter Three that individuals with an "internal locus of control" participate in determining the contents of their lives and live more happily. Summarizing the University of Michigan's nationwide surveys, Angus Campbell (2007) commented that "having a strong sense of controlling one's life is a more dependable predictor of positive feelings of well-being than any of the objective conditions of life we have considered."

Other ingredients for happiness. Having a strong spiritual faith; having close, supportive friendships and marriages; and having work and other activities that enhance our identity and absorb us appear to be additional ingredients for happiness (Garcia, 2005).

Being really happy, according to psychologist Mihaly Csikszentmihalyi (2016) is **living in a state of flow**—that is, being totally absorbed in an activity, whether at work or play. Complete immersion in an experience could occur while you are singing in a choir, dancing, playing bridge, or reading a good book. If you enjoy your job, it could happen during a task. It may occur in a social interaction, when talking with a good friend, or while playing with a baby. Moments such as these provide flashes of intense living against the dull background of everyday life. *Flow* goes beyond mere contentment; it entails active participation, a sense of mastery, and the use of all or most of your skills. Using too few skills generates boredom, which Dr. Csikszentmihalyi warns may be the biggest threat to happiness.

There are no small parts, only small actors.
—KONSTANTIN STANISLAVSKI

You must first be who you really are, then, do what you need to do, in order to have what you want.
—MARGARET MEAD

Of all the things we do, interaction with others is the least predictable. At one moment we experience flow; the next apathy, anxiety, relaxation, or boredom. Over and over, however, our findings suggest that people get depressed when they are alone, and that they revive when they rejoin the company of others. The strong effects of companionship on the quality of experience suggest that investing energy in relationships is a good way to improve life (Csikszentmihalyi, 2016).

The ancient Greeks described charisma as a "gift of grace," an apt descriptor if you believe likability is a trait that comes naturally to some but not others. The truth is that charisma is a learned behavior, a skill to be developed in much the same way that we learned to walk or practice vocabulary when studying a new language. Olivia Fox Cabane, a charisma coach and the author of the book *The Charisma Myth* says we can boil charismatic behavior down to three pillars.

Ways to Be Happy

Many of us might think "I will be happy when ..." Why not start making happiness a habit right now? In her book *Simple Abundance,* Sarah Ban Breathnach (2019) writes of our need to adopt a new state of mind about happiness. She encourages us to stop thinking that things outside our control will bring us happiness.

Certainly, specific events, such as the semester being over and making an "A" in Human Relations, getting a new and exciting job, or finding that special someone can make us feel—at least momentarily—happier. But the seeds of contentment are planted deep within our outlook on life (McGowan, 2005). Although the pursuit of happiness is an inalienable right guaranteed by the Declaration of Independence, we have to be willing to *pursue* it.

In *Notes on How to Live in the World and Still Be Happy,* Hugh Prather (2011) says, "You must make the effort—the struggle to be happy now—and not first gain what you need in order to be happy." Dr. Myers (2018) agrees by saying, "happiness is less a matter of getting what you want—money, possessions, success, etc.—than of wanting what you have."

Ultimately, genuine happiness can only be realized once we commit to making it a personal priority in our lives.

Bonnie Ware worked in palliative care, spending time with patients who had only a few months to live. The most common regret that they expressed to her was, "I wish I'd had the courage to live a life true to myself, not the life others expected of me" (Haden, 2016).

WHAT OTHER PEOPLE THINK—ESPECIALLY PEOPLE YOU DON'T EVEN KNOW—DOES NOT MATTER. WHAT OTHER PEOPLE WANT YOU TO DO DOESN'T MATTER.

In *Life is So Good*, George Dawson (2002), who died at the age of 103, tells of how he became bored with fishing at the age of 98 and found time to do the one thing he was never able to in his younger days—he learned to read. "Don't worry about what someone else thinks," Dawson writes in his autobiography. "Just do the right thing and take pride in yourself."

Martin Seligman, founder of the Positive Psychology movement, which focuses on strengths rather than weaknesses, asserts that it is not happiness we should be seeking, but a "life of well-being." In Dr. Seligman's books *Authentic Happiness* (2004) and *Flourish* (2012), he explains a life of well-being has four parts:

1) *a pleasant life*—a life that successfully pursues the positive emotions about the present, past, and future;

2) *a good life*—using your strengths to obtain abundant gratification in the main realms of your life;

3) *a meaningful life*—using your strengths and virtues in the service of something much larger than you are; and

4) *a life of fostering good, important relationships.*

Well-being theory: Well-being is a construct; and well-being, not happiness, is the topic of positive psychology. Well-being has five measurable elements (PERMA) that count toward it:

Positive emotion (Of which happiness and life satisfaction are all aspects)
Engagement
Relationships
Meaning and purpose
Accomplishment

No one element defines well-being, but each contributes to it. Some aspects of these five elements are measured subjectively by self-report, but other aspects are measured objectively. Perhaps the words of Dr. Russ Harris (2008) in his book *The Happiness Trap* are worth remembering:

> If you are not living according to your values, you will not be happy, no matter how much you are achieving.

BECOMING AWARE OF TECHNOLOGY
BEING AWARE IN DIGITAL LIFE

The Pew Research Center and Elon College found that the following insights from participants in the Digital Life and Wellbeing conference in 2018 focused on the following themes of digital life which will possibly be helpful in the future:

Themes About the Future of Connection Digital life links people to people, knowledge, education, and entertainment anywhere globally at any time, in a nearly frictionless manner.

Commerce, Government, and Society Digital life revolutionizes civic, business, consumer, and personal logistics, opening a world of opportunity and options.

Crucial Intelligence Digital life is essential to tapping into an ever-widening array of health, safety, and science resources, tools, and services in real time.

Contentment Digital life empowers people to improve, advance, or reinvent their lives, allowing them to self-actualize, meet soul mates, and make a difference.

Continuation Toward Quality Emerging tools will continue to expand the quality and focus of digital life; the big-picture results will continue to be a plus overall for humanity.

The conference also focused on the following themes that may not be helpful in the future:

Digital Deficits People's cognitive capabilities will be challenged in multiple ways, including their capacity for analytical thinking, memory, and focus.

Digital Addiction Internet businesses are organized around dopamine-dosing tools designed to hook the public.

Digital Distrust/Divisiveness Personal agency will be reduced and emotions such as shock, fear, indignation, and outrage will be further weaponized online, making divisions and doubts.

Digital Duress Information overload and declines in trust and face-to-face skills and poor interface design = rises in stress, anxiety, depression, inactivity, and sleeplessness.

Digital Dangers The structure of the Internet and the pace of digital change invite ever-evolving threats to human interaction, security, democracy, jobs, privacy, and more.

(Pew Research Center and Elon University's Imagining the Internet Center, 2018. pewresearch.org)

TIPS FOR HAPPINESS

Jeff Haden writes that, when planning your life, remember the bottom line—you want your plan to reflect your own vision of happiness!

Good news and bad news: Unfortunately, approximately 50% of your happiness, your "happiness set-point," is determined by personality traits that are largely hereditary. Half of how happy you feel is basically outside your control.

But, that means 50% of your level of happiness is totally within your control: relationships, health, career, etc. So even if you're genetically disposed to be somewhat gloomy, you can still do things to make yourself a lot happier.

Like this:

- **Seek out good friends.** It's easy to focus on building a professional network of partners, customers, employees, connections, etc., because there is (hopefully) a payoff. But there's a way to make real (not just professional or social media) friends. Increasing your number of friends correlates to higher subjective well-being; doubling your number of friends is like increasing your income by 50% in terms of how happy you feel.
- **Actively express thankfulness.** According to one study, couples that expressed gratitude in their interactions with each other resulted in increases in relationship connection and satisfaction the next day—both for the person expressing thankfulness and (no big surprise) for the person receiving it. (In fact, the authors of the study said gratitude was like a "booster shot" for relationships.) Of course the same is true at work. Express gratitude for an employee's hard work, and you will both feel better about yourselves.
- **Actively pursue your goals.** Goals you don't pursue aren't goals; they're dreams, and dreams make you happy only when you're dreaming. Pursuing goals, though, does make you happy. According to David Niven, author of *100 Simple Secrets of the Best Half of Life*, "People who could identify a goal they were pursuing were 19 percent more likely to feel satisfied with their lives and 26 percent more likely to feel positive about them."
- **Do what you do well.** Everyone has at least a few things they do incredibly well. Find ways to do those things more often. You'll be a lot happier. And probably a lot more successful.
- **Give.** While giving is usually considered unselfish, giving can also be more beneficial for the giver than the receiver. Providing social support may be more beneficial than receiving it.
- **Don't single-mindedly chase "status."** Money is important. Money does a lot of things. (One of the most important is to create choices.) But after a certain point, money doesn't make people happier. After about $75,000 a year, money doesn't buy more (or less) happiness, just many things. Chase a few experiences instead.
- **Live the life you want to live.**

—Jeff Haden, author of *The Motivation Myth: How High Achievers Really Set Themselves Up to Win* (2019), Penguin Random House.

Breathe Easy to Increase Happiness and Health

> *I've learned that if you pursue happiness, it will elude you. But if you focus on your family, your friends, the needs of others, your work, and doing the very best you can, happiness will find you.*
> —K. Wert

We have all been told to "take a deep breath." Andrew Weil, MD, recommends we take that one step further with this exercise: "4–7–8 breath." "Doing this daily will induce a feeling of serenity," says Dr. Weil (2011). Dr. Weil also adds, "Over time, it will give you greater emotional resilience—especially in hard moments."

- **Step 1.** Rest the tip of your tongue on the mouth, behind your top teeth.
- **Step 2.** Exhale completely through your mouth, with your lips slightly pursed, to make a whoosh sound.
- **Step 3.** Close your mouth and inhale deeply and slowly through your nose to a silent count of 4.
- **Step 4.** Keep your mouth closed and gently retain your breath for a silent count of 7.
- **Step 5.** Exhale slowly through your open mouth for a count of 8, making the same whoosh sound.
- **Step 6.** Repeat steps 3, 4, and 5 for a total of four breaths. Perform this twice daily for optimal results.

Chapter Review

If you are going to get serious about life planning, you will have to take risks. The purpose of life planning is to be certain that the risks you take are the right ones, based on careful thought.

- **Basic Law of Life** For everything you get in life, you have to give up something.
- **Intelligent risk taking** involves knowing your motivations, defining success, looking at best and worst outcomes, making a timetable, focusing on benefits, getting started, and doing what matters to you.
- Needs and drives cause us to consider life planning. A **need** is a condition that exists when we are deprived of something we want or require. When a need exists, it creates a drive that pushes (motivates) us to satisfy the need. One of the greatest insights in the field of **human motivation** is that satisfied needs do not motivate. It's only the unsatisfied need that motivates.
- Four fundamental human needs, according to Stephen Covey, are to live, to love, to learn, and to leave a legacy.
- Abraham Maslow's **Hierarchy of Needs** is based on the principle that there are certain survival needs that must be met before we can become concerned with the satisfaction of other needs. The hierarchy of needs encompasses: physiological, safety and security, love and belonging, self-esteem, and self-actualization, the fullest development of our potentialities.
- Our lives are divided into three periods: 1) getting an education, 2) going to work and earning a living or working in the home and community, and 3) living in retirement. It is important that we consider each period when we consider life planning. A **plan** is a goal or aim for satisfying the needs and wants of your life. In short, **goals** give purpose and meaning to our lives.
- Authorities generally write of at least seven different kinds of goals: physical, financial, spiritual, career, family, mental, and social.
- Some guidelines or criteria for identifying personal goals and making them work are: your goals must be your own, the goal must not be in conflict with one's personal value system, goals need to be specific and written down, start with short-range goals, goals must be realistic and attainable, and goals should contain specific time deadlines.
- **Success** might be defined as the progressive realization of a worthwhile, predetermined personal goal. Contributors to success are: a sense of direction, a feeling of self-confidence, a healthy mental attitude, a belief in perseverance, an understanding of others, and learning lessons.
- A basic tenet of all individuals who wish to succeed in any endeavor is "I have to be willing to fail." And, the magic word to success has been referred to as "work"—working hard and long to accomplish goals.
- You cannot manage time, but you can learn to manage yourself within the time you have. Discovering your **time wasters**—anything preventing you from achieving your objectives most effectively—is the key to managing yourself in relation to time. The essence of effective time and life management is to organize and execute around balanced priorities. When we direct either too little or too much time to the important areas in our life, our chair of life is out of balance.
- The **80-20 principle** states that 20% of what we do yields 80% of the results; and conversely, 80% of what we do yields 20% of the results.
- In **monochronic cultures**, time is organized sequentially, and schedules and deadlines are valued over people. In **polychronic cultures**, time is organized horizontally, and people tend to do several things at once and value relationships over schedules.
- The key to successful life planning is the willingness to take responsibility for ourselves. As we take control of our lives in various situations, we have three choices: change it, enjoy/tolerate it, or leave it.

- Four questions to ask yourself about the arena of life and work planning are: 1) Who am I?, 2) What am I up to?, 3) Where am I going?, and 4) What difference does it make anyway?
- One mistake people commonly make in seeking happiness is to try to wipe out all the sources of displeasure in their life, but we cannot have one without the other. Happiness is a sense that life is good—a state of well-being that outlasts yesterday's moment of elation, today's buoyant mood, or tomorrow's feeling of sadness. It is **contentment**.
- Psychologists have defined **happiness** as a combination of life satisfaction and the relative frequency of positive and negative affect.
- Several truths about happiness are: happiness is not an illusion or a delusion, happiness and marriage may go together, happiness knows no gender, happiness does not depend on age, and wealth does not beget happiness.
- Several traits that seem to be shared by happy people are: self-esteem, optimism, extroversion, and personal control. Having a strong spiritual faith; having close, supportive friendships and marriages; and having work and other activities that enhance our identity and absorb us into the flow appear to be additional ingredients to happiness. Living in a state of **flow** is being totally absorbed in an activity, whether at work or play, with a sense of mastery, and the use of all or most of one's skills.
- We can learn to adopt a new state of mind about happiness: making the effort to be happy now, rather than first gaining what we want or need in order to be happy.
- Contentment is the goal.
- Seligman says a **life of well-being** has four parts: a pleasant life, a good life, a meaningful life, and a life of fostering good, important relationships.
- In positive psychology, well-being has five measurable elements (PERMA) that count toward it:
  Positive emotion (Of which happiness and life satisfaction are all aspects)
  Engagement
  Relationships
  Meaning and purpose
  Accomplishment

Learning Outcomes Review

1. Explain what the Basic Law of Life means and how it applies to risk taking.
2. Explain how needs and drives cause us to consider life planning or take various directions for our life. In the field of human motivation, which needs motivate, and which needs do not motivate?
3. Explain the four fundamental human needs, as outlined by Stephen Covey.
4. Explain the concept of Maslow's Hierarchy of Needs. List and discuss the needs at each level in the hierarchy.
5. According to Richard Boles, into what three periods are our lives divided? Explain how these three periods should be considered in life planning. Discuss the purpose of goal setting.
6. List at least five different kinds of goal areas, as discussed in the text.
7. Discuss the guidelines or criteria for identifying personal goals and making them successful.
8. Explain the contributors to success. What is the magic word to success?
9. Identify and explain the significance of the basic tenet of all individuals who wish to succeed in any endeavor.
10. Explain why it is impossible to manage time. What is the essence of effective time and life management?

Explain the chair of life concept. Is your chair of life in balance or out of balance—why?

11. Discuss the meaning of the 80-20 principle as it applies to establishing priorities in one's life.
12. Distinguish between monochronic and polychronic cultures in relation to the way time is organized.
13. Identify and explain the key to successful life planning. What three choices do we have as we learn to take control of our lives in various situations?
14. Discuss four questions you can ask yourself about the arena of life and work planning.
15. Define happiness, and discuss why pleasure and displeasure are "two sides of the same coin."
16. Intelligent risk taking involves which steps?
17. Explain the term, "living in a state of flow," as it relates to happiness.
18. Explain how we can learn happiness.
19. Define contentment.
20. Discuss Seligman's parts of a life of well-being. What is SWB? Define it.
21. What is the purpose of the Breathe Easy exercise suggested by Dr. Andrew Weil?
22. List three (3) characteristics of intelligent risk-taking.
23. What does PERMA mean?
24. What digital elements are important for the future?

Key Terms

Altruism	Flow (Living in a state of)	Polychronic Cultures
Basic Law of Life	Goals	PERMA
Chair of Life	GRIT	Risk
Contentment	Happiness	Safety and Security Needs
Digital Deficits	Intelligent Risk Taking	Self-Actualization Needs
Digital Distrust/Divisiveness	Love and Belonging Needs	Success
Digital Duress	Maslow's Hierarchy of Needs	SWB
Drive	Monochronic Cultures	Time Waster
Esteem Needs	Need	80-20 Principle
FLOW	Physiological Needs	Well-being

Reflections: Critical Thinking Activity

Individually answer these questions or get into groups of 3 and share answers with a discussion of your findings.

1. What risks are you afraid of taking right now in your life?
2. What are you going to have to give up to have what you want?
3. What do you think are the basic needs and wants of human beings?
4. Identify some of the needs and wants you have established right now in your life. What are you doing now to satisfy them?

5. Of Maslow's five basic needs, which one seems most important for you to satisfy right now?
6. What does success mean to you?
7. What determines success in our society?
8. Discuss this statement: Each of us becomes what we think about.
9. What is your greatest time waster? How much of your time do you spend on this activity?
10. Diagram and discuss your chair of life. Is it in balance? If not, why?
11. Discuss, giving examples, how the 80-20 principle has applied to your life.
12. What is your definition of happiness?
13. Discuss this statement: if you can't appreciate what you have, your achievements will feel hollow.
14. What would a life of well-being look like to you?
15. What is your definition of contentment?
16. What motivates you?
17. What is intelligent risk-taking?
18. What is SWB?
19. Why learn a breathing exercise?
20. What is pure altruism? What is pseudo altruism? and what is nurturing altruism? And egoism?
21. Define Wellbeing. What is PERMA?

Technology Resources and Activities

https://www.youtube.com/watch?v=XdoyMswtNUk&feature=youtu.be

Sanjiv Chopra explores the tenets of happiness, the critical importance of friends, the ability to forgive, being of service to others, and expressing gratitude.

http://ggia.berkeley.edu

Greater Good in Action: Science-based Practices for a Meaningful Life.

https://www.bigspeak.com/makes-good-life-robert-waldinger-three-lessons/

What makes a good life? Lessons from the longest study on happiness.

www.motivation123.com/

A psychological view of motivation and happiness.

https://positivepsychology.com/positive-psychology-com-podcast-out-of-your-mind-into-your-life/

A podcast on positive psychology.

https://www.psychologytoday.com/us/basics/decision-making

Expert guidance through step-by-step decision making.

http://angeladuckworth.com/grit-scale/

The Grit Scale measures the character strength of perseverance.

http://www.ted.com/read/ted-studies/psychology

TED Studies and coursework on Psychology: Understanding Happiness.

www.authentichappiness.sas.upenn.edu/testcenter.aspx

The Authentic Happiness Inventory measures overall happiness.

VIDEOS

http://www.upworthy.com/researchers-studied-the-ways-spending-money-can-affect-happiness-e-results-are-eye-opening

Researchers studied the ways spending affects our happiness. The results are eye-opening.

http://www.npr.org/2012/05/02/151881205/the-pursuit-of-happiness

Being happy is a universal human yearning, but this simple goal often eludes us. If we're truly able to attain happiness, then how do we find it? Three TED speakers offer some big ideas for achieving happiness.

https://www.bigspeak.com/makes-good-life-robert-waldinger-three-lessons/

What makes a good life? Lessons from the longest study on happiness.

https://www.upworthy.com/here-are-5-things-you-may-regret-at-the-end-of-your-life-from-a-nurse-who-works-with-the-dying

Here are 5 things you may regret at the end of your life, from a nurse who works with the dying.

http://www.upworthy.com/science-found-4-categories-of-independence-in-young-adults-where-do-you-belong

Science found 4 categories of independence in young adults. Where do you belong?

https://www.youtube.com/watch?annotation_id=annotation_385315229&feature=iv&src_vid=NUslk-3jiooU&v=yux_m8AdzwY

Personal Goal Setting: How to set SMART goals to boost confidence and achieve your dreams.

http://www.ted.com/talks/emilie_wapnick_why_some_of_us_don_t_have_one_true_calling

Career coach Emilie Wapnick celebrates the "multipotentialite": those of us with many interests, many jobs over a lifetime, and many interlocking potentials.

https://www.youtube.com/watch?v=HTfYv3IEOqM

Daniel Goleman on Focus: The secret to high performance and fulfillment.

https://www.drweil.com/videos-features/videos/breathing-exercises-4-7-8-breath/

Breathing exercise for better health.

Name _____ Date _____

Your Life's Activities

PURPOSE

To demonstrate how your activities make up your life.

Current Life

Three Years Ago

Ideal Life

INSTRUCTIONS

1. **Draw three circles in a row.** Divide the circle on the left, as a pie, into parts that represent your current life. Label each part: for example, home life, work, personal, education, leisure, and whatever else represents your current life.
2. Divide the circle in the center into parts that represent your life three years ago. Use the same labeling as in the first circle or add others as needed.
3. For the third circle, divide it in a way that represents the ideal way you'd like your life to be. Label each part as in previous circles.
4. Complete the answers to the questions below and be prepared to discuss them in small groups.

DISCUSSION

Let us compare and contrast the three circles.

1. What is keeping your present circle of activities from being like the ideal circle?

2. What can you do within the next six months to make the ideal circle like your real life?

3. Is your ideal circle realistic for you? Why or why not?

4. What did you learn about yourself from this activity?

Think About it ...

Brené Brown, in her 2017 book *Braving the Wilderness*, said "True belonging is the spiritual practice of believing in and belonging to yourself so deeply that you can share your most authentic self with the world and find sacredness in both being a part of something and standing alone in the wilderness. True belonging doesn't require you to change who you are; it requires you to be who you are."

What is your reaction to this quote?

Write about this in your learning journal.

What Do You Want?

PURPOSE

To establish three sets of goals and to examine what you are really working toward accomplishing.

INSTRUCTIONS

1. Write down what goals you would like to accomplish in the following areas. If you do not have a goal in a particular area, that is okay. You decide.

    FAMILY:

    a.

    b.

    PHYSICAL:

    a.

    b.

    MENTAL:

    a.

    b.

    SOCIAL:

    a.

    b.

    SPIRITUAL/RELIGIOUS:

    a.

    b.

    FINANCIAL:

    a.

    b.

    CAREER:

    a.

    b.

Next, select the three things you want most to accomplish within the next six months.

    a.

    b.

    c.

Now, select from your goals the three things you want most to accomplish in the next year.

    a.

    b.

    c.

Now, select your three most important life goals.

    a.

    b.

    c.

Write down why you want to achieve the goals. List all the ways you will personally benefit from achieving the goals.

    a.

    b.

    c.

Now, write down anything, large or small, you have done within the past month to accomplish any of these goals.

What are you doing to increase your happiness? What is your happiness plan?

DISCUSSION

1. Are you presently working toward what you say is important to you? If not, why?

2. Do you really want these things?

3. Review the seven areas of possible goals and write down what goals you really want to start working on now.

Name _____ Date _____

Lifeline

PURPOSE

To take a look at where you have been, where you are, and where you want to go.

INSTRUCTIONS

1. If you are keeping a journal for the class, include this in your journal. If done in class for a class activity, on a piece of heavy poster board or construction paper, start with the year in which you were born and depict the significant experiences and people who have helped shape your life.
2. Your lifeline will be dated in terms of the years these significant experiences or people appeared in your life.
3. Make notations above or below each year to remind you of exactly what occurred.
4. When completed, your lifeline will appear like a graph: "highs and lows," "hills and valleys," and "steady" periods of your life. You may use pictures, words, or whatever you wish to depict these significant time periods in your life.
5. The last dot on your lifeline should be on a "hill," a high point in the future. Fantasize and jot some words down to describe what you would like to have happen in your life in the next five or ten years. What will you be doing, where will you be, and who will be with you?
6. After you have completed your lifeline, you will divide into small groups and explain your lifeline. Be prepared to give a 3 to 5 minute presentation.

DISCUSSION

1. How do you feel about the quality of your life at the present time?

2. What experiences are primarily responsible for where you are today?

3. What experiences are primarily responsible for what you want to accomplish in the future?

4. What goals are implied as you picture yourself 5 to 10 years in the future?

Name _____ Date _____

My Future Autobiography

PURPOSE

To think about the quality of your life and to demonstrate that you still have a life ahead with which to do whatever you choose.

INSTRUCTIONS

1. In the space below, write at least a two or three paragraph autobiography for yourself. Include things that you would like to have said or written about you near the end of your life. Write about things that you would like to accomplish and what contributions you want to make. Write about what character strengths you want to have, and what qualities you want to develop.

2. Have someone else read your autobiography and complete the first discussion question.

DISCUSSION

1. What long-range goals are implied in this autobiography? Write them below, even if they are vague.

2. Do you see any similarity in the goals implied here and in the goals you listed in the previous activity?

Connection to Humanity Quiz

Some people feel a strong sense of kinship with all members of humankind, no matter what differences or distances might exist between them; others have a tendency to keep those feelings closer to home.

The quiz below assesses how deeply you identify with all of humanity, independent of your identification with your country or community. It is a simplified, adapted version of a scale recently developed by Sam McFarland, Matthew Webb, and Derek Brown, psychologists at Western Kentucky University.

For the first 18 items, select the answer that best describes how you feel. There are no right or wrong answers, so please answer as honestly as possible. The last seven questions will be used by the research team to better understand how identification with humanity relates to factors like income level and political orientation.

When you're done, you'll get your score, along with ideas for increasing your feelings of connection to humankind.

TAKE THE QUIZ

(Adapted from: McFarland, S., Webb, M., & Brown, D. (2012). "All humanity is my ingroup: A measure and studies of identification with all humanity." http://www.ncbi.nlm.nih.gov/pubmed/22708625 *Journal of Personality and Social Psychology*, 103(5), 830-853.

The Greater Good Science Center studies the psychology, sociology, and neuroscience of well-being, and teaches skills that foster a thriving, resilient, and compassionate society. http://www.berkeley.edu/ Berkeley: University of California. © 2019 The Greater Good Science Center at the University of California, Berkeley

COPING EXERCISE—When You Should Help Your Coworkers—and When to Think Twice

Research offers some guidance on how to be more helpful at work—for everyone's benefit.

By Shanna B. Tiayon | June 10, 2019

When was the last time you helped a colleague at work?

Helping in the workplace can take various forms—for example, training an intern, comforting a colleague in distress, or taking on extra work to complete a team project.

If your organization has a competitive work culture—or if you're anything like the 35 percent of working Americans who feel overwhelmed by their workload—helping others in the workplace may not be at the top of your priority list. However, research suggests that more helpful workplaces actually perform better; they produce better-quality products and have increased sales. And helping others at work feels good.

If you can't recall the last time you lent a hand to a coworker, the three questions below may help you start thinking about your interactions at work and how you could be of more service to others in the workplace.

1.   When are you most likely to help others at work?

Are you more likely to help when a colleague asks you for help (called reactive helping) or when you perceive the need for help without being asked (proactive helping)?

Surprisingly, proactive helping can sometimes be problematic. A recent study surveyed 51 employees from diverse industries on their proactive and reactive helping behaviors. They rated how much they helped coworkers make progress, deal with problems, or avoid potential problems either without being asked or when their coworkers explicitly requested help.

The study found that when people engaged in reactive helping—helping when asked—they received more gratitude. In turn, the helpers perceived that they had a greater impact and felt more engaged at work the next day. Put simply, reactive helpers felt good after helping.

But that wasn't the case for proactive helpers. Proactive helpers didn't receive as much gratitude, which seemed to diminish the psychological returns for them.

Rather than jumping in and fixing something, you can help a colleague come up with their own solutions. Even better, you can encourage reactive helping by communicating to colleagues that you're willing to help if needed, increasing the likelihood that they will ask for help directly.

2.   Why do you help others at work?

Motivation is a key driving force of behavior. The first step in understanding how you help others is to get clear on what motivates you.

A 2014 study provides some insight on why motives matter. The study surveyed 174 professionals, from diverse industries, about their helping behaviors in the workplace. Respondents were asked about how much they helped fellow colleagues by sharing work-related knowledge, helping with work problems, explaining a regulation or procedure, or helping a colleague after they were absent.

They found that how much people helped depended on their motivation. Individuals who reported altruistic motives—based on personal values or a desire to contribute to the team—helped more than employees who reported helping others under specific conditions (if it wouldn't interfere with their work, the person asking for help was perceived to be worthy, or they had the knowledge and skills to help).

People motivated by altruism are less concerned with their reputation and status when helping others. They help because they believe it's the right thing to do, even if there's a personal cost in doing so, like lost time.

If your reasons for helping others in the past have been less altruistic, be on the lookout for the next opportunity to support your work team. Then, try focusing more on making a meaningful contribution to the group and less on the benefits you hope to gain. It will take some pressure off of you, and chances are you'll be appreciated anyway (because your helping signals to the group your motivation to contribute to the common good).

3. Whom do you tend to help at work?
Think back to the last several people you helped at work. Who were they?

Chances are they shared many characteristics with you, like race, gender, or socioeconomic status. Research shows that homophily, the tendency to connect to people who are similar to us, structures our social networks at work. As a result, your helping may be restricted to a homogenous group of work colleagues, limiting your efforts.

In fact, research suggests that people are less helpful in more diverse work groups. A 2009 study of 1,762 employees from a large electronics company in Korea, representing 96 separate work units, found that in more diverse groups (in terms of gender and education), respondents observed fewer of the following behaviors among coworkers: 1) going out of their way to help others with work problems, 2) showing genuine concern and courtesy toward others, and 3) voluntarily helping new employees settle into the job.

In addition to homophily, this pattern is likely linked to intergroup bias, as well. Intergroup bias causes us to subconsciously evaluate those who are similar to us more favorably than those who are not—for example, when determining the perceived worthiness of someone who needs our help. Or when deciding who is trustworthy, which also greatly impacts our likeliness to help others.

One way to break this subconscious pattern is to expand your work network to be inclusive of those who are different from you and to be cognizant of your personal biases that may come into play when making decisions at work. Practicing mindfulness is a good starting point.

While many efforts to boost workplace productivity today focus on increasing employee satisfaction and well-being, helping merits more attention. Helping could be the missing link that explains why employees in a better mood perform better—happier employees are more likely to help others, and workplaces with helping cultures see better employee performance. And who wouldn't want to work in a happy, helpful, and productive workplace?

Becoming *Aware*

COPING EXERCISE—ACCEPTANCE WITH ICE CUBES

Acceptance is an essential positive coping technique. This exercise will allow you to notice your sensations and accept their existence without trying to control or change them. There are four steps in this exercise, and you can learn more about it from the https://positivepsychology.com/tools/practicing-acceptance-with-ice-cubes/ Practicing Acceptance with Ice cubes exercise.

Step 1 – **Take one or two ice cubes and hold them gently in your palm. Try to keep holding them for the next couple of minutes.**

Step 2 – After a few seconds, you will start feeling extreme cold on your skin. At this point, you might have thoughts about letting go of the ice cubes to restore warmth and comfort. **Your goal at this stage would be to notice these thoughts without trying to act on them.**

Step 3 – **The third stage is about tuning into your emotions.** You may notice feelings such as fear or discomfort. Try to see how you are feeling and what thoughts are popping into your mind while you continue holding the ice cubes.

Step 4 – **The fourth step of this exercise is about offering kindness and gratitude to yourself.** While you may continue experiencing extreme sensations, try to comfort and remind yourself that this is not harmful to you.

Step 5 – **Finally, release the ice cubes and warm your hands with a dry towel or cloth.**

When you feel the cold sensation fading away, try to recall the experience and ask yourself:

- What did I learn from this exercise?
- What thoughts and emotions did I experience while I was holding the ice cubes?
- How did I react to my emotions? Can I use a similar approach to my life problems?

Adapted from Positive Psychology.com

COPING EXERCISE—Tasks You Want to Accomplish Today

Remember a tool called the Johari Window, the tool created for use in social sciences by the two psychologists Joseph Luft and Harrison Ingham?

Use this tool to evaluate the tasks you want to accomplish today. Put each task in the box that represents how you feel about it: Important/Unimportant and Urgent/Not urgent. Some things may end up close to a line, but every task must fit entirely inside a box—no crossing lines.

IMPORTANT	UNIMPORTANT

URGENT

NOT URGENT

The upper left box is the high priority box, and the other boxes are lower priority. The lower left and upper right are where you must make a judgement: is urgent + unimportant a higher priority than important + not urgent? The lower right is likely the lowest priority. Be careful not to categorize things as unimportant because others believe that—this is about importance to you, your life, your goals, your sense of well-being.

Name _____ Date _____

Goal Development

PURPOSE

To further understand yourself and to define your goals.

INSTRUCTIONS

1. List your strengths, based on questionnaires, personal assessments, assignments, and personal experiences gained in or out of class this term.

2. List your weaknesses, based on questionnaires, personal assessments, assignments, and personal experiences gained in or out of class this term.

3. Re-evaluate your responses to the exercises in this chapter and what you now know about yourself. List the five most important things in your life at the present time.

   a.

   b.

   c.

   d.

   e.

4. Review your lifeline and what you know about yourself and list at least three peak experiences that have been meaningful to you.

   a.

   b.

   c.

5. What other peak experiences would you like to have in the future?

6. Review your autobiography and your lifeline and list the tentative goals implied in each activity.

7. Review your responses to the activity "What Do You Want?" and your responses to the previous questions in this activity and write down at least three goals that you want to start working on now.

   MY GOALS:

   a.

   b.

   c.

Goal Project

PURPOSE

To develop a plan of action for what you want to accomplish.

INSTRUCTIONS

1. From the previous exercise, select two goals and develop a plan of what you can do this next year to achieve these goals.

Goal Number One

1. I want to:

2. What obstacles must I overcome?

3. How do I plan to overcome these obstacles? Be specific.

4. What behaviors must I change?

5. How do I plan to change these behaviors? Be specific.

6. When will I achieve this goal? Be specific.

Goal Number Two

1. I want to:

2. What obstacles must I overcome?

3. How do I plan to overcome these obstacles? Be specific.

4. What behaviors must I change?

5. How do I plan to change these behaviors? Be specific.

6. When will I achieve this goal? Be specific.

DISCUSSION

1. How do you feel about the goal project you have just completed?

Life Planning

LEARNING JOURNAL

Select the statement below that best defines your feelings about the personal value or meaning gained from this chapter and respond below the dotted line.

I learned that I . . .   I was surprised that I . . .

I realized that I . . .   I was pleased that I . . .

I discovered that I . . .   I was displeased that I . .

· ·

Glossary

5-to-1 Ratio A five-to-one ratio of positive interactions to negative interactions is vital to a happy relationship.

80-20 Principle 20% of what we do yields 80% of the results; and conversely 80% of what we do yields 20% of the results.

Ableism Discrimination in favor of able-bodied people.

Accommodating Strategy A lose-win strategy in which individuals attempt to resolve the conflict by passively giving in to the other party.

Acceptance is defined as agreement with or belief in an idea, opinion, or explanation. (2019 Merriam Webster Dictionary)

Acting A process of clarifying values, whereby an individual follows a pattern of taking action on a chosen value.

Active Listening Seeing the expressed idea or problem from the speaker's point of view. Also, active listening implies listening with a purpose.

Addiction The state of being enslaved to a habit or practice or to something that is psychologically or physically habit-forming, such as narcotics, to such an extent that its cessation causes severe trauma.

Advising Response Responding to others by offering a solution.

Agender *(adj.)* Describes a person who does not identify with any gender identity.

Agreeableness One of the "big five" dimensions of personality: ranges from good-natured, cooperative, trusting at one end to irritable, suspicious, uncooperative at the other.

Aggression Any behavior that is intended to hurt someone, either verbally or physically. Aggression is a deliberate and repeated attempt to cause harm to others of lesser power.

Aggressive Moving against another with an intent to hurt.

Alarm Stage The stage in which the body recognizes the stressor and prepares for fight or flight, which is done by a release of hormones from the endocrine glands.

Alienation the act of alienating, or of causing someone to become indifferent or hostile: as through indifference or disaffection:

Ally *(noun)* A person who does not identify as LGBTQ, but stands with and advocates for LGBTQ people.

Alcoholism A chronic disorder characterized by dependence on *alcohol*, repeated excessive use of *alcoholic*.

Altruism Feelings and behavior that show a desire to help other people and a lack of selfishness.

Anger The feeling of extreme displeasure, usually brought about by interference with our needs or desires.

Appreciation is defined as a recognition and enjoyment of the good qualities of someone or something.

Androgynous *(adj.)*, **Androgyne** *(noun)* Used to describe someone who identifies or presents as neither distinguishably masculine nor feminine.

Annoyance A mild form of anger.

Anxiety An unpleasant, threatening feeling that something bad is about to happen; the basis of the fear is not generally understood.

Anxiety Disorders Everyone experiences anxiety sometimes, but when it becomes overwhelming and repeatedly impacts a person's life, it may be an anxiety disorder.

Aromantic *(adj.)* A romantic orientation generally characterized by not feeling romantic attraction or a desire for romance.

Assertiveness Response to conflict situations that involves standing up for yourself, expressing your true feelings, and not letting others take advantage of you; however, assertiveness involves being considerate of others' feelings.

Asexual relationship Some people are asexual, meaning they don't experience sexual desire or attraction to others, but they still want to participate in a romantic relationship. While asexual people often choose to date each other to create a purely asexual relationship, this is not always the case. When an asexual person and a sexual person enter into a relationship, it can take a few different forms, according to the Asexuality Visibility & Education Network. The couple can choose to be completely sexless, or the asexual partner can "compromise" by engaging in sex occasionally under certain circumstances, or partners can experiment with "pseudosexual behavior," such as cuddling, to find an arrangement that works for both. See https://asexuality.org/

Assigned sex *(noun)* The sex that is assigned to an infant at birth based on the child's visible sex organs, including genitalia and other physical characteristics. Often corresponds with a child's assigned gender and assumed gender.

Assume *or* **Assumptions in Communication** To accept as fact without any evidence of proof.

Attention economics Is a management approach which views an individual's attention as a scarce commodity, and one which must be acquired to achieve effective marketing. Attention economics is of particular importance in the current age of the internet. Consumers in the modern age have access to overwhelming amounts of information, and this has caused them to become skimmers rather than readers. The internet is full of meaningless content as much as it is filled with relevant information Attention economics considers awareness, recognition, and action thereof to be integral to economic decision making (World Atlas, 2019).

Attentive Listening One of the four levels of normal listening; paying attention and focusing energy on the words that are being said.

Attitudes Positive or negative orientations toward a certain target.

Attribution Error The tendency to overemphasize internal explanations of other people's behavior.

Attribution Theory An explanation that suggests we frequently overestimate the influence of an individual's personality and underestimate the impact of his or her situation.

Authentic Self True to one's own personality, spirit, or character. The authentic self is the you that can be found at your absolute core. It is the composite of all your skills, talents, and wisdom. It is all of the things that are uniquely yours and need expression, rather than what you believe you are supposed to be and do.

Autonomy vs. Doubt Erikson's psychosocial crisis at the second stage of the human life cycle; the two- and three-year-old develops independence and self-reliance in proportion to positive parental encouragement and consistency of discipline.

Avoidance Response to conflict situations that involves being passive and removing yourself from the conflict.

Avoiding Strategy A lose-lose strategy in which individuals attempt to passively ignore the conflict rather than resolve it.

Awe Mixed emotion of reverence, respect, dread, and wonder inspired by authority, genius, great beauty, sublimity, or might: We felt awe when contemplating the works of Bach. To be inspired with awe is to be **awestruck.**

Basic Law of Life For everything you get in life, you also have to give up something.

Behavioral Contract An agreement (commitment) made to change your behavior.

Belief The acceptance of some thought, supposition, or idea.

Behavioral confirmation is a type of self-fulfilling prophecy whereby people's social expectations lead them to behave in ways that cause others to confirm their expectations.

Bias Definite opinions—positive or negative feelings about a social group; prejudice.

Biological sex *(noun)* A medical classification that refers to anatomical, physiological, genetic, or physical attributes that determine if a person is assigned male, female, or intersex identity at birth. Biological sex is often confused or interchanged with the term "gender," which encompasses personal identity and social factors, and is not necessarily determined by biological sex.

Binary system *(noun)* Something that contains two opposing parts; binary systems are often assumed despite the existence of a spectrum of possibilities. Gender (man/woman) and sex (male/female) are examples of binary systems often perpetuated by our culture.

Biphobia The fear or hatred of bisexual people or people who do not meet society's gender role expectations.

Bisexual Relating to, or characterized by, sexual or romantic attraction to members of both sexes; also, engaging in sexual activity with partners of more than one gender.

Bisexual, Bi *(adj.)* A person emotionally, romantically or sexually attracted to more than one sex, gender, or gender identity, though not necessarily simultaneously, in the same way, or to the same degree.

Blended Families A family system consisting of stepchildren and stepparents.

Blind Area of Johari Window Information about you of which you are unaware but is easily apparent to others.

Body dysmorphic disorder is a mental disorder in which you can't stop thinking about one or more perceived defects or flaws in your appearance—flaws that, to others, are either minor or not observable.

Body Leakage Where body postures rather than the face leak the truth.

Broken-Record Technique Calmly repeating your assertive message without getting sidetracked by irrelevant issues.

Bullying is a form of aggressive behavior in which someone intentionally and repeatedly causes another person injury or discomfort. Bullying can take the form of physical contact, words, or more subtle actions. Studies show that bullies lack prosocial behavior, are untroubled by anxiety, and do not understand others' feelings. Bullying is a distinctive pattern of harming and humiliating others, specifically those who are in some way smaller, weaker, younger, or in any way more vulnerable than the bully. Bullying is not garden-variety. A bully can be an aggressive juvenile, an intimidating boss or colleague, a controlling romantic partner, an unruly neighbor, a high pressure sales/business representative, a condescending family member, a shaming social acquaintance, or those in a variety of other types of abusive relationships, and some of this has moved to the Internet (https://www.psychologytoday.com/us/basics/bullying).

Casual sex relationship is when both partners agree to have sex with each other on a regular basis—and that's it. Those in casual sex relationships can be physically and/or emotionally intimate with others as well, so long as both people are OK with it. Casual sex relationships can also be "exclusive"—meaning neither person sleeps with anyone else—which is similar to monogamous relationships, without the emotional connection.

Categorizing Placing people into groups—by race, sex, physical attractiveness, height, etc.

Catharsis An emotional release through talking.

Chair of Life An analogy, representing four valuable parts of life. The "chair" (our life) can either be in balance or out of balance, based on the amount of time we devote to each of these important parts of life.

Character Composed of personal standards of behavior, including honesty, integrity, and moral strength.

Character Ethic A style of living based on principles and values rather than on techniques.

Character Trait An enduring characteristic of a person that is related to moral and ethical behavior and shows up consistently.

Charismatic Being likeable. The Oxford dictionary defines is as a compelling attractiveness or charm that can inspire devotion in others.

Choosing Freely Consciously and deliberately making a value choice without any pressure from significant others.

Cisgender or Cissexual *(adj.)* Describes a person whose gender identity aligns with the sex assigned to them at birth; a person whose sense of personal identity and gender corresponds with their birth sex; (e.g., someone born with a penis identifying as a man). It's the opposite of transgender. Cis is the abbreviation for cisgender or cissexual.

Cissexism *(noun)* A system of discrimination and exclusion that oppresses people whose gender and/or gender expression falls outside of normative social constructs. This system is founded on the belief that there are, and should be, only two genders—usually tied to assigned sex.

Becoming *Aware*

Class The system of ordering a society in which people are divided into sets based on perceived social or economic status.

Classical Conditioning A type of learning in which a neutral stimulus acquires the capacity to evoke a response that was originally evoked by another stimulus. Many of our emotions, feelings (like love, hatred), biases, phobias, and fears are obtained by classical conditioning.

Classism Also known as **Class discrimination**, is *prejudice* or *discrimination* on the basis of *social class*.

Classism Prejudice against or in favor of people belonging to a particular social class.

Closed Questions Questions that often result in yes, no, or a very short response.

Codependent Relationship A dependency on people—on their moods, behavior, sickness, well-being, and their love.

Code-switch When adults often or sometimes feel the need to talk differently around different races and ethnic groups, especially Black college graduates under 50 years old.

Cognitive behavior is the theory that behaviors and emotions are the result of negative patterns of thinking which have adapted over time. It is the basis of the counseling approach called **Cognitive Behavioral Therapy** (CBT).

Cognitive Dissonance A concept (theory) that accounts for reactions to inconsistencies in attitudes and beliefs.

Cognitive Restructuring The process of modifying thoughts, ideas, and beliefs.

Cognitive Theory Our mental processes turn our sensations and perceptions into organized impressions of reality.

Cohabitation A situation in which couples live together outside of marriage.

Collaborating Strategy A win-win strategy in which parties attempt to jointly resolve the conflict with the best solution agreeable to all parties.

Collaborative Problem Solving The win-win approach to conflict resolution whereby conflicts are resolved with no one winning and no one losing. Both win because the solution must be acceptable to both.

Collectivism Putting group goals ahead of personal goals and defining one's identity in terms of the groups to which one belongs.

Colorism The discrimination of African Americans by skin tone in their own community, usually subconsciously done, as most Blacks do not realize they're doing it until a rapper or famous person makes a stupid, untrue statement about darker toned women (urban dictionary.com). For more information see https://www.tedxvienna.at/blog/colourism-bias-social-inequality/

Coming out *(verb)* A lifelong process of self-acceptance and revealing one's queer identity to others. This may involve something as private as telling a single confidant or something as public as posting to social media.

Commitment A joint decision to begin a relatively long-lasting, more intimate relationship that to some extent excludes other close intimate relationships.

Communication The process of conveying feelings, attitudes, facts, beliefs, and ideas between individuals, either verbally or nonverbally, and being understood in the way intended.

Communication Barriers Things that stop, block, prevent, or hinder the communication process.

Communication Channels The medium through which a message passes from sender to receiver.

Communication Process A process involving three parts: 1) a sender of the message, 2) a receiver of the message, and 3) the content of the message.

Companionate Love Commitment and intimacy, but no passion.

Compensation This involves efforts to overcome imagined or real inferiorities by developing one's abilities.

Competing/Forcing Strategy A win-lose strategy in which an individual uses aggressive behavior to satisfy one's own needs at the expense of the other person.

Complementary Needs One person's strengths compensate for the others' weaknesses.

Compromising Strategy A lose-lose strategy that attempts to resolve the conflict through assertive give-and-take concessions or cooperation.

Conditioned Response (CR) A learned reaction to a conditioned stimulus that occurs because of previous conditioning.

Conditioned Stimulus (CS) A previously neutral stimulus that has, through conditioning, acquired the capacity to evoke a conditioned response.

Confidant A significantly close personal friend with whom one can safely share one's deepest concerns and joys.

Confidence The feeling or belief that one can rely on someone or something; firm trust. The state of feeling certain about the truth of something or a feeling of self-assurance arising from one's appreciation of one's own abilities or qualities.

Conflict An expressed struggle between at least two people who perceive the situation differently and are experiencing interference from the other person in achieving their goals.

Conflict resolution Also known as reconciliation, is conceptualized as the methods and processes involved in facilitating the peaceful ending of conflict.

Conflicting Stimuli Things that are in conflict with your beliefs and values.

Conscientiousness One of the "big five" dimensions of personality: ranges from well organized, careful, responsible at one end to disorganized, careless, unscrupulous at the other.

Consequences The results of your behavior—positive reinforcement, negative reinforcement, or punishment.

Continuum model of impression formation In social psychology, according to this model of impression formation, impressions are formed when individuals automatically categorize others into social categories.

Consummate Love Commitment, intimacy, and passion.

Contentment An internal state of well-being that's independent of what you have or don't have, or life's ups and downs.

Cooperativeness The degree to which one is concerned about maintaining the relationship or satisfying the concern of others in conflict resolution.

Coping Refers to active efforts, either positive or negative, to master, reduce, or tolerate the demands created by problems and/or stress.

Covert bullying or passive-aggressive bullying behaves appropriately on the surface, but takes you down with subtlety. Passive-aggressive behavior can be intensely frustrating for the target because it's hard to identify, difficult to prove, and may even be unintentional (World Atlas, 2019).

Craftfulness A combination of the words "crafting" and "mindfulness," this wellness technique promotes creativity as a form of self-care. Coined by Rosemary Davidson and Arzu Tahsin.

Cultural Difference To be highly skilled in interpersonal relations you must recognize and appreciate individual and demographic (group or category) differences as well as cultural differences. People from the same demographic group often come from many different cultures. Cultural sensitivity can also be known as political correctness, also called "PC." Cultural intelligence shows respect for all workers and cultures.

Cultural Display Rules in Emotions Norms about when, where, and how much individuals from different cultures should show emotions.

Cultural Fluency is the ability to conduct business in a diverse international environment, relating well to people from different cultures and knowing a second language; having knowledge of international environments and the ability to adapt and work well with people from other cultures.

Cyber A combining form meaning "computer," "computer network," or "virtual reality," used in the formation of compound words (cybertalk; cyberart; cyberspace) and by extension meaning "expressing visions of the future" (cyberfashion).

Cyberbullying The act of harassing someone online by sending or posting mean messages, usually anonymously.

Cyberpsychology The study of the impact of emerging technology on human behavior "Cyber" refers to any technology, from Bluetooth to mobile intelligence and networked devices, gaming, virtual reality and more.

Daily Hassles Irritating and frustrating incidents that occur in our everyday interactions with the environment.

Debilitative Emotions Emotions that prevent a person from functioning effectively.

Decoding The process in which a receiver attaches meaning to a message.

Defense Mechanisms Behavior patterns used to protect one's feelings of self-esteem and self-respect.

Delight The earliest pleasant reaction (emotion), appearing in the form of smiling, gurgling, and other babyish sounds of joy.

Demisexual *(adj.)* Used to describe someone who feels sexual attraction only to people with whom they have an emotional bond—often considered to be on the asexual spectrum.

Denial A defense used when we refuse to recognize or acknowledge a threatening situation.

Depression Depression is more than just feeling sad or going through a rough patch: it's a serious mental health condition that requires understanding and treatment.

Desensitization Method of behavioral modification whereby the individual's fear of an object or person is replaced by relaxation.

Disabilities are the consequence of an impairment that may be physical, cognitive, intellectual, mental, sensory, developmental, or some combination of these that results in restrictions on an individual's ability to participate in what is considered "normal" in their everyday society. Many people would rather be referred to as a person with a disability instead of handicapped.

Discrimination Treatment or consideration of, or making a distinction in favor of or against, a person or thing based on the group, class, or category to which that person or thing belongs rather than on individual merit: racial and religious intolerance and discrimination.

Dismissive positivity Also known as toxic positivity; having an unhelpful cheerful attitude.

Displacement A defense used when the person redirects strong feelings from one person or object to another that seems more acceptable and less threatening.

Distress Negative or harmful stress that causes a person to constantly readjust or adapt.

Diversity The inclusion of individuals representing more than one national origin, color, religion, socioeconomic stratum, sexual orientation, etc.; diversity in the workplace.

Diversity umbrella is appreciating cultural diversity in organizations, and was original aimed at assisting women and minorities—it includes more people as the workforce encompasses a greater variety of people.

Divorce A complete, legal breaking up of a marriage.

Domination An aggressive technique of resolving conflict, characterized by moving against another with the intent to hurt.

Door Openers Short responses inviting the other person to share his/her ideas, judgments, or feelings.

Double Bind in Communication A situation in which the nonverbal message contradicts the verbal message.

Drive An internal tension or force that pushes (motivates) us to satisfy a need.

Eating Disorders When you become so preoccupied with food and weight issues that you find it hard to focus on other aspects of your life, it may be a sign of an eating disorder.

Ego The rational, logical, and realistic part of the personality that attempts to maintain balance between the id and superego.

Ego identity is the conscious sense of self that we develop through social interaction, which is constantly changing due to new experiences and information we acquire in our daily interactions with others.

Emotion is a feeling state that involves certain components like physiological changes, subjective cognitive states, and expressive behaviors.

Emotional Attachments Feelings that there is someone around to take care of us or help us out.

Emotional Bank Account Continuing to make small, everyday sacrifices and making efforts to notice and appreciate the kindness of your partner.

Emotional Debt A condition of imbalance in which feelings are trapped instead of expressed.

Emotional Intelligence The ability to monitor, access, express, and regulate one's own emotions; the capacity to identify, interpret, and understand others' emotions; and the ability to use this information to guide one's thinking and actions.

Emotion-Packed Phrases Phrases that, when combined with different mood levels, can cause an individual to verbally react in inappropriate ways.

Emotions Feelings that are experienced.

Empathetic Listening The fifth level, known as the highest form of listening to others; listening with the intent to understand. (See Active Listening and the Understanding Response.)

Empathy An active process in which you try to learn all you can about another person rather than having only a superficial awareness.

Empty Love A form of love that includes commitment, but no intimacy or passion.

Encoding The process of putting thoughts into symbols, most commonly words.

Envy The thoughts and feelings that arise when our personal qualities, possessions, or achievements do not measure up to those of someone relevant to us.

Esteem Needs The need to feel worthwhile, which is often satisfied by maintaining a healthy self-image, through status, prestige, a good reputation, or titles; also referred to as one of Maslow's Hierarchy of Needs.

Ethnicity The fact or state of belonging to a social group that has a common national or cultural tradition.

Ethics Our standards of conduct or behavior.

Eustress Good stress or short-term stress that strengthens individuals for immediate physical activity, creativity, and enthusiasm.

Exhaustion Stage In a three-stage reaction to stress, the stage in which continuous stress will not enable the important resistance step to take place, and an individual will go from step one, alarm, directly to step three, exhaustion.

Expectations The perceived possibilities of achieving a goal.

Explanatory Style The story you construct about why things happen.

Exposure Effect A phenomenon that states the more we are exposed to novel stimuli, a new person, or a new product, our liking for such stimuli increases.

External Locus of Control A characteristic of individuals who see their lives as being beyond their control; they believe what happens to them is determined by external forces—whether it be luck or fate, or other people.

External Noise includes such elements in the physical environment as temperature, a show on television, music on a stereo, loud traffic, or any other external event or distracting influences.

Extraversion One of the "big five" dimensions of personality: ranges from sociable, talkative, fun-loving at one end to sober, reserved, cautious at the other.

Extraversion (E) or Introversion (I) A preference on the MBTI covering how you get energized as a person.

Facilitative Emotions Emotions that contribute to effective functioning.

Fatuous Love Commitment and passion, but no intimacy.

Fear The feeling associated with expectancies of unpleasantness.

Feedback The process by which the sender clarifies how his or her message is being received and interpreted.

Feminism The advocacy of women's rights on the basis of the equality of the sexes.

First Impressions One of the factors that seems to influence our social perceptions. (See Social Perceptions.)

Flow (living in a state of) Being totally absorbed in an activity, whether at work or play, with a sense of mastery, and the use of all or most of one's skills.

Forgiveness A healing process involving six stages, whereby painful past experiences are put into perspective and one gets on with life, unencumbered by excess emotional baggage.

Friend A person attached to another by respect or affection.

"Friends with benefits" relationship is similar to a casual sex relationship, but with one important difference—an established, platonic friendship. Often, "friends with benefits" relationships begin when two friends agree to act on a mutual sexual attraction. Outside of the sexual relationship, the partners behave purely platonically. Usually, a "friends with benefits" relationship ends when one or both partners start to date someone else.

Full Value A value that meets all of the criteria that have been established by Value Clarification theorists.

Gay *(adj.)* Used to describe people (often, but not exclusively, men) whose enduring physical, romantic, and/or emotional attractions are to people of the same sex.

Gay/Lesbian Relationships Same sex relationships.

Gender either of the two sexes (male and female), especially when considered with reference to social and cultural differences rather than biological ones. The term is also used more broadly to denote a range of identities that do not correspond to established ideas of male and female.

Gender *(noun)* A set of social, physical, psychological and emotional traits, often influenced by societal expectations, that classify an individual as feminine, masculine, androgynous, or other. Words and qualities ascribed to these traits vary across cultures.

General Adaptation Syndrome The stages of a chain of reactions to stress.

Gender Violence Violence as a human rights issue; gender-based violence.

Generativity vs. Self-Absorption Erikson's psychosocial crisis at the seventh stage of the human life cycle; conflict between concern for others and concern for self.

Gender dysphoria *(noun)* Clinically significant distress caused when a person's assigned birth gender is not the same as the one with which they identify.

Gender expression *(noun)* External appearance of one's gender identity, usually expressed through behavior, clothing, haircut, or voice, and which may or may not conform to socially defined behaviors and characteristics typically associated with being masculine or feminine.

Gender-fluid *(adj.)* A person who does not identify with a single fixed gender and whose identification and presentation may shift, whether within or outside of the male/female binary.

Gender identity *(noun)* One's innermost feeling of maleness, femaleness, a blend of both, or neither. One's gender identity can be the same or different from their sex assigned at birth.

Gender neutral *(adj.)* Not gendered, usually operating outside the male/female binary. Can refer to language (e.g., pronouns), spaces (e.g., bathrooms), or identities.

Gender nonconforming *(adj.)* A broad term referring to people who do not behave in a way that conforms to the traditional expectations of their gender or whose gender expression does not fit neatly into a category. Also, gender expansive.

Genderqueer *(adj.)* Describes a person who rejects static categories of gender (i.e., the gender binary of male/female) and whose gender expression or identity falls outside of the dominant social norms of their assigned sex. They may identify as having aspects of both male and female identities, or neither.

694

Gender roles *(noun)* The social behaviors and expression that a culture expects from people based on their assigned sex (e.g., girls wear pink; boys don't cry; women care for home and child; men are more violent), despite a spectrum of various other possibilities.

Generation X Born between 1965–1980.

Generation Z The generation born in the late 1990s and early 2000s. Anyone born from 1997 onward is part of a new generation (also called Post Millenials, iGeneration and Homelanders). (Pew Research Center 2019)

Genuineness This means being honest and open about one's feelings, needs, and ideas—being what one really is without front or facade. A person who is true, unaffected, open, honest, and forthright is authentic.

Goal An aim or purpose—a plan or something that you are trying to do or achieve.

Goal efficacy Refers to how likely an individual is to succeed in achieving their goal.

Good Grief The process of working through the stages of grief so that it becomes a positive growth experience.

Gratitude Expressing thanks may be one of the simplest ways to feel better.

Grief and Bereavement To be deprived of someone or something very important; sometimes referred to as mourning.

Grief Work The process of freeing ourselves emotionally from the deceased and readjusting to life without that person.

Grit Is defined as mental toughness and courage, also. Grit also ties in with *positive psychology* and in particular, with perseverance. The ability to stick with and pursue a goal over a long period is an important aspect of grit.

Guilt The realization of sorrow over having done something morally, socially, or ethically wrong.

Habit A settled or regular tendency or practice, especially one that is hard to give up. An acquired mode of behavior that has become nearly or completely involuntary.

Happiness A sense that life is good—a state of well-being that outlasts yesterday's moment of elation, today's buoyant mood, or tomorrow's feeling of sadness.

Hardiness A cluster of characteristics that seem to distinguish stress-resistant people from those who are more susceptible to its harmful effects. These characteristics are commitment, control, and challenge.

Hate May be thought of as intense anger felt toward a specific person or persons.

Heteronormativity *(noun)* Coined by social critic Michael Warner, the term refers to a societal assumption of certain norms: 1) that there are two distinct sexes; 2) that male and female functions and characteristics are distinctly different; and 3) that traits such as attraction and sexual behavior correspond to anatomy. Those who do not fit these norms—be it through same-sex attraction, a non-binary gender identity or nontraditional gender expression—are therefore seen as abnormal, and often marginalized or pressured to conform to norms as a result.

Heterosexism *(noun)* The assumption that sexuality between people of different sexes is normal, standard, superior or universal while other sexual orientations are substandard, inferior, abnormal, marginal, or invalid.

Heterosexual *(adj.)* Used to describe people whose enduring physical, romantic and/or emotional attraction is to people of the opposite sex. Also straight.

Heterosexual/cisgender privilege *(noun)* Refers to societal advantages that heterosexual people and cisgender people have solely because of their dominant identities. This can include things as simple as safely holding hands with a romantic partner in public or having safe access to public bathrooms. This can also include systemic privileges such as the right to legally donate blood, to adopt children without facing possible rejection because of your sexual orientation, or to play organized sports with others of the same gender identity.

Hearing The physiological sensory process by which auditory sensations are received by the ears and transmitted by the brain.

Hidden Agenda Entering a conversation or situation with a special interest in mind, a grudge that we are wanting to bring into the open, or even a "chip on our shoulder."

Hidden Area of Johari Window Information and personal feelings that you keep hidden from others.

High-Context Culture Those cultures that value self-restraint, avoid confrontation, rely heavily on nonverbal systems, and give a great deal of meaning to the relationships between communicators. Examples are the Japanese, Chinese, Asian, and Latin American cultures.

Homophobic The fear of hatred of homosexual people or people who do not meet society's gender role expectations.

Homosexuality 1: sexual attraction or the tendency to direct sexual desire toward another of the same sex; 2: sexual activity with another of the same sex.

Homophobia* *(noun)* A fear or hostility toward lesbian, gay and/or bisexual people, often expressed as discrimination, harassment, and violence.

Honeymoon Period Any time from the wedding day to a year or so from that day.

Hostility A mild form of anger/hate directed to a specific person or group.

Human Relations The art of developing relationships that improve personal skills and life effectiveness. The study of Human Relations offers insight to how you fit into the world and feel about race, class and gender issues. Human relations can be defined as the art of developing relationships that improve personal skills and life effectiveness. It offers insight into how you fit into the world and feel about race, class, and gender issues. Basically, you have to understand yourself before you can understand others effectively, and "become aware" of how you fit into the world.

Hyperstress An overload that occurs when stressful events pile up and stretch the limits of a person's adaptability.

Hypostress An overload that occurs when a person is bored, lacking stimulation, or unchallenged.

"I" Message An I-message or I-statement is an assertion about the feelings, beliefs, values etc. of the person speaking, generally expressed as a sentence beginning with the word "I", and is contrasted with a "you-message" or "you-statement," which often begins with the word "you" and focuses on the person spoken to, or a message that describes the speaker's position without evaluating others.

Id The part of the personality composed of the basic biological drives that motivate an individual.

Identity vs. Role Confusion Erikson's psychosocial crisis at the fifth stage of the human life cycle, in which the 12- to 18-year-old adolescent must integrate his experiences to develop a sense of ego identity.

Ignoring while Listening One of the four levels of general listening, better known as not really listening at all.

Immune System The body's defense and surveillance network of cells and chemicals that fight off bacteria, viruses, and other foreign or toxic substances.

Implicit Bias: Implicit is unquestioning or unreserved; absolute: implied, rather than expressly stated: implicit agreement. **Bias** is a particular tendency, trend, inclination, feeling, or opinion, especially one that is preconceived or unreasoned: unreasonably hostile feelings or opinions about a social group; prejudice: So **implicit bias** would be an unquestioning preconceived or opinion of a social group; prejudice.

Impression management is a conscious or subconscious process in which people attempt to influence the perceptions of other people about a person, object or event.

Inclusion True meaning of valuing diversity is to respect and enjoy a wide range of cultural and individual differences. Appreciating these differences is often referred to as inclusion, to emphasize unity rather than diversity.

Intercultural Communication is a form of communication that aims to share information across different cultures and social groups. It is used to describe the wide range of communication processes and problems that naturally appear within an organization or social context made up of individuals from different religious, social, ethnic, and educational backgrounds.

Individualism Putting personal goals ahead of group goals and defining one's identity in terms of personal attributes rather than group memberships.

Individuation The establishment of one's identity, based on experiences, rather than following parents' dreams.

Industry vs. Inferiority Erikson's psychosocial crisis at the fourth stage of the human life cycle; the 6- to 11-year-old whose curiosity is encouraged develops a sense of industry, as opposed to the child whose curiosity is disparaged and who develops a sense of inferiority.

Infatuation An irrational feeling or passion for someone or something. Passion, but no commitment or intimacy.

Inferiority Complex A concept that underlies and motivates a great deal of human behavior. A striving for superiority is a universal drive to adapt, improve oneself, and master life's challenges.

In-Group—Out-Group Bias Refers to our tendency to perceive people differently depending on whether they are members of our in-group or out-group.

Initial Response Level Every response of the targeted behavior that occurs within a specific period of time prior to conditioning.

Initiative vs. Guilt Erikson's psychosocial crisis at the third stage of the human life cycle; the 4- or 5-year-old either is encouraged to go out on his own or is restricted in his activities.

Integrity This is exhibited when you achieve congruence between what you know, what you say, and what you do.

Integrity vs. Despair Erikson's psychosocial crisis at the eighth stage of the human life cycle; a response that depends on how an old person remembers his life.

Intelligent Risk Taking Intelligent risk-taking, means having a process for making good risk decisions.

Intense Emotions Emotions that are debilitative—they disrupt our overall functioning.

Interactional Possibilities Considering the situation and the possible options before making a response.

Internal Locus of Control The state in which individuals who feel that what happens to them and what they achieve in life is due to their own abilities, attitudes, and actions.

Internal Noise Includes such things as a headache, lack of sleep, daydreaming, preoccupation with other problems, or even a preconceived idea that the message is going to be unimportant or uninteresting.

Internal Psychological Filter A filter through which all information received is processed. This filter consists of prejudices, past experiences, hopes, and anxieties.

Interpersonal communication is the process by which people exchange information, feelings, and meaning through verbal and non-verbal messages: it is face-to-face communication.

Interpersonal Conflict The term used to describe the disagreement between two people in respect to values and attitudes; also a difference that prevents agreement: disagreement between ideas, feelings, etc.

Interpersonal Relations Our interactions with others—how they relate to us and how we relate to them.

Interpretative Response A response in which the receiver tries to tell the sender what his or her problem really is and how the sender really feels about the situation.

Intersex *(adj.)* An umbrella term describing people born with reproductive or sexual anatomy and/or a chromosome pattern that can't be classified as typically male or female.

Intimacy The feeling that one can share all of one's thoughts and actions with another.

Intimacy vs. Isolation Erikson's psychosocial crisis at the sixth stage of the human life cycle; the young adult either is able to relate to others or feels isolated.

Intimate Distance One of Hall's four distance zones, ranging from skin contact to 18 inches.

Intracultural Interactions is a form of communication that aims to share information across different cultures and social groups.

Irrational Beliefs Beliefs that result in inappropriate emotions and behaviors.

Jealousy The state of demanding complete devotion from another person; being suspicious of a rival or of one believed to enjoy an advantage.

Johari Window A model that describes the relationship between self-disclosure and self-awareness.

Judging Response A response that shows that the receiver is making a judgment about the motive, personality, or reasoning of the sender.

Judgment (J) or Perception (P) A preference on the MBTI covering the kind of lifestyle you prefer to live.

Kinesics The science of study of nonverbal communication.

Labeling Assignment to a category, especially inaccurately or restrictively; often based on perception of others and stereotyping.

Latinx *(adj.)* A gender-expansive term for people of Latin American descent used to be more inclusive of all genders than the binary terms Latino or Latina.

Law of Effect Behaviors followed by possible consequences are more likely to be repeated and behaviors followed by negative consequences are less likely to be repeated.

Learned Helplessness The assumption—based on past failures—that one is unable to do anything to improve one's performance or situation and gives up.

Learned Optimism A learned way of explaining both good and bad life events that in turn enhance our perceived control and adaptive responses to them.

Learning A relatively permanent change in behavior as a result of experience or practice.

Lesbian *(adj.)* Used to describe a woman whose enduring physical, romantic, and/or emotional attraction is to other women.

LGBTQ "LGBTQ" is an acronym that originated in the 1990s and replaced what was formerly known as "the gay community." The acronymn was created to be more inclusive of diverse groups. An acronym for "lesbian, gay, bisexual, transgender and queer." Less often, the Q stands for "questioning." Acronyms like LGBTQIA also include the intersex, allied, and asexual communities, while acronyms like LGBTQ attempt to envelop an entire community of people who hold identities that are not cisgender or heterosexual.

Liking A fondness or preference for someone or something. Intimacy, but no commitment or passion.

Listening An intellectual and emotional process that integrates physical, emotional, and intellectual inputs in a search for meaning and understanding.

Listening with the Third Ear Listening to what is said between the lines and without words, what is expressed soundlessly, and what the speaker feels and thinks.

Living Together Loneliness (LTL) The results of a discrepancy between expected and achieved contact.

Loneliness A feeling of longing and emptiness, which is caused by the lack of emotional attachments and/or social ties.

Long-distance relationship occur when partners have a long amount of distance separating them. Due to the lack of physical intimacy caused by the couple's physical separation, some choose to open their relationship while they live far apart. While the "long-distance" part of this relationship type is often temporary, some couples choose to live happily ever apart indefinitely.

Lose-Lose An approach to conflict resolution in which neither party is happy with the outcome.

Lose-Win The result of the accommodating strategy in conflict resolution, with low concern for self and a high concern for others.

Love When the satisfaction, security, and development of another person is as important to you as your own satisfaction, security, and development (Harry Stack Sullivan); also referred to as the desire to see another individual become all they can be as a person—with room to breathe and grow.

Love and Belonging Needs The need to feel loved, included, and accepted; this need usually assumes importance after the safety and survival needs have been met; also referred to as one of Maslow's Hierarchy of Needs.

Low-Context Culture Those cultures that use more explicit language, are more direct in their meanings, rely less on nonverbal systems, and stress goals and outcomes more than relationships. Examples are the German, Swedish, American, and English cultures.

Lust An intense physiological attraction for another person.

Marriage A close union of two people who decide to share their lives, dreams, and goals with each other.

Maslow's Hierarchy of Needs The arrangement of needs in order of basic importance as established by Abraham Maslow: physiological needs, safety needs, belongingness and love needs, esteem needs, and self-actualization needs.

Matching Hypothesis A concept that proposes that people of similar levels of physical attractiveness gravitate toward each other.

Mental Illness Mental illness is a condition that affects a person's thinking, feeling or mood. Such conditions may affect someone's ability to relate to others and function each day. Each person will have different experiences, even people with the same diagnosis. Research suggests multiple, linking causes. Genetics, environment and lifestyle influence whether someone develops a mental health condition. A stressful job or home life makes some people more susceptible, as do traumatic life events like being the victim of a crime. Biochemical processes and circuits and basic brain structure may play a role, too.

Mere-Exposure Effect The more familiar we become with someone or something, the more accepting we will become.

Microaggresssions A subtle, often unintentional form of prejudice Rather than an overt declaration of racism or sexism, a microaggression often takes the shape of an offhanded comment, an inadvertently painful joke, or a pointed insult, offensive comment, or action directed at a minority or other non-dominant group that is often unintentional or unconsciously reinforces a stereotype, such as "I don't see you as Black."

Microexpressions Fleeting facial expressions that last only a fraction of a second.

Mid-Life Crisis Occurring somewhere between the ages of 40 and 45; may be characterized by a painful and disruptive struggle with one's identity and satisfaction of personal needs.

Mid-Life Transition Stage One of Levinson's developmental stages occurring between the ages of 40 and 45; characterized as the period when individuals realize their life is half over and they reevaluate their life and what they want out of the remainder of their life.

Mild Emotions Emotions that are facilitative—they assist us in preparing for the future, solving problems, and in doing what is best for us.

Millennials People born between the early 1980s and 2000.

Mindful Valuing a certain orderliness and sense of there being an appropriate time and place for everything. Mindful people do not value interruptions. They like to concentrate on the job at hand and take time commitments very seriously.

Mindfulness is knowing yourself, to be centered and grounded. It's about increasing self-awareness so you can make better decisions.

Minimal Encourages Brief indicators to the speaker indicating that the receiver is still listening.

Misgender *(verb)* To refer to someone in a way that does not correctly reflect the gender with which they identify, such as refusing to use a person's preferred pronouns or name.

Mixed Emotions Emotions that are combinations of primary emotions. Some mixed emotions can be expressed in single words (such as awe, remorse), whereas others require more than one term (such as, embarrassed and angry, relieved and grateful).

Modeling Imitating a behavior one observes.

Monochronic Cultures Cultures in which time is organized sequentially; schedules and deadlines are valued over people.

Monogamous relationships Those in monogamous relationships only have one sexual/romantic partner at a time.

Moods A general feeling tone.

Morality Includes a set of principles or ideals that help a person distinguish right from wrong and act on this distinction.

Move Against Being aggressive and responding to conflicting situations with the intent to hurt.

Moving Toward Responding to conflicting situations by moving toward your opposition until you are either closer together or on the same side.

Mutual Reward Theory (MRT) States that a relationship between two people is enhanced when there is a satisfactory balance of rewards between them.

Myers-Briggs Type Indicator (MBTI) A questionnaire consisting of 16 basic personality types and four dimensions.

Narcissism The tendency to regard oneself as grandiosely self-important.

Need A condition that exists when we are deprived of something we want or require.

Negative Reinforcement Anything that increases a behavior by virtue of its termination or avoidance.

Neurotic Anxiety Anxiety experienced when the quality of the threatening experience is blown out of proportion to the actual danger posed, and to the point that the anxiety hinders daily functioning.

Neuroticism One of the "big five" dimensions of personality: ranges from calm, secure, and self-satisfied at one end to anxious, insecure, self-pitying at the other.

Neutral Stimulus (NS) Classical conditioning begins with a stimulus that does not elicit a response. The neutral stimulus will eventually become the conditioned stimulus (CS).

Noise Anything that interferes with communication and distorts the impact of the message.

Nonbinary *(adj.)* An umbrella term that refers to individuals who identify as neither man or woman, or as a combination of man or woman. Instead, nonbinary people exhibit a boundless range of identities that can exist beyond a spectrum between male and female.

Nonverbal Communication Messages expressed by other than linguistic means.

Novel Stimuli People, places, or things that are new, different, unique, or original.

Nurturing altruism Doing kind things with the goal of inspiring others to pay it forward.

Obsessive-compulsive Disorder causes repetitive, unwanted, intrusive thoughts (obsessions) and irrational, excessive urges to do certain actions (compulsions).

Observational Learning Learning that occurs when an individual's behavior is influenced by the observation of others—modeling.

One-Way Communication Communication in which a receiver provides no feedback to a sender.

Open Area of Johari Window An area that represents information, feelings, and opinions that you know about yourself and that others know about you.

Open Communicator One who is willing to seek feedback from others and to offer information and personal feelings to others.

Openness Trust and mutual sharing of information and feelings.

Openness Trait One of the "big five" dimensions of personality: ranges from imaginative, sensitive, intellectual, at one end to down-to-earth, insensitive, crude at the other end.

Open Questions Questions that provide space for the speaker to explore his or her thoughts.

Open relationships are a hybrid of monogamous and polyamorous relationships. While an open relationship allows both partners to share physical intimacy with anyone they want, they reserve their emotional intimacy for each other. So each person can have as many sexual partners as they want, but only one romantic partner.

Operant Conditioning Conditioning based on the principle of reinforcement; the consequences of a response determine whether that response will persist.

Operant Level The number of responses prior to conditioning or baseline of behavior prior to conditioning.

Optimism A general tendency to envision the future as favorable.

Optimistic Explanatory Style Using external, unstable, and specific explanations for negative events.

Outing *(verb)* The inappropriate act of publicly declaring (sometimes based on rumor and/or speculation) or revealing another person's sexual orientation or gender identity without that person's consent.

Pansexual *(adj.)* Used to describe people who have the potential for emotional, romantic, or sexual attraction to people of any gender identity, though not necessarily simultaneously, in the same way or to the same degree. The term panromantic may refer to a person who feels these emotional and romantic attractions, but identifies as asexual.

Paralinguistics Nonlinguistic means of vocal expression: tone, rate, pitch, and so on.

Paraphrase Stating the essence of the other person's spoken words in your own words.

Parenthood The role of being a mother or father.

Parroting To repeat exactly the speaker's words.

Partial Lose-Lose The result of the compromising strategy in conflict resolution, where nobody gets all that he or she wants, but everyone gets something.

Parts of a Communication Transaction Six steps commonly referred to as the idea, encoding, transmission, receiving, decoding, and understanding.

Passion An intense physiological desire for another person.

Passive Avoiding or removing yourself from the conflicting situation by leaving, shutting up, placating, concealing your feelings, or postponing a confrontation until a better time.

Passive-aggressive or covert bullying is a less frequently mentioned form of bullying, but in some ways it's the most insidious. A passive-aggressive or covert bully behaves appropriately on the surface, but takes you down with subtlety and the attention economy of the Internet has been a good thing for passive-aggressive trolls, and people that hide behind the Internet.

Passive/Aggressive Being marked by, or displaying, behavior characterized by the expression of negative feelings, resentment, and aggression in an unassertive passive way, such as through procrastination and stubbornness.

Passive Listening Not listening actively; pretending to listen "to be nice." See One-Way Communication

People Perception The study of how we form impressions of others.

Perceptual Awareness Process The means by which we interpret or misinterpret the world around us.

Personal Distance One of Hall's four distance zones, ranging from 18 inches to 4 feet.

Personality Ethic A style of living based on having the right image and doing the right things, defined by the right kind of special techniques and a positive mental attitude.

Personal Self-Image The part of the self that includes physical, behavioral, and psychological characteristics that establish uniqueness.

Pessimism A general tendency to envision the future as unfavorable.

Pessimistic Explanatory Style Using internal, stable, and global explanations for negative events.

Phubbing A word for phone snubbing.

Physical Attractiveness Our perception of the beauty of another person.

Physiological Needs Our most basic and fundamental needs, such as food, water, sleep, clean air to breathe, exercise, and sex; also called our primary or survival needs; also referred to as one of Maslow's Hierarchy of Needs.

Pillow Method A technique used to gain empathy and understanding of another's position and frame of reference when disagreements exist.

Platonic Relationship Of, relating to, or having a close relationship in which there is no romance or sex.

Polyamorous relationships A polymorous relationship has more than one romantic relationship at a time. Often, polyamorous couples have a primary partner, a secondary partner, etc. with the understanding that these "rankings" can change as their individual needs do. Others treat every simultaneous relationship they are engaging in as perfectly equal.

Polychronic Cultures Cultures in which time is organized, cyclical; people tend to do several things at once and value relationships over schedules. People are their main concern (particularly those closely related to them or their function) and they have a tendency to build lifetime relationships.

Positive Reinforcement Anything that increases a behavior by virtue of its presentation.

Pot of Self-Worth Virginia Satir's view of how much self-worth we have at any given time; the amount in the pot is constantly changing based on the different experiences we have, as well as the feedback we get from others.

Prejudging When we prejudge a person or group of people prior to having all known information and facts. Also thought to be unreasonable feelings, opinions, or attitudes, especially of a hostile nature, regarding an ethnic, racial, social, or religious group.

Prejudice A preconceived opinion, feeling, or attitude, either positive or negative, which is formed without adequate information.

Preferred pronouns *(adj.)* The pronoun or set of pronouns that an individual personally uses and would like others to use when talking to or about that individual. Can include variations of he/him/his, she/her/hers, they/their/theirs, among others. This term is being used less and less in LGBTQ circles, as it suggests one's gender identity is a "preference" rather than innate. *Recommended replacement: "Your pronouns, my pronouns, their pronouns, etc."*

Preparation Anxiety Anxiety that helps individuals get energized to deliver their best, such as mild tension before going for a job interview.

Pretending while Listening One of the four levels of normal listening. Some examples are "Yeah. Uh-huh. Right."

Primacy Effect Occurs when the first impression carries more weight than subsequent information.

Primary Emotions Basic emotions identified by R. Pluchick as joy, acceptance, fear, surprise, sadness, disgust, anger, and anticipation; identified by Gary Emery and James Campbell as mad, sad, glad, and scared.

Primary Groups Primary groups come together for expressive reasons - to provide emotional support, love, companionship, and security. It is through these groups that one begins to develop the sense of self.

Primary Reinforcers Reinforcers to which we respond automatically, without learning (food, drink, heat, cold, pain, physical comfort or discomfort).

Privilege Societal privilege that in some countries benefits some people over another people, particularly if they are otherwise under the same social, political, or economic circumstances. A right or benefit that is given to some people and not to others. A special opportunity to do something that makes you proud. The advantage that wealthy and powerful people have over other people in a society. (Gender & Equity Center OU 2017)

Prizing Cherishing and being happy with the choice (value), as well as being willing to affirm the choice (value) publicly.

Projection A defense mechanism used when an individual attributes their own feelings, shortcomings, or unacceptable impulses to others.

Proximity Geographical nearness, location.

Psychological Reactance The tendency to protect or restore one's sense of freedom or social control, often by doing the opposite of what has been demanded.

PTSD A severe anxiety disorder characterized by symptoms of intense fear and avoidance behavior, resulting from an unusually distressing event.

Public Distance One of Hall's four distance zones, ranging outward from 12 feet.

Public self/Private self So much information about individuals is currently public on social media that some think they have no private self; the experience of true solitude or a sense of privacy because of the popularity of social media.

Punishment Anything that decreases a behavior by virtue of its presentation.

Queer *(adj.)* Once a pejorative term, a term reclaimed and used by some within academic circles and the LGBTQ community to describe sexual orientations and gender identities that are not exclusively heterosexual or cisgender.

Questioning *(adj.)* A term used to describe people who are in the process of exploring their sexual orientation or gender identity.

Questioning Response A response that indicates that the receiver wants to probe the sender for additional information and to discuss the issue further.

Race—(human category) Is a grouping of humans based on shared physical or social qualities into categories generally viewed as distinct by society. Modern scholarship regards race as a *social construct*, an *identity* which is assigned based on rules made by society. While partially based on physical similarities within groups, race is not an inherent physical or biological quality.

Racism Prejudice, discrimination, or antagonism directed against someone of a different race based on the belief that one's own race is superior. **Racism** as "individual- and group-level processes and structures that are implicated in the reproduction of racial inequality." **Systemic racism** happens when these structures or processes are carried out by groups with power, such as governments, businesses or schools (*Sociology of Racism,* Clair & Denis).

Rage Uncontrolled, intense anger; implies that the anger is expressed through violent physical activity.

Rational Beliefs Beliefs that result in appropriate emotions and behaviors.

Rationalization A defense mechanism consisting of reasonable, rational, and convincing explanations, but not real reasons.

Reacting to Others A situation in which the emotional, feeling, and irrational characteristics of a person are communicated.

Reaction Formation A defense mechanism in which impulses are not only repressed, they are also controlled by emphasizing the opposite behavior.

Real Self The person you really are, not who you think you are; a situation in which the belief system is accurate, rather than distorted.

Reciprocal Determinism The interacting influences between, person, behavior, and environment.

Reciprocity The tendency to like individuals who tend to like us.

Recovery 1. The regaining of or possibility of regaining something lost or taken away. 2. Restoration or return to health from sickness. 3. Restoration or return to any former and better state or condition.

Regression A defense used when we psychologically retreat to a form of behavior characteristic of an earlier stage of development.

Reinforcement The effect of applying reinforcers.

Reinforcers Pleasant or unpleasant stimuli that strengthen behavior.

Remarriage Marrying for the second, third, or subsequent time.

Repression A defense mechanism consisting of the exclusion of painful, unwanted, or dangerous thoughts and impulses from the conscious mind.

Repulsion Hypothesis People are initially spontaneously repulsed by strangers who are very dissimilar to themselves.

Resentment Chronic anger resulting from unresolved anger at an injustice.

Resistance Stage The period of recovery and stabilization, during which the individual adapts to the stress.

Responding Reflectively Paraphrasing the essence of the speaker's content and mirroring back to the speaker the emotions which he/she is communicating.

Responding to Others A situation in which the rational, thinking, logical part of a person is communicated.

Risk To reach for something you are not entirely sure of but believe is better than what you now have, or is at least necessary to survive (David Viscott).

Role Confusion An uncertainty experienced by individuals during the ages of 12 and 18 about who they are and where they are going.

Role Expectations Beliefs about a man and woman's roles in marriage.

Romantic Love A form of love that includes intimacy and passion, but no commitment.

Romeo and Juliet Effect Same as psychology reactance—when love is intensified, not weakened, by their families' opposition.

Safety and Security Needs The need to protect oneself from danger and to keep safe from harm; on a psychological level, safety needs might relate to safety and security, such as finding and keeping a job; also referred to as one of Maslow's Hierarchy of Needs.

Search for Meaning Viktor Frankl's idea that our task in life is to create a life that has meaning and purpose.

Secondary Reinforcers Stimuli to which we have attached positive or negative value through association with previously learned conditioned reinforcers.

Selective Listening One of the four levels of normal listening, known as hearing only certain parts of the conversation.

Self-Actualization The fulfillment of one's own completely unique potential.

Self-Actualization Needs The need for self-fulfillment; the need to become all that one is capable of becoming; also referred to as one of Maslow's Hierarchy of Needs.

Self-Awareness The capability to reflect and decide and become aware of our responsibility for choosing the way we live and thus influence our own destiny.

Self-Change Program A five-step program to self-change.

Self-Control A person's sense of their ability to control their own behavior.

Self-Disclosure The process of deliberately revealing information about oneself that is significant and that would not normally be known by others.

Self-Discovery The process of getting to know yourself as a person—the person within yourself.

Self-Efficacy Our belief about our ability to perform behaviors that should lead to expected outcomes.

Self-Esteem An overall evaluation of oneself, whether one likes or dislikes who one is, believes in or doubts oneself, and values or belittles one's worth.

Self-Evaluation How you compare yourself with others.

Self-Fulfilling Prophecy A prediction or expectation of an event that makes the outcome more likely to occur than would otherwise have been the case.

Self-Image A mental blueprint of how we see ourselves and how we feel about ourselves.

Self-Perception How you evaluate your "self"—physically and psychologically.

Self-Serving Bias A person's tendency to evaluate their own behavior as worthwhile, regardless of the situation.

Self-Talk A person's beliefs or what they say to themselves.

Self-Theory Carl Rogers' theory, defining the development of the self in terms of self-actualization.

Self-Validation Disclosing information with hopes of obtaining the other person's approval.

Self-Worth Virginia Satir's idea that our individual worth is our perception of what happens between people and inside people.

Semantics The study of the meaning and changes of meaning in words.

Same-gender loving *(adj.)* A term coined in the early 1990s by activist Cleo Manago, this term was and is used by some members of the Black community who feel that terms like gay, lesbian, and bisexual (and sometimes the communities therein) are Eurocentric and fail to affirm Black culture, history, and identity.

Sensing (S) or Intuition (N) A preference on the MBTI covering what you pay attention to when you gather information.

Sex Roles People are born male or female but are taught how to be masculine or feminine also called sex-role stereotyping.

Sexism Prejudice, stereotyping, or discrimination, typically against women, on the basis of sex. synonyms:sexual discrimination, chauvinism, gender prejudice, gender bias.

Sexting Sending, receiving, or forwarding sexually explicit messages, photographs, or images, primarily between mobile phones, of oneself to others is considered sexting. It may also include the use of a computer or any digital device.

Sexual orientation *(noun)* An inherent or immutable emotional, romantic or sexual attraction to other people; oftentimes used to signify the gender identity (or identities) to which a person is most attracted.

Shame A painful emotion caused by consciousness of guilt, shortcomings, or impropriety.

Shyness The feelings, physical reactions, and thoughts that create a state of anxiety, discomfort, and inhibition.

Significant Others The important people in our lives.

Significant Stimuli Anything directly related to another person's needs, wants, interests, and desires.

Similarities The process of selecting friends because of comparable interests, income level, educational beliefs, and so on.

Singlehood The decision not to marry.

Situational Shyness Specific environmental circumstances that develop feelings, physical reactions, and thoughts that create a state of anxiety, discomfort, and inhibition.

Social categories Classifying people into social groups often based on characteristics such as race, ethnicity, class, and gender.

Social Comparison How a person evaluates themself in relation to others.

Social Control Revealing personal information may increase your control over other people and sometimes over the situation. Social control, within sociology, refers to the many ways in which our behavior, thoughts, and appearance are regulated by the norms, rules, laws, and social structures of society. Social control is a necessary component of social order, for society could not exist without it.

Social Dominance The social dynamics of school bullying: the necessary dialogue between the blind man and the elephant social dominance theory.

Social Distance One of Hall's four distance zones, ranging from 4 to 12 feet.

Social Emotional Learning Social Emotional Learning (SEL) is composed of the skills we use to recognize and manage our own emotions and being able to recognize emotions in others. This concept arose out of research about "emotional intelligence. Methods for improving SEL emphasize learning personal and social skills and setting personal goals.

Social Exchange Theory We measure our actions and relationships on a cost-benefit basis. People maximize their rewards and minimize their costs by employing their resources to gain the most favorable outcome.

Social Justice Justice in terms of the distribution of wealth, opportunities, and privileges within a society.

Social Learning Theory The theory that suggests that personality development occurs through observational learning.

Social Networking The development of social and professional contacts; the sharing of information and services among people with a common interest. Using digital technology for networking; the use of websites or other online technologies to communicate with people and share information, resources, etc.: "I found my current job through social networking."

Social Perception The way we perceive, evaluate, categorize, and form judgments about the qualities of people we encounter.

Social Ties The feeling that we are part of a group or have an identity.

Spranger's Six Value Systems Relates to six different types of people based on their types of value systems, or their frameworks for developing their own beliefs.

Stages of Psychosocial Development Eight stages of Erikson's human life cycle; the stages are trust vs. mistrust, autonomy vs. doubt, initiative vs. guilt, industry vs. inferiority, identity vs. role confusion, intimacy vs. isolation, generativity vs. self-absorption, and integrity vs. despair.

Stepfamilies Remarriages involving children from one or both spouses.

Stereotyping A process of making generalizations by categorizing an object, person, or situation—a widely held but fixed and oversimplified image or idea of a particular type of person or thing.

Stigma A mark of disgrace or infamy; a stain or reproach, as on one's reputation.

Stonewalling When one partner wants to discuss troubling issues in the relationship, sometimes people defensively stonewall, or refuse to talk or listen to their partner.

Strengths-Based Psychology Focusing more on what's right with people rather than focusing more on people's shortcomings.

Stress The nonspecific response of the body to any demand placed on it, whether that demand be real, imagined, pleasant, or unpleasant.

Stressor A stressful event.

Sublimation A defense whereby an individual redirects their basic desires toward a socially-valued activity.

Success The outcome of setting a goal and achieving that goal, whatever that goal may be; accomplishing an aim or purpose.

Subjective well-being (SWB) is perhaps the most important concept in Positive Psychology. Simply put, subjective well-being is defined as your evaluations of a) your own life, and b) your moods and emotions—hence the label "subjective." This refers to how people experience the quality of their lives and includes both emotional reactions and cognitive judgments. Subjective well-being consists of a person's cognitive and affective evaluations of their life.

Superego The part of the personality that consists of our values, morals, religious beliefs, and ideals of our parents and society; sometimes referred to as our conscience.

Supportive Response A response that shows the receiver's intent is to reassure, comfort, or minimize the intense feelings of the sender.

Suppression A defense mechanism in which people are conscious of their emotions, but deliberately control rather than express them.

Survivors guilt Is a mental condition that occurs when a person believes they have done something wrong by surviving a traumatic event when others did not, often feeling self-guilt.

Symbols in Communication Such things as the selection of words, tone and pitch of voice, nonverbal method, or even types of supportive materials.

Sympathy An involuntary feeling—the passive experience of sharing another person's fear, grief, anger or joy.

Target Behavior The goal you have set for yourself—your behavioral goal.

Technoference Technology Interfering with life.

The Aesthetic Person Beauty, form, and harmony are most important to this type of individual.

The Economic Person Personal needs, production, marketing, credit, and wealth are more important to this type of person than are social or artistic values.

The Political Animal This type of person is very power motivated, with values centered on influence, fame, and power.

The Religious Person To this individual, the highest value is unity; he or she tries to understand the universe as a whole and relates to it meaningfully.

The Social Person This person values and loves other people, with kindness and unselfishness as very important values.

The Theoretical Person This individual seeks to discover truth and observes happenings and thinks them through, trying whenever possible to put ideas into a system.

Thinking (T) or Feeling (F) A preference on the MBTI covering how you make decisions.

Third Gender 1. A gender classification in societies that recognize a gender other than male or female. 2. A person who identifies as a gender other than male or female or as neither male nor female.

Thought Stopping Concentrating on the unwanted thoughts and, after a short time, suddenly stopping and emptying the mind of all stressful thoughts.

Time Waster Anything preventing you from achieving your objectives most effectively.

Tolerance is a fair, objective, and permissive attitude toward those whose opinions, beliefs, practices, racial or ethnic origins, etc., differ from one's own; freedom from bigotry **Tolerance** is also defined as sympathy or indulgence for beliefs or practices differing from or conflicting with one's own (2019 Merriam Webster Dictionary).

Toxic positivity Having an unhelpful cheerful attitude ialso called "dismissive positivity."

Toxic relationship A relationship that is a relationship characterized by behaviors on the part of the toxic partner that are emotionally and, not infrequently, physically damaging to their partner. A toxic relationship is characterized by insecurity, self-centeredness, dominance, control, and drama.

Trait A relatively stable and consistent personal characteristic.

Transgender Being a person whose gender identity differs from the sex the person was identified as having at birth.

Transsexual *(adj.)* A less frequently used term (considered by some to be outdated or offensive) which refers to people who use medical interventions such as hormone therapy, gender-affirming surgery (GAS) or sex reassignment surgery (SRS) as part of the process of expressing their gender. Some people who identify as transsexual do not identify as transgender and vice versa. *Only use this term if someone who specifically identifies as such asks you to.*

Transphobia The fear or hatred of transgender people or people who do not meet society's gender role expectations. Transphobia is closely linked to homophobia and biphobia.

Transitioning *(verb)* A process during which some people strive to more closely align their gender identity with their gender expression. This includes *socially transitioning*, during which a person may change their pronouns, the name they ask to be called, or the way they dress to be socially recognized as another gender. This includes *legal transitioning*, which may involve official name change and modified IDs and birth certificates. And this includes *physically transitioning*, during which a person may undergo medical interventions to more closely align their body to their gender identity. Transgender and nonbinary people transition in various ways to various degrees; self-identification alone is enough to validate gender identity.

Troll In internet slang, a troll is a person who starts quarrels or upsets people on the internet to distract and sow discord by posting inflammatory and digressive, extraneous, or off-topic messages in an online community (such as a newsgroup, forum, chat room, or blog) with the intent of provoking readers into displaying emotional responses and normalizing tangential discussion, whether for the troll's amusement or a specific gain.

Trust vs. Mistrust Erikson's psychosocial crisis at the first stage of the human life cycle; the subsequent response of a person to the way he is treated as an infant.

Two Spirit *(adj.)* An umbrella term in Native culture to describe people who have both a male and female spirit within them. This encompasses many tribe-specific names, roles and traditions, such as the *winkte* of the Lakota and *nadleeh* of the Navajo people. This term often describes Native people who performed roles and gender expression associated with both men and women. This term should be used only in the context of Native culture.

Two-Way Communication An exchange of information in which the receiver deliberately provides feedback to a sender.

Type A Behavioral Pattern A behavioral pattern characterizing individuals who live a competitive, aggressive, ambitious, and stressful lifestyle.

Type B Behavioral Pattern A behavioral pattern characterizing individuals who live a more relaxed and less hurried lifestyle.

Unconditional Positive Regard The situation in which love is given freely and does not depend on any specific aspects of behavior.

Unconditioned Response (UCR) An unlearned reaction to an unconditioned stimulus that occurs without previous conditioning.

Unconditioned Stimulus (UCS) A stimulus that evokes an unconditioned response without previous conditioning.

Understanding Response This response indicates that the receiver is seeking to fully understand what the sender is actually saying. This is the most effective way of responding to others and requires the skills of active listening, sometimes referred to as empathetic listening. (See active listening and empathetic listening.)

Unknown Area of Johari Window Information about you that is unknown to self or others.

Value The personal worth placed on an object, thought, or idea.

Value Indicators Partial values, such as desires, thoughts not acted on, opinions, interests, aspirations, goals, and so on, which are in the process of being formed.

Value System The personal blueprint or guidelines for one's life, based upon one's values. Values are extensions of ourselves. They are what define us.

Values Clarification A process that helps people distinguish between full values and partial values.

Verbal Communication The expression of words; language.

Wellness- the quality or state of being healthy in body and mind, especially as the result of deliberate effort.

Well-being theory well-being is a construct; and well-being, not happiness, is the topic of positive psychology. Well-being has five measurable elements (PERMA) that count toward it: Positive emotion (Of which happiness and life satisfaction are all aspects), Engagement, Relationships, Meaning and purpose, and Accomplishment. No one element defines well-being, but each contributes to it. Some aspects of these five elements are measured subjectively by self-report, but other aspects are measured objectively.

Win-Lose An approach to conflict resolution in which one person gets his or her way, and the other does not.

Win-Win An approach to conflict resolution in which conflicts are resolved with no one winning and no one losing. Both win because the solution must be acceptable to both.

"You" Messages Messages creating a feeling of blame and accusation.
Many words have been defined by https://www.dictionary.com/browse/online-dictionary or the Random House Unabridged Dictionary, © Random House, Inc. 2019.

*University of California-Davis's LGBTQIA Resource Center offers this note on words like this: We've been intentionally moving away from using words like "transphobic," "homophobic," and "biphobic" because (1) they **inaccurately describe systems of oppression** as irrational fears and (2) for some people, phobias are a very distressing part of their lived experience and co-opting this language is disrespectful to their experiences and perpetuates ableism.

Words to avoid
Homosexual (n.); homosexual (adj.)
Sexual preference
Tranny/transvestite

Preferred terms
Gay man/person (n.); gay (adj.)
Sexual orientation
Transgender person or trans person (if they so identify)

Definition sources
Note: Not all definitions are used word-for-word, but were inspired by meanings
     provided by the following sources.
PFLAG National Glossary of Terms
Human Rights Campaign Glossary of Terms
University of California Davis, LGBTQIA Resource Center Glossary
Glossary of Terms, from the GLAAD Media Reference Guide
Asexuality.org
The Trevor Project Glossary
Lambda Legal, Glossary of LGBTQ
Oxford English Dictionary
UC Davis
International Encyclopedia of the Social Sciences
Tony Enos, "8 Things You Should Know About Two Spirit People," Indian Country
     Today. 2017
Teaching Tolerance Newsletter

References

CHAPTER 1

Aberson, C., Healy, M., & Romero, V. (2000) Ingroup bias and self-esteem: A meta-analysis. *Personality and Social Psychology Review,* 4, (2): 157-173.

Adler, R., & Proctor, R. (2016). *Looking Out Looking In*. Boston, MA: Wadsworth (2016) Cengage Learning.

Allan, G. (2008). Flexibility, friendship, and family. *Personal Relationships*, 15, 1–16. doi: 10.1111/j.1475-6811.2007.00181.x

Antony, Martin PhD, Swinson, Richard MD(2017) The Shyness and Social Anxiety Workbook: (3rd edition)New Harbinger Publications Inc. Oakland,CA

Aonson, E., Wilson, T., & Akert, R. (2018). *Social Psychology*. Upper Saddle River, NJ: Pearson Education, Inc.

Au, Sara(June 11, 2019) Four Boundaries Children Need to Understand. *Psychology Today.*

Asatryan, K. (2016). *Stop Being Lonely: Three Simple Steps to Developing Close Friendships and Deep Relationships.* Novato, CA: New World Publishing

Baron, R., Branscombe, N. (2017). *Social Psychology*. New York: Pearson Publishing.

Baumgarte, R. (2002). Cross-gender friendship: The troublesome relationship. In R. Goodwin & D.Cramer (Eds.). *Inappropriate Relationships* (pp.103-124). Mawah, NJ: Lawrence Erlbaum Associates.

Bernardo Carducci, HarperCollins e-books; Reprint edition (October 13, 2009) *Shyness: Understanding, Hope, and Healing.*

Berscheid, E. (2010). Attraction. In A. Kazdin (Ed.), *Encyclopedia of Psychology*. Washington, DC and New York: Wiley Publishing.

Berscheid, E., & Reis, H.T. (2010). Attraction and close relationships. In D.T. Gilbert, T. Fiske, & G. Lindsey (Eds.), *The Handbook of Social Psychology* (4th ed.), vol. 2. Boston, MA: McGraw Hill, 193–281.

Bolton, E. (2014). AAUW: What we can do to combat stereotypes and bias. http://www.aauw.org/2014/08/13/why-stereotypes-are-bad/

Brown, B. (2010). *The Gifts of Imperfection*: Center City, MN: Hazelden.

Brownell, Kelly et al., eds(2005). *Weight Bias: nature, consequences, and remedies*, Guilford Press.

Brown, Brene (2016) *Dare to Lead*. Random House Publishing

Bryant, J. (2009). *Love Leadership: The New Way To Lead In A Fear-Based World.* San Francisco: Jossey-Bass.

Buscalia, L. (1983). *Living, Loving and Learning:* New York: Ballantine.

Byers, E. S., & Demmons, S. (2010). Sexual satisfaction and sexual self-disclosure within dating relationships. *Journal of Sex Research, 36*, 180-189. doi:10.1080/00224499909551983

Cacioppo, John; Patrick, William, *Loneliness: Human Nature and the Need for Social Connection*, New York: W.W. Norton & Co., 2008.

Carducci, Bernardo (2016) Shyness: The New Solution. *Psychology Today*

Carducci, Bernard (2019) APA Speaking of Psychology//Speaking of Psychology: Born bashful? Learning how to manage shyness. Episode 41

Carducci, B., & Zimbardo, P. (2018). The cost of shyness. *Psychology Today.*

Carducci, B. (2009). *Shyness—Understanding, Hope and Healing.* New York: Harper-Collins.

Carducci, B. (2009) *Shyness: Understanding, Hope and Healing.* Harper Collins ebook.

Casriel, E. (2007). Stepping out. *Psychology Today, 40,* 69–75.

Christakis, N.A. & Fowler, J.H. (2009*). Connected: The surprising power of our social networks and how they shape our lives.* New York, NY: Little, Brown and Company.

Creole, H. (2016). *Overcoming Depression and Loneliness.* Self published.

Davis, E. (2014). *Connected: Curing the Pandemic of Everyone Feeling Alone Together.* Nashville, TN: B&H Publishing.

Davis, Nicola (2018) Loneliness linked to major life setbacks for millennials, study says. *The Guardian.*

DuBrin, A. (2016). *Human Relations for Career and Personal Success.* Upper Saddle River, NJ: Pearson Education, Inc.

Duckworth, A. (2016). *Grit: The Power of Passion and Perseverance.* NY: Scribner.

Duffy, K. (2007/2008). *Annual Editions: Personal Growth and Behavior.* Dubuque, IA: McGraw Hill Contemporary Learning Series.

Duffy, K., & Atwater, E., et al (2013). *Psychology for Living.* Upper Saddle River, NJ: Pearson.

Eastwick, P. W., Eagly, A. H., Finkel, E. J., & Johnson, S. E. (2011). Implicit and explicit preferences for physical attractiveness in a romantic partner: A double dissociation in predictive validity. *Journal of Personality and Social Psychology,* 101(5), 993–1011. doi:10.1037/a0024061

Eastwick, P. W., & Finkel, E. J. (2008). Sex differences in mate preferences revisited: Do people know what they initially desire in a romantic partner? *Journal of Personality and Social Psychology,* 94(2), 245–264. doi:10.1037/0022-3514.94.2.

Fehr, B. (2008). Friendship formation. In S. Sprecher, A. Wenzel, & J. Harvey (Eds.), *Handbook of relationship initiation* (pp. 29–54). New York, NY, US: Psychology Press.

Fiske, Susan (2012) Envy Up, Scorn Down: How Status Divides Us. Russell Sage Foundation

Fisk S., Cuddy, A., Glick, P., & Xu, J. (2002). A model of (often mixed) stereotype content: competence and warmth respectively follow from perceived status and competition. *Journal of Personality and Social Psychology,* 82 (6), 878–902.

Fiske, S. (2018). *Social Beings* (4th ed.). New York: Wiley.

Fiske, S. (2012). Social structures and neural maps of inter-group processes. *British Journal of Social Psychology,* 70, 491–512.

Fiske, S. T., Lin, M., & Neuberg, S. (2018). The continuum model: Ten years later. In *Social Cognition: Selected Works of Susan Fiske* (pp. 41-75). Taylor and Francis. https://doi.org/10.4324/9781315187280

Flora, C. (2004). Snap judgments. *Psychology Today,* May/June, 60–66.

Fugère, M. A., Cousins, A. J., & MacLaren, S. (2015). (Mis)matching in physical attractiveness and women's resistance to mate guarding. *Personality and Individual Differences*, 87, 190–195.

Fuerdi, F. (2015) How the Internet and social media are changing culture. The Aspen Institute

Fugere, M. (2017) Why Physical Attraction Matters, and When It Might Not- Research into why our actions don't match our words when it's time to pair up. *Psychology Today,* January Online

Gale, T. (2007). *Prejudice in the Modern World Reference Library.* Detroit, MI: UXL.

Garis, Mary G.(2019). A psychologist's satisfying take on why you should lean into your bad moods, MSN lifestyle MSN.com

Giddens, A. (2013). *Sociology.* Cambridge, UK: Polity Press.Gosling, S. (2016). Mixed signals. *Psychology Today*, 42, 61–71.

Gilligan,Carol (2016) *In a Different Voice: Psychological Theory and Women's Development.* Harvard University Press.

Griffin, A. M., & Langlois, J. H. (2006). Stereotype directionality and attractiveness stereotyping: Is beauty good or is ugly bad? *Social Cognition*, 24(2), 187–206. doi:10.1521/soco.2006.24.2.187

Gudino, O., & Lau, A. (2010). Parental cultural orientation, shyness, and anxiety in Hispanic children: An exploratory study. *Journal of Applied Developmental Psychology* 31, 3: 202-210.

Gudykunst, W., & Ting-Toomey, S. (1991). *Culture and Interpersonal Communication.* Newbury Park, CA: Sage.

Hafen, B.Q., Karren, K.J., Frandsen, K.J., & Smith, N.L. (2005). *Mind/Body Health.* Boston, MA: Allyn & Bacon.

Hanna, S., Suggett, R., & Radke, D. (2008). *Person to Person–Positive Relationships Don't Just Happen.* Upper Saddle River, NJ: Pearson.

Henderson, G., & Long, W. (2016). *Introduction to Human Relations Studies.* Springfield, IL: Charles Thomas Publisher LTD.

Henderson, Lynne & Zimbardo, Phil. (2010). Shyness, Social Anxiety, and Social Anxiety Disorder. *Social Anxiety*. 65–92. 10.1016/B978-0-12-375096-9.00003-1.

Hewstone, M., Rubin, M., & Willis, N. (2002). Intergroup bias. *Annual Review of Psychology*, 53, 575–604.

Huong, B. T. (2010). 'Let's talk about sex, baby': Sexual communication in marriage in contemporary Vietnam. *Culture, Health & Sexuality, 12*, S19-S29. doi:10.1080/13691050903072025

Hutson, M. (2009). Best face forward. *Psychology Today*, 42, 20.

Hutson, M. (2016). Relationships: Best face forward. *Psychology Today*, 42, 20.

Karbo, K. (2016). Friendship: The laws of attraction. *Psychology Today,* 39, 91–95.

Kansas Health Foundation, (2019). Community Toolbox. University of Kansas: https://ctb.ku.edu/en retrieved 1/11/2020

Kazden, A. (2000). Editor in Chief. Encyclopedia of Psychology, APA Reference Books Collection

Kilmartin, C. (2015). *The Masculine Self.* Cornwall-on-Hudson, NY: Sloan Publishing.

Kleiman, E. and Liu, R. (2013). Social support as a protective factor in suicide: Findings from two nationally representative samples. *Journal of Affective Disorders*, 150(2), 540–545.

Kleman, E. (2008). *Journaling for the world to see: A proposed model of self disclosure intimacy in blogs.* Paper presented at the annual meeting of the National Communication Association, Chicago, IL.

Kraus, L.A., Davis, M.H., Bazzini, D., Church, M., & Kirchman, C.M. (1993). Personal and social influences on loneliness: The mediating effect of social provisions. *Social Psychology Quarterly*, 56, 37–53.

Kruglanski, Arie W.; Higgins, E. Tory; Van Lange, Paul A.M. (2012). *Handbook of theories of social psychology.* Los Angeles: SAGE. pp. 267–288

Kurzban, R., & Weeden, J. (2005). HurryDate: Mate preferences in action. Evolution and Human Behavior, 26(3), 227–244. doi:10.1016/j.evolhumbehav.2004.08.012

Lamberton, L. (2014). *Human Relations—Strategies for Success.* New York: McGraw Hill.

Lamberton, L. & Minor-Evans Leslie, McGraw (2018) *Human Relations* Hull Education; 6 edition

Lanning, Carly (2019) The Vlogging Cure. *Psychology Today*

Leahy, R.L. (2006). *The Worry Cure: Seven Steps to Stop Worry from Stopping You.* New York: Three Rivers Press.

Li, N. P., Valentine, K. A., & Patel, L. (2011). Mate preferences in the US and Singapore: A cross-cultural test of the mate preference priority model. *Personality and Individual Differences*, 50(2), 291-294. doi:10.1016/j.paid.2010.10.005

Lippa, R. A. (2007). The preferred traits of mates in a cross-national study of heterosexual and homosexual men and women: An examination of biological and cultural influences. *Archives of Sexual Behavior*, 36(2), 193–208. doi:10.1007/s10508-006-9151-2

Loehr A. (2016). *Eight Quick Tips for Interpersonal Communication and Relationship Building.* Huffington Post blog US edition: April 12.

Luo, S., & Zhang, G. (2009). What leads to romantic attraction: Similarity, reciprocity, security, or beauty? Evidence from a speed-dating study. *Journal of Personality*, 77(4), 933–964. doi:10.1111/j.1467-6494.2009.00570.x

Lynch, C., & Daniels, V. (2000). *Patterns of Relationships.* https://www.sonoma.edu/users/d/daniels/lynch.html

Markman, A. (2018) Ulterior Motives-Confidence and Certainty From Advisors We like experts who exude confidence.

Markman, A (2018) We like experts who exude confidence. But what does that mean? Posted May 02, 2018 *Psychology Today*

Mitchell, Terence R.; Daniels, Denise (2003). "Motivation". In Walter C. Borman; Daniel R. Ilgen; Richard J. Klimoski (eds.). *Handbook of Psychology* (volume 12). John Wiley & Sons, Inc. p. 229.

Monsour, M. (2002). *Women and Men as Friends.* Mahwah, NJ: Erlbaum.

Montoya, R. (2008). I'm hot, so I'd say you're not: The influence of objective physical attractiveness on mate selection. *Personality and Social Psychology Bulletin*, 34(10), 1315–1331. doi:10.1177/0146167208320387

Myers, D.G. (2015). *Social Psychology.* McGraw Hill Higher Education New York: Worth.

Nelson, S. (2016). *Frientimacy: How to Deepen Friendships for Lifelong Health and Happiness.* Berkeley, CA: Seal Press.

Nevid, J. (2017). *Essentials of Psychology: Concepts and Applications.* New York: Cengage Learning.

National Institutes of Health. (2009). *News in Health Newsletter.*

Nicholaisen, M., Thorsen, K, (2016). What are friends for? Friendships and loneliness over the lifespan—From 18 to 79 years, *International Journal of Aging and Human Development, 84,* 126-158.

Norris, A.R. (2011). Impression management: Considering cultural, social, and spiritual factors. *Inquiries Journal,* 3 (7): 1.

Patrick, W. L. (July 2019) The Most Powerful Non-Physical Trait That Attracts Others. *Psychology Today* online

Pegg, Mike (2018) The Transparent Self pdf. http://www.sidneyjourard.com/

O'Connel, A., & O'Connel, V. & Kuntz, Lois-Ann (2005). *Choice and Change.* Upper Saddle River, NJ: Pearson.

Pelusi, N. (2007). The privacy paradox. *Psychology Today, 40,* 68–69.

Perilloux, C., Fleischman, D. S., & Buss, D. M. (2011). Meet the parents: Parent-offspring convergence and divergence in mate preferences. *Personality and Individual Differences,* 50(2), 253–258. doi:10.1016/j.paid.2010.09.039

Pittman, M.; Reich, B. (2016). "Social media and loneliness: Why an Instagram picture may be worth more than a thousand Twitter words". *Computers in Human Behavior.* 62: 155–167.

Plight, J., & Vliek, M. (2017). The Psychology of Influence: *Theory, research and practice.* Routledge Press.

Plous, S. (2003). *Understanding Prejudice and Discrimination.* New York: McGraw Hill.

Punches, B. (2010). *What You Say and Do Next Matters!* Dubuque, IA: Kendall Hunt Publishing Co.

Reeder G.D. (2013). Attribution as a gateway to social cognition. *Journal of Personality and Social Psychology,* 69.

Reiss, I. L. (2006). *An Insider's View of Sexual Science since Kinsey.* Lanham, MD: Rowman & Littlefield.

Resnick, B (2019) 22 percent of millennials say they have "no friends." Vox.com

Rippon, Gina. (2019) *Gendered Brain: The new neuroscience that shatters the myth of the female brain.* Vintage Publishing, UK.

Roberts, J. (2019) Kids, Sex & Screens: Raising Strong, Resilient Children in the Sexualized Digital Age. *Psychology Today*

Rodgers, J. (2006). Altered ego. *Psychology Today, 39,* 72–75.

Rosen, L. (2011). Is Constant "Facebooking" Bad for Teens? Research presented at the American Psychological Association meeting, Washington DC, August 5, 2011.

Rosen, Larry (2016) *The Distracted Mind: Ancient Brains in a High-Tech World.* MIT Press

Rosenthal, R., & Jacobson, L. (2003). *Pygmalion in the Classroom.* Norwalk, CT: Crown Publishing Co.

Rosling, H & Rosling-Ronnlund, A (2018) *Factfulness: Ten Reasons We're Wrong About the World—and Why Things Are Better Than You Think.* Macmillan Publishers.

Santrock, J. (2006). *Human Adjustment*. New York: McGraw Hill.

Schafer, J. (2015). Self-disclosures increase attraction: Talking about yourself is not always a bad thing. *Psychology Today* blog. https://www.psychologytoday.com/blog/let-their-words-do-the-talking/201503/self-disclosures-increase-attraction

Schultz, W & Oskamp, S (2005) *Attitudes and Opinions*. Psychology Press NY

Shane, Scott (2017) The Fake Americans Russia Created to Influence the Election. *NYTimes* Sept 7.

Sheldon, P. (2008). The relationship between unwillingness to communicate and students' Facebook use. *Journal of Media Psychology, 20*, 67-75.

Sheldon, P. (2013). Examining gender differences in self-disclosure on Facebook versus face-to-face. *The Journal of Social Media in Society* 2(1).

Shenk, J.W. (2009). What makes us happy? *The Atlantic Magazine*, June 1.

Smock, A. D., Ellison, N. B., Lampe, C., & Wohn, D. Y. (2011). Facebook as a toolkit: A uses and gratification approach to unbundling feature use. *Computers in Human Behavior, 27*, 2322-2329.

Stein, M., & Walker, J. (2009). *Triumph over Shyness and Social Anxiety*. New York: Anxiety Disorders Association of America.

Taliaferro, et al. (2009). Association between physical activity and reduced rates of hopelessness, depression and suicidal behavior among college students. *Journal of American College Health*, 57(4), 427–435.

Tenney, E.R., Meikle, N.L., Hunsaker, D., Moore, D.A., & Anderson, C. (2019). Is overconfidence a social liability? The effect of verbal versus nonverbal expressions of confidence. *Journal of Personality and Social Psychology*, 116(3), 396–415

Thao, H., Overbeek, G., & Engels, R. E. (2010). Effects of attractiveness and social status on dating desire in heterosexual adolescents: An experimental study. *Archives of Sexual Behavior*, 39(5), 1063–1071. doi:10.1007/s10508-009-9561-z

Vitelli, R. (2013). Painfully shy: Can shyness lead to problems with depression and anxiety? *Psychology Today*, 12, 23.

Weeden, J., & Sabini, J. (2005). Physical attractiveness and health in Western societies: A review. *Psychological Bulletin*, 131(5), 635–653. doi:10.1037/0033-2909.131.5.635

White, V., & Demarais, A. (2007). *First Impressions: What You Don't Know About How Others See You*. New York: Bantam.

Wills, T. A., & Ainette, M. G. (2012). Social networks and social support. In A. Baum, T.A. Revenson & J. Singer (Eds.), *Handbook of Health Psychology* (2nd ed.). New York, NY: Psychology Press.

Wilson, J. (2008). The conflation of public and private identity: The notion that privacy is a "right" is likely lost on the Millenial. *Psychology Today*, Dec 2008.

Wilson, R. (2007). Loneliness increases risk of dementia. *Bottom Line Personal*, 28, 15.

Winch, G. (2013). Together but still lonely. *Psychology Today*. June 2013

Wiseman, H., Mayseless, O., & Sharabany, R. (2006). Why are they lonely? Perceived equal quality of early relationships with parents, attachment, personality, predispositions and loneliness in first-year university students. *Personality and Individual Differences*, 40, 237–238.

Wood, J.T. (2017). *Communication Mosaics*. Belmont, CA: Wadsworth.

Wood, W., Wood, E., & Boyd, D. (2013). *Mastering the World of Psychology*. New York: Pearson.

Worchel, S., Cooper, J., Goethals, G., & Olson, J. (2000). *Social Psychology*. Belmont, CA: Wadsworth.

Yum, Y., & Hara, K. (2005). Computer-mediated relationship development: A cross-cultural comparison. *Journal of Computer-Mediated Communication, 11*(1). Retrieved from http://jcmc.indiana.edu/vol11/issue1/yum.html.

Zebrowitz, L. A., Wang, R., Bronstad, P., Eisenberg, D., Undurraga, E., Reyes-García, V., & Godoy, R. (2012). First impressions from faces among U.S. and culturally isolated Tsimane' people in the Bolivian rainforest. *Journal of Cross-Cultural Psychology*, 43(1), 119–134. doi:10.1177/0022022111411386

Zimbardo, P. (1990). *Shyness, What It Is, What to Do about It*. Reading, MA: Addison-Wesley.

Zhou, X., Sedikides, C., Wildschut, T., Gao, D.-G. (2008). Counteracting loneliness: On the restorative function of nostalgia. *Psychological Science 19* (10), 1023–9. doi:10.1111/j.1467-9280.2008.02194.x. PMID 19000213.

CHAPTER 2

Adler, A. (1998). *What Life Could Mean to You*. Boston, MA: Martino Fine Books.

Adler, R., & Proctor, R. (2011). *Looking In Looking Out*. Boston, MA: Cengage.

Bandura, A. (2009). Failures in self-regulations: Energy depletion or selective disengagement. *Psychological Inquiry, 7*, 20–24.

Bandura, A. (2006). *Toward a Psychology of Human Agency*. A paper presented at the meeting of the American Psychological Society, Chicago, IL.

Benveniste, Daniel (2000). "Erik H. Erikson: An Outsider at the Center of Things" in Benveniste, D. (2000) Book Review of Identity's Architect: *A Biography of Erik Erikson* by Lawrence J. Friedman. *The Psychoanalytic Review*. Vol. 87, No. 6. p. 5.

Branden, N. (2015). *The Psychology of Self-Esteem*. New York: John Wiley & Sons.

Brody, N., & Ehrlichman, H. (1998). *Personality Psychology: The Science of Individuality*. Upper Saddle River, NJ: Prentice Hall.

Bronson, P. (2007). How not to talk to your kids: The inverse power of praise. *New York Magazine*, August 3.

Brown, Brene (2018) *Dare to Lead: Brave Work. Tough Conversations. Whole Hearts*. Random House Publishing

Carver, CS & Scheir, MF.(2011) *Perspectives on Personality*. Needham Heights, MA: Allyn & Bacon.

Cloninger, S. (2013). *Theories of Personality*. Upper Saddle River, NJ: Prentice Hall.

Cole, M., Field, H., & Harris, S. (2004). Student learning motivation and psychological hardiness: Interactive effects on students' reactions to a management class. *Academy of Management Learning and Education*, March, 64–85.

Crain, W. (2005). *Theories of development: Concepts and applications* (5th Ed.). Upper Saddle River, NJ: Pearson Prentice Hall.

Davidson, T. (2014). STRENGTH: A system of integration of solution-oriented and strength-based principles. *Journal of Mental Health Counseling*, 36, 1-17.

Deary, Matthews G, Whiteman, MC (2003). Personality Traits (PDF) (2nd ed.). Cambridge University Press.

Deckers, Lambert (2018). *Motivation: Biological, Psychological, and Environmental.* New York: Routledge. pp. 423–425. ISBN 978-1-138-03632-1.

Dweck, C. (2013). *Mindset: The New Psychology of Success.* NY: Random House

Dweck, C. (2013). *Mindset: How You Can Fulfill Your Potential.* Penn: Robinson Publishing

Eder, R.A., & Mangelsdorf, S.C. (1997). The emotional basis of early personality development Implications for the emergent self-concept. In R. Hogan, J. Johnson, & S. Briggs (Eds.), *Handbook of Personality Psychology.* San Diego: Academic Press, 209–324.

Elliott, C. (2004). Putting your best face forward. *Psychology Today,* May/June, 49–50.

Erikson, E. (1993). *Childhood and Society.* New York: W.W. Norton.

Erikson, EH & Erikson, JM. (2011) The Life Cycle Completed. New York: Norton.

Feldman, R.S. (2016). *Development Across the Life Span.* Upper Saddle River, NJ: Prentice Hall.

Festinger, L. (1954). A theory of social comparison processes. *Human Relations,* 7, 117–140.

Fleming, James. (2019) "Erikson's Psychosocial Developmental Stages". *Psychological Perspectives on Human Development.*

Flora, C. (2005). The measuring game: Why you think you'll never stack up. *Psychology Today,* 38, 42–50.

Frankl, V.E. (2006). *Man's Search for Meaning.* New York: Washington Square Press.

Freud, S. (1965). *New Introductory Lectures on Psychoanalysis.* New York: W.W. Norton.

Gibbs, N. (2005). Midlife crisis? Bring it on. *Time,* May 16, 53–63.

Goodman, W. (2019) https://www.psychologytoday.com/us/therapists/whitney-goodman-miami-fl/258231

Hardy, B (2019) Personality isn't permanent-Break free from self-limiting beliefs and rewrite your story. https://medium.com/@benjaminhardy

Helgoe, L. (2010). Revenge of the introvert. *Psychology Today,* 43, 54-61.

John, O.P., & Srivastava, S. (2008). The big five-trait taxonomy: History, measurement, and theoretical perspectives. In L.A. Pervin, & O.P. John (Eds.), *Handbook of Personality: Theory and Research* (3rd ed.). New York: Guilford Press, 102–138.

Kassin, S., Fein, S., Markus, H. (2016). *Social Psychology.* Boston: Cengage Learning.

Keemanovic, Jelena (2019) It's not just you, American adults are increasingly anxious. *Washington Post.*

Keirsey, D. (1998). *Please Understand Me II.* Del Mar, CA: Prometheus Nemesis Book Company.

Kerpin, D. (2016). *11 Simple Skills That Will Get You Everything You Want.* New York: Crown Publishing Random House.

Kimmel, M., & Aronson, A. (2011). *Sociology Now.* Boston, MA: Pearson.

Krueger, J., & Vohs, K. (2003). Does high self-esteem cause better performance, interpersonal success, happiness, or healthier lifestyles? *Psychological Science in the Public Interest,* 4, 1–44.

Krueger, R., & Johnson W. (2008). Behavioral genetics and personality. In O.P. John, R.W. Robbins, & L.A. Pervin (Eds.), *Handbook of Personality Theory and Research.* New York: Guilford, 287–310.

Langer, E. (2014). *Mindfulness 25th Anniversary edition*. Boston: DaCapo Press.

Larsen, R., & Buss, D. (2014). *Personality Psychology Domains of Knowledge about Human Nature*. Upper Saddle River, NJ: Prentice Hall.

Levinson, D. (1986). A conception of adult development. *American Psychologist*, 41, 3–13.

Livingston, G. (2019) The way U.S. teens spend their time is changing, but differences between boys and girls persist. Pew Research Center

Marano, H. (2008). The making of a perfectionist. *Psychology Today*, 41, 81–86.

Malone JC, Liu SR, Vaillant GE, Rentz DM, Waldinger RJ.(2016) Midlife Eriksonian psychosocial development: Setting the stage for late-life cognitive and emotional health. *Dev Psychol*.; 52(3): 496-508. doi:10.1037/a0039875

Matsumoto, D. (2007). Culture, context and behavior. *Journal of Personality*, 75, 1285–1320.

McCrae, R.R., & Costa, P.T., Jr. (2005). *Personality in Adulthood*. New York: The Guilford Press.

McCrae, R.R., & Costa, P.T., Jr. (2008). A five-factor theory of personality. In L.A. Pervin, & O.P. John (Eds.), *Handbook of Personality: Theory and Research* (3rd ed.). New York: The Guilford Press, 139–153.

McGraw, P. (2003). *Self Matters*. New York: Free Press.

McKay M., & Fanning, P. (2016). *Self-Esteem*. Oakland, CA: New Harbinger.

Mischel, W. (2008). *Introduction to Personality*. New York: Worth.

Myers, D.G. & DeWall, C.N. (2017). *Psychology*. New York: Worth.

Myers, I., & Myers, P. (1995). *Gifts Differing*. Palo Alto, CA: Consulting Psychologist Press.

Newton, P. (1994) Daniel Levinson and His Theory of Adult Development: A Reminiscence and Some Clarifications Journal of Adult Development, Vol L No. 3, 1994

Nevid, J., & Rathus, S. (2019). *Psychology and the Challenges of Life*. New York: Wiley.

Nier, J. (2004). Why does the above average effect exist? *Teaching of Psychology*, 31, 53–54.

Pastorino, E., & Doyle-Portillo, S. (2019). *What is Psychology?* Boston, MA: Cengage Learning.

Pollard, M.W., & McKinney, C. (2016). Parental physical force and alcohol use in emerging adults: Mediation by psychological problems. *Journal of Interpersonal Violence*. 2016, Jul 25. pii: 0886260516659654

Rath, T. (2013). *StrengthsFinder 2.0*. New York: Gallup Press.

Rogers, C. (1995). *On Becoming a Person: A Therapist's View of Psychotherapy*. Boston, MA: Houghton Mifflin.

Rosenberg, M. (1965). *Society and the Adolescent Self-image*. Princeton, NJ: Princeton University Press.

Rosling H. & Rosling-Ronnlund A. (2018) *Factfulness: Ten Reasons We're Wrong About the World—and Why Things Are Better Than You Think*. Macmillan Publishers

Sanford, L., & Donovan, M. (1993). *Women and Self Esteem*. New York: Penguin Books.

Satir, V. (1988). *New Peoplemaking*. Palo Alto, CA: Science and Behavior Books.

Satir, V. (2004). *Self Esteem*. Berkeley, CA: Celestial Arts.

Schacter, D., Gilbert, D., Wegner, D. (2016). *Psychology* (2 ed.). New York, NY: Worth Publishers.

Schretlen et al, 2010 Personality/five-factor-model-big-five-personality; Psychologist World.

Sheehy, G. (2006). *Passages: Predictable Crises of an Adult Life.* New York: Ballantine Books.

Sullivan, H.S. (2016). *The Interpersonal Theory of Psychiatry.* New York: Norton.

Tallon, R., & Sikora, M. (2004). *Awareness to Action: The Enneagram, Emotional Intelligence and Change.* Scranton, PA: University of Scranton Press.

Turkle, S. (2012) *Alone Together: Why We Expect More From Technology and Less From Each Other.*

Weiten, W., Dunn, D., & Hammer, E. (2014). *Psychology Applied to Modern Life.* Stamford, CT Cengage Learning.

CHAPTER 3

Aamodt, M., & Raynes, R. (2001). *Human Relations in Business.* Belmont, CA: Wadsworth.

Ackerman, J., Goldstein, J., Shapiro, J., & Bargh, J. (2009). You wear me out: The vicarious depletion of self-control. *Psychological Science*, 20, 326-332.

Allen, David M. (2014). Mindfullness or Mindlessness? Stress tolerance skills are great, but why remove the source of stress? *Psychology Today* online, February.

Aronson, E., Wilson, T., & Akert, R. (2013). *Social Psychology.* Upper Saddle River, NJ: Pearson Education, Inc.

Bandura, A. (2008). *Self-efficacy in Changing Societies.* West Nyack, NY: Cambridge University Press.

Baron, A. Robert (2004), *Social Psychology* (Tenth ed.) Upper Saddle River, NJ: Pearson Education, Inc P144

Baron-Cohen, S. (2003) *The Essential Difference: men, women and the extreme male brain.* Penguin, Allen Lane/ Basic Books.

Buscaglia, L. (1985). *Living, Loving and Learning.* New York: Ballantine Books.

Chowdhury, S.F., Pychyl, T.A. (2018) A critique of the construct validity of active procrastination. *Personality and Individual Differences*, Volume 120

Cline, F., & Fay, J. (2014). *Parenting with Love and Logic: Teaching Children Responsibility.* Carol Stream, IL: Tyndale House Publishers.

Deaner, R.O., Geary, D.C., et al (2012). A sex difference in the predisposition for physical competition: Males play sports much more than females even in the contemporary U.S. *U.S. PLoS ONE,* 7(11), e49168. doi:10.1371/journal.pone.0049168

Dreher, D. (2014) How Much Control Do You Have in Your Life? The power of locus of control. *Psychology Today* online

Duckworth, A.L., Peterson, C., Mathews, M.D. & Kelly, D.R. (2007). Grit: Perseverance and passion for long- term goals. *Journal of Personality and Social Psychology,* 92(6), 1087–1101.

Flora, C. (2016). You 2.0. *Psychology Today,* June 9.

Gardner, R. (2002). *Psychology Applied to Everyday Life.* Belmont, CA: Wadsworth.

Goldberg, S. (2002). The 10 rules of change. *Psychology Today,* 35, 38–42.

Guffey, M. E. (1996). *Five steps to better critical thinking, problem solving, and decision-making skills.*

Hahn, S. E. (2000). The effects of locus of control on daily exposure, coping and reactivity to work interpersonal stressors: A diary study. *Personality and Individual Differences*, 29, 729–748.

Kemmis, Sam(2019) Secrets of the most productive people https://www.fastcompany.com

Joelson Richard B. (2017), Locus of Control-How do we determine our successes and failures? *Psychology Today*

Judge, T. A., & Bono, J. E. (2001). Relationship of core self-evaluations traits—self-esteem, generalized self-efficacy, locus of control, and emotional stability—with job satisfaction and job performance: A meta-analysis. *Journal of Applied Psychology*, 86, 80–92.

Korb, A., Seigel, D. (2015) *The Upward Spiral: Using Neuroscience to Reverse the Course of Depression, One Small Change at a Time.* New Harbringer Publisher.

Kormanik, M.B., Rocco, T. S. (2009). Internal versus external control of reinforcement: A review of the locus of control construct. *Human Resource Development Review*, 8, 4, 463-483.

Leahy, R. (2006). *The Worry Cure.* New York: Three Rivers Press.

Martin, G., & Pear, J. (2015). *Behavior Modification.* New York: Routledge. Hall.

Matsumoto,David & Hwang, Hyi-Sung September (2011) *Cultural Display Rules* Volume Cross-Cultural Psychology.

Martin Robert D (2019) No substitute for sex. *Psychology Today,* online

Mayo Clinic (2019) Positive thinking: Stop negative self-talk to reduce stress. https://www.mayoclinic.org/healthy-lifestyle/stress-management/in-depth/positive-thinking/ retrieved 1/11/2020

Mischel, W. (2004). Toward an integrative science of the person. *Annual Review of Psychology*, 55, 1–22.

Moscovici, S., & Markova, I. (2006). *The Making of Modern Social Psychology.* Cambridge, UK: Polity Press.

Myers, D.G.(2013) *Social Psychology.* New York:Worth

Neimark, J. (2007). The optimism revolution. *Psychology Today,* 40, 88–94.

Nelson, D. (2018) Stimulation of The Prefrontal Cortex Found To Reduce Violent Impulses. *Science Trends*

Orma, Steve (2019) Stop Worrying and Go to Sleep. https://drorma.com/wp-content/uploads/2015/01/StopWorryingAndSleep.pdf ebook

Pychyl, T. (2008). Procrastination: A strategy for change. *Psychology Today* online.

Pychyl, T. (2010). Implementation intentions facilitate action control: One of the most effective anti-procrastination strategies I know. *Psychology Today.* Posted Jan 21, 2010.

Roden, J. (2004). Revisiting the health belief model. *Nursing Health and Science*, 6, 1–10.

Rotter, J.B. (1990). Internal versus external control of reinforcement: A case study of a variable. *American Psychologist*, 45, 489–491.

Santrock, J. (2006). *Human Adjustment.* New York: McGraw Hill.

Seligman, Martin (2018) *The Hope Circuit: A Psychologist's Journey from Helplessness to Optimism.* Hachette Book group NY.

Scheier, M., Carver, C., & Bridges, M. (1994). Distinguishing optimism from neuroticism (and trait anxiety self-mastery, and self-esteem.): A re-evaluation of the life orientation test. *Journal of Personality and Social Psychology*, 67, 1063–1078.

Schmitt David (2017) The Truth About Sex Differences, *Psychology Today online*

Scholtz, U., Gutierrez-Dona, B., Sud, S., & Schwarzer, R. (2002). Is perceived self-efficacy a universal construct: Psychometric findings from 25 countries. *European Journal of Psychological Assessment*, 18(3), 242–251.

Schultz, D., & Schultz, S. (2016). *Theories of Personality*. Belmont, CA: Wadsworth.

Scott, Gwen (2013) Revisiting-External-vs-Internal-Locus-of-Control. http://gwen-scottcounselling.com/wp-content/uploads/2013/04/

Seligman, M.E.P. (2006). *Learned Optimism*. New York: Knopf.

Skinner, B.F. (2002). *Beyond Freedom and Dignity*. New York: Hackett Publishing.

Tamashiro, Tim (2019) *How to Ikigai: Lessons for Finding Happiness and Living Your Life's Purpose*; Kindle Edition

Twenge, J. M., Zhang, L., & Im, C. (2004). It's beyond my control: A cross-temporal meta-analysis of increasing externality in locus of control, 1960–2002. *Personality and Social Psychology Review*, 8, 308-319.

Vaughan, S. (2000). Optimists live better lives than pessimists. *Bottom Line*, December 15, 13–14.

Wargo, E. (2009). Resisting temptation: Psychological research brings new strength to understanding willpower. *Observer*, 22, 10-15.

Watson, D.L., & Tharp, R.G. (2014). *Self-Directed Behavior*. Belmont, CA: Wadsworth.

Webber, R. (2010). Make your own luck. *Psychology Today*, 43, 63-68.

Weiten, W., Dunn, D., & Hammer, E. (2014). *Psychology Applied to Modern Life*. Belmont, CA: Wadsworth

Worchel, S., Cooper, J., Goethals, G., & Olson, J. (2000). *Social Psychology*. Belmont, CA: Wadsworth.

Chapter 4

Adler, R., & Proctor, R. (2016). *Looking Out Looking In*. Boston, MA: Cengage.

Aiken, M. (2016). *The Cyber Effect: A Pioneering Cyberpsychologist Explains How Human Behavior Changes Online*. New York: Spiegel & Grau.

Amen, D. (2015). *Change Your Brain, Change Your Life: The Breakthrough Program for Conquering Anxiety, Depression, Obsessiveness, Lack of Focus, Anger, and Memory Problems*. New York: Harmony Publishers.

Anderson, C.A., Gentile, D.A., & Buckley, K.E. (2007). *Violent Video Games Effects on Children and Adolescents: Theory Research and Public Policy*. New York: Oxford University Press.

Anderson, M.(2018) A Majority of Teens Have Experienced Some Form of Cyberbullying. Pew Research Center

Anderson, J and Rainie. L (2018) "The Future of Well Being in a Tech-Saturated World." Pew Research Center

Bandura, W. (2008). *Self-efficacy in Changing Societies*. West Nyack, NY: Cambridge University Press.

Baskin, T.W., & Enright, R. D. (2004). Intervention studies on forgiveness: A meta-analysis. *Journal of Counseling and Development, 82*, 79–90.

Batcho, K. I. (2017). What will your children remember about you? Psychology Today. https://www.psychologytoday.com/blog/longing-nostalgia/201506/what-will-your-children-remember-about-you-0

Bradberry, T & Greaves, (2019) *Emotional Intelligence 2.0*, Talent Smart publishers, SanDiego, CA

Brooks, D. (May 30, 2019) When Trolls and Crybullies Rule the Earth-How technology reshapes consciousness. *New York Times*.

Brown, B. (2018). *Daring Greatly.* New York: Avery.

Brown, B. (2019). *I Thought It Was Just Me (but it isn't): Telling the Truth about Perfectionism, Inadequacy and Power.* New York: Gotham Publishers.

Burns, D. (2008). *Feeling Good: The New Mood Therapy.* New York: William Morrow and Co.

Buscaglia, L. (1996). *Love: What Life is all About.* New York: Holt, Rinehart and Winston.

Daniel J. Dickson, Brett Laursen, Olivia Valdes, Håkan Stattin. (2019) Derisive Parenting Fosters Dysregulated Anger in Adolescent Children and Subsequent Difficulties with Peers. *Journal of Youth and Adolescence.*

Carlson, R. (2007). *Don't Sweat the Small Stuff . . . and it's all small stuff.* New York: Hyperion.

Cline, F.W., & Fay, J. (2006). *Parenting with Love and Logic: Teaching Children Responsibility* (CD). Colorada Springs, CO: NavPress.

Cose, E. (2005). *Bone to Pick: Of Forgiveness, Reconciliation, Reparation and Revenge.* New York: Atria.

DeSilver, D. (2019) The concerns and challenges of being a U.S. teen: What the data show. Pew Research Center.

Dienes, K.A., Torres-Harding, S., Reinecke, M.A., Freeman, A., Sauer, A. (2019). Cognitive therapy. In S. B. Messer and A. S. Gurman (Eds.), *Essential Psychotherapies: Theory and Practice* (3rd ed.). New York, NY: The Guilford Press. pp. 143–160.

Dickenson, G., & Leming, M. (2020). *Annual Editions: Dying, Death, and Bereavement.* New York: McGraw Hill/Dushkin.

Duffy, K. (2007/2008). *Annual Editions: Personal Growth and Behavior.* Dubuque, IA: McGraw Hill Contemporary Learning Series.

Duffy, K., & Atwater, E. Kirsh, SJ (2014). *Psychology for Living: Adjustment, Growth and Behavior Today.* Englewood Cliffs, NJ: Pearson.

Ellis, A. (2016). *How to Control Your Anxiety Before it Controls You?* North Hollywood, CA: Wilshire Books.

Ellis, A. (2001). *Feeling Better, Getting Better, Staying Better.* New York: Impact Publishers.

Ellis, A., & Harper, R. (1998). *A Guide to Rational Living.* New York: Impact Publishers.

Emery, G. (2000). *Overcoming Depression.* Oakland, CA: New Harbinger Publications.

Enright, R. (2019). *Forgiveness Is a Choice: A Step-by-Step Process for Resolving Anger and Restoring Hope.* Chicago, IL: American Psychological Association.

Evans, C., & Chapman, M. (2014). Bullied youth: The impact of bullying through lesbian, gay, and bisexual name calling. *American Journal of Orthopsychiatry, 84,* (6) 644–652.

Felmlee, D., & Faris, R. (2016). Toxic ties: Networks of friendship, dating, and cyber victimization. *Social Psychology Quarterly, 79*(3), 243–262.

Feuerman, M, (2016). *21 Warning Signs of an Emotionally Abusive Relationship.* World of Psychology psychcentral.com

Foltz-Gray, D. (2002). Anger with no hurt. *Reader's Digest,* July, 130–135.

Freeman, S. (2005). *Grief and Loss. Understanding the Journey.* Belmont, CA: Brooks/Cole.

Fromm, E. (2006). *The Art of Loving.* New York: Perennial.

Gardner, R. (2002). *Psychology Applied to Everyday Life.* Belmont, CA: Wadsworth.

Gibbs, N. (2001). The EQ factor. *Time, 2,* 60–68.

Ginott, H. (2003). *Between Parent and Child.* New York: Three Rivers Press.

Goldsmith, D.J., & Fulfs, P.A. (1999). You just don't have the evidence: An analysis of claims and evidence in Deborah Tannen's you just don't understand. In M.E. Roloff (Ed.), *Communication Yearbook 22.* Thousand Oaks, CA: Sage, 1–49.

Goleman, D. (2006). *Emotional Intelligence: 10th Anniversary Edition—Why It Can Matter More Than IQ.* New York: Bantam Books.

Goleman, D. (2007). *Social Intelligence: The New Science of Human Relationships.* New York: Bantam Books.

Goleman, D. (2011). *The Brain and Emotional Intelligence: New Insights* (1st ed.). Northampton, MA: More than Sound.

Gorman, C. (2002). The science of anxiety. *Time,* June 10, 45–53.

Greenberg, M. (2003). Good grief: The different ways to cope after loss. *Psychology Today, 36,* 44.

Gudykunst, W.B., & Young, Y.K. (2003). *Communicating with Strangers.* New York: McGraw Hill.

Hall, Sue Parker (2009). *Anger, Rage and Relationship: An Empathic Approach to Anger Management.* New York: Routledge.

Howie, P. (2015). *Meditations for Angry People.* www.Amazon/kindle.

John-Roger, & McWilliams, P. (1994). *Life 101.* Wilton, CT: Consolino & Woodward.

Jung, C.G. (2016). *Psychological Types.* New York: Harcourt Brace.

Kagan, J. (2009). *What is Emotion? History, Measures and Meanings.* New Haven, CT: Yale University Press.

Keemanovic, Jelena (2019) It's not just you, American adults are increasingly anxious. *Washington Post.*

King, L. (2020). *The Science of Psychology.* New York: McGraw Hill.

Kübler-Ross, E. (1997). *Death: The Final Stage of Growth.* New York: Simon & Schuster.

Kushner, H. (2004). *When Bad Things Happen to Good People.* New York: Anchor.
_____(2007). *Overcoming Life's Disappointments.* Portmoody, BC: Anchor.

Kushlev, Kostadin, Drummond, Danielle M, Heintzelman, Samantha J. & Diener, Ed (Jul 2019) Do happy people care about society's problems? *Journal of Positive Psychology.*

Larsen, E. (1992). *From Anger to Forgiveness.* New York: Ballantine Books.

Lazarus, R. (2000). Reason and our emotions: A hard sell. *The General Psychologist, 35,* 16–20.

Leahy, R. (2011). The way of the worrier. *Psychology Today, 38,* 68–72.

Lerner, H.G. (2014). *The Dance of Anger.* New York: Harper Collins.

Luskin, F. (2007). *Forgive for Love*. New York: Harper.

May, Cindi (2017). A large multinational study provides some surprises. *Scientific American*

Mayer, J., & Salovey, P. (2004). *Emotional Intelligence: Key Reading on the Mayer and Salovey Model*. Port Chester, NY: Dude Publishing.

Mayer, J., Salovey, P., & Caruse, D. (2009). Emotional intelligence: New ability or eclectic traits. *American Psychologist*, 63, 503–517.

Myers, David (1993) *Pursuit of Happiness* William Morrow publishers.

Nay, W. (2010). Overcoming anger. *Psychology Today Blog*, Jan. 31, 2010.

Ng'andu, J. (2015). Life long success starts with social—emotional learning. *Edutopia, December*.

Ni, Preston M.S.B.A (2017) 5 Ways That Adults Bully Each Other-Five types of bullying tactics. *Psychology Today* Jan 22, 2017.

Ni, Preston (2014) *How to Handle Aggressive, Intimidating, and Controlling People* Ebook http://nipreston.com

Ong, Walter J. (1982) *Orality and Literacy: The Technologizing of the Word*. Routledge Press NY.

Orloff, Judith (2011). *Emotional Freedom: Liberate Yourself From Negative Emotions and Transform Your Life*. Three Rivers Press.

Petrov, Christo(February 28, 2019) *Disturbing Cyberbullying stats*. https://techjury.net/

Plutchik, R. (2003). *Emotions and Life: Perspectives from Psychology, Biology, and Evolution*. Washington, DC: American Psychological Association.

Preidt, R. (2019). *HealthDay*; Healthday.com

Preidt, Robert (2019) Does Bullying start at home? *HealthDay News*

Reidbord, S. (2016) Choose Your Actions, Not Your Feelings. *Psychology Today*. May 08, 2016.

Reiner, A. (2016). Teaching men to be emotionally honest. *New York Times*, April 10.

Rogers, C. (1995). *On Becoming a Person: A Therapist's View of Psychotherapy*. Boston, MA: Houghton-Mifflin.

Rolls, G. (2010). *Women Can't Park, Men Can't Pack: The Psychology of Stereotypes*. London, England: Hodder & Stoughton.

Rosenthal, A. (2009). Shame on me. *Psychology Today*, 42, 16.

Schmidt, B. (2002). Fear not. *Psychology Today*, 35, 46–54.

Silk, S., Goldman, B. (2016). We've all been there, stumbling for words at a bedside or funeral. The ring theory helps you know what to say. *Los Angeles Times*, April 20.

Simon, S. (2005). The lion tamer. *Psychology Today*, 38, 54–60.

Simon, S., & Simon, S. (1991). *Forgiveness: How to Make Peace with Your Past and Get on with Your Life*. New York: Warner Books.

Simonini, R. (2011). The terminator. *Psychology Today*, 44, 28–29.

Sisemore, B. (2009). Lessons in forgiveness. *The Dallas Morning News*, August 8, 2009.

Smedes, L. (2007). *Forgive & Forget: Healing the Hurts We Don't Deserve*. New York: Harper Collins Paperback.

Spencer Scott, P. (2016). Feeling awe may be the secret to health and happiness. *Parade*, October 17.

Suttie Jill (September 11, 2019) Happiness Doesn't Make You Ignore Social Problems. *Greater Good Magazine* UC Berkley.

Tavris, C. (1989). *Anger: The Misunderstood Emotion*. New York: Simon & Schuster, Inc.

University at Buffalo. (2019, May 9). For teens, online bullying worsens sleep and depression: Nearly 15 percent of high school students report being bullied online. *ScienceDaily*. Retrieved August 15, 2019 from www.sciencedaily.com/releases/2019/05/190509142707.htm

Viscott, D. (1990). *The Language of Feelings*. New York: Pocket Books.

Walton, D. (2013). *Emotional Intelligence: A Practical Guide*. Kindle.

Weiten, W. (2016). *Psychology-Themes and Variations*. Pacific Grove, CA: Brooks/Cole.

Welshons, J., & Dyer, W. (2012). *Awakening from Grief: Finding the Road Back to Joy*. Novato, CA: New World Library.

Westburg, G. (2019). *Good Grief*. Minneapolis, MN: Augsburg Publishers.

Wood, S., & Wood, E. (2014). *Mastering the World of Psychology*. Needham Heights, MA: Allyn & Bacon.

Wright, 2014. Death and the Internet: The implications of the digital afterlife. Firstmonday.org Volume19, 6–2 June 2014

Ybarra, M., & Mitchell, K. (2006). Cyberbullies increasingly target peers online. *APA Monitor*, 37, No. 9.

Chapter 5

Adler, R., Rosenfeld, L., & Proctor, R. (2015). *Interplay—The Process of Interpersonal Communication*. New York: Oxford University Press.

Anderson, M & Kumar, M.(May 7, 2019) Digital divide persists even as lower-income Americans make gains in tech adoption

Anderson, M. and Kumar, M. (May 7, 2019) *Digital divide persists even as lower-income Americans make gains in tech adoption* Pew Research FactTank https://www.pewresearch.org

Atkinson, D.R. (2004). *Counseling American Minorities*. New York: McGraw Hill.

Bajracharya, Shraddha(J anuary 7, 2018) "Why is Non-verbal Communication Important?," iBusinesstopia, Jhttps://www.businesstopia.net/communication/why-non-verbal-communication-important.

Barker, L., & Watson, K. (2000). *Listen Up: How to Improve Relationships, Reduce Stress, and Be More Productive by Using the Power of Listening*. New York: St. Martin's Press.

Baruth, L.G., & Manning, M.L. (2016). *Multicultural Counseling and Psychotherapy: A Lifespan Perspective*. Englewood Cliffs, NJ: Prentice Hall.

Berne, Eric (1996) *Games People Play: The Basic Handbook of Transactional Analysis*. Ballentine Publishing.

Berne, Eric (2011). *Games People Play*. Audible Books.

Blanchard, K. (2006). *Putting the One Minute Manager to Work: How to Turn the Three Secrets into Skills*. New York: William & Morrow.

Bolton, R. Dorothy Grover Bolton(2009). *People Styles at Work—and Beyond: Making Bad Relationships Good and Good*. Harper Collins NY

Bradberry, T. (2016) Seven Tricks For Reading Body Language Like A Pro. *Forbes Magazine online*

Brown, Anna (2019) Couples who meet online are more diverse than those who meet in other ways, largely because they're younger. June 24, 2019 Pew Research FactTank

Burgoon, J., Guerrero, L.K., & Floyd, K. (2016). *Nonverbal Communication*. New York: Routlege.

Burgoon, J., & Levine, T. (2010). Advances in deception detection. In S.W. Smith, & S.R. Wilson (Eds.), *New Directions in Interpersonal Communication Research*. Thousand Oaks, CA: Sage.

Carnegie, D. (2011). *How to Win Friends and Influence People*. New York: Simon & Schuster.

C. Cambell & S.Clarke (2019)*The Beauty of Conflict for Couples*. Mango Media

Ciaramicoli, A. and K. Ketchen (2001). *The Power of Empathy: A Practical Guide to Creating Intimacy, Self-understanding and Lasting Love*. New York: Dutton.

Cline, F.W., & Fay, J. (2006). *Parenting with Love and Logic: Teaching Children Responsibility* (CD). Evergreen, CO: Love and Logic Press.

Communication Research Associates. (2016). *Communicate! A Workbook for Interpersonal Communication*. Dubuque, IA: Kendall Hunt Publishing Co.

Covey, S.R. (1998) *First Things First*. Franklin Covey NY Simon Shuster

Covey, S.R. (2005). *Principle-Centered Leadership* (CD-Audiobook). Prince Frederick, MD: Your Coach in a Box.

Covey, S.R. (2013). *The Seven Habits of Highly Effective People* (CD). New York: Free Press.

Coyne, S (February 2016) Smartphones interfere in romantic relationships, psychologists find. *Family Relations: An Interdisciplinary Journal of Applied Family Studies* Vol 47, No. 2 Print version: page 55

Coyne, S. M., Stockdale, L., Busby, D., Iverson, B., & Grant, D. M. (2011). "I luv u :)!": A descriptive study of the media use of individuals in romantic relationships. *Family Relations: An Interdisciplinary Journal of Applied Family Studies*, *60*(2), 150–162.

Dean, A. (1996). *Caring For The Family Soul*. New York: USA Penguin Group Inc.

De Vito, J.A. (2015). *The Interpersonal Communication Book*. Reading, MA: Addison Wesley.

Drago, E. (2015). The effect of technology on face-to-face communication. *The Elon Journal of Undergraduate Research in Communications*.

Dresser, N. (2005). *Multicultural Manners: New Rules of Etiquette for a Changing Society*. New York: John Wiley & Sons, Inc.

Dunn, A. (September 24, 2019) Younger, college-educated black Americans are most likely to feel need to 'code-switch.' Pew Research Fact-tank.org

Eckman, P. (2007). *Emotions Revealed: Recognizing Faces and Feelings to Improve Communication and Emotional Life*. New York: Owl Books.

Emanuel, R., et al. (2008). How college students spend their time communicating. *Interpersonal Journal of Listening*, 22, 13–28.

Englander-Golden, P., & Satir, V. (1991). *Say It Straight*. Palo Alto, CA: Science and Behavior Books, Inc.

Fisher-Sykes, J. (2005). Bite your tongue! 10 ways to be an effective listener. *Living Magazine*, June, 54–58.

Gordon, T. (2000). *Parent Effectiveness Training*. New York: Three Rivers Press.

Hall (1968) Proxemics Current Anthropology. 9 83–108. doi:10.1086/200975. JSTOR 2740724 retrieved Sept. 5, 2019.

Hall, E.T. (1992). *The Hidden Dimension*. Garden City, NY: Anchor Books.

Hamilton, C. (2017). *Communicating for Results*. Belmont, CA: Wadsworth.

Hamilton, C. (2014). *Essentials of Public Speaking*. Belmont, CA: Wadsworth.

Hanna, S., Suggett, R., & Radtke, D. (2008). *Person to Person*. Upper Saddle River, NJ: Prentice Hall.

Heslin, R., & Alper, T. (1983). Touch: A bonding gesture. In J.M. Wiemann, & R.P. Harrison (Eds.), *Nonverbal Interaction*. Beverly Hills, CA: Sage Publishing Co.

Horn, S. (1997). *Tongue Fu! How to Deflect, Disarm and Defuse Any Verbal Conflict*. New York: St. Martins Press.

Internet Activities. (2019). *Pew Internet and American Life Project*, January 6.

Johnson, D. (2014). *Reaching Out*. Needham Heights, MA: Allyn & Bacon.

Kassian, M. (2014). *Conversation Peace*. Nashville, TN: LifeWay Press.

Kirwan Institute. (2019). *Implicit Bias Report* http://kirwaninstitute.osu.edu

Knapp, M., & Hall, J. (2014). *Nonverbal Communication in Human Interaction*. New York: Wadsworth Publishing Co.

Lerner, H. (2002). *The Dance of Connection*. New York: HarperCollins.

McFarland, S., Webb, M., & Brown, D. (2012). All humanity is my ingroup: A measure and studies of identification with all humanity. *Journal of Personality and Social Psychology*, 103(5), 830–853.

MacGeorge, E., Graves, A., Feng, Gilliham, S., & Burleson, B. (2004). The myth of gender cultures. *Sex Roles*, 50, 143–175.

Marano, H. (2016). Love interruptus. *Psychology Today*, July/August, 58-59.

Matsumoto, D. (2004). Paul Ekman and the legacy of universals. *Journal of Research in Personality*, 38, 45–51.

Menninger, K., & Holzman, P. (Eds.). (2010). *Theory of Psychoanalytic Technique*. Northvale, NJ: Jason Aronson.

Milliken, M.E. and Honeycutt, A. (2017). *Understanding Human Behavior*. Albany, New York: Dalmar Publishers, Inc.

Nonviolent Communication. (2019). https://www.cnvc.org/ retrieved 12-3-19.

O'Neill, S., & Chapman, E. (2008). *Your Attitude Is Showing: A Primer on Human Relations*. Englewood Cliffs, NJ: Pearson.

Pachter, B. (2006). *When the Little Things Count . . . and They Always Count*. Cambridge, MA: De Capo Press.

Perina, K. (2006). Distinct emotional dialects. *Psychology Today*, 39, 5.

Perina, K. (2011). Secrets of special agents. *Psychology Today*, 44, 56–73.

Piercy, F., Sprenkle, D. Wetchler, J., et al. (1996). *Family Therapy Sourcebook*.

Reece, B., & Brandt, R. (2014). *Effective Human Relations in Organizations*. Boston, MA: Houghton Mifflin Co.

Rogers, C. (1957). The necessary and sufficient conditions of personality change. *Journal of Counseling Psychology*, 22, 95–110.

Rogers, C. (1995). *On Becoming a Person: A Therapist's View of Psychotherapy*. Boston, MA: Houghton Mifflin.

Rosenberg, M. (2015). *Nonviolent Communication.* Encinitas, CA: Puddledancer Press.

Rosen, Larry (2009) *The Distracted Mind: Ancient Brains in a High-Tech World.* MIT Press, 2016.

Santrock, J. (2006). *Human Adjustment.* New York: McGraw Hill.

Satir, V. (1995). *Making Contact.* Millbrae, CA: Celestial Arts.

Sbarra, David (2019) How Smartphones Are Affecting Our Relationships *Perspectives on Psychological Science* https://www.psychologicalscience.org/journals/pps

Schaeffer, Katherine (August 2019) Most U.S. teens who use cellphones do it to pass time, connect with others, learn new things. Pew Research Center Fact Tank.

Smith, Aaron(2016) 15% of American Adults Have Used Online Dating Sites or Mobile Dating Apps. Pew Research Center

Smith, A. & Anderson, M. (April 2019) Social Media Use in 2018/2019 Fact Tank Pew Research Center

Tannen, D. (2007). *You Just Don't Understand.* New York: Ballantine Books.

Tavris, C., & Wade, C. (2011). *Invitation to Psychology.* Englewood Cliffs, NJ: Prentice Hall.

Turkle, S. (2017). *Alone Together: Why We Expect More from Technology and Less from Each Other.* New York: Basic Books.

Turkle, S. (2016). *Reclaiming Conversations: The Power of Talk in the Digital Age.* New York: Penguin Publishing.

Weir, K (March 2017) *Seven ways to overhaul your smartphone use* Vol 48, No. 3 Print version: page 48

Weir, K.,(March 2017), (Dis)Connected Psychologists' research shows how smartphones are affecting our health and well-being, and points the way toward taking back control https://www.apa.org/monitor/2017/03/index 03 Vol 48, No. 3

Wing Sue, D. (2010). Racial microaggression in everyday life: Is subtle bias harmless? *Psychology Today* blog, October 5.

Wing Sue, D. (2019). *Microaggressions in Everyday Life:* Hoboken, NJ: John Wiley & Sons.

Wood, J. & Fixma-Oraiz, N (2018). *Gendered Lives.* Boston, MA: Wadsworth.

Chapter 6

Abrams, A.(Nov 17, 2019). Divorce rate in U.S. drops to nearly 40-year low. *Time Magazine USA Time.com* retrieved 12-3-2019.

Alkon, A. (2010). The truth about beauty. *Psychology Today,* 43, 54–65.

Amato, PR (2005) The impact of family formation change on the cognitive, social, and emotional well-being of the next generation. *The Future of Children Journal*

Amato, PR (2010) *Research on divorce: Continuing trends and new developments* Journal of marriage and family 72 (3), 650-666

Amato, PR & Booth, A (2009) *A generation at risk.* Harvard Publishing.

Amato, P.R., & De Buer, D.D. (2001). The transmission of marital instability across generations: Relationship skills or commitment to marriage? *Journal of Marriage and Family,* 63, 103–1051.

Amato, P.R., & Previti, D. (2003). People's reasons for divorcing: Gender, social class, the life course, and adjustment. *Journal of Family Issues,* 24, 602–626.

Anderson, M. (2015). For teens, phone calls are reserved for closer relationships. Pew Research Center.

Anderson, M.(2018) A Majority of Teens Have Experienced Some Form of Cyberbullying, Pew Research Center.

Anderson, R.E. (2003). Envy and jealousy. *American Journal of Psychotherapy*, 56, 455–479.

Bahrampour, T. (2016). Why more millennials are avoiding sex: 'There isn't really anything magical about it' *Washington Post,* Aug. 2.

Baron, R., Branscombe, N., & Byrne, D. (2017). *Social Psychology.* Boston, MA: Allyn & Bacon.

Masci, D, Brown, A and Kiley, J. (June 24, 2019) *5 facts about same-sex marriage* Pew Research Center Fact Tank

Beattie, M. (2011). *Co-Dependent No More Workbook.* New York: HarperCollins.

Belsky, J. (2018). *Experiencing the Lifespan.* New York: Worth Publishers.

Berastain, P. (2016). Domestic Violence in LGBT Communities: *US edition Huffington Post* February 2.

Besen-Cassino,Yasemin & Cassino, Dan (2014) Division of House Chores and the Curious Case of Cooking: The Effects of Earning Inequality on House Chores among Dual-Earner Couples. Vol.3 N.6 AG AboutGender *https://riviste.unige.it/aboutgender/article/view/176*

Booth, A., & Amato, P.R. (2004). Parental pre-divorce relations and offspring post-divorce well-being. *Journal of Marriage and Family,* 63, 197–212.

Bordens, K., Horowitz, I. (2013). *Social Psychology, Fourth Edition.* Solon, OH: Academic Media Solutions.

Brown, B. (2014). *I thought it was just me (but it isn't); Making the journey from what will people Think to I am enough.* New York: Penguin Random House.

Bumpass, L., & Hsien-Hen L. (2000). Trends in cohabitation and implications for children's family contexts in the U.S. *Population Studies,* 54, 29-41.

Bureau of Labor Statistics. (2019). *American Time Use survey* BLS.gov/tus/

Buss, D.M., et al. (1999). International preferences in selecting mates: A study of 37 cultures. *Journal of Cross Cultural Psychology*, 21, 5–47.

Buss, D.M. (2016). *The Evolution of Desire.* Jackson, TN: Basic Books.

Buss, D.M. (2019). *Evolutionary Psychology.* Boston, MA: Allyn & Bacon.

Buss, D.M. (2016). *The Mating Crisis Among Educated Women.* Edge.Com

Buss, D.M., Shackelford, T.K., Kirkpatrick, L.A., & Larsen, R.J. (2001). A half century of mate preferences: The cultural evolution of values. *Journal of Marriage and Family,* 63, 491–503.

Center for Disease Control (Aug. 2019) *National Intimate Partner Survey* https://www.cdc.gov/violenceprevention/pdf/cdc_nisvs_victimization_final-a.pdf)

Centers for Disease Control and Prevention. (2019). *Cohabitation.* Atlanta, GA: cdc.gov.

Chapman, G. (2015). *The Five Love Languages.* Northfield, MN: Northfield Publishing.

Chatterjee, C. (2016) *The Science of a Good Marriage- Why the best marriages are based on deep friendship.* Psychology Today

Chatterjee, C. (2016). Can men and women be friends? *Psychology Today,* June 9, 61–67.

Cherlin, A. (2010). Demographic Trends in the United States: A Review of Research in the 2000s. *Journal of Marriage and Family, 72*, 1-17.

Cherlin, A. (2010). *The Marriage-Go-Round: The State of Marriage and the Family in America Today.* New York: Vintage.

Coontz, S. (2006). *Marriage, a History: How Love Conquered Marriage.* New York: Penguin Group.

Daugherty, J., & Copen C. (2016). Trends in attitudes about marriage, childbearing, and sexual behavior: United States, 2002, 2006–10, and 2011–13. National Health Statistics Reports, no. 92. Hyattsville, MD: National Center for Health Statistics.

De Angelis, B. (2004). *Are You the One for Me?* (CD). New York: Macmillan Audio.

Degges-White S. (2015). The 13 essential traits of good friends. *Psychology Today,* March.

DiGiulio,Sarah(2019) Meeting someone online is fundamentally different than meeting someone IRL (in real life). https://www.nbcnews.com/better/lifestyle/how-be-better-online-dating-according-psychology-ncna979791?cid=eml_better_20190319

Dixit, J. (2009). You're driving me crazy. *Psychology Today, 42*, 66–74.

Dresser, N. (2005). *Multicultural Manners: New Rules of Etiquette for a Changing Society.* New York: John Wiley & Sons, Inc.

Duffy, K., & Atwater, E. (2013). *Psychology for Living.* Upper Saddle River, NJ: Pearson.

Elder, S. (2005). The Emperor's new woes. *Psychology Today.*

Evans, F. Barton (2006). *Harry Stack Sullivan: Interpersonal Theory and Psychotherapy.* London: Routledge.

Fry, R. (2016). *For First Time in Modern Era, Living With Parents Edges Out Other Living Arrangements for 18- to 34-Year-Olds.* Pew Research Center.

Fry, R. (2016). *The evolving landscape of young adult living arrangements.* Pew Research Center.

Fulwiler, M. (2014). *The Six Things that Predict Divorce.* The Gottman Institute Blog, October.

Gadoua, S.P. and Larson,V. (2014) *The New I Do: Reshaping Marriage for Skeptics, Realists and Rebels questions to ask in your relationship.* Seal Press

GEIGER, A.W. AND LIVINGSTON, (Feb. 2019) 8 facts about love and marriage in America https://www.pewresearch.org/fact-tank/2019/02/13/8-facts-about-love-and-marriage/

Godek, G. (1997). *Love.* Markham, ON: Sourcebooks Trade.

Gottman, J. (1995). *Why Marriages Succeed or Fail.* New York: Simon and Schuster, Inc.

Gottman, John Ph. D. (October 10, 2014) *The 6 Things That Predict Divorce* https://www.gottman.com/blog/the-6-things-that-predict-divorce/.

Gottman JM, Levenson RW, Swanson C, Swanson K, Tyson R, Yoshimoto (2003) Journal of Homosexuality; 45(1): 65–91 https://www.ncbi.nlm.nih.gov/pubmed/14567654

Gottman, J., & Carrere, S. (2000). Welcome to the love lab. *Psychology Today, 23*, 42–47.

Gottman, J., & Declaire, J. (2007). *Ten Lessons to Transform Your Marriage.* New York: Three Rivers Press.

Gottman, J., & Silver, W. (2015). *The Seven Principles of Making Marriage Work (CD)*. Harmony Publishing.

Grolnick, W.S., Gurland, S.T., DeCourcey, W., & Jacob, K. (2002). Antecedents and consequences of mothers' autonomy support: An experimental investigation. *Developmental Psychology, 38*, 143-155.

Hetherington, E., & Kelly, J. (2003). *For Better or For Worse: Divorce Reconsidered.* New York: W.W. Norton.

Hetherington, E.M., et al. (1998). The role of individual differences and family relationships in coping with divorce and remarriage. In P.A. Cowan, & E.M. Hetherington (Eds.), *Family Transition.* Hillsdale, NJ: Erlbaum.

Hyde, J., & DeLamater, J. (2019). *Understanding Human Sexuality.* New York: McGraw Hill.

Jedege, A. (2019) Top Ten Countries with Highest Divorce Rate in the World. Trendr.net

Katz, J. (2016). Ten Things Men Can Do to Prevent Gender Violence. www.jacksonkatz.com

Katz, J. (2015). Engaging men in prevention of violence against women. In Johnson, H., Fisher, B., Jaquier, V., *Critical Issues on Violence Against Women: International Perspectives and Promising Strategies*, London: Routledge, 233–243.

Katz, J. (2006). *The Macho Paradox: Why Some Men Hurt Women and How All Men Can Help.* Naperville, IL: Sourcebooks.

Khan, K Chaudhry, S. (February, 2015) An evidence-based approach to an ancient pursuit: systematic review on converting online contact into a first date. *Evidence Based-Medicine Journal*, BMJ.com.

Kelly, J. (2004). Divorce: The adult perspective. In B.B. Walman (Ed.), *Handbook of Developmental Psychology.* Englewood Cliffs, NJ: Prentice Hall.

Khazan, Olga (Oct 24, 2016) *Emasculated Men Refuse to Do Chores—Except Cooking.* The Atlantic Magazine

Konigsberg, R. (2011). Chore wars. *Time*, August 8, 2011.

Kreider, R. (2009). *Number, Timing, and Duration of Marriages.* 2001 U.S. Census Bureau, Household Economic Studies. Washington, DC: Department of Commerce.

Lague, L. (2001). How honest are couples really? *Reader's Digest*, August, 2001, 88–99.

Livingston, Gretchen and Brown, Anna (May 2017) Intermarriage in The U.S. 50 Years After Loving V. Virginia. Trends and patterns in intermarriage. Pew Research Center Social and Demographic Trends

Livingston, G. (2014). *Four-in-Ten Couples are Saying "I Do," Again Growing Number of Adults Have Remarried.* Pew Research Center.

Lucas, R. (2005). Time does not heal all wounds; a longitudinal study of reaction and adaptation to divorce. *Psychological Science, 16*, 945–950.

Marano, H. (2006). Relationships. *Psychology Today, 39*, 48–49.

Marano, H. (2016). Love and Power. *Psychology Today, June 9.*

Masci, David, Brown, Anna and Kiley, Jocelyn (2019) *5 facts about same-sex marriage* Pew Research Center FactTank.

Masci, David, Brown, Anna and Kiley, Jocelyn (June 24, 2019) *5 facts about same-sex marriage* Pew Research Center

Matsumoto, D., & Juang, L. (2016). *Culture and Psychology.* Florence, KY: Wadsworth.

McGraw, P. (2007). *Relationship Rescue*. New York: Hyperion.

Myers, D.G. (2017). *Exploring Social Psychology*. New York: McGraw Hill.

National Domestic Violence Hotline (2019) https://www.thehotline.org/

Nevid, J., & Rathus, S. (2019). *Psychology and the Challenges of Life*. Hoboken, NJ: John Wiley & Sons, Inc.

NNEDV.org/census. (2019) *National Domestic Violence Counts*,.

O'Meara, J. D. (1989). Cross-sex friendships: Four basic challenges of an ignored relationship. *Sex Roles*, 21, 525-543.

Overstreet, L. (2007). *Gaining Perspective*. Dubuque, IA: Kendall Hunt Publishing Co.

Parker-Pope, T. (2011). *For Better: The Science of a Good Marriage*. New York: Dutton Adult.

Parker, K. (2015). *Parenting in America and Running a Household: How Working Parents Share the Load*. Pew Research Center.

Perina, K. (2016). The Success of a Marriage. *Psychology Today*, June 9.

Pew Internet & American Life Project. (2009). *Online dating*. Washington, DC.

Pew Research Center. (2019). *Millennials in adulthood: Detached from institutions, networked with friends*. Retrieved March, 7, 2014 from http://www.pewsocial-trends.org/2014/03/07/millennials-in-adulthood/.

Pew Research Center. (2015). *More Millennials living with family despite improved job market*. Retrieved July 29, 2015 from http://www.pewsocialtrends.org/2015/07/29/more-millennials-living-with-family-despite-improved-job-market/.

Pew Research Center(2019) *Generation Z Looks a Lot Like Millennials on Key Social and Political Issues*. January 14,2019.retrived October 2019. https://www.pew-socialtrends.org/2019/01/17/generation-z-looks-a-lot-like-millennials-on-key-social-and-political-issues/psdt_1-17-19_generations-10/

Pew Research Center. (2018). *Millennials Overtake Baby Boomers as America's Largest Generation*.

Pew Research Center Staff. (2009). *Survey: Working moms wish for part-time jobs*. Pew Survey, people-press.org.

Psychology Today (2019) What Is Sexual Orientation https://www.psychologytoday.com/us/basics/homosexuality

Psychology Today. (2019) Science of Mating. https://www.psychologytoday.com/us/basics/mating

Rao, Aliya Hamid (June 2017) Stand By Your Man: Wives' Emotion Work During Men's Unemployment. *Journal of Marriage & Family*

Regnerus, M., & Uecker, J. (2011). *Premarital Sex in America: How Young Americans Meet, Mate and Think about Marrying*. Oxford, England: Oxford University Press.

Rodrigues, A., Hal, J., & Fincham, F. (2006). *What predicts divorce and relationship dissolution?* In M.A. Fine, & J.H. Harvey (Eds.), *Handbook of Divorce and Relationship Resolution*. Mahwah, NJ: Erlbaum.

Rosen, L. (2010). Welcome to the iGeneration. *Psychology Today*.

Schaeffer, K (August 23, 2019) Most U.S. teens who use cellphones do it to pass time, connect with others, learn new things. Pew Research Center

Schwartz, P. (2003). Love is not all you need. *Psychology Today*, 35, 57–62.

Schwartz, Pepper (2016) Love Is Not All You Need- What makes a relationship work? The importance of listening, teamwork and flexibility. *Psychology Today*

ScienceDaily (2008, June 4). Are People More Likely To Become Friends Based on Proximity Or Shared Values and Interests? Retrieved 12-3-2019 from www.sciencedaily.com/releases/2008/06/080602163842.htm

Seltzer, J. A. (2004), Cohabitation in the United States and Britain: Demography, kinship, and the future. *Journal of Marriage and Family*, 66, 921–928. doi:10.1111/j.0022-2445.2004.00062.x

Siegel, D. (2007). Two people, one breadwinner. *Psychology Today,* 20, 46–48.

Smith A., (2016). *15% of American Adults Have Used Online Dating Sites or Mobile Dating Apps.* Pew Research Center.

Smock, P. (2000). Cohabitation in the United States: An appraisal of research themes, findings, and implications. *Annual Review of Sociology,* 26.

Stack, S., & Eshleman, J. (1998). Marital status and happiness: A 17-nation study. *Journal of Marriage and the Family,* 60, 527–536.

Stepler, Renee (April 6, 2017) Number of U.S. adults cohabiting with a partner continues to rise, especially among those 50 and older. PEW Research Center *FactTank*

Sternberg, R.J. (2004). A Triangular Theory of Love. In H.T. Reis, C. Rusbult, *Close Relationships*. New York: Psychology Press, p. 258.

Sternberg, R.J. (2007). Triangulating love. In T.J. Oord, (Ed.,) *The Altruism Reader: Selections from Writings on Love, Religion, and Science.* West Conshohocken, PA: Templeton Foundation, p. 332.

Strong, B., & Cohen, T. (2014). *The Marriage and Family Experience.* Belmont, CA: Cengage.

Sullivan, H.S. (1968). *The Interpersonal Theory of Psychiatry.* New York: Norton.

Tang, S. M., & Zuo, J. P. (2013). Dating attitudes and behaviors of American and Chinese college students. *The Social Science Journal,* 37, 67-78. doi:10.1016/S0362-3319(99)00066-X

Taylor, S.E., & Peplau, L.A. (2009). *Social Psychology.* Upper Saddle River: NJ: Prentice Hall.

Twenge, Jean in There isn't really anything magical about it': Why more millennials are avoiding sex By Tara Bahrampour August 2, 2016 *Washington Post.*

Twenge J., Sherman, R.A., Brooke, R., & Wells B.E. (2017). Sexual inactivity during young adulthood is more common among U.S. millennials and iGen: Age, period, and cohort effects on having no sexual partners after age 18, *Archives of Sex Behavior,* 46, 433. doi:10.1007/s10508-016-0798-z

U.S. Bureau of the Census. (2019). *Median Age of First Marriage:1890-2019.* Washington, DC: U.S. Government Printing Office.

Vranglova, Z, Bukverg, R, Riegir, G (2014). Birds of a feather? Not when it comes to sexual permissiveness.*Journal of Social and Personal Relationships,* 31, 93–113.

Wartik, N. (2005). The perils of playing house. *Psychology Today,* 38, 42–52.

Weiten, W., Dunn, D., & Hammer, E. (2017). *Psychology Applied to Modern Life.* Belmont, CA: Wadsworth.

Wood, S., Wood, E., & Boyd, D. (2014). *Mastering the World of Psychology.* New York: Pearson.

Wong, Brittany (December 27, 2016) Eleven Qualities Every Truly Happy Relationship Has In Common—Marriage therapists share their top relationship must-haves. Huffington Post

CHAPTER 7

Ablon, Stuart (2018) *Changeable: How Collaborative Problem Solving Changes Lives at Home, at School, and at Work.* Penguin Publishing

Adler, R., & Proctor, R. (2016). *Looking Out Looking In.* Boston, MA.

Adler, R., & Rodman, G. (2016). *Understanding Human Communication.* Fort Worth, TX: Harcourt Brace.

Alberti, R.E., & Emmons, M.L. (2008). *Your Perfect Right: A Guide to Assertive Living* (6th ed.). San Luis Obispo, CA: Impact Publishers, Inc.

Atwater, E., & Duffy, K. (2013). *Psychology for Living: Adjustment, Growth and Behavior Today.* Englewood Cliffs, NJ: Prentice Hall.

Baskin, T.W., & Enright, R. D. (2011). Intervention studies on forgiveness: A meta-analysis. *Journal of Counseling and Development, 82,* 79-90.

Bolton, R. (1986). *People Skills.* New York: Simon & Schuster, Inc.

Bower, S.A., & Bower, G.H. (2004). *Asserting Yourself.* Philadelphia, PA: DeCapo Press.

Breitman, P., Hatch, C., & Carlson, R. (2001). *How to Say No without Feeling Guilty: And Say Yes to More Time, More Joy, and What Matters Most to You.* New York: Broadway.

Burgess, H., & Burgess, G. (1999). *Encyclopedia of Conflict Resolution.* Santa Barbara, CA: ABC-Clio.

Buscaglia, L. (1994). *Born for Love.* New York: Ballantine.

Cambell, C. & Clarke, S.(2019) *The Beauty of Conflict for Couples.* Mango Media

Chapman, Gary (2015) *The 5 Love Languages: The Secret to Love that Lasts.* Northfield Publishing: Chicago

Cloud, H. and Townsend, J. (2017) *Boundaries Updated and Expanded Edition: When to Say Yes, How to Say No To Take Control of Your Life.* Zondervan publishers

Collier, M.J. (1991). Conflict competence within African, Mexican, and Anglo-American friendship. In S. Ting-Toomey, & F. Korzenny (Eds.), *Cross-Cultural Interpersonal Communication.* Newbury Park, CA: Sage.

Communication Research Associates. (2016). *Communicate! A Workbook for Interpersonal Communication.* Dubuque, IA: Kendall Hunt Publishing Co.

Coyne, S. M., Stockdale, L. Busby, D., Iverson, B., & Grant, D. M. (2011). I luv u:): A descriptive study of the media use of individuals in romantic relationships. *Family Relations,* 60, 150–162. doi: 10.1111/j.1741-3729.2010.00639.x

Davis, M., Eshelman, E., & McKay, M. (2019). *The Relaxation and Stress Reduction Workbook.* Oakland, CA: New Harbinger Publications.

DeCenzo D., & Silhanek B. (2002). *Human Relations Personal and Professional Development.* Upper Saddle River, NJ: Prentice Hall.

Deutsch, M., Coleman, P., & Marcus, E. (2014). *Handbook of Conflict Resolution.* New Haven, CT: Yale University Press.

Dubrin, A. (2016). *Human Relations for Career and Personal Success.* Upper Saddle River, NJ: Prentice Hall.

Emmons RA, et al. (Feb. 2019). "Counting Blessings Versus Burdens: An Experimental Investigation of Gratitude and Subjective Well-Being in Daily Life," *Journal of Personality and Social Psychology*: Vol. 84, No. 2, pp. 377–89.

Fememenia, N., & Warner, N. (2015). *The Silent Marriage: How Passive Aggression Steals Your Happiness.* New York: Creative Conflict Resolution Inc.

Firestone, Lisa (2013) How your attachment style impacts your relationship. *Psychology Today*, https://www.psychologytoday.com/us/blog/compassion-matters/201307/how-your-attachment-style-impacts-your-relationship)

Fisher, R., & Ury, W. (2011). *Getting to Yes: Negotiating Agreement without Giving In*. New York: Simon & Schuster Audio.

Fontaine, G. (1999). Cultural diversity in intimate intercultural relationships. In D.D. Cahn (Ed.), *Conflict in Intimate Relationships*. New York: Guilford.

Green, R. (2001). *Human Aggression*. Pacific Grove, CA: Brooks/Cole.

Gordon, T. (2008). *Parent Effectiveness Training*. New York: New American Library.

Gottman, John and Silver, N. (2015) *The Seven Principles for Making Marriage Work: A Practical Guide from the Country's Foremost Relationship Expert*. Harmony Books: NY, NY.

Gudykunst, W. (2005). *Theorizing About Intercultural Communication*, Thousand Oaks, CA: Sage Publications.

Hammond, J., Keeney, R., & Faiffa, H. (2002). *Smart Choices: A Practical Guide to Making Better Decisions*. Cambridge, MA: Harvard Business School Press.

Harrison, D.D. (1978). *Some Things Are Better Said in Black and White*. Fort Worth, TX: Branch Smith, Inc.

Heinrichs, J. (2017). *Thank You For Arguing*. New York: Three Rivers Pres.s

Hendrix, Harville Ph.D., Hunt, Helen LaKelly PhD (2019) *Getting the Love You Want: A Guide for Couples: Third Edition* St. Martins Press: NY, NY.

Hocker, J., & Wilmot, W.W. (2017). *Interpersonal Conflict*. New York: McGraw Hill.

Johnson, D.W. (2014). *Reaching out: Interpersonal effectiveness and self-actualization* (12th ed.). Boston: Allyn & Bacon.

Johnson, D.W. (2015). Are you a conflict positive person? Research shows benefits of being conflict positive. *Psychology Today*. December.

Kottler, J. (2003). *Beyond Blame*. San Francisco: CA: Jossey-Bass.

Kirsh, Steven J., Duffy, Karen Grover et al. (2013) *Psychology for Living: Adjustment, Growth, and Behavior Today*. Pearson Publishing.

Kruschewsky, G.(2017). 14 Beautiful Experiences That Make Your Cross-Cultural Relationship Truly Special. *http://www.huffingtonpost.com/2014/02/19/inter-cultural-relationship_n_4800492.html*. Feb 19, 2014

Lamberton, L., & Minor, L. (2018). *Human Relations: Strategies for Success*. New York: McGraw Hill.

Lerner, H.G. (2002). *The Dance of Connection*. New York: HarperCollins.

Lerner, H.G. (2014). *The Dance of Anger*. New York:Harper Collins Publications.

Maine, M., & Kelly, J. (2005). *The Body Myth: Adult Women and the Pressure to be Perfect*. Hoboken, NJ: Wiley.

Marano, H. (2000). The eight habits of highly popular people. *Psychology Today,* 33, 78.

Markway PhD, Barbara, Celia Ampel, et al. (2018) *The Self Confidence Workbook: A Guide to Overcoming Self-Doubt and Improving Self-Esteem*. Emeryville, Calif.: Althea Press.

McDaniel, B. T., & Coyne, S. M. (2014). Technoference: The interference of technology in couple relationships and implications for women's personal and relational well-being. *Psychology of Popular Media Culture*. doi: 10.1037/ppm0000065

Morin, R. (2008). Who Makes the Decisions in Your Home? Pew Research Center. Washington, DC.

O'Neill, S., & Chapman, E. (2008). *Your Attitude Is Showing: A Primer on Human Relations*. Englewood Cliffs, NJ: Prentice Hall.

Phelps, S., & Austin, N. (2002). *The Assertive Woman: A New Look*. San Luis Obispo, CA: Impact Publishers.

Puhn, L. (2012). *Fight Less, Love More: 5-Minute Conversations to Change Your Relationship without Blowing Up or Giving In*. New York: Rodale Books.

Punches, B. (2010). *What You Say and Do Next Matters!* Dubuque, IA: Kendall Hunt Publishing Co.

Przybylski, A. K., & Weinstein, N. (2012). Can you connect with me now? How the presence of mobile communication technology influences face-to-face conversation quality. *Journal of Social and Personal Relationships, 30,* 237–246. doi: 10.1177/0265407512453827

Pychl, T. (2013) *Solving the Procrastination Puzzle*. Penguin Random House, NY.

Rahim, M., & Magner, N. (1995). Confirmatory factor analysis of the styles of handling interpersonal conflict. *Journal of Applied Psychology, 80,* 122–132.

Reece, B., & Brandt, R. (2010). *Effective Human Relations in Organizations*. New York: Cengage Learning.

Roberts, J. A., & David, M. E. (2016). My life has become a major distraction from my cell phone: Partner phubbing and relationship satisfaction among romantic partners. *Computers in Human Behavior*, 54, 134-141. doi:10.1016/j.chb.2015.07.058

Scott, E. (2019). Confllict Resolution Mistakes to Avoid. VeryWell.com

Seider, B. (2010). Couples who use the pronoun we. Independent co.uk 10-10-2018.

Smith, M. (2000). *When I Say No I Feel Guilty: For Managers & Executives*. New York: A Train Press.

Stone, D., Patton, B., & Heen, S. (2010). *Difficult Conversations*. New York: Penguin Putnam.

Tannen, D. (2007). *The Argument Culture: Stopping America's War of Words*. New York: Ballantine Books.

Tannen, D. (2001). *You Just Don't Understand*. New York: Ballantine Books.

Telushkin, J. (2019). *Words That Hurt, Words That Heal, Revised Edition: How the Words You Choose Shape Your Destiny*. New York: William Morrow and Company, Inc.

Ting-Toomey, S.T., & Oetzel, J. (2002). *Managing Intercultural Conflict Effectively*. Thousand Oaks, CA: Sage Publications.

Verderber, K., MacGeorge, E. (2015). *Inter-Act: Interpersonal Communication Concepts, Skills and Contexts*. New York: Oxford University Press.

Watanabe, K. (2009). *Problem Solving 101*. London, England: Penguin Books.

Weiten,W. (2017) *Psychology Themes and Variations*. Cengage Learning 10th edition

Weiten, W., Dunn, D., & Hammer, E. (2017). *Psychology Applied to Modern Life*. Belmont, CA: Thompson Wadsworth.

CHAPTER 8

Almeida, D. (2005). Resilience and vulnerability to daily stressors, assessed via diary methods. *Current Directions in Psychological Science, 14,* 64–68.

APA report on Stress retrieved 12-3-2019. David S. Krantz, PhD, Beverly Thorn, PhD, and Janice Kiecolt-Glaser, PhD.

Beck, A., Freeman, A., & Davis, D. (2015). *Cognitive Therapy of Personality Disorders*. New York: The Guilford Press.

Benson, H. (2009). *The Relaxation Response*. New York: Harper Collins.

Bernstein, A. (2016). *The Myth of Stress*. Tampa, FL: Free Press.

Bernstein, E. (2016). Steps to turn off the nagging self-doubt in your head most of us lose time to negative thoughts; reframe your thinking and feel more positive. *The Wall Street Journal*, June 13.

Bottos, S., & Dewey, D. (2004). Perfectionist's appraisal of daily hassles and chronic headache. *Headache, 44*, 772–779.

Brown, B. (2015). *Daring Greatly: How the Courage to Be Vulnerable Transforms the Way We Live, Love, Parent, and Lead*. New York: Gotham.

Brown, B. (2018) *Dare to Lead: Brave Work. Tough Conversations. Whole Hearts*. Ebury Digital Publishing

Brown, S., & Vaughn, C. (2010). *Play: How it Shapes the Brain, Opens the Imagination, and Invigorates the Soul*. New York: Avery.

Burns, D. (2006). *The Feeling Good Handbook*. New York: William Morrow and Co.

Burns, D. (2007). *When Panic Attacks: The New Drug-Free Anxiety Therapy That Can Change Your Life*. New York: Random House.

Castillo, L. G., Schwartz, S. J. (2013). Introduction to the special issue on college student mental health. *Journal of Clinical Psychology, 69*(4), 291-297

Ciaramicoli, A. (2016). *The Stress Solution: Using Empathy and Cognitive Behavioral Therapy to Reduce Anxiety and Develop Resilience*. Novato, CA: New World Library.

Davis, M., Eshelman, E.R., & McKay, M. (2019). *The Relaxation and Stress Reduction Workbook*. Oakland, CA: New Harbinger Publications.

Dembling, S. (2017). How to deal with the emotional triggers that stress you out. *The Dallas Morning News*.

Duffy, K., & Atwater, E. (2014). *Psychology for Living*. Upper Saddle River, NJ: Pearson.

Ellis, A. (2001). *Overcoming Destructive Beliefs, Feelings and Behaviors: New Directions for Rational Emotive Behavior Therapy*. New York: Prometheus Books.

Ellis, A. (2002). *Overcoming Resistance: A Rational Emotive Behavior Therapy Integrated Approach*. New York: Springer Publishers.

Ellis, A. (2006). *How to Stubbornly Refuse to Make Yourself Miserable about Anything—Yes, Anything*. New York: Carol Publishing Group.

Ellis, A., & MacLaren, C. (2005). *Rational Emotive Therapy: A Therapist's Guide*. New York: Impact Publishers.

Epstein, R. (1999). On the real benefits of eustress: A conversation with Hans Selye. *Psychology Today Reader*. Dubuque, IA: Kendall Hunt Publishing Co.

Freud, S. (2013). *The Problem of Anxiety*. New York: Norton.

Friedman, M., & Rosenman, R.H. (1982). *Type A Behavior and Your Heart*. New York: Fawcett.

Gallwey, W., Hanzelik, E., & Horton, J. (2009). *The Inner Game of Stress*. New York: Random House.

Hanna, H. (2014). *Stressaholic: 5 Steps to Transform Your Relationship to Stress*. Hoboken, NJ: Wiley.

Hanna, H. (2013). *The Sharp Solution: A Brain-Based Approach for Optimal Performance*. Hoboken, NJ: Wiley.

Harvard Health (2019) Anxiety & Physical Illness Health. Harvard. edu/staying healthy/anxiety

Jacobs, G. (2004). How to stay upbeat and stay healthy. *Bottom Line,* March 1, 12–13.

Kemmis-Zapier, Sam (May 2019) Procrastination is an emotional problem. https://www.fastcompany.com/

Kleinke, C. (2002). *Coping with Life Challenges.* Pacific Grove, CA: Brooks/Cole Publishing Co.

Lazarus, R.S. (2000). Toward better research on stress and coping. *American Psychologist,* 55, 665–673.

Lazarus, R.S. (2006). *Stress and Emotion.* New York: Springer Publishing.

Maddi, S. R. (2006). Hardiness: The courage to grow from stresses. *Journal of Positive Psychology.* 1 (3), 160–168. doi:10.1080/17439760600619609

McLeod, S. (2017). *Type A and B Personality.* Retrieved from www.simplypsychology.org/personality-a.html

Mueller, M. (2001). *Taking Care of Me: The Habits of Happiness.* Sevierville, TN: Insight, Inc.

Nairne, J. (2013). *Psychology: The Adaptive Mind.* Belmont, CA: Wadsworth/Thomas Learning.

Orma, S. (2016). *Stop Worrying and Go to Sleep: How to Put Insomnia to Bed for Good.* eBook. https://drorma.com/overcome-insomnia/

Pastorino, E., & Doyle-Portillo, S. (2018). *What is Psychology?* Belmont, CA: Thompson Wadsworth.

Paul, A. (2011). The uses and abuses of optimism. *Psychology Today,* Nov./Dec., 5–63.

Paulus, P., Seta, C., & Baron, R. (2000). *Effective Human Relations: A Guide to People at Work.* Needham Heights, MA: Allyn & Bacon.

Peale, N.V. (2003). *The Power of Positive Thinking.* New York: Simon and Schuster.

Peruttzi, B L. (2016). *Transition House Wellness Newsletter,* Fall edition.

Plotnik, R. Koyoumdjian, H. (2014). *Introduction to Psychology.* Pacific Grove, CA: Wadsworth.

Pychyl, T. (2011). Oops, where did the day go? *Psychology Today,* Sept./Oct., 58–61.

Raeburn, P. (2006). A case for double-edged optimism. *Psychology Today,* 39, 74–79.

Rayl, A. (2007). The price of a broken heart. *Psychology Today,* 40, 96–102.

Barr, V., & Krylowicz, B. (2016). The Association for University Annual Survey. Washington, D.C..

Rosch, P. (2016). The American Institute of Stress. Young Adults Are Most Stressed Generation: Survey. Retrieved from http:www.stress.org

Rudolph, K., Sánchez, B., Stuart, E., Greenberg, B., Fujishiro, K., Wand, G., Shrager, S., Seeman, T., Diez Roux, V. & Golden, S. (2016). Job strain and the cortisol diurnal cycle in MESA: Accounting for between- and within-day variability. *American Journal of Epidemiology,* 183(5), 497–506.

Sbarra, David (February 11, 2019) How Smartphones Are Affecting Our Relationships https://www.psychologicalscience.org/journals/pps Perspectives on Psychological Science

Sifferlin, A. (2013). The Most Stressed Out Generation? Young Adults. Retrieved from Healthland.Time.com/2013

Schultz, D., & Schultz, S. (2009). *Psychology and Work Today.* Upper Saddle River, NJ: Prentice Hall.

Scott, E. Elizabeth (2016). Attitude, Self Talk and Stress. Retreived from https:www. VeryWell.com

Seguin, A. (2015). *Negative Thoughts: Discover How to Stop Negative Thoughts by Changing the Way You Think*. Lexington, KY: Miafn, LLC.

Seligman, M. E., Steen, T. A., Park, N., & Peterson, C. (2005). Positive psychology progress: empirical validation of interventions. *American Psychologist*, 60(5), 410.

Smith, T., & Ruiz, J. (2002). Psychosocial influences on the development and course of coronary heart disease: Current status and implications for research and practice. *Journal of Consulting and Clinical Psychology*, 70, 548–568.

Southwick, S., Vythilingam, M., & Charney, D. (2005). The psychobiology of depression and resilience to stress. *Annual Review of Clinical Psychology*, 1, 255–291.

Stone, A., Smith, J., Kaell, A., & Hurewitz, A. (2000). Structured writing about stressful events. *Health Psychology*, 19, 619–624.

Surveys.ap.org (2008). Stress and Mental Health high. A survey conducted Feb. 28–March 6 by Edison Media Research.

Tannen, D. (2007). *You Just Don't Understand: Women and Men in Conversation*. New York: Harper Collins.

Taylor, S.E. (2004). Commentary in Taylor takes on fight-or-flight. *American Psychological Society*, 17, 21.

Time Magazine Special Edition (2019) *The Science of Happiness*. Meredith Corporation NY. NY.

Underwood, A. (2005). The good heart. *Newsweek*, October 3, 49–55.

Weiten, W., Dunn, D., & Hammer, E. (2017). *Psychology Applied to Modern Life*. Belmont, CA: Wadsworth.

Wolpe, J. (1992). *The Practice of Behavior Therapy*. Elmsford, NY: Pergamon Press.

CHAPTER 9

Albom, M. (2002). *Tuesdays with Morrie*. New York: Broadway.

Allport, G.W. (1979). *The Nature of Prejudice*. 25th Anniversary, Perseus Book publishers Reading, MA: Perseus.

Alper, B. (2015). *Millennials are less religious than older Americans, but just as spiritual*. Pew Research Center: Nov. 23, 2015 FactTank

Anderson, M., & Hitlin, P. (2016). *Social Media Conversations About Race*. Pew Research Center.

Aronson, E. (2018). *The Social Animal*. New York: Worth Publishers.

Aronson, E., Wilson, T., & Akert, R. (2018). *Social Psychology*. Upper Saddle River, NJ: Pearson Education, Inc.

Brooks, D. (2016). The power of altruism. *New York Times*, July 8.

Begley, S., & Kalb, C. (2000). Learning right from wrong. *Newsweek*, March 13, 30–32.

Character Education: An Historical Overview(2019) http://cnx.org

Ciccarelli, S., & Noland, J. (2016). *Psychology*. Upper Saddle River, NJ: Pearson.

Cohen, R. (2004). *Negotiating Across Cultures: International Communication in an Interdependent World* (rev. ed.). Washington, DC: United States Institute of Peace.

Coleman, P. (2016). Racism and Violence in America, What are white allies to do? Online The Five Percent blog

Coontz, S. (2016). *The Way We Never Were: American Families and the Nostalgia Trap.* New York: Basic Books.

Compton, W. (2005). *An Introduction to Positive Psychology.* New York: Wadsworth.

Corey, G., & Corey, M. (2013). *I Never Knew I Had a Choice.* Pacific Grove, CA: Brooks Cole Publishing Co.

Cory Collins (Fall 2018) What Is White Privilege, Really? Issue 60, *Teaching Tolerance*

Covey, S.R. (2013). *The Seven Habits of Highly Effective People*—Anniversary Edition. New York: Free Press

Covey, S.R. (2008). *The Speed of Trust-The One Thing that Changes Everything.* New York: Free Press.

DeCenzo, D., & Silhanek, B. (2002). *Human Relations: Personal and Professional Development.* Upper Saddle River, NJ: Prentice Hall.

Devine, P. (1989). Stereotypes and prejudice: Their automatic and controlled components. *Journal of Personality and Social Psychology*, 56, 680–690.

Dimock, M. (2019) *Defining generations: Where Millennials end and Generation Z begins.* Pew research Center Fact tank.

Dovidio, J. F., Glick, P. S., & Rudman, L. A. (2005). *On the Nature of Prejudice: Fifty Years After.* Allport. Malden, MA: Blackwell Pub.

Dubrin, A. (2016). *Human Relations for Career and Personal Success.* Upper Saddle River, NJ: Prentice Hall.

Epstein, R. (2002). M. Scott Peck wrestling with God. *Psychology Today*, 35, 68–73.

Fazio, R., Jackson, J., Dunton, B., & Williams, C. (1995). Variability in automatic activation as an unobtrusive measure of racial attitudes: A bona fide pipeline? *Journal of Personality and Social Psychology*, 69, 1013-1027.

Festinger, L. (1957). *A Theory of Cognitive Dissonance.* Stanford, CA: Stanford University Press.

Fiske, S. (2018) Stereotype Content: Warmth and Competence Endure tps://journals.sagepub.com/home/cdp

Fiske, S. T., & Durante, F. (2016). (See References). Provides an in-depth review of the stereotype content model, with an emphasis on cross-cultural similarities and a few differences.

Frankl, V.E. (2006). *Man's Search for Meaning.* New York: Washington Square Press.

Freiberg, K. (2014). *Annual Editions: Human Development.* Dubuque, IA: McGraw Hill/Dushkin.

Grossman, C. (2010). 72% of millennials more spiritual than religious. *USA Today*, April 27, 2010.

Hecklinger, F., & Black, B. (2012). *Training for Life.* Dubuque, IA: Kendall Hunt Publishing Co.

Henslin, J. (2016). *Essentials of Sociology.* New York: Pearson.

Hetherington, C. (2008). *Choose Happiness: Pay Attention to Co-Dependent Patterns.* Iowa City, IA: Hetherington and Associates.

Howard, P. (2016). *The Values Toolkit: Application Manual for the Owner's Manuel for Values at Work.* Charlotte, NC: CentACS Press.

Humbert, P. (2016). Living a great life from Goal Setting 101 Manual. http://www.philiphumbert.com/index.htm

Johnson, D. (2014). *Reaching Out: Interpersonal Effectiveness and Self-Actualization*. Boston: Pearson.

Josephson, M. (2004). The Power of Character. Unlimited publishing.

Jung, C.G. (1976). *Psychological Types*. New York: Harcourt Brace.

Kardaras, N. (2017). *Glow Kids: How Screen Addiction Is Hijacking Our Kids-and How to Break the Trance*. New York: St. Martins Press.

Kardaras, N. (2017). It's digital heroin: How screens turn kids into psychotic junkies. http://nypost.com/2016/08/27/its-digital-heroin-how-screens-turn-kids-into-psychotic-junkies/

Kluckhohn, F. (1967). Value orientations. In R.R. Grinker, Sr. (Ed.), *Toward a Unified Theory of Human Behavior: An Introduction to General Systems Theory*. New York: Basic Books, Inc.

Kohlberg, L. (1981). *The Philosophy of Moral Development: Moral Stages and the Idea of Justice*. San Francisco, CA: Harper and Row.

Lamberton, L., & Minor, L. (2014). *Human Relations: Strategies for Success*. New York: McGraw Hill.

Lampe, C., Ellison, N. (2016). Social Media in the Workplace. Pew Research Center, June.

Lenhart, A. (2018). Teens, smartphones and texting. http://www.pewinternet.org/2012/03/19/teens-smartphones-texting/

Lenhart, Amanda (2015) Teens, Technology and Friendships. Pew Research Institute

Lewis, H. (2007). *A Question of Values*. New York: Harper and Row.

Madigan, Tim. (2005). *I'm Proud of You, my friendship with Fred Rogers*. Ubuntu Press, Los Angeles, CA.

Myers, D.G. (2017). *Psychology*. New York: Worth.

Mynatt, C., & Doherty, M. (2013). *Understanding Human Behavior*. Upper Saddle River, NJ: Pearson Education.

Nosek, B. (2007). Implicit-explicit relations. *Current Directions in Psychological Science,* 16, 65-69

Park, C. (2013). The meaning making model: A framework for understanding meaning, spirituality, and stress-related growth in health psychology. *European Health Psychologist,* 15, 40-17.

Pattakos, A. et al. (2017). *Prisoners of Our Thoughts*. San Francisco, CA: Berret-Kohler Publishers, Inc.

Pausch, R. (2008). *The Last Lecture*. New York: Hyperion Books.

Peck, M. (2003). *The Road Less Traveled,* 25th Anniversary Edition. New York: Simon & Schuster.

Pennebaker & Bealle (1986) *Confronting a Traumatic Event. Toward an Understanding of Inhibition and Disease* Journal of Abnormal Psychology, 95(3): 274–81.

Pew Research Center, Religion and Public Life (March 2016) Gender gap in worship service attendance differs between Muslim-majority and Christian-majority countries.

Pojman, L.P. (2016). *Ethics: Discovering Right and Wrong*. Belmont, CA: Wadsworth.

Rathus, S., & Nevid, J. (2015). *Psychology and the Challenges of Life*. New York: Wiley.

Reece, B., & Brandt, R. (2016). *Effective Human Relations in Organizations.* Boston, MA: Cengage Learning.

Ricard, M. (2016). *Altruism: The Power of Compassion to Change Yourself and the World.* New York: Little Brown Publishers.

Rokeach, M. (2000). *Understanding Human Values.* New York: The Free Press.

Schwartz, B. (2000). Waking up from the American Dream. *Psychology Today, 32,* 74.

Spranger, E. (2013). *Types of Men.* New York: Harcourt Brace Jovanovich (Johnson Reprints).

Stahl, L. (2010). SMU moves to emphasize ethics in all fields of study. *Dallas Morning News*, December 25, 2010.

Tolerance.org A project of the Southern Poverty Law Center retrieved 12-4-19

Values. (n.d.). *Dictionary.com Unabridged.* Retrieved 12-14-19 from Dictionary.com website http://www.dictionary.com/browse/values

Vandeveer, R., & Menefee, M. (2009). *Human Behavior in Organizations.* Upper Saddle River, NJ: Pearson.

Wert, K. (2016). *Ten Essential Character Traits for a Happier Life.* Retrieved from Meant to be Happy.com website

Wyer, N. (2004). Value conflicts in intergroup perception: A social cognitive perspective. In G.V. Bodenhausen, & A.J. Lambert (Eds.), *Foundation of Social Cognition.* Mahwah, NJ: Erlbaum.

Yalom, I.D. (2006). *Momma and the Meaning of Life.* Dunmore, PA: HarperCollins.

Zuckerman, P. (2016). LA Times Op-Ed: How secular family values stack up. *LA Times* Sept. 18.

CHAPTER 10

Allen, D. (2015). *Getting things Done: The art of Stress Free Productivity.* New York: Penguin Press.

Anderson,J and Rainie L. (2018) The Future of Well Being in a Tech-Saturated World. Pew Research Center

Ash, M.K. (2008). *The Mary Kay Way: Timeless Principles from America's Greatest Woman Entrepreneur.* New York: Wiley.

Boles, R.N. (2011). *How to Find Your Mission in Life.* Berkeley, CA: Ten Speed Press.

Boles, R.N. (2019). *What Color Is Your Parachute?* Berkeley, CA: Ten Speed Press.

Breathnach, S. (2019). *Simple Abundance.* New York: Warner Books.

Campbell, A. (2007). *The Sense of Well-Being in America.* New York: McGraw Hill.

Campbell, D. (2007). *If You Don't Know Where You're Going, You'll Probably End Up Somewhere Else.* Niles, IL: Thomas More Press.

Canfield, J. (2015). *The Success Principles.* New York: Collins Living.

Clark, et al (2008) Corey, G., & Corey, M. (2013). *I Never Knew I Had a Choice.* Pacific Grove, CA: Brooks Cole Publishing Co.

Covey, S.R. (2016). *Primary Greatness: The 12 Levers of Success.* New York: Simon and Schuster.

Covey, S.R. (2014). *The Leader in Me.* New York: Simon & Schuster.

Covey, S.R. (2013). *The Seven Habits of Highly Effective People.* New York: Simon & Schuster.

Covey, S.R., Merrill, A.R., & Merrill, R. (1998). *First Things First.* New York: Fireside edition Simon and Schuster.

Csikszentmihalyi, M. (2016). Finding flow. *Psychology Today,* June edition.

Davis, M., Eshelman, E., & McKay, M. (2019). *The Relaxation & Stress Reduction Workbook.* Oakland, CA: New Harbinger Publications, Inc.

Dawson, G., & Glaubman, R. (2013). *Life Is So Good.* New York: Penguin USA.

Diener, E., Lucas, R. E., & Oishi, S. (2018). Advances and Open Questions in the Science of Subjective Well-Being. *Collabra. Psychology,* 4(1), 15. doi:10.1525/collabra.115

Doskoch, P. (2005). The winning edge. *Psychology Today,* 38, 42–52.

Drafke, M., (2018). *The Human Side of Organizations.* Upper Saddle River, NJ: Pearson Education, Inc.

Duckworth, A. (2018). *Grit: The Power of Passion and Perseverance.* New York: Simon and Schuster.

Epstein, M. (2016). Opening up to happiness. *Psychology Today June edition online.*

Figler, H. (2013). *The Complete Job Search Handbook.* New York: Owl Books.

Flora, C. (2016). The pursuit of happiness. *Psychology Today,* 42, 60–69.

Garcia, L. (2005). Happiness Is . . . *The Dallas Morning News,* May 24.

Gasca, P. (2015). *Become a Better Leader With These 5 Cultural-Awareness Tips.* WorkforceDiversityNewwork.com

Green, K. (2013). *4 Steps to Self-Actualization and Becoming the Best Version of You.* Huffington Post.

Guillebeau, C. (2016). *Born for this: How to find the work you were meant to do.* New York, NY: Penguin Random House LLC

Haden, J. (2016). Seven things to remarkably happy people do more. Inc.com blog, March 24.

Harris, R. (2008). *The Happiness Trap.* Boston, MA: Trumpeter.

Hecklinger, F., & Black, B. (2012). *Training for Life.* Dubuque, IA: Kendall Hunt Publishing Co.

Helmstetter, S. (2014). *Who Are You Really, and What Do You Want.* New York: Park Avenue Press.

Johnson, D. (2012). *Reaching Out.* Needham Heights, MA: Allyn & Bacon.

Johnson, S. (2002). *Who Moved My Cheese?* New York: G. P. Putnam's Sons.

Kaplan, J. (2010). Buddhism and psychotherapy: An interview with Dr. Mark Epstein. *Psychology Today,* October edition.

Kashdan, T. (2016). Three ways culture shapes happiness and well-being. *Psychology Today,* February edition online.

Lakein, A. 2008). *How to Get Control of Your Time and Your Life.* New York: New American Library.

Mackenzie, A. (2009). *The Time Trap.* New York: AMACOM (Division of American Management Association).

MacKay, H. (2019-January 24). How to take risks effectively. Posted to Unexpress Blog http://www.unexpress.com/harvey-mackay/

Manzoni, A. (2016). Conceptualizing and measuring youth independence: A multi-dimensional approach using latent class analysis. *Acta Sociologica,* June 29.

Maslow, A. (1998). *Maslow on Management.* New York: John Wiley & Sons.

McCullough, M. (2005). *Rules for Success: Time Tested Keys for Developing Excellence in Your Life.* Colorado Springs, CO: River Oak Publishing.

McGowan, K. (2005). The pleasure paradox. *Psychology Today,* January/February, 52–53.

McWilliams, John-Roger & McWilliams, P (2004) Do It Los Angeles; Prelude Press.

Myers, D.G. (1993) The Pursuit of Happiness. What Makes a Person Happy and Why. Avon Books

Myers, D.G. (2008). *The American Paradox: Spiritual Hunger in an Age of Plenty.* New Haven, CT: Yale University Press.

Myers, D.G. (2018). *Myers Psychology for AP.* New York: Worth Publishing.

Pavot, W., & Diener, E. (2008). The Satisfaction With Life Scale and the emerging construct of life satisfaction. J*ournal of Positive Psychology*, 3, 137–152

Peck, M.S. (2003). *The Road Less Traveled,* 25th Anniversary Edition. New York: Simon & Schuster, Inc.

Prather, H. (2011). *Notes on How to Live in the World and Still Be Happy.* Boston, MA: RedWheel/Weiser.

Rosling H. & Rosling-Ronnlund A. (2018) *Factfulness: Ten Reasons We're Wrong About the World—and Why Things Are Better Than You Think.* Macmillan Publishers

Schreiber, K. (2011). Ego in full bloom. *Psychology Today*, 44, 18.

Seligman, M.E. (2012). *Authentic Happiness: New Positive Psychology to Realize Your Potential for Lasting Fulfillment.* New York: Free Press.

Seligman, M.E. (2011). *Flourish.* New York: Free Press.

Siegel, B. (2015). *Love, Medicine and Miracles: Lessons Learned about Self-Healing from a Surgeon's Experience with Exceptional Patients* (Kindle Edition). New York: William Morrow Paperbacks.

Viscott, D. (2003). *Finding Your Strength in Difficult Times.* New York: McGraw Hill.

Weil, A. (2013). *Spontaneous Happiness.* New York: Little Brown & Co.

Worchel, S., Cooper, J., Goethals, G., & Olson, J. (2000). *Social Psychology.* Chicago, IL: Nelson-Hall.

Yang, Y. (2008). Social inequalities in happiness in the United States. *American Sociological Review,* 73, 204–226.

Ziglar, Z. (2000). *See You at the Top.* Nashville, TN: Thomas Nelson Publishers.

Ziglar, Z. (2019) *Goals: How to Get the Most Out of Your Life.* Nightingale Conant publisher

Index

NOTE: Page references in *italics* refer to figures and tables.

I

J

K